THE
WORLD *of the* HAITIAN REVOLUTION

T0323762

THE
WORLD *of the* HAITIAN
REVOLUTION

EDITED BY

David Patrick Geggus
Norman Fiering

Indiana University Press
BLOOMINGTON AND INDIANAPOLIS

Published with the cooperation and support of the
John Carter Brown Library, Providence, Rhode Island

This book is a publication of

Indiana University Press
601 North Morton Street
Bloomington, IN 47404-3797 USA

http://iupress.indiana.edu

Telephone orders: 800-842-6796
Fax orders: 812-855-7931
Orders by e-mail: iuporder@indiana.edu

Publication of this book is made possible in part with the
assistance of a Challenge Grant from the National Endowment
for the Humanities, a federal agency that supports research, education,
and public programming in the humanities.

The paper used in this publication meets the minimum requirements
of American National Standard for Information Sciences—
Permanence of Paper for Printed Library Materials, ANSI Z39.48-1984.

Manufactured in the United States of America

Library of Congress Cataloging-in-Publication Data

The world of the Haitian Revolution / edited by David Patrick Geggus and Norman Fiering.
p. cm. — (Blacks in the diaspora)
Includes bibliographical references and index.
ISBN 978-0-253-35232-3 (cloth : alk. paper) — ISBN 978-0-253-22017-2 (pbk. : alk. paper)
1. Haiti—History—Revolution, 1791–1804—Causes.   2. Haiti—History—Revolution,
1791–1804—Influence.   I. Geggus, David Patrick.   II. Fiering, Norman.
F1923.W67 2008
972.94'03—dc22

2008022420

1 2 3 4 5 14 13 12 11 10 09

Contents

PREFACE AND ACKNOWLEDGMENTS

Norman Fiering

T HE STORY OF HAITI IN THE REVOLUTIONARY ERA IS A PRISM THROUGH
WHICH IS DRAMATICALLY REVEALED AND EXPOSED MOST OF THE HIS-
TORICAL FORCES OF THAT MOMENT: REVOLUTION AND COUNTER-
revolution, slavery and antislavery, imperial ambition and colonial resistance,
racism and equality, capitalist growth and capitalist wreckage.

At the John Carter Brown Library it was a logical step to want to commemorate in 2004 with a scholarly conference the bicentennial of Haiti's
declaration of independence. The library has nearly incomparable holdings of
primary printed materials relating to the French colony of Saint-Domingue
and its transformation into Haiti at the beginning of the nineteenth century.
A conference and the subsequent publication of essays were sure to spark
new research in the collection.

Despite the upsurge of interest in the Haitian Revolution associated with
various bicentennials, it is a topic that is hardly overwritten. The concatenation
of events on the island, the wide ramifications of the revolution, and the sheer
complexity of the narrative continue to demand further research and reflection.
Indeed, the current fashion of "Atlantic history" brings Haiti to the forefront
with renewed urgency. If the newly imagined domain of the "Atlantic World"
in the early modern era has a capital, it is surely Saint-Domingue. Before the
upheaval, the colony was hailed as the major exporter of wealth from the
Americas, and at its height Saint-Domingue was the main destination of the
African slave trade.

For the revolutionary period, the island is a laboratory for the study of
race relations like nowhere else, and the debate over the enduring crime of
slavery in the hemisphere was fundamentally transformed by the revolution,
which sucked into its vortex not only metropolitan France, but England,
Spain, and the United States as well. Haiti's struggle for racial equality and
emancipation gave rise to some of the French Revolution's most radical land-
mark reforms, and some scholars now claim for it an important place in the

vii

histories of democracy and modernity. Everywhere one looks, Haiti is the beacon that can throw new light on the era.

Yet for all this, one of the great historical works of the second half of the twentieth century, R. R. Palmer's *Age of the Democratic Revolution* (1959–1964), failed even to mention Haiti. The nation of France, ordinarily so brilliantly attentive to its own national history, eschewed until very recently giving extensive consideration to the cruel and tragic history of Saint-Domingue, and textbooks in the United States also typically found it convenient to avoid the subject, perhaps because of our shameful diplomacy regarding this would-be "sister republic." It was not until the administration of Lincoln that the United States even recognized Haiti as an independent nation. No matter, the Haitian Revolution was one of the great junctures in human history, not for its generation of imperishable new ideas and principles, as occurred in the American Revolution and the French Revolution, but for the imposition of harsh justice on an unprecedented scale. If any of the above is intriguing, dear reader, you will find here a feast of revelation.

I turn back, however, to the moment in July 2001 when it was decided at the library that we could not let 2004 pass without paying due homage to the suffering and achievements of the Haitian Revolution. The precipitating factor in that decision, the inspiration, was the urging of Ashli White and Malick Ghachem, both graduate students at the time—Ashli at Columbia and Malick at Stanford—who were also research fellows at the John Carter Brown Library and were in the midst of writing dissertations on Haiti. When they offered their energy and expertise, how could we not then forge ahead?

My first assignment was to find funding for the venture, and we received a substantial part of what we needed immediately from Mrs. Jane Gregory Rubin, via her organization InterAmericas and its affiliate the Reed Foundation. With Mrs. Rubin's active sponsorship and involvement, we were able to form an expanded Planning Committee for the conference, which met over a two-day period in New York City in February 2002. That committee—consisting of Ashli and Malick plus Philip Boucher, David Brion Davis, David Geggus, and Philip Morgan—created the structure of the conference, isolated the central topics, more or less chose who was to be invited to present their work, and invited session chairs and commentators.

It is my pleasure to list here the names and affiliations (at the time) of all those who were present as contributors to the conference, held June 17 to June 20, 2004: Bernard Bailyn, Harvard University; David Bell, Johns Hopkins University; Madison Smartt Bell, Goucher College; Yves Benot, Paris; Robin Blackburn, University of Essex; Philip Boucher, University of Alabama in Huntsville; Christopher Leslie Brown, Rutgers University; Jean Casimir, ambassador of the Republic of Haiti to the United States, 1991–1997; Elizabeth Colwill, San Diego State University; Seymour Drescher,

University of Pittsburgh; Laurent Dubois, Michigan State University; Ada Ferrer, New York University; Carolyn Fick, Concordia University; Norman Fiering, John Carter Brown Library; Malick Ghachem, Stanford University; and John D. Garrigus, Jacksonville University.

Also: David Geggus, University of Florida; Léon-François Hoffmann, Princeton University; Rhett Jones, Brown University; Stewart R. King, Mt. Angel Seminary; Jane Landers, Vanderbilt University; Sidney Mintz, Johns Hopkins University; Philip Morgan, Johns Hopkins University; Gene Ogle, John Cabot University (Rome); Sue Peabody, Washington State University; Jeremy Popkin, University of Kentucky; João José Reis, Universidade Federal de Bahia; Dominique Rogers, Université des Antilles et de la Guyane, Martinique; Pierre Saint-Amand, Brown University; Vertus Saint-Louis, Ecole Normale Supérieure, Haiti; Julie Saville, University of Chicago; Julius Scott, University of Michigan; Alyssa Goldstein Sepinwall, California State University, San Marcos; Mimi Sheller, Lancaster University (U.K.); Ashli White, Columbia University.

All of these contributors, whether or not they are represented in print in this book, have influenced its shape and contents, as did many of those who attended the conference simply as registered participants. So rich was the intellectual environment that no one present over those three days could possibly have come away without fresh information about Haiti and without new perspectives on the revolution. The conference, in that sense, provided the first round of editing of this book.

Two of the essayists in the book, Jacques de Cauna and Carlos Célius, both French scholars, were unable to attend the conference but submitted papers that were read aloud by others. Yves Benot, a legendary figure in the field, who traveled from France and was present, died not long after the event, much mourned. His contribution is posthumous, and this volume is dedicated to his memory.

I must single out as a stirring presenter at the conference the prizewinning novelist Madison Smartt Bell, whose superb trilogy on the Haitian Revolution has probably lured more people into serious study of the colony's history than any monograph could.

The conference included an excursion one afternoon to Newport, Rhode Island, where there is much to reflect on regarding the slave trade and other matters pertaining to the inter-relations of Africa and New England in the eighteenth century. One session was held in the so-called Colony House there, a meeting hall constructed in 1739 (in part by African American slaves) that served as Rhode Island's state house until 1901. It is one site that still stands, among others in Newport, in close proximity to where slaves were actually bought and sold. We thus assembled that afternoon on what might be called sacred ground. Before the session, Daniel Snydacker, formerly director of the Newport Historical Society, led our group on a "Black History" walking tour of the city.

If the conference was well organized and logistically flawless, much is owed to the Administrative Office at the John Carter Brown Library, where Carolyn Anderson, Valerie Andrews, Valerie Krasko, Maureen O'Donnell, Nan Sumner-Mack, and Vivian Tetreault all performed splendidly. Andrew Romig, a Brown University graduate student in history, served as my all-around assistant during the conference and during the run-up to it; his work was invaluable.

The initial grant support from the Reed Foundation was eventually augmented by two other large subventions: from the Florence Gould Foundation, led by John R. Young, who on many occasions has helped underwrite John Carter Brown Library projects; and from the Discretionary Fund of Brown University's president, Ruth Simmons, a remarkable educational leader by any measure, who, as it happens, has had for many years a scholarly interest in Haiti.

The conference also received help, thanks to Françoise Oldcorn, from Air France, which covered the travel expenses of several of the contributors, and from the C. V. Starr Center at Washington College, led at the time by Ted Widmer. To all of these supporters, beginning with Mrs. Rubin, we are forever grateful.

Two offshoots of the conference deserve mention, both intended to call attention to the holdings of the John Carter Brown Library. Prior to the opening of the conference, we commissioned Malick Ghachem to prepare an exhibition of primary sources in the John Carter Brown collection that, in Dr. Ghachem's words, would "provide a running narrative of the Haitian Revolution." The contents of that excellent exhibition, which was for three months on view in the Library Reading Room, have been published as a 40-page pamphlet entitled simply *The Haitian Revolution, 1789–1804*. Copies may be purchased from the library.

In addition, with the support of the Florence Gould Foundation, the library has put up on its Web site "A Checklist of John Carter Brown Library Holdings Relating to Saint-Domingue and the Haitian Revolution, 1735–1834" (http://www.brown.edu/Facilities/John_Carter_Brown_Library/pages/jcbl_haiti/index.html), which contains over 500 contemporary titles. The initial work on that online source was undertaken by another Brown University graduate student, Yarí Pérez Marín.

It seemed evident to me that the 2004 conference had to be captured, selectively, in print, and not long after the event I asked David Geggus, recognized by all as the preeminent authority on the Haitian Revolution, to serve as the editor of the book with me in an ancillary role. He generously agreed, and together we have labored to make this volume serve its noble ends as effectively as possible.

PROLOGUE

FROM SAINT-DOMINGUE TO HAITI:
TO LIVE AGAIN OR TO LIVE AT LAST!

Jean Casimir

I N THE TRANSFORMATION OF SAINT-DOMINGUE INTO HAITI, THE POPU-
LATION CONVERTED A "PLANTATION ISLAND" INTO A SOCIETY ORIENTED
TOWARD THE SATISFACTION OF ITS OWN NEEDS. THE INHABITANTS OF
the colony did not choose to cultivate sugar cane and other export commodities;
the cultivation of such commodities required a high degree of social organization and control. This organization, compared to autochthonous societies built
on time-honored traditions, was sudden in its development, and social relations
within it did not flow as normal and natural sets of behaviors.

Whites, mulattoes and blacks, planters and tradesmen, freed men and
women, and captives were not linked by lifelong habits. The social fabric of
the colonial territory took shape as a result of efforts by the local population,
regardless of the policies that emanated from the state. This contradiction
between the actual society of the island and the concepts of the metropolis, together with the internal conflicts arising from the "racialization" of the
emergent society and from the exploitation of the enslaved, combined to create an unstable milieu.

To function properly, the plantation system needed financial, commercial, and industrial enterprises as well as state institutions. Its two main social
categories, planters and slaves, were supposed to follow the prescriptions of
a social project that the enslaved ignored, since it was of no benefit to them.
Without coercion, daily behaviors rarely coincided with the dictates of the
law. The slave depicted in the Black Code was not the slave found on the
plantation, and the social order was constantly questioned.

The Black Code of Louis XIV invented an ideal slave that the state and
the dominant classes endeavored to replicate in reality. Macandal was a runaway slave or a deserter according to his master, Le Normand de Mézy. But
he moved around fully armed because he had not acknowledged that he was

somebody's property. To speak of fugitives and deserters is to think like the slave trader and the planter. On no scientific basis can one favor their opinion and perceptions over the overt opposition of those they enslaved. No traditional relationship of subordination linked one group to the other.

Captives "became" slaves only after their numbers had been thinned by the pruning of those who died refusing to accept the injunctions of positive laws. The sacrifices the survivors had to make in order to adapt to or to overcome the regime of plantation servitude cannot be ignored. Slavery was essentially a relationship of domination and exploitation, since relations of subordination did not achieve any significant degree of institutionalization. To be sure, in private life and interpersonal relations, this preeminence of relations of domination may have diminished, but this happened in limited areas of contact between social actors who belonged to each of the main categories.

A reading of the history of Haiti from this standpoint produces a picture quite different from that obtained in traditional historiography.[1] The slave trade was the first institution of modern times in which labor power was bought and sold on a large scale. The Haitian nation emerged from the plantation labor market, but it did so in direct contradiction to the values propounded by this very Western institution. Exactly how Haitians evolved principles for social cohesion out of the early international division of labor that brought their country into existence is an obscure process and the object of unfortunate distortions that deserve to be clarified.

The Colonial Worker of Saint-Domingue

The slave trade, or the commercial traffic in black people, was a project of France and the other colonial powers. The bookkeepers of the slave ships and plantations would sell or buy a standardized product: the black person. How that person was treated varied according to the state of the market. A historical analysis that as a starting point simply accepts the servile condition of the population concerned endorses such a condition as normal and necessary and erases from the pages of history a world of social relations lived beyond the horizons of the owners of the market and the merchandise.

The behavior of the captives and their need for "seasoning" show that they did not live slavery as a necessary and normal form of existence. It follows that there was no logical common ground where the assumptions underlying their servitude could be shown to be superior to those underlying their resistance or revolt. The revolt of colonial laborers in Saint-Domingue was not conceived and expressed as a form of bargaining over or negotiating around the value of the merchandise—that is, the labor power being traded. It was not carried out within the context of economic theory; it ignored altogether the tenets of Western social thought.

The deportees from Africa, who were generally adults, could not free themselves from the body of knowledge and ethnic characteristics that defined them. But even in the case of the creole (that is, locally born) captives, there are no grounds for arguing that they accepted the Western ideas that fashioned their fate and that they surrendered under the weight of the evidence that suggested that they were impotent in the market place. Whatever testimony they may have produced to the contrary is not admissible. The colonial social organization was too recent to have embedded itself deeply, and it relied too much on coercion instead of the pressures that normally emanate from significant institutions or social relations.

The state, metropolitan traders, and planters could never complete their modeling of the slave as a social category or completely force this category on the mind of the captive. Investments to achieve this result increased steadily during the colonial period, ending with the expensive expedition that Napoleon entrusted to his brother-in-law. Choosing to ignore the mounting weight of these considerable expenses means enclosing oneself in the mindset of the slave traders.

The Negro as defined by the Code Noir of Louis XIV was not a historical necessity. It was simply one option among several. Plantation slavery cannot be conceived of as a moment in the life of these Negroes and, by the same token, as a fortunate introduction to Western civilization. In such a line of thinking, the Negroes' contribution to their own well-being—that is to say, to their life before and after the plantation system—would become invisible or would be discarded because it was contrary to the supposed well-being of humanity as defined by Louis XIV.

The population of Saint-Domingue that broke with the West consisted mostly of African-born individuals. Around 1790, it was estimated that these enslaved Africans made up roughly two-thirds of the total labor force of the colony. Both the processes by which their culture was attacked and their efforts to formulate an alternative to Western culture were more overt in Saint-Domingue than elsewhere in the Caribbean. Moreover, two generations separated the creoles who cast off their chains in Saint-Domingue from those who later did the same in the English and other French territories. Not only was the process of creolization deeper in the neighboring plantation societies, but because the slave trade had come to an end or substantially diminished well before the slaves on the neighboring islands experienced emancipation, planters on those islands and the authorities were obliged to ensure that the labor force reproduced itself. Planters in other colonies replaced unbridled torture with bargaining methods that tended to conceal exploitation and create more space for compromise and understanding. In Saint-Domingue, by contrast, resources, such as land and crops, were not on the table for negotiation. Haiti removed itself from the international division of labor, and ethnic markers or categories filled the role labor and capital played elsewhere to mediate conflicts.

Whites, Mulattoes, and Blacks in Saint-Domingue

A "Negro" is the result of a socialization process. Except for the few Ladinos who landed in the time of Christopher and Diego Columbus, "Negroes" as such never disembarked in Saint-Domingue. In the societies where so-called Negroes came from, skin color was not a marker of social ranking or even of ethnicity. "Black" social actors were unknown in Africa; the raw material offered on the slave market was a stock of Ibos, Aradas, Mandingas, Yorubas, Ashantis, or Hausas who had to be converted into "Negroes."

The success of plantation society depended on getting the captives to behave like "Negroes"—that is, like people born to be slaves. The unforeseen consequence of this achievement was that to protect themselves and to survive, prisoners formed themselves into a new community unrelated to the legal fiction outlined by Louis XIV.

The international labor market was created simultaneously with the invention of the "Negro" as a slave. The Western world systematically manufactured his or her inferiority and made it operational and productive. He or she became a movable asset and his or her emancipated descendants could only reach the rank of second-class citizens.

The success of the eighteenth-century plantation system bears witness to this accomplishment, whose source was the oppression of those who occupied subordinate social layers. But it was proved only after the fact, at the end of a process of struggle of which the outcome was uncertain. For the population—Europeans, Africans, and creoles—the superiority or inferiority of one or another stratum was not a given. The conflicts within plantation society show that its social hierarchy, which was contested by the subaltern groups, was enforced only because of constant pressure from public authorities.

The racialization of the society and the alleged superiority of whites were an end product, not a starting point. The different actors did not have a common history and did not share traditions that institutionalized this stratification as the natural order of things. The sums invested in imposing such inequality demonstrate that the success or failure of the colonial project was neither necessary nor inevitable. They also suggest that the oppressed had social power in dealing with the limitations imposed on them. The state had to reeducate each new group of captives and each new generation.

The analysis of colonial society based on the categories white, black, and mulatto uses as a hypothesis the very results of the processes observed. Whites had to live fully armed in order to enforce their superiority. Racializing plantation society was the process of accepting as a given the specific racial anthropology underlying that society.

The results of the Haitian Revolution were foreshadowed in the initial cleavage which the imposition of white people's racial supremacy made inevitable. France never had total control over the thought processes of the subordinate classes in Saint-Domingue. Between 1790 and 1804, the dislocation inherent in "plantation society" worsened following the arrival of huge numbers of deported Africans. The renewed opposition of the oppressed groups to the road map prepared by Louis XIV led to the emergence of a new black who made his official appearance in the 1805 constitution proclaimed by Jean-Jacques Dessalines.

The 1805 constitution took note in article 13 of the presence of naturalized white women and their children as well as naturalized Germans and Poles. In article 14, it stipulated that all Haitians were to be included under the generic denomination "blacks." This new "black" encompassed the various ethnic groups that had been involved in the struggle against the Western vision of mankind. Victory in adversity gave birth to this new character, which was a synthesis not only of Ibos, Aradas, and Hausas but also of French, Germans, and Poles. The concept of the slave by birth who was called "Negro" left the colony with the remnants of the French expeditionary army. To mark the occasion, it was also decided that the country would revert to its Amerindian name of Haiti, closing the chapter in its history when it was known as Hispaniola or Saint-Domingue.

The new "Negro" was not a creation of the 1804 elite. One finds him in the vernacular language, where the word designates all human beings. In contrast, the term *blanc* ("white") is used—at least today—to refer to all foreigners, regardless of their color. The Negro, a central figure of Haitian thought, is not part of the international labor market, nor does he have a place in the Industrial Revolution or in the epics of imperialism. He made his way alone, and his success, unglamorous by Western standards, did not attract much attention.

Settlers and City Dwellers in Haiti

Before this period of social upheaval concluded with the defining of the Haitian in article 14 of Dessalines's constitution, there was a period of increased rivalry among the members of the intermediate strata of colonial society. These conflicts continued after independence, and traditional historiography normally describes the political evolution of the country in terms of the infamous "question de couleur."

Information on rivalries between "mulattoes" and "blacks" refers exclusively to struggles for influence and quarrels among *anciens libres* (those already free before slavery was abolished). If the rebellion of Ogé and Chavanne concentrates attention on the status of these colored leaders as themselves slaveholders, subsequent conflicts between blacks and mulattoes do not seem to express, even at the level of their protagonists, any antagonistic political positions. Toussaint, Rigaud, Dessalines, Christophe, and Pétion were surrounded by political clientele whose quarrels were related to social projects that had common goals. Their agendas, although derived from divergent social experiences and standpoints, did not correspond to unbridgeable ideological orientations. Their shared opposition to the policies of General Leclerc and his expeditionary army are one example. The friendship between Goman and André Rigaud and the loyalty that the fiercest maroon of his time vowed to Dessalines illustrate my point.

The racialization of the island population was a requirement of the plantation economy that did not disappear after 1804. However, it became obsolete as the peasant economy developed or as individuals left the limited circle of the *anciens libres* and their heirs—"blacks" or "mulattoes." After the "whites" and the plantations had been eliminated, the various components of society had to be reshuffled. The early efforts to convert the subordinate classes into *cultivateurs*, that is to say, into barely disguised indentured servants (at best), occurred at a time when the "indigenous army" could still boast of its military professionalism. Yet the fear that the French expeditionary army would return or that other great powers would become aggressive did not materialize. As the metropolitan countries turned elsewhere to develop their colonial empires, Haiti became more and more insignificant, while its army together with its fortresses lost their raison d'être.

If one classifies the territories of nineteenth-century America into settlement colonies and exploitation colonies, Haiti belongs to the first group. The year 1804 marked the turning point from exploitation colony to settlement colony. Settlement colonies are built by their inhabitants. The word *habitant*—in English, "settler"—appeared in Saint-Domingue at the end of the seventeenth century and the beginning of the eighteenth before it was replaced by the concept of planter, which was central to the evolving exploitation colony. The concept of *habitant* surfaced again as the conflicts leading to independence intensified, when it usually meant "creole." In fact, the free creoles sometimes called themselves "American colonists." This term doesn't seem to have included white creoles, however, or captives born in the colony.

It never occurred to the country's historians to think of it as a settlement colony. While the leaders bickered over the spoils of colonial power, the bulk of the population appropriated the term "settler." The demobilization of the indigenous army and the establishment of the peasantry were in fact the same process. In the same way, and especially after the last eastern campaign of Soulouque, when the colonial powers were occupied elsewhere, the army no longer needed to measure itself against aggressors. So it busied itself with the tasks entrusted to any governmental bureaucracy. Especially from 1860 onward, it increasingly took care of regional development and the arbitration of local conflicts. It administered the peasant world that by then had taken over the entire national landscape.

The sociopolitical structure put in place after 1804, which focused on defending the territory and managing public affairs, had the same prestige as in colonial times. The structure was based, as was foreign trade, in the seaports. A social stratum emerged during the nineteenth century that replaced both the political authorities and the traders of the metropole. In the process, it differentiated itself from the settlers or *habitants*. It consisted of city-dwellers, or *gens de la ville*, as opposed to those that lived outside the city, or *moun an deyò*.

The cleavage between these two social layers has been rarely questioned in Haitian social sciences, but it would be useful to revisit it, taking into account the upward mobility of the *notables* from the provinces. The fracture seems to have been much less deep during the nineteenth century than it is today after the occupation by the United States (1915–1934). Small towns, known as *bourgs* or *bouk*, mushroomed as administrative centers between the scattered settlements and the city-dwellers. They were places of residence for the *notables* and as intervention points of the political structure.

As they shed their indenture-like condition of *cultivateurs*, the *habitants* became upwardly mobile, as evidenced by the partisans of Acaau at the century's beginning or those of Mérisier Jeannis at its end. The rural-urban divide diminished because of the importance of the provincial towns. During the nineteenth century, most heads of state and members of their cabinets came from the humblest townships, a fact that contradicts the alleged divorce between city and countryside. In fact, not until the end of the nineteenth century did the government bureaucracy begin to concentrate in Port-au-Prince.

Conclusion: To Govern in a Hostile World

It is impossible to appreciate the country's achievements after 1804 without referring to the international context. Haiti's nineteenth-century elite were caught between the unbridled imperialism of the time and pressure from the peasant society. The genocide of the Amerindians of the western United States, the horrors of the European conquest of Africa, the countless abuses that waves of European migrants experienced wherever they landed were all accomplished under the banner of a racist ideology backed by scientific pretensions. Out of conviction or to cajole a decidedly hostile world opinion, Haiti's elite implemented various Eurocentric and anti-nationalist cultural policies. It entrusted the French clergy with "educating" the countryside and invited the population to deepen its cultural dependence on France. On the other hand, the elite bluntly challenged the racist theories in use in the contemporary world.

Moreover, even though various political groups competed for the support of external powers in their quest for economic and political dominance, in the end no foreign state achieved a clear predominance in the affairs of Haiti before the uninvited intervention by the United States in 1915.

The political elite showed remarkable skill in managing the nation. In addition to the lengthy administrations of Christophe, Pétion, Boyer, Soulouque, and Geffrard during the first half of the century, Haiti experienced thirty-four years of republican stability at the end of the century. From 1874 to 1888, three presidents from the south governed, followed by four others from the north from 1888 to 1908. Their tenure in office lasted on average five years each.

By the end of the century, the national territory was divided into subregions, each centered on a seaport. When grievances arose, the *notables* would raise a local army and march on the nation's capital to state their demands. This anti-plantation, anti-colonialist, anti-racist, anti-imperialist state did not and could not organize itself according to the Western patterns of the time. As everywhere else, democratic elections were rare. However, no general who was winning a civil war could seize power without having Parliament "elect" him to the supreme command. This suggests that the chambers of deputies operated as negotiating venues for the political powers in play rather than as a legislature, as expected in the Western world.

Finally, during the nineteenth century very few countries could teach Haiti any lesson concerning respect for the fundamental rights of human beings. Haiti was among the rare places on earth where a worker, especially if he or she was not white, had full access to the product of his or her labor.

But with the blossoming of the second colonial empires, Haiti's elite gradually lost its ascendancy in the country. At the turn of the twentieth century, the living conditions of the masses deteriorated and the United States occupied the country with little effort. The occupation of 1915 put an end to a century during which the deportees from Africa could live again and could bequeath to their descendants a homeland where they could finally know what it was to thrive without limitations imposed by foreign powers. After 1915, the standard of living of the Haitians again became dependent on the international division of labor.

Note

1. Sidney W. Mintz, *Sweetness and Power: The Place of Sugar in Modern History* (New York: Viking Penguin, 1985), 19ff. See particularly John Stuart Mill's statement on page 42: "[The West Indies] are hardly to be looked upon as countries, carrying on an exchange of commodities with other countries, but more properly as outlying agricultural or manufacturing estates belonging to a larger community." See also Octavio Ianni, *As metamorfoses do escravo, Apogeu e crise da escravatura no Brasil Meridional* (São Paulo: Difusão Européia do Livro, 1962), 233ff.

PART ONE

SAINT-DOMINGUE
ON THE
EVE OF REVOLUTION

Saint-Domingue on the Eve of the Haitian Revolution

David Geggus

T HE HAITIAN REVOLUTION IS AN EVENT OF GLOBAL SIGNIFICANCE PARTLY BECAUSE OF *WHERE* IT TOOK PLACE. EIGHTEENTH-CENTURY SAINT-DOMINGUE REPRESENTED THE APOGEE OF THE EUROPEAN colonizing process begun three centuries earlier. In the late 1780s, it was the world's major exporter of sugar, coffee, and, till shortly before, of indigo as well. These were not the cheap bulk commodities they later became but were valuable staples, the lifeblood of Atlantic commerce. Saint-Domingue's exports were worth far more than the gold of Brazil or the silver of Mexico, and they kept an entire navy in business.[1] The colony's enslaved population was then almost as large as that of the United States south of the Potomac. It had become the single main destination of the Atlantic slave trade. When the French Revolution broke out, Saint-Domingue was home to almost half a million slaves, about 30,000 white colonists, and a roughly equal number of free people of color.

The French and Haitian Revolutions' simultaneity and intertwined narratives inevitably have led historians to ask in what degree the colonial revolution was caused by the metropolitan one. Had there been no upheaval in France, might Haiti be nowadays a French *département?* Or was the Saint-Domingue of the 1780s hurtling toward its destruction whatever might happen in France?

Those colonists who gathered in Paris in 1789 were warned by the marquis de Mirabeau that they were sleeping at the foot of a volcano. One of them, the marquis de Rouvray, had himself written a few years earlier that, as slave-owners, they "walked on barrels of gunpowder." Another stated in a government report that "sooner or later" Saint-Domingue's overworked and underfed slaves would "rush headlong into the horror of terminal despair." Raynal's already famous *Histoire des deux Indes* had predicted a black Spartacus, and the triumph of such a figure was foreseen in Louis-Sébastien Mercier's frequently republished 1771 novel, *L'an 2440*. Even proslavery writers were willing to respond that if their own reform projects were ignored, such predictions might come true.[2]

To my mind, such premonitions raise some doubt about categorizing the Haitian Revolution as an "unthinkable event," as Rolph Trouillot memorably called it.[3] It is particularly difficult to explain the widespread fears of slave revolt that struck colonists, merchants, and officials at the very beginning of the French Revolution if contemporaries were incapable of imagining a massive or successful rebellion.[4] Yet it is certainly true that those commentators (mostly physiocrats) who, from the 1750s, had forecasted or approved a future separation of France and Saint-Domingue generally envisaged secession as being carried through by the planter class, not the enslaved.[5] Both slaves and slave-owners, therefore, were seen in some quarters as potential threats to the colonial status quo.

Of course, such prognostications were rare. Predictions of environmental ruin were perhaps more common.[6] The surviving correspondence of colonists is largely filled with family matters, work, and weather. The major preoccupations of Saint-Domingue's administrators in these years were administrative, judicial, and fiscal reform; trade regulation; and public works. They did not see the slave revolution coming, even if they did not exclude the possibility. Whether we think they should have been more attentive to the rumblings of the volcano partly depends on how much smoke we can detect at its summit when looking through the lens of the historical record. Personally, I do not find the view very clear.

Let us start with slave rebellions. Although Saint-Domingue possessed the Caribbean's largest slave population for most of the eighteenth century, historians have been hard put to discover rebellions and conspiracies prior to that of 1791. Pierre de Vaissière, one of the few historians to work through the full range of pre-revolutionary administrative archives, believed that there were none after 1704. Charles Frostin, another such historian, concluded contentiously that Saint-Domingue's whites were the most rebellious part of the population.[7] Yet there are references here and there in eighteenth-century sources to localized revolts or plots, and we need to know more about them. Nonetheless, it is obvious that Saint-Domingue was not like Jamaica with its long record of collective violent resistance. Some colonists attributed this difference to the colony's authoritarian government, others to its large free colored militia.[8]

Perhaps more plausibly, the paucity of rebellions might be related to the feasibility on this large island of escaping from slavery, especially across the frontier into sparsely populated Santo Domingo. The study of such "maroonage" has been a battleground, notably between Haitian scholars who have read it as a protorevolutionary development in which Haitian independence was already implicit and European empiricist historians who seek to delimit its dimensions and generally see it as a safety valve within the system. Each side has accused the other of either romanticizing or "banalizing" the subject—and with good reason.[9] Maroonage certainly was banal, in the sense of being an everyday event, although the short-term and localized *petit marronage* was infinitely more common than the eye-catching activities of armed bands that novelists and Caribbean nationalists have found so appealing. On the other hand, all fugitives risked brutal retribution and had to live by their wits, be it for years or just days. Behind every banal statistic was a personal drama.

For our purposes, the following points seem most relevant.[10] Clashes between maroon communities of more than a hundred people and major expeditions continued, even in the densely settled North Province of Saint-Domingue, into the mid-1770s, but they were always a frontier phenomenon, and ten years later they were a thing of the past everywhere in the rapidly developing colony. The total number of fugitives undoubtedly continued to increase with the slave population, but plantation documents generally suggest that the proportion missing at any given time was about 1 percent; maybe one in thirty or forty adult slaves went missing in any year, and the great majority returned or were recaptured in a few weeks or months. Proportionately, the colonial garrison lost far more of its soldiers to desertion.[11] Not all of those missing were outside the system: some passed as free in the towns, others were employed under conditions resembling the exploitation of illegal immigrants today. Finally, the common claim that the main leaders of the 1791 uprising were maroons is, with one important exception, demonstrably untrue.

That exception was the dashing young coachman Jean-François, who became the slave revolution's main leader. We know he had been a fugitive for the previous four years, though we do not know if he lived in a maroon community.[12] Although his fellow leaders Biassou, Jeannot, and Boukman were not maroons, one can find a few lesser figures who were and who subsequently played minor roles in the uprising.[13] This might be a promising line of investigation and could substantiate Robin Blackburn's and Carolyn Fick's argument that the experience gained in *petit marronage* contributed to the revolution's success. It is unlikely, however, that most of those who took up arms in 1791 had ever been fugitives.

The likeliest connection between maroonage and the uprising might in fact be a negative one. The rapid clearing of mountain forests in Saint-Domingue that made it progressively more difficult to become a successful maroon may have made outright rebellion more likely. In this view, maroonage was an alternative to violent revolt rather than a precursor.

A similar argument can be made about Vodou and whether it defused anomic tensions in the slave population as much as it contributed to the coming revolution.[14] That contribution came in several forms but especially through providing leadership and an organization that overcame the ethnic divisions of slave society. Faulty translations of surviving religious chants have exaggerated the specifically anti-white nature of an association that primarily promised its followers protection. Belief in the protective power of amulets, however, was to prove a powerful mobilizing device. As with maroonage, many revolutionary leaders have been unjustifiably claimed as Vodou priests, but contemporary evidence does exist in the case of Boukman and, less certainly, Jeannot, although modern claims about a network of Vodou priests are very implausible.[15]

Above all, we do not really know when the umbrella structure of the present-day religion came into existence and thus united the different ethnically based religions that were its components. It is possible that it was forged by the unifying experience of participating in a successful revolution rather than being a major element in that revolution's causation. Ethnic identities, and tensions, certainly continued until after independence. Pre-revolutionary evidence is largely limited to the accounts of the colonists Moreau de Saint-Méry and Drouin de Bercy. Mixing Kongo chants with apparently West African blood oaths and snake worship, these accounts may simply conflate different stories their authors had heard. Yet it is tempting to see in them the first concrete evidence that by the 1780s slaves from different religious traditions were worshipping together in the same forum.

Moreau de Saint-Méry also testifies to the recent appearance in Saint-Domingue of the violent, conflict-centered Petro cult, which colonists regarded as particularly dangerous. It was evidently linked with the growing numbers of Kongolese in the colony and, because of its apparent association with the famous Bois-Caïman ceremony that preceded the slave uprising, it may be regarded as at least a shower of sparks shooting from the colonial volcano.[16]

According to C. L. R. James, the slaves' main weapon of resistance was poison.[17] Most histories of the Haitian Revolution tell the story of the charismatic sorcerer Macandal, who was executed in 1758 for distributing poison and who quickly became a legend. Many writers quote the novelette-like account of his life published thirty years later in the *Mercure de France*, but few have used the report by the judge that examined Macandal's case. Historian Pierre Pluchon interpreted the contemporary sources as revealing no revolutionary conspiracy. Instead, he found a network of sorcerers and clients that spanned several parishes (not the colony) that killed many more blacks than whites and for personal, not political, motives.[18] Since panic-stricken colonists confused both disease and sorcery with poison and gathered evidence by using torture, distinguishing fact from fiction in the affair may be impossible. Room certainly remains for interpretation, and what is perhaps most important about Macandal is that by 1789 he had already become a mythical figure, remembered by slaves, as Moreau de Saint-Méry tells us, for his supernatural powers. The terrible poisoning scares of the period 1757–1779 appear to have abated in the pre-revolutionary decade. This reflected the growth of a more modern mindset among colonists, who became more willing to interpret livestock epidemics as natural events and less inclined to believe confessions extracted with torture. Trends in the actual use of poison, however, are impossible to discern.

Pre-revolutionary developments in slave resistance, therefore, offer no strong clues about the approach of the 1791 uprising. What about changes in colonial demography or the conditions under which slaves lived? Do we find there signs of destabilization, weakening social control, or mounting pressures?

Saint-Domingue's demography leads one immediately into a thicket of contradictory statistics and questionable sources, at both the plantation and colonial levels. Simply identifying official census figures for a given year can be an impenetrable mystery, let alone assessing their reliability or estimating more arcane figures such as contraband slave imports or birth and death rates.[19] Fortunately, as the "hardest" data available concern the legal slave trade, we do know that more than 220,000 enslaved Africans arrived in Saint-Domingue during the postwar economic boom years of 1784–1790. During the five years before the uprising, the colony absorbed nearly two-fifths of all the Africans being brought to the Americas, breaking all records for the Atlantic slave trade. Then, in the year 1790, imports jumped by 45 percent above their already high level, and close to 20,000 Africans arrived in just the single port of Cap-Français, which the following year became the center of the zone of insurrection. The proportion of young males among them was higher than ever before.[20] The figures are so compelling that it might seem that one need look no further than the demography of the slave trade to understand why there was a Haitian Revolution.

However, this upsurge in immigration did not greatly change the overall shape of Saint-Domingue's already populous society. Because the white and free colored populations also grew rapidly in this period, the balance between slave and free and between black and white remained fairly stable and within the norms of the non-Hispanic Caribbean. The remarkable population growth reported in the late colonial censuses was partly due to improved record-keeping. Saint-Domingue underwent an extraordinary boom, but other slave societies (Cuba, Guadeloupe) knew similar spurts of growth and several Caribbean colonies (Grenada, Antigua, Tobago, Suriname) had even more unbalanced populations,[21] although the combination of a highly unbalanced *and* a rapidly expanding population was much more unusual.

One need also note that the fastest-growing of Saint-Domingue's three provinces in the 1780s was not the North, the home of the 1791 uprising, but the underdeveloped South Province.[22] Between the 1775 and 1789 censuses, the North grew far more slowly than both the South and West.[23] The great majority of new migrants, moreover, were absorbed into the rapidly expanding coffee sector and went to live in the mountains of Saint-Domingue,[24] precisely those areas that were drawn most slowly into the Haitian Revolution. This was especially true of the Kongolese, whom John Thornton has arrestingly depicted as exiled soldiers.[25] While this depiction significantly reshapes understanding of the 1791 insurgents, it is not evident that such military captives were more prominent in the slave trade of the 1780s than earlier. Most important, the slave revolt of 1791 broke out amid the most creolized part of the slave population and was led by locally born slaves. Thus it remains far from clear that the rapid expansion of the slave trade made the Haitian Revolution more likely.

One could argue that the demographic ratio most relevant to social control was that between slaves and the European soldiers of the garrison. Although the logic is perhaps a little too elementary to appeal to all scholars, the colonial garrisons were the last line of defense against revolts, and an extensive body of evidence shows that slave conspiracies and rebellions in the Americas often occurred at times of declining garrison strength.[26] The French Caribbean was more strongly garrisoned than the British until the mid-1780s. Saint-Domingue's peacetime garrison apparently maintained a ratio close to 100 slaves for every soldier, and in wartime it was far lower.[27] During the American Revolutionary War more than 8,000 French troops as well as Spanish forces were stationed in the colony.[28] In the British West Indies, troop levels were maintained after the war and then increased, but the concentration of soldiers in Saint-Domingue was abruptly dispersed in the mid-1780s, just when the slave population was growing most rapidly.

The ratio of slaves to soldiers shot up to more than 150 to 1, even with a garrison at full strength, and began climbing sharply. In January 1788, the garrison was in fact 16 percent under strength.[29] Furthermore, although the slave population roughly doubled during the 1770s and 1780s, the number of rural police (200) remained unchanged.[30] The situation became even more precarious after the outbreak of the French Revolution, when the garrison had difficulty maintaining its numbers. It is true that the South was always the most lightly garrisoned part of Saint-Domingue. Yet the greatest absolute and relative declines in troop levels, the most likely to encourage slaves' reassessment of the balance of power, occurred in the North. This took place in the mid-1780s when the wartime military buildup, which was concentrated in that province, came to a belated end. Even before the disruption of the French Revolution, therefore, slaves in the North Province had good cause to feel that the prospects for successful resistance were improving.

Access to freedom through legal channels, on the other hand, was clearly diminishing in the late ancien régime. Manumission, the freeing of slaves by legal instrument, has often been regarded as a safety valve for slave regimes that encouraged compliance by offering hope. In Saint-Domingue, however, alarm at the growth of the free black population caused the administration after 1775 to make the freeing of slaves more difficult, and after brief improvements in 1779 and 1785, the number of manumissions declined precipitously on the eve of the revolution (see table 1.1).[31]

Although the odds of being freed were good compared with those of a modern lottery, the great majority of those emancipated were women and children of white fathers. Black males, including children, made up merely 14 to 16 percent of the manumitted. They had never been favored for manumission, but black slaves' access to freedom was evidently being limited by increasing competition from those of mixed racial descent.[32] Scarce regional data suggest that slaves in the North Province had similar chances of being freed to those in the rest of the colony but that the situation there for men, after improving somewhat, declined sharply. In 1789, only seven black males were freed out of a regional population of more than 190,000.

How important this trend may have been in disappointing the expectations of the enslaved depends on whether this restriction of official manumission encouraged masters to de facto free slaves without paying the fees that legalized the change of status. Slave-owners may have increasingly evaded the requirement. It is also plausible that the rising cost of slaves in these years discouraged all types of manumission.[33] Uncertainty about the extent of unofficial emancipation mandates caution, therefore. Yet it would seem that if manumission did strengthen the slave regime in Saint-Domingue, it was through co-opting enslaved women, typically domestic servants, who hoped that they or their children would one day be freed. It had much less impact on the black males who made up the majority of the slave population, and insofar as it was a safety valve, it appears to have been almost closed shut before the outbreak of the revolution.

Changes in other aspects of slave treatment are much harder to discern. The historians who assert that conditions on Saint-Domingue's plantations worsened in the late colonial period collectively make three assertions: that atrocities increased in response to fears caused by population imbalance; that workload also increased, in response either to soil exhaustion or to booming demand; and that food supplies became inadequate for the growing population. The reasoning is always a priori and without supporting evidence. Empirical investigation of these issues in a colony with 8,000 plantations is, however, a daunting task and fraught with methodological problems. At a very general level, it is unlikely that, by Caribbean standards, Saint Domingue was an exceptionally deadly place for slaves. By 1790, it had imported about as many Africans as had neighboring Jamaica (and its African immigrants had a man-to-woman ratio that was less favorable to reproduction than that of Jamaica's

Table 1.1.	Official Manumissions		
Year	Total Freed	Female Percent	Black Percent
1785	739	65	45
1786	411	64	na[1]
1787	273	na	na
1788	297	67	43
1789	256	63	41

[1] na = "not available."

Sources: C9A/159, f.183, C9A/158, f.37, C9A/156, manumission statistics for 1785 (corrected), and C9B/37, letter of January 16, 1787, all in CAOM; Barbé-Marbois, État des finances (Port-au-Prince, 1789), table 5; Proisy, État des finances (Port-au-Prince, 1790), 31 and table 4.

African immigrants), yet it had a much larger slave population.[34] This, however, does not exclude the possibility that conditions worsened through time.

Insofar as a trend can be perceived in the incidence of atrocities against slaves, it was apparently toward diminution. Contemporaries remarked that by 1770 they were becoming less common as slave-owners' mores became more civilized.[35] Official executions were fewer and the administration was, according to some, more willing to intervene against "private justice."[36] Heinous acts of cruelty persisted, without any doubt, but the gradual humanizing of European culture in these decades (and perhaps the rising price of slaves) make it unlikely that atrocities were really more common, especially as no contemporary seems to have thought so.

Two general reasons for doubting that the conditions of slave life worsened after 1750 are the increasing percentage of locally born slaves in the population and the increasing proportion that worked on coffee and cotton plantations. Creoles lived healthier and socially more complete lives than transplanted Africans, and their growing numbers progressively brought down the imbalance between men and women from 18 to 10 in 1730 to about 12 to 10 in the 1780s.[37] Coffee and cotton, the colony's main growth sectors after 1750, were considerably less demanding on their workforces than sugar, which by 1791 employed less than one-third of the enslaved population.[38] Technological advances, moreover, went some way in these years toward eliminating the most exhausting tasks in both coffee and indigo production.[39] The growth of these secondary crops also increased the presence of resident owners among the planter class, which colonists and historians have generally thought positive for slaves. Certainly the grueling labor involved in creating new plantations offset these factors, to an unknowable degree, but by the 1780s land clearance had become a diminishing proportion of the slaves' work.[40]

On sugar estates an increasing ratio of slaves to caneland seems to indicate that workloads were diminishing in the last two decades of slavery, but it may simply reflect the long-term trend toward producing semi-refined sugar, which demanded more workers in the manufacturing stage than did muscovado. It may also reflect a tendency to replant cane more frequently and ratoon less frequently.[42] These factors may explain the seemingly higher workload on northern estates. However, the generally lower fertility rates of enslaved women on northern estates suggest that the work regime there was harsher and that it perhaps grew worse during this 20-year period (see table 1.2).

Low fertility, of course, can be related to poor nutrition as well as overwork. Although there is reason to believe that slaves were better fed in the north than elsewhere in Saint-Domingue, pressure on locally grown food supplies was most likely to be felt on Northern Plain estates because they had the smallest reserves of new land and were the most affected by soil depletion.

Table 1.2	TRENDS IN WORKLOAD ON SUGAR PLANTATIONS		
Region	Time Period	Acres of Caneland per Slave	Number of Plantations
North	1770s	1.73	23
	1780s	1.66	43
	1790–1791	1.53	9
West and South	1770s	1.40	12
	1780s	1.30	26
	1790–1791	1.31	11

Table 1.3	TRENDS IN FERTILITY ON SUGAR PLANTATIONS			
Region	Time Period	Mean Fertility Index[1]	Median Fertility Index	Number of Plantations
North	1770s	.309	.314	21
	1780s	.333	.303	36
	1790–1791	.215	.222	7
West and South	1770s	.364	.356	7
	1780s	.368	.290	14
	1790–1791	.408	.443	6

[1.] Fertility index = children 0–4 years/women 15–44 years.

Sources: Personal database. Most of the sources for Tables 1.2 and 1.3 are listed in Geggus, "Sugar and Coffee Cultivation in Saint Domingue and the Shaping of the Slave Labor Force," in Cultivation and Culture: Labor and the Shaping of Slave Life in the Americas, ed. Ira Berlin, Philip Morgan (Charlottesville: University Press of Virginia, 1993), 95–96; and Geggus, "The Sugar Plantation Zones of Saint Domingue and the Revolution of 1791–1793," Slavery & Abolition 20 (1999): note 8. Additional sources include Archives départementales de l'Eure et Loire, Chartres, 24 J art. 145 (Peyrac); 92APC/5/16 (Gérard), Notsdom 405 (Des Varrennes), Notsdom 934 (De Luynes), Notsdom 1396 (Minière de Tressain), Notsdom 1712, d.14 (Chantelot), and Notsdom 1713 d.7 (La Serre), all in CAOM; HCA 30/273 (Caillau/D'Orlic and Laugardière), Public Record Office, London; Greffe 3:17 (Foäche), Jérémie Papers, University of Florida, Gainesville; Slavery and Plantations in Saint Domingue Collection (Rocheblave, and Molie/Villeneuve), University of Florida, Gainesville; Affiches Américaines (Port-au-Prince): July 1786 (Dubreuil de Fontroux), April 1787 (Duburqua/Durocher), and August 1787 (Audubon); Bernard Foubert, "L'Habitation Leroux," Revue de la Société Haïtienne d'Histoire 212 and 213 (2002) (Leroux); Jean-Louis Donnadieu, "Entre Gascogne et Saint-Domingue" (Thèse de doctorat, Université de Pau, 2006) (Noé).

Most had highland provision grounds, but soil erosion and declining rainfall were already impacting the northern mountains, and the 1787 and 1788 censuses show a 5 percent decline across the colony in the acreage devoted to food crops, although the reliability of these statistics is admittedly dubious.[43] The opening of new free ports brought improved access to imported foodstuffs, particularly at Cap-Français, but contemporaries disagreed about whether this was an adequate solution.

Besides population pressure and environmental decline, natural disasters were the other main threat to the food supply. These were, however, a regular feature of Caribbean life. In Saint-Domingue, the most drought-prone plantation zones (the northeast and northwest) were not the most prompt to rebel in the 1790s. It may be significant, even so, that the drought of 1790 was the worst in living memory. As in 1776 and 1786, some slaves were left to fend for themselves, to scavenge and seek out odd jobs in return for food. Such abandonment in the basic matter of subsistence must have undermined whatever paternalist claims were made by the slave-owners concerned.[44] It would also have facilitated contact between slaves over a wide area and thus the mobilization of the discontented.

Gabriel Debien devoted the final chapter of his magnum opus on French West Indian slavery to the question of whether the slave regime became less harsh during the years after 1770. He found evidence of better treatment of new arrivals, the sick, pregnant women, and newborns, but he concluded that such improvements were piecemeal and affected only a minority of plantations.[45] Such a scenario of scattered improvements might have encouraged a sense of relative deprivation among the majority of slaves who did not benefit and thus increased levels of discontent.[46] The same is perhaps true of the royal government's attempted reforms of 1784–1785, which created a storm of protest among colonists and a flurry of strike action by slaves and apparently remained a dead letter.[47] This effort by the late ancien régime administration to intervene between slave and slave-owner is perhaps most important, however, for its having created a plausible basis for the royalist ideology that the slave insurgents would adroitly use in 1791, when they claimed to be acting in the name of the king.

This brings us to the white population of Saint-Domingue. While it seems appropriate to devote most attention to the slaves, the Haitian Revolution began nonetheless at the apex of colonial society as a pursuit of self-government and free trade by both resident and absentee sections of the planter class. White settler autonomism had a long history in the colony. The 1670s, 1720s, and 1760s had each seen brief rebellions against the agents of royal authority. The 1780s brought much to encourage and alarm wealthy slave-owners who identified with the French *pays d'état* and envied British colonists their cheap slaves and self-government. The independence of the

United States had shown that a colonial rebellion could be successful and respectable, and trade relations with the new mainland republic expanded in the postwar period, when Yankee merchants opened businesses in Le Cap and Port-au-Prince. Probably only the wildest dreamers imagined that an easily blockaded island whose colonists were greatly outnumbered by slaves could emulate the mainland colonies' secession, but to others a British protectorate may have seemed feasible.[48]

In some quarters, the cultural adaptation of planters to the tropical milieu perhaps reinforced the sense of separate identity forged by divergent interests. So many young whites spoke Creole better than French that a newspaper editor suggested replacing the Latin Mass with a French one to teach them the mother tongue. Some colonists preferred cassava to wheaten bread. Young white women copied women of color in dress and mannerisms.[49] But all this is easily exaggerated.

A far more immediate threat to imperial ties was the battery of reforms launched by the late ancien régime government that alienated a wide spectrum of the white population. Slave-owners and plantation employees were angered by the 1784–1785 decrees and bursts of judicial activism and administrative intervention that sought to limit their abuse of slaves and punish atrocities.[50] The abolition of the Cap-Français appeal court, whose role paralleled that of the *parlements* in France, earned the enmity of its numerous lawyers and was a blow to all North Province colonists.[51] Mercantilist trade laws were relaxed somewhat, but efforts to combat smuggling were stepped up. Finally, the intendant Barbé-Marbois (1785–89) reclaimed a mountain of debts from lax officials, ran roughshod over the colonists' few fiscal privileges, and initiated reform of sensitive issues such as debt law and land grants. A paragon of vigorous efficiency, he became one of the revolution's first casualties.[52]

This conflict between the administration and colonial whites fits quite well with R. R. Palmer's concept of an "aristocratic reaction." The revolution would take a democratic turn in 1789 only because of the explosive militancy of the *petits blancs*, the artisans, clerks, seamen, and plantation personnel of European origin. They burst on the scene, in the minds of some observers, "as if from underground."[53] As the main colony of Europe's most populated country, Saint-Domingue had always attracted indigent young males seeking employment, but migration seems to have surged with the economic crisis in France of the late 1780s. The net inflow of passengers (which was 85 percent male) together with deserting seamen exceeded 1,950 in the period 1788–1789, and the rate of arrival increased in the first half of 1790.[54] This presumably explains why some contemporaries (and later historians) were surprised at the later prominence in the revolution of the white working class and unemployed.

The role they played was marked by an extreme hostility to the free people of color, the colony's third major population group, with whom they competed for jobs. These *gens de couleur libres* grew rapidly during the decades before the revolution, not just in numbers but also in wealth. Although many historians have exaggerated their ownership of land and slaves, they were exceptional by American standards for including a substantial group of middling planters as well as urban proprietors.[55] They stood out all the more in Saint-Domingue because the wealthiest whites were absentees. The government's response to this upward mobility was a growing body of discriminatory legislation and an increasingly punctilious policing of the color line. After 1760, race relations quickly lost the flexibility they had once had. Banned from certain jobs and from wearing certain clothing and segregated in public venues, people of color also suffered extralegal harassment that ranged from petty humiliation to vicious assaults.[56]

This combination of upward mobility confronted by repression was potentially explosive because free men of color made up about half of the colonial militia by 1789 and most of the rural police. During the War of American Independence, two free colored battalions had seen service overseas, which provided military experience to several future revolutionary leaders. The experience encouraged some of the wealthiest men of color to lobby the colonial ministry about reforming the regime of racial discrimination. Their arguments were sympathetically heard by the minister, de Castries, but officials in Saint-Domingue continued to discourage any innovation through the 1780s. Debate went on in the corridors of power whether a policy of humiliating or co-opting free people of African descent would do least to destabilize the slave regime.[57] As white opinion was not monolithic, it is uncertain how that debate would have developed.

Also uncertain is how explosive the racial question was in Saint-Domingue. Some contemporaries thought harassment of *gens de couleur* was worsening. But Dominique Rogers has recently argued that the overall picture was one of increasing integration.[58] Moreover, although their numbers and sense of identity were growing, the free people of color were a very diverse and fragmented group, and they would behave with similar diversity in the revolution.

Separate channels of lava beneath the colonial volcano, free colored activism, white settler autonomism, and slave resistance all had complex prehistories quite independent of the French Revolution. Their explosive potential seems obvious in hindsight, as it did to many eighteenth-century observers. But that potential was realized only through the seismic tremors that issued from revolutionary France. How we read the balance between stress and stability in late colonial Saint-Domingue will ultimately depend on our individual susceptibility to materialist and idealist arguments and to local and external factors. Regrettably, the facts do not suggest a coherent picture of either mounting pressure or steady equilibrium.

Were it possible to construct a "misery index" for the slave population, it is debatable whether it would have been higher in 1789 than in 1750. There are, nevertheless, several indications that if slaves were being worked harder than in the past and going hungrier, it was probably in the Northern Plain. Moreover, if objective conditions were not worse in the aggregate, the scattered attempts some planters made to improve conditions may have provoked a sense of relative deprivation among slaves. The ineffective reform efforts of the administration may have produced a similar result and may have revealed cracks in the power structure that could be exploited. On the other hand, the revolutionary potential of the slave population's dramatic growth is not as obvious as it first seems, although its relation to the military component of social control and to trends in manumission warrant further investigation.

Slave resistance, in my view, was chiefly important for keeping alive a spirit of contestation. The popular picture of massing bands of maroons linked to a network of Vodou priests is entirely mythical, although of the four main leaders of the 1791 uprising, one was a maroon and perhaps two were Vodou priests. The documentary evidence does hint at a religious organization that was bringing together different ethnic groups before the revolution, but as long as it promoted magical rather than political remedies to real-world problems, its revolutionary potential was limited. Maroon band activity clearly diminished in the 1780s, and it may be that decreasing opportunities for maroonage made armed revolt more likely.

If the French Revolution had occurred two or three decades earlier, one might wonder if the slave, or indeed white, populations would have behaved any differently than in 1789. Only among free people of color, then a community in embryo, might a different reaction have been expected. Even so, the autonomist leanings of the planter class were undoubtedly strengthened by the United States example and the late ancien régime's program of colonial reform. By the time the French state went bankrupt in the summer of 1788, colonists were already concerting opposition to the colonial administration, drawing inspiration from the reform movement in France, and they quickly picked up the demand for representation in the States-General that was to link the colonial and metropolitan revolutions inextricably.

Notes

1. Despite considerable uncertainty about price levels and the dimensions of contraband commerce, there can be little doubt that exports were worth at least 22 million dollars, easily twice as much as the private bullion shipped from Brazil or Mexico, i.e. excluding royal taxes, and were equivalent to the average annual amount of silver coined in Mexico around 1790. See David Geggus, "Urban Development in Eighteenth Century Saint Domingue," *Bulletin du Centre d'Histoire des Espaces Atlantiques* 5 (1990): 228;

Fernando A. Novais, *Portugal e Brasil na crise do antigo sistema colonial (1777–1808)* (São Paulo, 1979), 306–390; John Fisher, *Commercial Relations between Spain and Spanish America in the Era of Free Trade, 1778–1796* (Liverpool, 1985), 61; Leslie Bethell, ed., *Colonial Spanish America* (Cambridge, 1987), 139–141; David Brading, *Miners and Merchants in Bourbon Mexico* (Cambridge, 1971), 131.

2. Jean Philippe Garran Coulon, *Rapport sur les troubles de Saint-Domingue*, 4 vols. (Paris, 1797–1799), 4:18; Paul Vaissière, *Saint-Domingue: la société et la vie créoles* (Paris, 1909), 174, 230; Yves Benot, *La Révolution française et la fin des colonies* (Paris, 1987), 26–29; Paul Ulric Dubuisson, Julien-Antoine Dubuc-Duféret, *Lettres critiques et politiques sur les colonies et le commerce des villes maritimes de France, adressées à G.T. Raynal* (Geneva, 1785).

3. Michel-Rolph Trouillot, *Silencing the Past* (Boston, 1995), ch. 3.

4. For an example of each: Commission des Colonies, *Débats entre les accusateurs et les accusés dans l'affaire des colonies*, 9 vols. (Paris, 1795), 1:100–103; entry for September 5, 1789, C 4364, Archives départementales de la Gironde, Bordeaux; letters of October 1789, C9A/162, Centre des Archives d'Outre-mer, Aix-en-Provence (hereafter CAOM).

5. Benot, *La Révolution française*, 26–27; Prosper Boissonnade, "Saint-Domingue à la veille de la Révolution," *Mémoires de la Société des Antiquaires de l'Ouest* 29 (1905): 555–556.

6. Jacques-François Dutrône de Couture, *Précis sur la canne* (Paris, 1790), 343–346; *Les j'ai vu d'un habitant du Cap. Nouvelle edition* (Cap-Français: 1790), 2; *Histoire des désastres de Saint-Domingue* (Paris, 1795), 17–18, 81–85; Gabriel Debien and Charles Frostin, "Papiers des Antilles III," *Cahiers des Amériques Latines* 1 (1968): 203.

7. Vaissière, *Saint-Domingue*, 232–234.

8. "Réflexions sur la position actuelle," F3/192, CAOM (also in John Carter Brown Library, Providence, Codex Fr 19); *Histoire des désastres*, 52.

9. David Geggus, *Haitian Revolutionary Studies* (Bloomington, 2001), ch. 5.

10. This section draws on many collections of plantation papers; see below, note 41. Relevant published studies include Geggus, *Haitian Revolutionary Studies*, ch. 5; Geggus, "Une famille de La Rochelle et ses plantations de Saint-Domingue," in *France in the New World*, ed. D. Buisseret (East Lansing, 1998), 119–136; Bernard Foubert, "Le marronage sur les habitations Laborde à Saint-Domingue dans la seconde moitié du XVIIIe siècle," *Annales de Bretagne* 95 (1988): 277–310 (whose figures I have adjusted).

11. Regimental statistics in CAOM: D2C/99 and 105 (1786–1791), C9B/37 (1787), and F3/160, f. 116 (1765).

12. See the "wanted" ad in *Affiches Américaines, Feuille du Cap*, November 3, 1787.

13. For example, one source identifies as a maroon François Dechaussée, who participated in the Lenormand plantation meeting and subsequent attack on the Chabaud estate in August 1791: Limbé municipality report, Government Papers 8:5, Fisher Collection, New York Public Library.

14. David Geggus, "Haitian Voodoo in the Eighteenth Century: Language, Culture, Resistance," *Jahrbuch für Geschichte von Staat, Wirtschaft und Gesellschaft Lateinamerikas* 28 (1991): 21–51; Geggus, *Haitian Revolutionary Studies*, ch. 5.

15. *Procès-Verbaux des Séances et Journal des Débats* (Cap-Français), November 15, 1791. Historians have failed to recognize that the leader known as Médecin-Général was not Toussaint Louverture but Jeannot. Vodou was still acephalous in the twentieth century.

16. However, the significance of the Bois-Caïman ceremony of August 1791 has been much exaggerated, and according to West African historian Robin Law was not necessarily a Petro ceremony: Geggus, *Haitian Revolutionary Studies*, ch. 6.

17. C. L. R. James, *The Black Jacobins* (New York, 1963), 16.

18. Pierre Pluchon, *Vaudou, sorciers, empoisonneurs: de Saint-Domingue à Haïti* (Paris, 1987), 165, 170–182, 208–219, 308–315; M.-R. Hilliard d'Auberteuil, *Considérations sur l'état présent de la colonie française de Saint-Domingue*, 2 vols. (Paris, 1776–1777), 1:137–138.

19. Geggus, "The Major Port Towns of Saint Domingue in the Late Eighteenth Century," in *Atlantic Port Cities*, ed. Franklin Knight and Peggy Liss (Knoxville, 1991), 101–104.

20. Geggus, "The French Slave Trade: An Overview," *William and Mary Quarterly* 58 (2001): 119–138; David Eltis, *The Trans-Atlantic Slave Trade: A Revised and Enlarged Database, 1500–1867*, forthcoming.

21. These comments hold true even for high estimates of the slave population of up to 600,000, which I believe are exaggerated.

22. Report of June 28, 1789, C9A/163, CAOM, which shows a growth rate nearly 50 percent higher there than in the rest of the colony. The figures for 1788 and 1789 in the introduction to Ducoeurjoly, *Manuel des habitants de Saint-Domingue* (2 vols. [Paris, 1802]), show 4 percent growth in the north and 9 percent elsewhere.

23. By 50 percent as compared to 78 percent. See G1/509, CAOM; Vincent-René de Proisy, *État des finances de Saint-Domingue* (Port-au-Prince, 1790), table 10.

24. Morange to Foäche, July 19, 1789, 505 Mi 85, Archives Nationales, Paris (hereafter AN); Félix Carteau, *Soirées bermudiennes* (Paris, 1802), 299; *Histoire des désastres*, 81–85.

25. John Thornton, "African Soldiers in the Haitian Revolution," *Journal of Caribbean History* 25 (1993): 58–80.

26. David Geggus, "The Enigma of Jamaica in the 1790s," *William and Mary Quarterly* (1987): 292–299. For additional data, see Geggus, "Slavery, War, and Revolution in the Greater Caribbean," in *A Turbulent Time: The French Revolution and the Greater Caribbean*, ed. D. Gaspar and D. Geggus (Bloomington, 1997), 35n31; Jean-Claude Nardin, *La mise en valeur de l'isle de Tabago (1763–1783)* (Paris, 1969), 211.

27. A scattering of (sometimes contradictory) military data from the 1720s onward can be found in F3/160, f. 109–117, CAOM; 195 Mi 1, dossier 8/16, AN; M. L. E. Moreau de Saint-Méry, *Description . . . de la partie françoise de l'isle Saint-Domingue*, 3 vols. (1979, repr., Paris, 1958), 2:1006–1007, 1013; and Beauvais Lespinasse, *Histoire des affranchis de Saint-Domingue*, 143–144, 159–160, 168–170, 180–183. Colonial censuses are in G1/509, CAOM.

28. 195 Mi 1, dossier 8/16, AN. According to J. Abeille, *Essai sur nos colonies* (Paris, 1805), 42, the total reached between 15,000 and 20,000 troops. Some, expelled from the east Caribbean, stayed only briefly.

29. Garrison statistics, C9A/161, CAOM.

30. Stewart King, *Blue Coat or Powdered Wig: Free People of Color in Pre-Revolutionary Saint Domingue* (Athens, 2001), 59. King notes that the *maréchaussée* compensated by using unpaid supernumerary troopers, who could number six per regular *cavalier*. In the North, however, they were rare, "impossible to find," according to Moreau de Saint-Méry, *Description*, 1:441.

31. Barbé to Castries, January 16, 1787, and Barbé to Montmorin, December 13, 1787 , C9B/37, CAOM. For reasons unknown, Peytraud, *Esclavage*, 492, gives a slightly higher figure for 1785 manumissions, and Moreau de Saint-Méry, in *Considérations présentées aux vrais amis du repos et du bonheur de la France* (Paris, 1791), 36, states that 1,765 (instead of 1,976) people were freed in 1785–1789. The peak in 1785 was partly due to the decision of the departing intendant, de Bongars, to waive the manumission tax for numerous administrative colleagues. Although a subset of the total, the 1,630 notarized acts of manumission from the period 1776–1789 studied in Dominique Rogers, "Les libres de couleur dans les capitales de Saint-Domingue: fortune, mentalités et intégration à la fin de l'Ancien régime (1776–1789)" (Thèse de doctorat de l'université, Université de Bordeaux III, 1999), 69–80, 274–289, are particularly valuable.

32. See the samples of manumittees from earlier periods in Gautier, *Les soeurs de Solitude* (Paris, 1985), 172; John Garrigus, "A Struggle for Respect: Free Coloreds in Pre-Revolutionary Saint Domingue" (Ph.D. diss., Johns Hopkins University, 1988), 422–423; King, *Blue Coat or Powdered Wig*, 44, 108; and Rogers, "Les libres de couleur," 71. Service with the *maréchaussée*, nonwhite militia, and the Chasseur battalions of 1779 and 1780 did offer men an exclusive avenue to freedom and helped boost the male percentage of manumittees around 1780.

33. The average price of Africans disembarked from slave ships rose by 28 percent to 2,134 livres from 1783 to 1789. See Geggus, "The French Slave Trade," note 38; La Luzerne, *Mémoire envoyé le 18 juin 1790* (Paris, 1790), 70. The manumission tax for women was 2,000 livres.

34. This assumes that 15,000 Africans reached Saint-Domingue in the seventeenth century and that the inter-island trade supplied an additional 10 percent beyond the data in David Eltis, Stephen Behrendt, David Richardson, and Herbert Klein, *The Transatlantic Slave Trade: A Database on CD-ROM* (Cambridge, 1999); and David Eltis, *The Rise of African Slavery in the Americas* (Cambridge, 2000).

35. F3/90, f. 155, 268, CAOM; "Remarques sur la colonie" (ca. 1780), Ms. 3453, f. 36–37, Bibliothèque Mazarine, Paris; Peynier and Marbois to La Luzerne, September 25, 1789, C9A/162, CAOM; Vaissière, *Saint-Domingue*, 192–194.

36. F3/150, f. 78–83, CAOM.

37. Censuses 1681–1788, G1/509, CAOM; "Tableau de la population . . . 1789," Special Collections, University of Florida. Overall sexual imbalance was lower, since censuses tended to omit the elderly (who were mostly women).

38. The author of *Histoire des désastres* is unusually critical of coffee plantations for their negligent planters and inhospitably cold climate but still accepts that the work regime was worse on sugar estates (pp. 65–66). He is conspicuously weak on demography.

39. On the grinding and winnowing mills that extracted coffee beans, see Carteau, *Soirées bermudiennes*, 297; *Histoire des désastres*, 105–106. On the mechanical paddles

used in indigo basins, see Geggus, "Indigo and Slavery," in *Slavery without Sugar*, ed. Verene Shepherd (Gainesville, 2001), 21.

40. This is probably the main reason the premium paid for adult male slaves declined after the 1760s.

41. Most of the sources are listed in Geggus, "Sugar and Coffee Cultivation in Saint Domingue and the Shaping of the Slave Labor Force," in *Cultivation and Culture: Labor and the Shaping of Slave Life in the Americas*, ed. Ira Berlin and Philip Morgan (Charlottesville, 1993), 95–96; and Geggus, "The Sugar Plantation Zones of Saint Domingue and the Revolution of 1791–1793," *Slavery & Abolition* 20 (1999): 44. Additional sources include 24 J art. 145 (Peyrac), Archives départementales de l'Eure et Loire, Chartres; CAOM: 92APC/5/16 (Gérard), Notsdom 405 (Des Varrennes), Notsdom 934 (De Luynes), Notsdom 1396 (Minière de Tressain), Notsdom 1712, d.14 (Chantelot), and Notsdom 1713 d.7 (La Serre); HCA 30/273 (Caillau/D'Orlic and Laugardière), Public Record Office, London; Greffe 3:17 (Foäche), Jérémie Papers, University of Florida, Gainesville; Slavery and Plantations in Saint Domingue Collection (Rocheblave and Molie/Villeneuve), University of Florida; *Affiches Américaines* (Port-au-Prince), July 1786 (Dubreuil de Fontroux), April 1787 (Duburqua/Durocher), and August 1787 (Audubon); Bernard Foubert, "L'Habitation Leroux," *Revue de la Société Haïtienne d'Histoire* 212 & 213 (2002) (Leroux); Jean-Louis Donnadieu, "Entre Gascogne et Saint-Domingue" (Thèse de doctorat, Université de Pau, 2006) (Noé).

42. Geggus, "The Sugar Plantation Zones of Saint Domingue," 31–46. Using the erroneous equivalence of 1 *carreau* = 1.137 hectares (it should be 1.292 hectares), colonial historians, including myself, have hitherto understated land areas. The error, which may have resulted from confusing the English foot and the French *pied*, apparently derives from the 1958 edition of Moreau de Saint-Méry, *Description*, 1:16, which has misled two generations of scholars. Ratoon canes grew from the roots of harvested canes. They yielded less than "plant canes" but obviated the back-breaking work of planting.

43. C9A/160, f. 335–336, CAOM. According to Matts Lundahl, *The Haitian Economy: Man, Land, and Markets* (New York, 1983), the environmental impact of food crops is particularly deleterious.

44. James C. Scott argues that access to subsistence and reciprocity between subordinate and dominant classes have been central to peasants' sense of social justice (*Moral Economy of the Peasant: Subsistence and Rebellion in Southeast Asia* [New Haven, 1976], 157–160, 165–179) and that the gap between ideology and reality prevents the achievement of hegemony and stimulates resistance (*Weapons of the Weak: Everyday Forms of Peasant Resistance* [New Haven, 1985], 317, 336–338).

45. Gabriel Debien, *Les esclaves aux Antilles françaises aux XVIIe et XVIIIe siècles* (Basse Terre, 1974), 471–495.

46. Although the concept of relative deprivation as an explanation for group behavior fell from academic favor after T. R. Gurr's controversial *Why Men Rebel*, it has since regained popularity. See Iain Walker and Heather Smith, eds., *Relative Deprivation: Specification, Development, and Integration* (Princeton, 2001).

47. Letters of March–November 1785, 505 Mi 85, AN; F3/126, f. 417–418, CAOM.

48. Gabriel Debien, *Les colons de Saint-Domingue et la Révolution française: essai sur le Club Massiac* (Paris, 1953); Charles Frostin, "L'Histoire de l'esprit autonomiste colon

à Saint-Domingue aux XVIIe et XVIIIe siècles" (Thèse de doctorat d'état, Université de Paris I, 1972).

49. *Affiches Américaines, Feuille du Port-au-Prince*, July 1790; Ms 3453, f. 71, Bibliothèque Mazarine; Justin Girod de Chantrans, *Voyage d'un Suisse dans différentes colonies d'Amérique*, ed. Pierre Pluchon (Paris, 1980), 152–155.

50. Pierre Pluchon, *Nègres et Juifs au XVIIIe siècle* (Paris, 1984), 164–188; Malick Ghachem, "Sovereignty and Slavery in the Age of Revolution: Haitian Variations on a Metropolitan Theme" (Ph.D. diss., Harvard University, 2001), 120–142, 156–170, 255–298; note 47 above.

51. The court's abolition in 1787 looks like a dry run for the government attack on the *parlements* the following year. It was touted twenty years later as a model for future metropolitan reforms in Guillaume Lamardelle, *Réforme judiciaire* (Paris, 1806).

52. See especially letters of February 17, May 4, September 11, and December 23, 1788, C9A/161, CAOM.

53. Robert R. Palmer, *The Age of the Democratic Revolution*, vol. 1 (Princeton, 1959); Geggus, *Slavery, War and Revolution* (Oxford, 1982), 34–35; Anne-Louis Tousard, *Tousard, Lieutenant-colonel* (Paris, 1793), 8; Lincoln to Stanislas Foäche, July 5, 1792, 505 Mi 80, AN.

54. Shipping statistics in *Affiches Américaines*, 1788–1790; Gabriel Chastenet-Destère, *Considérations sur l'état présent de la colonie française de Saint-Domingue* (Paris, 1796), 47.

55. They were almost entirely absent from the sugar sector. As coffee planters, they appear in the notarial archives infrequently, usually as very small-scale proprietors. However, a study of the Artibonite plain, where free coloreds were numerous, is critically needed.

56. Yvan Debbasch, *Couleur et liberté: le jeu du critère ethnique dans l'ordre juridique esclavagiste* (Paris: Dalloz, 1967); King, *Blue Coat or Powdered Wig*; John Garrigus, "Colour, Class and Identity on the Eve of the Haitian Revolution: Saint Domingue's Coloured Elite as *Colons Américains*," in *Against the Odds: Free Blacks in the Slave Societies of the Americas*, ed. Jane Landers (London, 1996), 20–43; letters of March 11 and September 25, 1786, C9B/36, CAOM.

57. John Garrigus, "Catalyst or Catastrophe? Saint Domingue's Free Men of Color and the Battle of Savannah," *Revista/Review Interamericana* 22 (1992): 109–125; Debbasch, *Couleur et liberté*, 108–131.

58. T650/1/5, f. 9, AN; Rogers, "Les libres de couleur," 589–594.

Vestiges of the Built Landscape of Pre-Revolutionary Saint-Domingue

Jacques de Cauna

EVEN MORE SO THAN IN THE ENGLISH, SPANISH, AND PORTUGUESE COL-ONIES, THE LARGE PLANTATION (*HABITATION*) HAS BEEN THE CRUCIBLE OF THE CREOLE SOCIETY OF THE "FRENCH ISLANDS OF AMERICA."[1] It was a place of interracial blending where a specific sociocultural identity was formed, principally in the eighteenth century with the tremendous expansion of the sugar agro-industry and the massive influx of Africans.[2] Far more than the ephemeral maritime exploits of the buccaneers, the failed attempts to settle whites using indentured servitude, or the weak efforts at urban development, the large-scale plantation has left an indelible mark on the land, particularly in Haiti, the former Saint-Domingue, "queen of the West Indies" and "pride of France in the New World."[3] In Haiti, to this day a country that has remained very rural, plantations are still a central reference point and have profoundly marked the people's mindset. The first question asked by peasants meeting for the first time is: "*Ki bitasyon nou sòti?*" (Which plantation are you from?)

Saint-Domingue can be taken to represent the Caribbean experience because of the size of its territory (twenty-five times that of Martinique), the size of its population (six times that of Martinique, receiving eight out of ten passengers sailing to the French islands), and because of its output (six or seven times that of Martinique or Guadeloupe, more than all the British and Spanish West Indies combined, more than a third of France's entire foreign trade). It is notable that Gascons made up 40 percent of Saint-Domingue's colonists, and their influence is particularly evident on the colony's architecture, its place-names and family names, and its mentality.[4]

In spite of its continued presence in the everyday life of Haiti, which is apparent even in individual behavior and is especially visible in the rural areas that are the heart of the country, the colonial heritage has been little studied in Haiti itself and hardly at all outside, although it is a living museum of colonial plantation society.

Haiti's first-rank architectural heritage is exceptional but has been under serious threat since the 1980s, when it suffered considerable damage, and the problem has only increased since the fall of the Duvalier regime in 1986. In the capital, the old cathedral has been destroyed, but a few forts are still standing and the massive promenade of the Intendancy with its staircases and fountains remains. Elsewhere, churches, houses, bridges, paved roads, and various fortifications survive, particularly in Cap-Haïtien, which contains an entire district comparable to New Orleans's Vieux Carré, featuring houses with balconies, squares with fountains ornamented with the royal crown, and a grid of streets still bearing their ancien régime names.

In the Haitian countryside can be found remains of some of the 8,500 eighteenth-century plantations that made up the West Indies' most important network of rural businesses.[5] These ruins, which the rural *habitant* calls *vye mazi* or *bagay ansyen testament* (very old buildings, from the French *vieilles masures*; things from the olden times, i.e. before independence), are difficult to find and difficult to get to. They are progressively deteriorating due to the luxuriant vegetation that invades them and the effects of human negligence and depredation. They were left for a long time in a state of abandonment and ruin after the revolution, and their deterioration has accelerated since the beginning of the twentieth century. Population growth and the changes brought about by modernization, such as urbanization and the arrival of modern central sugar factories in the large plains, HASCO in the Cul-de-Sac and the Dessalines factory at Les Cayes, are among the causes. But whatever the causes, Haiti's colonial heritage is at the present time in great danger.

In the course of two lengthy stays in Haiti totaling thirteen years, I systematically visited the sites of more than 300 plantations (mainly sugar estates, but also coffee, indigo, and cotton plantations; distilleries; market gardens; lime kilns; tile factories; and so forth). These sites were located in the west (in the plains of Cul-de-Sac, l'Arcahaye, Léogane, and l'Artibonite and the hills of Pétionville, Saint-Marc, and Montrouis), in the north (the plain and mountains of Le Cap and Milot and Tortuga Island), and in the south (the Rochelois plateau, the plain of Les Cayes, and the little plains of Aquin, Jacmel, and the two Goâves). Employing the methodology of industrial archaeology, I first engaged in systematic research and inventorying of public archives, particularly cartographic resources but also the papers of notaries and public registrars, land surveys, and so forth in France—at the Centre d'Accueil et de Recherche des Archives Nationales in Paris and the Centre des Archives d'Outre-mer in Aix-en-Provence, in departmental and local archives, and especially in private collections, notably in the Aquitaine region. The latter are a mine of first-hand information about the daily life and management of plantations that include accounts, inventories, and managers' correspondence, as Gabriel Debien demonstrated. At the same time, I explored physical sites, made inquiries (in Creole), described the terrain (taking photographs, drawing plans), and undertook critical analysis of oral history and of contemporary Haitian perceptions in a manner similar to Nathan Wachtel's research on Peru.[6] The findings have been summarized in a number of articles, reports, and books.[7]

This body of research allowed me to relate the plantation system to its environment and to reach certain conclusions regarding typology, chronology, and function. The tenacious retention by Haitians of the memory of names reveals great resistance to change notwithstanding a tendency toward simplification in the names' creolized form.

The earliest agricultural ventures—annatto, cacao, tobacco, and market gardens—were relatively small and gave way to the beginnings of large-scale production on cotton and indigo plantations. With the first stable group of *habitants* early in the seventeenth century, food crops (manioc, sweet potatoes, bananas) occupied the greatest area. Three crops were exported: annatto, an indigenous plant inherited from the Arawaks whose grains produce a red dye; cacao, brought by the Spanish from Mexico to Hispaniola in 1525 and which Governor Bertrand d'Ogeron tried to develop in 1665 around Port Margot before it almost entirely disappeared in 1717 (none survives today); and above all tobacco, or *pétun*, whose use by the Indians Columbus noticed on his first voyage.

Only tobacco production passed beyond an artisanal stage of development, notably between 1660 and the peace of Nijmegen in 1697, thus fairly late and well after its introduction around the 1620s into St. Kitt's, Barbados, and the Chesapeake. Semi-wild in cultivation, tobacco required a large cleared land area and substantial numbers of white indentured servants to harvest, dry, and roll the leaves, but this work took place on relatively small plantations that used little equipment (mostly artisanal wooden mills for twisting). Tobacco cultivation has left very few traces. The drying sheds that can be seen in the plain of Les Cayes or near Jacmel, Gonaïves, and Le Cap (where artisanal cigars are still made) are reminders of this crop, and peasant women still smoke short white meerschaum pipes like those of the buccaneers.

The other types of places that existed at that time were brickworks, lime kilns (of which some examples survive), potteries (which have entirely vanished), and market gardens. The other export products were timber (the nineteenth century would see major destruction of ancient forests of ironwood and mahogany), hides from primitive tanneries, tortoiseshell, and a few spices and medicinal plants, notably cassia.

Cotton was one of the oldest export crops, dating from the early sixteenth century. At first it was neglected because of its mediocre quality and vulnerability to insects, but it revived with the Industrial Revolution of the late eighteenth century to become the colony's third most important export. It then accounted for about 5 percent of cultivated land area and was often grown in dry regions together with indigo. The cotton was picked from bushes six or seven feet high planted in staggered rows. The separation of seeds from the fibers (*épeluchage*) was performed using a wooden gin with two fluted wheels worked by a foot pedal. It was then packed into sacks of crude cloth (*balles*) weighing 300 pounds.[8] Plantation storehouses and sheds were typically made of wood and have left no trace, although a few fields of semi-wild cotton can still be seen around Gonaïves and Jacmel. (Fig. 2.1.)

Indigo, of the *franc* and *bâtard* varieties, was introduced into Saint-Pierre du Moustique in the North Plain in 1676 by French refugees from Samaná. It is a grass whose seeds sprout in two or three days and which adapts to drought better than sugar but not as well as cotton. Its most favorable environment was the clay soil of small plains and narrow valleys between the mountains, but it quickly exhausted the soil and was abandoned in the large plains. Indigo nonetheless still accounted for 22 percent of the land under cultivation on the eve of the revolution; these were dry lands that were unsuitable for sugar. A complicated preparation in vats made of masonry produced a dark blue dye that was very popular at that time, especially for the *gros bleu* cloth (the forerunner of blue denim) that was given to slaves. Indigo was, before sugar, the colonists' first source of wealth produced on large plantations. The slaves' work mainly consisted of cutting and carrying the plant, draining the paste in baskets called *couleuvres*, and packing it first in boxes and then in barrels after it had been dried and cut into pieces. The sole vestiges of these plantations, such as they can be seen on the Rival estate at Le Cap, or Glaize de Maisoncelle at Grand-Goâve, are the three stone vats: the *trempoire*, where the salts were dissolved; the *bouilloire* or *batterie*, where the dyestuff coagulated; and the *diablotin*, where the starchy matter floated to the surface. (Fig. 2.2.)

The large sugar plantations of the second half of the eighteenth century needed blocks of land of at least 100 *carreaux* (300 acres) and workforces that often reached 200 to 300 slaves, a heavy investment the profitability of which was much more long term. On the eve of the revolution, the nearly 800 sugar estates represented 40 percent of all the capital invested in the colony (including the nearby distilleries that manufactured the other product derived from sugar cane, rum), although these estates occupied no more than 14 percent of cultivated land. The main areas of sugar cultivation were the plains of the north, especially around Cap-Français, which were the longest established and produced three-quarters of the colony's semi-refined sugar (*sucre terré* or *blanc*); the Cul-de-Sac, near Port-au-Prince, and the adjoining plains of l'Arcahaye and

[FIG. 2.1] COTTON PLANTATION.

From left to right: Slaves picking and cleaning cotton; sailboats at the wharf; bales waiting to be shipped; a slave ginning cotton with a pedal machine. M. Chambon, *Traité général du commerce de l'Amérique* (Amsterdam, 1783). Courtesy of the John Carter Brown Library at Brown University.

INDIGOTERIE.

1. la Trempoire. 2. la Batterie. 3. le Diablotin ou reposoir. 4. Plantes d'Indigo. 5. Negres qui portent l'Indigo dans la trempoire. 6. Cassons a sécher l'Indigo. 7. Negres qui portent l'Indigo aux cassons. 8. Indigo qui egoute. 9. Cierge Epineux. 10. Commandeur. 11. Bois de trompette.

[FIG. 2.2] INDIGO PLANTATION.

From left to right: The planter's house; the three masonry basins; storage shed and thatched huts of the slave quarters. *In the foreground:* Slaves making the paste and carrying it in baskets to be dried. Jean Baptiste Labat, *Nouveau voyage aux isles de l'Amérique* . . . (Paris, 1742), vol. 2. Courtesy of the John Carter Brown Library at Brown University.

Léogane, which produced three-quarters of the muscovado sugar (*sucre brut*); and the plain of Les Cayes in the south, the Artibonite, and a few other plains of lesser importance (Jean-Rabel, Jacmel, Jérémie, Saint-Marc, Nippes, Aquin, Cavaillon, Saint-Louis). (Figs. 2.3 and 2.4.)

These plantations were the greatest source of wealth and social prestige, places of technical innovation (by Father Labat and Belin de Villeneuve), and they had the finest buildings, both domestic dwellings and, in particular, industrial buildings. Almost all followed the same architectural model. (Fig. 2.5.)

The residential area of the plantation had at its center the *grand-case*, the planter's house. Where possible, it overlooked the other buildings for surveillance purposes and was upwind of the industrial buildings to avoid the risk of fire and unpleasant smells and noise. Single-storied and surrounded by a veranda, the "big house" was, except in the north, generally built of wood on a masonry foundation with walls made of daubed wattles between posts. Roofs were covered with shingles or, for the wealthiest, slate or tile; floors were tiled; and occasionally there was a vaulted cellar. A simple kitchen stood separately, detached to avoid the risk of fire. A dispensary, grandiloquently called "the hospital," conformed to a traditional model: divided into three parts, it had one room for men and one for women separated by an examination room and was equipped with iron rings attached to a bar to immobilize the patients. This building was usually made of wattle and daub mounted on wooden posts and had a tiled floor and a roof of thatch, shingles, or tile. Separate huts were used to isolate slaves with contagious diseases.

Nearby stood lodgings for the nurse, domestic servants, and the cook, and often a building for guests. There were also a chicken coop, a dovecote, sheds and storehouses; the lodgings of white distillers and stewards; a bell tower to call the slaves to work; occasionally a vaulted masonry dungeon; a lime kiln; buildings containing a forge and the coopers' and wheelwright's workshop; corrals for horses, mules, and cattle; a well; and water troughs. In the north especially, a long avenue lined with trees led to a large wrought-iron gate mounted on imposing pillars. A fine-looking entrance was an object of pride for the colonist. (Fig. 2.6.)

The industrial buildings, located downwind, were laid out in accordance with the different stages of sugar manufacture. First, if the supply of water was sufficient, there would be a long aqueduct with solid arches stretching a hundred yards or more. Fed by canals, it brought water to the mill along its *dalle*, or mill race, closed in by its *mâchoires*, where it fell onto the great wheel and was evacuated through the *taillevanne*, an opening at the end of the *fosse*, or mill pit. A staircase gave access to the sluice-gate at the top that controlled the flow of water. A mill house built of stone sheltered the three rollers that crushed the cane, and adjacent to it was a cane "park." From the

[Fig. 2.3]   DUPATY SUGAR PLANTATION.

From left to right: The village church; the drying tower, of which the roof had burned; the animal-powered mill with its access ramp and cane park; the boiling house with its chimneys, aqueduct, and water mill. *In the right background:* The Bay of Acul and the Morne du Cap. *In the foreground:* An ox cart loaded with cane. Located in Acul-du-Nord, the estate belonged to the Mercier-Dupaty family of La Rochelle.

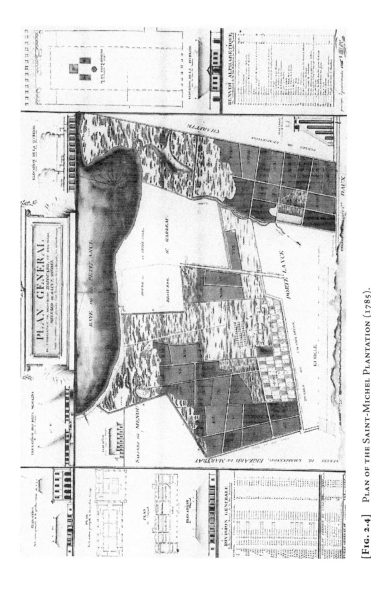

[**Fig. 2.4**]　Plan of the Saint-Michel Plantation (1785).

Left panel: Elevation and plan of the guest house and planter's house; elevation and plan of the hospital. *Middle panel*: Twin animal-powered mills; a slave hut; main plan of the cane pieces, provision grounds, and buildings; rear view of the boiling house (the side with the furnaces and chimneys); the drying tower. *Right panel*: Plan of the boiling house, curing house, and drying tower; front view of the boiling house. The Saint-Michel Plantation was close to Le Cap, in Quartier-Morin parish. Private collection. © J. de Cauna, *Au Temps des Isles à Sucre* (1987).

[FIG. 2.5] SUGAR PLANTATION.

From left to right: The slave quarters and slave-driver's hut; the planter's house and guest house; the cane pieces with their hedges; provision grounds in the hills; curing house and drying tower; boiling house, water mill and spillway, aqueduct, and trash house. *In the foreground:* The savanna. *Il gazzettiere Americano* . . . (Livorno, 1763), vol. 2. Courtesy of the John Carter Brown Library at Brown University.

[FIG. 2.6] ENTRANCE OF THE VAUDREUIL PLANTATION.
Located near Cap-Français, this sugar estate belonged to the marquis Joseph-Hyacinthe Rigaud de Vaudreuil. © J. de Cauna, 1984.

mill house, the *vesou*, or cane juice, flowed along a pipe or gutter toward the two ranges of five or six cauldrons, set in brickwork, in the *sucrerie*, or boiling-house, that was always recognizable by its chimneys and furnaces fueled by *bagasse* (crushed cane). A little further on, in the shape of a U or an L, was the *purgerie*, where the sugar was purified in clay molds, or *formes*. These curing-houses were usually wooden, which explains the rarity of their ruins today. Finally, the sugar was carried into the *étuve*, a sort of tall, closed-in tower, of which there were generally two, occasionally topped with a pinnacle. There the sugar loaves were dried for about two weeks on rows of shelves warmed by a parallel-piped cast-iron oven that was kept continuously in operation. (Figs. 2.7 through 2.12.)

On plantations that lacked water, or to supplement the power of the water mill, there was often an animal-driven mill (*moulin à bêtes*) and some-times a double one. With an access ramp for the animals, it had a raised circular pathway set on a masonry base that was pierced with elegant vaulted openings through which the cane was brought. The roof was conical in shape and the cane "park" formed a semi-circle. The rollers, mounted on a stone base, were either horizontal (*à l'anglaise*) or vertical. The *guildiverie* (distill-ery), where the rum was made, was as a rule a stone building that backed on to the aqueduct. Most of the *guildives* to be seen in modern Haiti have been built on the ruins of a colonial structure (Figs. 2.13 and 2.14).

Slave quarters, situated a good distance downwind, consisted of sym-metrical rows of wattle huts, rarely wooden ones. Almost none have been preserved. On the other hand, in the large sugar-growing plains of Haiti there can still be seen today the vestiges of many boiling-houses, aqueducts, and *étuves*. Some, especially in the north and west, are imposing. Yet it is very unusual for a complete plantation to have survived, particularly one for which plans still exist.

Chronologically the last export crop to be established (but the second most important in value) was coffee. Its cultivation began late, essentially in the second half of the eighteenth century, well after its appearance in the Lesser Antilles. After the successive reigns of tobacco, indigo, and sugar cane, it became the premier pioneer activity.

The first coffee bushes were introduced by the Jesuits in 1725 on their plantation at Terrier-Rouge in the north. The following year, Monsieur de Nolivos planted coffee on his estate in the west, at Léogane, but it was not until 1738 that the first trees appeared in the mountains of Dondon, where the crop really took off beginning about 1770. Whereas production amounted to only 7 million pounds in 1755, it had reached 77 million pounds in 1789, a little more than that of sugar. By then, coffee occupied 60 percent of the colony's cultivated land.

[FIG. 2.7] AQUEDUCT.

Prince sugar estate, Boucassin, which belonged to a governor of Saint-Domingue, Louis-Armand-Constantin de Rohan, prince de Montbazon. © J. de Cauna, 1984.

[FIG. 2.8] CARADEUX PLANTATION, BELLEVUE.

Aqueduct, archway, and surveillance tower. Located in the Cul-de-Sac plain, this sugar estate belonged to the marquis Jean-Baptiste de Caradeux, known as "Caradeux the cruel." © J. de Cauna, 1984.

[FIG. 2.9]   DELUGÉ SUGAR PLANTATION, MONTROUIS.

On the left: The aqueduct with its mill-dam; the mill house. *On the right*: The boiling house with its chimneys. A channel for carrying cane juice runs from the mill to the factory. Piles of crushed cane lie in the yard. © J. de Cauna, 1984

[Fig. 2.10] Guillon Sugar Plantation.

General view showing the aqueduct and spillway, the water mill, and distillery. The boiling house is hidden. The plantation belonged to a family from La Rochelle.©J. de Cauna, 1984.

[FIG. 2.11]   WATER MILL.

Sugar estate of Edmé-Félix Pivert, Hauts de Saint-Marc. In 1986 this was one of the last three colonial mills in operation, along with those of the Guillon and Delugé plantations. © J. de Cauna, 1984.

[**Fig. 2.12**] Drying Tower.

Located on the Dagout sugar estate at Croix-des-Bouquets in the Cul-de-Sac plain, which formerly belonged to a colonial governor, Comte Robert d'Argour. © J. de Cauna, 1984.

[**Fig. 2.13**] Animal-Powered Mill.

Santo sugar estate at Croix-des-Bouquets in the Cul-de-Sac plain, which belonged to the Santo-Domingo family of Nantes. © J. de Cauna, 1984.

[FIG. 2.14] LAMARDELLE SUGAR PLANTATION.

Situated in the Cul-de-Sac plain, the estate belonged to Guillaume-Pierre François de La Mardelle, attorney-general of the Port-au-Prince Conseil supérieur. ©J. de Cauna, 1984.

Coffee trees, about six or seven feet in height, were planted at roughly 1,000 per acre in staggered rows on a previously cleared patch of land, called a *bois neuf*. The tree did best in the mountains at altitudes of between 1,000 and 3,000 feet. The crop needed less in the way of buildings than did sugar estates, and coffee planters were in general less rich and less respected than sugar planters. However, the availability of stone in the mountains, the need to protect against the cold, and the multiple operations of washing, crushing, and drying involved in coffee's preparation led to the construction of numerous stone buildings on these plantations.

Living quarters consisted usually of a *grand-case* situated in a commanding position on a hilltop. Not far away but separate, to avoid the risk of fire, was the kitchen with its chimney and bread oven. These tend to have survived. The slave quarters were generally made up of one or two stone buildings divided into little family units, and there was a hospital divided into three parts. The preparation of the coffee berries began in a "pulping" or decorticating mill (*moulin à grager*). Such mills were made of wood and were turned by hand by a crew of twelve slaves. The coffee was then washed in a circular basin where the impurities were carried away by running water, and it was drained for twenty-four hours spread out on a platform. On most plantations these operations were carried out in a large industrial building divided into three parts corresponding to these three operations. Frequently well preserved, these buildings are easy to recognize by their basins and gutters. The next phase consisted of drying the beans, still covered in their "parchment," on masonry platforms, or *glacis*. At their center were small circular basins called *bassicots* into which the beans were pushed in the evening and covered to protect them from the humidity of the night air. The beans were then put into a pounding mill (*moulin à piler*) whose vertical wheel, worked by mules, separated the beans from their parchment without crushing them by turning them in a circular stone pit ten or twelve feet in diameter. These mills were occasionally protected by a building. Finally, a hand-operated winnowing mill (*moulin à vanner*) was used to blow away the parchment before the beans were sorted on long tables. These wooden installations have not survived. Storehouses and sheds, which sometimes have been preserved, completed the group of buildings. (Figs. 2.15 and 2.16.)

Most of the remains of coffee plantations are to be found in the mountainous regions, mainly the Northern Massif (Dondon, Marmelade, Grande-Rivière); in the Matheux and Cahos mountain chains of the center; on the Rochelois plateau; and in the Macaya mountains of the south.

Important road-building projects accompanied the development of the plantations from the beginning of the eighteenth century, thanks to compulsory *corvée* labor, but they were constructed piecemeal, as need arose, without a general plan. In addition to the main roads or royal roads, whose width was fixed at ten feet by a 1781 decree that was little obeyed, there were also parish

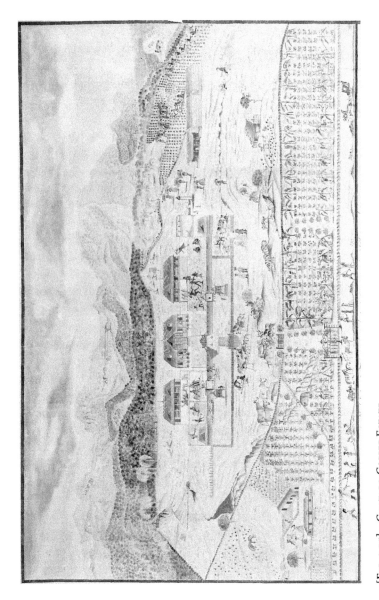

[**Fig. 2.15**] Chatard Coffee Estate.

Plantation of the Apothecary-Royal, Pierre-François Chatard, at Plaisance. The planter's house flanked by industrial buildings. *Foreground:* Slaves drying coffee on the glacis; storehouses and dovecotes on stilts; the savanna. From an eighteenth-century painting, private collection. ©J. de Cauna, 1984.

[Fig. 2.16] Moneyron Coffee Plantation.

View from the planter's house of the ruins of the mill, drying platform, and covered cistern. Located on the Rochelois plateau, the plantation belonged to Antoine-Joseph Monneron. © J. de Cauna, 1984.

roads and private roads that linked plantations to wharves. As early as 1740, Governor Larnage opened some difficult routes in the south, and in 1751 Vaudreuil improved the road between Port-au-Prince and Le Cap. There remained, however, a two-kilometer section at the Puilboreau pass called "the staircase" that was difficult even on horseback, and it was not until 1788 that it was circumvented with a detour that could be used by coaches. Some traces of this road system, segments of which were made of stones or paving, have persisted, especially in the mountains.

The crossing of rivers and ravines was for a long time accomplished by fords or ferries, as at Petite-Rivière de l'Artibonite. The first stone bridge, built at Saint-Marc in 1785, spanned 28 feet and was 33 feet wide. The Larnage bridge, or Pont-Rouge, at the entrance to Port-au-Prince followed in 1786, but the great canal bridge over the Artibonite, which was intended to replace the ferry in 1790, was not completed. The Bréda bridge at Haut-du-Cap, which was rebuilt after independence and is still there today, remained the largest bridge in the colony. The Charrier bridge in the Cul-de-Sac was one of the little masonry bridges that planters in the plains were obliged to construct by the decree of 1788 regarding drainage and irrigation ditches.

Larnage and Maillard encouraged the creation of a remarkable irrigation network consisting of canals, dams, and distribution basins. Special officials (the *syndics des eaux*) oversaw the redirecting and canalization of streams and the storage and distribution of the water to plantations. This system changed the fate of many reputedly sterile lands in the great sugar-growing plains of Les Cayes, where the d'Avezac dam and canal have kept their names, and in the Cul-de-Sac, where the main basin of the Grande-Rivière, which was begun in 1773 and completed in 1784, watered some 24,000 acres that belonged to fifty-eight sugar estates. It is still functioning today, along with the Bassin Joly on the Rivière Blanche that served about 15,000 acres. In the Artibonite plain, Bertrand de Saint-Ouen installed a steam pump and siphon—the remains are stamped "Perrier frères, Chaumont"—that watered 6,000 acres. In the north, around Le Cap, the abundance of rainfall and rivers meant that planters needed only diversion dikes erected in river beds. At l'Arcahaye and Léogane, they used diversions and drainage ditches that involved only simple constructions. After several experiments, the engineer Ricord decided in 1739 that it was impossible to irrigate the Aquin plain, and other attempts in the Savane Désolée of the plain of Gonaïves were also abandoned.

In order to supply towns with drinking water, sources were diverted (as at Turgeau, Martissant, and La Charbonnière in the hills above Port-au-Prince) and fountains were built on the public squares. Three of these remain: two at Le Cap, the fountain in Toussaint Louverture Square (formerly Place Royale) and the very fine Ducommun fountain with its basin and coat of arms, and one at Port-au-Prince on the Promenade de l'Intendance.

Cap-Haïtien, the former Cap-Français, is the best-preserved example of colonial town planning in spite of the historic fires of 1793 and 1802 and the earthquake of 1843. Its grid of streets, some of which have retained their old name-plaques, form blocks made up of four corner houses grouped around a shared courtyard, each with its own well, bread ovens, staircases, paving, and period buildings. Decorated chimneys, monuments, and public buildings, including the Hôtel de la Marine, the Providence du Cap (the hospital), and the colonial barracks (which have become the Saint-Justinien Hospital) can still be seen, as well as bridges, the royal bakery, and some faint traces of the ramparts. Port-au-Prince has recently lost the surviving wing of its Hôtel de la Marine and its public water trough (Bassin Cheval).

Fine colonial coastal defenses can be found at Fort-Liberté (Fort La Bouque and Fort Dauphin, which includes a powder magazine); Port-de-Paix (Grand-Fort and Petit-Fort on the Pointe des Pères); Môle Saint-Nicolas, the Gibraltar of the Caribbean (barracks, a massive powder magazine, various batteries); and most notably Le Cap (Forts Saint-Joseph, Aux Dames, and Picolet, all of which are well preserved). Port-au-Prince has Forts l'Islet, Bizoton, and Mercredi but other forts and batteries have disappeared (Sainte-Claire, Bel-Air, À Rebours, and Saint-Joseph). In the bay of Saint-Louis-du-Sud, the ruins of the Grand-Fort Saint-Louis stand on an island in the harbor, and the Compagnie battery stands on the Pointe des Oliviers. Reminders of the age of the buccaneers can be found on Tortuga Island: the walls of the upper battery rebuilt by Labatut in 1776, some abandoned cannons in the harbor batteries and the D'Ogeron tower, and a few rows of stones that trace the bastions around the famous Refuge rock (Fort Levasseur).

The most splendid example of religious architecture, the old cathedral of Port-au-Prince, was recently lost in a criminal fire. Erected after the 1770 earthquake, the cathedral contained an elegant marble altar donated by Louis XVI, pillars made of solid mahogany, and, among its masterpieces of carpentry and cabinet-making, a staircase and a throne. However, some provincial churches are still standing at Torbeck, Petite-Anse, and around Cap-Haïtien. A ruined hexagonal tower from the ancient cathedral, Gascon in style, stands near the new church of Saint-Marc, and the floor of Le Cap's cathedral, which has a similar façade to that of Montauban, is preserved. Some remarkable cemeteries survive at Jacmel, which contains the tombstone of Horace-Camille Desmoulins and two others engraved "native of Africa," and at Port-au-Prince, where the Cimetière Intérieur (in the courtyard of the present Ecole Saint-Anne) houses both the mausoleum of Governor Thérèse Charpentier d'Ennery and the tomb of Jean-Jacques Dessalines. The French revolutionary Billaud-Varenne is buried beneath the present church of Saint Anne.

Beyond its purely aesthetic value and its emotional impact, this exceptional and irreplaceable architectural patrimony is rich in reminders of the long common history of France and Haiti and of a pioneering, preindustrial, and primarily agro-commercial type of society. This creole plantation society, which was characteristic of the entire Caribbean region, reached its highest point of development in Saint-Domingue. As a result of the diaspora of its refugee colonists, the French model was spread after the revolution to neighboring Cuba, to Jamaica, and to New Orleans, giving a transnational character to the Dominguan diffusion of French influence that invites comparison with other countries of the region.[9]

Notes

1. See in particular the outstanding works of Barry Higman, *Jamaica Surveyed: Plantation Maps and Plans of the Eighteenth and Nineteenth Centuries* (Kingston: University of the West Indies Press, 1988); Manuel Moreno Fraginals, *El ingenio: el complejo económico-social cubano del azúcar, 1760–1860* (Havana: Editorial de Ciencias Sociales, 1978); and Gilberto Freyre, *Maîtres et esclaves* (Paris: Gallimard, 1952).

2. Jacques de Cauna, *Au temps des Isles à sucre. Histoire d'une plantation à Saint-Domingue au XVIIIe siècle* (Paris: Karthala, 1987), which is an abridgement of "Une habitation de Saint-Domingue au XVIIIe siècle: la sucrerie Fleuriau de Bellevue" (thèse de 3me cycle, Université de Poitiers, 1983); Pierre Pluchon, "L'économie d'habitation à Saint-Domingue," *Revue d'Histoire Maritime* 1 (1995): 197–241; Paul Butel, "L'essor de l'économie de plantation à Saint-Domingue dans la seconde moitié du XVIIIe siècle," *Bulletin du Centre d'Histoire des Espaces Atlantiques* 7 (1995): 61–76. For slaves on large plantations, see the numerous studies of Gabriel Debien, which he synthesized in *Les esclaves aux Antilles françaises* (Basse-Terre: Société d'Histoire de la Guadeloupe, 1974); and David Geggus, "Les esclaves de la plaine du Nord à la veille de la Révolution française," *Revue de la Société Haïtienne d'Histoire et de Géographie* nos. 135 (juin 1982): 8–107; no. 136 (sept. 1982): 5–32; no. 144 (sept. 1984): 15–44; and no. 149 (1985): 16–52.

3. M. L. E. Moreau de Saint-Méry, *Description topographique, physique, civile, politique et historique de la partie française de l'isle Saint-Domingue*, ed. Blanche Maurel et Étienne Taillemite (1797; repr., Paris: Société de l'histoire des colonies françaises, 1958), 1:4.

4. Jacques de Cauna, "La colonisation française aux Antilles. Les Aquitains à Saint-Domingue (XVIIe–XVIIIe siècles)" (thèse d'État, Université de Paris IV–Sorbonne, 2000), published as *L'Eldorado des Aquitains. Gascons, Basques et Béarnais aux Îles d'Amérique* (Biarritz: Atlantica, 1998).

5. In 1789, the Intendant listed 793 sugar estates, which were producing semi-refined and muscovado sugar; 54 cacao walks; 3,151 indigo plantations; 789 cotton plantations; 3,117 coffee plantations; 182 distilleries; 370 lime kilns; 26 brickworks or tile factories; and 29 potteries, along with 40,000 horses, 50,000 mules, and 250,000 cattle

and smaller livestock. The total value of the property was estimated at a billion and a half livres, and its annual output was estimated at 180 million. François Barbé de Marbois, *État des finances de Saint-Domingue* (Paris, 1790).

6. Nathan Wachtel, *La vision des vaincus. Les Indiens du Pérou devant la conquête espagnole* (Paris: Gallimard, 1971).

7. Jacques de Cauna, "Vestiges de sucreries dans la Plaine du Cul-de-Sac," *Conjonction* no. 149 (1981): 63–104 and no. 165 (1985): 4–32. These articles set in their historical and contemporary contexts some thirty sugar estates in the Cul-de-Sac plain near Port-au-Prince. After first identifying the estates in colonial maps and other documents, I photographed their remains and made a general description of their location and accessibility, their soil quality and production, their enslaved workforces, and the condition of the architectural remains. I researched the origin of the name, the names of the owners from colonial times to the present, and historical events that took place on the plantation.

Jacques de Cauna, *Haïti, Route 2004, Éomusée du Nord* (PNUD/UNESCO, 1996), which summarizes field research from 1984 to 1986, in particular the discovery of two locations for the famous Bois-Caïman on the Choiseul and Lenormand de Mézy plantations. The report describes about twenty large plantations (mainly sugar estates) in the plain around Cap-Haïtien (former parishes of Petite-Anse, Quartier-Morin, and Haut-du-Cap). This region is rich in historical sites, such as the Vertières plantation and Charrier hill; Galliffet, a focal point of the insurrection; Bréda, the birthplace of Toussaint Louverture; sites associated with King Christophe such as Duplaa, a.k.a. Les Délices de la Reine; and Grand-Pont, formerly known as Macnemara.

"Parc Historique National," report by Institute de Sauvegarde du Patrimoine National and PNUD/UNESCO, 1986, which is partly summarized in Jacques de Cauna, "Mémoire des lieux, lieux de mémoire: quelques apercus sur la toponymie haïtienne et ses racines historiques," *Chemins Critiques* (Port-au-Prince) 4 (1990): 125–140. This study inventories the plantations (mainly coffee estates) of the Parc Historique National, which covers five parishes around the historical sites of the Citadel and the Sans-Souci palace of King Christophe. The research technique was one of microtoponymy. I extracted place names from oral tradition through questions to residents and compared them with data collected from colonial sources such as period maps, the *Description topographique* of Moreau de Saint-Méry (for districts and cantons), and the *État de l'indemnité de Saint-Domingue* (for names of landowners and properties).

Didier Pillot and Jacques de Cauna, *Paysans, systèmes et crises. Travaux sur l'agraire haïtien* (Pointe-à-Pitre: SACAD, 1993), which surveys the plantations of the Madian-Salagnac-Aquin "transect" in the southern peninsula. Some seventeen sites of coffee estates on the Rochelois Plateau were photographed, studied, and mapped.

De Cauna, *L'Eldorado des Aquitains*; de Cauna, "L'habitation d'un Béarnais à Saint-Domingue: la sucrerie Nolivos à la Croix-des-Bouquets," *Revue de Pau et du Béarn* 12 (1985): 213–232; de Cauna, "Indigoteries à Saint-Domingue: Les habitations Gandérats et Pascal," *Cahiers du Centre de Généalogie et d'Histoire des Isles d'Amérique* 47 (1994): 25–31; de Cauna, "A Plantation on the Eve of the Haïtian Revolution," *Plantation Society in the Americas* 2 (1993): 31–49; de Cauna, "Une caféière du Rochelois à la fin du xviiie siècle: l'habitation Viaud," *Revue de la Société Haïtienne d'Histoire et de Géographie* no. 142 (1984): 44–59; De Cauna, "Les propriétés Navailles à Saint-Domingue: caféières du Petit-Saint-Louis et de la Montagne du Port-de-Paix, 1777–1814," *Revue de Pau et du Béarn* 15 (1988): 291–304. For the most part based on family papers of colonists from Aquitaine, these works include studies of plantations and their rural or urban environments on Tortuga Island and at Cap-Haïtien, Port-au-Prince, Léogane, Les Cayes, Saint-Louis-du-Sud, Jacmel, Aquin, Grand- and Petit-Goâve, Boucassin, Arcahaye, Montrouis (Les Sept Moulins), Saint-Marc (Les Hauts), Gonaïves, Artibonite, route du Nord, Morne du Cap, Port-Français, Haut-du-Cap, Petite-Anse, Quartier-Morin, Morne Rouge, and Fort-Dauphin.

8. S. J. Ducoeurjoly, *Manuel des habitants de Saint-Domingue* (Paris: Lenoir, 1802), 2: 28–31; Jean Barré de Saint-Venant, *Des colonies modernes sous la zone torride et particulièrement de celle de Saint-Domingue* (Paris: Brochot, 1802), 317–319. The cotton gin is illustrated in Denis Diderot et Jean D'Alembert, eds., *L'Encyclopédie: Recueil de planches sur les sciences, les arts libéraux et les arts mécaniques avec leur explication* (1762; repr., Paris: Hachette, 1985), 40.

9. A useful first step toward scholarly exchange would be a quadrilingual glossary in French, Spanish, Creole, and English of the typical terms of the plantation lexicon, accompanied by a listing of sources and their whereabouts. One might then bring together different research to achieve a Caribbean-wide synthesis and obtain a finer focus on the various European and local contributions to the creolization process.

Saint-Domingue's Free People of Color and the Tools of Revolution

John D. Garrigus

To evaluate the role that Saint-Domingue's free people of color played in the Haitian Revolution, we should first define our terms. Was the slave uprising of 1791 "the Haitian Revolution"? Although freedmen like Toussaint Louverture would eventually lead Saint-Domingue's black armies, it is difficult to find *gens de couleur libres* who in 1791 were openly sympathetic to the slaves' revolt against their masters.[1] If we instead define the revolution as the events surrounding Haiti's 1804 declaration of independence, then we find former free men of color playing a far more prominent role.[2] From the mid-1790s, André Rigaud and Toussaint created autonomous states that claimed loyalty to France but set their own internal policies. In 1803, Dessalines's secretaries, freeborn men of color like Louis Boisrond Tonnerre, appear to have been the first to articulate the even-more-radical idea of an indigenous and independent Haitian nation.

This chapter argues that this claim of Haitian indigenousness was rooted in white colonists' formulation of a specific kind of "creole patriotism" in the 1750s. Over the next forty years, Saint-Domingue free men of color resisted and reworked this idea so that they, and not whites, would emerge as the true "creole patriots." They possessed three advantages, or tools, that allowed them to redefine creole patriotism: an unprecedented level of economic success, a leadership deeply familiar with French political culture, and an important but still obscure regional pattern of military service. These were not the weapons that destroyed or even directly challenged slavery. However, they were the implements that forged an emerging sense of New World nationhood.

Why was Saint-Domingue's free population of color so unusually large, wealthy, and self-confident on the eve of the French Revolution? In his 1986

49

survey of Latin American and Caribbean slavery, Herbert Klein notes, "This was apparently the only significant group of free colored planters known to have existed in any slave society in America."[3] Overviews of colonial society frequently describe the group as owning one-third of Saint-Domingue's land and one-quarter of its slaves in 1789, a claim probably first advanced by Julien Raimond, a free colored indigo planter and self-appointed political spokesman in Paris.[4]

However, data that I have culled from thousands of colonial contracts illustrate that this claim was exaggerated. In his native parish of Aquin, far from Saint-Domingue's greatest colonial estates, Raimond's wealth and that of his free colored friends and neighbors was much more prominent than it would have been in Cap-Français or Port-au-Prince. And even in Aquin, the total property of free colored brides and grooms amounted to just 18 percent of the property of all 122 couples who signed marriage contracts in this parish from 1780 to 1789.[5] Raimond's friend and supporter Claude Boisrond was one of the wealthier men of color in the southern peninsula.[6] But a 1783 road-building assessment showed that, with forty slaves, Boisrond ranked just below the median in slave-holding size for his district. Together Boisrond and his two free colored neighbors owned only 114 out of 1,422 slaves owned by all twenty assessed proprietors.[7]

Yet Raimond—and Klein—were correct to point out the extraordinary wealth some free families of color controlled. In a society based on the brutal enslavement of African men and women, free people of African descent were responsible for approximately one-third of the wealthiest 10 percent of Aquin marriage contracts in the 1780s. Raimond's 1782 marriage to the free colored widow of a white planter created a household worth over 300,000 livres, more than the property of a neighboring militia officer who married a notary's daughter, whose household was worth 227,200 livres.[8] Raimond's neighbors, the three Depas-Medina brothers, signed marriage contracts worth between 60,000 and 143,200 during this decade, similar in value to that of a militia officer who married an indigo planter's daughter (93,700 livres).[9]

Such prosperity, as I have suggested, was probably noticed more in the poorer South Province than anywhere else in Saint-Domingue. Real estate there was generally less valuable than in the West and North Provinces. Nevertheless, the average value of free colored land sales in the south in the 1780s was 7,797 livres, about one-third higher than the average 5,793 livres Stewart King found in selected parishes of the north and west in the 1770s and 1780s.[10]

Yet Saint-Domingue's wealthiest families of color were all at about the same economic level by the 1780s, regardless of region. King found that the Laporte family of Limonade parish in the North Province had 300 slaves and over 2,000 acres of land, approximately the combined wealth of Raimond and his seven siblings. King describes other wealthy free colored families in the West Province—the Baugés of Croix des Bouquets parish, the Nivards or Rossignols of Mirebalais, the Turgeaus of Port-au-Prince—as worth about 100,000 livres in the 1780s.[11]

So why did French colonists allow, as Klein phrases it, "freedmen ... to enter the class of plantation owners from the beginning," unlike slave owners in the rest of the hemisphere? Many historians have understood Saint-Domingue's large free colored population to be a material phenomenon produced by an extraordinarily dynamic plantation economy, mountainous terrain, and massive slave imports.[12] These conditions were, indeed, quite different from those that shaped France's other mature plantation colonies, Martinique and Guadeloupe. Yet they were not unique.

Eighteenth-century Jamaica and Brazil also had large enslaved populations working under murderous conditions to produce sugar and other commodities. In the eighteenth century alone, these two territories and Saint-Domingue together absorbed over 40 percent of the trans-Atlantic slave trade.[13] By 1768, slaves constituted about 50 percent of Brazil's population and 90 percent of those of Jamaica and Saint-Domingue. In all three societies, European colonists and their American-born sons commonly freed the children they had produced with enslaved women and recognized their paternity.[14] All three had the kind of undeveloped interior land that was unavailable in most of the islands of the Lesser Antilles. These open frontiers allowed free people of color as well as new European immigrants to establish farms and ranches, some of which eventually became full-blown slave plantations. In Jamaica and Brazil, even more than in Saint-Domingue, these interiors also sheltered semi-permanent communities of escaped slaves. Finally, all three colonies relied on free people of African descent to police the slave population.[15]

Eighteenth-century Brazilian society was deeply racist, excluding persons of up to one-eighth African ancestry from public office. Yet nearly all observers agreed that in practice, colonial officials were flexible about these racial laws, especially for wealthy light-skinned persons.[16] Jamaican law and custom excluded free people of African descent from proper colonial society, but influential planters used the Colonial Assembly to carve out exceptions on a case-by-case basis. From the late 1600s through the 1700s, this body granted civil rights to more than 200 free persons of color.[17] Consequently, by the 1760s, Jamaica's population included numerous individuals who, despite their partial African ancestry, enjoyed the rights of full citizenship, a kind of honorary "whiteness." William Cunningham, perhaps the wealthiest, owned 160 slaves in an estate worth 16,780 pounds at his death in 1762.[18]

In conditions like those found in Jamaica, Saint-Domingue, and parts of Brazil, where enslaved people outnumbered owners ten to one, where many of the slaves were African rather than locally born, and where there were many more male than female colonists, it is not surprising that free property-owning men and women formed a united master class. What is surprising is that in Saint-Domingue at mid-century the colonial elite began categorically to exclude planters and merchants who Brazilian or Jamaican elites might have considered "white."

The post-1763 triumph of white racial "purity" over slave-owner solidarity in Saint-Domingue, described below, explains why free colored leaders during the revolution were so familiar with elite French culture; they had been raised in it, much like other creole children of successful colonists. To re-examine Klein's formulation, Saint-Domingue's free colored planters were not "freedmen" who "entered the class of plantation owners from the beginning"; they were established creole colonists of mixed ancestry. It was a change in colonial culture, specifically, a new concept of "American patriotism," that redefined them as *affranchis*, or ex-slaves.

By 1763, the demands of Saint-Domingue's colonists for a liberalized economic and administrative regime had become a difficult political issue, as Charles Frostin, Malick Ghachem, and others have described.[19] Saint-Domingue's island-born elite, who were increasingly prosperous and articulate as the island's plantations flourished, pressed Versailles to replace mercantilist restrictions with free trade and replace the "arbitrary" power of military governors with the rule of law.

What has largely escaped historians' notice is that this emerging "creole" identity had an ethnic or racial undertone. Not only were European authors like Cornelius De Pauw speculating about the biological inferiority of New World species[20] but in 1750 Emilien Petit, a colonial judge in Saint-Domingue's Léogane Council, offered an implicitly racial definition of creole identity in his book *Le Patriotisme américain*. As he described how French administrators could construct a more loyal and prosperous colonial society, Petit warned that if Saint-Domingue's free people of color were not separated from island-born whites, the common culture they shared might spawn an anti-imperial form of "American patriotism."

Petit was himself born in Saint-Domingue in 1713. His stated goal in *Patriotisme américain* was to encourage Versailles to take measures that would guarantee Saint-Domingue's prosperity and safety within the empire. What he had in mind, specifically, was a complete reformulation of island government to suit the new kind of colonist.

For Petit, the greatest danger to French authority in Saint-Domingue was Versailles's refusal to acknowledge that colonial society had changed. He argued that France's harsh military rule in Saint-Domingue was creating, not restraining, colonial rebels. Caribbean colonists had once been rude and rebellious buccaneers, but they were now productive subjects. Successful planters left the island as soon as they could afford to, while French immigrants with potentially valuable skills quickly despaired after arriving. The exodus of colonists inured to tropical conditions meant France did not have enough loyal and acclimated subjects to defend the colony; instead, the crown had to garrison expensive soldiers in the Caribbean.[21]

Colonists would stay in Saint-Domingue, Petit argued, if they were guaranteed that they would not be "gratuitously exposed every day to the most violent effects of an arbitrary power ... to the caprices of the smallest local commander, who uses the needs of the government to justify his own pride and stupidity and demand absolute and passive obedience."[22]

The colonial ministry was receptive to Petit's argument that political reforms could instill creole patriotism and hired him in 1759. Until the 1780s he worked at Versailles, helping write laws, writing more books, briefing newly appointed colonial governors, and helping sponsor other, better-known writers on colonial affairs, like Hilliard d'Auberteuil and Moreau de Saint-Méry.[23]

Petit's liberal critique of the authoritarian colonial state may have appealed to metropolitan administrators because it did not challenge French mercantilism the way many colonists did. Instead *Patriotisme américain* drew on French "patriot" authors, who argued that love of one's country, which for Petit included both France and Saint-Domingue, was strongest when it was rooted in liberty and prosperity.[24]

In *Patriotisme américain*, Petit acknowledged the danger that creole colonists would lose their French identity. He did not expound on the sensuality of creole women, as later writers did, but he identified the emigration of French women to Saint-Domingue as critical to the development of creole patriotism.[25] Colonists' strong attachment to the New World, Petit suggested, might be dangerous to the crown if it drew in other groups. Describing Saint-Domingue's emerging free population of color, Petit warned that familiarity leading to marriage between whites and free people of color was undesirable because "were they to develop common interests, the consequences might be dangerous, even irreparable."[26] To eliminate this possibility, he proposed a kind of Caribbean apartheid. Free people of color would be exiled to the mountains of the interior, leaving plantation jobs, urban trades, and planters' marriage beds for French immigrants.

Petit grasped an issue that would haunt Saint-Domingue until Haitian independence. Life in the colony had produced a new kind of Frenchman, the creole, whose productivity and attachment to his New World fatherland would create a more prosperous colony. Though he did not use racial terminology, Petit nevertheless believed that colonists' cultural ties to Europe had to be reinforced or "American patriotism" would weaken France's hold on the territory. If the government wanted island-born planters to love both

France and Saint-Domingue, it needed to separate them from the free people of color with whom they shared a common homeland. Indeed, in 1755 the Port-au-Prince Council entertained a proposal to require the city's free mulattoes to relocate to the mountains of the interior, much as Petit had suggested five years before.[27]

Since the seventeenth century, Saint-Domingue had had an acknowledged free population of color. The royal census of 1754 counted 2,907 whites and 997 free people of color.[28] But for many individuals, status as "white" or "non-white" was still determined as much by social as physical criteria. At least this was the argument that a 17-year-old named Pierre Braquehais made in 1760 when he appeared before the *sénéchaussée* judge in Saint-Louis.[29] In the next forty years, Braquehais would become a prosperous planter, a charter member of the province's free colored revolutionary correspondence committee,[30] and the uncle by marriage of the author of the Haitian Declaration of Independence.[31] Yet in 1760s he came before the Saint-Louis court with a petition and the testimony of four men to establish that he was "neither mulatto nor a quadroon." None of this evidence referred to his ancestry or appearance.

Braquehais's petition informed the judge that he had been born in Aquin to parents who were legitimately married and that the militia captain of nearby Jacmel was his godfather. He had faithfully completed an apprenticeship as a carpenter. Beaulieux, his current employer, swore that he was hardworking, quiet, and calm, "never having heard him offer any offensive word or swearing of any kind, skillfully doing the work given him." Surean and Bauvery independently testified that Pierre, son of the planter (*habitant*) Joseph Braquehais, "is neither a quadroon nor a mulatto; is a boy who leads a good life and has the best moral character, working hard at his profession, never uttering a single curse or filthy word." A fourth witness, Michel, did not say whether he thought Braquehais was a man of color but noted that he was "incapable of insulting anyone" and that he "knew him better than anyone since I taught him to read and write."

Around the same time, Claude Gellée, another creole in the same parish, successfully rejected allegations that he was a man of color. In 1767 the Port-au-Prince Council delayed the registration of Gellée's nobility due to a rumor that his maternal grandmother from Saint-Christophe might have been black. Assembling nine of the oldest residents of the parish, Gellée, a wealthy planter, convinced the high judges that his ancestor was instead an Amerindian, not an African. He went on to serve as an infantry officer and a prominent member of the several Masonic lodges in the province.[32]

Such legal debates over racial identity suggest the influence of Petit's warning about the "dangerous, even irreparable" consequences of a creole patriotism that commingled free people of color with island-born whites.[33] In 1769 a six-week revolt in this very parish, during which wealthy white creoles like Gellée directed men of color like Braquehais as well as poor whites to resist a new militia system, led to a major hardening in racial attitudes.

The Seven Years' War (1756–1763) convinced Versailles that it needed to strengthen bonds between Saint-Domingue and France, as Petit had suggested. The war had devastated French Caribbean commerce, and the surrender of Guadeloupe to the British in 1759 provoked concern about Saint-Domingue's loyalty. In 1761, a remonstrance by the Port-au-Prince Council, which was dominated by creole judges who shared Petit's "patriotic" views, had described Saint-Domingue's "barbaric laws, violent and meaningless administration" and had blamed the "ambitious spite of [local] commanders."[34]

When the war ended, therefore, Versailles gave Saint-Domingue's "patriotic" colonists what they had been asking for: an end to the military government and onerous militia duties. In March 1763, imperial officials dissolved the militia, whose officers had administered local government. Parish commanders passed their responsibilities to new civilian officials. The new law transformed colonial government in ways magistrates and their supporters had long argued would guarantee colonial prosperity and loyalty.

Then Versailles abruptly reversed its decision. It cost too much to defend Saint-Domingue's coastline without a militia. The colonial minister Choiseul believed that the colonies needed a military government to defeat Britain in the next war. Colonists, who had just paid a special tax of four million livres to be rid of militia duty, were incredulous. Few would accept a return to the old system, and the kinds of "patriotic" arguments Petit mustered were widely cited as justification.[35]

But Choiseul and the reformers who surrounded him were convinced that France and its colonies needed a new kind of patriotism. The anti-authoritarian writers who had inspired Petit emphasized "liberal" virtue, the positive behavior that developed naturally when the rule of law protected subjects from a despot's arbitrary decisions. Choiseul's writers, on the other hand, identified patriotism with ancient Greek and Roman examples of civic virtue, stressing obedience and discipline for the greater good of the community. Saint-Domingue needed to accept a return of the militia in the name of this kind of patriotism, officials insisted.[36]

It took two governors and five years to force the Council of Port-au-Prince to sign a law reestablishing the militia. In the South Province, where wartime military administrators had been especially resented, whites and free men of color refused to appear at the first musters. In February 1769, they held armed meetings and circulated letters discussing the possibility of appealing for help to British Jamaica.[37] Groups of whites and free men of color kidnapped pro-militia colonists and publicly humiliated militia officers. Only by bringing in troops from the West Province could the governor intimidate the rebels into submission.[38]

The revolt of 1769 marked the last time that Saint-Domingue's old creole families turned to free people of color to fight royal authority, a coalition that seemed to validate Petit's 1750 warning about too much "American patriotism." The following years brought a wave of laws that required respected men like Braquehais and Raimond to declare their African ancestry and prove their freedom at every turn. Such island-born men would no longer be considered "creoles," but foreigners. By the 1780s, colonists were calling these freeborn slave-owners *affranchis*, or freedmen—ex-slaves.

Julien Raimond described discrimination against free people of color as a minor aspect of colonial life until this moment.[39] By his account, it was a speech by the attorney of the Port-au-Prince Council in 1770 welcoming a new governor after the militia revolt that signaled the change. In what amounted to a compromise between the "liberal" patriotism espoused by militia opponents and the "civic" patriotism advocated by Versailles, the council's representative called for harsher laws against the class "which still bears on its forehead the mark of slavery."[40]

But as Saint-Domingue's mixed-race planters and merchants passed from the class of "colonists" into the newly rigid caste of "nonwhites," they found themselves in a larger but poorer group of free people. These included artisans, small merchants, ranchers, peasants, and plantation employees, many of whom were former slaves. This group, which had never belonged to the elite, produced many of the leading military figures of the Haitian Revolution, Toussaint, Rigaud, and Henri Christophe among them.

Because militia service was at the heart of conflicting definitions of patriotism in Saint-Domingue, there are few reliable sources describing the pre-revolutionary militia service of the colony's free people of color.[41] As the colony's newly installed Governor La Luzerne complained in 1786, "either there have never been any comprehensive militia records kept here, or each governor has taken away those that he created. There are no archives in the government offices, no trace of what happened."[42]

For this reason, Stewart King's portrait of a rising "military leadership group" that was self-consciously distinct from established free colored families is a tantalizing hypothesis for understanding the issue of free colored patriotism after 1769. These men were artisans and urban entrepreneurs serving as noncommissioned officers in the colonial militia. King depicts them as avoiding the social connections with whites that many free colored planters maintained even after discrimination became intense. Instead, they developed extensive social connections in the slave world.

Yet King's own evidence suggests that this free colored military leadership class existed only in Saint-Domingue's North Province. For example, fifteen of the nineteen elite men of color he describes as associated with the military were from the North Province, thirteen of them from Cap-Français.

Thirty-eight of his forty-four non-elite "military leaders" lived in the North Province. He explains this striking concentration as the result of regional differences in how notaries in Cap-Français recorded militia rank.[43]

But it seems more likely that King has found a regional subculture, fostered in Cap-Français by the city's military and commercial role in the French empire.[44] Since the late seventeenth century, this port had launched a number of military expeditions in which slaves had won their liberty. It was here, in 1697, after a successful attack on Cartagena, that ex-slaves formed a separate free black militia company, the first in the colony.[45] In 1780 at least two distinguished free black veterans of that Cartagena campaign still lived in the North Province, Vincent Olivier in Cap-Français and Etienne Auba in Fort-Dauphin. Publicly celebrated by white creoles and the royal government, these living symbols of free black military honor had no counterparts in the West and South Provinces.[46]

What we know about the 1779 expedition from Saint-Domingue to Savannah, Georgia, supports this thesis of regional concentration. Between the revision of militia laws in 1769 and the French Revolution in 1789, the Savannah campaign was the most important example of men of color trying to show their patriotism by adopting the metropolitan ideal of self-sacrifice.

Patriotism was the central theme of the literature published in early 1779 to draw volunteers for an attack on British North America. "At this moment what Frenchman does not experience a reawakening of his courage and ardor to fight against the enemies of the State?" Recruiters called on "the zeal and the good will of Citizens of every condition [espèce]. Good Frenchmen, without a doubt, will not need much encouragement to show their natural valor."[47]

Perhaps drawn by this appeal to "citizens of every condition," 941 free men of color came to Cap-Français to enlist and 545 sailed with the expedition. In contrast, only 156 whites joined. In fact, leading colonists refused to acknowledge that such participation was virtuous or patriotic. Even as volunteers enrolled, the colonial newspaper announced: "To the honor of humanity, surely one will never again see a ferocious and barbarian mother send her son to his death with a dry eye, without emotion, see him again pale and bleeding and believe she owes this horrible sacrifice to the fatherland. . . . These awful traits, so long admired by our fathers, are unnatural and make any respectable and sensitive soul tremble."[48]

The colonial elite, on the other hand, stressed its "liberal" patriotism. Colonists would support France and, at the same time, their own natural commercial interests by subscribing to a fund to purchase a new ship for the royal navy. The colonial broadsheet contrasted this less bellicose generosity with the ancient Greek and Roman ideals military leaders constantly invoked. "Compared to us, what are those superb cities of antiquity, whose citizens have been so praised for their great feats and worthy souls?" The ancients were "harsh" and "severe."

Who were these 545 free colored "patriots" of 1779? The only nomina-
tive record unearthed to date is a list of ninety free colored volunteers who
sailed from the French military port of Brest to Saint-Domingue in 1780
and 1781.[49] While it is highly likely that these men served in Savannah, none
of their names exists in a database of nearly 3,000 notarial contracts from
the South Province in the period 1780 to 1803.[50] If any were from the south,
they may not have returned home. The only identifiable names were Auba
and Olivier, prominent men from the North Province who appear in King's
book.[51] This partial evidence supports the thesis that the North Province
had a regional military subculture that had no counterpart in the south.

Though King was able to find fifteen men who identified themselves as
Savannah veterans in notarial contracts in the North Province, neither he
nor Dominique Rogers found any such men in the west.[52] Nor did veterans
identify themselves in the South Province, including men who are known to
have served. Neither André Rigaud nor Guillaume Bleck mentioned their
service in pre-revolutionary documents.[53] In 3,000 notarial contracts from
the South Province from 1780 through 1803, only two documents mentioned the unit that served at Savannah. Both of those cases involved men
who were leaving the region to serve in Cap-Français.[54] There is no evidence
that either ever returned.

The available evidence, then, suggests that King's "free colored military
leadership class" was centered on Cap-Français. Nothing in the South Province
suggests a distinction between a dark-skinned urban "blue coat" class and a
rural "powdered wig" planter group. Julien Raimond, as much of a "powdered
wig" as existed in Saint-Domingue, served as quartermaster sergeant (fourrier)
of his parish's mulatto dragoons in 1780 and 1781.[55]

If the Savannah free colored volunteers were hoping French officials
or white colonists would take them seriously as civic-minded patriots,
their expedition was a disaster. Upon their return in 1780, officials in Cap-
Français tried to conscript them into a permanent unit, nearly producing a
revolt.[56] In 1781, the crown formally dissolved the unpopular company and
sent a new governor and intendant.[57] About the same time, a rumor spread
that the new administrators were bringing racial reforms.[58] Encouraged by
this prospect, Julien Raimond appears to have asked the new governor if he
and his neighbors could join the colonial subscription campaign and collect
patriotic donations.[59] Contributing to the colony's ship fund would illustrate
that Saint-Domingue's free people of color possessed the same "liberal" virtues claimed by white colonists.

As Raimond pursued this project, he began to correspond with the colonial ministry. In 1784, as white colonists and the royal government continued
to feud over the kind of liberalization Petit had advocated in 1750, Julien
Raimond described his class to Versailles: "They conduct their moral and civil

affairs with the approval of the government; they are truly attached to the state by their religion, their possessions and by their feelings of patriotism."[60]

If Raimond had not read Petit's *Patriotisme américain,* he had absorbed its main premises. His own proposals paralleled Petit's except for his argument that light-skinned families of color should be classified as "new whites." This inclusiveness, he contended, would generate more colonial patriotism than the current racial regime. Removing the rigid color line would allow poor French immigrants to marry into families of color without shame. Ignoring the omnipresence of African slaves, Raimond predicted that inter-marriage would eventually do away with the color line in Saint-Domingue. Though he avoided the word "creole," Raimond echoed Petit, contending that a colonial population reinvigorated by intermarriage would be more attached to the land than temporary residents from France.

These pre-revolutionary letters to the colonial ministry illustrate that Raimond shared colonists' "patriotic" hatred of arbitrary authority. The object of whites' protests was the tyranny of French military administrators, but Raimond directed his patriotic rhetoric against the arbitrary nature of racism, at least in its effects on wealthy men like himself, the sons of Frenchmen. He criticized the militia system not because it required sacrifice but because despotic whites used it to humiliate men of color.[61] Recognizing that Dominguan racism had developed a rigidity not found in similar societies, he urged the ministry to institute a hierarchy like that found in Brazil.[62]

Lack of space makes it impossible to trace into the revolutionary period the twin discourses of civic and liberal "patriotism" in Saint-Domingue. But Raimond's claims in 1786 show how he positioned himself to take advantage of both styles of patriotic language.

During the early years of the revolution, "Patriot" became the label adopted by those colonists who believed that the tyranny of royal and military government was the colony's greatest problem. From 1789 to 1791, such "Patriots" attacked royal government. They identified Saint-Domingue's free men of color as a threat to liberty because of their ongoing militia service to the crown. Yet the pre-revolutionary "liberal" patriotism that Emilien Petit had espoused in 1750 adapted poorly to the events of the revolution. Its anti-authoritarian stance was nearly impossible to integrate into a proslavery vision of Saint-Domingue after the slave uprising of 1791.

After 1791, the colony's white "Patriots" stood for little more than opposition to the political power of men of color. Their positions did not represent deep loyalty to France or to a colonial homeland. By 1792, supporters of the men of color were using the term "creole patriot" to signify loyalty to the unity of the metropole and colony around revolutionary ideals.[63] By 1802 and 1803, when France withdrew its commitment to those ideals, Raimond was dead. Another man of color from the southern peninsula, the nephew of one of his closest neighbors and supporters, Louis Boisrond Tonnerre, would write a declaration of independence that defined a new Haitian patriotism.[64]

Notes

1. See the discussion in David P. Geggus, "The 'Swiss' and the Problem of Slave/Free Colored Cooperation," in Geggus, *Haitian Revolutionary Studies* (Bloomington: Indiana University Press, 2003), 99–118.

2. They were known as *anciens libres*, "former freemen," after the slaves were freed in 1793.

3. Herbert S. Klein, *African Slavery in Latin American and the Caribbean* (New York: Oxford University Press, 1986), 237.

4. For example, Carolyn E. Fick, *The Making of Haiti: The Saint Domingue Revolution From Below* (Knoxville: University of Tennessee Press, 1990), 19. On Raimond, see John D. Garrigus, "Julien Raimond: Planter, Revolutionary and Free Man of Color, 1744–1801," in *The Human Tradition in the Atlantic World 1500–1850*, ed. Karen Racine and Beatriz Gallotti Mamigonian (New York: Scholarly Resources, 2005). See the inconsistent use by one of Raimond's Parisian supporters in Abbé A. de Cournand, *Requête présentée à nosseigneurs de l'Assemblée Nationale, en faveur des gens de couleur de l'île de Saint-Domingue* (n.p., [1790]), 1. Vincent Ogé attributed the formula to Raimond, according to Yvan Debbasch in *Couleur et liberté: Le jeu du critère ethnique dans un ordre esclavagiste* (Paris: Dalloz, 1967), 161n3.

5. See Garrigus, "Redrawing the Colour Line: Gender and the Social Construction of Race in Pre-Revolutionary Haiti," *Journal of Caribbean History* 30 (1996): 28–50, for other conclusions based on this data.

6. The Boisronds are described in greater detail in Garrigus, "Color, Class and Identity on the Eve of the Haitian Revolution: Saint-Domingue's Free Colored Elite as *colons américains*," *Slavery & Abolition* 17 (1996): 35.

7. Dossier Boisrond, Greffe 168, Centre des Archives d'Outre-mer, Aix-en-Provence (hereafter CAOM).

8. Monneront reg. 1417 (this and all notarial register numbers below use the CAOM's post-1990 numbering system), February 10, 1782, CAOM; Gaudin reg. 751, November 19, 1785, CAOM.

9. Monneront reg. 1428, January 14, 1789, CAOM; Paillou reg. 1465, January 10, 1785, CAOM; Paillou reg. 1465, April 11, 1785, CAOM; Gaudin reg. 747, October 15, 1782, CAOM; Scovaud reg. 1597, January 16, 1781, CAOM.

10. Stewart R. King, *Blue Coat or Powdered Wig: Free People of Color in Pre-Revolutionary Saint Domingue* (Athens: University of Georgia Press, 2001), 133.

11. King, *Blue Coat or Powdered Wig,* 144–145, 189, 196, 205, 208, 223–234.

12. Gwendolyn Midlo Hall, *Social Control in Slave Plantation Societies: A Comparison of St. Domingue and Cuba* (Baltimore, Md.: Johns Hopkins University Press, 1971); Michel-Rolph Trouillot, "Motion in the System: Coffee, Color, and Slavery in

Eighteenth-Century Saint-Domingue," *Review* 5 (1982): 331–388; King, *Blue Coat or Powdered Wig.*

13. David Eltis, Stephen D. Behrendt, David Richardson, and Herbert S. Klein, *The Trans-Atlantic Slave Trade: A Database on CD-ROM* (London: Cambridge University Press, 1999).

14. Barbara Bush, "White 'Ladies,' Coloured 'Favorites,' and Black 'Wenches': Some Considerations on Sex, Race and Class Factors in Social Relations in White Creole Society in the British Caribbean," *Slavery and Abolition* 2 (1981): 245–262; Kathleen J. Higgins, "Gender and the Manumission of Slaves in Colonial Brazil: The Prospects for Freedom in Sabará, Minas Gerais, 1710–1809," *Slavery & Abolition* 18 (1997): 1, 12–13; Herbert S. Klein, "The Colored Freedmen in Brazilian Slave Society," *Journal of Social History* 3 (1969): 34, 41; Linda Lewin, "Natural and Spurious Children in Brazilian Inheritance Law from Colony to Nation: A Methodological Essay," *The Americas* 48 (1992): 363–368.

15. Herbert S. Klein, "The Colored Freedmen in Brazilian Slave Society," *Journal of Social History* 3 (1969): 31–32; A. J. R. Russell-Wood, *The Black Man in Slavery and Freedom in Brazil* (New York: St Martin's Press, 1982), 84–87; Samuel J. Hurwitz and Edith F. Hurwitz, "A Token of Freedom: Private Bill Legislation for Free Negroes in Eighteenth-Century Jamaica," *William & Mary Quarterly* 24 (1967): 427; Douglas Hall, "Jamaica," in *Neither Slave nor Free: The Freedman of African Descent in the Slave Societies of the New World*, ed. David W. Cohen and Jack P. Greene (Baltimore, Md.: Johns Hopkins University Press, 1972), 193–213.

16. Russell-Wood, *The Black Man in Slavery and Freedom in Brazil*, 69–75; Carl N. Degler, *Neither Black Nor White: Slavery and Race Relations in Brazil and the United States* (New York: Macmillan, 1971), 84.

17. Trevor Burnard, "The Sexual Life of an Eighteenth-Century Jamaican Slave Overseer," in *Sex and Sexuality in Early America*, ed. Merril D. Smith (New York: New York University Press, 1998), 57–58; Hurwitz and Hurwitz, "A Token of Freedom," 424–430.

18. Linda Sturz, "'A Very Nuisance to the Community': The Ambivalent Place of Freeds in Jamaican Free Society in the Eighteenth Century" (1999), paper prepared for the 31st annual conference of the Association of Caribbean Historians, Havana, April 11–17, 1999, 25.

19. Charles Frostin, *Les révoltes blanches à Saint-Domingue aux xvii et xviiie siècles (Haïti avant 1789)* (Paris: Editions de l'Ecole, 1975); Jean Tarrade, "L'administration coloniale en France à la fin de l'Ancien Régime: Projets de réforme," *Revue historique* 229 (1963): 103–123; Gabriel Debien, "Gouverneurs, magistrats et colons: L'opposition parlementaire et coloniale à Saint-Domingue (1763–1769)," *Revue de la société haïtienne d'histoire, de géographie et de géologie* 59 (October 1945): 1–50; and Malick W. Ghachem, "Montesquieu in the Caribbean: The Colonial Enlightenment between *Code Noir* and *Code Civil*," *Historical Reflections/Réflexions Historiques* 25 (1999): 183–210.

20. For example, Cornelius De Pauw, *Recherches philosophiques sur les américaines* (Berlin, 1768). See also Michèle Duchet, *Anthropologie et histoire au siècle des lumières: Buffon, Voltaire, Rousseau, Helvétius, Diderot*, ed. Claude Blanckaert (Paris: Maspéro, 1971), 202–205.

21. Emilien Petit, *Le patriotisme américain ou mémoires sur l'établissement de la partie française de l'isle de Saint-Domingue, sous le vent de l'Amérique* (N.p.: 1750), 9.

22. Petit, *Patriotisme américain*, 130.

23. Emilien Petit, *Traité sur le gouvernement des esclaves* (Paris: Chez Knapen, 1778); Emilien Petit, *Droit publique ou gouvernement des colonies françoises d'après les loix faites pour ces pays* (1771; repr., Paris: Geuthner, 1911); Ghachem, "Montesquieu in the Caribbean," 194–195; Tarrade, "L'administration coloniale," 104–106.

24. Jacques Godechot, "Nation, patrie, nationalisme et patriotisme en France au xviiie siècle," *Annales historiques de la révolution française* 43 (1971): 485.

25. See Garrigus, "Redrawing the Colour Line," 35–37.

26. Petit, *Patriotisme américain*, 118–119.

27. Debbasch, *Couleur et liberté*, 102, cites Pierre de Vassière, *Saint-Domingue (1629–1789): La société et la vie créoles sous l'ancien régime* (Paris: Perrin, 1909), 223–234.

28. G1/509, no. 28, CAOM.

29. Dossier Braquehay, Greffe 168, CAOM.

30. Either Braquehais or his son was an inaugural member of free colored committee of Les Cayes in 1790. He was one of those sent by the Provincial Assembly of the South to negotiate with rebel slaves in August 1792 and was listed as a "notable of the commune" of Les Cayes in November 1792. He served as the free colored municipal attorney of Les Cayes in 1793. See Françoise Thésée, "Les assemblées paroissiales des Cayes à St. Domingue (1774–1793)," *Revue de la société haitienne d'histoire et de géographie* no. 137 (1982): 67, 163.

31. Paillou reg. 1465, February 15, 1784, CAOM; Scovaud reg. 1601, 11 January 1785, CAOM. One Braquehais described as a "mulatto from the south" was aide-de-camp for Martial Besse in 1797 and secretary for Henri Christophe in 1802. After Christophe's surrender, he fought pro-French forces in his home district of Les Islets just outside Les Cayes. He was one of the opposition leaders drowned by Berger, the commander of the city. See Beaubrun Ardouin, *Etudes sur l'histoire d'Haïti suivies de la vie du général J.-M. Borgella*, ed. François Dalencour (Port-au-Prince, 1958), 5:7, 77.

32. E 201, CAOM; see also Elisabeth Escalle and Mariel Gouyon Guillaume, *Francs-maçons des loges françaises aux Amériques, 1750–1850* (Paris: Edition E. Escalle, 1992), 499.

33. See, for example, the Chapuiset controversy in E 71, CAOM, described in Debbasch, *Couleur et liberté*, 69.

34. "Lettre de M. Bart gouverneur général . . . au ministre touchant les remontrances du conseil du Port-au-Prince au Roi contre lui. Au Port-au-Prince ce 27 janvier 1762," F3/175, 67, CAOM.

35. See the letters of Galbaud du Fort in Debien, "Gouverneurs, magistrats et colons," 15–21.

36. Edmond Dziembowski, *Un nouveau patriotisme français, 1750–1770: La France face à la puissance anglaise à l'époque de la guerre de sept ans* (Oxford: Voltaire Foundation, 1998), 488–489; [d'Estaing], "Objets principaux que j'ai en vue dans la réédition de l'ordonnance des milices de St Domingue," 15 janvier 1765, C9B/17, Archives Nationales, Paris (hereafter AN).

37. D'Argout to Versailles, February 24, 1769, F3/182, CAOM; d'Argout to Rohan, March 2, 1769, F3/182, CAOM; d'Argout to Rohan, 5 March 1769, F3/182, CAOM.

38. Col. C9A rec. 135, AN, cited in Frostin, *Les révoltes blanches*, 401; also E 57, dossier "Buttet (André)," CAOM.

39. F3/91, f. 192–197, CAOM.

40. F3/91 f. 189, CAOM.

41. Moreau de Saint-Méry's *Description* of Saint-Domingue, completed on the eve of the Revolution, does include population and militia numbers for each of the colony's fifty-five parishes. But most of these data appear to be drawn from royal censuses. At best, numbers can be contradictory. Stewart King reports that "colored and black militia companies numbered 104 out of 156 of the total force in 1789," citing Moreau de Saint-Méry, *Description*, 1:451. This is a typographical error, according to the author, and the evidence actually comes from Col. D2/115, Troupes et personnel civil, CAOM. However in 1786, La Luzerne claimed that Saint-Domingue had 223 militia companies. See D2c/114, Troupes et personnel civil, CAOM.

42. "Etat des Mémoires en demande des graces que Mre de La Luzerne fait passer avec son travail de revues," D2c/114, CAOM.

43 King, *Blue Coat or Powdered Wig*, 276–277.

44. His appendix includes a table showing that there were relatively six to ten times as many notarial deeds featuring free colored militia figures in the North Province as in the West Province. King, *Blue Coat or Powdered Wig*, 278–279.

45. Debbasch, *Couleur et liberté*, 51.

46. Moreau de Saint-Méry, *Description*, 186, 229.

47. *Affiches Américaines*, April 6, 1779.

48. *Affiches Américaines*, March 30, 1779.

49. The list of free colored soldiers is in Xi carton 1, Service Historique de l'Armée de la Terre, Vincennes.

50. After the Battle of Savannah, some free colored units were sent to France before returning to the colony. Dossier "Lenoir de Rouvray," 54 and 55, E 278, CAOM; "Régiment des chasseurs volontaires de St Domingue," D2/341, CAOM.

51. King, *Blue Coat*, 62.

52. King, *Blue Coat*, 277–278; Dominique Rogers, "Les libres de couleur dans les capitales de Saint-Domingue: Fortune, mentalités et intégration à la fin de l'Ancien Régime (1776–1789)" (Doctoral thesis, Université de Bordeaux III, 1999), 425.

53. For Rigaud's service history, see dossier 484, Dxxv50, AN; for Rigaud in the notarial record, see Scovaud reg. 1600, May 3, 1784, CAOM; for Bleck in the notarial record, see Carré reg. 335, June 12, 1786, CAOM.

54. Scovaud reg. 1596, December 2, 1780, CAOM; Belin Duressort reg. 103, July 10, 1769, CAOM; dossier "Nommé Fossé," E 189, CAOM.

55. F3/91, CAOM.

56. "Lettre de M. Le Commandant général par interim à M. L'Intendant . . . du 26 mai 1780," F3/189, CAOM; D2c/41, Troupes et personnel civil, CAOM. See Garrigus, "Catalyst or Catastrophe? Saint-Domingue's Free Men of Color and the Battle of Savannah, 1779–1782," *Revista/Review Interamericana* 22, nos. 1–2 (1992): 109–125.

57. Debbasch *Couleur et liberté*, 126–127.

58. Julien Raimond, in F3/91, f. 197, CAOM.

59. F3/91, f. 189, CAOM.

60. F3/91, f. 186, CAOM.

61. F3/91, f. 190–191, CAOM.

62. F3/91, f. 182, CAOM.

63. See the story of Milscent de Musset, a creole white and former captain of a mulatto militia unit living in France during the revolution. He published five issues of a newspaper entitled *Le Créole Patriote* beginning in June 1792, as men of color were given citizenship. Jean-Daniel Piquet, "*Le Créole Patriote,* apôtre de l'insurrection de Saint-Domingue," *Annales historiques de la révolution française* (1993): 519–521; Florence Gauthier, "Comment la nouvelle d l'insurrection des esclaves de Saint-Domingue fut-elle reçue en France (1791–1793)," *L'insurrection des esclaves de Saint-Domingue (22–23 août 1791)*, ed. Laënnec Hurbon (Paris: Karthala, 2000), 22; and especially Yves Benot, "L'Affaire Milscent," *Dix-huitième siècle* 21 (1989): 311–327.

64. Raimond probably knew Boisrond Tonnerre. See Julien Raimond, *Correspondance de Julien Raimond avec ses frères* (Paris, 1793), 46, in which his friend Louis-François Boisrond asks Raimond to oversee the education of his family in France in 1791.

On the Road to Citizenship
The Complex Route to Integration of the Free People of Color in the Two Capitals of Saint-Domingue

Dominique Rogers

"CITIZENSHIP" AND "INTEGRATION" ARE TWO TERMS THAT MAY SEEM OUT OF PLACE PRIOR TO 1789 AND EVEN SHOCKING WHEN APPLIED TO PEOPLE OF COLOR LIVING IN A SLAVE SOCIETY. THE ACCOUNTS of European travelers from the late eighteenth century, just like the famous memoranda the *quarteron*[1] Julien Raimond sent to the colonial ministry in the 1780s, have long established the idea that Saint-Domingue's free people of color lived in a society where no integration was possible.[2] Because of color prejudice, the whites seemed always superior to the blacks and the lightest-skinned *métis* remained, nevertheless, always a black person or, in short, a vile human being. Historians have asserted, therefore, that despite the Black Code of 1685, the *libres de couleur* of French Saint-Domingue enjoyed only a "second-class citizenship" and a partial freedom ("une liberté surveillée"). European travelers, however, were not always the most appropriate persons for understanding such a complex colonial society, and my argument here is that this conventional point of view lacks a true grasp of what citizenship meant in an ancien régime context and fails to perceive how legal norms differed from daily practice. Drawing on a corpus of 7,000 documents, mainly from notarial and judicial archives, I will try to demonstrate that another interpretation is possible for which the words "citizenship" and "integration" are relevant when applied to the *libres de couleur*.

Citizenship and Free Colored City-Dwellers

For the French, as for Americans, no doubt, the concept of citizenship is tightly linked to the exercise of political rights—to the idea that each individual can participate in shaping the direction of his or her country. Yet in the context of the ancien régime, such possibilities existed for only a few. Only the members of the nobility and the *haute bourgeoisie* could assume the responsibilities of governance. Before 1789, women, domestic servants, Jews (to a certain degree), Protestants, and ordinary urban and rural folk could not aspire to participate in the political life of their city or country. Consequently, citizenship in the ancien régime did not represent, as Diderot phrased it, participation "in juridical life" (*la judicature*) or the expectation of passing "from the state of mere bourgeois to the highest ranks of the magistracy."[3] For most French people, it meant simply enjoying full possession of their civil rights. In Saint-Domingue, where no such society of orders existed, the likelihood of participating in the political life of the colony was no greater than in France: the few seats of *conseillers* on the appeal courts were reserved for magistrates trained in the metropole, members of the five-yearly advisory assemblies were essentially officials appointed by the king, and the chambers of agriculture each had only nine members, who were chosen from the richest *habitants* of the colony. Consequently, for the majority of the *libres de couleur*, as for most white people, citizenship was only realized in the civil domain. Real political rights remained the terrain of struggle for an elite that scarcely concerns us here, even if in 1789 the entourage[4] of Julien Raimond included two very important free colored merchants in Port-au-Prince: the mulatto Chanlatte the elder and the quadroon Jean-Charles Haran, called l'Africain. The vast majority of citizens of color never attained a comparable position and do not seem to have had such ambitions.[5]

Under the ancien régime, the most basic civil rights were the *conubium* (the right to marry), the *commercium* (the right to draw up various contracts), and lastly the right to bequeath and to inherit property[6]—all legal rights that *libres de couleur* fully enjoyed in Saint-Domingue. The right to inherit and bequeath property was important for two reasons: first, because it reminds us that *libres de couleur*, whether they were free by birth or by manumission, were considered by legal authorities to be *régnicoles* (a juridical term meaning "nationals of a country"), not foreigners; and second, by exempting them from the *droit d'aubaine*, it made possible the accumulation of wealth.[7]

Unlike the practice in many other colonies, *libres de couleur* were also accorded free choice in marriage. Mixed marriages, often perceived as misalliances, were nevertheless found in all social ranks and remained quite common. At the end of the ancien régime, such marriages accounted for 17 percent of legitimate unions in the south, 7 percent of marriage contracts in Port-au-Prince, and 11 percent in Cap-Français.[8] Finally, the right of *commercium* guaranteed freedom in the economic realm for free people of color. They could thus acquire, sell, and lease as they wished. According to contemporaries, they owned between a quarter and a third of immovable and movable property on the island.[9] They could work and associate with whomever they chose. Despite official decrees, they were found in all trades. The notaries of Cap-Français mention a midwife (Marie Guérineau), a surgeon (the *mulâtre* Toussaint Lavallé), and several goldsmiths (the *nègre libre* Joseph dit Aubry and the *mulâtres* Pierre dit Cabarin and Laurent Sequin).[10]

The exercise of citizenship, in fact, even at the civil level, implied more: it assumed the possibility of obtaining legal protection for one's goods and one's person. The existence of this right, however, has not been without controversy in the historical literature. The oft-cited memoranda of Julien Raimond affirmed that it was impossible for a *libre de couleur* to bring a lawsuit against a white. "In Saint-Domingue, persons of color who dare to strike a white are rigorously punished, even when they are struck first: such is the force of prejudice against them that their death, in such a case, is not considered too great a punishment,"[11] and in 1789, the unidentified author of *Précis des gémissements des sang mêlés des colonies françaises* asserted that as soon as the racial identity of litigants was announced to a court, "our fate was sealed."[12] The actual decisions issued by the Conseil supérieur (court of appeals) and the *sénéchaussée* (lower court) of Port-au-Prince allow us to test these claims.[13]

The response of the courts, it should be noted, constituted a final judgment. In civil matters, I found that not only did the *libres de couleur* dare to summon whites before the seneschal or the Conseil supérieur, or even the Conseil du Roi, but they were also heard by the magistrates. In one-third of the "ordinary" judgments (36 percent of the cases), the seneschal of Port-au-Prince found in favor of the free people of color. This was also the outcome for 39 percent of the judgments by default and 62 percent of the judgments without appeal. In the Conseil supérieur, the judges went even farther, siding with the *libres de couleur* in almost 60 percent of the cases.

The minutes of the clerk's office do not always mention the details of the cases; nevertheless, the explanations given for judicial decisions demonstrate the fairness of the judges. They based their decisions upon legalities and upon evidence: that is, the existence of a legal document (a work contract, bill of sale, or marriage settlement) or a private agreement recognized and accepted as "full proof" (such as an account book containing signatures verified as genuine). Their procedures followed in every detail those practiced in the metropole, where all of the colony's judges had been trained. For instance, when one party in a suit failed to appear, his or her case was systematically dismissed, just as in metropolitan France, whatever the color of the parties. Perhaps even more important, the *serment à main levée* (solemn oath), which was common practice in the ancien régime, was also in use between whites and free people of color. Contrary to the suggestion of the author of *Précis des gémissements des sang mêlés*, the word of a *libre de couleur* was considered the legal equivalent of—indeed sometimes superior to—that of a white. In 1789, in the case of César the elder, *libre de couleur*, against the sieur Vaisse, merchant of Port-au-Prince, the judges affirmed: "Ruling in favor of César the elder for the oath taken before us in execution of the sentence of 16 March 1788. The court condemns the sieur Vaisse to bear expenses of the case and requires him to execute the sentence of 16 March 1788."[14] In July 1789, Suzette dit Turgeau, *mulâtresse libre*, confronted her tenant, le sieur Courtin, who insisted that he had given her the keys to her apartment before his departure. She swore to the contrary and obtained a favorable verdict. Such verdicts concerned white legal opponents of every background and level of wealth. The cases brought by the *receveur des aubaines* (a tax collector) were regularly dismissed, and Barré de Saint-Venant, an illustrious member of the Cap-Français Chamber of Agriculture, did not fare better before the justices. Considering this equal treatment of legal opponents and the possibility of a favorable verdict against a white, how can one affirm that whites and *libres de couleur* were *not* treated equally, at least by the judges?

The cases I have cited concern only civil law; I have not treated cases of assault and battery. The majority of such cases of violence were dealt with, insofar as they were, by the *commandants de quartier*, who did not leave written records. In 1786, the intendant Barbé de Marbois proposed to bring all cases between whites and *libres de couleur* before the tribunals because of the militia officers' inequitable handling of cases. This step, which suggests an administrative will to improve the situation, appears to have been effective. In 1789, the *cahiers de doléances* submitted to the States-General by Saint-Domingue's wealthy whites confirmed this point *a contrario* by demanding that free coloreds be subjected to the *grande police* "as in the past."[15] Even so, in the few cases of assault considered at the level of the Conseils supérieurs, the view of Raimond and others is substantiated. Acts committed against a white were defined as "crimes," whereas the same acts against *libres de couleur* were described simply as misdemeanors (*délits*).[16] Nevertheless, such offences were punished by a fine—at times, a considerable sum. In 1783, the sieur Chanche was obliged to pay 3,000 livres for striking the *mulâtre* Charles Marcombe "in such a manner that he risked the loss of an eye." Yet the same behavior earned a colored perpetrator the iron collar and temporary banishment. This punishment was reduced by the end of the period to the iron collar and just a fine, although the small number of trials of this type does not allow us to confirm there was a definite evolution in the direction of less severity.

The fundamental distinctions in criminal cases prevent us from claiming that free people of color enjoyed full citizenship at the end of the ancien régime, even when the equal treatment they received in the civil sphere and their numerous civil rights might suggest otherwise. Should we therefore assume, as is often done, that the process of assimilation, or at least integration, of *libres de couleur* was decisively blocked in Saint-Domingue?

The Integration of Free Colored City-Dwellers

"Integration" is a concept not often used by American historians, who prefer the term "assimilation." It therefore requires some explanation. For French sociologists, being integrated is different from being assimilated. Assimilation is a process that results in a foreigner being viewed and fully accepted as an ordinary member of the community.[17] Being integrated, on the other hand, only means that one is allowed to enjoy the same rights and advantages as other members of a society but without being viewed as one of them. The many civil rights granted to the free coloreds of Saint-Domingue are an illustration of what integration can be. Nevertheless, true integration also implies the peaceful enjoyment of rights within a community that respects differences. The humiliations suffered by people of color that were observed by visitors to Saint-Domingue plus the discriminatory regulations of the 1750s to 1770s seem incompatible with this vision, although the colonists did discuss even the assimilation of free coloreds.

The ordinances (*ordonnances*) and the regulations often cited by historians to demonstrate that French colonial society was segregationist were not fundamental laws and for this reason proved to be optional in application.[18] For instance, the sumptuary law of 1779 directed at free coloreds was intended to be temporary. Analysis of a few inventories and of the trousseaux of free colored women confirms that this rule was obsolescent at the end of the old regime. Furthermore, although the judgments of 1761 and 1762 forbade free colored men to carry a sword except on militia or *maréchaussée* service, colored noncommissioned officers were allowed to do so at least during the American Revolution, on the mainland and in the colony.

Those discriminatory laws are clearly related to a particular period of Saint-Domingue history when the French metropolitan administration saw the free coloreds as enemies of the whites. It was the time of the Macandal conspiracy and of the successful rebellions of the Suriname maroons.[19] In order to maintain the slave system, the ministry thought the only solution was to affirm the inferiority of the blacks and demean free coloreds in every way possible.[20] The instructions given to the administrators specified that "it would be impossible to put too much distance between the two species, or to instill in the *nègres* too much respect for their masters. This harsh discrimination, even after manumission, is the principal line of subordination, because of the resulting idea that the *nègre's* color dooms him to servitude and that nothing can make him equal to his master."[21]

In the 1780s, the general context changed. Under the influence of the philosophes, the colonial ministry had begun to view blacks differently. Free coloreds were not primarily seen as former slaves but, on the contrary, as slave-owners and therefore potential allies of the whites. They were said to be "the strongest barrier against any rebellion of the enslaved."[22] The new government did not abolish the old discriminatory regulations, but it also did not create new ordinances that discriminated against *libres de couleur*. In addition, the naval and colonial minister, the Maréchal de Castries, enjoined the new administrators to favor "those [free colored people] who owned an estate for they have a style of life which merits reward."[23]

From 1782, new administrators were asked to seek the advice of "the high court judges, the members of the chambers of agriculture, and of land-owners (*habitants*) whom they thought the most trustworthy, in order to temper the policy of degradation that had been established, and to put an end to it."[24] Some symbolic gestures, military pensions, for instance, were proffered to free colored people. Julien Raimond was received by the administrators and then by the naval and colonial minister. Nevertheless, the new policy was not successful. Although the local elite had long contemplated the true assimilation of free coloreds (as distinguished from their integration, which already existed), they continued to suggest long-term solutions that favored only light-skinned individuals rather than the numerous and wealthy free blacks and mulattoes.[25] In 1788, Governor Duchilleau's instructions asserted that the discriminatory policy against the free coloreds could come to an end only "when the signs of their [African] origin had disappeared, that is when they could pass for white people."[26] When, at the beginning of the French Revolution, the administrators and the colonists claimed that most of those discriminatory regulations had fallen into abeyance, they were thought by historians to be stretching the facts.[27] A close analysis of the practice of Conseils supérieurs and of the notaries allows us to perceive a little more of this complex reality.

According to the ordinances on the civil governance of the colonies, the Conseils supérieurs had two functions: to register the local administrators' *règlements de police* (regulations regarding public order) and, as a court of appeals, to interpret local laws by issuing *règlements de justice* (judicial rulings).[28] In 1781, the registration of the discriminatory ordinances of Intendant Alexandre Lebrasseur gave rise to a serious conflict between him and the high court judges.[29] In a dispute concerning goldsmiths, the judges issued explicit directives. "The regulations allow free colored people to work," they asserted, "[a right which is] certainly included in article 59 of the edict of 1685, by which the King accorded to emancipated slaves the same rights, privileges, and immunities enjoyed by those free from birth." The intendant's decree, they continued, was "a direct attack on the status of freedmen." Did the administrators think they were authorized to overturn the intention of an edict?[30] The ministry followed the high court judges. In 1782, Alexandre Lebrasseur was recalled to Paris and none of the new rules were registered, except for one related to poisons. A minister added sarcastically: "The desire to legislate, although it may stem from a good principle, sometimes blinds a person to the point that he will find bad the wisest laws of the king and find good only what he himself does."[31]

The Conseils supérieurs of Saint-Domingue regularly interpreted laws in a manner favorable to the economic assimilation of illegitimate free colored children. The judges systematically favored such children (especially *enfants naturels simples*[32]) over legitimate, but less closely related, heirs residing in France. They also ratified legacies and settlements well beyond the usual living allowance of 400 to 600 colonial livres a year. In 1782, Cap-Français's high court judges allowed "free colored illegitimate children half of a succession[,] including an estate."[33] In 1777, the magistrates of Port-au-Prince permitted a legacy of 40,000 livres to go to Marie-Thérèse Livet dite Dutapion, *mulâtresse libre* of Saint-Marc, whereas the lower court had found an allowance of 10,000 livres to be sufficient.[34]

The notaries, who were supposed to enforce the new identification laws directed against persons of color, also chose to resist. The explicit aim of the new regulations was to reinforce racial segregation by creating a racialized naming system (*une onomastique de couleur*). The 1773 regulation forbade free coloreds to use the name of a white person and forced freedpersons and illegitimate children to adopt a nickname related to Africa ("tiré de l'idiome africain"). Two decisions of the Cap-Français Conseil supérieur in 1783 completed the plan by confirming the practice of using the terms *sieur*, *dame*, and *demoiselle* in the public records solely for white people.[35]

Notaries in both Port-au-Prince and Cap-Français respected neither the letter nor the spirit of the law. Although they did insert a nickname in 95 percent of the manumission deeds they registered between 1776 and 1789, the nicknames were chosen from a wide variety of domains, for instance the Bible, European flora and fauna, or geography. However unusual the nicknames Castor (beaver), Tulipe, or Mouton (sheep) were, they certainly did not link the future *affranchi* to Africa. Moreover, the Christian names and diminutives that were adopted were not distinctive at all. In addition, the practice of giving a personal nickname to each family member prevented apparently African nicknames (Mambo, Mabia, Zilia, Tollo, Quicambe) from becoming surnames in the next generation. Finally, the choice of an anagram of the master's name poses the fundamental question of the extent to which masters were implicated in the process of resistance. When the widow Gazin accepted "Nizag" as the nickname of her slave or when le Sieur Cairou approved the name "Raucoi," they fooled nobody.[36] So why did they do it? Let us recall that in the early colonial period, as in antiquity, a freedman remained tied to his former master in a patron-client relationship and often adopted his name. By inserting an anagram of his name, the master was actually expressing his desire to maintain, and publicize, his personal link to the ex-slave. Finally, if the recently freed generally adopted the new nickname, although sometimes only for a few years or months, those who had been freed before the law resisted, sometimes with great determination. Between 1776 and 1789, 61 percent of free coloreds who had a marriage contract in Port-au-Prince had a family name that had no relation to the 1773 regulations, and 30 percent had only a Christian name.

With regard to the color and status labels, the notaries of the two capital cities proceeded differently. In Port-au-Prince, where the high court took a hard line with those who were recalcitrant, notaries strictly enforced the new regulations. In 90 percent of marriage contracts and testaments, they demanded the birth or the manumission certificate of their free colored clients. In Cap-Français, on the other hand, notaries largely ignored the regulation. In most marriage contracts or wills, they identified free colored clients in the same way as they did white clients. If they did indicate their color, they hardly ever mentioned their precise status, and ascertained that a person was free simply by reference to his or her reputation, specifically their *possession d'état de libre* (the fact that a person was considered by others to be free).

We will touch only briefly on the question of the titles *sieur, dame,* and *demoiselle,* which raise issues more complex than we can fully analyze here.[37] On the whole, notaries used these terms of respect sparingly. Exceptions for people of color were rare, but in this, the notaries simply followed common practice. Contrary to what is often believed, the decrees of 1783 concerned public acts exclusively. Private agreements, account books of metropolitan ship captains, and correspondence of the era all attest that in everyday life whites did use these forms of address for free people of color, at least for the wealthiest or the most highly regarded of them.[38] The question is complicated because although the lightest *métis* generally received such respect, this terminology was also applied on occasion to *nègres libres.*

The decisions of the notaries and judges did more than merely express the will of French jurists. Registering nonconforming surnames, using the titles *sieur* and *dame,* or applying the names of European families to illegitimate children required, at a minimum, the tacit agreement of some segment of the white population. Free people of color were familiar figures in the day-to-day existence of many white colonists; they were their neighbors, their economic partners, sometimes their former slaves, and sometimes their children, concubines, or spouses. Their refusal of segregation testifies to the reality of integration and perhaps to the beginning of an assimilation.

At the end of the eighteenth century, Saint-Domingue's capitals provided a setting that was particularly favorable to this normalization of relations—a fact that is most evident in the absence of residential segregation. Whites and free coloreds lived in the same neighborhoods, shared kitchens and wells in the same courtyards, and sometimes lived under the same roof without necessarily having more intimate relations.[39] If neighborly conflicts occasionally added spice to daily life, whites and *libres* also learned to speak to one another, to resolve problems, and to compromise rather than to allow disputes about racial superiority embitter relations. The verbal and sometimes physical aggression that we often hear about was probably not the ordinary mode of behavior of the white population as a whole or even of those grouped under the name *petits-blancs* but was rather an expression of racism by those who were excluded from the system, the "moutons-France" who arrived each year by the hundreds and who, lacking money, support, and sometimes even skills, failed to succeed. Mistrusted by the locals, they formed an urban proletariat that was restless and particularly sensitive to the dominant racist discourse, since their whiteness was their sole social advantage. But alongside them a number of urban artisans and merchants and even small and middling planters lived on good terms with the free colored population. They were competitors with one another, but also clients and sometimes associates.

Wills and gifts reveal that solidarity and even friendship were possible between whites and free people of color. Traditionally such relationships were cases of love, or actual matrimony, or concubinage. While these bonds across racial lines do suggest a certain acceptance of difference and are thus significant, they were not the only form of connection possible between whites and *libres* at the end of the eighteenth century. For instance, Dame Marie-Françoise Sarget bequeathed 6,600 livres to the housekeeper (*ménagère*) of her son, Françoise dite Francillette, to facilitate the establishment of the young woman.[40] In 1786, Bernard Lamouroux gave a 9-year-old *petite négrille* slave to the legitimate daughter of two *mulâtres* who were his neighbors.[41] In 1780 and in his will of 1782, Port-au-Prince police officer François Noël Leprestre made bequests to two of his work companions: to Pierre dit Gerbau, *mulâtre libre* and a trooper in the *maréchaussée*, he gave a small plot of land in the town, and to his former troop commander, Labastille, "for his good and affectionate services," he gave a Congo slave.[42] At the moment of death, a number of *petits-blancs*, in other respects ill-tempered, avowed their emotional debts to women of color who had cared for them when whites had abandoned them. Such gestures speak of daily practices far removed from segregationist discourse.

Professional competence was also a fundamental means of integration and, in a certain sense, of assimilation. In Cap-Français, wealthier artisans and tradespeople of color won respect across the racial divide with their efficiency. Whites did not hesitate to give important construction projects to the most talented colored artisans. From 1776 to 1786, the business log of the *mulâtre* entrepreneur Joseph Rouanet is among the most impressive: besides several rich free colored families (Desrouleaux and Laporte), he counted among his clients the notary Arnault Lacaze; Sieur Jullian, a bourgeois of

Le Cap; and Pierre Joseph Laborie, high court lawyer and member of the Chamber of Agriculture. The sums in question are quite significant, with just five large contracts amounting to a total of 334,909 livres. In a larger sense, the artisans of Cap-Français provided technical education for young freemen of color as well as the training of slaves. In one exceptional case, the *quarteron* Joseph Pironneau even trained a white child, Bernard Thenot Lachenez.[43] Moreover, the artisans of color of Le Cap were customarily solicited to appraise work that had been entrusted to whites or *libres*. At the request of individuals of one or the other group, they intervened as experts and *surexperts*. In 1788, the seneschal of Le Cap named three *libres de couleur*, Etienne Chavileau, Joseph Rouanet, and Claude Imbert, to decide a dispute between the *mulâtre libre* Jean-Baptiste Lagarde and the *demoiselle* Geneviève Hébert, a midwife who was the widow of Sieur Lemoine.[44] In spite of prejudice, no one dreamed of calling into question the impartiality of the chosen experts. Finally, Le Cap's notaries regularly solicited forty or so *libres de couleur* to authenticate official acts, even when they did not know how to write. In Port-au-Prince, however, where the artisans were less active and the population of color generally was less wealthy, notaries only rarely summoned free coloreds for appraisals or to authenticate a notarial act.[45]

Beyond these differences in the behavior of notaries, the urban centers of Saint-Domingue integrated their free colored populations in quite different ways. At this stage of my research, it seems that in Port-au-Prince relations between whites and *libres de couleur* evolved within more traditional structures, in which the white family—whether legitimate or illegitimate—and relations of patronage played a determining role in the economic and social promotion of individuals. In the absence of a true community based on solidarity of color, the former master or the *bienveillant*[46] was often the sole guardian of the most vulnerable. From 1776 to 1789, some fifty women of color designated a white person to execute their wills; twelve male testators of color did the same. To manage their affairs, wealthy urbanites of color similarly preferred to place their trust in a white in nearly three-quarters of the cases (73.8 percent). Port-au-Prince free coloreds regularly chose whites to build their homes or to be their tenants (80 percent of a total of 90 contracts signed between 1777 and 1789). If this suggests real trust, it nonetheless also reveals the dominant lineaments of power within the city. The white was always in a dominant situation: it was the white who manumitted, the white who helped free coloreds get settled, find work, or survive on a daily basis. The rare white persons who approached a free person of color to execute their wills were isolated Frenchmen who called upon the services of a professional like the merchant Jean-Charles Haran dit l'Africain. Consequently, other than the rich *métis*, the townspeople of color in Port-au-Prince were often integrated in a subaltern position. If the *libres de couleur* in the western countryside were very quick to make political claims early in the revolution, the majority of urban residents of color were harassed and mistreated by the *petits-blancs*, who refused men of color the full citizenship they themselves were denied.

In Cap-Français, on the other hand, it seems that the integration of free people of color was accompanied by more egalitarian relations with whites. The existence of an elite corps of rich or comfortable artisans of color, whose competence and social standing was widely recognized by whites, seems to have been one of the fundamental reasons for this situation. The presence among them of numerous *nègres libres* (free blacks) also appears to have been an important element in changing the attitude of the white population, although more research on the matter is needed. On a general level, men participated in the elaboration of a true community of *hommes de couleur* that was open to all without regard to shades of complexion or status. Consequently, free people of color ordinarily approached one of their own to construct their houses, manage their goods, execute their wills, or educate their children, most often one of the wealthier artisans in the community. Bonds with whites were not severed, however. When they drew up their wills, free black women chose someone of their own color in 60 percent of the cases, but in 17 percent of the cases they turned to whites. This indicates a real trust, since they had never legally contracted with these whites, as they would have with a professional. Finally, whites were still 42 percent of the proxies named by Le Cap's residents of color to manage their goods, against, it is true, 74 percent in Port-au-Prince.[47] However, because free people of color truly had an alternative, one can suppose that their choice represented a positive step that expressed a feeling of integration. Significantly, free people of color in Cap-Français were never harassed by the white population before 1791, and they never rebelled.[48]

I am not suggesting here that Saint-Domingue society was not racialist. Until the very end of the ancien régime, the idea of black inferiority, based on color prejudice, remained the basis of local society. Nevertheless, the economic rise of the *libres de couleur* compelled part of the white community to view them differently and therefore to contemplate not only their integration (which was already occurring) but also their assimilation. Those whites most often favored the wealthiest and the lightest-skinned people of color, but their attitudes also changed toward free blacks, especially in Cap-Français. A more detailed study of the attitudes of various segments of the white community toward people of color is still needed, but the general trend seems already clear. Finally, although the *libres de couleur* of Saint-Domingue were not quite equal citizens according to present-day criteria, they enjoyed as many rights as most French people in the metropole or in Saint-Domingue, and they enjoyed greater equality than free colored people in the other French colonies. If the discriminatory regulations were never formally abolished, by the late eighteenth century many of them were no longer being enforced. The *libres de couleur* were bold enough to ask for political rights in 1789, not because their social status was deteriorating, as scholars have often claimed, but because their heightened social integration gave them new confidence, as did the increasing wealth of the whole group.

Notes

1. Quadroon. Typically a person whose grandparents included three whites and one black.

2. Alexandre-Stanislas de Wimpffen, *Haïti au XVIIIeme siècle, richesse et esclavage dans une colonie française*, ed. P. Pluchon (Paris: Karthala, 1993); Justin Girod de Chantrans, *Voyage d'un Suisse dans différentes colonies d'Amérique pendant la dernière guerre*, ed. P. Pluchon (Paris: Taillandier, 1980); Memoranda by Julien Raimond, 1784–1787, F3/91, Centre des Archives d'Outre-mer, Aix-en-Provence (hereafter CAOM).

3. "Citoyen," in *Encyclopédie ou dictionnaire raisonné des sciences, des arts et des métiers*, ed. Denis Diderot and Jean D'Alembert (Paris, 1753), 3:488.

4. André Maistre du Chambon, "Acte notarié relatif aux doléances des gens de couleur de Saint-Domingue; 29 juillet 1789," *Mémoires de la société archéologique et historique de la Charente* (1931), 5–11.

5. On the wealth of the free colored city-dwellers, see Dominique Rogers, "Les Libres de couleur dans les capitales de Saint-Domingue: Fortune, mentalités et intégration à la fin de l'Ancien Régime, (1776–1789)" (thèse de doctorat, Université de Bordeaux III, 1999), chapter 2.

6. Anne Lefebvre-Teillard, *Introduction historique au droit des personnes et de la famille* (Paris: P.U.F., 1996), 23.

7. The *droit d'aubaine* permitted the king to appropriate possessions left by foreigners.

8. Jacques Houdaille, "Trois paroisses de Saint-Domingue au XVIIIe siècle," *Population* 1 (1963): 93–110.

9. Pierre Pluchon, ed., *La Révolution de Haïti* [Pamphile de Lacroix, *Mémoires pour servir à l'histoire de la Révolution de Saint-Domingue*] (Paris: Karthala, 1995), 48.

10. See Rogers, "Les Libres de couleur dans les capitales de Saint-Domingue," annexes chapter 3.

11. Julien Raimond, *Réclamations adressées à l'Assemblée Nationale par les personnes de couleur de Saint-Domingue* (Paris, 1790), 2.

12. J. M. C., Américain de sang mêlé, *Précis des gémissements des sang mêlés des colonies françaises* (Paris, 1789), 5.

13. Appeals court cases, 1776 to 1788; lower court "ordinary judgments," November 29, 1783, to March 27, 1784; lower court "decisions rendered without appeal" and "judgments by default," July 21, 1789, to December 1, 1789, Greffe 1–3, 6, 8–9, CAOM.

14. Case no. 37, Greffe 9, CAOM.

15. Blanche Maurel, ed., *Cahiers de doléances de la colonie de Saint-Domingue* (Paris: E. Leroux, 1933), 267.

16. See *livre journal* containing fourteen decisions (*arrêts*) of the Conseil supérieur of Cap-Français from 1785 to 1786, C9A/165, CAOM; M. L. E. Moreau de Saint-Méry, *Loix et constitutions de l'Amérique française sous le vent*, 6 vols. (Paris, 1784–1790).

17. Assimilation is a social process that leads to homogeneity (cultural, linguistic, and political) and is promoted, more or less, by the members of a group.

18. François-Olivier Martin, *Les Lois du Roi* (Paris: Loysiel, 1988). The fundamental laws were meant to limit the king's power and could not be abridged or changed in any way.

19. Between 1749 and 1772, they obtained the recognition of their independence, just like the maroons of Jamaica had in 1739 and 1740.

20. See in particular Emilien Petit, *Traité sur le gouvernement des esclaves* (Paris, 1777). As president of the first Committee on Legislation, Petit was officially responsible for overseeing colonial administration.

21. See instructions to Fieldmont and Malouet, 1776, F3/91, f. 209, CAOM.

22. F3/72, especially f. 46, CAOM.

23. F3/278, 341, CAOM.

24. F3/72, especially f. 46, CAOM.

25. Barré de Saint-Vénant, "Mémoire sur les affranchis," October 3, 1776, F3/125, d124(44), CAOM; Hilliard d'Auberteuil, *Considérations sur l'état présent de la colonie française de Saint-Domingue* (Paris, 1777), 2:82–96.

26. F3/72, 241, CAOM.

27. Yves Benot, *La Révolution française et la fin des colonies* (Paris: La Découverte, 1987).

28. See ordinances on the administration of the colonies of 1766, 1775, and 1785 in Moreau de Saint-Méry, *Loix et constitutions*, vol. 4; and F3/120, 26–46, CAOM.

29. Ordinances on poisons, midwives, and goldsmiths.

30. C9A/151, May 4, 1781, CAOM.

31. F3/78, 249, CAOM.

32. Children born to parents who were not married to each other or to anyone else.

33. M. L. E. Moreau de Saint-Méry, *Loix et constitutions de l'Amérique française sous le vent* (Paris, 1784–1790), 6: 252.

34. Judgment of June 11, 1777, Greffe 1, 84–86, CAOM.

35. Decision of the Conseil supérieur of Cap-Français, February 22, 1783, F3/276, 246, CAOM.

36. Manumission act for Jeanne, October 9, 1778, Notsdom 169, CAOM.

37. On the complex question of identification, see Rogers, "Les Libres de couleur," ch. 5.

38. Dominique Rogers, "Contribution à la recherche sur les réseaux commerciaux des Bordelais à Saint-Domingue dans la deuxième moitié du XVIIIe siècle" (TER, Université de Bordeaux III, 1989).

39. Rogers, "Les Libres de couleur," ch. 7.

40. Deed of April 22, 1788, Notsdom 1554, CAOM.

41. Deed of June 19, 1786, Notsdom 1522, CAOM.

42. Deed of May 6, 1780, Notsdom 436, CAOM.

43. Apprenticeship contract of October 12, 1779, Notsdom 176, CAOM.

44. Deed of March 4, 1788, Notsdom 200, CAOM.

45. Only five *libres de couleur* were requested to authenticate a notarial deed from 1776 to 1789 in Port-au-Prince.

46. A sponsor, sometimes different from the master, who attended to of all the formalities needed to manumit a slave.

47. 37 proxies out of 88 for Cap-Français; 31 proxies out of 42 for Port-au-Prince.

48. See "Adresse des commissaires nationaux-civils aux colons et habitants, hommes de couleur et nègres libres de la ville du Cap-Français, des paroisses du Terrier Rouge, Port-Margot, Plaisance, La Marmelade, le Borgne, le Petit-Saint-Louis, le Port-de-Paix, le Gros Morne, Jean Rabel, le Môle Saint-Nicolas et le Port-à-Piment," cited in Yvan Debbasch, *Couleur et liberté. Le Jeu du critère ethnique dans un ordre juridique esclavagiste* (Paris: Dalloz, 1967), 205.

THE TRANS-ATLANTIC KING AND IMPERIAL PUBLIC SPHERES
EVERYDAY POLITICS IN PRE-REVOLUTIONARY SAINT-DOMINGUE

Gene E. Ogle

L'ÉTAT, C'EST MOI," LOUIS XIV IS SUPPOSED TO HAVE SAID, AND WHETHER HE DID OR NOT, THE PRINCIPLES, IF NOT THE EVERYDAY REALITIES, OF OLD REGIME POLITICS COULD NOT BE SUMMED up better. In theory, French kings reserved all legislative, judicial, and executive power to themselves. They not only represented divine authority on the earth, their persons encompassed the entire French political order. As the Sun King's successor, Louis XV, declared in 1766, "It is in my person alone that sovereign power resides. . . . The whole system of political order emanates from me."[1]

During the seventeenth and eighteenth centuries, the political order of which Louis XV spoke grew to include colonial territories oceans away from France. By 1789, the king's subjects had come to number hundreds of thousands of enslaved and free Africans, African Americans, and South Asians as well as millions of Europeans. Colonial social and economic structures may have differed radically from those of the metropole, but the same political principles were applied to ruling them. As the *domingais* jurisconsult Émilien Petit noted in 1778, "The government of the French colonies is entirely in the hands of the king."[2]

Such an application of French absolutism to distant slave-based plantation colonies raises several questions. How could French political culture, dependent as it was upon the charisma of an individual and his lineage, be transferred to islands thousands of miles from France? As the manifest presence of the king in his territory remained important to the monarchy's legitimacy, how could the king's rule be preserved in lands upon which no

French ruler had ever set foot or would ever do so? Perhaps most important, as Jacky Dahomay has asked, "What then would become of . . . diverse
forms of [traditional] legitimization among men of different cultural origins
reunited in the artificial and violent space of the colonial slave societies?"[3] In
other words, what could France's absolute monarchs mean in the Caribbean
to the heterogeneous groups of Kongos, Bretons, Aradas, Alsatians, Igbos,
Provençals, Nagos, Irish, Mandingoes, and creoles of European, African,
and mixed descent who, together with others, composed the populations of
Guadeloupe, Martinique, and Saint-Domingue?

This chapter approaches these questions by looking at how royal authority was represented and translated into everyday political interaction in
Saint-Domingue. For the king's free colonial subjects, two distinct if overlapping political cultures developed over the course of the Old Regime. Both
were dominated by the king's local agents: military officers, administrative
officers, and magistrates. The first may be defined as "traditional" absolutism, in which local power came from symbolically representing or speaking
for the king. Power was personal in nature and, as Montesquieu suggested,
honor was the "principle," or the "human passion," that drove its workings.[4]
The second political culture, which began taking shape in the era of the
Seven Years' War, was associated with new approaches to government that
frequently have been called "Enlightened" absolutism. Within this imperial
political culture, claims to distinction were in theory based on the cultivation
of useful knowledge. Competing attempts to shape, mobilize, and represent
public opinion increasingly dominated it in practice.

The ways in which the king's enslaved subjects understood, experienced,
and shaped these two political cultures remain unclear. Much of the colony's
African majority brought models of kingship with them from their home-
lands, and enslaved creoles and Africans witnessed French representations
of their king. Both "traditional" and "Enlightened" absolutism shaped slaves'
lives, since a key issue that was disputed through these political idioms was
the relative authority of their masters and the king over them. If the meanings
the French king held for Saint-Domingue's African and African American
masses are difficult to decipher, they are of extreme importance, for when
the North Province's slaves revolted in 1791, they claimed that they did so
in his name.

The King's Trans-Atlantic Bodies

Within the framework of "traditional" absolutism, the monarchy's Caribbean
agents manifested royal claims to sovereignty and asserted the king's control
much as they did in most of France's provinces. Symbolic bonds of authority
and assent were maintained by oaths of allegiance and royal commissions that

delegated portions of the king's power to his officers.[5] More important, those commissioned officers represented the king to his other subjects. In part, they did so by materially establishing the king's presence. The royal symbol of the fleur-de-lys was omnipresent; it decorated official buildings and fountains and, more brutally, was branded onto the flesh of convicts.[6] Portraits of the king in his splendor hung on the walls of important public spaces, such as the court rooms of Cap-Français.[7] During the last years of the Old Regime, popular entertainments reproduced images of the king or symbols representing him. A 1785 fireworks display began with a "salute to the king" that included a triumphal arch with his coat of arms. In 1787, a wax museum at Port-au-Prince featured "the royal family dressed for court [and] the king holding his *lit de justice*, accompanied by his guards in uniform."[8]

Saint-Domingue's toponymy and ritual calendar marked colonial space and time with the presence of the monarch. Place names, such as those of the towns Saint-Louis, Port-au-Prince, and Fort-Dauphin, tied the contours of colonial geography to the royal family.[9] Public celebrations of royal victories and rites of passage connected colonial time to the royal family's life histories. Processions and special masses celebrated royal births such as that of "Madame Royale" in 1779 and mourned royal deaths such as that of Louis XV in 1774.[10] Royal battlefield victories and declarations of peace between the king and foreign princes were celebrated with *te deums*, bonfires, and cannon salutes.[11]

Most significant, the king's officials represented him in their own persons. Invested with varying portions of royal sovereignty, these officials embodied the king in the sphere over which they were given power, much as the king embodied God's authority on earth. The king's most direct representative in Saint-Domingue was the governor-general, whose commission made him the fullest recipient of royal power in the colony.[12] This manifestation of royal authority was regularly put on display in places of honor, such as the central *fauteuil* (chair) in the Conseils supérieurs from which the governor overlooked the council's president. Special seats inside the choirs of churches that in France would have been reserved for the king (or his provincial governors) were reserved for the colonial governor.[13]

However, the governor was not the king's sole representative, nor could he be. As Keith Baker has pointed out, one of the theoretical foundations of the absolute monarchy was the belief that only the king could possess full sovereignty due to the fact that he alone could reunite and represent in his person the entirety of the "particularistic society of orders and estates that was the ancien regime."[14] In fact, the governor and the military officers beneath him received only one element of royal sovereignty, the power of the sword. A body of civilian officials headed by the intendant represented and oversaw the king's fiscal claims and his beneficence through public works.

The intendant, as chief justice, and the colony's magistrates also received the king's power to judge his subjects according to his laws. Composed of these three governmental orders, military, fiscal, and judicial, the structure of Saint-Domingue's administration was not significantly different from that of the provinces of the hexagon.[15]

Ideally, as the rhetoric of numerous ministerial dispatches suggested, these three orders were to work together in "perfect harmony" and "perfect concert." If they represented different aspects of the king's majesty, they were united through his person and their service to him. In a political culture in which authority was unitary, there simply was no space for legitimate contestation, at least according to this rhetorical ideal. Thus, when difficulties arose, officers of the different orders were told to show the respect and/or the submission they owed to one another and limit themselves to their respective rights and duties.[16]

The rhetoric of "perfect harmony" suggested not only balance but also hierarchy, mirroring the society over which France's absolute monarchs ruled. The relationship of the three orders to one another was more or less one of parity, but subtle distinctions existed between their highest officers. Colonial governors, representing as they did the fullest part of the royal person, were to have their way when they and intendants disagreed. In such cases, the maintenance of "perfect concert" required the intendant to defer publicly to the governor's wishes and then confidentially inform the minister of the navy of the reasons for his disagreement.[17] Further, elaborate but sometimes uncertain hierarchies ranked officers within each order, and lower officers of any order were considered to owe deference to higher ones of the others.[18]

This hierarchized harmony was one of the principal messages that public ceremonies such as processions and bonfires were supposed to convey to both the officers participating in them and the crowds watching them. A Fête-Dieu celebration held at Cap-Français in 1769 illustrates how processions, when they went according to script, enacted this model of the political order. According to the Conseil supérieur's clerk, upon arriving at the Church of Notre-Dame, the conseil was escorted to its official pews by the churchwardens.

> The officiating priests arriving forthwith at the altar, the procession
> set out; the court followed immediately after the holy sacrament, which
> was carried by the . . . apostolic prefect and the priest with two curates
> assisting him. The canopy was carried by two grenadiers of the Legion
> of Saint-Domingue on its right side, and by two grenadiers of this town's
> militia on its left; its cords were held by the two current churchwardens
> along with the two who had exercised the charge last year; the grenadier
> company of said legion, their officers in front, formed a double line to the
> right, and the grenadier company of the militia a double line to the left
> of the canopy, inside which the Conseil's bailiffs marched in two lines in

front of the court with the first bailiff, baton in hand, at their center. After the Conseil, the lower court of Le Cap marched in the same order, similarly between two double lines of soldiers, followed by the company of the *maréchaussée* . . . and finally by that of the police. In front of the holy sacrament, all of the troops of the town's militia marched in two double lines in the following order: the Legion of Saint-Domingue, the Gendarmes, the Carabiniers, the Foot Dragoons, and the companies of *Sieurs* Papillon, Crebassa . . . and the company of mounted dragoons. . . . When the procession had returned to the church, high mass was performed.[19]

The entire display emphasized balance between the military and judicial orders. The military, represented in this case by militia officers, marched on one side of the host and the magistracy on the other, each escorted by the troops under their command. The arrangement of participants within each order suggested the relative status of the different officers and bodies composing it.

This hierarchical harmony occurred less frequently than church bells rang in Saint-Domingue. Members of the military, judicial, and administrative orders were often in conflict with one another, and the public ceremonies that were supposed to affirm their unity were disrupted by their disputes. Ministerial rhetoric notwithstanding, authorities in Versailles appear to have counted on and encouraged such conflict as a way of maintaining control across the ocean. Magistrates were allowed to accumulate property, which itself created local interests and bases of power. The colony's administrative and military officers were discouraged and even banned from doing so, with the result that their futures were more strongly wed to the imperial bureaucracy.[20] As a result, the greatest amount of conflict between royal officers tended to be between magistrates and those of the other two orders.[21]

Nonetheless, Saint-Domingue's high politics was by no means reducible to conflict between locally rooted magistrates and centralizing imperial authorities, for allegiances and interests were not always so clearly defined. Military and civilian officers, including governors and intendants, acquired plantations and married into creole families throughout the Old Regime despite the monarchy's attempts to limit their doing so. As a result, some of those officers espoused local causes, just as magistrates did.[22] Moreover, key officers such as intendants and attorneys general (*procureurs généraux*) at times sided with the colony's governor (and as such with the colony's military order) to affirm their loyalty to the king's foremost agent, but at other times they stood by Saint-Domingue's magistracy in the name of civilian rule and professional solidarity.[23] Such disputes between civilian and military officers were long-standing and had origins in rivalries that grew out of the nobility of the sword's disparagement of the more recent ancestry of the nobility of the robe and of the pen, the very different professional cultures of these orders, and everyday conflicts that arose over authority and influence.[24]

The subjects of disputes between the governmental orders were myriad, ranging from disagreements over who should have control of the colony's police forces to arguments over taxation and militia service to disputes about titles, forms of address, and place in public ceremonies. They were always about power, whether it was control over coercive force and financial resources or the manifestation of authority within the political hierarchy during public festivities. Notably, the longest and most persistent political struggles that took place in the colony were specifically over symbolic markers of status and power.[25] A few examples will suffice as illustrations. More than once in the 1730s, military officers refused to give judicial officers torches to light bonfires, and on one of these occasions a judge's insistence resulted in his suffering the "ignominy" of being arrested in his courtroom and dragged to the military jail "in front of all the troops and the people assembled."[26] Royal officers fought over the decoration of their church pews—in 1743 and 1761 disputes arose when military officers and magistrates, respectively, made their pews more imposing in size and decoration than those of their rivals.[27] Throughout the eighteenth century, the members of the Conseils supérieurs fought with colonial and metropolitan administrators over titles and forms of address as they sought to assimilate themselves to the status of metropolitan *parlements*. More generally, over the course of Saint-Domingue's existence as a royal colony, no fewer than sixty-six court decisions, administrative orders, ministerial dispatches, and royal laws established, contested, and reestablished precedence in seating arrangements and public ceremonies.[28]

The energies royal officials devoted to such struggles resulted from the importance of form and the personal nature of politics in "traditional" absolutism. As the colony's administrators wrote to the Cap-Français conseil in 1769, "In public affairs, one cannot weigh and measure titles [and] expressions too much [before employing them]; they are true debts, and with debts of honor as with debts of money, it is an insult to voluntarily pay more than what is due."[29] As this quote suggests, titles were more than superficial signs of respect. In the honor-bound political culture of "traditional" absolutism, they were claims regarding the place of addressers and addressees in hierarchical political relationships. They had to be "weighed and measured" with such care not only for fear that they might insult, but also because they could rearrange hierarchies, and in doing so, transform those relationships.

New Bodies Politic:
Imperial and Colonial "Public Spheres"

The last thirty years of the Old Regime witnessed the beginnings of significant changes in French imperial political culture that affected both the empire's overall structure and the ways in which the king's agents claimed and contested local authority. At base, these changes had the same root causes—the imperial crisis that arose from the costs of fighting and losing the Seven Years' War and the increasing influence of Enlightenment thought on the king's agents on both sides of the Atlantic. These two developments, along with the rise of a literate urban public culture, led to the creation of two interlocking public spheres, the first of which was imperial in scope and the second more rooted in the colony.[30] As metropolitan administrators solicited advice from royal agents in the Caribbean, as some of those agents became increasingly influenced by Enlightened political thought, and as all branches of the government began to appeal to the forces of public opinion to support their causes, new possibilities for claiming power and legitimization emerged. This was particularly the case for Saint-Domingue's most locally rooted political elite—men of law.

Fighting the Seven Years' War across the globe stretched the capacities of the eighteenth-century imperial powers to their limits. In the war's aftermath, the British, Spanish, and French governments began experimenting with reforming their empires. French officials felt the need for reform all the more due to the losses the Treaty of Paris imposed on the French crown. Since better knowledge about the colonies and their government was considered fundamental to formulating reforms, the ministry of the navy and colonies embarked upon a program of collecting information. This research began before the war was over. In December 1761, the king's Conseil d'État established a Commission on the Legislation of the French Colonies to collect information regarding colonial administration and propose changes.[31] While this particular commission was abolished by royal order in 1768, other such bodies continued to be created throughout the remainder of the Old Regime.[32]

One of the chief tasks of these commissions was to prepare the way for a codification of colonial law, which was to serve as the centerpiece of imperial reform. The commissions solicited proposals for reform but saw their main task as that of collecting and compiling the legislation and jurisprudence that had developed piecemeal and contradictorily during the seventeenth and eighteenth centuries. This program, as Malick Ghachem has argued, required metropolitan authorities to ask for the help of colonial men of law, as they were in the best position to amass such information.[33] In doing so, these metropolitan officials created a new terrain on which colonial magistrates and other interested parties could continue their struggles to achieve greater status and authority within colonial and imperial power structures. Some men of law, such as Petit, Hilliard d'Auberteuil, and Moreau de Saint-Méry, seized upon this invitation as an opportunity to further their careers and play a role in reshaping the political order in a more fundamental manner than engaging in everyday contests over titles, ceremonial precedence, and the registration of individual pieces of legislation.

Becoming advocates of Enlightened reform appears to have come naturally to significant numbers of Saint-Domingue's men of law for two reasons. First, the Enlightenment's most basic practices involved reading, writing, and oration—skills central to the everyday activities of lawyers and magistrates. Moreover, the 1760s and 1770s coincided with the era in which learning became the essential hallmark of the colonial legal profession.[34] The practices of Enlightenment were but a variation on the more general claim to authority men of law made on the basis of their learning. As a result, lawyers and magistrates, along with members of the medical profession, made up the greater part of the cultural elite associated with Saint-Domingue's Enlightenment.[35] Second, certain aspects of Enlightenment thought proved especially meaningful to colonial lawyers and jurists because they allowed them to make greater claims for their own authority. Lockean contract theory and Montesquieu's insistence on the importance of local conditions in defining political arrangements provided them with new theoretical backing for their claims to power. These arguments offered new and more convincing foundations for the claims magistrates had long made to represent the colony as the only permanently resident group among the king's officers in Saint-Domingue.[36]

The importance of knowledge of local conditions, and thus of its possessors, to reform projects had long been recognized in both the metropole and the colony.[37] However, during the last half of the eighteenth century, the convergence of the economic and cultural growth of Saint-Domingue, the imperial need for reform, and the ways in which Enlightenment thought linked political legitimacy to empirical knowledge and rational discussion transformed the importance and effects of this recognition. Significantly, this meant that the process of gathering the information needed for colonial reform was carried out not only within a trans-Atlantic public composed of royal officers but also before and in interaction with a literate public composed of Saint-Domingue's colonists.

That colonial public sphere was the product of the extension to Saint-Domingue of broad-based metropolitan cultural change (especially increasing literacy and the taste for Enlightened reading) and government efforts. Metropolitan authorities solicited information regarding the colony primarily from the king's local officers, but they also went further by appealing to the colony's reading public. In some cases, they did so by encouraging the publication of potentially controversial works. For instance, the former intendant of Guadeloupe and Martinique, Mercier de la Rivière, encouraged the publication of Hilliard d'Auberteuil's controversial *Considérations sur l'état présent de la colonie française de Saint-Domingue* (1776). He argued that by provoking public debates among "enlightened or interested men," the book's publication would contribute to "the reestablishment of good order in Saint-Domingue."[38] To pave the way for reform, the monarchy also created chambers of commerce and agriculture, which quickly became organs for the formulation and exposition of colonial opinion. More generally, the French government encouraged the development of a reading public by allowing the establishment in the 1760s of printing presses and a newspaper.[39]

The development of this local public sphere, like that of the larger trans-Atlantic one, further encouraged Saint-Domingue's men of law to play a role in the process of reform. As in France, participation in the public spheres gave lawyers and magistrates experience in a developing political culture based on Enlightened knowledge and appeals to "public opinion."[40] Men trained in law played key roles in many of the institutional settings associated with the colonial public sphere—the secretary of the Chamber of Agriculture was always a lawyer, as were the first two writer-editors of the colony's newspaper.[41] Further, colonial lawyers, like their metropolitan peers, increasingly took their cases before the reading public by publishing their judicial *mémoires*.[42] With the experience of debating before and appealing to the colonial public, men of law such as Moreau de Saint-Méry gained confidence in the support that their projects had in the colony and in their abilities to act in the public sphere. As a result of the willingness of metropolitan authorities and local civilian and judicial officers to participate in these new spaces for politics, a new political culture built upon the cultivation of useful knowledge and the mobilization of public opinion began to transform the traditional one based on representing the monarchy and rituals of deference.

It should be noted that this Enlightened political culture by no means triumphed over the older one in which status and hierarchy defined political relationships. The divergent careers of Hilliard d'Auberteuil and Moreau de Saint-Méry suggest that if enlightened thought and practices opened new routes to legitimacy and advancement, they did so only on the condition that those who took these new paths did not abandon the earlier system. While the two men made similar arguments regarding the need to reform Saint-Domingue's government in ways that would grant greater power to colonial magistrates and prove more favorable to colonial interests, the legal clerk Hilliard d'Auberteuil, a Breton immigrant, ended up as a Grub Street figure ghost-writing judicial *mémoires* for other lawyers while Moreau de Saint-Méry became a member of the Conseil supérieur of Cap-Français and played a significant role in imperial politics during the revolution's early years. More often than not, the difference between their arguments was one of style, not substance. Hilliard d'Auberteuil, with his heated language and willingness to publicly criticize individual administrators, failed to conform to the political culture based on deference that still held sway. In contrast, Moreau de Saint-Méry carefully nurtured his patronage networks and took care not to incur the disfavor of the king's administrators on either side of the Atlantic.[43] His writings contained many ideas similar to those of Hilliard d'Auberteuil but they were presented in a less vociferous tone, and in his pre-revolutionary writings he expressly avoided criticisms that could be read as implicating individual royal agents.[44]

If the transformation of Saint-Domingue's political culture was incomplete, it nonetheless destabilized colonial society and politics during the last years of the Old Regime and the first years of the colonial French Revolution. In acknowledging that the king's person was not the sole source of legitimate political opinion, the expansion of the imperial and colonial public spheres weakened the ideological glue that bound colony to metropole and the different orders of colonial society to one another. By appealing to a rational public opinion, the monarchy's bureaucracy and colonial advocates weakened the authority of the absolutist king, and by doing so, they raised the question of what might take his place.[45] Competing answers to that question, along with the very process of gathering information and instituting reform, exacerbated tensions between colony and metropole and within the colony itself.

First, the combination of gathering information and proposing reforms, followed by the disillusionment that occurred when the reforms actually arrived, contributed greatly to the emergence of an ideology of "colonial autonomism."[46] Participation in the process of reform allowed the formulators of this ideology to refine their arguments. Then, the disappointment they felt when the monarchy implemented reform measures that in the end strengthened the imperial bureaucracy at the expense of the local Conseils supérieurs radicalized their positions.[47] This "autonomist" ideology was intensified by cultural developments within the institutions of the colonial public sphere. Participation in the latter led colonists to reflect upon and elaborate the differences between their society and that of the metropole. Such manifestations of an emerging creole consciousness can be seen in cultural productions such as poetry by white creoles in the Creole language and the performance of locally authored plays such as *Lundi du Cap, ou les Recouvrements, Les amours de Mirebalais,* and *Arlequin mûlatresse protégée par Macanda.*[48]

Second, the development of the public sphere raised fundamental questions regarding colonial identity as groups within the colony disputed the right of others to participate in the public arena. Fights over participation crossed all of the fault lines that divided the colony's free society, including those between wealthy and poor whites, military men and men of law, white creoles and European immigrants, men and women, and so on. Yet for many colonists and royal agents, the most troubling demands regarding participation in the new public spaces and forums came from free people of color. Not only did the members of these castes claim seats in Saint-Domingue's theaters, their most articulate representatives demanded civil equality with the colony's whites.[49] As John Garrigus has argued, these contests resulted in the further elaboration of both the colony's regime of racial discrimination and of protests against it, setting up the battles over racial equality that would rage in the colony and in Paris after 1789.[50]

The White Flag of Revolt: Slaves and the French King

Ironically, just as France's absolute monarch was becoming less potent as the symbol that held free imperial society together, his image may very well have served to help enslaved creoles and Africans of varying backgrounds unite in opposition to slavery. When the slaves of the North Province rose up in August 1791, beginning the transformation of the French Revolution in Saint-Domingue into the Haitian Revolution, they did so under the white flag of the monarchy.[51] The royalism of these revolutionary slaves has been a rich subject for historical debate and has remained one of the most problematic features of the Haitian Revolution for scholars using interpretive schemes based upon European and North American historical experiences.[52] Arguing against Eurocentric interpretations, John Thornton has shown how African monarchist ideologies, which included frameworks for both absolute and limited monarchies, were the sources of this royalism for the African-born majority of the enslaved population.[53] However, his interpretation does little to explain the royalism of enslaved creoles, who composed most of the high-level leadership of the slave revolutionaries and whose understandings of kingship likely grew as much out of the colonial context as out of creolized African traditions. To gain a fuller understanding of slaves' royalism, we need to take into account the fact that slaves' political cultures were as varied as their geographical and cultural backgrounds and built upon a wide range of cultural and political traditions.[54]

Let us begin with the creole population. The few pieces of evidence from the Old Regime that indicate how slaves viewed the French monarchy reveal an ambiguous picture.[55] On one hand, crowds of slaves frequently jeered at and even physically assaulted colonial executioners. For these slaves, such actions were probably a way of attacking the colony's authorities by proxy, although they may have defined those authorities in purely local terms.[56] On the other hand, as Malick Ghachem and Laurent Dubois have suggested, slaves likely saw the king as a potential protector or, if nothing else, the possessor of a power greater than that of their masters.[57] Slaves certainly had opportunities to observe public manifestations of the image of the king and his power. They also appear to have been aware of the king's paternalist claims that he would protect them as he did all of his subjects. While rarely acted upon, clauses of the 1685 Code Noir and the 1784 and 1785 royal ordinances that reformed the slave regime on plantations with absentee owners clearly stated the king's official wishes that slaves be adequately fed and clothed and that they not be subject to torture or bodily mutilation.[58] On a number of occasions, slaves appealed to royal magistrates for protection from their masters, as those law codes permitted.[59] Notably, this view of the king as protector and liberator played a role in the August 22, 1791, uprising. Rumors had earlier circulated throughout the colony that the king had enacted further reforms of slavery, and during the August 14 meeting to plan the revolt, its leaders presented forged documents stating that the king had granted slaves three days of freedom per week.[60]

While enslaved creoles probably put together much of their understanding of the French king by appropriating the paternalistic elements of French imperial political culture, the colony's African-born majority brought models of kingship with them across the Atlantic. Those models appear to have varied greatly both in their theoretical foundations and in the kinds of authority they conferred on kings. For instance, Thornton has pointed out that Kongolese captives possessed two models of kingship—violent conqueror kings whose authority was defined as absolute and conciliatory blacksmith kings whose authority was limited.[61] While more research needs to be done on the political ideologies captives from other parts of Africa brought with them to the Americas, preliminary investigation suggests much variation within cultural groups as well as across them.[62] These models of kingship may have been undergoing creolization by 1789. Moreau de Saint-Méry believed that this was the case, at least in the ways that "kings" and "queens" appeared in Vodou ceremonies. According to him, Vodou "kings" and "queens" presided over such ceremonies "according to usages they may have brought from Africa, and to which Creole customs have added several variants, and some features that indicate European ideas."[63]

Put together, the varied meanings and traditions attached to kingship by Saint-Domingue's slaves can help explain why the North Province's enslaved insurgents donned the white cockade in August 1791. The royalist banner and the distant French king's name provided symbols around which slaves from many different backgrounds could unite in opposition to the slave regime.[64] To the extent that understandings of kingship had become creolized, their application to the French monarch provided a meeting ground of shared meanings for creoles and Africans of varied ethnicities. Perhaps more important, since the rapid influx of unwilling African immigrants in the 1770s and 1780s renders such thorough creolization unlikely, rallying in the name of the French king allowed enslaved insurgents to paper over differences within their own ranks. Much of the revolt's creole leadership did not necessarily envision an end to the plantation system so much as an end to their own personal enslavement or, if they were more ambitious, a more elevated place for themselves in the plantation hierarchy. In contrast, the rank and file of the insurgent forces appear to have had a wide range of goals, almost all of which entailed the end of forced plantation labor.[65] The distant king and his white flag served as multivalent symbols to which different groups among the insurgents could attach their own meanings as they claimed to fight together in his name.

Notes

1. Quoted in C. B. A. Behrens, *Society, Government, and the Enlightenment: The Experiences of Eighteenth-Century France and Prussia* (New York: Harper & Row, 1985), 25.

2. Émilien Petit, *Dissertations sur le droit public des colonies françoises, espagnoles, et angloises, d'après les loix des trois nations, comparées entr'elles* (Geneva, 1778), 168. All translations are by the author unless otherwise noted.

3. Jacky Dahomay, "L'esclave et le droit: les légitimations d'une insurrection," in *Les abolitions de l'esclavage de L.F. Sonthonax à V. Schoelcher: 1793, 1794, 1848*, ed. Marcel Dorigny (Vincennes: Presses Universitaires de Vincennes and Editions UNESCO, 1995), 36.

4. Charles-Louis de Secondat, baron de Montesquieu, *De l'esprit des lois*, 2 vols. (1748; repr., Paris: Gallimard, 1995), 1:114, 122–124.

5. Gene E. Ogle, "Policing Saint Domingue: Race, Violence, and Honor in an Old Regime Colony" (Ph.D. diss., University of Pennsylvania, 2003), 255–256.

6. Arrêts du Conseil Supérieur de Léogane, July 6, 1705, and June 15, 1711, F3/269, Centre des Archives d'Outre-mer, Aix-en-Provence (hereafter CAOM); Médéric-Louis-Élie Moreau de Saint-Méry, *Loix et constitutions des colonies françoises de l'Amérique sous le vent*, 6 vols. (Paris, 1784–1790), 5:417–418; Moreau de Saint-Méry, *Description topographique, physique, civile, politique et historique de la partie française de l'Isle Saint-Domingue*, 3 vols., ed. Blanche Maurel and Etienne Taillemite (Philadelphia, 1797; repr., Paris: Société de l'histoire des colonies françaises, 1958), 1:311, 327–328.

7. Moreau de Saint-Méry, *Description*, 1:373.

8. *Affiches Américaines*, quoted in Jean Fouchard, *Plaisirs de Saint-Domingue: notes sur la vie sociale, littéraire et artistique* (1955; repr., Port-au-Prince: Éditions Henri Deschamps, 1988), 102–103, 113.

9. In 1731, the town of Bayahá was renamed Fort-Dauphin in honor of the birth of Louis XV's first son. The history of the naming of Port-au-Prince is less clear. According to Charlevoix, it was named after a ship that found harbor there in 1706. Moreau de Saint-Méry claimed that the name was older and was originally attached to nearby islands. Whatever its origins, the name itself recalled the monarchy as did that of nearby Port-Royal with which it merged. The site of Saint-Louis had been called Cromwell's Bay prior to 1677 when a militia captain and *conseiller* in the colony's first *conseil* gave it its lasting name. Moreau de Saint-Méry, *Description*, 1:128–129; 2:973–974; 3:1241, 1449.

10. Moreau de Saint-Méry, *Loix et constitutions*, 3:10; 5:227–230, 513, 885; 6:239.

11. Moreau de Saint-Méry, *Loix et constitutions*, 1:584–585, 595; 3:636; 6:396.

12. The comte d'Estaing's commission even declared that he "represent[ed] Our Person" in its fullness, a privilege formerly restricted to viceroys and ambassadors. Moreau

de Saint-Méry, *Loix et constitutions*, 4:632–634; "Discours de M. Le Comte d'Estaing au Conseil de Cap," May 7, 1764, Département de l'Armée du Terre, Service Historique de la Défense, A/1/3674, Vincennes.

13. They also had a reserved loge in colonial theaters. In churches and theaters, the intendant also had a seat of honor. Moreau de Saint-Méry, *Description*, 1:332, 358, 374; 2:986, 1001; Moreau de Saint-Méry, *Loix et constitutions*, 1:376; 3:258, 751.

14. Keith Michael Baker, "Representation," in *The Political Culture of the Old Regime*, vol. 1, *The French Revolution and the Creation of Modern Political Culture*, ed. Keith Michael Baker (Oxford: Pergamon Press, 1987), 469–472.

15. It differed only in two significant ways. First, the number and variety of political authorities were more limited due to the absence of preexisting provincial and communal authorities and the fact that the proliferation of different offices within the three royal orders was more restrained. Second, due to the delays inherent in trans-Atlantic communication, Saint-Domingue's governor and intendant shared in the king's legislative faculties, if only provisionally. Guillaume Thomas Raynal, *Essai sur l'administration de Saint-Domingue* (1785), 144.

16. To encourage colonial officers to live up to this ideal, metropolitan authorities mobilized the principle of emulation, for the governor and intendant were supposed to provide models of this "perfect harmony." Ducasse to Conseil Supérieur, May 15, 1692, F3/269, CAOM; Ministre to M. de Fayet, December 16, 1732, and June 29, 1734, F3/270, CAOM; Ministre to le comte d'Autichamp, July 26, 1781, F3/275, CAOM; Ministre to officiers de la juridiction des Cayes, July 26, 1781, F3/275, CAOM; Moreau de Saint-Méry, *Loix et constitutions*, 4:159–161; Ministre to de la Rochalard and de Montholon, September 12, 1724, F3/270, CAOM. Colonial officers of the different orders also mobilized the ideal of "harmony" in their interactions with one another and the metropolitan bureaucracy. See "Arrêté du Conseil Supérieur de Cap-Français sur les garnisons employées par les Administrateurs pour faire payer dettes civiles," May 14, 1784, F3/276, CAOM.

17. Raynal, *Essai sur l'administration*, 144.

18. For a discussion of these ambiguities among men of law, see Ogle, "Policing Saint Domingue," 210–215.

19. This ceremony took place at a moment when unity was particularly needed— order had just been reestablished in the South and West Provinces following rebellions against the reestablishment of militia service in 1768–1769, and Port-au-Prince's *conseillers* had been arrested and deported for their ties to these rebellions less than three months before this procession occurred. Moreau de Saint-Méry, *Loix et constitutions*, 5:245–246. Additional details can be found in ibid., 5:227–230, which describes the Conseil's attendance at a funeral service for the queen a few months earlier. Seating arrangements in other settings functioned in a similar manner. Ibid., 5:251–253.

20. Moreau de Saint-Méry, *Loix et constitutions*, 2:512, 655; 3:117; 4:277–279, 644–705, 835; 5:489–490; "Lettre du Ministre à Marbois touchant la permission de l'Intendant pour les mariages de ceux qui sont employés sous ses ordres," April 6, 1786, F3/277, CAOM; "Lettre du Ministre à Luzerne sur le mariage des officiers," September 25, 1786, F3/277, CAOM.

21. For interpretations of Saint-Domingue's political history that emphasize these features, see Charles Frostin, "Histoire de l'autonomisme colon de la partie fran-

çaise de St.-Domingue aux XVIIe et XVIIIe siècles: contribution à l'étude du sentiment américain d'indépendance" (Thèse, Université de Paris I, 1972); and Frostin, *Les révoltes blanches à Saint-Domingue aux XVIIe et XVIIIe siècles (Haïti avant 1789)* (Paris: L'École, 1975).

22. Frostin, *Les révoltes blanches*, 146–147, 266.

23. Moreau de Saint-Méry, *Loix et constitutions*, 2:97–98 and 3:158–159; Pierre de Vaissière, *Saint-Domingue: la société et la vie créoles sous l'Ancien Régime (1629–1789)* (Paris: Perrin et Cie, 1909), 131, 136, 138–143.

24. The disrespect of nobles of the sword for those of the robe was strong enough to disrupt the everyday operation of colonial government. Occasionally, the navy minister had to intervene to reinforce the authority of an officer who belonged to the nobility of the robe. See Moreau de Saint-Méry, *Loix et constitutions*, 1:163, MS note; Ministre to Larnage, November 11, 1744, F3/271, CAOM. For conflicts between officers of the sword and officers of the pen, see Moreau de Saint-Méry, *Loix et constitutions*, 5:859; Ministre to Rohan and de Bongars, September 3, 1766, F3/273, CAOM; Ministre to Administrateurs, July 16, 1773, F3/273, CAOM. References marked by "MS note" are drawn from manuscript notes in Moreau de Saint-Méry's hand in the margins of a copy of his *Loix et constitutions* at the CAOM.

25. On the importance of "fine [symbolic] distinctions" to structures of rule, see Lauren Benton, *Law and Colonial Cultures: Legal Regimes in World History, 1400–1900* (Cambridge: Cambridge University Press, 2002), 2.

26. Moreau de Saint-Méry, *Loix et constitutions*, 3:412–415; "Procès-verbal du procureur du roi de Cap-François du refus de lui donner un flambeau au feu de St. Jean," June 23, 1730, F3/91, CAOM.

27. Moreau de Saint-Méry, *Loix et constitutions*, 3:740; 4:391.

28. For a fuller treatment, see Ogle, "Policing Saint Domingue," 264–282.

29. Moreau de Saint-Méry, *Loix et constitutions*, 5:222–223.

30. Jürgen Habermas, *The Structural Transformation of the Public Sphere: An Inquiry into a Category of Bourgeois Society*, trans. Thomas Burger (1962; repr., Cambridge: MIT Press, 1991). For useful syntheses of research on the development of publics in eighteenth-century Europe, see James Van Horn Melton, *The Rise of the Public in Enlightenment Europe* (Cambridge: Cambridge University Press, 2001); and Dorinda Outram, *The Enlightenment* (Cambridge: Cambridge University Press, 1995), 14–30.

31. Moreau de Saint-Méry, *Loix et constitutions*, 4:438–439.

32. Jean Tarrade, "L'administration coloniale en France à la fin de l'Ancien Régime: projets de réforme," *Revue historique* 229 (1963): 103–122.

33. Malick Ghachem, "Montesquieu in the Caribbean: The Colonial Enlightenment between *Code Noir* and *Code Civil*," *Historical Reflections/Réflexions historiques* 25 (1999): 183–210.

34. Ogle, "Policing Saint Domingue," 196–206.

35. On doctors and the Enlightenment in Saint-Domingue, see James E. McClellan, III, *Colonialism and Science: Saint Domingue in the Old Regime* (Baltimore, Md.: Johns Hopkins University Press, 1992).

36. Ghachem, "Montesquieu in the Caribbean"; Ogle, "Policing Saint Domingue," 285–287.

37. For instance, in preparing the 1685 Code Noir, metropolitan ministers requested information from Caribbean authorities, including the Conseils supérieurs of Martinique and Guadeloupe. Malick W. Ghachem, "Sovereignty and Slavery in the Age of Revolution: Haitian Variants on a Metropolitan Theme" (Ph.D. diss., Stanford University, 2001), 34.

38. Mercier de la Rivière, quoted in Michel-René Hilliard d'Auberteuil, *Considérations sur l'état présent de la colonie française de Saint-Domingue: ouvrage politique et législatif,* 2 vols. (Paris: Chez Grangé, 1776), 1:xii–xiii.

39. Metropolitan authorities also recognized a local scientific society by giving it the status of an *académie.* Moreau de Saint-Méry, *Description,* 1:490–492; McClellan, *Colonialism and Science,* 181–258. On the development of a "public sphere," see John Garrigus, "'Sons of the Same Father': Gender, Race, and Citizenship in French Saint-Domingue, 1760–1792," in *Visions and Revisions of Eighteenth-Century France,* ed. Christine Adams, Jack R. Censer, and Lisa Jane Graham (University Park: Pennsylvania State University Press, 1997), 141–144.

40. For the metropole, see David A. Bell, *Lawyers and Citizens: The Making of a Political Elite in Old Regime France* (New York: Oxford University Press, 1994).

41. Moreau de Saint-Méry, *Description,* 1:443–444, 491.

42. See for instance, Darracq, *Mémoire pour Mme Marguerite-Rose Bedout* (1787), F3/279, CAOM; and Baudry des Lozières, *Précis pour le sieur Pierre Dumas, habitant à la Marmelade* (Port-au-Prince: Mozard, 1788), Bibliothèque Moreau de Saint-Méry, 87/miom/4, CAOM. On France, see Sarah Maza, *Private Lives and Public Affairs: The Causes Célèbres of Prerevolutionary France* (Berkeley: University of California Press, 1993).

43. Ogle, "Policing Saint Domingue," 290–294.

44. Instead, Moreau de Saint-Méry leveled his critiques against almost purely structural problems such as the rapid turnover of royal administrators and the contradictory legislation to which that led. Moreau de Saint-Méry, *Loix et constitutions,* 1:x–xi. The difference between the careers of Hilliard d'Auberteuil and Moreau de Saint-Méry also reflected the different social bases from which they began. Moreau de Saint-Méry was a third-generation member of the French Caribbean magistracy; his father and grandfather had been magistrates in Martinique. In contrast, Hilliard d'Auberteuil's background was less distinguished, and his only introduction to the official life of Saint Domingue was his uncle, who was a notary. Since many elements of magisterial culture were communicated as patrimony, this difference of origins probably also resulted in different understandings of how Old Regime political culture worked and different levels of attachment to it. Ogle, "Policing Saint Domingue," 199–202.

45. My argument here builds upon a large body of scholarship on political culture and the French Revolution. See especially Keith Michael Baker, *Inventing the French Revolution: Essays on French Political Culture in the Eighteenth Century* (Cambridge: Cambridge University Press, 1990); and Lynn Hunt, *Politics, Culture, and Class in the French Revolution* (Berkeley: University of California Press, 1984).

46. Frostin, *Les révoltes blanches;* Ghachem, "Montesquieu in the Caribbean."

47. For instance, after the 1787 suppression of Cap-Français' Conseil, the once cooperative Moreau de Saint-Méry became, according to his one-time patron Barbé de Marbois, "the champion of the judiciary vermin." Barbé de Marbois, quoted in Moreau

de Saint-Méry, *Description*, 1:xvii. For discussions of these reforms, see Ghachem, "Sovereignty and Slavery," 156–170; and Ogle, "Policing Saint Domingue," 294–299.

48. Moreau de Saint-Méry, *Description*, 1:81–83, 364; McClellan, *Colonialism and Science*, 95; Lauren Reynolds Clay, "Theater and the Commercialization of Culture in Eighteenth-Century France" (Ph.D. diss., University of Pennsylvania, 2003).

49. The legal category "free people of color" included all free people recognized as having at least some African ancestry. They were by no means a homogeneous group socially, ranging from African-born freedmen and women to legitimate children of Saint Domingue's most successful white colonists, but they were tied together by an ever-increasing body of discriminatory legislation and social prejudice. John D. Garrigus, "A Struggle for Respect: The Free Coloreds of Pre-Revolutionary Saint Domingue, 1760–69" (Ph.D. diss., Johns Hopkins University, 1988); Yvan Debbasch, *Couleur et liberté: le jeu du critère ethnique dans un ordre juridique esclavagiste* (Paris: Librairie Dalloz, 1967); Stewart R. King, *Blue Coat or Powdered Wig: Free People of Color in Pre-Revolutionary Saint Domingue* (Athens: University of Georgia Press, 2001). Regarding theater seats, see Moreau de Saint-Méry, *Description*, 1:361–362. On demands for equality, see the four *mémoires* Julien Raymond addressed to the minister of the navy in September 1786, F3/91, CAOM.

50. Garrigus, "'Sons of the Same Father'"; Garrigus, "Race, Gender, and Virtue in Haiti's Failed Foundational Fiction: *La mulâtre comme il y a peu de blanches* (1803)," in *The Color of Liberty: Histories of Race in France*, ed. Sue Peabody and Tyler Stovall (Durham, N.C.: Duke University Press, 2003).

51. David Patrick Geggus, *Haitian Revolutionary Studies* (Bloomington: Indiana University Press, 2002), 12.

52. John K. Thornton, "'I Am the Subject of the King of Congo': African Political Ideology and the Haitian Revolution," *Journal of World History* 4 (1993): 181–183.

53. Thornton, "'I Am the Subject of the King of Congo,'" 181–214.

54. For a similar treatment of insurgent "royalism" that follows the phenomenon on through the Haitian Revolution, see Laurent Dubois, *Avengers of the New World: The Story of the Haitian Revolution* (Cambridge, Mass.: Belknap Press, 2004), 106–109.

55. For clarity of argument, I am making an overly clear-cut distinction between creoles and Africans. This distinction should be read as representing overall tendencies within various components of Saint-Domingue's enslaved population. Creolization was a process. Not only could African-born individuals develop the attitudes suggested here for creoles, but as Afro-creole cultures developed over the course of the eighteenth century, they incorporated and reworked a wide range of African traditions along with European and American ones.

56. Gene E. Ogle, "Slaves of Justice: Saint Domingue's Executioners and the Production of Shame," *Historical Reflections/Réflexions historiques* 29 (Summer 2003): 287–291.

57. Laurent Dubois, "An Enslaved Enlightenment: Notes on the Political Culture of Slave Revolution in Saint-Domingue," paper presented to the 36th Annual Meeting of the Association of Caribbean Historians, Christ Church, Barbados, May 17–21, 2004, 7, cited with permission of the author; Ghachem, "Sovereignty and Slavery."

58. Robert Chesnais, ed., *Le code noir* (Paris: L'Esprit frappeur, 1998), 20, 25–27, 32, 34; Moreau de Saint-Méry, *Loix et constitutions*, 6:655–667, 918–928.

59. "Extrait du registre de la siège royale de Jérémie," November 6, 1786, F3/277, CAOM; Ghachem, "Sovereignty and Slavery," 120–133, 157, 262–268; Chesnais, ed., *Le code noir*, 26.

60. Carolyn Fick, "Emancipation in Haiti: From Plantation Labour to Peasant Proprietorship," *Slavery and Abolition* 21 (2001): 14–15. Such rumors circulated throughout the Caribbean from the 1780s to the 1820s. See David Patrick Geggus, "Slavery, War, and Revolution in the Greater Caribbean, 1789–1815," in *A Turbulent Time: The French Revolution and the Greater Caribbean*, ed. David Barry Gaspar and David P. Geggus (Bloomington: Indiana University Press, 1997), 7–8.

61. Thornton, "'I Am the Subject of the King of Congo,'" 190–191.

62. In addition to Thornton's article, see Edna G. Bay, *Wives of the Leopard: Gender, Politics, and Culture in the Kingdom of Dahomey* (Charlottesville: University of Virginia Press, 1998); Robert S. Smith, *Kingdoms of the Yoruba*, 3rd ed. (1969; repr., Madison: University of Wisconsin Press, 1988), 6–9, 91–92; and Robin Law, "'My Head Belongs to the King': On the Political and Ritual Significance of Decapitation in Pre-Colonial Dahomey," *Journal of African History* 30 (1989): 399–415.

63. Moreau de Saint-Méry, *Description*, 1:65.

64. Another probable reason for this "royalism" was the fact that rebelling in the name of the king allowed the insurgents to try to claim a place for themselves in the dominant imperial political culture.

65. Thornton, "'I am the Subject of the King of Congo,'" 201–206; David Geggus, "Slave Society in the Sugar Plantation Zones of Saint Domingue and the Revolution of 1791–1793," *Slavery and Abolition* 20 (1999): 40–41.

PART TWO

THE UNFOLDING OF THE SLAVE REVOLUTION

The Insurgents of 1791, Their Leaders, and the Concept of Independence

Yves Benot[1]

T HE INDEPENDENCE OF HAITI GREW OUT OF THIRTEEN YEARS OF STRUGGLE WHOSE POINT OF DEPARTURE WAS THE SLAVE INSUR-RECTION IN NORTHERN SAINT-DOMINGUE THAT BEGAN IN THE parishes of Acul and Limbé during the night of August 22/23, 1791. For this reason, it was crucial that the insurrection should succeed and that the repression that would result would fail in its attempts to stop it from spread-ing. Spread it did, over a vast area of the richest part of what was then the Caribbean's richest colony. This made it possible, in modern terms, for the slaves to commit to a long struggle. We need to ask, however, whether inde-pendence was already their goal. To get a better idea, it is necessary to go back to the earliest days of the insurrection, to its preparation and organization. We will look for answers in some documents that are in no sense unknown but that deserve a rereading.

While it was in progress, in fact from the outset, the insurrection was sometimes attributed to the influence of *mulâtres,* a term that at the time included all free people of color, both free blacks and those of mixed racial descent, and sometimes it was attributed to royalists and counterrevolution-aries, as if the slaves could not make up their minds for themselves. Whether or not one uses the definite article is important. If it is a matter of *the* mulat-toes or *the* royalists as a whole, it is evidently wrong. Yet it is quite another matter to speak of *certain* mulattoes and *certain* royalists.

In November 1790, before the slave insurrection, there had already taken place the failed revolt by Vincent Ogé in the districts of Grande-Rivière and Dondon. This revolt sought equality for the people of color—that is, the politi-cal rights that were denied them by both the colonists and the Constituent Assembly in Paris. It was not until eight months after the outbreak of the slave insurrection, on April 4, 1792, that the Legislative Assembly would right these wrongs. Ogé publicly proclaimed that he was not seeking the abolition of slavery and that he wanted nothing more than rights for mulattoes. Free people of color had slaves, just as whites did. This right at least was not denied them. When the revolt collapsed fairly quickly, Ogé and some of his companions took refuge in the Spanish colony of Santo Domingo. From there they were handed over to the colonists, tortured, condemned, and executed in conformity with the laws of Louis XIV that the colonial assemblies continued to apply completely illegally. However, a large number of those who took part in the Ogé revolt escaped arrest, were condemned in absentia, and lived in hiding from December 1790 to the end of August 1791.

At this point Jean-Baptiste Cap, one of the people living undercover, emerged. His father-in-law was at this time receiving much praise in France in Lavallée's 1789 novel *Le nègre comme il y a peu de blancs* and later in 1793 in a play called *Le nègre aubergiste*. The father-in-law was a free black named Desrouleaux who had financially assisted his former master when the master's business had been ruined. Desrouleaux's daughter had married Jean-Baptiste Cap, another free black and one of the men condemned in absentia in the Ogé affair. It seems that by this time the couple had separated, but J.-B. Cap was in any event quite a wealthy man. One of our sources, an unpublished book manuscript written by the attorney of the Clément plantation in Acul, the same estate where Boukman lived and where everything began on August 22, mentions J.-B. Cap's involvement in an attempted slave rebellion to free Ogé in February 1791.[2]

> At about the same time, that is during the night of 5/6 February, there was a movement in the Acul district where I lived that was nothing less than an insurrection of blacks and mulattoes led by Jean-Baptiste Cap, a free black complicated [he meant implicated] in the Ogé affair. As I learned the next morning, this leader had planned to come to Le Cap and, joined by the mulattoes of the town, open the jails to his accomplices. The rivers that overflowed that evening prevented . . . ten to twelve thousand blacks from gathering and rebelling. All the plantations' slave drivers had been warned since the beginning of the year.

The same author also claims, however, that one of the drivers supposedly informed his owner. The author himself and several *habitants* (a term that meant "planters") were said to have written to Le Cap to send warning. Was the failure due to the informant or the overflowing rivers? It is not clear, but the fact remains that this attempt is mentioned in the report on the interrogation of Ogé's brother, who was also arrested, tortured, and executed.[3]

Here then we have an example of the role of certain free people of color operating underground in preparing the insurrection. J.-B. Cap was still linked with the slaves in August, since on September 1 he attempted to incite the slaves of the town. He was denounced by one of them, whom he trusted, and was arrested, tortured, broken on the wheel, and paraded for hours through the town in agony. By a remarkable turn of events, the police-man who arrested Cap was captured by the insurgents three weeks later and executed on the orders of Jeannot, who was then one of their main leaders. This was in spite of the intercession of several young black women, according to the Clément manuscript.

Other underground figures appear at the earliest moments of the insurrec-tion in charge of certain rebel camps, such as the Godard brothers, free blacks who were violently hated by the colonists. Although J.-B. Cap is the only name known to us from the preparatory phase, nothing prevents us from thinking he was surely not alone. The well-known meeting of August 14, 1791, at which the insurrection was planned for the following days, must have been preceded by many others in which supporters of Ogé participated. Above all, we know that Jeannot listed among the goals of the uprising (after the goal of the return of the king to his throne) revenge for Ogé. This is what he told a small planter, François Blaise Laroque, who was his prisoner from August 27 until Jeannot's death on November 1. And mulattoes led the column of Jeannot's army that took Dondon on September 10, which guaranteed access to the Spanish part of the island, from where the insurgents drew supplies. This group of *mulâtres* could have shared their military skills and knowledge with the slaves, since they formed the majority of the colonial militia and some of them had even taken part in the American Revolutionary War.

We certainly find, therefore, *individual* mulattoes side by side with the slaves at the beginning of the insurrection, but not *the* mulattoes, who took up arms at the same time but in the West Province and for different motives. Their demand was for equality among all free persons, whites, mulattoes, and blacks, and they were in alliance with a few major white planters. In the north, the mulattoes of the city of Le Cap, where they were quite numer-ous, far from supporting the slaves, volunteered to go and reestablish order, despite the fact that overexcited whites killed about fifteen of them.

As regards the royalists, an initial insight is provided by the Clément man-uscript which gives us the source of the often-cited words of Boukman when he declared he had been betrayed by Lt.-Col. Tousard, who had promised him that the royal troops would not fire on the insurgents and that they would have to fight only the colonists. This statement was reported by "a mulatto woman of M. Estève who saw this leader every day." Estève was able to flee from Acul on August 25, two days after the start of the insurrection. Tousard, lieutenant-colonel of the Cap-Français regiment, is, along with its colonel, Cambefort, one of the individuals most commonly mentioned by those who blame the royal-ists for causing the uprising. It may seem far-fetched at first sight that these two high-placed guardians of law and order could have been the instigators of an insurrection that overturned the entire social structure. Yet there is a later episode that might explain the matter.

As early as October 1789, as soon as news reached Saint-Domingue of the revolution in France, a plan was concocted to simulate a "Negro" insurrection. Bacon de la Chevalerie, a relative of Barnave and one of the most influential colonists, came up with this idea, with the intention of creating alarm in Paris and demonstrating to everyone the necessity of maintaining the colonial status quo, including slavery. It was feared that enthusiasm for the rights of man might lead the Constituent Assembly to abolish the slave trade and slavery. So a revolt was planned for October 23 as a massive exodus of slaves into the hills where whites rarely went. Some mention of this did in fact reach France, but it was quickly known that nothing serious had happened and nothing more was said about it. The surgeon Dalmas, who has left us the earliest account of the Bois-Caïman Vodou ceremony, points out that Bacon de la Chevalerie called on "Jeannot à Bullet" to act as his guide in the mountains—the same one who would later appear among the very earliest leaders of the slaves.[4]

In light of these events, it is possible to imagine that Tousard might have wanted the insurrection to break out, not only so he could crush it and eliminate any desire for another one, but especially to alarm Paris by giving it the aim of restoring the king to his throne at a moment when the National Assembly had just suspended him following the flight to Varenne. Boukman, one may imagine, had other objectives, but he must have been encouraged by the support of such a high-placed officer.

We have a few other pieces of information about Boukman. Leclerc, the *procureur-syndic* of the Limbé town council at the time of the insurrection and later, from October 1792 to June 1793, the government delegate to the Le Cap law court, drew up some notes that inform us that Boukman had been a slave on his family's plantation and that he was considered a "bad slave."[5] He ran away but did not go far; he came back to the plantation at night to get food. After being discovered one night by Leclerc's brother, he was shot and wounded, then sold. This is how he ended up on the Clément plantation in Acul, a parish next to Limbé. He cannot have been considered all that "bad" a slave, since he was employed in the trusted position of coachman. It provided him with the opportunity to go to Le Cap and make contacts there while waiting for his master. We know that he went there on the morning of Monday, August 22. That Tousard might have passed a message to him, either directly or indirectly, is therefore not an absurd hypothesis.

Another document by the same Leclerc concerns the week before the insurrection, those few days during which it was discovered and yet everything continued as normal. It shows a slave of mixed racial descent named Dechaussée naming not Tousard, but Cambefort.[6] There would also be later attempts, in November, to contact Tousard and get him to intervene in their favor.

The theme of reestablishing the king, which was mentioned by all the slave leaders, is the revealing trace that remains of the involvement of certain royalists in an affair whose future dimensions they could not foresee. They did not realize that the insurrection would sweep away their own property. One needs to remember, nevertheless, that the aura of the king had earlier appeared in disturbances among slaves in Guadeloupe and Martinique (though not in Guyane). It was thought that he had decreed freedom for the slaves and that the colonists were blocking the decree by refusing to have it promulgated. Occasionally, he was supposed to have granted the famous three days a week of rest from slavery.[7] In any event, the king was a remote figure for the slaves; unlike the colonists and the local administration, he had not done them any harm. In 1791, there was not yet any talk of a republic, which was an even more remote notion. Perhaps one should recall that in Brazil, associations of slaves were allowed, or at least tolerated, that had at their head a king and a queen.

Independently of the two officers who were quite certainly implicated in a Machiavellian plot that they failed to control, Governor Blanchelande has occasionally been suspected, too, in particular by the marquis de Rouvray.[8] Blanchelande was clearly a royalist at heart, but that was not a sufficient reason. We will simply take note that he wrote to the minister that on August 22 he had been given warning of the insurrection, just after the attempt to kill Mossut, manager of one of the Galliffet plantations to the south of Cap-Français. On that Monday, Le Cap was buzzing with rumors of an imminent insurrection. However, there is some reason to believe that Blanchelande had been warned since August 18. Why the pretense?

We need to return to the parish of Limbé, to that Thursday, August 17, when the secrets were revealed and follow the narrative of Leclerc, who was one of the main protagonists among the whites.[9] Early that morning, he received a warning message from the colonist Chabaud. The previous evening around 10 P.M., his "housekeeper" (the slave who acted as a maid) had gone to take a bath in an irrigation canal when she suddenly saw flames and woke him up shouting "Fire!" A small group had already set fire to the trash house. When Chabaud arrived, they ran off, but he wounded and captured one, whose name was Jacques. A slave driver from the nearby Desgrieux estate, Jacques, ended up revealing the meeting of August 14 and the decision to organize the insurrection. The fire was intended to announce it, and he did not know why it had not broken out that very night. He was certain, nonetheless, that neither the delay nor his arrest and his confession would make any difference and that the insurrection would take place in a few days everywhere.

Leclerc arrived and took down the confession of Jacques, which included names that would crop up again later: Barthélémy, Paul, Boukman, and a few others. With the help of some white neighbors, Leclerc had some of them arrested if they were close at hand. When they set out with the prisoners, the plantation slaves tried to stop them and free the prisoners. By threatening to shoot, the whites opened up a path amidst them. It was by now no longer a matter of a few ringleaders, as they are usually called, but of a movement that whole workforces had joined. Once Jacques was brought to the local village and confined, first in the presbytery, then in the jail, the interrogation continued. The next day, an urgent message was sent to Le Cap with a request to send 100 soldiers so that preventive measures could be taken. Blanchelande sent only six men with a noncommissioned officer. The Limbé town council sent warning to Acul, which was the parish most immediately threatened, and went on with the investigation. It was in the course of these inquiries that Leclerc learned from the mouth of a slave that the insurgents were counting on the complicity of Colonel Cambefort.

The governor's attitude can be explained in several ways. A few months earlier, Blanchelande had been able to save his life only by a desperate escape from Port-au-Prince during a riot of white so-called Patriots who put Colonel Mauduit to death. The new Colonial Assembly was Patriot in tendency, and after meeting in Léogane in the West Province it decided to move to Le Cap, opting thereby to not leave the governor in peace. For the self-proclaimed Patriots of Saint-Domingue, any representative of the central government was a despot. Blanchelande had every reason to be concerned by the installation of this troublesome assembly that was planned for August 25. In addition, as regards the threat posed by the insurrection, he may have judged the greatest danger to be an alliance between town slaves and those on the plantations. He in fact took pains to prevent any revolt in the town by increasing surveillance, making preventive arrests, and transferring other slaves to ships in the harbor. Blanchelande, moreover, like most whites and the colonists in general, and like even people of mixed racial descent, did not believe that the blacks were capable of organizing a large-scale uprising. In short, nothing allows us to confirm Rouvray's suspicions.

After excluding Blanchelande, it remains the case that two external interventions, each of them very different, played a role in the outbreak of the insurrection. One group consisted of free blacks and men of mixed race. They had their own grievances, and although some of them may have sincerely supported universal freedom, most were willing to abandon the insurgents when the first civil commissioners promised them the amnesty voted by the Constituent Assembly in Paris, which was not granted to the insurgent slaves. A second, very small, group of royalists incorporated a slave revolt into a Machiavellian plan to restore the old regime. They alternated between attractive promises and repressive action and occupied much more important positions than those in the first group. But what of the thoughts and aspirations of the insurgents themselves? Certainly they adopted the slogan of restoring the king's power. On the oldest surviving written document from the insurrection, Jean-François and Biassou call themselves "generals of the king's armies" and under their signatures are the words "general of the armies" and "marshal."[10]

We cannot, however, take these expressions at face value, as has often been done. The civil commissioner Philippe Roume, for example, did so during the revolution, which gave rise to the dubious label "the black Vendée."[11] In certain of our documents, it is possible to come across statements made by the slaves, albeit already translated into French whereas they were originally spoken in Creole. In Leclerc's account of the days preceding the uprising, we learn that Jacques told Chabaud that they wanted "to take over the country." When he was facing Leclerc, Jacques certainly invoked the theme of reestablishing the king, but for him, evidently, the one goal did not exclude the other. The same was true of the *griffe* Dechaussée, who was interrogated by Leclerc on Sunday, August 21. After talking about the king, he went on: "All the blacks in the colony know the plan; it is to burn the plantations, kill the whites, and take over the country." At the same time, he saw no contradiction in claiming that there were whites with them; it was he who implicated Cambefort.

Clément's attorney, who was a prisoner of the insurgents for several hours during the night of August 22/23 and the following morning, recorded the comments of the two men whom Boukman had charged with guarding him (and who were nonetheless killed when he was freed by Tousard's dragoons). They too said that "their aim was to punish us because we had destroyed the king, because we had neither, faith, law, nor religion, had burned Port-au-Prince, and because of the king's decree that granted three days." They added that without the orders of the wealthy whites, they would not have gotten involved in "such an extensive plot that consisted of nothing less than destroying all the whites with the exception of some of the priests, surgeons, and women, burning all the plantations, and making themselves masters of the country."[12] In a document that is later, from about May 1792, but that comes directly from the insurgent Joseph Fourré, we can again read, "My idea was that, if I died in combat, I would die for our good king Louis XVI, king of the French. Liberty or death!" and further on, "Long live freedom for all the Swiss of Saint-Domingue!"[13]

The interpretation is thus not as simple as it may have seemed to Civil Commissioner Roume, and not the least because here and there a second theme appears without canceling out the others, that of the rights of man. Slaves, at least those who had access to the big house, the master's dwelling—servants and cooks, for example—had heard whites talking about revolution and the rights of man. The slave gangs could not be unaware of all this, despite the censorship that prevented the establishment of radical newspapers in Saint-Domingue and the repression that forbade informing the slaves of the declaration. Yet we find an interesting piece of information in the papers of the future vicomte Lainé, then a young man, who was in Saint-Domingue trying to obtain payment of unpaid rents that were part of his father's inheritance and was forced to serve in the national guard in the area around the besieged town of Cap-Français. On August 28, "the leader of a group of insurgents boldly came up to us saying he wanted the rights of man or a general pardon from Monsieur the governor." Lainé had previously mentioned the arrest of a young man from the Gironde who, living on a plantation, liked to read the newspapers of the "Jacobins and other philosophical enemies of the whites."[14] The Clément manuscript also records the execution of this white along with four insurgents without mentioning the reason for it. But the same manuscript does mention, referring to September 26th, that Father Cachetan, the priest of Petite-Anse parish, remained among the insurgents "to preach to them the declaration of the rights of man and the gospel of liberty." He, too, would be captured and executed.[15]

In these fragments of sentences, we begin to see layers of discourse of different value. On top is the language of the leaders, which acquired a sort of official status and played the role of a password: we are fighting for the king, who, let us note in passing, was still very legally France's head of state. There was in the rapid and durable dissemination of this idea a reasoning that the Clément manuscript makes apparent. After seeing so many rebellions or simple acts of disobedience drowned in blood, the slaves felt the need to seek allies who would give them the hope of succeeding. Even if the behavior of these so-called allies was disappointing, their purported existence allowed the slaves to throw themselves into the great adventure of the uprising without excessive fear. The invocation of the king, therefore, was not just a display for the benefit of outsiders but also gave courage to those on the inside.

Underneath this, the plan of campaign, with its killing of white masters and burning of plantations, reveals a quite different vision that was much more deeply rooted in the rebels' aspirations. It can be summed up in the slogan that was recorded on several occasions: take over the country. If it succeeded, what could the king do about it? Perhaps they would pay allegiance to him as long as he remained far away and did not hinder their taking over the country, their country. In a basic sense, this was a slogan that would have led directly to independence as early as 1791 if total victory had been achieved straightaway. The invocation of the rights of man, often expressed with the slogan "general liberty"—to distinguish it from the individual and uncertain manumissions granted according to the whims of the colonists—was in no sense incompatible with this profound desire for independence. Neither was the concern for sparing priests and surgeons, who were useful in various ways.

The military operations of the first weeks of the insurrection tend to confirm the view that the attainment of universal liberty and independence was the driving force behind the uprising. While the revolt was gaining ground in almost all of the north, destroying 165 sugar plantations in less than a month, the town of Le

Cap was besieged until about September 21, and we have already seen that Jean-Baptiste Cap had earlier attempted to organize a revolt of town slaves that perhaps had formed part of the original plans. In fact, if it had been possible to pull off these simultaneous insurrections and put the insurgents in control of the capital, the slaves would have been, so to speak, at home in most of the North Province. Taking the capital at the outset would have been a major step along the road to independence. Circumstances forced the insurgents to commit to a prolonged struggle. It was a decision that their leaders did not make without a certain hesitation.

We need to ask if all the insurgents' leaders shared the goal of independence. The names of five leaders emerged during the insurrection's first weeks. Boukman was chronologically the first without any doubt. Paul was his counterpart in Limbé. Jeannot, by capturing Dondon on September 10, gave the insurgents access to the Spanish part of the island, from where they could draw supplies. Jean-François and Biassou were the only ones still living after November.[16] As soon as these two found themselves alone as leaders, they attempted to negotiate, as if the insurrection's only aim had been to open up discussions from a position of strength. Whom did they approach, even before the arrival of the first civil commissioners? Tousard—and not only did they write to him but they also ordered their troops to cease offensive operations. At Christmas, when Jean-François met the civil commissioners (in a four-hour interview, according to the Clément manuscript), these leaders were willing to be satisfied with the freeing of fifty people and amnesty for the insurgents, whom they would, in return, force back to the plantations.

The negotiations were broken off solely because of the secret intervention of a royalist officer, Captain Poitou, who convinced the two leaders that the commissioners were misleading them and wanted to have them all massacred. Meanwhile, when the white prisoners were freed and handed over in accordance with an initial agreement, their escort commanded by Toussaint, in an assertion of power, had to push back or face down the insurgent masses who opposed the measure.[17]

As for the three others, Paul was supposedly put to death by the insurgents themselves. According to Dalmas, they reproached him for failing to protect them from Tousard's column that had regained a foothold in Limbé at the end of October. Boukman died in combat when Cambefort's column retook Acul at the beginning of November. He had remained behind alone to make a stand on the same Clément plantation where it had all started. But what are we to make of the report given in the Clément manuscript that on September 19th there had been found on the body of an insurgent an order signed by Jean-François to kill Paul and Boukman?[18] This is a complete mystery.

Jean-François, however, certainly did execute Jeannot on November 1. The reason was that the latter was much too cruel. It is true that Jeannot made white prisoners suffer everything that so many slaves had already suffered, and still were suffering at this time, such as those who were being tortured and broken on the wheel in Le Cap.[19] There is no reason to doubt Jean-François's sincerity; he did not approve of these methods. But bearing in mind the events of November–December, it is fairly clear as well that Jeannot was an obstacle to negotiations and that his execution was perhaps an affirmation that henceforward the insurgents would treat white prisoners humanely.

It is tempting to see a distinction between leaders such as Boukman, Paul, and probably Jeannot, who had given some thought to taking over the country, and the duo Jean-François and Biassou, who expected to deal with the whites as equals but also to negotiate (with all that word implies) with regard to making concessions. They, along with Toussaint and Charles Belair, already had what one would call nowadays a sense of "government culture." We have a few letters from Biassou to the abbé Delahaye in 1792 and another to Delahaye from Fayet, the free black commandant of Dondon.[20] By then an ardent defender of the demand for universal liberty, Biassou asked the cleric to draw up a sort of constitution for him. He adopted the role of a man in power who is anxious to provide law and order for his people. A fairly extensive liberated zone existed at this time that included several small towns. It happens, however, that the abbot still had several slaves in his service, both male and female, with the acceptance of Biassou. Only toward the end of the year, when the military situation had grown worse, did he free them. Fayet's letter is even more eye-opening. He was concerned about a rumor that accused Delahaye of having preached to the blacks that they should not work—which was no doubt false. In any event, for Fayet the end of slavery did not mean the right to do what one wanted. The leaders were serious; they intended to establish their authority according to recognized norms.

Of course, as long as universal liberty had not yet been won, first by defeating the French and then the Spanish and the English—that is, until 1798—differences of opinion and values had to take second place to the necessity of unity in the struggle. Yet such differences were already present in embryo. My intention here has not been to speculate what black independence in 1791 or 1792 might have led to or to judge in any way what the leaders conceived to be good government. My intention is simply to make clear that the aspiration toward independence was present from the beginning, although the leaders would not take that step until Bonaparte's attempted restoration left them no other choice.

Notes

1. Translated by David Geggus.
2. "Révolution de Saint-Domingue contenant tout ce qui s'est passé dans la colonie depuis le commencement de la révolution jusqu'au départ de l'auteur pour la France le 10 8bre 1792" (hereafter Clément manuscript), F3/141, f. 165–432, Centre

des Archives d'Outre-Mer, Aix-en-Provence (hereafter CAOM). It was used in Jacques Thibau, *Le temps de Saint-Domingue* (Paris, 1989), but only from the insurrection onward and only in extracts. The author paints a perfectly racist portrait of blacks in his preface but admits all the same to some exceptions, such as Boukman.

3. Dxxv/79, Archives Nationales, Paris (hereafter AN).

4. Dalmas, *Histoire de la Révolution de Saint-Domingue* (Paris, 1814). The text, at least the part concerning the insurrection, was written some twenty years before its publication.

5. "Extrait des notes de M. Leclerc, procureur-syndic du Limbé, commissaire du gouvernement près du tribunal criminal du Cap français, sur la brochure de M. Gros," CC9A/5, CAOM.

6. "Détails sur la révolte des nègres à Saint-Domingue depuis le jeudi 24 août jusqu'au [blank] 1791, par M. Clerc," F3/267, f. 311–342, CAOM. He obviously should have put "jeudi 17" and not "24," and in the blank, "4 septembre."

7. Slaves in the south of the colony had sought to gain three free days per week to devote to the cultivation of their provision grounds, hence to themselves.

8. Letter from the marquis to his daughter, dated December 6–7, 1791, in "Lettres du marquis et de la marquise du Rouvray," *Revue d'Histoire des Colonies* (1958): 153, 155.

9. The following is based on Leclerc's manuscript entitled "Détails sur la révolte."

10. Order dated September 15, 1791, promoting a certain Lamant lieutenant-colonel, Dxxv/78, AN.

11. The peasant rebellion in the Vendée region during the mid-1790s has often served as a symbol of fanatical conservatism. See chap. 9 in this volume.

12. Thibau, *Le temps de Saint-Domingu*, 281. Thibau extensively cites the manuscript F3/141 for the period following August 22.

13. The term "Swiss" referred to blacks who had taken up arms in March 1792 to support the claims not only of the mulattoes but also their own, as we see in this text. This was in the region of Gros Morne and Jean-Rabel, where the insurrection failed to break out in August 1791, owing to a betrayal followed by preventive executions.

14. Lainé's papers have been published on two occasions by Émile de Perceval, in *Le vicomte Lainé* (Paris, 1926) and in *Dans les archives du vicomte Lainé* (Paris, 1929). The same texts appear in the two volumes but with variations and interpretations that are not always reliable. The quote comes from the 1926 volume, p. 75.

15. Here we have the question of the whites found in the insurgent ranks, who, although few, did exist. The Clément manuscript allows for a count of about fifteen, some of whom were among those found dead after battles, including deserters, and some of whom were artillerymen. A letter dated September 19 by Mossut, the manager on the Galliffet estates who was wounded the evening of August 21, says this: "Various whites from the most wretched class, captured bearing arms and leading the slaves, have been brought to justice. Many slaves have also been executed, among them ten from our plantations. Both groups have kept stubbornly silent when interrogated about the nature and originators of this odious plot, although they admitted being guilty and participating in it." See 107AP/128, AN. The deserters, who are no doubt included in the category "the most wretched social class," might also have helped spread ideas of the rights of man.

16. At this time, Toussaint was Biassou's secretary but he also commanded a detachment of cavalry.

17. For these events we have only the narrative in Gros's *Récit historique sur les événements qui se sont succédés dans les camps de la Grande Rivière, du Dondon, de Sainte Suzanne et autres depuis le 26 octobre 1791 jusqu'au 24 décembre de la même année*, which was published in France with Verneuil's help in early 1793. The first edition appeared in Le Cap at the beginning of 1792 and created such a scandal that the author was forced to flee to the United States. There is another text by Gros that the Bibliothèque Nationale has catalogued among its anonymous works with the call mark Lk12 438.

18. Thibau, *Le temps de Saint-Domingue*, 302.

19. Without going further into the matter, it should be noted that an eyewitness account exists that gives a rather different picture of Jeannot. It was written by the lower-class colonist François Blaise Laroque, who was Jeannot's prisoner from August 27 to November 1. Jeannot had promised Laroque's mother, who was gravely ill, that he would spare her son's life, and in fact he was not killed.

20. CC9A/7, CAOM. These are transcriptions by Chanlatte. The originals are in Dxxv, AN.

Avenging America
The Politics of Violence in the Haitian Revolution[1]

Laurent Dubois

I N September 1791, a plantation manager named Pierre Mossut wrote to his employer, the Marquis de Gallifet, describing his narrow escape from the slave insurgents who had overrun half of the Northern Plain of Saint-Domingue the month before. Mossut provided several details in his description of the attack on one of Gallifet's plantations: the futile resistance of Gallifet's employees; the death of one of them, Odeluc; and the generosity of a slave who saved Mossut's life by presenting him with the horse he rode to safety. The account is as interesting for what it fails to include as for what it does describe: nowhere does Mossut write anything about a white baby impaled on a stake.[2]

In November 1791, however, a chronicle of the slave insurrection in Saint-Domingue claimed that, as the rebels approached the Gallifet plantations, they had as their standard "the body of a white child impaled upon a stake." This chronicle was published by Saint-Domingue's colonial assembly and was clearly aimed at generating sympathy and support for the planters, who dominated this political body. It drew on a stock accusation of the time, and in the case of Saint-Domingue, the image of blacks killing a white child seems to have been believable to many readers. The assembly's report was quickly translated into English, and the impaled white child became one of the most lasting images of Saint-Domingue's slave uprising. In Paris in 1792, the leading revolutionary journalist Camille Desmoulins attacked the abolitionist Brissot by saying that he was to blame "if a child carried on the end of a pike served as the standard of the blacks."[3]

The image continues to resonate in present-day representations of the revolution. Yet the dissonance between the assembly's text and the eyewitness account written by Mossut—who would probably have included such a detail if he had indeed witnessed it—forces us to ask whether this haunting picture was called into being by individuals haunted by something quite different from what they represented—not an onslaught of atavistic barbarism, but an organized and strategic revolution of slaves.

The era of revolutionary transformation in Saint-Domingue was a profoundly violent one. It emerged in a society saturated by and structured around daily violence and was shaped by a series of interlocking episodes of insurrection and political violence as well as by a global war in which the Caribbean colony played a crucial role. The revolution generated new structures of coercion which were justified by the threat of a return of older forms of violence, and its leaders often spoke of vengeance for old brutalities they had suffered as they justified new ones against their enemies. At the same time, the course of the Revolution was influenced in profound ways by representations of violence: political projects for the future were justified through evocations of past atrocities. To write about the politics of violence in the Haitian Revolution, then, is necessarily to write about the politics of representation, since the very accounts we depend on to understand the forms of violence employed during the revolution were themselves shaped by the political context they sought to describe and by the racialized world into which they were issued. But we also must seek to understand how the leaders of revolutionary Haiti sought to channel and contain revolutionary violence as they confronted the complexities involved in destroying plantation slavery and creating a new regime in its place. As they did so, these leaders found themselves confronting an imperial order that could be shaken but not altogether destroyed.

Slavery in Saint-Domingue was sustained by a regime of terror and torture. While the 1685 royal Code Noir placed limits on the physical violence that could be meted out to slaves and instituted punishments for masters who murdered slaves, in practice these provisions were rarely enforced. Slaves repeatedly brought complaints before local administrators about burning, mutilation, and murder on the plantations, but even when these were well documented, planters were almost never punished. Masters effectively protected their plantations from any intervention on the part of the state, banding together as a community to defend their right to use violence without restraint as a means of control. One visitor to the colony in 1775 described how every plantation had a stake at which slaves suspected of using poison were burned alive in front of the assembled residents as both a punishment and a deterrent.[4]

Planters justified their use of violence by arguing that in a society in which white masters were a tiny minority, the threat of atrocity was the only way to prevent slave insurrection. This was an interpretation shared by the

British abolitionist James Stephens, who in 1802 noted of the French plantation societies of the West Indies that what had "secured in great measure the tranquillity of these colonies before their revolutions" was "the nameless and undefined idea of terror, connected in the mind of a negro slave, with the notion of resistance to a white man and a master." But throughout the late eighteenth century, many colonial administrators, along with reformers in Paris, made the opposite argument: they worried that the unchecked violence of masters would incite revolution among the slaves. They advocated various reforms meant to rein in planter violence, some of which were incorporated into royal decrees in the mid-1780s. These reformers acknowledged that coercion was a necessary part of any slave system but argued that it had to be channeled and limited by the state. One defender of the royal reforms, for instance, argued that although because of their "composition," the colonies were based on a state of violence that could only be "maintained by force," there was a difference between "the absolute power that is necessary" and the "abuse of this power." The laws had to prevent "subaltern employees" from treating "350,000 slaves" with a cruelty that "revolted nature." Reformers ultimately failed to rein in planter violence, in part because their opponents successfully deployed the argument that intervention on the part of the state into slave-master relations would shatter the entire plantation system.[5]

Once the revolution had begun, contemporaries who tried to describe it often provided highly bifurcated accounts of the violence. One finds in them both descriptions of extreme brutality and incidents of loyalty and pity on the part of the slaves who had suddenly gained power over their masters. Bryan Edwards, who traveled to Saint-Domingue soon after the uprising and whose English-language writings on it profoundly shaped subsequent interpretations of the event, wrote that the uprising had produced "horrors of which imagination cannot adequately conceive nor pen describe" and a "picture of human misery" that "no other country, no former age, has exhibited." "Upwards of one hundred thousand savage people," Edwards wrote, "habituated to the barbarities of Africa, avail themselves of the silence and obscurity of the night, and fall on the peaceful and unsuspicious planters, like so many famished tygers thirsting for human blood." But he also described the "unexpected and affecting" act of one slave who, though he was part of the conspiracy that preceded the uprising, saved the life of his master and his family once it began. Interestingly, while Edwards gives no indication of what sources he relied on for his stories of black atrocities, he did provide a footnote explaining where he had heard the story of the slave who saved his masters. Accounts of barbarity, it would seem, required no corroboration, while accounts of the humanity of the slaves did. The same impulse apparently influenced the anonymous writer of the 1795 *Histoire des désastres de Saint-Domingue*, who, as Jeremy Popkin has argued, used "his first-person experiences" of being saved by several of his slaves to "nuance a more hostile portrait of black insurrectionists."[6]

This pattern of doubleness also shaped the various versions of one of the most important sources we have on the early months of the slave insurrection, the *Précis historique* of a writer named Gros. He was taken prisoner by the insurgents and ultimately served as the secretary of Jean-François during a series of negotiations with the French administration in late 1791. Gros's account was quite popular at the time. It was reissued by a printer in Cap-Français in February 1793 after its first printing in Saint-Domingue in mid-1792 and was printed in France in 1793. An English translation was also produced, under the title *Historick Recital*, in Baltimore in 1792 or 1793. It is highly valued by historians of the revolution, for it provides a rare glimpse of the activities and debates within the insurgent camps.[7]

As Popkin shows, while Gros's account details a number of tortures and executions he witnessed by insurgents under the command of Jeannot, it also speaks quite admiringly of Jean-François and several other insurgent leaders. Gros's text "highlights not only the humanity he experienced among the insurgents but also their intelligence." It tells a story of how the intervention of Jean-François and later Toussaint Louverture saved him and other prisoners, and it tells of his own service to Jean-François. Gros unsurprisingly presented his ascent from prisoner to secretary of Jean-François as the result of his own skillful maneuvers, which he claims were aimed at influencing the choices of the insurgents. But even this narrative strategy cannot hide the basic fact that, as Popkin writes, "a white man could come to identify himself with a black 'master,' even to the point of admiring his taste in clothing," as Gros indeed did.[8]

In preparing the English translation of his narrative, Gros took some steps to present a rather different, and less sympathetic, view of the insurgents. An overview of the insurrection of 1791, seemingly written by Gros himself, was appended to the work. As Popkin writes, it "includes the most lurid descriptions of atrocities supposed to have been committed during the insurrection, although Gros did not claim to have personally witnessed the most horrifying incidents he reported." Gros in fact acknowledged that there was "a great Contradiction" between his own first-hand account and the chronicle he provided. He explained the difference by noting that when he first wrote his account in mid-1792, the law of April 4—which had granted equal rights to free people of color—was being enforced in the colony and he wished to play down the "multiple crimes" of the "Banditti" of color in the colony.[9]

Gros's explanation seems to me rather spurious, however, since the intention of the April 4 decree was to crush the insurrection by uniting free people of color and whites against the slaves. Although there certainly may have been good reasons to play down the role of free coloreds in the insurrection—Gros portrayed those who were in the numerous insurgent camps as essentially

prisoners—there would have been little political pressure upon him to present positive portrayals of the insurgents themselves, who were the target of
several military campaigns sent by the French commissioners during 1792.
The change in tone, or the "contradiction," between the two texts—like the
dissonance between the first-person accounts provided by Edwards and the
anonymous author of the *Histoire des désastres* and like the difference between
Mossut's account of the taking of Gallifet and that presented by the Colonial
Assembly—strikes me as the result of a broader set of pressures that shaped
how the violence of the insurrection was portrayed. Those whites who directly
experienced the violence of the insurrection presented complex texts that spoke
of atrocities and kindnesses, of vengeance and forgiveness on the part of insurgents. As the narratives move a bit further from the first-hand accounts and
become chronicles and simultaneously charters for interpreting and responding to the insurrection, they tend to repeat representations that focused on
atrocities. In the case of Edwards and in other contemporary texts, the lurid
details were usually accompanied by claims that it was impossible to represent
their horror adequately. But what was in fact impossible to represent was more
the ambiguity and complexity of insurgent violence than its actual effects. The
politics of counterrevolution, strengthened by the politics of racial discourse,
tended to discourage the ambiguity of interpretation present in the direct
accounts written by Gros and a few others.

Terror was an important part of the first days of the uprising of 1791. It made
possible the initial advances of the insurgents, who sent many white residents
of the Northern Plain fleeing toward Cap-Français and thereby gained control
of a swath of territory south of the town. The counterattacks of French troops
and rapidly mobilized residents against the insurgents then became what
Edwards described as an "exterminating war." In their sorties against occupied
plantations, the troops were often indiscriminate in their attacks against slaves
they suspected of being involved with or supporting the uprising. In several
cases—notably at the Gallifet plantations—troops took over insurgent camps
after most warriors had departed and only noncombatants remained, including many children and elderly slaves. They nevertheless massacred those they
captured. Many slaves who might otherwise have opted for the relative safety
of their plantations were thus pushed into the insurgent camps. Both sides
used the corpses of their enemies as symbols of their willingness to fight all-out
war. "The country is filled with dead bodies, which lie unburied," one newspaper reported. When they passed through, the insurgents left whites with
stakes "driven through them into the ground," and "white troops . . . [took] no
prisoners, but killed everything black or yellow, leav[ing] the negroes dead
upon the field." "The heads of white prisoners, placed on stakes, surrounded

the camps of the blacks," another contemporary wrote, "and the corpses of black prisoners were hung from the trees and bushes along the roads that led to the positions of the whites."[10]

The insurgent leaders knew, however, that ultimately they could not win a war against an empire without external support. From early on, some understood that atrocities against whites, though they played a crucial role in the early phases of the uprising, needed to be contained in order to open the way for negotiation. Sometimes, they realized, particular individuals needed to be controlled. This was the case of the insurgent leader Jeannot, whose acts of torture were described by Gros in his captivity narrative but were also described and criticized by other insurgent bands who were operating in the same area as he was but disapproved of his tactics. Jeannot's acts of violence were carried out in front of both white prisoners and insurgents and mirrored those long used on slaves in the colony: whipping, burning, mutilation. At times he invited former slaves to torture and kill their former masters. He was not, however, left free to continue with these actions for very long. Alarmed by reports of Jeannot's atrocities, his superior Jean-François had him arrested, tried, and executed. This act of authority, and humanity, by the insurgent leader is worth highlighting. It contrasts with the history of the French administration in Saint-Domingue which, despite certain attempts, never succeeded in containing the violence of planters against their slaves. Unlike the planters in Saint-Domingue and in other slave colonies, the insurgents chose, at least at some moments, to pursue a comparatively humane set of policies towards those whose lives they controlled. Whether they did so simply for strategic reasons or for moral ones—or for some combination of the two—is of course difficult to know.[11]

Gros's account offers other examples of the divisions within the insurgent camps over the use of violence. While sometimes his captors treated prisoners quite harshly, he wrote, there were also several insurgents who went out of their way to treat the prisoners humanely. Gros described the hospitality he received—in the form of food and mattresses—from one insurgent leader, a domestic slave who had lived for several years in France and for this reason was nicknamed "the Parisian." He also tacitly acknowledged the link between the anger expressed toward white prisoners and the experiences of the formerly enslaved insurgents at the hands of their masters. Those who had labored on sugar plantations, he claimed, were more "enraged" than those who had been on the mountain coffee plantations, which were smaller. Furthermore, Gros singled out women as being particularly thirsty for vengeance. The insurgent leader Biassou also claimed that insurgent women were particularly harsh toward whites. These observations were not presented with a great deal of sympathy, of course, but taken together they suggest that attitudes toward insurrectionary violence were shaped by the diverse experiences individuals had had in the system it sought to destroy.[12]

Other personal histories apparently shaped how insurgents viewed the goals of the war they had begun. Some of these differences in perspective became apparent only after the insurgents had successfully gained control over territory through their military successes, forcing a divided and disoriented colonial administration to begin negotiating with them. The plan insurgent leaders discussed with the French administrators would have granted liberty to only several hundred leaders, while their followers would have been obliged to return to the plantations. As the leaders admitted, however, such plans would hardly satisfy the "multitude" of Africans who constituted their forces and who shaped the "general will" of the insurrection. This "multitude" demanded reforms in the practice of slavery and limits on punishment, and many spoke out forcefully against both compromise and mercy. As Gros recounted, when Jean-François, accompanied by Toussaint Louverture, led some white prisoners to Cap-Français to release them as part of the negotiations, they had to confront a group of insurgents who demanded that the whites' heads be brought to town on pikes instead. Negotiations between insurgents and colonial officials fell through, mostly because of the intransigence of local planters. Yet the pressures placed upon insurgent leaders by the "multitude" in the camps also certainly placed limits on how much negotiation was possible. The war, therefore, continued, until a new turn of violence—this one incited by developments across the Atlantic—created new openings for the revolutionary movement of the slaves.[13]

The stalemate between the administration and the insurgents would likely have continued for years had it not been for the onset of foreign war in early 1793, which opened the way for a dramatic set of transformations in Saint-Domingue. When Britain and Spain declared war against France, each sought to conquer the valuable colony. The Spanish did so by recruiting insurgents as "auxiliaries," promising them freedom if they would fight against the French. Many, including Louverture and Jean-François, responded positively. The French administration, battling the Spanish "auxiliaries" and the British, who had recruited planter allies, similarly offered freedom to those who would serve the Republic. When such measures proved insufficient, they took a much bolder step and abolished slavery outright in a desperate bid to save the colony for France. The strategy was a success. The forces France gained through emancipation stalled the advances of the British and Spanish and ultimately reversed them. The emancipation decreed locally in Saint-Domingue in 1793 was ratified in Paris in 1794 and extended to the entire French empire.

The decision of the Republican administrators effectively appropriated and channeled the violence of the slave uprising into the war between France and its enemies. The colonial administration embraced the cause of liberty, transforming its greatest internal threat into the foundation for the defense of the colony. In the place of stories of insurgent atrocities, the defenders of emancipation celebrated the heroism and idealism of their new, formerly enslaved, recruits. In the process they opened the way for the ascendancy of a new group of leaders, many of them ex-slaves, who would ultimately take control of the task of transforming Saint-Domingue into a post-emancipation society. But these leaders, foremost among them Toussaint Louverture, also understood from the beginning that they faced a dangerous counterrevolution. The planters who had been defeated and fled Saint-Domingue were not going to accept the abolition of slavery, and they had at their disposal a powerful and widespread tradition of racism on which to draw in criticizing and belittling the former slaves who had made the revolution. To save emancipation, the revolutionary leadership would have to hold at bay the counterrevolution in an Atlantic world dominated by empires and nations deeply invested in slavery. Doing so required that they counter the many representations of black barbarism that brought comfort to this counterrevolution by providing their own alternative representations of the revolutionary violence of Saint-Domingue.

"If, because some blacks have committed cruelties, it can be deduced that all blacks are cruel," declared Toussaint Louverture in 1797, "then it would be right to accuse of barbarity the European French and all the nations of the world." He was writing in response to a speech by a former slave-owner from Saint-Domingue, Viénot de Vaublanc, who painted a picture of a chaotic colony overrun by lazy and violent former slaves. Vaublanc's speech focused on the "barbarities" committed during the 1791 insurrection as a way of delegitimizing the emancipation it had brought about. In his response, Louverture conceded that "terrible crimes" had been committed by ex-slaves in Saint-Domingue. But, he insisted, the violence in the colony had been no greater than that in metropolitan France. Indeed, he noted ironically, if the blacks of Saint-Domingue were as "ignorant" and "gross" as Vaublanc proclaimed, this should excuse them for their actions. The same was not true, he suggested, of the numerous Frenchmen who, despite "the advantages of education and civilization," had committed horrific crimes in continental France during the Revolution. Pursuing his own attack against Vaublanc's attempt to reject an entire political project by pointing to particular atrocities committed in its pursuit, he noted that if the treason and errors of some in Saint-Domingue justified a return to the old order there, then the same would be true in France. Would it not be justified to claim, on the basis of the violence of the French Revolution, that the French were "unworthy of liberty" and "made only for slavery" and that they should be once more put under the rule of kings? How, he further insisted, could Vaublanc—a onetime owner of slaves—gloss over "the outrages committed in cold blood by civilized men like himself" who had allowed "the lure of gold to suppress the cry of their conscience"? "Will the crimes of powerful men always be glorified?"[14]

Louverture was acutely aware of the importance of countering European prejudices against the ex-slaves who were the majority in the colony. Since his days in the insurgent camps, he had been conscious of the potential negative ramifications of violence and had distinguished himself for the clemency he showed counterrevolutionary whites. Indeed, Louverture's lack of vengeance against whites contrasted sharply with the actions of white administrators in the region during the same period. In Guadeloupe in 1794, for instance, several hundred counterrevolutionaries who had fought with the British were massacred by the French colonial administrator Victor Hugues. When Louverture captured areas controlled by the British, meanwhile, he typically gathered together in a local church the whites who had supported the enemy and told them that, following Catholic teachings, he would forgive them if they repented for what they had done. Such magnanimity went against French policy, which tended to treat those who had supported the British quite harshly, and it earned him harsh criticism from French administrators in the colony and in continental France. Some went so far as to portray him as a tool of the counterrevolution.[15]

Louverture's policy toward former slave-owners was one piece of the complicated and at times extremely difficult balancing act through which he sought to consolidate and sustain emancipation. The twists and turns of his regime were the by-now-familiar set of compromises and ironies facing revolutions that sought independence in the midst of empire: in order to make sure Saint-Domingue never reverted to the slave colony it had been, he chose to maintain the central institution of the old system—the plantation—as a way of negotiating with a threatening set of powers, all of which were invested in slavery. Maintaining the plantation order served two purposes for Louverture. It was an attempt to appease the French regime by proving that even without slavery, the colonies could produce sugar and coffee for France and continue to sustain its economy as they had before abolition. At the same time, however, the production of sugar and coffee was also a way of making sure Louverture had an alternative if the French government and the Saint-Domingue planters were not appeased by the continuing production of tropical produce. Plantation commodities provided Louverture with a source of foreign exchange, and his ability to trade with British and North American merchants made it possible, among other things, for him to build up supplies of weapons so that he might have the capacity to resist potential attempts to unseat him and rebuild the old order in the colony.

While Louverture's guiding goal was to protect emancipation, the emphasis on plantation production seriously constrained the possibilities of ex-slaves, many of whom refused his demands that they continue to labor on the plantations. Ultimately, in a draconian decree he passed in 1800 and then in his 1801 constitution, Louverture created an order in which he used his military to coerce former slaves into continuing to work on the plantations. Where the violence of slavery had been privatized and controlled by individual masters, the violence of Louverture's regime was regimented and delivered by state representatives, and it was defended as a necessary part of a broader project of liberation.[16]

Despite Louverture's willingness to use coercion to maintain plantation production, Bonaparte and his advisors came to view him as an obstacle to their designs, and in 1802 they sent a mission to the colony with the intent of reestablishing metropolitan control and destroying the autonomous regime Louverture had constructed in the colony. This decision created a new situation, one in which warfare ultimately defined the terms through which a new nation was imagined.

Bonaparte's attempt to destroy Louverture's regime broke apart the alliance between former slaves and the French revolutionary regime that had stabilized and protected Saint-Domingue during the previous years and ultimately transformed the revolution in Saint-Domingue into a war for national liberation. Despite an initial, though costly, military victory over Louverture, the French were unable to vanquish resistance in the colony, which was sustained throughout the island by small groups of fighters, often led by African-born leaders. Dependent on the black soldiers of Saint-Domingue to fight these rebels, the French became increasingly paranoid about the prospect of desertions to the enemy side. Seeking to prevent and punish disloyalty through the threat and exertion of violence, the French helped solidify the resistance. The fear of subversion drove the French to brutal excess, and they began massacring whole units of black soldiers, gassing them in the holds of ships, drowning them in the harbors, executing officers and their families.[17]

Both sides increasingly came to identify their enemies primarily according to skin color rather than political or ideological criteria. Vengeance once again surfaced as a motivation for violence. Already in 1802, troops under the command of Jean-Jacques Dessalines, one of Louverture's leading generals, had massacred whites, inspired, according to one survivor, the writer Michel Etienne Descourtilz, by the memory of the brutality white masters had once exercised against slaves. These actions represented a break with Louverture's policies of the previous years. They were driven not only by the memory of past violence but by the very real fear that a counterrevolution might resurrect slavery in the colony.[18]

A major turning point in the battle against the French was the creation of a solid alliance between the ex-slave Dessalines and a group of officers who came from the class known before the revolution as "free people of color." As numerous as the white population of the island before 1789, many of these individuals were of mixed European and African descent, and many were owners of land and slaves. Over the course of the revolution, some members of this group had sought to separate themselves from the mass of the formerly enslaved, and the divisions between these two groups had animated a series of violent conflicts. The unity achieved in 1802 between blacks and people of color was predicated on opposition to a common enemy who was no longer making distinctions among those of African descent, whether loyal or rebellious, rich or poor, former slave or former slave-owner. The joining of the two groups was symbolized most clearly in the flag the leaders of the "indigenous army" chose in early 1803 that removed the white from the French tricolor. The gesture—one used the previous year by revolutionaries fighting a doomed battle against the French in Guadeloupe—had a clear meaning: through their brutality, whites had forfeited their right to be included in the new political community being forged in Saint-Domingue.[19]

But once they had successfully united a diverse and divided population and defeated the French under this new flag, revolutionary leaders had to find a language through which to define this new community. The nationalist language they chose emerged from the violence of the war. The declaration was meant both to evoke the horrors that French control had wrought on the colony and to exorcise them. It proclaimed a new Haitian national identity by focusing on the need to erase, and avenge, the past of French colonialism.[20]

The declaration not only asked for a permanent rejection of France but also for a kind of purification. The survivors of the war who looked around them for dead brothers, sisters, wives, and husbands instead saw everywhere the French "vultures" who had killed them. It was their responsibility to take revenge; if they did not do so, the disgusted spirits of their relatives would reject them. Moreover, revenge would not only assuage the spirits of the dead, it would send a message to those who might threaten the new country. The generals who had won a military victory for independence would have "done nothing" until they had given "to the nations" a "terrible, but just, example of the vengeance that a people proud of having won back its liberty, and ready to jealously preserve it, must exercise."[21]

Dessalines's 1804 proclamation was shaped by the racialized war out of which it emerged. But its mobilization of vengeance was also a response to a particularly challenging problem he faced in proclaiming the birth of a new nation. Dessalines referred to the "indigenous" people of the colony in his 1804 proclamation and called his troops the "indigenous army." But the people of African descent in Haiti were no more indigenous to the land than the whites whose destruction Dessalines demanded, and indeed most were African-born. They were exiles, brought to Saint-Domingue on slave vessels, often still speaking their African languages and drawing on their religious and military traditions in their battle for liberty. How could Africans and descendants of Africans claim a territorial right to the colony of Saint-Domingue, one that superseded the claims of the French empire that had made the colony what it was? How could this claim be legitimized?

Dessalines's answer was to portray the expulsion of the French as an act of vengeance not only for their recent brutality but for all the violence of the European colonizers in the Americas. The name Dessalines and his officers chose for the new nation was, according to early accounts of the conquest of the Caribbean (which were very likely known to members of Dessalines's staff), the name given to Hispaniola by the original inhabitants of the island. By choosing this name, the Haitian revolutionaries presented themselves as surrogates for and descendants of the vanished indigenous inhabitants. Dessalines had opted for a similar message when he briefly termed his forces the "Army of the Incas" (before changing to the simpler "indigenous army"), mobilizing the symbolism, revived by South American indigenous rebellions in the 1780s, of the Inca as enemies of European conquest. In claiming the mantle of the long-defeated indigenous peoples of the island, they infused their own struggle against the French with a broader historical significance, adding to their list of grievances those of the inhabitants brutalized by the Spanish centuries before and pre-senting themselves as their avengers of a violent history.[22]

In an April 1804 proclamation, Dessalines asserted that the violence of the revolution had purified Saint-Domingue (and the Americas as a whole) by taking revenge for the suffering of generations of the dead. "Yes, we have paid these true cannibals back crime for crime, war for war, outrage for outrage," he thundered. "I have saved my country. I have avenged America." Having created the first independent nation in Latin America, he imagined it as the negation of European colonialism and its attendant brutalities, as a state that would channel the centuries of suffering of the colonized into a new political commu-nity that guaranteed the eternal freedom of its scarred constituency.[23]

Notes

1. This chapter draws on my narrative history of the Haitian Revolution, *Aveng-ers of the New World: The Story of the Haitian Revolution* (Cambridge: Cambridge Uni-versity Press, 2004). An earlier version of the chapter was presented under the title "Avenging America: Violence and Vengeance in the Haitian Revolution" at the confer-ence Rethinking Latin America's Century of Revolutionary Violence, Yale University, May 2003. I thank the participants of that conference, particularly Greg Grandin, Gilbert Joseph, and Rebecca Scott, for their responses to this earlier version. A French translation of this essay, entitled "La revanche de l'Amérique: La politique de violence dans la révolu-tion haïtenne," was published in *Revue de la Société haïtenne d'histoire et de géographie* 79, no. 219 (December 2004): 15–51.

2. Mossut to Gallifet, September 19, 1791, dossier 3, 107 AP 128, Archives Nationales, Paris (hereafter AN). Antoine Dalmas, who had also worked on the Northern Plain during the early days of the insurrection and may have witnessed the attack on La Gossette, did not mention this detail in his memoir of the uprising, penned in 1793–1794; see his *Histoire de la Révolution de Saint-Domingue* (Paris, 1814), esp. 1:120–123.

3. *A Particular Account of the Commencement and Progress of the Insurrection of the Negroes of St. Domingo* (London, 1792), 4–5; Camille Desmoulins, *J. P. Brissot démasqué* (Paris: 1792), 40, quoted in Eléni Varkis, preface to Olympe de Gouges, *L'esclavage des noirs, ou l'heureux naufrage* (1792; reprint, Paris, 1989), 25.

4. Pierre de Vassière, *Saint-Domingue: La société et la vie créoles sous l'ancien régime, 1629–1789* (Paris, 1909), 189–194; Pierre Pluchon, *Vaudou, sorciers, empoisonneurs: de Saint-Domingue à Haïti* (Paris, 1987), 176.

5. James Stephens, *The Crisis of the Sugar Colonies; or, an Enquiry into the Objects and Probable Effects of the French Expedition to the West Indies* (1802; repr., New York, 1969), 72; "Mémoire rélatif à l'ordonnance du 4 Décembre 1784 sur les gérens [sic] et la police des noirs," box 1, series III, folder 32, Gen MSS 308, Documents Relating to the French Participation in the American Revolution, Beinecke Rare Book and Manuscript Library, Yale University, New Haven, Connecticut. For an excellent general study of these debates, see Malick Walid Ghachem, "Sovereignty and Slavery in the Age of Revolution: Haitian Variations on a Metropolitan Theme" (Ph.D. diss., Stanford University, 2001).

6. Bryan Edwards, *The History, Civil and Commercial, of the British Colonies in the West Indies* (London, 1801), 3:67, 79; Jeremy Popkin, "Facing Racial Revolution: Captivity Narratives and Identity in the Saint-Domingue Insurrection," *Eighteenth-Century Studies* 36, no. 4 (2003): 523. A now-classic discussion of European reactions to the Haitian Revolution is presented in Michel-Rolph Trouillot, *Silencing the Past: Power and the Production of History* (Boston, 1996), chapter 2.

7. See Popkin, "Facing Racial Revolution," 528–529n5. For the French version of Gros, see Gros, *Isle de Saint-Domingue: Précis Historique* (Paris, 1793). On the reprint in Saint-Domingue, see *Moniteur Général de Saint-Domingue*, February 8, 1793, 336.

8. Popkin, "Facing Racial Revolution," 516.

9. Popkin, "Facing Racial Revolution," 523.

10. Edwards, *History*, 3:82; *Philadelphia General Advertiser*, October 10 and November 14, 1791; Pamphile de Lacroix, *La Révolution de Haïti* (Paris, 1987), 95.

11. See Gros, *Précis Historique*. For an account by a group of *gens de couleur* insurgents that corroborates Gros's account of Jeannot's actions and notes that the insurgent leader also tortured and killed blacks in his camp, see "Adresse à l'assemblée générale . . . par MM. les citoyens de couleur, de la Grande Rivière," folder 4, no. 4, DXXV 1, AN.

12. Biassou to Commissioners, December 23, 1791, folder 4, no. 20, DXXV 1, AN.

13. Jean-François and Biassou to Commissioners, December 12, 1791, folder 4, no. 6, DXXV 1, AN; Gros, *Précis*.

14. Toussaint Louverture to the Directory, October 27, 1797, in *Toussaint Louverture*, ed. George Tyson, Jr. (Englewood Cliffs, N.J., 1973), 36–43.

15. On Louverture, see Beaubrun Ardouin, *Etudes sur l'histoire d'Haïti* (1853–1865; repr., Port-au-Prince, 1958), 3:99. On Guadeloupe, see Laurent Dubois, *A Colony of*

Citizens: Revolution and Slave Emancipation in the French Caribbean, 1787–1804 (Chapel Hill, 2004), chapter 7.

16. See Claude Moïse, *Le projet nationale de Toussaint Louverture et la Constitution de 1801* (Port-au-Prince, 2001).

17. The best history of the 1802 expedition is Claude Bonaparte Auguste and Marcel Bonaparte Auguste, *L'expédition Leclerc, 1801–1803* (Port-au-Prince, 1985).

18. Michel Etienne Descourtilz, *Voyages d'un naturaliste, et ses observations* (Paris, 1809), 3:279–281.

19. Ardouin, *Etudes sur l'histoire d'Haïti*, 5:83–84. On the flag in Guadeloupe, see Dubois, *A Colony of Citizens*, 158–159 and 400.

20. Ardouin, *Etudes sur l'histoire d'Haïti*, 6:7–8.

21. Ardouin, *Etudes sur l'histoire d'Haïti*, 6:8–9.

22. David Geggus, *Haitian Revolutionary Studies* (Bloomington, 2002), 207–220.

23. Ardouin, *Etudes sur l'histoire d'Haïti*, 6:17.

"Fêtes de l'Hymen, Fêtes de la Liberté"
Marriage, Manhood, and Emancipation in Revolutionary Saint-Domingue

Elizabeth Colwill

Three Scenes from a Marriage

In early December 1793, Citoyen Robquin, devoted associate of Commissioner Sonthonax and captain in the 92nd regiment of the French infantry, sent his father news of the "most beautiful gift" that revolutionary France had granted Saint-Domingue: general emancipation. Robquin's construction of liberty as a gift spoke volumes, for it ascribed to the French a beneficence that incurred obligations, specifically the obligation of former slaves to serve in the French military and on colonial plantations. Robquin then turned to more intimate matters. "It may surprise you that in the midst of such afflicting scenes, I was able to choose a worthy and respectable companion." On "22 July '93, with the approval of the civil commissioners and the military leaders, I offered my hand to citoyenne Laure Castaing . . . of the class of citizens of 4 April"—a free woman of color.[1]

As Robquin posted his letter, Guillaume-François Mahy, baron de Cormeré—erstwhile French financial official and twice an émigré—penned a several-hundred-page denunciation of the commissioners, their retinue, and the entire course of emancipation. Brother of a resident proprietor in Saint-Domingue, de Cormeré abandoned revolutionary France for Saint-Domingue in March 1792 in the wake of the execution of his more famous brother, the marquis de Favras, convicted of a plot to rescue Louis XVI. His manuscript, which framed his eyewitness account of the months preceding general emancipation within a tidy conspiracy theory, rejected the notion of liberty as a gift and the possibility of the "regeneration" of slaves through military service and marriage.[2]

On August 4, less than two weeks after Robquin and Laure Castaing exchanged their vows, Citoyen Jean Petour, "formerly belonging to Citoyen LaCroix," and "Marie," "belonging to Citoyen La Croix," came before the General Council of Fort Dauphin to register their intent to marry. The ceremony occurred in the wake of the French commissioners' proclamation of July 11, 1793, which encouraged "warriors" fighting for the Republic to emancipate their families through republican marriage.[3] After a lifetime of labor, Citoyen Petour and Citoyenne Marie would not have considered liberty a gift.

I open with these three "scenes from a marriage" to suggest the diverse meanings of a single ritual—marriage—and of slave emancipation itself to persons widely separated by privilege, position, and perspective who lived the revolution in Saint-Domingue. This chapter offers a microscopic view of the revolution, layering three distinct narratives that chronicle episodes in the revolutionary year that preceded emancipation in the North Province on August 29, 1793. This technique of narrative montage involves "stepping in the same waters" thrice, to use Joan Dayan's evocative phrase—for it provides three different windows on the process of emancipation, each of which frames encounters, or collisions, between historical actors who sought to define the parameters of freedom in Saint-Domingue.[4] To a greater degree than we have heretofore understood, they did so in gendered terms.[5]

In Frame I, "The Second Commission and the 'Gift of Liberty,'" the correspondence and official proclamations of French civil commissioners Léger Félicité Sonthonax and Étienne Polverel and their republican allies are read anew through the lens of gender. This perspective, in certain respects, defamiliarizes the political narrative, discovering the ways in which the process of emancipation in Saint-Domingue involved a ritual struggle in which the rights and duties of man were fought and secured through military service and, equally important, republican marriage. In Frame II, "The Conspiracy of Emancipation," de Cormeré's little-known *Histoire de la révolution de la partie française de St. Domingue* breaks in upon the commissioners' narrative of emancipation, using insult, irony, and the specter of miscegenation to reframe the political struggle as a cultural battle in which the stakes were aristocratic privilege, masculine honor, and racial purity. In Frame III, the stories of slave women, fractured and discontinuous, cut across and dramatically recast these two more unified narratives. It would have been logical, perhaps, to have partnered the commissioners and de Cormeré with their most powerful political and military allies and combatants: the free men of color, the armies of insurgents, and their male leaders.[6] But this strategy would be to confirm their own conception of the process of emancipation as one fought primarily on the battlefield and in public office, on the terrain of masculine honor and male citizenship. Instead, I tack a subterranean course through the archives, finding in the traces of enslaved women's lives a striking counterpoint to more familiar, and heroic, narratives of emancipation—stories that highlight both the toll of war on community and kin, and women's diverse and distinct pathways to freedom.

As Jill Lepore has written: "War twice cultivates language: it requires justification, it demands description."[7] My aim is to suggest some of the ways that gender shaped debates over race and war, the process of emancipation, and the meanings of freedom to those who fought to define, claim, or constrain it in revolutionary Saint-Domingue. In that effort, the structure of this chapter as narrative collage is not simply a literary alternative to a more linear, unified history but conveys the argument itself; discrete images of the revolutionary process, superimposed, provide an interpretative vantage point inaccessible through any single narrative lens. All of the historical actors who appear in these pages wove gendered narratives of revolution. But how gender mattered in revolutionary Saint-Domingue varied, depending on who was telling the story.

Frame I: The Second Commission and the "Gift of Liberty"

Emancipation was a process, not a single decree, and Civil Commissioners Sonthonax and Polverel could have predicted neither its course nor its outcome in a period in which change repeatedly outstripped contemporaries' ability to imagine or assimilate it.[8] As emissaries of revolutionary France, their charge was not to emancipate the slaves but rather to suppress a slave revolution while forging equality among all free men, regardless of color. Their personal and political commitment to the law of April 4, 1792, which had granted free men of color rights of citizenship, set the commissioners in immediate conflict with the supporters of the old colonial order; their war against the insurgents etched a sharp divide between republican France and the slave population of Saint-Domingue.[9] Transposed from France to a deeply divided political landscape, invested with an internally contradictory mission, the commissioners first directed their tenuous authority toward efforts to "regenerate" free men.[10]

The new commissioners disembarked on the pier in Le Cap in September 1792 to formal fanfare that only thinly veiled the intense anxiety of most white residents. Their entry speech paired reassurance and threat: they promised to preserve slavery and the prerogatives of planters but explicitly disjoined the exercise of rights from color—that is, from the increasingly elaborate system of classification that linked rights and privileges to racial bloodline in the last decades of the eighteenth century. "Henceforth we recognize only two classes of men . . . : free, without any distinction of color, and slaves."[11]

The commissioners were highly conscious of the importance of ritual as they moved swiftly to implement the law: dissolving the existing colonial assemblies, abolishing racial terminology in the État Civil, appointing a racially integrated Intermediary Commission, and establishing procedures for electing new municipal governments without regard to color.[12] In keeping with their charge, the entry ceremonies, military assemblies, and political festivals under the Second Commission assumed a relentlessly masculine and militaristic cast.[13] The commissioners' bellicose proclamations—confiscations of émigré estates, deportations, requisitions—provide a register of their increasing isolation from the white population of all social levels and their dependence on free men of color as a political and military bulwark of republicanism in Saint-Domingue.[14]

Occasionally, the commissioners received indications that principles of equality had penetrated the hearts of some colonial whites. When Sonthonax, suffering from fever, sought to regain his health at the Charrier plantation, the hospitable proprietor "seized the moment" of his arrival to reenact the fall of the monarchy by toppling a large statue of Louis XVI from its pedestal on the stairway.[15] Nonetheless, by late spring Sonthonax and Polverel faced political isolation, treason, international war, new incursions, racial conflict—and word that the newly appointed Governor-General Galbaud had moved to usurp their own powers.[16] Faced with this grave threat, the commissioners, previously engaged in the pacification of the west and south, reversed course and returned precipitously toward Le Cap, accompanied by several hundred armed men of color.

Yet, astonishingly, in the midst of this new crusade, they paused on June 7 in Saint-Marc long enough to attend the first celebration of republican marriage in the colony.[17] Delivered by Mayor Savary, the marriage discourse was composed, claimed one antagonist, by Polverel himself. Republican marriage and martial fraternity would serve as twin pillars of the commissioners' vision of racial equality.

Regeneration, Race, and Revolutionary Intimacies:
A Cultural History of the Burning of Le Cap, I

Just over a fortnight after this first republican marriage, the city of Cap-Français burned to the ground. The conflict between the commissioners and Governor-General Galbaud, both emissaries of the French Republic, is a story most often told as a conflict among political elites. Yet political intrigue in the early days of June also unfurled as cultural theatre, in which a processional path, the refusal of a gift, a dinner invitation, a familial spectacle, and the composition of one's personal retinue furnished the immediate impetus to the military conflagration. The stage on which these scenes unfolded was not merely in the realm of high politics and the battlefield but of culture and sociability, not merely on the terrain of racial ideology but of gendered intimacies.

In the intricate ritual negotiations surrounding the commissioners' second entry to Le Cap,[18] the two men recast political loyalties and reordered the body politic on the grounding of racial equality by flouting ceremonial conventions. Although Galbaud preserved older honorific forms by greeting the commissioners at their entry to Haut-du-Cap, the commissioners, with "republican" regard for principles over rank, treated him "with the greatest coldness" and refused to grant him a private audience.[19] The following day they attended a ceremony with the civil and military corps that concluded, in an atmosphere rife with suspicion, with an "oath of sincerity."[20] An elaborate dinner hosted by Galbaud expressly in their honor was to have followed. The commissioners, however, spurned the invitation and with it Galbaud's gift of hospitality and the obligations that it incurred.[21]

The commissioners' supporters justified their flouting of protocol on the grounds of race prejudice, gender inversion, and violations of republican sociability: specifically, Galbaud's reluctance to accept the "citizens of 4 April" into his own, and his wife's, personal entourage. According to Boucher, president of the Intermediary Commission, after the commissioners' refusal to attend Galbaud's dinner, Galbaud unleashed a torrent of racial and sexual invective against "the Mulattoes," claiming that "even the women" had turned against him since he had refused to make "all the concubines of the city the social equals of his wife." In this race war, the commissioners, their allies, and their opponents all appealed to the sexual imaginary to etch the divide between virtue and vice on the body politic. In Boucher's account, Galbaud's wife played the part of a colonial Marie-Antoinette, fanning the flames of racism and fomenting discord. Indeed, in Boucher's representation, Madame Galbaud urges her own son to seek revenge for his father's humiliating dismissal. "Let the Mulattoes rule under their despots," she exclaimed. "Go my son: a word from you to the National Convention will unmask them."

A few days later, amidst looming financial disaster and the imminent threat of white insurrection, the commissioners announced their own "small civic fête" for June 19. Governor-General Galbaud was not among the guests, for by that time Sonthonax and Polverel had boldly stripped him of office and confined him aboard the *Normande* for deportation to France.[22] That the commissioners should have inserted into the cascading violence a night of feasting and theatre *en famille* reveals something of the significance of the spectacle of interracial sociability across gender lines, in which revolutionary intimacies provided the path toward republican regeneration. Reportage in the *Moniteur Général de la Partie Française de Saint-Domingue* highlighted the ways that the gender intermixture at the gathering served as a harbinger of racial equality: "Yesterday there was a dinner and concert at the civil commissioners'; the mélange of colors and of diverse classes of *citoyens* and *citoyennes* formed a happy ensemble where harmony and equality presided."[23]

The next day sailors and colonial whites under the leadership of the escaped Galbaud rose in insurrection. The ensuing conflict has often been recounted: the initial military confrontations between Galbaud, supported by most of the white troops and National Guard, and the commissioners, backed by the free coloreds; the white residents' rebellion checked only by the commissioners' offer of liberty to insurgents who would join French republican forces; the influx of reinforcements under the black generals Pierrot and Macaya; and finally, the sack of Le Cap.[24] Witnesses agreed that the commissioners' proclamation of June 21, which emancipated insurgent slaves who agreed to fight for the Republic, was a watershed in the prosecution of the war and the course of emancipation.[25]

As described by Sonthonax, the transformation of the loyalties of the armed insurgents was effected through a ritual of political conversion, in which the commissioners played the role of republican tutors to the students of liberty. "Stripping off the signs of royalism," they "donned the tricolor ribbon," the symbol of the French republic, then swore a military oath.[26] The staging of masculinity through militarism had long served as an important locus of the commissioners' campaign to imprint the citizenship of free colored men on the government and military.[27] Martial ceremonies featured masculinity in ways that obscured racial division in gender difference; simultaneously they legitimized slavery by displacing the notion of class as color by distilling class to a simple binary: free/unfree.[28] But in June 1793, manhood displayed as military prowess, put to the service of the state, served as a rationale not only for rights for free men of color but also for the emancipation of male slaves.[29] From the perspective of the commissioners, the military oath of obedience taken by the black insurgents on June 21 served as a ritual through which the republic gave birth to *hommes nouveaux* (new men)—an identity as free men and citizens, for the "regenerated citoyens of 21 June" as for the "citoyens of 4 April," rooted directly in military service.[30]

Significantly, even republican accounts intimated that the "gift of liberty" was not altogether freely given. As Citoyen Robquin later recalled the course of emancipation, the beleaguered commissioners could no longer "resist the storm": black men "felt their strength and their rights." "It was thus necessary to attach this mass of men so precious to the interests of the Republic, and the most beautiful gift that they could be given was general liberty." Robquin's language reflects what had become by then the standard formula of French officials and their deputies as they sought to justify emancipation as a gift through which they gave birth to "new men." But to bestow the gift of liberty was simultaneously an act of possession, specifically a claim on the bodily labor—military and agricultural—of the new citizens. As Pierre Bourdieu has written, a man "possesses by giving. A gift that is not returned can become a debt, incur a lasting obligation; and the only recognized power—recognition, personal loyalty or prestige—is the one that is obtained by giving." While the usurer exerts his power through overt economic violence, the gift, through the moral and emotional obligations it generates, exerts a "symbolic violence, censored, euphemized."[31] However fervent the belief of Sonthonax and Polverel in the redemptive possibilities of regeneration, emancipation would remain a "gift" that incurred a debt on the part of the former slaves.

The Making of "New Men," I

To create "new men" in Saint-Domingue was not, to the minds of the commissioners, a simple task. Their challenge was not only to sculpt citizens from former slaves but also to ensure that those new citizens performed the labor of colonial subjects. To this end, French officials linked the obligations of the new citizen within the French empire to manhood itself, a manhood born of military service yet anchored in family life. Precisely because the boundaries of manhood and the meanings of citizenship were at issue, the commissioners' proclamations regarding labor, land, and military service were permeated with discussions of family, marriage, and morality.[32] Even the brief June 21 decree, written under the spur of military necessity, sought to win the insurgents to the republican cause with the promise of an amelioration of conditions for slave families, including pregnant women and nursing mothers, and of land sufficient to support freedmen and their families.[33] Indeed, the justification for successive emancipations and the invention of "new men" was inseparable in the minds of the commissioners from the creation of "legitimate" nuclear family units under masculine authority. The dilemma of emancipation, from the standpoint of French officials, was intimately interwoven with the problem of matrimony.

Feminist scholars have established the public and political significance of the purportedly "private" ritual of heterosexual marriage: headship of a family, in conjunction with property ownership, has long defined men's entitlement to rights.[34] Republican France, as it embraced more inclusive definitions of citizenship, severed, in some respects, the exclusive historical linkages between property, political rights, and paternal power and invested legal authority in the husband—a status that carried rights of possession that were more veiled and contradictory but no less politically significant. Granted, this tendency conflicted with revolutionary legislation that abolished illegitimacy, authorized divorce, and reinvented marriage as a civil contract—an assault on clerical and noble privilege that had the unintended consequence of eroding the coercive powers of some husbands over their dependents. Nonetheless, French republicans continued to view the family as the foundation of political and moral order.[35] Quite logically, then, republican representatives of the French government in revolutionary Saint-Domingue extended the same philosophy to the colonies by inventing "new men" in the body of the husband. In the eyes of Sonthonax and Polverel, the position of husband and father together with military service provided the public proof of manhood that enabled the male slave to shed the status of chattel and claim the title of citizen. It followed that women would win their freedom by virtue of their relationship to men.

And so it was that one week after the reentry to Le Cap, as the commissioners courted and threatened the insurgents,[36] sought provisions, reorganized government, and fought the Republic's foreign and domestic foes, they issued in Creole and French the proclamation of July 11, which authorized free men to emancipate their families through marriage.[37] Their action was not, in a sense, unprecedented: John Garrigus, Dominique Rogers, and Stewart King have demonstrated that free men—white, colored, and black—and, less frequently, women had long used Article IX of the Code Noir to free their spouses through marriage.[38] The commissioners, however, prescribed the civil procedures required to emancipate a spouse through the republican ritual of marriage and offered to assume in the name of the French Republic the costs of indemnities to slave women's owners. The emancipation thus took the form of a purchase (indemnity) that transferred women slaves from the hands of masters to those of their husbands through the intervention of the Republic. Citizenship for "new men" was thus secured by granting them the "gift" constitutive of manhood: the prerogatives of husbands.

Importantly, under the provisions of the decree, the Republic assumed the costs of indemnities only for free men who registered with municipal authorities their intention to marry slave women within the prescribed period of fifteen days. While Article XIV did permit free women to marry, and thereby manumit, slave men, the Republic would not assume the burden of the associated indemnity. Designed, in part, to secure the loyalties of the "citizens of 21 June" and win new recruits for the republican armed forces, the decree fostered a vision of family constructed through masculine initiative and under paternal authority.[39] In practice, of course, the fabrication of marital authority as a foundation of French citizenship had profoundly different implications for white citizens and former slaves. For enslaved men, stripped of the legal underpinnings of paternal authority by their own status as property, the status of husband after emancipation would serve as substitute for, rather than guarantor of, full equality and economic autonomy. For freedwomen, denied political rights by their sex and denied the prerogatives of (bourgeois) domesticity by their class and race, the status of wife would remain linked to the demand for labor under the French Republic.[40] For the commissioners, however, the July 11 decree—a foundational republican moment in what Stephanie McCurry has recently christened "the marital path to emancipation"—epitomized the dream of regeneration: family affections, gently cultivated through republican marriage, would foster love for the "great family" of citizens.[41]

Frame II: Mahy de Cormeré and the "Conspiracy" of Emancipation

Guillaume-François Mahy de Cormeré, baron and émigré, was not of the opinion that men could be made anew. Safely arrived in Baltimore in August 1793, the flames of Le Cap fresh in mind, de Cormeré superimposed upon the commissioners' proclamations a competing colonial narrative. His *Histoire* reads as epistolary assault, a fulmination against republican principles so passionate that the formal history at times occupies barely two lines, followed by a full page of vitriolic footnotes. Casting himself in these pages as omniscient historian, eyewitness, interlocutor, financial expert, and arbitrator, de Cormeré fashions himself in heroic discursive duel with the two French officials. Presenting their proclamations verbatim the better to interrupt and castigate them, de Cormeré's *Histoire* never realizes its explicit goal: a "final explanation" of the disaster of the colonies. Only seven of the twelve letters that compose the epistolary narrative were ever published; the rest found their way into the obscurity of Moreau de Saint-Méry's personal archives. Indeed, the text itself, in which the specter of family disintegration and sexual disorder serves as foil to the commissioners' narrative, recounts the end of the world as he has known it. While the curtain opens on the France of de Cormeré's birth and terminates, not incidentally, with the salutary cession of Jérémie to His Britannic Majesty, the emancipation decree functions as the nadir of the dramatic conflict, the realization of a dystopian vision incontrovertibly opposed to his version of aristocratic manhood, in which the rights of man, severed from republicanism, forever remain the prerogative of whites.

De Cormeré rejected the commissioners' construction of the gift of liberty on the grounds of the illegality of this assault on the "rights of property," the irrationality of exacting labor from former slaves, and the impossibility of animating "property" as free men. Masculinity and marriage, in the commissioners' texts, the medium for the erasure of race, appear in de Cormeré's *Histoire* as the jousting field on which "regeneration" battles with honor, anarchy with privilege, and claims to freedom with rights of property.[42]

Insult, Shame, and Honor:
A Cultural History of the Burning of Le Cap, II

In de Cormeré's account, the "conspiracy" of emancipation in general and the burning of Le Cap in particular unfold not as family romance but as a ritualized assault on the cultural prerogatives of race, masculinity, and privilege (10/34–35).[43] The commissioners' public entertaining disgusted him. "In order to excite universal discontent," he recounted, "[Sonthonax and Polverel] announced . . . that it was time that . . . the theatre be reopened" (10/40). The choice of comic operas passed without comment[44] but the spectacle of racial mixing struck de Cormeré as both "insolent" and indecent (10/40–41nn1–2). Citizens' wives were forced to attend the commissioners' courtesans, respectable women compelled to perform for the commissioners' pleasure. Deploying, in the words of John Garrigus, "the cliché of corrupt feminine sexuality that delineated the colonial public sphere," de Cormeré denounced the festive evening as a "brothel" of republican sociability.[45] The republican dinner on the 19th, lauded elsewhere as a pinnacle of civic-mindedness, appears in the *Histoire* as the insulting prelude to the theatre of "courtesans" planned for the 23rd and as the final act in the cultural war that preceded the military contest.

For de Cormeré, the racial and sexual integration of the officials' entourage, its suspicious overlapping ties of politics, patronage, sociability, and sex, bespoke illegitimacy in their very intimacy:

> The society of the commissioners was composed of the mulatto Castaing, his mother, and his two sisters, married to the *nommés* Garnot et Robequin . . . the courtesan Eugénie—the favorite of the salacious Sonthonax—currently pregnant through the work of that wretch, and proud that in a few months she'll be bringing into the world a little Jacobin like him; an old, disgusting creature *nommée* La Vernet . . . a former *vivandière* who made a fortune from the thefts of blacks and other illicit trades. This woman has a daughter, whom she intends for Polverel's son; while waiting, she is the declared mistress of the father.[46]

In de Cormeré's *Histoire*, the interracial intimacies of the commissioners' entourage announce the racial apocalypse to come. "Events of this nature were well suited to cause an insurrection. The harbor rose in revolt" (10/42–43).

But the rebellion, which began on June 20, soon fell victim, from de Cormeré's perspective, to the "weakness" and "incompetence" of its general (10/44–45 and n1). In his narrative of defeat, de Cormeré took one of his more interesting authorial liberties: a political and discursive volte-face in which, chameleon-like, he shed the skin of the ultras only to emerge as diplomat.[47] Indeed, de Cormeré claimed that on several occasions, as hostilities escalated, he made his way to government authorities to mediate the conflict (10/46–47n1; 10/51–52n2). Thrice refused—by Galbaud, the commissioners, and the municipality—de Cormeré emerged from the fray with honor intact while Le Cap moved inexorably toward disaster.

For de Cormeré to inhabit these seemingly incompatible positions, even if only in his text, is to be reminded of the complexities of identity formation in the heat of revolution. Immigrant to Saint-Domingue at the very moment when emigration lists were swelling, ultra-royalist transposed to an autonomist milieu in a colony in the throes of republican and racial revolution, de Cormeré exhibited an unusual imbrication of identities.[48] His (temporary) volte-face is consistent with this political mélange: his birth identity as French aristocrat; his identification, both economic and familial, with the white elite of Saint-Domingue; and the thin veneer of revolutionary *citoyen* invested with rights. This collage of identities authorized both insurrection and conciliation, as dictated by political expediency, in defense of honor and hierarchy, rooted variously in bloodline, estate, race, and citizenship—and always in masculinity.

In any case, his tenure as diplomat was as brief as his advocacy of the rights of man. In the race war that provides the tragic denouement of de Cormeré's *Histoire*, the battle lines are drawn "caste" against "caste," and honor, ever a white prerogative in his text, consists in the loyalties enacted or abjured by white men. De Cormeré's chronicle of the fall of Le Cap thus reads as a protracted indictment of the commissioners, who had betrayed the rules of "civilized" warfare and masculine honor (9/45n1). In de Cormeré's construction, the disaster prepared by the commissioners place the colonial elite not in honorable contest with equals but pitted them against a "caste of mulattoes" bent on vengeance, disloyal domestics, slaves "stolen" from their masters, and "criminals" jailed in Le Cap. Finally, when this motley force of 4,000 "scoundrels" (10/39n1) proved insufficient to defeat Galbaud, the commissioners slipped out of town "with their seraglio" to a "lair at Haut-du-Cap" as rivers of white refugees, warned by loyal slaves that Le Cap was to be burned, streamed from their homes (10/55). When dawn broke, the "two tigers," "indignant at the humanity of the slaves of the city," devised a devil's pact—freedom and the sack of Le Cap for the "brigands" in exchange for military aid (10/53–54).

While in Sonthonax's telling, the proclamation of June 21, which emancipated insurgents who agreed to fight for the Republic, was an honorable military oath sworn by courageous "new men," in de Cormeré's *Histoire*, the proclamation's prelude is a sinister promise by the prison concierge to release brigands and slaves on death row in order to exterminate the "white race."[49] The proclamation of liberty, read solemnly "in negro idiom," struck de Cormeré as a "tissue of falsehoods" (10/55).[50] His insistent usage of the insulting racial terminology that had demarcated pre-revolutionary identities in Saint-Domingue—*le nommé, mulâtre, nègre*—and his sarcasm toward the new republican vocabulary of race served as a defense against the inversion of the natural order and as a linguistic denial of the possibility of regeneration.

The Making of "New Men," II

As the smoke rose from the ashes of Le Cap, Sonthonax and Polverel, still at Haut-du-Cap, made overtures to insurgent leaders to bring the insurgent slaves permanently under the flag of the French Republic (10/57–58, 61,

64–65). De Cormeré claims to have been present on the afternoon of June 26 for the commissioners' first meeting with the insurgent general Macaya and his brother. De Cormeré's account revises the political narrative offered by Pamphile de Lacroix, for in his rendering, the spectacle becomes a mixed-gender burlesque of republican ritual. "I ventured toward the den of brigands. . . . I was in the middle of their court composed of negroes and mulattoes. Among them appeared the *vivandière* concubine of Polverel, the *mulâtresse* Eugénie, mistress of Sonthonax, the *mulâtresse* Garnot, sister of the mulatto Castaing, and the Sénéchal Vergniaux" (10/64n3).[51]

In the *Histoire*, the participation of women, and particularly the presence of "*mulâtresses*"—wives and mistresses of white men—serves as a register of the indecency of the commissioners' negotiations with the insurgents; indeed, the feast appears to be a reincarnation of the indecorous interracial civic fête that had preceded the military debacle by just one week. The ritual opened with a formal introduction by Officer Robquin himself, who "arrives, holding the two Macaya brothers by the hand." The commissioners and their "courtesans" proceeded to effect the regeneration of the uncomprehending "slaves." After Polverel proclaimed Macaya's rebirth as "free man and French officer," "an old white rosette attached to the hats of the two Macaya brothers" was torn off. "Princess Sonthonax then adorned them with an enormous tri-color ribbon." The ceremony struck de Cormeré as absurd in its attempt to confer masculine honor across the boundaries of caste, gender, and race. "Polverel made a sign; at that instant a bottle and two glasses were brought. Polverel filled them," but scarcely had Macaya begun to drink than "Polverel seized him in his arms, grabbed the glass, and concluded with a kiss. 'There, brave Macaya, the pact of union is contracted between us.'" De Cormeré, "rendered mute with astonishment," concluded by reasserting the futility of this ritual of regeneration: "The hope of booty had brought this chief of the bandits; the commissioners had just interrupted the pillage" (10/63–66).

As the "conspiracy" of emancipation moved toward its inexorable conclusion, de Cormeré also found himself in a textual duel with the commissioners concerning their program of making "new men" from marriage. While male insurgents, particularly free men of color, had repeatedly fought their way into his *Histoire* as military combatants and political rivals, slave women constituted the absent category. The proclamation of July 11, which offended de Cormeré as "the height of absurdity, insanity, and despotism," brought enslaved women into his text for the first time. "These inconceivable men, guilty of the most foul debauchery, the most scandalous concubinage, dare to borrow the language of virtue; . . . they authorize blacks to marry slave *négresses*; they control the compensation of the masters of these wives and their children; finally, they allocate this indemnity to the national treasury, which they believe they can dispose of, just like the wealth of Saint-Domingue" (11/83–84).

Returning to his primary strategy of argumentation, de Cormeré painstakingly copied the commissioners' proclamation line by line, the better to raise again the specter of miscegenation and to interject his own sarcastic commentary. Even a brief excerpt conveys the tenor of the debate:

> **Sonthonax:** "The spirit of family is the first tie of political societies; the free man who has neither wife nor children can be only a savage or a brigand."
>
> **de Cormeré:** "Sonthonax, for example, justifies this maxim: he has neither wife nor children. It is true that the quarteronne Eugénie, his concubine, will soon make him a father; it's said that he must marry her and claim as his own three fatherless children." ...
>
> **Sonthonax:** "We have made some free; we will make more,"
>
> **de Cormeré:** "And by what right?"
>
> **Sonthonax:** "but we want to make them into citoyens, who, through the habit of family affections, become accustomed to cherishing and defending the large family, composed of all citoyens."
>
> **de Cormeré:** "They should have added, with the exception of whites." (11/83–86)

For the republican commissioners, to "gift" black soldiers with marriage and their wives with liberty was to bestow the morality that was the foundation of liberty.[52] De Cormeré, on the other hand, ridiculed their gesture as a profligate gift, bestowed without legal sanction. An assault on the foundations of aristocratic hierarchy, the proclamation legitimized the progeny of previous unions, no matter who the biological father, and upset racial hierarchy in allowing the rights of black husbands to trump those of masters. In sum, for de Cormeré, manhood could never be born of military service or marriage, just as citizenship could not be invented through the "extralegal" actions of "despots." The bitter contention over the proclamation of July 11 reveals gender, once again, as central to the process and meanings of emancipation.

Frame III: Enslaved Women's Emancipation

To return to the third "scene from a marriage" with which this essay began: on the very day that Jean Petour and Marie registered their *promesse de mariage* in the Maison Commune of Fort Dauphin, five other couples also appeared before the same republican officials to register their intention to marry. Since the records reveal only three marriages in that parish in the previous seven months, the arrival of these couples en masse would have been an unusual event—all the more so because five of the six brides appear to have been slaves. In the wake of the proclamation of July 11, their marriages to free men—four of whom were currently serving in the republican armed forces—would have constituted legal grounds for the emancipation of both the brides and the couples' children.[53] On August 12, Marie and Jean Petour returned to the Maison Commune, legitimizing through the ritual of marriage their seven children—"Etienne, age 20, Gillot, age 16, 13-year-old twins Antoine and Pierre, Marie Louise and Jean, also twins, 8 years old, and Marie-Josephe, 4 years." Their marital union represented a living challenge to de Cormeré's assumptions about the desires and dignity of people of African descent and a renunciation of servitude. It was likely the first time that Marie had appeared in the public record as *citoyenne*.

Women's emancipation disrupts the two narratives traced to this point, for it follows different pathways and offers different chronologies than those charted by republican officials and their colonial opponents. For enslaved women in Saint-Domingue, emancipation was neither gift nor conspiracy. Women's emancipation is not readily knit into a grand narrative of the sort that emerges from the proclamations of Sonthonax or de Cormeré's *Histoire*. Multiple rather than singular, the stories of women's emancipation are accessible only as fragments, hidden within texts written by others and for other purposes. Yet even a few of these fragments are sufficient to demonstrate that women's diverse experiences of emancipation fit poorly, if at all, within the gendered frames of emancipation offered thus far. The republican commissioners' concern with republican marriage, like de Cormeré's rage at the racial and sexual integration of the commissioners' dinner, would have seemed profoundly removed from women's quest for freedom—a disjunction I have tried to reflect in my own rendition of this final narrative. For enslaved women, the year that stretched between the summers of 1792 and 1793 was significant as a profound dislocation of power relations that reconfigured and often severed bonds of family and community and altered the calculus of risk, danger, and hope involved in taking one's liberty.

In Insurrection

In the most schematic sense, the commissioners fought the struggle over racial hierarchy and slavery on the terrain of masculinity, rights, labor, and citizenship; de Cormeré, in contrast, fought that battle on the terrain of masculinity, property, and honor. In both cases, masculinity had important military referents—a fact that contributed to the tendency of white and colored men across a wide range of the political spectrum to construct the slaves in insurrection as exclusively male. As a case in point, one document from the Galliffet plantation listing the plantations burned in seven regions, estimates "40,000 blacks in insurrection, from which one must subtract three quarters for the children, women, and old people, leaving 10,000."[54]

But no war is ever only a man's war, and this revolution, which cut vast swaths of destruction through the colony, drew men, women, and children into the vortex of conflict.[55] True, the fighting troops among the insurgents were largely men, particularly as troop structure formalized—a fact that would sustain the commissioners' construction of the citizen-soldier and long constrain the meanings of liberty for women.[56] Yet fragments from newspaper reports and correspondence, like the plantation inventories studied by David Geggus, tell a more complex story of women's relationship to the insurrection. In the winter and spring of 1793, chroniclers of the insurgency wrote reports in which the fact of women's resistance, suppressed from white consciousness, wafts unbidden into the text:[57]

> 9 March 1793: "On 10th February, at the Camp des Mornets, commanded by the brave Dubuisson, the war counsel executed a free *négresse* [wife of a rebel leader]. . . . This *négresse* was a very bad subject, whom it was necessary to destroy promptly."[58]
>
> [Late May] 1793: "Camp des Mornets was attacked night before last by a considerable number of brigands. The brave Dubuisson, having heard the shot fired by the sentinel, opened his door to discover his house surrounded by the villains' cavalry; he closed it immediately and, falling silent, overheard the *négresses* saying: 'zaute monte vite sus platon là, vous va trouve toute blancs la io après droumi, et vous va prend io comme vous va v'le'" (Quickly, go up there to the plateau, where you'll find all the whites asleep, and you can take them easily).[59]
>
> Pamphile de Lacroix: "One can judge what the revolt in the North has been, and the terror that it has spread, by the number of women who came to beg forgiveness: we counted up to 14,000."[60]

For those men, women, and children who by choice or necessity had found their way to the insurrectionary camps in the hills and plains, the commissioners' promise on June 21 of amelioration of the conditions of slaves, including protection for pregnant women and nursing mothers, would have been profoundly remote. Of the thousands who died from hunger, smallpox, or enemy fire, we can never know how many were women. In the months that de Cormeré interpreted as the forward march of conspiracy and Sonthonax as the forward march of racial equality, emancipation came too late for many women as well as men.

Servitude and the Slave Market

"Citoyen Durand is leaving for France, he requests that those who owe him, pay him, and those whom he owes, present themselves to be paid; he is selling a *nègre*, tailor, as well as a *négresse*, huckster and laundress, six-months pregnant."[61]

While emancipation was framed by the commissioners and their republican allies in marital terms—strong families the foundation of strong morals—in practice, the cataclysmic changes wrought by revolution and war disrupted the tenuous stability, such as it was, painstakingly forged by enslaved women. Advertisements for slave sales in the *Moniteur* from the commissioners' arrival in 1792 to July 1793, when the newspaper ends, while in no sense an accurate guide to the numbers of slaves actually sold, provide one window on the experiences of enslaved women and men in the year prior to general emancipation in the north.[62] The single most striking feature of the ads is the number of liquidations not just of plantations but of small businesses and workshops: shoemakers, bakers, carpenters, fishermen, merchants, tailors, weavers, and hotel keepers, including proprietors of color, sold entire lots of skilled slaves along with foundries, hotels, boats, and businesses. The pattern of sales displays a high ratio of men to women, since men dominated the skilled trades. Nonetheless, ads for laundresses, seamstresses, wet nurses, housekeepers, and female domestics pepper the *Avis Divers* column.[63]

"For sale. A *négresse*, with her daughter who has a three-month-old infant."[64] To read these notices against the swelling lists of white and free colored emigrants departing for New England and France, many in the company of their slaves, is to glimpse, however imperfectly, the revolutions in daily existence which affected increasing numbers of enslaved men and women, whose position might, formerly, have provided some modicum of security.[65] A striking 56 percent of the total 138 ads explicitly state either succession or emigration as the reason for the sale; the content of the ads suggests that the real percentage was likely much higher.[66]

The notices display a cool disregard for women's bonds with their husbands, partners, relatives, or fictive kin and, often, for their maternal responsibilities. Twenty of a total of ninety-five women advertised for sale were pregnant or nursing a child under age two; in the following ad, a woman "just delivered" is nonetheless advertised "childless": "To sell or to rent, a young, pretty *négresse*, wet nurse, without children, gave birth the sixth of this month, good laundress, and recognized as a very good subject."[67] Law and custom dictated that women and their young children should remain together, and many ads seem to reflect this practice. "For sale. . . . A *négresse*, laundress, ironing woman, good seamstress, and cook, with a five-year-old *négritte*. A *négresse*, good wet nurse, laundress and ironing woman with her two children, of which one is newborn and the other aged 6. . . . For cash or goods." Yet sales notices like these announced a profound dislocation in the intimate terrain of women's lives.[68] The impact of revolution and an owner's emigration on the stability of slaves' situations may also have altered the balance sheet of risk and hope involved in the decision to flee.

"Désirée, nation Misérable, rather powerful body, medium height, red skin, age 28–30, having some marks of smallpox and a mark below an eye, stamped L. N. Meteyé, walking with stomach stuck out and feet far behind, having a scar on one leg and a slightly elongated chin. . . . She is suspected to be in the region of Trou; provide information to mademoiselle Meteyé, rue des Marmouzets."[69] Crafted to etch the slave-owner's claim to his or her property in the minds of the reading public, advertisements for escaped slaves followed a thoroughly formulaic script.[70] While notices for runaways in the *Moniteur* represented only a fraction of those who had left their owners in the wake of the slave revolution, such ads, interspersed among emigration lists, notices of plantation and slave sales, and reports of new incursions by the insurgents, would have carried a force out of proportion to their numbers: each a reminder to slaveholders of the tens of thousands of insurgents at large and a reminder also to the cooks and wet nurses and laundresses in Le Cap of the changing political landscape and the pull of freedom. Enslaved women in Le Cap would have heard rumors of escapes. Some would have known Reine, who walked away from her master's home wearing an iron collar on the very day the new commissioners disembarked in Saint-Domingue. Others would have heard of Hortense, a *mulâtresse* from Martinique who proudly departed her owner's household in the company of her grown son, "both subjects calling themselves free," with another man, "Jean-Louis," who claimed that he was their slave.[71]

If the year before emancipation was one of turmoil and often loss for enslaved women in Le Cap, one can occasionally also glimpse the wedge of opportunity that the revolutionary upheaval provided individual women. There was, for instance, Marie-Joseph, "formerly belonging to the now-deceased widow Cottin," whose ad in *Avis Divers* announced her independent business as midwife.[72] The growing lists of manumissions in the *Moniteur* in 1793 are consistent with the high female-to-male sex ratio of manumissions in previous decades, while the elimination of the "liberty tax" gave masters added incentives to emancipate "loyal" slaves.[73]

The Burning of Le Cap, III

One such woman, "the *négresse* Penelope," who was manumitted with her four children in "repayment for good services rendered," remained with them in the household of her former master, Citoyen Isnard, on the night that Le Cap burned. According to Isnard's testimony, on June 19, 1793, he attended the commissioners' civic dinner in the company of his wife and their young children. When fire overtook the city on the 21st, the families of Penelope and Isnard fled together toward Haut-du-Cap in the dead of night. Although the story of the destruction of Le Cap is told most frequently as the realization of a white colonial nightmare, it was not only white families who wondered and waited, gathered their children, abandoned their homes, searched for refuge. The trope of the "loyal black" pervades the pages of white memoirs from this period, yet one can easily discern a credibility gap between the testimony of de Cormeré, who read the "loyalty" of slaves as proof of the legitimacy of slavery, and the testimony of Isnard, whose narrative is replete with personal examples of generosity on the part of blacks toward whites. It was, Isnard revealed, two women of color from Port-au-Prince who gave food to the hungry children—four black, three white—in his party. Isnard's family also found protection under Penelope's escort: by his report, she explained her presence to a black man who challenged them as follows: "[Isnard] gives food to us, and his wife raised [my] children." On July 29, when Isnard attempted to board with a ship bound for Charleston with Penelope, her children, and insufficient resources, the captain refused her passage. "She confided her child to me," states the narrative. "It was an act of mercy that [the captain] allowed me to bring the little *citoyenne*, whom my wife and I have adopted as our child."

We will never know how Penelope would have recounted her choice. But if Isnard's narrative here exposed Penelope's vulnerability, his text clearly contained a different subscript, one in which the lives of whites were dependent on blacks.[74] For all the highly mediated testimony about loyal slaves, the revolution of Le Cap for slave women must also have signified opportunity. As the doors of the prisons opened on the 21st, women as well as men who had been incarcerated as runaways or at the request of their owners would have walked free; women numbered among the domestic servants who saw their opportunity that same night and took their freedom.[75] Women, like men, would have experienced the irreversible alteration of identities that occurred during those mid-June nights.[76] If the revolution of Le Cap ended for many white residents at the harbor, it did not for the many black and colored women who returned to the city, reclaiming it for their children. How did they experience the visible inversions of power so bitterly denounced in the memoirs of the white elite: the sight of white men disarmed at Haut-du-Cap, whites clearing cadavers from the streets of Le Cap, black families taking up residence in homes that had once housed whites? How many "loyal slaves," women who had long served white and brown families in the region, joined the victorious processional entry back into Le Cap on July 4, 1793, singing the Marseillaise?[77]

Fêtes de l'Hymen, Fêtes de la Liberté: Three Perspectives on Freedom

Women were also among the celebrants at the Fête de la Fédération on July 14, hastily planned by the new governor-general as a colonial elaboration of the French federation, the ritual of fraternal unity first celebrated in France in 1790. Thousands who had fled against the backdrop of Le Cap in flames joined the crowd that gathered on the "place de la Fédération, formerly Champ de Mars" where a liberty tree capped by a *bonnet rouge* was planted before the "altar of the nation." Despite the familiar contours of French republican ritual, the federation presented an unprecedented spectacle.[78] Staged amidst the ruins of Le Cap, the altar surrounded by military battalions largely composed of men of color, this colonial fraternity of "100 whites, 200 mulattoes, and 6,000 blacks" offered a distinctive vision of racial equality constructed on the grounding of martial and marital ritual.[79]

For the commissioners, the ceremony raised the standard of the French Republic before its enemies—white creoles, counterrevolutionaries, and kings—and consecrated the new contours of the French body politic. For de Cormeré, the entire affair was a humiliating "vexation," the penultimate act in the colonial tragedy of emancipation, designed to let the "blacks understand their superiority over the whites and mulattoes" (11/82 and n1). He also claimed that the July 11 decree, which legally emancipated women who married free men, was devised explicitly "to prepare spirits for the Federation of 14 July" (11/84n1). Be that as it may, by July 14 word of the July 11 decree, published in both French and Creole, would have traveled widely through the region.[80] For women, in the wake of the decrees of June 21 and July 11, the ceremony would have been a celebration of the prospect of their own liberty and that of their children.

Sonthonax and Polverel issued the proclamation of July 11 only a week after their reentry to Le Cap. Both de Cormeré and the commissioners represented the decree as an attempt to domesticate and civilize the insurgents, although they reached different conclusions about its efficacy. Commentators hostile to the commissioners concluded that slaves lacked the racial pedigree necessary to benefit from the masculine privilege that the decree bestowed.[81] The author of *Histoire des désastres de Saint-Domingue*, for instance, deplored the edict: "It produced no effect on these beings who, perhaps incapable of feeling the full extent of this favor, preferred to deliver themselves to their bloodthirsty inclinations."[82]

Nonetheless, to retrace the process of successive emancipations in the summer of 1793 is to glimpse the ways that July 11, like the proclamation of general emancipation in the North Province on August 29, was a response to the demand of black men and women themselves.[83] The destruction of notarial and civil registers from this period, especially in the North Province, means that we are unlikely to know the number of couples who married under the provisions of the decree. Sonthonax himself—hardly a disinterested party—reported on July 30 that celebrations were happening at the rate of thirty per day, adding "fêtes de l'hymen deviennent pour eux celles de la liberté" (wedding festivals are for them festivals of liberty).[84] The État Civil of Fort Dauphin and Port-de-Paix reveal several republican marriages that appear to fall within the purview of the edict.

Given the unreliability of the quantitative evidence, a proclamation by Sonthonax on August 21, 1793, little noticed by historians, may provide one of the strongest indications of the interest in the July 11 decree of men newly freed and of women still enslaved. Evidently, couples had complained that they had encountered problems when they attempted to marry under the provisions of the new law. The commissioners had intended, explained Sonthonax, to favor the soldiers, "the most vital section of the citizenry at this moment." However, many soldiers, unable to leave their posts, were prevented from marrying during the specified fifteen-day period. To complicate matters further, some notaries had apparently refused to register these marriages on the grounds that only free persons could enter into contracts. Clearly there had been enough complaints to convince Sonthonax to extend the deadline. Ordering a week's extension to the state's pledge to indemnify slave-owners, Sonthonax directed notaries to register marriages between soldiers and women slaves.[85]

Those women who married under the provisions of July 11, which was extended to the South Province on July 25 and to the West Province on August 28, sought practical and incalculably precious legal protections: legitimacy for their children under the law, public recognition of a spousal relationship, and, above all, freedom papers for themselves and their children. To pursue this strategy would not have required that they share the commissioners' assumptions about masculinity, citizenship, marriage, and morality. Indeed, my preliminary efforts to follow the traces of marriage through the État Civil suggest that the pursuit of marriage in 1793 was a highly strategic goal for a limited number of couples. As Laurent Dubois has recently argued, freedwomen regularly marked their claims to public identities for themselves and their families in the État Civil in the years that followed emancipation.[86] Yet in the decade following emancipation, freedwomen in Fort Dauphin were more likely to inscribe their children in civil registries than to marry before the municipal officer or the parish priest.[87] Regardless of the commissioners' script, marriage did not provide the legal road to freedom for the vast majority of women in Saint-Domingue.

The fragments of lives encountered in these pages suggest something of how gender mattered in revolutionary Saint-Domingue. They offer as well a perspective on how change occurred: the small gestures and symbolic acts—encounters cultural as well as military—through which identities were reinforced, challenged, and forged. Power was reconfigured, on the one hand, through intimate relationships and private gestures that held public meaning; on the other, through formal public behaviors that, through specific bodily acts, restructured hierarchy. When Sonthonax deported white troops who refused to swear a loyalty oath, when de Cormeré recoiled before the spectacle of republican marriage, when a woman stood before the man who called himself her owner and called herself free, all served as measures of the centrality of ritual in creating a new world or defending the old.[88]

I will conclude with two brief episodes that signal the significance of gender, marriage, and ritual to the process of emancipation in Saint-Domingue. The great assembly of the commune of Le Cap occurred on August 25, 1793, the immediate inspiration for the general emancipation proclamation of the North Province. Guillaume Henri Vergniaud, the white republican who drafted the famous petition in favor of abolition, delivered the keynote address. He devoted his speech to the rights of man and the "sacred bonds of marriage." As the colony's delegates to the Convention reported on the meeting of the commune, the demand for general emancipation was framed around liberty for women and children. Strikingly, women were advocates on their own behalf. Preceded by the "liberty cap, carried in triumph" as a "symbol of unity," "an immense crowd of women dragging their children with them followed the petitioners crying with emotion: 'Vive la république française! vive la liberté!'"[89]

The transition from slave to *citoyen* after general emancipation in Saint-Domingue long remained a site of struggle.[90] So too did the transition from slave to *citoyenne*. While neither de Cormeré's notion of masculine honor through racial purity nor Sonthonax's vision of republican regeneration through labor and marriage would triumph in Saint-Domingue, both left a legacy. The stories of women who helped to forge the meanings of freedom in the years that followed—in the État Civil, in the courts, in their families, in their bids for economic independence on plantations, and in cities—are just beginning to be told.[91] Enslaved people, men and women, fought for freedom; the commissioners decreed it and sought to fix its meanings. It remained for freedpeople—*citoyens* and *citoyennes*—to claim liberty, its meanings fired within the crucible of work, revolution, and war.

Postscript

Six days after the Fête de la Fédération Mahy de Cormeré surfaces in the *Affiches Américaines* on the list of departures for New England.[92]

On June 8, 1794, the corvette *l'Espérance* pulls into harbor, carrying word of the Convention's 16 Pluviôse decree of General Emancipation and a deportation order for Sonthonax and Polverel.

On February 1, 1798, "Marie Joseph Négresse" appears in the État Civil of Port-au-Prince, manumitted with four children and infant granddaughter by Jean Kina, the black royalist who won fame and freedom fighting against the insurgents—a reminder that for many women, liberty was long in coming.[93]

Notes

I would like to thank Peter Arnade, Aimee Lee Cheek, William Cheek, Stephanie McCurry, Jeremy Popkin, and Margaret Waller for their inspiration and insightful comments.

1. Robquin [son] from New York, December 8, [1793], to Robquin [father] in Paris; see also Castaing Robquin [to Robquin père], December 9, 1793, Dxxv/80/786, docs. 13–14, Archives Nationales, Paris (hereafter AN). The term *citoyens du 4 avril* (citizens of April 4) refers to free people of African descent, who were granted rights of citizenship by a French law promulgated on April 4, 1792. To highlight the gender-specific meanings of citizenship in the revolutionary era, I have used the French terms *citoyen* and *citoyenne* rather than the gender-neutral English equivalent, "citizen."

2. The first seven letters of this epistolary history were published as G. F. Mahy de Cormeré, *Histoire de la révolution de la partie française de St. Domingue. Développement exact des causes et principes de cette révolution. Manoeuvres, intrigues employés pour son exécution* (Baltimore, 1794). The five additional letters that complete the volume were never published due to lack of funds and eventually found their way into the hands of Moreau de Saint-Méry; I discovered a microfilm copy of the full manuscript in F3/193, AN. Although de Cormeré's text places him at the center of political activity, he surfaces only rarely in the press. A "citoyen de Cormeré" employed at the "General Bureau of Administration in Le Cap" does appear in *Moniteur Général de la Partie Française de Saint-Domingue* (hereafter *Moniteur Général*), June 3, 1793, 79. According to Gabriel Debien (*Les colons de Saint-Domingue et la Révolution: Essai sur le Club Massiac* [Paris, 1953], 185), Mahy de Cormeré was also a former member of the Massiac Club. The only study of de Cormeré that I am aware of is David Geggus, "Saint-Domingue and the British Government in 1794: A Memoir by Mahé de Cormeré," *Archives Antillaises* 3 (1975): 27–38. According to the *Annuaire de la noblesse de France* (Paris, 1894), 484, Mahy de Cormeré was a descendant of an old noble family from Orléans. His father, Guy-Guillaume Mahy, baron de Cormeré, married Thérèse Charpentier; Guillaume-François married Jeanne-Charlotte de Fredefond on November 22, 1770. De Cormeré, a financial official in France, wrote prolifically on the colonies and on financial affairs, e.g. *Recherches et considérations nouvelles sur les finances* (London, 1789); and *Mémoire sur les finances et sur le crédit, pour servir de suit aux recherches & considérations nouvelles sur les finances* (Paris, 1789). He also published a defense of his brother, *Testament de Mort de Messire Thomas de Mahy de Favras* (Paris, 1790).

3. The commissioners' assault on racial prejudice included a ban on the use of racial terminology in civil registries. Consequently, for the historian, it is often difficult to determine race with any precision in the État Civil of 1793. In this particular register from Fort Dauphin, the continued (though infrequent) use of the terms *sieur* or *demoiselle* to designate some individuals served to demarcate people of color from whites. Of the seventeen marriages or *promesses de mariage* registered in 1793 in Fort Dauphin, three entries in the index or the registers themselves identified either the bride or groom or both as "Sieur" or "Demoiselle." Of those remaining, twelve occurred in August and September soon after the commissioners' decree. In none of these cases was a surname listed for the bride. According to Article IX of the Code Noir and the commissioners'

proclamation of July 11, women could be manumitted through the act of marriage to a free man. However, marriages registered in the Bureau Municipal of Fort Dauphin do not specifically state that women received their liberty. Mariages 1793–1802, Régistres de l'État Civil, vols. 73–74, Fort Dauphin, Microfilm 1094191, Family History Research Center, Church of Jesus Christ of Latter-day Saints, Poway, California.

4. See Joan Dayan's study of ritual, hybridity, and gender, *Haiti, History, and the Gods* (Berkeley, 1995), xv.

5. For pioneering scholarship on women, slavery, and gender in Saint-Domingue, see John Garrigus, "Race, Gender, and Virtue in Haiti's Failed Foundational Fiction: La mulâtre comme il y a peu de blanches (1803)," in *The Color of Liberty: Histories of Race in France,* ed. Sue Peabody and Tyler Stoval (Durham, N.C., 2003), 73–94; Garrigus, "Redrawing the Colour Line: Gender and the Social Construction of Race in Pre-Revolutionary Haiti," *Journal of Caribbean History* 30 (1996): 28–50; Arlette Gautier, *Les soeurs de Solitude: la condition féminine dans l'esclavage aux Antilles du XVIIe au XIXe siècle* (Paris, 1985); David P. Geggus, "Slave and Free Colored Women in Saint Domingue," in *More Than Chattel: Black Women and Slavery in the Americas,* ed. David Barry Gaspar and Darlene Clark Hine (Bloomington, 1996), 259–278; Judith Kafka, "Action, Reaction, and Interaction: Slave Women in Resistance in the South of Saint-Domingue, 1793–94," *Slavery and Abolition* 18, no. 2 (1997): 48–72; Bernard Moitt, *Women and Slavery in the French Antilles, 1635–1848* (Bloomington, 2001); Sue Peabody, "Négresse, Mulâtresse, Citoyenne: Gender and Emancipation in the French Caribbean, 1650–1848," in *Gender and Slave Emancipation in the Atlantic World,* ed. Pamela Scully and Diana Paton (Durham, N.C., 2005), 56–78; Dominique Rogers, "Les libres de couleur dans les capitales de Saint-Domingue: Fortune, mentalités et intégration à la fin de l'Ancien Régime (1776–1789)," (Thèse de doctorat, Bordeaux III, 1999); Mimi Sheller, "Sword-Bearing Citizens: Militarism and Manhood in Nineteenth-Century Haiti," *Plantation Society in the Americas* 4 (Fall 1997): 233–278.

6. This narrative choice is in no way meant to deny the complex and vitally significant political, economic, and ideological roles of the free population of African descent or enslaved men on all sides of the conflict.

7. Jill Lepore, *The Name of War: King Philip's War and the Origins of American Identity* (New York, 1998), x.

8. On Sonthonax and Polverel, see Marcel Dorigny, ed., *The Abolitions of Slavery: From Léger Félicité Sonthonax to Victor Schoelcher, 1793, 1794, 1848* (New York, 2003); and Robert Stein, *Léger-Félicité Sonthonax: The Lost Sentinel of the Republic* (Rutherford, N.J., 1985). Stein emphasizes the commissioner's abolitionist commitments even before his arrival in Saint Domingue. Other scholars have placed greater emphasis on factors such the role of the slave revolution and/or the threat of British and Spanish invasion in provoking the emancipation decree of August 29, 1793.

9. "Relation officielle des événements arrivés au Cap, 1–8 Dec. 1792," Dxxv/5/43, doc. 1, AN.

10. On the complex pathways of "regeneration," see Alyssa Goldstein Sepinwall, *The Abbé Grégoire and the French Revolution: The Making of Modern Universalism* (Berkeley, 2004).

11. "Discours prononcé par M. Sonthonax . . . 20 septembre dans l'église du Cap," *Affiches Américaines,* October 4, 1792, 3–4, ADxxa/6, AN. On the process of strict racial

codification as it developed after the Seven Years' War, see John Garrigus, *Before Haiti: Race and Citizenship in French Saint-Domingue* (New York, 2006).

12. The registry of births, marriages, and deaths, long the province of parish priests, was formally transferred from religious to civil authorities in September 1792; parish records were supplanted by the État Civil. For a detailed political chronology of the early months of the Second Commission, see Stein, *Sonthonax*, 41–62; and Laurent Dubois, *Avengers of the New World: The Story of the Haitian Revolution* (Cambridge, Mass., 2004), 132–151.

13. After independence, argues Mimi Sheller, "a martial image of the male citizen took on a special salience" for the construction of Haitian national identity ("Sword-Bearing Citizens," 233).

14. On émigrés, see "Circulaire. L'Adjoint aux Administrateurs de Cayenne et St. Domingue. Paris le 8 jour du 2e mois de la 2e année républicaine," B 228, doc. 6, Centre des Archives d'Outre-mer, Aix-en-Provence (hereafter CAOM).

15. Apparently Charrier was less than sanguine about the future prospects of the republic, for he "had the replica stored under the staircase," to be restored to its rightful position in case of counterrevolution. *Moniteur Général*, January 16, 1793, 243.

16. For the crises faced by the commissioners, see Civil Commissioner to the Ministry of the Marine, June 18, 1793, CC9a/8, CAOM; Geggus, *Haitian Revolutionary Studies* (Bloomington, 2002), 14–15; Sonthonax to the President of the National Convention, December 18, 1792, Dxxv/5/43, no. 2, AN; *Moniteur Général*, February 7, 1793, 329.

17. De Cormeré, *Histoire*, letter 9/48 and note 2.

18. As Garran-Coulon reports in the first official French history of emancipation, the commissioners "were preceded by a troop of conquerors from Port-au-Prince; men, women, and children of color from Le Cap led the way, the air ringing with their cheers. They made a distressing contrast with the icy demeanor of the whites." J. Ph. [Jean Philippe] Garran-Coulon, *Rapport sur les troubles de Saint-Domingue* (Paris, 1798–1799), 3:396–397; and *Moniteur Général*, May 8, 1793, 690–691.

19. Garran-Coulon, *Rapport*, 3:396–397.

20. *Moniteur Général*, June 11, 1793, 703–704.

21. Boucher, president of the Intermediary Commission, claimed to have had no less than three meetings with the governor-general on the subject of the reception. See "Galbaudiana, ou Anecdotes sur Galbaud cy-devant Gouverneur Général de St. Domingue, recueillies par Boucher Président de la Commission intermédiaire, avant l'arrivée de ce général au Cap & jusqu'après son départ & déposée aux Archives de la Commission Civile par forme de declaration authentique le 1 Juillet 1793," Manuscrits, Nouvelles acquisitions françaises (hereafter n. a. fr.) 6846, "Papiers de Sonthonax Relatifs à Saint-Domingue," vol. 1, Correspondance, f. 50–51, Bibliothèque Nationale (hereafter BN).

22. The commissioners signed the deportation order on June 13. *Moniteur Général*, June 14, 1793, 123–124.

23. Civil Commissioners to the Ministry of the Marine and the Colonies, June 18, 1793, CC9a/8, CAOM. On the celebration, see *Moniteur Général*, June 20, 1793, 147.

24. Republicans, royalists, and colonial elites tested the justice or injustice of black citizenship on the proving ground of race and masculinity. See *Histoire des dés-*

astres de Saint-Domingue, précédée d'un tableau du régime et des progrès de cette colonie, depuis sa fondation, jusqu'à l'époque de la Révolution française (Paris, 1795). On the *Histoire*, see Jeremy D. Popkin, "Facing Racial Revolution: Captivity Narratives and Identity in the Saint-Domingue Insurrection," *Eighteenth-Century Studies* 36 (2003): 523–524. H. D. de Saint-Maurice's more moderate recital ends with a plea for general emancipation: "Récit historique du malheureux évenement qui a reduit en cendres la ville du Cap Français," manuscript bound at end of the *Moniteur Général* at the BN. See also [Louis] Dufay, *Compte Rendu sur la situation actuelle de Saint Domingue, 16 pluviôse an II* (Paris, 1794). P.-M. Duboys distills the meanings of the reversal of racial hierarchy into an archetypal image:"Even the women and children are not spared. One of these cannibals was seen stabbing a child at its mother's breast with a bayonet and carrying it as a trophy at the end of his gun.""Précis historique des annales de la colonie française," 1:110, Manuscrits, n. a. fr. 14878, BN.

25. "Proclamation, Polverel, Sonthonax," Haut-du-Cap, June 21, 1793, Dxxv/9/90, doc. 12, AN. Madame de Rouvray describes the June 21 decree and its consequences for her family's slaves, who were "seduced" by the commissioners' promises, in a letter to her daughter on August 13, 1793: "It's the end of the world, my child, and the end of *honnêtes gens.*" Laurent François Le Noir Rouvray, *Une correspondance familiale au temps des troubles de Saint Domingue; lettres du marquis et de la marquise de Rouvray à leur fille, Saint-Domingue-Etats-Unis, 1791–1796* (Paris, 1959, 101–102).

26. At the same time, in his account, the treachery of Galbaud served to highlight the "fearlessness" and heroism of the "nouveaux citoyens" (the ex-slaves). Sonthonax to the Convention Nationale, July 10, 1793, Dxxv/5/52, doc. 6, AN.

27. Thus, when the Régiment du Cap refused to take an oath integrating free men of color into a color-blind military corps, Sonthonax announced that he would deport anyone who resisted. *Moniteur Général*, December 8, 1792, 87. On this ceremonial challenge to the commissioner's authority, which soon led to military conflict, see Dubois, *Avengers*, 146; and Stein, *Sonthonax*, 59–60. The right to bear arms had long been a critical link in the claim of free men of color to political rights. For the colonial period, see Stewart R. King, *Blue Coat or Powdered Wig? Free People of Color in Pre-Revolutionary Saint Domingue* (Athens, 2001), esp. 52–77; Garrigus, "Catalyst or Catastrophe? Saint-Domingue's Free Men of Color and the Savannah Expedition, 1779–1782," *Review/ Revista Interamericana* 22 (1992): 109–125; and Garrigus's rich analysis of free colored participation in the militia and *maréchaussée* in *Before Haiti*, 195–225. Concerning the revolutionary period, John Garrigus has argued that free men of color "built their political strategy around [the] masculine image" of the "citizen soldier," brought to prominence in France in 1789; "Race, Gender, and Virtue," 79.

28. Consistent with this vision, the commissioners sought to garner the support of *petits blancs* with the argument that counterrevolutionaries who opposed racial equality also defended class privilege; *Moniteur Général*, June 1, 1793, 71. Joan Wallach Scott has noted that "men's difference from women served to eradicate differences of skin color and race among men" in the context of the French National Convention's abolition of slavery in *Only Paradoxes to Offer: French Feminists and the Rights of Man* (Boston, 1996), 9.

29. Polverel and Sonthonax, June 2, 1793, Dxx7/61, docs. 6 and 10; and June 3, 1793, doc. 27, all in AN. David Geggus explains that the arming of slaves that followed

the slave revolution fell into distinct genres, ranging from the use of plantation guards and informal corps to the Second Commission's alliances with slave insurgents and creation of formal corps; see "The Arming of Slaves in the Haitian Revolution," in *Arming Slaves: From Classical Times to the Modern Age*, ed. Christopher Leslie Brown and Philip D. Morgan (New Haven, Conn., 2006), 209–232. See also in the same volume Laurent Dubois, "Citizen Soldiers; Emancipation and Military Service in the Revolutionary French Caribbean," 233–254; and Dubois, *Avengers*, 134–142. General Pamphile de Lacroix provided his own succinct summary of his perception of the threatening linkage between military service, manhood, and authority: to make slaves into auxiliary military units was to "suggest to the slaves the idea of becoming masters themselves"; Lacroix, *La révolution de Haïti*, ed. Pierre Pluchon (1819; repr., Paris, 1995), 158–159. See also *Créole patriote*, 8 February Year II (1793), 114, ADxxᵃ/176, AN.

30. Saint-Maurice, "Récit"; Sonthonax to the National Convention, July 10, 1793, Dxxv/5/52, doc. 6, AN.

31. Pierre Bourdieu, *The Logic of Practice*, trans. Richard Nice (1980; repr., Stanford, 1990). This interpretation complicates both the heroic narrative of republican emancipation and more critical views that suggest that the emancipation decrees were the result of either necessity or self-interest.

32. See "Loi qui détermine les causes, le mode et les effets du Divorce," Dxxv/9/90, doc. 6, AN; and *Moniteur Général*, December 30, 1792, 173–174, and January 8, 1793, 109–110.

33. Sonthonax and Polverel, June 21, 1793, Dxxv/9/90, doc. 12. See also Saint Maurice's discussion of the decree in "Récit."

34. For one pioneering example of this argument, see Carol Pateman, *The Sexual Contract* (Stanford, 1988).

35. On familial order and the French Revolution, see Lynn Hunt, *The Family Romance of the French Revolution* (Berkeley, 1992); Suzanne Desan, *The Family on Trial in Revolutionary France* (Berkeley, 2004); Elizabeth Colwill, "'Women's Empire' and the Sovereignty of Man in *La Décade Philosophique*, 1794–1807," *Eighteenth-Century Studies* 29 (1996): 265–289.

36. [Civil Commissioners to] Commandant Pierrot, July 13, [1793], Dxxv/7/66, doc. 55, AN; to Citizen Genet, July 8, 1793, CC9a/8, CAOM; to the grenadiers of the 84th Regiment, July 1, 1793, Dxxv/7/64, doc. 8, AN.

37. Stein, *Sonthonax*, 86–87, and Peabody, "Négresse," 64, both quote the letter to the Convention in which Sonthonax describes the decree.

38. John D. Garrigus discusses this phenomenon in *Before Haiti*, 198–201, as does Stewart King, (*Blue Coat or Powdered Wig*, 183). Dominique Rogers found that such marriages represented 12 percent of the total contracts in Cap-Français and 39 percent in Port-au-Prince in the period she studied ("Les libres de couleur," 557–559, 545). On the provisions of Article IX of the Code Noir, which both authorized free men to emancipate slave women through marriage and delineated punitive measures for masters who fathered children with slave women outside the bonds of marriage, see Peytraud, *L'esclavage aux Antilles françaises avant 1789* (Pointe-à-Pitre, 1973), 197–206; and Louis Sala-Molins, *Le Code Noir, ou le calvaire de Canaan* (Paris, 1987), 106–117.

39. Sonthonax and Polverel, "Proclamation," Cap-Français, July 11, 1793, Dxxv/9/91, doc. 7, AN. The Creole translation of the July 11 decree (Doc. 9 in the same folder) was published in venues as diverse as the republican *Affiches Américaines* in Le Cap and the counterrevolutionary *Radoteur* in Philadelphia. The proclamation of July 25, 1793, best known as a declaration of amnesty for the insurgents and liberty for those slaves armed by their masters, also extended the marriage law of July 11 to the soldiers of the south; Dxxv/9/91, doc. 25, AN. On August 28, the law was extended to the West Province. Laurent Dubois attributes the success of the commissioners in winning over insurgent leaders in Les Cayes in part to the extension of this decree to the south; *Avengers*, 160–161.

40. On the state's demand for labor and the "gift of liberty," see "André Rigaud, gouverneur général du départment du Sud et quartiers y annexés et Louis Gavanon, ordonnateur civil dudit département, Fait aux Cayes, le quartidi de la premiere décade de Vendémiaire, l'an 3," CC9a/9, doc. 65, CAOM. On blacks' claims to liberty and republican labor regimes, see Fick, *The Making of Haiti: The Saint Domingue Revolution from Below* (Knoxville, 1990), 163–203. On the "militarization of agriculture" after emancipation and under the black generals, see Fick, "Emancipation in Haiti: From Plantation Labour to Peasant Proprietorship," in *After Slavery: Emancipation and Its Discontents*, ed. Howard Temperley (London, 2000), 26.

41. Stephanie McCurry has argued that in the context of the American South, the "marital path to emancipation" of republicanism, widely disseminated in the nineteenth century, has been reproduced in twentieth-century historiography of the Civil War in ways that powerfully constrain our understandings of political history in general and the process of emancipation in particular; see "War, Gender, and Emancipation in the Civil War South," in *Lincoln's Proclamation: Race, Place and the Paradoxes of Emancipation*, ed. William Blair and Karen Younger (Chapel Hill, University of North Carolina Press, forthcoming).

42. On the French debates over race and slavery prior to the revolution, see Sue Peabody, *"There Are No Slaves in France": The Political Culture of Race and Slavery in the Ancien Régime* (Oxford, 1996).

43. In-text page-number citations are to letter numbers and page numbers of de Cormeré, *Histoire*.

44. Jean-Jacques Rousseau, *Le devin du village: intermède représenté à Fontainebleau devant leurs majestés les 18 et 24 octobre 1752, Et à Paris par l'Académie royale de musique le 1ᵉʳ mars 1753* (Paris, [1753]); and Pierre Baurens, *La servante maîtresse: comédie en deux actes* (n.p., 173–?).

45. Both Garrigus ("Race, Gender, and Virtue," 73–94, 80) and Dayan (*Haiti*, esp. 165–182) have shown that the colonial sexual metaphor remained a site of contestation after the revolution.

46. *Vivandière*, a woman who accompanies troops selling liquor, food, supplies, and, in the context of this text, sex. The insulting term *"nommé/e"* ("so-called"), commonly employed within the racial nomenclature of pre-revolutionary Saint-Domingue to stigmatize individuals of African descent, is employed here indiscriminately as epithet.

47. On de Cormeré's efforts to foment insurrection prior to the commissioners' second entry, see de Cormeré, *Histoire*, 10/18–19n1.

48. Geggus aptly describes de Cormeré's views as a "curious mixture of anglophilia and counter-revolution" in "Saint Domingue and the British Government," 32. Charles Frostin's study of the white elite, *Les révoltes blanches à Saint-Domingue aux XVIIe et XVIIIe siècles* (Paris, 1975), emphasizes the autonomist leanings of some sectors of the colonial elite.

49. The editor of the *Radoteur* in Philadelphia parodied the decree in "Notes instructives sur la catastrophe du Cap," July 30, 1793, 78, ADxxa/604, AN.

50. "No one can be dispossessed of his property, even for public utility, without prior indemnity; this principle embedded in the rights of man forms the basis of the constitution of 1789 and that of all civilized peoples" (10/54n1). His formulation starkly poses the central contradiction of the Second Commission in particular and republicanism in general: how to defend the universal rights of man, rooted in property, in a world in which persons are property. See Robin Blackburn, *The Overthrow of Colonial Slavery* (London, 1988); and David Brion Davis, *The Problem of Slavery in Western Culture* (Oxford, 1966).

51. Lacroix, *La Révolution de Haïti*, 167.

52. According to de Cormeré, in the absence of a municipal government, the commissioners formed an interracial Bureau Municipal—"citoyens Rouge (*blanc*), Fluiry (*mulâtre*), l'Haviteau (*nègre*), and Richebourg (*blanc*) in the position of *syndic municipal*"—specifically to implement the law (de Cormeré, *Histoire*, 11/88 and n1). The Intermediary Commission had approved the decree (de Cormeré, *Histoire*, 11/86).

53. The registers specify neither race nor dates of manumission, but they do provide surnames for five of the men and indicate that several were enrolled in the Compagnie du Citoyen Hylaire Gaston (a Ouanaminthe free colored), which increases the likelihood that one or more were free men of color prior to the revolution. I would like to thank Dominique Rogers for her help in interpreting these documents.

54. "Liste des habitations incendiées dans sept quartiers," in "Lettres et mémoires sur l'insurrection de St. Domingue 1790–1807," AP107/128, folder 1, AN.

55. *Moniteur Général*, February 16, 1793, 368.

56. Arlette Gautier suggests that women participated in the insurgency but in roles different than men's and in ways that would work to women's disadvantage (*Soeurs*, 241–244).

57. Geggus, "Slave and Free Colored Women," 272–273; Moitt, *Women*, 126–132; "Lettre de la municipalité du Port-au-Prince à la municipalité du Cap," *Moniteur Général*, 10 March 1793, 454.

58. N.a. fr., 9 March 1793, Dxxv/80/782, doc. 24, AN.

59. "Nouvelles du Cap," *Moniteur Général*, June 4, 1793, 83. My thanks to Laurent Dubois and David Geggus for their help with interpretation and translation.

60. Lacroix, *La Révolution de Haïti*, 157.

61. *Moniteur Général*, February 26, 1793, 408.

62. Although the traditional public auction had been suspended in Le Cap for some months, notary M. Voisin alerted the public on December 13, 1791, that it would resume its daily operations; *Moniteur Général*, December 13, 1791, 118. Slave women, of course, were owned by mistresses as well as masters who were free black, colored, and white. Dominique Rogers has shown that in the period 1776–1789, free women of African descent bought and possessed women more frequently than men and purchased

slaves in small groups of two to seven persons in over a third of the cases in Le Cap. In most cases the familial groupings that she cites were mothers and children, although she discovered two cases of married couples sold together (Rogers, "Libres," 1:121–123).

63. Geggus, "Slave and Free Colored Women," 260, reports the sex ratio of 120:100 in the 1780s. The total number of men and women advertised, excluding ads in which sex or number is unspecified, is 333:95; for slaves in groups of five or less, the ratio drops to 116:73. It is lower still for sales of only one or two slaves.

64. *Moniteur Général*, April 4 1793, 556.

65. For instance, *Moniteur Général*, May 18, 1793, Supplement, 2.

66. I excluded from this sample of 138 total ads thirty-four in which either the number or the sex of slaves was not specified. Of the remainder, seventy-seven specified "succession" or emigration as reason for sale.

67. Several owners, whether motivated by marketing strategy or emotional ties, testified to the good character of the slaves to be sold, particularly to their "good conduct since the insurrection" (*Moniteur Général*, March 16, 1793, 480; and January 22, 1793, 268).

68. Among many examples, see *Moniteur Général*, November 27, 1792, 52; and February 16, 1793, 368.

69. *Moniteur Colonial*, August 20, 1791, 1168, 4-Lc12-2, BN.

70. David Geggus's study of the *Affiches Américaines* in 1790 shows 2,020 escaped slaves jailed and 632 advertised "en marronnage." In the *Moniteur Général*, by contrast, from July 1, 1792, to June 20, 1793, once duplicate ads are eliminated, only 62 adults (45 men, 17 women), were advertised as escaped slaves, primarily from the urban region of Le Cap. In addition to these adults, nine children were listed as "lost," "kidnapped," or "en marronnage"; three were girls, ages 3 to 6, one of whom was found in the company of her mother (*Moniteur Général*, January 28, 1793, 292). The small number of ads in the *Moniteur* in no sense mirrors the number of escaped slaves in this period. The paper featured no column for "nègres marrons entrés à la geôle," the site of the most complete lists for escaped slaves in colonial papers such as the *Affiches Américaines*. Furthermore, Geggus and others have demonstrated that prior to the slave revolution, the ads for escaped slaves reflected only a small percentage of escaped slaves; see "On the Eve of the Haitian Revolution: Slave Runaways in Saint Domingue in 1790," in *Out of the House of Bondage: Runaways, Resistance, and Marronage in Africa and the New World*, ed. Gad Heuman (London, 1986): 112–128, esp. 115.

71. *Moniteur Général*, September 21, 1792, 428; January 31, 1793, 304; January 16, 1793, 244.

72. *Moniteur Général*, February 5, 1793, 324.

73. On the day of the commissioners' celebration there appeared in the *Moniteur Général* (June 19, 1793, 143–144) a list of seventy manumissions, including fifty-three women. (I have excluded one entry of eight subjects, sex unspecified, from this calculation.) One of the entries, a woman named Barbe, is cited as self-manumitted. In a different list of twenty acts of manumission signed by Sonthonax, only three of those acts specified by sex were for men (*Moniteur Général*, March 31, 1793, 539). Rogers's pathbreaking work on manumission demonstrates that women represented 68.75 percent of the *affranchis* in Le Cap and 70.8 percent in Port-au-Prince from 1776 to 1789; nearly half of these were classified as *nègres*. Their manumission was not, therefore,

primarily dependent on white paternity (69–72). Geggus shows that the annual chances of manumission for women, "though better than a male's, never exceeded three in one thousand and were usually much less"; see "Slave and Free Colored Women," 268. See also Peabody, "Négresse"; and Gabriel Debien, "Les affranchissements aux Antilles françaises aux XVIIe et XVIIIe siècles," *Anuario de Estudios Americanos* 23 (1967): 1177–1203.

74. It was under the escort of Penelope; Pierre, her male partner; and four other black men, who all vouched for his "good citizenship," that Isnard reached their destination after an arduous journey. Dxxv/81/796, doc. 15, AN.

75. On March 26, 1793, the Intermediary Commission specified that the labor of both male and female prisoners would be requisitioned on behalf of the state; *Moniteur Général*, March 28, 1793, 526.

76. Saint-Maurice, "Récit," 12.

77. For the processional entry, see de Cormeré, *Histoire*, 10/66–67; on inversion, see *Histoire des désastres*, 302.

78. "Procès-Verbal de la Fête qui a eu lieu au Cap le 14 Juillet 1793," CC9a/8, doc. 38, CAOM; Sonthonax to the National Convention, Le Cap, July 30, 1793, Dxxv/5/52, doc. 11, AN.

79. The numbers are drawn from de Cormeré, who may well have inflated the disproportion between the races.

80. Sonthonax to the National Convention, July 30, 1793, Dxxv/5/52, doc. 11, AN; Stein, *Léger Félicité Sonthonax*, 86; "Procès-Verbal de la Fête," CC9a/8, doc. 38, CAOM; Civil Commissioners to Tronquet, July 13, [1793], Dxxv/7/66, doc. 39, AN; Governor to the Commissioners, July 13, 1793, Dxxv/7/66, doc. 42, [Sonthonax to Gignoux], July 13, [1793], Dxxv/7/66, doc. 46.

81. Also Lacroix, *Révolution*, 166; and de Cormeré, *Histoire*, 11/107n1. Haitian historian Beaubrun Ardouin follows suit in *Etudes sur l'histoire d'Haïti*, 2nd ed. (Port-au-Prince, 1958), 2:43.

82. *Histoire des désastres*, 307–308.

83. The delegation from Saint Domingue to the National Convention represented this demand for freedom in terms of masculine initiative and military might: "It was feared that these soldiers, in their ardor, would take up arms to free their women and children." ("Relation Détaillée," 72.)

84. Sonthonax to the National Convention, July 30, 1793, Dxxv/5/52, doc. 11, AN.

85. "Proclamation," Le Cap, au Carénage, August 21, 1793, Dxxv/10/92, doc. 12, AN.

86. Laurent Dubois presents striking evidence of women's use of the État Civil and notarial registers of Guadeloupe in *A Colony of Citizens: Revolution and Slave Emancipation in the French Caribbean, 1787–1804* (Chapel Hill, 2004), 249–276.

87. These are preliminary findings in my research in the État Civil of Port-de-Paix and Fort Dauphin for the years 1792 to Year 10. Garrigus, *Before Haiti*, and King, *Blue Coat* demonstrate the economic and social significance of the bonds of marriage for the free colored population in French Saint-Domingue. For a detailed discussion of marriage prior to the revolution, see Rogers, "Les libres de couleur," 544–589. For an overview of slave marriage in the French Antilles, see Moitt, *Women and Slavery*, 80–89.

88. This project thus searches, as Mark Johnson put it, for "the embodied origins of imaginative structures of understanding" (*The Body in the Mind: The Bodily Basis of Meaning, Imagination, and Reason* [Chicago, 1987], xv) and, in the words of Ann Laura Stoler, for the "'structures of feeling' in which race and colonial power were forged" (*Carnal Knowledge and Imperial Power: Race and the Intimate in Colonial Rule* [Berkeley, 2002], 216). On ritual and emancipation, see, Julie Saville, "Rites and Power: Reflections on Slavery, Freedom and Political Ritual," *Slavery and Abolition* 20 (April 1999): 81–102.

89. "Relation Détaillée," 73–74. See de Cormeré, *Histoire*, 11/107–108, on the speeches at the Commune.

90. Fick, *The Making of Haiti*; Sheller, *Democracy After Slavery: Black Publics and Peasant Radicalism in Haiti and Jamaica* (Gainesville, 2000).

91. Gautier, *Soeurs*, 221–258; Peabody, "Négresse." On women's resistance to Polverel's work code in 1794, see Fick, *Making of Haiti*, 170–182; and Kafka, "Action." On gendered narratives of race and nation, see Dayan, *Haiti*; Sheller, "Sword-Bearing Citizens"; and Garrigus, "Gender, Race, and Virtue."

92. *Affiches Américaines* (Cap-Français), July 20, 1793, 47, 87 MIOM 17, CAOM.

93. Registres de l'État Civil, vol. 190, Port-au-Prince, Libertés et Affranchissements, 1790–1798, February 1, 1798, Microfilm 1093914, LDS Family History Research Center.

"THE COLONIAL VENDÉE"

Malick Ghachem

> When the history of this war shall be written, before the eyes of
> the reader will be placed the horrible picture of men sawn in two,
> or mutilated in every limb, or burnt over a slow fire, or hung by
> the feet to a tree, and flayed alive. LA VENDEE alone offers some
> resemblance of the war, which for two years TOUSSAINT made
> on the Republicans of the colony.
>
> —Jean-Louis Dubroca, *The Life of Toussaint Louverture* (1802)

FRANÇOIS BARBÉ DE MARBOIS WAS THE LAST ROYAL INTENDANT OF FRENCH SAINT-DOMINGUE. IN BETWEEN TAKING OFFICE IN 1784 AND LEAVING IT IN 1789, HE CAME TO BE IDENTIFIED BY MANY PLANTERS in Saint-Domingue and the metropole as one of the leading conspirators in the plot known as "ministerial despotism." To his critics, Barbé de Marbois represented all that was wrong with Louis XVI's administration of the Caribbean colonies. He was far too exacting, they felt, in enforcing the mercantilist restrictions of the *exclusif*. Perhaps even worse, from the planters' point of view, he seemed to be overly sympathetic to the condition of slaves and free people of color. In 1787, Barbé de Marbois had disbanded the Conseil Supérieur of Cap Français, one of the colony's two high courts, after the tribunal's members refused to register a royal ordinance calling for stricter regulation of the treatment of slaves by abusive plantation managers.[1] After the convocation of the Estates General in 1788, not surprisingly, Barbé de Marbois became a favored object of denunciation in the *cahiers de doléances* and pamphlet literature sponsored by the planter community and generated by its journalistic hired guns.

In June 1790, Barbé de Marbois decided that the time had come to defend himself. That month, the publisher Knapen, who had earlier in the eighteenth century printed a number of important treatises and pamphlets by French colonial administrators, came out with Marbois's *Mémoire et observations du Sieur Barbé de Marbois . . . sur une dénonciation signée par treize de MM. les Députés de Saint-Domingue, et faite à l'Assemblée nationale au nom d'un des trois Comités de la Colonie.* Among his concerns in this pamphlet was to respond to the charge that the metropolitan *corvée*—the royal "tax" by which peasants were drafted for stints of forced labor on rural roads—was akin to the colonial version that Barbé de Marbois was responsible for enforcing as the chief judicial officer of Saint-Domingue. Given the radical unpopularity of the French *corvée* system in 1789 and 1790, as evidenced by the frequency of references to it in the provincial *cahiers de doléances*, it is easy to envision why he felt it necessary to respond to the planters' comparison. The metropolitan *corvée*, Barbé de Marbois acknowledged, had been rightly denounced by the nation for a simple reason: the French peasant could contribute to the building and maintenance of rural roads only at the expense of neglecting his daily responsibilities. Moreover, the metropolitan *corvée* was unjust as a matter of principle because those who profited from the existence of a road network in the countryside were not those responsible for the physical tasks of its upkeep.[2]

Barbé de Marbois went on to explain that in Saint-Domingue, by contrast, the roads existed only for the benefit of the planters, so it was fair for them to bear the expense of maintaining them. As for the slaves who actually did the work, according to Barbé de Marbois, it could hardly matter to them whether they were forced to cultivate sugar on the plantations or instead build the roads that linked them. It was thus "mal-à-propos," he insisted, for the planters to try to

> make us feel pity for the condition of corvée Negroes, and to apply to [these slaves] what has been said of laborers and peasants subject to the corvée [in France]: this is to try to accuse the administrators on the basis of a simple analogy of words.[3]

In so arguing, Barbé de Marbois was more revealing of colonial attitudes and conditions than even he himself may have been aware. In the first place, his comments reveal the extent to which even those administrators who were cognizant of the brutalities of slavery in Saint-Domingue and felt it necessary (for strategic as well as humanitarian reasons) to alleviate them could nonetheless dismiss the idea of the slave as a person. For the clear implication of Barbé de Marbois's comparison of peasant and slave *corvées* is that the peasant is an independent person with needs and responsibilities of his own, whereas the black slave is merely an extension of his master's will. As such, there could be no injustice in the colonial *corvée*, no question that the slave might be "prejudiced" by a regime of forced labor in the way that the metropolitan peasant was.[4]

In the second place, Barbé de Marbois's comments reveal an especially important and fateful dimension of colonial political culture on the eve of the French Revolution: the contest of analogies between metropolitan and colonial institutions, social categories, and conditions. These analogies encompassed all manner of fascinating and politically complicated comparisons in the eighteenth century: between domestic and overseas "provinces," nobles and masters, fiefdoms and plantations, sans-culottes and *petits blancs*, and so forth. Overshadowing all of these comparisons, arguably, was the analogy between peasants and slaves. It featured significantly in pre-revolutionary debates between abolitionists and their proslavery opponents, debates that were structured in part around comparisons of the relative penury inflicted upon the metropolitan peasant and the colonial slave.[5] During the opening two years of the French Revolution, as Barbé de Marbois's pamphlet suggests, this axis of comparison served as a powerful reference point in the to-and-fro over the future of French colonial policy. Here, as in other areas of colonial politics, there was a great deal of continuity between the Old Regime and the revolutionary period.

In particular, the analogy between peasants and slaves continued to play an important role in colonial debates well into the 1790s and resurfaced even in the early nineteenth century, on the eve of Haitian independence. Why did this analogy continue to resonate in the debate over the Haitian Revolution throughout these years? In part, it did so because it served to bridge the gap between the French and Haitian revolutions. That is to say, it served as a heuristic device for making sense of a political and cultural experience that was both familiar and foreign to many French observers: a revolution carried out in the name of French ideals by African slaves and their black and mixed-race descendants. But the analogy also had resonance because of the particular form it took in the years after 1793: a comparison between the Vendée war in France and the slave revolution in Saint-Domingue. Planter representatives in Paris insisted that the counter-revolutionary peasant uprising that broke out in the west of France in March 1793 and continued until it was fully and finally "pacified" in early 1796 was the political and military equivalent of the slave revolt unfolding in France's most important Caribbean colony. These representatives tried to establish an analogy between royalist and pro-British sympathizers among the clergy and nobility of the Vendée region, who were widely understood as responsible for instigating the "fanatical" Vendée rebellion, and the allegedly abolitionist, pro-British administrators and colonists who were believed to be playing a similar conspiratorial role in a "superstitious" Vodou-inspired slave revolution.

The shared suspicion (and reality) of British involvement in both the Vendée uprising and the Saint-Domingue slave revolution helps to explain the resonance of this analogy in post-1793 French colonial politics. The analogy also derived force from the shared position of peasants and slaves at the bottom of the metropolitan and colonial social hierarchies. The shared role of religious passions (perceived and real) in both the Vendée uprising, which was associated with an especially fanatical brand of peasant Catholicism, and the Saint-Domingue slave revolt, which was identified with an even worse form of anti-republican superstition (Vodou), must also be taken into account. Indeed, one of the principal effects of the comparison between the Vendée revolt and the slave revolt was to focus attention on the role of religion in the Haitian Revolution, an effect that would linger in metropolitan perceptions of that event for many decades to come.

Above all, the analogy's force was owed to the profound impact of the Vendée war on French revolutionary politics and society. Because of that impact, the Vendée exerted an influence over the contemporaneous understanding of colonial events. And it continued to do so well after the Vendée uprising had been pacified in early 1796. Over time, the analogy between the Vendée and the colonial slave revolt became more than a mere semantic game, and it eventually came to have a concrete impact on French strategies for "pacifying" the Haitian Revolution on the model of the "pacification" of the Vendée. In both the metropolitan and colonial contexts, this "pacification" came at the cost of tens of thousands of lives.[6] The word games of the French and Haitian revolutions were dangerous and fateful ones. Barbé de Marbois was correct to see in the "analogy of words" between peasants and slaves an instrumental tool of political contestation; he saw correctly that the planters were manipulating language in their attempt to defend slavery and he saw through these attempts to the underlying interests at stake in the debate (which included his own interests, of course). The proslavery politics and thrust of the peasant-slave analogy carried through to the analogy between the Vendée and the slave revolution. In that context, however, the analogy became more than a matter of mere words alone; it became part of a struggle over the actual outcome of the Haitian Revolution. The "analogy of words" became an arbiter of who would be free and who would remain slave.

The first part of this chapter discusses the earliest appearances and implications of the Vendée-slave revolt analogy in the period from late 1793 to 1795. The second section tracks the analogy as it surfaced with particular force in the debates over how to "restore order" to Saint-Domingue in the Council of Five Hundred (the lower house of the French legislature) in 1797. It was at this time that the decision to "pacify" the Haitian Revolution on the model of the "pacification" of the Vendée began to take shape, albeit in the context of a debate over whether the response should involve greater parts military-style repression or diplomatic conciliation. A brief concluding section suggests the concrete implications of that decision with reference to the diplomatic and military missions, respectively, of Gabriel Marie

Théodore Joseph d'Hédouville and Victor-Emmanuel Leclerc. The former was a seasoned veteran of the Vendée experience who became the Directory's agent in Saint-Domingue beginning in early 1798. The latter, Napoleon Bonaparte's brother-in-law, oversaw the final and most militarized phase of the Haitian Revolution, an avowedly exterminationist campaign that ended in both enormous loss of life and the liberation of Haiti.

The Beginnings of the Analogy

There are unmistakable traces of continuity between the peasant-slave comparison criticized by Barbé de Marbois in 1790 and the earliest appearances of the Vendée-slave revolt analogy. Barbé de Marbois's critique, it is worth reiterating, was not an abstract one but rather endeavored to highlight the analogical abuses employed by the planters in their denunciations of "ministerial despotism." Sometime during the second half of 1793 (the exact month is unclear), Deraggis, a former municipal official from the parish of Mirebalais in Saint-Domingue, published an "Address to the French People, Free and Sovereign." Purportedly written at sea while the author was on his way from Cap Français to refugee status in New York,[7] Deraggis's address opens with the following summary statement:

> The revolt of the blacks in Saint-Domingue is a veritable Vendée, sustained, nourished, and rewarded by the agents of the executive power, and by the civil commissioners Polvérel, Sonthonax, and Delpeche.[8]

The text then proceeds to denounce the "despotism" of the seventy-eight governors and intendants who had administered Saint-Domingue since it became official French territory in the late seventeenth century.[9] But the main point of this denunciation was to suggest that no matter how bad a century's worth of royal governors and intendants had been, their faults could not compare to the "atrocious crimes" and "enormous dilapidations" of the various members of the second civil commission sent by republican France to Saint-Domingue since the August 1791 slave revolt began.[10] Deraggis bemoaned what he described as the uncontrolled violence and massive destruction of human life that had come to the once-flourishing French colony. There was no question, in his view, where all of the blame for this violence lay: on the various civil commissioners and their "subaltern tyrants of all ranks" in the colonial administration, who had incited the slaves to seek revenge against their masters and indeed against whites of any kind. Together, these "tyrants" and their commissioner overlords were responsible for the "vastest, cruelest, and best organized conspiracy of which history could provide an example." Together, these figures had "exterminated one part of the human race, in order to subjugate the other, and make it wretched."[11]

Deraggis was, both explicitly and implicitly, invoking the imagery and language of the Vendée war. The only difference was that in the colonial context, the destruction of human life was the work of slaves rather than peasants, and it was instigated by republican representatives of the sovereign French legislature rather than by shadowy figures in the clergy and nobility of the Vendée. (The loss of life entailed in the "pacification" of the Vendée was not yet fully apparent at the time of this pamphlet's publication, but Deraggis's work was far from the last to leave this part of the Vendée war out of the picture.) In short, the defense of slavery and opposition to the conciliatory (if not emancipationist)[12] policies of Léger-Félicité Sonthonax and his fellow civil commissioners (particularly Étienne Polverel) lay at the origins of the Vendée analogy.

Two of Sonthonax and Polverel's most inveterate enemies throughout the revolutionary decade also chimed in with their own version of the analogy in 1793, emphasizing the common role that perfidious Albion played in the Vendée war and in Saint-Domingue. Pierre François Page was a planter from the southern town of Jérémie; Augustin Jean Brulley, his fellow commissioner from Saint-Domingue to the National Convention, hailed from la Grande-Rivière d'Ennery in the Northern Province. Like Deraggis, Page and Brulley took part in the general colonial outcry against "ministerial despotism." Unlike Deraggis, however, the two planter representatives also sought to associate Sonthonax and Polverel with British designs on Saint-Domingue. In their *Développement des causes des troubles et désastres des colonies françaises, présenté à la Convention nationale*, Page and Brulley argued that "to escape from the ruin of its trade and naval forces, England had only one means: the devastation of the French colonies." "The same hand that lit the first torch in the colonies," they elaborated, "has just begun to arm the Vendée rebels."[13] At the time this pamphlet was published, June 1793, British forces based in Jamaica were still three months away from beginning a five-year occupation of parts of the western and southern departments of Saint-Domingue. But France had already declared war on Britain in February 1793, and the effects of Britain's naval forces in the Caribbean were already being felt. During the summer of 1793, British forces made a number of attempts to provide, and the Vendée rebels made several attempts to receive, military support from France's archenemy across the Channel.

Page and Brulley were not alone in holding the British responsible for the domestic and overseas woes of revolutionary France. In September 1794, the administrators of the southwestern department of Haute-Garonne, from their capital in Toulouse, pronounced that in order to achieve the goals of the nation it was necessary to neutralize the "ferocious English, whose existence is the permanent scourge of humanity." The British were nothing less than "cannibals who have breathed life into and supported the Vendée war; who have committed ... the massacres, burnings, and pillaging in our colonies, the horrors of Toulon, etc."[14]

The reference to the "horrors of Toulon" was one of several attempts to link the Saint-Domingue slave revolt (and British involvement therein) not only to the Vendée war but also to the other main challenge to the authority of the National Convention in 1793–1794: the federalist revolt of Lyons, Toulon, and Marseilles. In July 1793, conflict between local Jacobins and dockyard workers from the city's sections sparked a more general revolt against Parisian authority, the longest and most significant such challenge against central authority during this period.[15] The polemics of Page and Brulley succeeded in convincing the National Convention to recall Sonthonax and Polverel to answer charges of having conspired to encourage the slave revolution. The two republican commissioners left Saint-Domingue in June 1794 to undertake their defense. After a series of delays and public hearings that lasted from January to August 1795, they were eventually acquitted. During the proceedings, the Saint-Domingue colonists (implicitly under the leadership of Sonthonax and Polverel) were accused of being the "authors of a system of independence" that sought to "federalize the colonies and withdraw them from France."[16]

Whether the issue was federalism or the Vendée, however, proslavery analogists were united in believing that the underlying problem was the capacity of an elite cabal to trigger an uncontrollably violent revolutionary social movement. Not far from the surface of this charge was the notion that just as peasants were incapable of appreciating their manipulation by a handful of fanatical clergymen and nobles, so too were the slaves of Saint-Domingue unaware of being misled by persons who were more interested in helping Britain and harming France than anything else. From this perspective, there could of course be no such thing as an autonomous desire for freedom on the part of the slaves, whose actions had nothing to do with the injustices of plantation slavery and everything to do with the self-interested exploits of a self-styled humanitarian vanguard. Just as Barbé de Marbois's critique of the peasant-slave comparison assumed that the slave was a mere extension of his master's will, so did too the authors of the Vendée-slave revolt analogy assume that any revolutionary efforts on the part of slaves could only be manifestations of a higher (and thus, by their definition, white) authority.

A prime example of such thinking is an August 1794 pamphlet by two planter representatives from Saint-Domingue to the National Convention, L. J. Clausson and F. A. Millet. After denouncing Sonthonax and Polverel's administration as the colonial equivalent of Robespierre's "despotism" during the Reign of Terror,[17] Clausson and Millet entered into an extended litany of the horrors inflicted on Saint-Domingue by the rebellious slaves, those "unfortunate instruments of [Sonthonax and Polverel's] crimes." "Like those of the Vendée," these enslaved "instruments" have "ever fought only for the tyrant [Louis XVI]":

> Like those of the Vendée, the names of *King* and *Brissot* were their rallying cry.
>
> Like those of the Vendée, seduced by priests, they slit the throats of your brothers and friends in the name of God.
>
> Like those of the Vendée, they fought under white flags embossed with the fleur-de-lys and tainted with the blood of patriots, and they carried as rosettes the ears of whites they had massacred.
>
> Like those of the Vendée, they have spread devastation, fire, and death everywhere in the name of the tyrant.
>
> Like those of the Vendée, they have solicited the help of the Republic's most implacable enemies.[18]

As this litany makes clear, the point of arguing that the violence of the Saint-Domingue slave revolution was ultimately attributable to the machinations of Sonthonax and Polverel was not to portray the slaves in an innocent or neutral light. On the contrary, Clausson and Millet wished to convince their audience that whoever committed such acts of violence could not be considered fully human. But precisely because they could not be considered responsible agents, it was all the more important to identify the members of the conspiratorial cabal who were supposedly behind all of the subaltern bloodletting.

Indeed, according to the proslavery analogists, the susceptibility to control from above was even greater in the case of the slave than in the case of the native-born French peasant. In 1794, J. B. Thounens, the public printer of Martinique and deputy to the National Convention from the colony of Sainte-Lucie, asked "why the African people, less enlightened in the colonies than is the white in France, would have been more clairvoyant in our [tropical] climates than a Frenchmen of the Vendée."[19] Thounens's question was part of a more general effort to paint the monarchy's representatives in the colonies during the first few years of the French Revolution as the counterparts of the "nobles and villainous priests" who preyed upon the unwitting peasants of western France.[20] In a similar vein, the Philadelphia-based *Courrier Français*, an exile paper published by refugees from Saint-Domingue, published an account in November 1794 equating the "secondary and passive role of the peasants of the Vendée" with that of the free people of color and slaves of the Caribbean. Like the Vendée peasants, the "unfortunate" rebels of Saint-Domingue were but the "stepping stones of a few intriguers positioned at this time between the altar and the scaffold."[21]

The following month, the same newspaper bemoaned the failure of "public opinion in France" to appreciate the lesson "before everyone's eyes of the example of the Vendée." If it had bothered to consult that lesson, the French nation would have realized that Saint-Domingue's slaves and free people of color would act no less horrendously than their peasant counterparts. "Led into all sorts of traps just as the men of the Vendée, their fanaticism was dreadful." The anonymous author went on to describe "the heads of government in Saint-Domingue" (by which he undoubtedly meant the civil commissioners) as "so many Mahomets" who "fanaticized the free people of color and the blacks . . . the former under the banner of the tyrants of London, the latter under the banner of a freedom without regulation and without laws." Lest there be any doubt that a war of the races was indeed unfolding in this distant province of France, the author asked whether it was not true that "all of the patriot blood that has been spilled in the flames and assassinations of Saint-Domingue is French blood? Is it not the same blood that flows in the veins of the Jacobins, the same blood by which France is securing her liberty?"[22]

Former slaveholding planters hoping to regain their colonial fortunes were not the only ones who found in the Vendée analogy a useful means to argue the putative justice of their cause. The *petit blanc* refugee population of Philadelphia also sponsored an article in the *Courrier Français* in January 1795 in which they sought to distinguish themselves from their more "decadent" fellow exiles. They complained of having been falsely equated in their search for refuge in the United States with the aristocratic metropolitan refugees who had taken shelter in Coblentz and other European cities where counterrevolutionary sentiment prevailed. "By what astonishing metamorphosis," they asked, "could these men [the *petits blancs*], upon whom the citizens of color and the blacks were set in 1791, just as the fanatics of the Vendée were set upon [their neighbors] in France, be confused with the clergy and nobility of France?" The *petits blancs* insisted that they had been "persecuted" since the beginning of the French Revolution, and that the "civil war of Saint-Domingue" was nothing other than the Vendée war. "These two scourges have been sustained by the counter-revolutionaries and the agents of the cabinet of Saint-James."[23] As these comments suggest, the Vendée analogy was something that could be put to work across lines of social division even as it remained firmly couched within a proslavery, white-versus-black (or white-versus-free people of color) framework.

At least one author found in the analogy a means of criticizing not only the "fanaticism" of the slaves but also the excesses of the French military response. In his *Précis de la Révolution de Saint-Domingue*, published in 1795, the planter Chotard observed that

> the war that has been waged against the rebels of the North only served to
> goad them on, and everything that the negroes had spared was set aflame by
> order of the government, on the pretext of not leaving them with a means

of retreat, while, as in the Vendée, those rebels who wanted to surrender were pursued, and the entire plain was destroyed in order to chase them into the mountains, and lead them to wreak even more havoc.[24]

Chotard's brief reference to the Vendée in this passage would not have been lost on anyone who was aware of the immense human toll that was entailed in the "pacification" of the Vendée in 1793 and 1794. Chotard's analogy was no doubt motivated, on the colonial side of things, by a concern with the loss of white rather than black or mulatto lives. Nonetheless, this acknowledgment that the official military reaction to the 1791 slave revolt had only caused the situation to worsen is revealing. It suggests that even some within the planter community were aware that French military tactics in Saint-Domingue were a major part of the cycle of uncontrollable violence that became the Haitian Revolution. And it highlights the shared role that counterinsurrectionary violence played in the unfolding of revolutionary history on both sides of the French Atlantic.[25]

Chotard's critique of the excesses of repression in the Vendée and Saint-Domingue alike was a rare but not unique intervention in the public debates over the 1791 slave revolt and its aftermath. During the colonial debates in the Council of Five Hundred in 1797, at least two other figures produced a similar critique of the excesses of counterinsurrectionary repression by way of linking the costs of the "pacifying" the Vendée to those of quelling the slave revolution. But despite these isolated wrinkles in the analogy and despite the variation developed by the *petits blancs* of Philadelphia, there was a great deal of thematic coherence to the arguments of those who invoked the Vendée with an eye toward Caribbean developments. The analogy was, at bottom, an instrument of counterinsurrectionary politics. Moreover, it was clearly the colonial "nobility," exiled planters in North America or Paris or those who risked continued residence in Saint-Domingue, who were most invested in the analogy and who did the most to feed its circulation.[26]

The 1797 Debates in the French Legislature

References to the Vendée analogy begin to fall away in the colonial pamphlet literature in 1795 and 1796. They return with a vengeance—both metaphorical and literal—in 1797. In that year, the French legislature (and particularly its lower house, the Council of Five Hundred) engaged in an extended debate over how to restore order to Saint-Domingue. This debate was characterized by the usual litany of planter denunciations of those held responsible for the "loss" of France's colonial crown jewel. Beneath the veneer of name-calling and blame-tossing, however, was a complicated and fateful discussion over the past, present, and future of French colonial policy. In that discussion the Vendée analogy occupied an important place at a time when the deputies of the Five

Hundred began to think about concrete steps that might be taken to bring Saint-Domingue back into the orbit of metropolitan control. Among the most important decisions to result from the 1797 debates was one that revealed the extent to which the Vendée war served as a formative context for thinking about the colonial revolution: the decision to send one of the generals responsible for neutralizing the Vendée rebellion to serve as the agent of France's executive Directory in Saint-Domingue.

The leading spokesperson for the slaveholders during the 1797 debates was a planter living in Paris named Viénot de Vaublanc. Having been elected a deputy to the Council of Five Hundred, Vaublanc used one of his earliest opportunities to address the lower house to pointedly defend the Directory's work in neutralizing the Vendée rebellion. In an April 1797 speech ostensibly concerning a petition to the Five Hundred from a group of refugees from Saint-Domingue, Vaublanc tempered his criticism of what he saw as the Directory's failure to apply a forceful policy of repression toward the slave revolt with some words of praise for its work in the Vendée. "I would be the first to acknowledge in fairness [the Directory's] pacification of the Vendée, the repression of the anarchist faction," he observed.[27]

Whether by "pacification" Vaublanc had in mind the more moderate concil-iatory approach of General Hoche in early 1795 or the ferocious scorched-earth policies of the military leaders who preceded him in 1794 was perhaps delib-erately left ambiguous (although the reference to "repression" is not encourag-ing). The distinction between the repressive and conciliatory phases of French policy toward the Vendée eventually found a counterpart in the development of policy toward Saint-Domingue, as shown in further detail below. For his part, however, Vaublanc stood for the proposition that Sonthonax's emancipa-tion had been a catastrophe for Saint-Domingue.[28] From this point of view, the disorders of the peasant rebellion in the Vendée and those of the slave revolt in Saint-Domingue posed the same kind of threat to the stability of France.

Vaublanc's sentiments were echoed in the upper house of the legislature, the Conseil des Anciens, in late March 1797 by Michel-Pascal Creuzé. Creuzé was responding to the abolitionist Garran de Coulon's famous report on the "troubles" of Saint-Domingue, commissioned by the National Convention as a kind of official history of the revolution there. "I regard the system of pillaging, torching, extermination, and agrarian law that has been pursued and that still reigns at this time in Saint-Domingue as a veritable conspiracy hatched against the Republic," opined Creuzé. "This infernal system," he continued, "is the same as the one that has devastated the Vendée, organized the civil war, stirred up feel-ings, and prevented reconciliation, while spreading fire and sword everywhere."[29] All that had happened in Saint-Domingue had a "major connection" with the travails of metropolitan France, he argued, such that events in the Caribbean were but a "branch of the vast conspiracy hatched against the Republic."[30]

Creuzé's intervention reflected a belief, as did the earlier polemics of 1793 and 1794, that the slaves of Saint-Domingue were merely puppets in the hands of higher forces—as Creuzé put it, an "evildoing spirit" was responsible for the parallel ills on either side of the Atlantic.[31] The conviction of the 1793–1794 analogists that foreign powers were directing events on the ground in Saint-Domingue was still powerfully present in 1797, some three years into the British occupation of parts of the colony's western and southern departments. In May 1797, Lazare Carnot, the presiding member of the five-man executive Directory, lamented to the Council of Five Hundred that "the colonial Vendée" had been "nourished" by the British and the Spanish.[32] The published version of Carnot's remarks included an appendix consisting of a letter from the colonial commissioners to the naval minister that singled out a slave leader named Malomba as "one of the most important leaders of the Vendée of la Grande Rivière." (La Grande Rivière was a parish in the northern department not far from where the 1791 slave revolt had begun.) Malomba's troops, the commissioners asserted, had been supplied with arms and munitions by the Spanish.[33]

That these were not simply polemical comparisons with little if any real-world consequences became clear as the summer of 1797 approached. In May, the deputies of the Council of Five Hundred began to take up in earnest the questions of what kind of military figure should be sent to restore "order" to the colonies and what the basis of his strategy should be. In deciding these questions, the veterans of the Vendée war were thought to provide both a source of strategic experience and a recruitment pool. Louis Thomas Villaret de Joyeuse, a deputy from Morbihan and a former military officer who would later serve under General Leclerc in the Napoleonic expedition to Saint-Domingue, delivered a speech "on the importance of the colonies and the means of pacifying them" in late May. He began by insisting that the first and most important task for the French government was to recall (and presumably discipline) "the Robespierre of the Antilles," Sonthonax.[34] He then reminded his audience that sending a new commission from France was the last thing that Saint-Domingue needed. "Have you forgotten that the Vendée war only took on greater force as more and more proconsuls were sent?" France needed only to do for Saint-Domingue "what [it] did with such success for the Vendée." "Saint-Domingue," he observed succinctly, "is also a Vendée to be reconquered," characterized by the same combination of civil and foreign war that made possible the devastation in the western French countryside. Villaret-Joyeuse argued that only the right combination of "the force of arms and energy mixed with gentleness and clemency" could bring the slave revolution to its knees.[35] The general to be chosen to represent the Directory in Saint-Domingue should be someone who could follow in the footsteps of General Hoche and his successful neutralization of the Vendée.[36]

Such comments undeniably reflected an awareness that what had ultimately served to quell the violence of the Vendée war was the conciliatory approach of General Hoche. Yet given the ferocity of the French response to the slave revolt from its outset, it would certainly have been reasonable to suspect that the Directory was likely to privilege "force and arms" over "gentleness and clemency" in attempting to restore "order" to Saint-Domingue. This at least was the impression of one deputy, Joseph Eschassériaux, who addressed the Council of Five Hundred in late May in a manner that vaguely echoed aspects of Chotard's 1795 pamphlet. Yet Eschassériaux displayed a skepticism about the Vendée analogy that no other white figure of the period seemed capable of evincing. "There is . . . no similitude in favor of military government between Saint-Domingue and the Vendée," he insisted.[37] If France were to attempt a Vendée-style pacification in the very different context and climate of Saint-Domingue, the colony would become a "tomb" of the French armies. It was much better to use the power of law and constitutionalism rather than brute force.[38]

In addition to this voice of caution emanating from within the French establishment, there were dissenting voices from a very different and no less important quarter. The arguments of Viénot de Vaublanc and his sympathizers in the Council of Five Hundred were answered by the most important voice of the slave revolution itself, Toussaint Louverture. In a refutation of Vaublanc's May 1797 speech that was published in late October of that year, Louverture defended himself and the black revolution from the "calumnies" of Vaublanc.[39] He countered the assertion of General Donatien Marie Joseph Rochambeau—who was evidently in league with Vaublanc and who in 1792 had served a stint as governor of Saint-Domingue—that France could subdue the slave revolution by applying overwhelming military force. If any such campaign was attempted, the liberated slaves of Saint-Domingue "would, with the [French] constitution in hand . . . defend the liberty that it guarantees." On a more conciliatory note, Louverture added that events in the colony over the past year had shown how unnecessary a French military expedition would be, given that agricultural discipline had been restored to the plantations during that period.[40] (Rochambeau would soon return to the colony as second-in-command under General Leclerc in 1802.)

More generally, Louverture noted that France was in no position to object to the violence the slaves of Saint-Domingue employed in the years since 1791. What, Louverture asked, might Vaublanc have to say about a French Revolution that had produced "the Marats, the Robespierres, the Carriers, the Sonthonaxes, etc. etc. etc., the traitors who delivered Toulon to the English . . . the bloody scenes of the Vendée, the massacres of September 2," and so forth?[41] Just as it was "indecent to accuse the black people of the excesses of a few of its members . . . so would it be unjust of us to accuse all of France of the excesses of a small number of partisans of the former system."[42]

Such rhetoric, despite its intensely provocative character, may also have been calculated to earn Louverture and the slave revolution some sympathy in the generally more conservative climate of French politics under the Directory regime. Whatever the case may be, however, the Vendée analogy had now been turned on its head by the leader of the slave revolution. Louverture was beginning to realize at least the possibility of an all-out military conflict with the French government even as he continued in his characteristic manner to work the diplomatic channels with the metropolitan representatives.

As 1797 came to a close, the winds of colonial policy in the metropole were beginning to shift in a more conciliatory and less proslavery direction as Etienne Laveaux and his allies gained more prominence. Before they had fully shifted, however, and while the conservative faction around Vaublanc was still the dominant influence on colonial policy, the Directory had named Gabriel Marie Théodore Joseph d'Hédouville, one of the generals responsible for "pacifying" the Vendée, as its agent in Saint-Domingue.[43]

From Conciliation to Extermination: Hédouville's Mission and the Leclerc Expedition

The course of French policy toward Saint-Domingue between 1798 and the end of the Haitian Revolution can be seen on the whole as a movement from conciliation to all-out repression. Although such a movement was in some respects the reverse of what had been witnessed in the Vendée, the Vendée experience continued to lurk not very far beneath the surface of events in the colony.

In early 1798, the Directory replaced Sonthonax with Hédouville, who had been in command of the Atlantic port city of Nantes during General Hoche's conciliatory experiment in the Vendeé region.[44] Significantly, Hédouville arrived in Saint-Domingue without an army,[45] and his association with the later "pacification" of the Vendée did not go unnoticed by Toussaint Louverture, who was attuned to the subtleties of French diplomatic policy. That same awareness, however, also predisposed Louverture to be exceedingly cautious in his dealings with the former general.

The ex-slaves of Saint-Domingue, for their part, very quickly began to suspect Hédouville, not without reason, of wanting to return them to the plantations. Groups of former slaves around the colony drew up petitions asking Louverture to assume full control of Saint-Domingue. In 1799, one such group from the parish of Petite-Rivière, in the West Province, drew up a petition that constitutes one of the rare examples of a Haitian Creole document from this period. The former slaves declared their refusal to work until Moïse, one of Louverture's military subordinates who had led his men in an uprising against French authority (and against Hédouville's mission in particular), was released from prison.[46]

Hédouville's mission turned out to be one of the pivotal events of the latter part of the revolution. His selection and the circumstances of his arrival were evidently motivated at least in part by a desire to appease the slave revolution rather than stoke further violence. Yet Hedouville's campaign to "restore order" consisted, in the end, of an effort to defeat Louverture by driving a wedge between him and the mulatto leader Rigaud—an effort that quickly backfired.[47] Hedouville's uncompromising rejection of emancipation of the slaves caused his relations with Louverture to sour and served to convince the black general that only an all-out conflict with France could guarantee freedom to Haiti.[48] Arguably conciliatory in its origins, Hédouville's mission ushered in a transition from the indeterminate status quo of 1797–1798, when the ascendant Louverture still pretended to be in the service of France, to the war of independence of 1802–1803.

That war began, on the French side, under the leadership of General Leclerc, whose strategy for subduing Louverture's black armies was plain and simple. It was necessary to fight a "war of extermination," Leclerc wrote to Denis Decrès, Bonaparte's colonial minister, on September 17, 1802.[49] A few weeks later, Leclerc wrote directly to Bonaparte that

> we must destroy all the blacks of the mountains—men and women—
> and spare only children under twelve years of age. We must destroy half
> of those in the plains and must not leave a single colored person in the
> colony who has worn an epaulette.[50]

After Leclerc's demise, Rochambeau continued this avowedly exterminationist strategy. In their different ways, both Hédouville's mission and the brutally repressive Leclerc-Rochambeau expedition ordered by Napoleon were products of the Vendée-slave revolt analogy and the worldview out of which it emerged.

To say this, however, is not to say that the violence of 1802–1803 can be attributed *solely* to the example of the metropolitan Vendée. Ferociously repressive French military tactics in Saint-Domingue, like the belief that Louverture's revolution was a religiously motivated royalist conspiracy, dated back to almost the first days of the slave revolt in 1791. Leclerc and Rochambeau did not invent the strategy of brutal and merciless military repression of the revolution out of thin air. What precise contribution the Vendée analogy made to the unfolding of the events of 1802–1803 is a question that, by its very nature, cannot be answered with certainty. What can be said with some confidence is that the Vendée analogy served to make more thinkable the explicitly exterminationist goals of the Leclerc-Rochambeau expedition and to highlight and perpetuate the element of peasant religious fanaticism in metropolitan perceptions of Haiti.

The continuing power of the analogy during the period of the war of independence is perhaps best reflected in Jean-Louis Dubroca's 1802 *Life of Toussaint Louverture*, a work that was commissioned by Napoleon's regime as part of a propaganda war against the slave revolution that accompanied the physical war. In that work, Dubroca observed that "LA VENDEE alone offers some resemblance of the war, which for two years TOUSSAINT made on the Republicans of the colony."[51] Thus, by the time of the war of independence, Toussaint Louverture had replaced Sonthonax as the principal personal target of the Vendée analogy. In this capacity, of course, Louverture served merely as a convenient symbol of a broader shift in the political and strategic terrain. Where the primary anxiety of the Vendée–slave revolt analogists had once been the efforts of all-controlling white "counterrevolutionary" authorities to emancipate the slaves, the new locus of concern was a black-led drive for independence. Far from putting an end to the analogy, the radicalization of the Haitian Revolution ushered in a new and more overtly racialist chapter in the analogy's history. For many years to come, the image of Haitians as "savage" and "fanatical" peasants who belonged to a different moral and racial universe than the rest of the Atlantic world would live on.

Some Alternative Contexts

Having traced the sources, unfolding, and impact of the Vendée analogy in its own time and place, it remains for me to suggest two of the broader contexts in which this history can be situated. The first of these contexts has to do with French revolutionary warfare, the second with Atlantic history.

Saint-Domingue was not the only territory outside France where the analogy to the Vendée war was used to justify decisive French military action against "subversive" populations. During the Napoleonic campaigns in Italy in 1806 and in Spain in 1809–1810, the Vendée was invoked to justify unprecedented ruthless measures for the pacification of local resistance. (In the Spanish case, these measures were captured nowhere more powerfully than in the art of Francisco Goya.) Indeed, the Napoleonic campaigns generally represent a turning point in the history of French warfare. Before Napoleon, with one major exception, French warfare, like warfare elsewhere in Europe, was seen as governed by the traditional laws of war—that is, by the *ius gentium*, or law of nations. The traditional laws of war required observance of the rules of proportionality and of respect for civilian life, which is to say that it mandated restraint rather than all-out uninhibited force. The chief exception to this understanding of warfare before Napoleon was, not surprisingly, the conduct of the Vendée war, which saw the abandonment of the classical rules of restraint and the embrace of an exterminationist style of warfare in which "the enemy" is not simply one's military opponent but a different kind of human being altogether: one more "fanatical" and more "savage" than "us," and hence more deserving of the most ruthless treatment possible. Napoleon's military campaigns made of this style of warfare the rule rather than the exception and so helped remove from European military history the sense of taboo and the practices of restraint that had hitherto marked (in theory if not always in practice) the conduct of warfare on the continent.[52]

Once this more unrestrained brand of warfare became legitimized on the continent, it became all the easier to deploy it outside Europe as well, against subject peoples who could be portrayed as different not simply in ideological terms but also in racial terms.[53] The war of Haitian independence is significant not only because it foreshadowed the patterns of nineteenth-century colonial warfare but also because it was, along with the Vendée (and partly because of the Vendée), one of the earliest exterminationist military campaigns in the new era of French revolutionary and postrevolutionary warfare. To read the accounts of the 1802–1803 Leclerc expedition in Saint-Domingue and its aftermath—including the Leclerc correspondence quoted above—is to bear witness to one of the most dramatic and radical examples in European history of this new willingness to exterminate the enemy rather than simply fight him to a peace.

A second context has to do with the role of analogies in Atlantic history. A kind of existential angst has hung over the recent rebirth of Atlantic history. Questions of definition and scholarly purpose have featured front and center: just what is Atlantic history? Does it have any concrete content and method, or is it just an urbane-sounding phrase for describing what historians of the early modern New World once did and are now doing again with renewed vigor and sophistication: exploring the connections between metropolitan and colonial developments, and between European and African history on the one hand, and the history of the Americas on the other? There is no recipe for doing Atlantic or any other kind of history, of course, but the Vendée analogy does suggest at least one concrete area of focus for Atlantic historians who believe, correctly, that the interrelatedness of developments on both sides of the Atlantic is what makes their work interesting and worthwhile. That area of focus is the articulation of analogies—between forms of government, social formations, cultural genres, military experiences, and so forth—by early modern citizens of the Atlantic world who tried to make sense of their everyday experience, to channel it in different directions, or to prevent it from escaping the realm of the familiar and the everyday. Atlantic history is in part the history of analogies. This does not mean that historians must accept these analogies at face value. But it does mean that analogies are historical forces in their own right and that the history of the Atlantic world between roughly 1500 and 1800 developed partly in the form of—and partly as a consequence of—a powerful will to compare the old with the new.

Notes

Earlier versions of this essay were presented at the John Carter Brown Library's bicentennial conference on the Haitian Revolution and the Johns Hopkins University History Department Seminar. I thank my interlocutors at both Providence and Baltimore, especially Chris Brown, Alyssa Sepinwall, David Bell, Jeremy Popkin, and Philip Morgan, for very helpful criticisms on those occasions. My title is a quotation from a 1797 speech by Lazare Carnot, a former member of the Committee of Public Safety and organizer of the French war effort in 1793–1794, to the lower house of the French legislature, the Council of Five Hundred. Carnot was the presiding member of the French Directory at the time of this speech. *Extrait du régistre des déliberations du Diréctoire exécutif, du 16 prairial, l'an 5 de la République française, une et divisible* ([Paris]: n.p., 1797), 2.

The epigraph: Jean-Louis Dubroca, *The Life of Toussaint Louverture* (London: H. D. Symonds, 1802), 11–12 (emphasis in the original). This is an English translation of a virulently polemical account of Louverture that was apparently commissioned by Napoleon's regime and was first published in French in the same year.

1. Michèle Oriol, *Histoire et dictionnaire de la Révolution et de l'indépendance d'Haïti* (Port-au-Prince: Fondation pour la Recherche Iconographique et Documentaire, 2002), 27.

2. François Barbé de Marbois, *Mémoire et observations du Sieur Barbé de Marbois . . . sur une dénonciation signée par treize de MM. les députés de Saint-Domingue, et faite à l'Assemblée nationale au nom d'un des trois Comités de la colonie* (Paris: Knapen, 1790), 8.

3. Marbois, *Mémoire*, 9.

4. Marbois, *Mémoire*, 8.

5. One of the more important contributors to these debates was Malouet. See Malick W. Ghachem, "Sovereignty and Slavery in the Age of Revolution: Haitian Variations on a Metropolitan Theme" (Ph.D. diss., Stanford University, 2002), chs. 1–2, 5.

6. As Lynn Hunt and Jack Censer note, "even today, controversy still rages about [the Vendée war's] death toll; estimates of rebel deaths alone range from about 20,000 to 250,000 and higher"; Jack R. Censer and Lynn Hunt, *Liberty, Equality, Fraternity: Exploring the French Revolution* (University Park: Pennsylvania State University Press, 2001), 99.

7. [Deraggis], *Adresse au peuple français, libre et souverain, par le citoyen Deraggis, ancien procureur-syndic de la commune de Mirebalais* (Paris: Pain, 1793), 14.

8. [Deraggis], *Adresse au peuple français*, 1.

9. Deraggis excepted only a handful of top administrators from his list of villains, including the governor of Saint-Domingue in 1789, Duchilleau, who had pleaded with the ministry of the navy and colonies to allow the importation of food from neighboring colonies despite the *exclusif*.

10. [Deraggis], *Adresse au peuple français*, 3–4. The original members of the second civil commission, dispatched in June 1792, were Léger-Félicité Sonthonax, Étienne Polverel, and Jean Antoine Ailhaud. Sonthonax and Polverel later promoted Olivier Ferdinand Delpeche, the commission's secretary, to take Ailhaud's place after the latter left Saint-Domingue in May 1793.

11. [Deraggis], *Adresse au peuple français*, 4–5.

12. It is unclear whether this pamphlet was published before or after Sonthonax decided to emancipate the slaves of the North Province on August 29, 1793. Given the pamphlet's florid rhetoric, it is quite likely that Deraggis was reacting in part to the emancipation proclamation.

13. Pierre François Page and Augustin Jean Brulley, *Développement des causes des troubles et désastres des colonies françaises, présenté à la Convention nationale, par les Commissaires de Saint-Domingue, sur la demande des comités de Marine et des Colonies* ([Paris]: n.p., 1793), 67.

14. *Invitation des Administrateurs du Directoire du Département du Haute-Garonne, à leurs concitoyens* ([Toulouse]: n.p., 1794), 1.

15. William Doyle, *The Oxford History of the French Revolution* (Oxford: Oxford University Press, 1989), 239–240.

16. *Débats entre les accusateurs et les accusés, dans l'affaire des colonies, imprimés en exécution de la loi du 4 pluviôse*, 11 vols. (Paris: [n.p.], 1795), 1&2:7. (This eleven-volume collection can be found, among other places, in the John Carter Brown Library.) A similar charge was directed against François Thomas Galbaud du Fort, who was appointed governor-general of Saint-Domingue in 1793. Galbaud was deported from the colony shortly after his arrival in May 1793 by the French civil commissioners on charges of seeking to undermine their authority. The deputies of the colony's northern department published an account accusing Galbaud and his fellow "agitators" of having allied themselves "during the federalist period, with all of the colonists, or aristocratic and royalist merchants, in our principal commercial cities." *Relation détaillée des événemens malheureux qui se sont passés au Cap depuis l'arrivée du ci-devant général Galbaud, jusqu'au moment où il a fait brûlé cette ville et a pris la fuite* (Paris: Imprimerie Nationale, 1794), 17.

17. [L. J. Clausson and F. A. Millet], *À la Convention nationale* (N.p.: n.p., 1794), 4–5. The text begins "Eh bien, citoyens, Saint-Domingue n'existe plus!"

18. [Clausson and Millet], *À la Convention nationale*, 6–7.

19. J. B. Thounens, *Compte rendu aux Comités de Marine et des colonies réunis, et au public* (Paris: n.p., 1794), 8.

20. Thounens, *Compte rendu aux Comités de Marine*, 7.

21. *Courrier Français*, November 29, 1794, 881, 883.

22. *Courrier Français*, December 3, 1794, 904–905.

23. *Courrier Français*, January 25, 1795, 1090.

24. Chotard, *Précis de la Révolution de Saint-Domingue, depuis la fin de 1789, jusqu'au 18 Juin 1794* (Philadelphia: Parent, 1795), 57.

25. It seems likely that Chotard's critique of the excesses of the repression of the Vendée was linked at some level to the example of General Lazare Hoche, who, beginning in early 1795, brought a more moderate, less militaristic approach to ending the Vendée revolt than was previously employed by the National Convention.

26. For some additional examples of planter invocations of the analogy in 1795, see Pierre François Page and Augustin Jean Brulley, "Notes fournies au Comité de Salut Public par les Commissaires de Saint-Domingue," in *Débats entre les accusateurs et les accusés, dans l'affaire des colonies*, 10:3, 12, 15, 57. These notes come from the hearings

held by order of the Convention in 1795 on the conduct of Sonthonax and Polverel. Page and Brulley's attacks on what they described as the conspiratorial violence of the slave revolt in these pages were part and parcel of their relentless campaign against the two civil commissioners.

27. Vincent-Marie Viénot de Vaublanc, *Opinion de Viénot-Vaublanc, sur la pétition des déportés de Saint-Domingue, détenus à Rochefort, et sur la compétence des conseils militaires (séance du 22 germinal, an V)* ([Paris]: [Imprimerie Nationale], 8.

28. Laurent Dubois, *Avengers of the New World: The Story of the Haitian Revolution* (Cambridge, Mass.: Harvard University Press, 2004), 209.

29. Michel-Pascal Creuzé, *Lettre de Michel-Pascal Creuzé, membre du Conseil des Anciens, à Jean-Philippe Garran, député de Loiret, sur son rapport des troubles de Saint-Domingue, distribué au corps legislatif* (Paris: Maret, 1797), 23.

30. Creuzé, *Lettre de Michel-Pascal Creuzé*, 62.

31. Creuzé, *Lettre de Michel-Pascal Creuzé*, 23.

32. *Extrait du régistre des déliberations du Diréctoire exécutif*, 1–2.

33. *Extrait du régistre des déliberations du Diréctoire exécutif*, 6. (The attachment is entitled "Extrait d'une lettre écrite au citoyen ministre de la Marine et des colonies.")

34. Louis Thomas Villaret de Joyeuse, *Discours de Villaret-Joyeuse, député du Morbihan, sur l'importance des colonies et les moyens de les pacifier (séance du 12 prairial an 5)*, ([Paris]: [Imprimerie Nationale], 1797), 5.

35. Joyeuse, *Discours de Villaret-Joyeuse*, 6.

36. Joyeuse, *Discours de Villaret-Joyeuse*, 8.

37. Joseph Eschassériaux, *Opinion d'Eschassériaux (aîné), sur les moyens de rétablir les colonies (séance du 16 prairial, an V)* ([Paris]: [Imprimerie Nationale], 1797), 10.

38. Eschassériaux, *Opinion d'Eschassériaux*, 12.

39. Toussaint Louverture, *Réfutation de quelques assertions d'un discours prononcé au corps législatif le 10 prairial, an cinq, par Viénot Vaublanc* ([Cap Français]: n.p., 1797), 1. It is not clear whether this document was published in Paris or Saint-Domingue, but Louverture's signature indicated "Au Cap, le 8 Brumaire, l'an sixième."

40. Louverture, *Réfutation de quelques Assertions*, 11.

41. Louverture, *Réfutation de quelques Assertions*, 26–27.

42. Louverture, *Réfutation de quelques Assertions*, 28.

43. Dubois, *Avengers of the New World*, 217.

44. Hédouville makes an appearance as the French military representative in charge of Nantes during the Vendée war in Alexandre Dumas's historical novel *The Companions of Jehu*, published in 1857. See, for example, Chapter 32 ("White and Blue").

45. Robin Blackburn, *The Overthrow of Colonial Slavery, 1776–1848* (London: Verso, 1988), 239–240.

46. *Arrêtés des différentes communes de la colonie de St. Domingue, adressées à l'Agent particulier du Directoire* [Hédouville], *au Général en chef* [Louverture], *et à l'Administration municipale du Cap* (N.p.: n.p., 1799), 19.

47. On this point, see Carolyn E. Fick, *The Making of Haiti: The Saint-Domingue Revolution from Below* (Knoxville: University of Tennessee Press, 1990), 109–201.

48. See generally Dubois, *Avengers of the New World*, 217–226.

49. Quoted in Dubois, *Avengers of the New World*, 290.

50. Quoted in Dubois, *Avengers of the New World*, 291–292.

51. Dubroca, *The Life of Toussaint Louverture*, 11–12 (emphasis in the original).

52. See David A. Bell, *The First Total War: Napoleon's Europe and the Birth of Warfare as We Know It* (Boston: Houghton Mifflin, 2007), esp. 154–185, 263–293.

53. On the importance of colonial warfare to European military history, see Jeremy Black, *Warfare in the Eighteenth Century* (New York: Harper Collins, 2005).

The Saint-Domingue Slave Revolution and the Unfolding of Independence, 1791–1804

Carolyn E. Fick

W HEN THE SLAVES OF SAINT-DOMINGUE TOOK UP ARMS IN 1791 TO WAGE WAR AGAINST THEIR MASTERS, THEY EMBARKED UPON A COLLECTIVE STRUGGLE FOR EMANCIPATION AND THE RIGHTS of man, but it was not framed in political theory. Notions of sovereignty, self-government, political independence, and modern nation-building were not among their first concerns as they put their torches to the plantations of the Northern Plain and destroyed the material foundations of their enslavement. Nor were the Bois-Caïman ceremony and war cry of liberty that announced the rebellion in August, in themselves, a formal declaration of independence. As one historian recently put it, the slaves were breaking new ground in a brave new world, and in so doing, "they took the Atlantic slave-based colonial complex and turned it upside down in search of fundamental human rights." Between 1791 and 1804, they "established a social and political conjuncture that significantly shaped the history of the Atlantic World."[1] The outcome of that struggle, of course, was the creation of an independent black state in which slavery was forever banished. Yet unlike their North American counterparts of a generation earlier, who had asserted in 1776 their intention to break from Great Britain and then fought to achieve their declared independence, the black revolutionaries of Saint-Domingue proclaimed independence *as a historical fact* only in 1804, at the end of thirteen arduous years of war and sacrifice in defense of their freedom, and only after the final defeat of Bonaparte's expeditionary army, which was sent in 1802 to break the black revolution and restore slavery. Independence for Haiti was therefore an unfolding process, subject to the contingencies of a world being reshaped and redefined in ways that neither the slaves nor the slave-owners, nor even the French revolutionary governments, could have predicted. That is what makes the Haitian revolution so extraordinary and until recently, even for historians, so inconceivable.[2]

But where, exactly, does the unfolding of independence begin? With the pre-revolutionary conspiracy of Macandal in 1757, with the insurrection of 1791, with general emancipation in 1793/94, or with the landing of Napoleon Bonaparte's expeditionary army in 1802? Undeniably, the slaves' struggle for independence had deep roots and many turning points along the way. What this study addresses is one segment of the *longue durée*, beginning with general emancipation in 1793/94 as a fundamental turning point that eventually revealed the necessity of political independence and culminated in its realization in 1804. The sinuous trajectory from slave emancipation to independence will be traced by examining the political conjunctures in France and Saint-Domingue that shaped its course. First, problematic constitutional issues arising from France's abolition of slavery are dealt with, as are Bonaparte's policies for its restoration. Also addressed is the political trajectory of Toussaint Louverture toward securing sovereign status for Saint-Domingue in response to changing metropolitan attitudes concerning freedom and citizenship in the colonies. Finally, focusing on the dynamics of popular movements and the crisis of leadership, the study seeks to examine the circumstances under which the initial resistance of Toussaint's army to the expeditionary force led by General Victor-Emmanuel Leclerc unfolded into a war of independence.

Consequences of Abolition in France and Saint-Domingue

When the revolutionary government of France declared that slavery was abolished in all French territory on February 4, 1794, it was actually ratifying the general emancipation proclamations that had already been issued throughout Saint-Domingue in 1793 by its civil commissioners, Léger-Félicité Sonthonax and Étienne Polverel, who were responding above all to the widespread and ongoing slave rebellions.[3] In abolishing slavery, the government also extended full French citizenship to the slaves, most of whom were African-born, and made the constitutional basis for equality in the colonies exactly the same as it was in metropolitan France. Unprecedented though this was, the abolition of slavery and the extension of civil equality to former slaves never brought into question the existence of the colonies themselves; they were, after all, the foundation of France's commercial and maritime strength. Thus, the abolition of slavery and the universal imposition of equality in the colonies required that the metropolitan government rethink the nature of its colonial empire. It would need to define a place for the colonies and the colonial populations within the French nation and somehow reconcile the unquestioned maintenance of market-driven colonial plantation production with the universalist principles of the rights of man as they should apply to the former slaves, who, in theory, had now become free French wage laborers.

Questions of colonial governance also needed to be addressed. Could, for example, the same laws by which French society was governed in Europe be applied to the plantation societies of the tropics? And if rights could be defined and circumscribed in France, how far could the rights of colonial blacks be restricted without undermining the legality of slave emancipation? In short, by abolishing colonial slavery, France was faced with the task of having to modernize its colonial system in keeping with revolutionary republicanism. None of these issues could be dealt with by the Jacobin government of 1794, which, less than six months after abolishing slavery, was overthrown and replaced with the conservative government of the Directory. Into its hands fell the unfinished task of confronting these issues and constitutionalizing slave emancipation.[4]

To its credit, the Directory maintained the integrity of the February 4 abolitionist law and therefore the principle of universal equality, when, in its Constitution of the Year III (1795), it formally declared the colonies to be "integral parts of the nation and subject to the same laws and the same constitution" as metropolitan France. It thereby assimilated them territorially and legislatively into the Republic, "one and indivisible."[5] The metropolis and the colonies would be unified under a single constitution that would guarantee equality and civil rights, the suppression of slavery, and establish uniform qualifications for suffrage throughout all French territory.[6] But what did this really mean? The republican deputy, Boissy d'Anglas, who headed the Directory's commission charged with defining the new relationship between metropolis and colony, delivered a report to the Directory's legislative body in 1795 in which he proposed to circumvent the universalist implications of the constitution. Without actually renouncing general emancipation, he used a discourse of pseudo-scientific racism and cultural and climatic determinism to justify the subordination of France's new African citizenry, who were deemed culturally inferior to European whites by virtue of the debilitating influence of the tropics and therefore incapable of self-government and self-determination. The colonies' assimilation into the Republic "one and indivisible" in essence meant that they should be governed by the central authority of the metropolis, that the colonial assemblies should be dissolved, and that the vast majority of the African citizens should be permanently tied to plantation agriculture.[7]

By opening the debate on the colonial question in such terms, the government of the Directory created a political climate in which the blatantly reactionary proslavery elements, consisting largely of exiled or émigré planters and port merchants, could maneuver with impunity to promote their own aims. Organized as the Société de Clichy (and known as the Clichyens), they were headed notably by Vincent Viénot de Vaublanc, François Barbé-Marbois, Louis Villaret de Joyeuse, and François Bourdon de l'Oise—all men of the ancien régime. Their victories in the 1797 legislative elections strengthened their position within the legislative body and emboldened them to launch an all-out offensive aimed at abrogating the February 4 law and suspending application of the Constitution of the Year III in the colonies, thereby opening the way for a restoration of the pre-1793 colonial regime.[8] Under heavy pressure from the colonialist lobby and with Saint-Domingue partly under British occupation, the government declared the colony under siege, placed it under military authority, and named General Gabriel Marie Théodore Joseph d'Hédouville, the "pacifier of the Vendée," as its agent.

In September 1797, the principal Clichyens were arrested and deported, but the colonial question addressed during the opening months of the Directory in 1795 still needed to be clarified and constitutionalized. On January 1, 1798, the Directory passed what it called the Law on the Constitutional Organization of the Colonies, which transformed the colonies into departments and assimilated them, along with their black and colored populations, into a unified egalitarian French republic in which slavery remained abolished.[9] But the damage had already been done. The mere fact that the Directory had appeared too weak to prevent a reactionary colonialist faction from gaining control of the legislature, if only temporarily, and from framing its position in racist terms reminiscent of the old slaveholding days, suggested the dangers that lay ahead for the emancipated blacks of Saint-Domingue.

This is where the Directory stood on the question of colonialism, and it was in this context that Toussaint Louverture, by now lieutenant-governor of the colony, expounded his own position unequivocally to the men of the Directory. In his famous letter of November 5, 1797 (when he evidently was unaware of the Clichyens' deportation), he masterfully denounced the perfidious aims of Vaublanc and his faction.[10] Eloquently defending republican virtues, he cautioned the Directory in no uncertain terms about the consequences it would face if the ambiguities it had tolerated regarding black emancipation should ever bring the government to revoke the February 4 law in order to reestablish slavery: "It would be to attempt the impossible: we have known how to face dangers to obtain our liberty, we shall know how to brave death to maintain it. . . . This, Citizen Directors, is the morale of the people of San Domingo [sic], those are the principles that they transmit to you by me."[11] The letter marked an unequivocal turning point in Toussaint's political itinerary, and it is certainly one of the keys, perhaps the primary one, to understanding his single-minded resolve, from that point on, to take personal control of the destiny of Saint-Domingue and its emancipated blacks.

The position he took with regard to the Directory in the face of the reaction-ary threat of a return to pre-abolitionist times also marked the definitive end of his deference to the French metropolis and its colonial commissioners, be they republican or not.

The unfolding of independence as a political option and a historical pro-cess is thus intimated in this letter of 1797. The steps that Toussaint took thereafter to consolidate his powers are well known. Having defeated the British occupation forces and personally negotiated the terms of evacuation with General Maitland in 1798, Toussaint forcibly expelled the French gov-ernment's agent, General Hédouville. In 1799–1800, with the aid of secret Anglo-American trade agreements favoring an economic blockade of the south, he engaged in civil war to crush the bid for power of the colony's for-mer free colored elite, led by the southern mulatto general, André Rigaud. With victory in August 1800, Toussaint effectively consolidated black rule throughout French Saint-Domingue. It remained to bring under his jurisdic-tion the neighboring Spanish colony of Santo Domingo (which was ceded to France in 1795 by the Treaty of Basle but never formally occupied) and thereby extend his military and political authority to the entire island. In December 1800, he announced to the Spanish authorities in Santo Domingo that he would take possession, in the name of France, of the eastern por-tion of Hispaniola. In defiance of explicit metropolitan prohibitions, he placed the territory under formal military occupation on January 21, 1801, and thereafter integrated it into a unified administrative structure of colo-nial departments. Finally, he imprisoned Philippe Roume, the only remain-ing commissioner of the French government at that point, for his refusal to approve the Spanish expedition.

Toussaint had by now traveled a tremendous distance since his letter to the Directory in 1797, and in 1801 his military and political authority was virtually hegemonic. At such unprecedented and vertiginous heights, he would need the stabilizing institutional force of a constitution to consolidate his powers and place them on solid ground:

> I have taken flight into the realm of the eagles, and I must be prudent as I descend to earth. I can no longer be placed but on a rock, and this rock must be the constitutional cornerstone that will guarantee my power for as long as I shall live.[12]

He first created a commission to draft a constitution and then on July 8, 1801, he officially promulgated it for all of Saint-Domingue. With the preservation of general emancipation underlying its principles, it established the internal institutions by which Saint-Domingue would be governed, thereby formal-izing the new relationship of the colony and its emancipated black citizenry to the French metropolis on *Toussaint's own terms*. He had taken the colony, if not to the brink of outright independence and separation from France—for he never declared independence—at the very least in the direction of self-determination as a black self-governing territory of the French empire.

By this time, it was no longer the Directory's equivocations and corruption and the ambiguities of its colonial policy that mattered; rather, it was Napoleon Bonaparte and the rehabilitated proslavery lobby of Vaublanc and his friends, pardoned and returned from exile, whose machinations Toussaint would have to anticipate. France's new Constitution of the Year VIII, hastily drafted and adopted in 1799 following the coup d'état of 18 Brumaire, had overturned the provisions in the constitution of the Directory that had assimilated the colonies into the French nation "one and indivisible" and stipulated that they would be governed by "special laws" that would take into account the specificity of each colony. This meant that general emancipation and the constitutional legality of citizenship that followed from it would no longer be guaranteed. The colonial citizens of Saint-Domingue would not be protected by the same laws that applied to French citizens in the metropolis. The constitutional impediments to overturning general emancipation that had been put into place under the tenuous republicanism of the Directory had effectively been removed, and the decree that abolished slavery and established the basis for a universal regime of French citizenship without regard to color no longer had constitutional validity. Henceforth, the February 4 law would be subject, as to its application or abrogation, to the uncertain intentions of the First Consul.

In this respect, Bonaparte's initial aims were purely pragmatic rather than ideological: restore the totality of French authority throughout the colonies, especially in Saint-Domingue, but deal with the question of slavery on a colony-by-colony basis. As for Saint-Domingue, he told his council of state, "I am convinced that this island would become British if the blacks were not tied to us by their concern for their freedom. They may make less sugar, but they will make it for us, and they will furnish us with soldiers as the need arises. . . . So I will speak of liberty in the French part of Saint-Domingue; I will confirm slavery in Ile-de-France, as well as the Spanish part of Saint-Domingue [and Martinique]; and I will reserve the prerogative of softening slavery where it will be maintained; and of reestablishing order and discipline where I shall maintain abolition."[13] Thus, for the citizens of Saint-Domingue, where general emancipation had been in effect since 1793, the regime of liberty and equality would apparently remain untouched, although the colony would be governed by laws other than those of metropolitan France. Bonaparte had already made these intentions known to the "citizens of Saint-Domingue" in his December 25, 1799, proclamation, issued immediately after the adoption of the Constitution of the Year VIII and directed primarily at Toussaint Louverture, who at the time was engaged in the civil war against Rigaud. In this proclamation Bonaparte announced that the Directory's Constitution of the Year III had been replaced by a new constitutional pact aimed at strengthening liberty. Article 91 of this new constitution concerns the French colonies, which will be governed by special laws. The reason for this derives from the nature of things and from differences in climate. The inhabitants of the French colonies situated in America, in Asia, and Africa cannot be governed by the same laws [as those of France]. Differences in customs, manners, interests, the soil, agriculture, and types of production all require various modifications. The consuls of the Republic, in announcing this new social pact, declare to you that the sacred principles of liberty and equality of the blacks shall never be modified. . . . Remember, brave Negroes, that only the French people recognize your freedom and the equality of your rights.[14]

He then designated three commissioners, General Jean-Baptiste Michel, army engineer Colonel Charles Vincent, and Julien Raimond, the former free colored leader who had accompanied General Hédouville to the colony in 1798, to deliver the proclamation and restore full metropolitan authority over the colony. But it was Toussaint's authority, not that of the French government, that was ultimately strengthened.

The Coming of Independence

The commissioners arrived toward the end of the civil war from which Toussaint and the black leadership emerged victorious. The outcome of the war and Toussaint's invasion of Santo Domingo in 1801 consolidated black rule over the entire island, at which point Toussaint created his commission to draft a constitution and thus preempt any "special laws" that might be issued from France. In effect, Toussaint aimed to replace article 91 of France's Constitution of the Year VIII (1799) with his own Constitution of 1801.

The constitution applied to the whole island, Saint-Domingue in its entirety, including "Samaná, Tortuga, Gonâve, Cayemittes, Ile-à-Vache, Saona, and all other adjacent islands, [which] form the territory of a single colony, which is part of the French empire, but is subject to particular laws."[15] It seemed that Bonaparte's "special laws" would now be superseded by Toussaint's "particular laws." Slavery, of course, was declared forever abolished: "There can be no slaves in Saint-Domingue. All men here are born, live, and die free and French."[16] Toussaint's powers as governor and commander-in-chief of the colonial army were confirmed and extended for life and, as an exceptional measure, Louverture was given the power to designate his own successor. The constitution explicitly gave the governor supreme and almost absolute legislative and executive authority. It was he who drafted and proposed the laws by which the colony and its inhabitants would be governed; such laws would be submitted to a handpicked central assembly for approval or rejection. Trade, commerce, the organization of agriculture and labor relations, the enactment of penal measures, the importation of new laborers, and above all the army were all under the authority of the governor.

Basic rights of citizenship, such as the right to personal security, the inviolability of one's domicile, the right to a trial in a law court, the writ of habeas corpus, the right to establish schools, and the right of petition, "especially to the governor," were all nominally guaranteed. Other rights, however, such as the right of public assembly or the right of association, were formally prohibited. The Catholic religion was declared official and its administrative divisions in the colony were to be determined by the governor. Finally, the sanctity and protection of private property were given special attention and would apply equally to white absentee planters in good standing, who needed only to produce legal title to reclaim their sequestered properties. In short, the place, the duties and responsibilities, and the rights of individuals—magistrates, the military, agricultural workers, landowners, urban laborers—were all clearly laid down in the constitution. The society that Toussaint was trying to forge was to be multiracial and juridically egalitarian, comprised of a mixture of civil and military authority, with military authority occupying a preponderant if not an omnipresent role. For the vast majority of the population, the plantation citizenry, it was an iron-clad regime of discipline and repression under the direct supervision and inspection of the military generals, to whom were leased sequestered plantations that had been become properties of the state.

Toussaint was attempting to fill the juridical void left by the absence of French constitutional law in the colony and to provide clear direction for Saint-Domingue but to do so under sovereign black leadership.[17] By creating the necessary administrative institutions and by reinforcing the social and economic structures of the colony, he sought to put Saint-Domingue back on the road to export crop production and, ultimately, to prosperity. Above all, with the powers invested in him by the Constitution of 1801, he aimed to protect the inviolability of general emancipation from the uncertain aims of the French government, whose own constitution now subjected Saint-Domingue to the specious device of "special laws." Indeed, the only function designated for the French government in Toussaint's constitution was that of sanctioning it. Even at that, it gave Toussaint the immediate freedom, "in the absence of such sanction and in the interests of reestablishing agricultural production and social order," to execute the constitution throughout the colony, which is to say, the entirety of Hispaniola.[18] Yet it was not a formal declaration of independence. Toussaint's final comment on it, pronounced in his public speech at the promulgation ceremony on July 8 was: "Forever live the French Republic *and* the colonial constitution."[19] As events proved, he could not have it both ways. Between Bonaparte and Louverture there were two constitutions; they were two heads of state.

Since 1797, the uncertain political climate in France after 9 Thermidor, coupled with the Directory's inability to defend unequivocally the principle of universal equality it had inherited from the revolutionary government of 1794 against the intrigues of a reactionary colonialist faction, had progressively pushed Toussaint toward a position of colonial self-determination. So long as France remained at war with Great Britain, Toussaint continued with impunity to enhance his power and move toward the realization of colonial sovereignty under his own autocratic governance. Even his forcible expulsion of Hédouville in 1798 went unchecked. By October 1801, however, with the preliminary peace agreements for the Treaty of Amiens concluded between Great Britain and France, Bonaparte could push ahead with his colonial design. He reiterated his policy: the inhabitants of Martinique and Sainte-Lucie as well as Ile-de-France would be advised that slavery would continue, while the blacks of Saint-Domingue should know that "whatever your origin or color, you are French; you are all free and are all equal before God and before the Republic."[20] Bonaparte's first objective with respect to Saint-Domingue, that of regaining metropolitan control over the colony, would therefore mean removing Toussaint and the colored generals from power and dismantling the Louverturian military-political structure, while at the same time reassuring the blacks of their freedom. The subsequent restoration of slavery and of the pre-1789 regime would be a matter of timing and pragmatism.

The plans for a military expedition were thus in the making even as Colonel Vincent arrived in Paris to deliver Toussaint's constitution to the First Consul. Although the constitution was not the determining factor in Napoleon's decision to send an expedition to restore French authority in Saint-Domingue, the revolutionary nature of the position Toussaint had taken and consecrated in his constitution intensified Bonaparte's resolve to deploy massive military force to destroy the black leadership and, ultimately, return the emancipated blacks to slavery. Saint-Domingue was, after all, the axis upon which France's colonial empire revolved, and Toussaint's constitution and the status it claimed for Saint-Domingue as a black self-governing polity were not only a direct challenge to Bonaparte's authority and to that of metropolitan France, they were close to being treasonable. But even more than that, coming from a former slave who had reached the summit of power and dared, as a black and as an equal, to confront the First Consul, the constitution struck a direct blow at the ontological foundations of white supremacy and, by its very existence, at the colonial foundations of the Atlantic colonial order.

Before the expedition set sail from Brest on December 14, 1801, Bonaparte gave its commander, General Victor-Emmanuel Leclerc, his brother-in-law, a set of secret instructions. The captain-general was first to deal with Toussaint and grant his every request in order to enter the colony and capture the strategic positions. The black generals, especially Toussaint Louverture, should be reassured of the good intentions of the metropolis. They should know that the 20,000 regular troops, the elite of the Napoleonic army; the 50-some ships and frigates;

and the division generals, brigade generals, and the whole array of lesser-ranking officers had come to Saint-Domingue simply to protect the colony from its enemies, preserve order, and suppress the few rebels that might emerge here and there. Above all, Leclerc should reassure Toussaint and the blacks that their freedom was safeguarded by France: "Never will the French nation place chains upon men whom she has recognized to be free."[21] These were Bonaparte's instructions, and the language was a masterpiece of duplicity. Leclerc had come to bring peace and security to the island, but at the point of bayonets. In Bonaparte's own threatening words, "Whosoever should refuse the authority of the captain-general shall be a traitor to the fatherland, upon whom the wrath of the Republic will descend just as swiftly as fire devours dry cane."[22]

So who were these enemies from whom Saint-Domingue needed protection? Was it not Toussaint's own army that had already defeated both the Spanish and the British occupation forces, thus driving from its borders the enemies of France? By now the negotiations between Great Britain and France had already established a temporary peace, as had the Treaty of Lunéville (signed in February 1801) on the continent. Toussaint's internal regime was one of authoritarian discipline and severe repression of resistance. Agricultural production and trade had resumed. The plantation labor regime was reinforced, and white owners were invited to reclaim their properties. Toussaint's policy clearly was to restore the colony's former prosperity. Why, therefore, should the government's new agent be accompanied by such massive military force merely to reintroduce metropolitan authority in the colony, which the French government had every right to do? Indeed, Toussaint's reaction upon first sighting the extent of the naval armada was that "we shall perish. All of France has come to overwhelm us."[23]

Bonaparte hoped the expedition would last only a few months. Toussaint would capitulate and be deported within two to three weeks. Should the governor refuse to submit, he would be declared a traitor and a war to the finish would be waged against him and his generals. Once captured, they would all be deported to France. With Louverture's army decapitated and its command structure dismantled, the black population would be left disoriented and demoralized, and ostensibly leaderless without recourse. Leclerc could thereupon proceed with the second stage of his mission, the general disarmament of the colonial population without regard to color. All of the blacks, once disarmed, would indiscriminately be thrown back into plantation agriculture and the colony would be restored to France. There was no question that Bonaparte intended to reinstate the pre-1789 regime of slavery and white supremacy throughout the empire. But it could not be done all at once, and much depended upon his ability to bring Saint-Domingue, the cornerstone—and the Achilles heel—of the empire, firmly under metropolitan control before restoring slavery where it had effectively been abolished.[24]

The actual events, as we know, did not unfold exactly as Bonaparte intended. The attempt to restore France's authority in the colony and ultimately to re-enslave the black population, backed by an initial array of more than 20,000 troops under leading generals of the Napoleonic army, escalated the struggle for black emancipation and transformed it into a war of independence. Deeply embedded in those early slave insurrections from 1791 to 1794 and in the successes of the slaves' struggle for emancipation lay buried the far greater historical burdens of independence-to-come, for the freedom they had fought so hard to win required that they defend it with every drop of their blood in a world that was not ready to accept the ending of slavery. One might even say that once the slaves had achieved their freedom, the struggle for independence was inevitable. Yet it was inevitable only to the extent that the restoration of slavery was inevitable. In the end, the revolution in France could not sustain one of its most revolutionary acts—the abolition of slavery. Faced with the realities of Leclerc's army, neither Toussaint nor the constitution would save the day. His visionary project of colonial autonomy and black self-government within the French empire had become irrelevant.

The course Toussaint had charted up to this point to preserve emancipation—creating a sovereign black state with himself at the helm—had taken him directly into the vortex of international politics and Atlantic capitalism. By engaging in international trade, negotiating treaties with the United States and Great Britain, driving the representatives of the metropolitan government out of the colony, and promulgating a constitution, Toussaint had already broken the bonds of colonialism and stepped into the world of nation-states. But what kind of a state was Saint-Domingue? And was it a nation? If so, what *kind* of a nation? Toussaint's concern had been to give Saint-Domingue an internal political economy that would revive agricultural output and enable it to recapture much of its former prosperity by competing in the international markets of the Atlantic economy. In pursuing this aim, Toussaint had created a military state in which the plantation complex was reinforced and white owners were courted and encouraged to reinvest in their properties. Sequestered plantations were leased to the high-ranking officers of Louverture's army, who also served as regional agricultural inspectors imposing military discipline and outright repression on the plantation laborers.[25] Toussaint's militarization of agriculture and the creation of a military landholding class empowered to implement his labor codes and mediate labor relations with force belied the individual liberties the black laborers understood to be concomitant with the abolition of slavery, notably the rights to become independent smallholders and to live their lives according to their own visions of freedom. When they rose in rebellion against the system in the north in October 1801, just months before Leclerc's landing, Toussaint's nephew, General Moïse, was held responsible. His opposition to Toussaint's agrarian policies was well known, and for his role in the rebellion and his challenge to the governor's supreme authority Toussaint arranged to have him shot. In sacrificing the most profound aspirations of the peasant masses to the strengthening of a state run by the military, Toussaint had in fact weakened the nation.

The civil war, too, had left particularly bitter wounds. Officers of the northern occupying army had committed horrible acts of reprisal against the mulatto faction in the south at the end of the war, in spite of the amnesty that Toussaint promised and his rhetorical insistence upon reconciliation. Dessalines was made military commander and therefore chief agricultural inspector of the south, where his military rule over the black laborers was notoriously cruel and his punishments were often harsher than any the blacks had ever known under the regime of Rigaud.[26] Such legacies cost Toussaint the support of the mulattoes and of popular African leaders like Lamour Dérance, who had fought with Rigaud during the civil war but retreated into the mountains rather than submit to Dessalines's command. At the head of independent bands of followers numbering in their thousands, Dérance initially welcomed Leclerc's army when Rigaud, who had been exiled by Toussaint at the close of the civil war, returned from France with the expedition to undermine support for the black general.[27]

In the process of shaping the emergent nation, Toussaint had alienated or removed those elements of society whose support he would need most at the time of Leclerc's landing. All the while he relied on his personal authority and the army, and by 1801, the constitution, to consolidate the state. Having taken charge of Saint-Domingue, he led the colony as if it were independent. In a sense it was (as long as France remained at war), although the society was critically fractured from within. This largely explains why Toussaint and his most loyal generals, notably Dessalines in the west and Christophe and Maurepas in the north, failed to do much more than hold out as long as possible during the first weeks after Leclerc's landing despite staunch defensive combat. But the war ahead would not be just an anticolonial struggle against metropolitan rule or against an invading army. It would become a total war against slavery that had to be fought with revolutionary measures by an entire nation in arms. No other objective than full independence could save them from slavery. And yet it is questionable whether Toussaint fully grasped the immediate imperatives facing him as Leclerc's army began to attack.[28] It was in the context of a fundamental crisis of leadership that the initial resistance to Leclerc was waged.

The War of Independence and Crisis of Leadership

A detailed account of the military engagements from the arrival of the expedition in February 1802 until the deportation of Toussaint in June the same year need not concern us here. What is important are the events during this critical period that expose the crisis of leadership. Of some significance in this respect is the fact that Christophe, Toussaint's brigade general in command at Cap-Français, not Toussaint himself, entered into negotiations with Leclerc when he arrived off the harbor on February 3. Instinctively, Christophe refused entry to the captain-general and his troops, and the following day he issued orders to evacuate the city and burn it to the ground. It was a bold and spectacular act of resistance, but Christophe made the decision alone, without direct orders from Toussaint (who at the time was still in the Spanish part of the island) and ironically after having burned the city, he opened it up to Leclerc. Other key generals of Louverture's army, with the notable exceptions of Dessalines in the west and Maurepas in the north, were left to vacillate. In spite of Toussaint's feverish attempts to deliver orders (all of which were intercepted) instructing his officers to employ scorched-earth tactics and take the resistance to the hills, a good number of his generals capitulated one after the other in the first weeks of February. The entire South Province was lost with the capitulation of its commander, General Laplume. With the capitulations of Toussaint's brother, Paul Louverture, who was in command at Santo Domingo, and that of the mulatto general Augustin Clervaux at Santiago, the entire eastern part of the island fell into French hands. While Christophe and Maurepas continued (more or less) to neutralize French attacks in the north and Dessalines shouldered the resistance in the west, roughly 8,000 of Toussaint's troops, almost half of his entire army, were by now under Leclerc's orders.

Yet during these first weeks, French losses were equally high, with 2,000 French troops already in hospital, of whom 1,500 were sick and another 500 were wounded. Within another week, the numbers rose to 2,000 sick, 1,500 wounded, and 600 dead in combat. Leclerc would need another 12,000 troops in addition to those already promised by Bonaparte if he was to complete his instructions.[29] By the end of April, nearly three months after his first attack, when the major objectives of the expedition should have been accomplished, a full one-third of Leclerc's initial army was incapacitated, not counting combat casualties, prompting the captain-general to speak of the need for at least 25,000 combat troops to consolidate his position in the north and west. "The government must not think of the costs it will need to incur in order to secure the world's prime colony and to keep those it already has in the Caribbean," he wrote to the First Consul, "for it is here, at this moment, that the question of whether Europe will be able to maintain colonies in the West Indies will be determined."[30] These were the stakes.

And yet the first three months ended in stalemate. At the end of April, when Toussaint could have begun to turn the French losses to his own advantage, even before the onset of yellow fever, he chose to negotiate with Leclerc, who at the beginning of May offered Toussaint and his generals full amnesty, asylum for Toussaint at a place of his choice within the colony, and the maintenance of general emancipation. The nineteenth-century Haitian historian Beaubrun Ardouin was particularly insightful with regard to Toussaint's potential for continuing the war at this point and (had Toussaint done so) for perhaps even avoiding the fratricidal strife that would accompany it for nearly another two years. Toussaint's position in the north was at the epicenter of the armed resistance that had been conducted since early March by mainly African insurgent leaders such as Sans-Souci, Petit-Noël Prieur, Sylla, and the fiercely independent Macaya, who held strategic positions across the mountainous interior at Limbé, Port-Margot, Dondon, Grande-Rivière, and particularly Plaisance. Toussaint maintained contact with them, and they all held commanding positions in his army: Sans-Souci was colonel and commander of the Grande-Rivière cordon; Sylla was battalion leader and commander at Mapou, in Plaisance; Petit-Noël Prieur, also a colonel in Toussaint's army, held military posts at Dondon and La Souffrière, while Macaya held Limbé and Acul.[31] All were able easily to mobilize the plantation laborers in these districts and, in Ardouin's opinion, they could have been under Toussaint's active command had he chosen to continue the war.[32] He did not.

At this point, Christophe, the first to resist Leclerc, became also the first to desert Toussaint. Tired of living like a rebel in the mountains, he accepted Leclerc's guarantees of good faith, the maintenance of his rank, and a specious promise that general emancipation would not be touched. With Christophe's defection, another 1,500 colonial troops as well as 4,000–5,000 armed plantation workers were delivered to Leclerc. Two days later, Toussaint accepted Leclerc's offer of amnesty and asylum, leaving Dessalines effectively isolated and with little alternative but to submit as well. By May 7, 1802, the formidable triumvirate of the black revolutionary army, Toussaint Louverture, Henri Christophe, and Jean-Jacques Dessalines, were in the hands of Leclerc. The rank and file of Louverture's army and the mass of the population were thus left to their own initiatives—and their own political wisdom—to organize and ultimately sustain the resistance as Leclerc attempted in early July to carry out the second phase of his instructions, a general disarmament of the population.

From this point on, the struggle for independence was fought from opposing camps. In the north, the African armies of Sans-Souci, Noël-Prieur, Sylla, and Macaya continued the insurgency in the form of guerilla warfare. Because their military posts had been under the jurisdiction of Christophe, who commanded the entire northern cordon, they all would have found themselves in Leclerc's army when Christophe defected were it not for their implacable refusal to submit. Sans-Souci was recognized as commander-general of the independent armies of the north. In the west, the core of the insurgency was under the command of the African leader Lamour Dérance.

He had initially supported Leclerc, but after witnessing Leclerc's deportation of Rigaud and other mulatto officers who had accompanied the expedition, he reorganized his troops in the mountains outside Léogane and Jacmel to combat the French. Within months they were 5,000 strong. In the south, resistance took the form of clandestine individual actions and collective conspiracies to revolt.[33] In their fierce determination not to be re-enslaved, the people and their own leaders, the foundation of the emerging Haitian nation, were pitted against both the French troops and the black and colored generals, whose leadership had thus far failed. In fact, by the end of July and early August, when news of Bonaparte's restoration of slavery in Guadeloupe had reached Saint-Domingue and when yellow fever was at a peak—that is, at the very moment when a combined offensive of popular insurrectionary forces and colonial troops under the command of Toussaint's regular army officers could have been decisive—the leading generals were fighting to crush the popular resistance.

Yet it was the strategies and instincts of the popular leadership, for the most part African, that would have allowed Toussaint to mount a cohesive resistance to Leclerc's forces in the first weeks of the expedition. Even Christophe acknowledged as much to the French general Pamphile Lacroix in July, when news of the restoration of slavery in Guadeloupe had transformed the popular resistance to Leclerc's army into a life-and-death struggle against slavery. When Lacroix asked him why, despite the influence he held over the blacks in the North, he could not manage to have Sans-Souci captured and delivered, Christophe spoke to the heart of the matter:

> If Sans-Souci were a soldier, I could flatter myself I would capture him, but he is an unpredictable and cruel brigand, who, without conscience, kills those whom he suspects. He knows how to flee and to cover his retreat with desert. He carries out his operations more effectively than we did at the time of your landing. If, instead of fighting you in open battle, our method of resistance had been to retreat and to raise the blacks by striking them with terror, you would never have been able to get to us. Old Toussaint kept saying so; no one wanted to believe him. We had the arms, but we were too vain to use them in such a way, and lost. These new insurgents appear to have adopted Toussaint's system: if they persist, we will have great difficulty in quelling them.[34]

These were the tactics and strategies the slave leaders had used at the outset of the revolution in 1791, when their task at hand had been to burn down the plantations and overthrow slavery. At the time of Leclerc's landing, hardened by ten years of armed struggle to sustain their freedom, the African masses and their leaders constituted the bedrock of Toussaint's forces because even though they were alienated by Toussaint's constitutional regime, they faced an expeditionary army that had come to restore slavery. And although Toussaint had the active support of most of the African leaders during the first couple months of the resistance, their support for his generals, especially Christophe and Dessalines, was far from certain. Dessalines had been notoriously brutal as agricultural inspector for the south, and it was he that Leclerc used in particular to carry out his most odious exactions against those who resisted his disarmament campaign. Leclerc called him the "butcher of the blacks."[35] The personal rivalry and hatred between Sans-Souci and Christophe in the north, which predated the war for independence, was deepened by the betrayal and resentment Sans-Souci felt when Christophe chose to join Leclerc and fight against him.[36] While they were in the service of Leclerc, both Christophe and Dessalines pursued an unrelenting war against these independent African leaders. Then, after they abandoned Leclerc in October 1802 to rejoin the independence movement and popular resistance was at its peak, they continued to harass, betray, and finally liquidate rather than accommodate those independent African leaders who refused to submit to the supreme authority of Dessalines as commander-in-chief of an amalgamated independence army.

The crisis of leadership that first appeared under Toussaint's governance and that characterized the military situation at the outset of the war against Leclerc had degenerated by the end of the war into a crisis of personal and political power struggles, all the more easily once Toussaint Louverture was out of the picture. In the end, the crisis of leadership was resolved by the implacable determination of the people and their own leaders never again to be enslaved. But the struggle for independence had been waged from opposing camps, and so, too, would be the unfolding struggle to define the nation once independence was won in 1804. The war bequeathed dire legacies that left the country critically fragmented as it faced the Herculean post-independence tasks of reconciliation and nation-building.

Notes

1. Hilary Beckles, "Divided to the Vein: The Problem of Race, Colour and Class Conflict in Haitian Nation-Building, 1804–1820," in *Caribbean Freedom: Economy and Society from Emancipation to the Present*, ed. Hilary Beckles and Verene Shepherd (Princeton: Markus Wiener, 1996), 494.

2. On this point, see Michel-Rolph Trouillot, "The Haitian Revolution as 'Unthinkable History': From Planters' Journals to Academia," *Journal of Caribbean History* 25, nos. 1/2 (1993): 81–99.

3. Among other factors that influenced the commissioners' decision to push ahead with their emancipation proclamations during the summer of 1793 were the looming threat of a British invasion, counterrevolutionary agitation, and the desire to win over the rebel slave leaders, notably Jean-François, Biassou, and Toussaint Louverture, who were fighting under the banner of Spain at that point. For a fuller discussion of the progressive

steps taken by the commissioners to achieve general emancipation throughout Saint-Domingue, see Robert L. Stein, *Léger-Félicité Sonthonax: The Lost Sentinel of the Republic* (London: Associated University Presses, 1985), 78–95. See also Carolyn Fick, "The French Revolution in Saint Domingue: A Triumph or a Failure?" in *A Turbulent Time: The French Revolution and the Greater Caribbean*, ed. David Barry Gaspar and David Patrick Geggus (Bloomington: Indiana University Press, 1997), 65–67.

4. The February 4, 1794, law did not provide any constitutional guidelines for assimilating the colonies and the emancipated slaves into the Republic. It merely stated that slavery was abolished in all French territory and that "all men, without distinction of color, residing in the colonies, are French citizens and will enjoy all of the rights [thereof] guaranteed by the Constitution." Quoted in French in Florence Gauthier, "Le rôle de la députation de Saint-Domingue dans l'abolition de l'esclavage," in *Les abolitions de l'esclavage: de L.F. Sonthonax à V. Schoelcher, 1793 1794 1848*, ed. Marcel Dorigny (Paris: Presses Universitaires de Vincennes/UNESCO, 1995), 205. (My translation; unless otherwise noted, all other translations from the French are mine.)

5. In Jouda Guetata, "Le refus d'application de la constitution de l'an 3 à Saint-Domingue, 1795–1797," in *Périssent les colonies plutôt qu'un principe! Contributions à l'histoire de l'abolition de l'esclavage, 1789–1804*, ed. Florence Gauthier (Paris: Société des études robespierristes, 2002), 81.

6. Guetata, "Le refus d'application de la constitution."

7. Guetata, "Le refus d'application de la constitution," 81–83. See also Bernard Gainot, "La constitutionnalisation de la liberté générale sous le Directoire (1795–1800)"; and Florence Gauthier, "Le rôle," in *Les abolitions de l'esclavage: de L.F. Sonthonax à V. Schoelcher, 1793 1794 1848*, ed. Marcel Dorigny (Paris: Presses Universitaires de Vincennes/UNESCO, 1995), 213–229 and 199–211, respectively.

8. Guetata, "Le refus d'application de la constitution," 87–90.

9. Laurent Dubois, *A Colony of Citizens: Revolution & Slave Emancipation in the French Caribbean, 1787–1804* (Chapel Hill: University of North Carolina Press, 2004), 299. For a full discussion of the dimensions of political citizenship that it prescribed, essentially leaving the black plantation laborers disenfranchized, see 299–304. See also Gainot, "La constitutionnalisation," 222–223.

10. Excerpts from the letter are cited in C. L. R. James, *The Black Jacobins: Toussaint L'Ouverture and the San Domingo Revolution* (1938; repr., New York: Vintage, 1963), 195–197.

11. Quoted in James, *The Black Jacobins*, 197 (emphasis in the original).

12. Quoted in Claude Moïse, *Constitutions et luttes de pouvoir en Haïti (1804–1987)*, 2 vols. (Montreal: CIDIHCA, 1988), 1:frontispiece.

13. Quoted in Thierry Lentz, "Bonaparte, Haïti et l'échec colonial du régime consulaire," in *Haïti, première république noire*, ed. Marcel Dorigny (Saint-Denis/Paris: Société Française d'Histoire d'Outre-Mer/Association Pour l'Étude de la Colonisation Européenne, 2003), 47–48.

14. Quoted in Lentz, "Bonaparte," 46–47. See also Jean-Marcel Champion, "30 Floréal an X: le rétablissement de l'esclavage par Bonaparte," in *Les abolitions de l'esclavage: de L.F. Sonthonax à V. Schoelcher, 1793 1794 1848*, ed. Marcel Dorigny (Paris: Presses Universitaires de Vincennes/UNESCO, 1995), 265–271.

15. In Claude Moïse, *Le projet national de Toussaint Louverture et la Constitution de 1801* (Montreal: CIDIHCA, 2001), 103 (article 1).

16. In Moïse, *Le projet national*, 104 (article 3).

17. "Law," Toussaint expounded, was "the guiding instrument [*la boussole*] for all citizens, and before the law all must succumb." In Moïse, *Le projet national*, 126.

18. In Moïse, *Le projet national*, 121–122 (article 77).

19. In Moïse, *Le projet national*, 127 (my emphasis).

20. Quoted in Champion, "30 Floréal an X," 267–268. Also see Lentz, "Bonaparte, Haïti et l'échec," in *Haïti, première république noire*, ed. Marcel Dorigny (Saint-Denis/Paris: Société Française d'Histoire d'Outre-Mer/Association Pour l'Étude de la Colonisation Européenne, 2003), 52.

21. In V.-E. Leclerc, *Lettres du Général Leclerc, commandant en chef de l'armée de Saint-Domingue en 1802*, ed. P. Roussier (Paris: E. Leroux, 1937), 269.

22. In Leclerc, *Lettres du Général Leclerc*, nos. 13 and 14, pp. 62–65.

23. Quoted in James, *Black Jacobins*, 288.

24. For the time being, Bonaparte maintained the legal status quo while proceeding under the auspices of the Leclerc expedition to prepare for the restoration of slavery in Saint-Domingue. His law of May 20, 1802 (30 floréal an X), which was issued four months into the Leclerc expedition and was promulgated—not coincidentally—on the same day as the Treaty of Amiens, declared the maintenance (not the reestablishment) of slavery in those islands where slavery had never effectively been abolished because of British wartime occupation. Therefore, slavery in Martinique, Ile-de-France, and Réunion would continue (contrary to the February 4, 1794, law) in conformity with pre-1789 law. The slave trade would be reopened and the colonial regimes would be subjected for the next ten years to new laws that the government might deem appropriate and that would supersede all previous ones, including that of February 4, 1794. Of note is the total absence of any reference to Saint-Domingue, Guadeloupe, or Guyana, where the regime of general emancipation had been effective since February 4, 1794. Bonaparte did, however, insert a reference in his instructions to Leclerc to the effect that "the blacks of Saint-Domingue shall continue to live as those in Guadeloupe." See Leclerc, *Lettres du Général Leclerc*, 269. It was only a question of time, however, before General Richepanse proclaimed slavery reestablished in Guadeloupe in July 1802. The law was issued five months after Leclerc's expedition left from Brest with Bonaparte's secret instructions to arrest and deport Toussaint Louverture, by which time he should have dismantled the political and military institutions put in place by the black leader, disarmed the entire colored population, and destroyed the black revolution. See Champion, "30 Floréal an X," 265–266. On the constitutional status of the February 4, 1794, law under the consular regime, see Yves Benot, *La démence coloniale sous Napoléon* (Paris: La Découverte, 1992), 21.

25. On the role of the military in implementing labor regulations and in running the daily lives of the workers, see Carolyn Fick, "Emancipation in Haiti: From Plantation Labour to Peasant Proprietorship," *Slavery & Abolition* 21, no. 2 (August 2000): 11–40. Dessalines, for his part, rented some thirty sugar plantations that yielded roughly 100,000 francs annually, while Christophe was believed to be worth close to $250,000 in personal wealth. See Mats Lundahl, "Toussaint Louverture and the War Economy of Saint Domingue, 1796–1802," in *Caribbean Freedom: Economy and Society*

from Emancipation to the Present, ed. Hilary Beckles and Verene Shepherd (Princeton: Markus Wiener, 1996), 6.

26. Fick, *Making of Haiti: The Saint Domingue Revolution from Below* (Nashville: University of Tennessee Press, 1990), 205, 324nn1–2.

27. A full biographical sketch of Lamour Dérance is presented in *Dictionnaire de la Révolution Haïtienne*, ed. Claude Moïse (Montreal: CIDIHCA and Les Éditions Images, 2003), 200–204.

28. C. L. R. James ascribes Toussaint's inability to recognize the imperatives of the situation to his political moderation and trust in the values of the French Revolution; see *Black Jacobins*, 289–291, 300, 310. Because of this, he failed to organize his forces to meet the type of war that Leclerc had brought to the colony. In a sense, history had passed him by.

29. In Fick, *Making of Haiti*, 212, 325nn22–24.

30. Leclerc, *Lettres du Général Leclerc*, 110 (February 27, 1802).

31. See in particular the articles on Makaya and Sans-Souci in *Dictionnaire de la Révolution Haïtienne*, 221–224, 288–291.

32. Beaubrun Ardouin, *Études sur l'histoire d'Haïti* [1853–1860], 11 vols., ed. François Dalencour (Port-au-Prince, 1958), vol. 5, book 6, 31. See also Leclerc, *Lettres du Général Leclerc*, 87 (February 15, 1802). On Toussaint's relations with these African leaders after the arrival of the expedition and before his capitulation, particularly during the month of March, see Claude B. Auguste and Marcel B. Auguste, *L'Expédition Leclerc 1801–1803* (Port-au-Prince: Henri Deschamps, 1985), 143–167.

33. On the popular movements of resistance in the south, see Fick, *Making of Haiti*, 215–226.

34. Cited in Général Pamphile de Lacroix, *La Révolution en Haïti*, ed. Pierre Pluchon (Paris: Karthala, 1995), 366–367.

35. Leclerc, *Lettres du Général Leclerc*, 230–231 (September 16, 1802).

36. On the personal war between Christophe and Sans-Souci, see Michel-Rolph Trouillot, *Silencing the Past: Power and the Production of History* (Boston: Beacon Press, 1995).

PART THREE

REVERBERATIONS

THE FRENCH REVOLUTION'S OTHER ISLAND

Jeremy D. Popkin

ISTORIANS HAVE OFTEN UNDERLINED THE WORLDWIDE IMPACT OF THE HAITIAN REVOLUTION, CITING ITS EFFECTS IN THE CARIBBEAN, THE FEAR IT CAUSED IN THE SOUTHERN UNITED STATES, ITS role in inspiring revolts against Spanish colonial rule in Central and South America, and its symbolic importance in world history. On this list, there is usually one curious blind spot: one rarely sees any discussion of the movement's importance for metropolitan France during the revolution.[1] It would be peculiar indeed if the destruction of the most productive colonial economy in the Americas and the first major abolition of African slavery had had no effects in the metropole of the empire in which they occurred. In fact, from the very start of the French Revolution, the existence of the slave colonies forced its leaders to confront the question of whether the revolution's promises of liberty and equality were truly universal, applying to people of all races, or whether they applied only to whites. From 1791 onward, when the great slave insurrection that would eventually lead to the island's independence broke out, the question of "who lost Saint-Domingue" bedeviled revolutionary politics, stoking the tensions that made its factional struggles so deadly and costing the lives of thousands of troops sent to maintain French rule as well as those of a number of generals, politicians, and publicists in France itself.

One reason we hear relatively little about the impact of colonial events on revolutionary France is that historians of the French Revolution continue to minimize or even ignore the revolution's colonial dimension. The tendency of historians to credit the revolutionaries for creating the first modern nation-state diverts attention from the fact that even in its radical republican phase, that nation-state also remained the center of an imperial system. This tendency to ignore France's colonial dimension is also encouraged because the revolution took place at a moment when the overseas empire seemed to have been reduced to geographic insignificance by comparison with what it had been before 1763 and what it would be by the end of the nineteenth century.

Although the revolutionary-era empire was admittedly small in geographic extent, France's colonies, especially the Caribbean sugar islands, were central to its economy. They loomed large in France's relations with the other European imperial powers, and they were the main reason why the country made the expensive effort to maintain a significant navy. A late-nineteenth-century historian, writing at the height of the "scramble for Africa," claimed that "it would not be an exaggeration to say that the colonial empire of 1789 was more important than that of today in international value."[2] The colonies involved France in the international nexus of slavery, and the issues this involvement posed fueled the interest that made Raynal's *Histoire des deux Indes* one of the great best sellers of the late eighteenth century. It might be going too far to put Saint-Domingue's relationship to France on the same level as Ireland's much closer relationship to England, but it is certainly worth remembering that revolutionary France had an "other island."

Understanding the impact of colonial events in the French metropole during the revolutionary era requires a comprehension of the dynamics of intra-imperial relationships of the sort that the sociologist Arthur Stinchcombe has attempted to construct in his *Sugar Island Slavery in the Age of Enlightenment*.[3] Overseas colonies, and Saint-Domingue in particular, were not simply provinces that happened to be separated from the metropole by a stretch of salt water. The sugar islands differed from their mother countries in every respect: in climate, in the racial composition of their population, and above all because of the "peculiar institution" of slavery that linked them to the rest of the New World but separated them from Europe. As a result, the ruling elites of colonial societies had their own interests that were different from those of their opposite numbers in the metropoles. At the same time, the existence of the colonial relationship allowed the colonists to influence decisions in the metropole in ways that foreigners could not. From the metropolitan point of view, the existence of the colonies was justified by the benefits they provided to the mother country, a utilitarian criterion that made their status very different from that of the European provinces of the kingdom. This unequal relationship was institutionalized in laws such as the Exclusif, the French navigation act that required the colonists to buy and sell only with the metropole, and in the royal administration's largely discretionary power in governing the colonies. The metropolitan groups that had strong interests in the colonies, notably the merchants engaged in colonial trade, had agendas that were not necessarily the same as those of the colonists. Given the sharp difference in outlook between the colonists and the metropole, conflict was inherent in their relationship.[4]

Revolutionary France confronted these issues more sharply than the pre-revolutionary monarchy because it was the modern world's first version of a constitutional or republican empire. Before 1789, Louis XVI, like other European monarchs, could rule over territories with widely differing legal systems and social structures without any feeling of contradiction. The adoption of the Declaration of the Rights of Man and Citizen in 1789 and the claim that the rights enumerated in that document were derived from human nature itself and therefore ought to apply uniformly throughout the nation radically changed the situation. From the beginning to the end of the revolutionary period, French political elites had to ask themselves whether a nation of rights-bearing citizens could govern overseas territories, especially if those territories were slave societies.

Colonial issues began to impact politics in France even before the summoning of the Estates-General with Jacques-Pierre Brissot's formation of the famous Société des Amis des Noirs in February 1788 and the formation of its proslavery counterpart, the Comité colonial de Saint-Domingue, later that year. As Catherine Duprat and Marcel Dorigny have emphasized, the Amis des Noirs was the incubator of the revolution's new political culture. Participation in it was, for many members, "a political apprenticeship without precedent in France at the time," as Dorigny has written.[5] It was the first group in France to propose reforms based on the principle of natural rights, and its debates had obvious implications for the metropole as well as for the colonies. The convocation of the Estates General forced an immediate decision about whether the slave colonies were part of the nation and thus deserving of representation in its assembly. The minutes of the Société des Amis des Noirs, recently published by Marcel Dorigny and Bernard Gainot, and corresponding documents from the proslavery camp make it possible to follow this debate, which involved many of the most prominent Patriot leaders, including Mirabeau, Condorcet, and (above all) Brissot, who was destined to become the revolutionary leader most identified with opposition to racial inequality.

Brissot pointed out as early as April 1789 the danger that the admission of deputies from the colonies would pose to "the unfortunate blacks," and after Necker mentioned the slavery issue in his inaugural discourse on May 5, 1789, the Société des Amis des Noirs launched a pamphlet exchange about his proposals.[6] A group of would-be representatives for Saint-Domingue succeeded in winning provisional acceptance from the Third Estate and joined in the Tennis Court Oath on June 20, 1789, but their status became the subject of a heated debate that occupied the newly formed National Assembly for three days during the tense interval between the king's acceptance of its claims on June 27 and the storming of the Bastille on July 14, 1789.[7] The Saint-Domingue deputies demanded a number of seats proportional to the colony's population, in the figure for which they included not only the whites but also the free colored population, who had been excluded from participation in the choice of deputies, and the black slaves. On June 27, several speakers explicitly objected to granting the white colonists the right to represent the rest of the colonial population. The duc de la Rochefoucauld referred to the antislavery bill then being considered by the British Parliament, mentioned the work of the Société des Amis des Noirs, and asked that "the Assembly debate freedom for the blacks before completing its work."[8] At this critical moment, when the colonial deputies had not yet been seated, a snap vote might have committed the assembly to an epochal decision by insisting that a free nation could not have slave colonies. But the discussion was suddenly interrupted by the arrival in the hall of the remaining noble and clergy deputies, obeying Louis XVI's injunction to accept the union of the three orders and providing a dramatic example of how colonial and domestic issues were to interfere with each other throughout the revolution.

The debate about Saint-Domingue resumed on July 3, when Mirabeau delivered his famous line to the effect that if the colonists were given deputies on the basis of their slaves, French provinces should be allowed to count their horses and mules. Equally significant for the future course of the revolution, however, voices were raised insisting that a viable relationship between the metropole and its overseas territories required the acceptance of differences between them. Carefully avoiding the word "slavery," Gouy d'Arsy, leader of the self-proclaimed Saint-Domingue deputies, insisted that "Saint-Domingue should not be compared to the provinces of the kingdom. The colony is very distant; it is isolated; the soil, the inhabitants, the method of farming, the resources, everything there is different." The deputy from Bordeaux, Pierre-Paul Nairac, objected that "the colonies should not be considered a part of the *patrie*. The colonies are provinces that are dependencies of it." The merchant interests he represented feared that colonial deputies would try to abolish the trade laws that made the colonies profitable to the metropole. The assembly's final vote was an awkward compromise: Saint-Domingue was limited to six deputies instead of the twenty it had requested or the twelve that the *comité de vérification* had suggested as an alternative. However, the assembly accepted the principle of representation for whites only and dropped the idea of committing itself to debate the issue of slavery.[9]

These debates of June 27 and July 3–4, 1789, show that the problem of reconciling France's new political principles with the existence of the empire and slavery preoccupied the revolutionaries during the movement's foundational moments. It is true that after this initial battle, the defenders of colonial slavery in the National Assembly managed to prevent any further legislative debate on the issue. When La Rochefoucauld suggested the abolition of slavery during the tumultuous session on the night of August 4, 1789, his proposition was ignored. Nevertheless, the contradiction between the revolution's fundamental postulates and the institution of slavery was too obvious to be overlooked. In the midst of the assembly's debate about the

Declaration of Rights, Mirabeau's *Courrier de Provence* published an article claiming that passage of the document would necessarily imply abolition: "What [the National Assembly] will say to the blacks, what it will say to the planters, what it will say to the whole of Europe, is that there are not and cannot be in France, or in any other land subject to French laws, any men other than *free men*, other than *men equal to each other*."[10]

Warding off these consequences required a constant mobilization on the part of the defenders of slavery and racial hierarchy. The Club Massiac, formed in August 1789 to defend slavery in the colonies, became a model for a kind of modern politics as important as that furnished by the Amis des Noirs, namely the single-issue lobbying group.[11] Whereas the Amis des Noirs operated in public, the Club Massiac understood that it would have more success if it stayed out of the limelight, cultivating contacts with ministerial officials, making sure that friendly legislators dominated the assembly's committee on colonial issues, and arranging for others, such as the chambers of commerce of France's port cities, to put forward its arguments instead of speaking in its own name. Despite the seemingly conclusive logic of arguments such as Mirabeau's, the defenders of slavery were not lacking in persuasive assertions of their own. A pamphlet published in early 1792 by the Cercle social, a club sympathetic to the principle of gradual emancipation, nevertheless accepted much of the proslavery case. To attempt abolition immediately, the author argued, would amount to abandoning the French colonies. "This would expose France to lose a debt of around 300 million [livres]; it would expose the colonies to invasion by foreigners who would impose harsh laws on us regarding the price of colonial goods, and deprive us of a market for our manufactures." The principles of the Declaration of Rights should indeed govern "all the individuals composing the empire," but they could not be abruptly implemented in the colonies "without violating the rights of citizens, rights equally guaranteed by the constitution."[12]

For the first two years of the revolution, the proslavery lobby was the most successful conservative force in France. While the National Assembly trimmed the king's powers, abolished the nobility altogether, and completely restructured the church, it left colonial slavery untouched. The colonial lobby's success was one of the first demonstrations in modern politics of how a small but wealthy and well-connected group with a focused agenda could effectively defend its interests in a parliamentary system. The slaveholders benefited also from the hesitancy of the abolitionist forces. Despite their reputation for principled intransigence, the Amis des Noirs had never really endorsed immediate emancipation. They had always asserted that some scheme could be found for reconciling the interests of slaves with those of the colonial planters and the metropolitan interests tied to the colonial system. By the fall of 1789, the Amis des Noirs were further distracted by their desire to work with the representatives of the free colored group in the colonies, led by the wealthy Saint-Domingue planter Julien Raimond, who, like many other members of this group, was himself a slave-owner. This group had addressed the Constituent Assembly on October 22, 1789, and it met with the Société des Amis des Noirs a month later, successfully urging that group to make the free colored issue its first priority and to put issues more directly related to slavery on the back burner.[13] Political realism appeared to favor this course, but it confused the issues to the point where Brissot, founder of the Amis des Noirs, would find himself arguing, in December 1791, that the free coloreds should be granted their rights because arming them was the most effective way of defending slavery.[14]

Until 1792, the issue of rights for free people of color in the colonies thus came to overshadow the questions of abolishing the slave trade and outlawing slavery itself. The Club Massiac succeeded in fending off the supporters of free colored rights until news of the brutal execution of the free colored insurrectionist Vincent Ogé reached France in early 1791. The Jacobin clubs launched a petition campaign for the rights of this group, generating perhaps the most broad-based movement around a colonial issue in the entire revolutionary decade,[15] and the assembly, after one of its most emotional debates, passed the decree of May 15, 1791, granting political rights to a fraction of the free colored population in the colonies.[16] In France itself, this debate was quickly overshadowed by the crisis caused by the king's flight to Varennes on June 20, 1791, which greatly intensified fears about the dangers to the revolution. The conservative backlash after Varennes allowed the proslavery forces to regroup and to benefit from the strategic position of their most powerful ally, Barnave, who was also the chief spokesman for the Feuillant group's strategy of maintaining the king's power within the new constitutional system as a protection against radicalism. On September 24, 1791, during the final revisions of the constitution, the proslavery forces succeeded in overturning the May vote and writing the white colonists' authority to define the rights of nonwhites into the new constitution.[17]

On paper, the colonial proslavery lobby had succeeded in its aim of getting the assembly to define the French empire as a differentiated space whose elements could have distinctive institutions, like the states of the new American republic. In exchange, the colonists had accepted the continuation of special regulations on colonial trade; in order to maintain a proslavery alliance with trading interests in France, they were willing to endorse the utilitarian notion that the colonies existed for the economic benefit of the metropole.[18] Unbeknownst to the deputies in Paris, however, the victory in September 1791 came too late: by the time it had been achieved, the slave insurrection in the island's North Province and the almost-simultaneous insurrection of the free colored population in parts of the west had been under way for a month. Once news of the insurrections did reach France at the end of October 1791, it completely changed the debate there about the colonial situation. For the rest of the revolutionary period, the abstract issue of whether the rights of man extended to the colonies would be inextricably linked to the explosive question of responsibility for the "disasters" afflicting Saint-Domingue.

In December 1791, just four months after the beginning of the Saint-Domingue insurrection, Edward Gibbon reported to his friend Lord Sheffield from his Swiss exile in Lausanne that "a Count d'Argout has just left us who possessed ten thousand a year in the island of St. Domingo, he is utterly burnt and ruined."[19] Not only the émigré count's life but that of the whole of France was sharply affected by events in the colony. The burning of the plantations in the island's North Province was the most spectacular act of physical destruction that had occurred since the outbreak of the revolution; the burning of the island's major city, Cap-Français, in June 1793 reinforced the perception that Saint-Domingue was suffering a veritable apocalypse. One cannot help thinking that events in Saint-Domingue had a good deal to do with creating the cliché of the revolution as a welter of *feu et flamme*, imagery that hardly reflected conditions in the metropole but that had a certain basis in reality in the colony.

Although we lack any comprehensive study of the subject, the shock to the French economy must also have been tremendous. Colonial trade had continued to boom during the first years of the revolution, but overnight the flow of sugar and coffee to the metropole was abruptly cut off, and with it France's lucrative re-export trade to other European markets. Considering that the entire colonial economy depended on credit from the mother country, there must have been thousands of lenders who suddenly realized that they had little chance of ever being repaid. The Club Massiac had no trouble rousing France's business circles to inundate the Legislative Assembly with demands for action. A typical letter from the *tribunal de commerce* of Orléans read, "From every part of the empire, there rises a cry, 'our colonies are ravaged, French trade is ruined.'"[20]

The political effects in France of the news of the insurrection were equally important, setting off a decade-long struggle over where to place the blame for the disaster. The first reports from Saint-Domingue arrived at a critical moment. In the newly elected Legislative Assembly, Jacobin radicals like Brissot were pushing for a preventive war against the foreign powers that were sheltering noble émigrés and threatening, in the Pillnitz declaration issued in August 1791, to take action on the king's behalf. Suddenly, reports arrived from the other side of the Atlantic that confirmed the radicals' worst fears: an outbreak of violence that the royally appointed local authorities, all of them nobles, seemed suspiciously unable to control and that provided an opening for foreign powers to involve themselves in French affairs, since the Colonial Assembly in Saint-Domingue had appealed to Jamaica and the Spanish in the Caribbean for aid before notifying Paris. Furthermore, the revolt threatened to force a diversion of French troops to the Caribbean at a moment when the Jacobin war hawks wanted them deployed on the Rhine. Brissot immediately voiced a suspicion that would poison French politics for years to come: "Don't we have here one branch of a great plan?"[21]

Fears of conspiracy had pervaded revolutionary politics since the movement's inception, but aside from the king's abortive flight to Varennes, the Saint-Domingue uprising was the most impressive piece of evidence of its reality. In a December 1791 speech, Brissot pointed out that the black revolt had started on August 22, 1791: "This date is full of meaning: they had just learned of the king's flight. Was it an accident that favored this rapprochement so favorable to the factious, of that flight so advantageous for them, of that so opportune revolt; or rather, didn't the news of the flight accelerate the revolt?"[22] The following month, Brissot gave his celebrated speech demanding a declaration of war against Austria, arguing that war would expose the counterrevolutionary plot and lead to its defeat. The news of the Saint-Domingue revolt thus provided French radicals with a crucial argument for their program of pushing the revolution at home forward by a preemptive strike against its enemies.

Just as the Saint-Domingue revolt initially helped Brissot defeat his Feuillant opponents and push France into war, the island's situation would continue to serve as a powerful tool in subsequent revolutionary political confrontations. In 1793, a strange alliance of "patriotic" colonial slaveholders and Montagnard radicals used the colonial issue against Brissot himself, blaming him and the Girondins for having brought about the destruction of Saint-Domingue by encouraging the slave revolt. In February 1794, the sudden arrival of deputies from the island, bringing news of the abolition of slavery there, broke that alliance: the Montagnards turned abolition into proof that their movement was truly devoted to the rights of man and gave them a powerful rhetorical argument against their enemies.

After Thermidor, however, the situation changed again. For a year in 1794–1795, the question of whether abolition would be defined as a touchstone of republicanism or stigmatized as one of the excesses of the Terror hung in the balance. Colonial policy proved to be the issue on which the republicans halted the right-wing offensive unleashed after Robespierre's fall. The acquittal of the revolutionary commissioner Sonthonax following six months of widely publicized hearings identified republicanism with the abolition of slavery. As counterrevolutionary forces gathered new strength in 1796 and the first half of 1797, they seized on the colonial issue once again and would have forced a radical change in French policy if the coup d'état of

18 Fructidor An V (4 September 1797) had not reinforced the republicans' grip on power. In the wake of that victory, the republicans once again made the granting of rights to people of color in Saint-Domingue one of the key symbols of their regime.

The antislavery movement's triumph was short lived, however. When Napoleon came to power at the end of 1799, the pro-slavery forces were once again able to turn the situation in the colonies against their opponents. Napoleon, determined to show that his regime had broken with the radical republican heritage, included the law of 30 Floréal An X (May 20, 1802) reauthorizing slavery in the French colonies in the panoply of measures taken that year (such as the Concordat with the Catholic Church and the creation of the Legion of Honor) that created a new order based on hierarchical institutions. Debates over the colonies, especially Saint-Domingue, were thus inextricably interwoven into every phase of the revolutionary drama in France.

In this chapter, it is impossible to present all the details of how the issue of Saint-Domingue entered into revolutionary politics after 1791. A few general points stand out, however. One of these is the distinctive character of the debate over the colonies during the radical phase of the revolution as opposed to the earlier and later parts of the movement. It is broadly accurate to say that in the years from 1789 to 1792 and again from 1795 to 1802, those in France who were on the political left believed that the universal principles of the Declaration of Rights should be extended to the colonies. On the other side, those who aligned themselves with conservative positions in metropolitan politics also defended the need for a colonial regime based on racial hierarchy and slavery. From 1792 to 1795, however, the situation was much less clear. The fact that the campaign for human rights in the colonies had been identified with Brissot, the most visible of the Girondins, drove his radical Jacobin enemies to make common cause with colonial lobbyists who accused him of encouraging disorder in France's valuable overseas territories.

That the Saint-Domingue colonists and their supporters were able to sell this story to many leading French revolutionaries, up to and including Robespierre, is difficult to understand at first, but in fact their narrative fit well with key aspects of the Jacobin mentality. The notion that every setback to the revolutionary cause had to be the result of a conspiracy was deeply ingrained in revolutionary political culture. Conspiracy fears had fanned the revolutionary violence of July 1789, and there were enough real conspiracies during the decade, from the Varennes affair to Babeuf's inept movement, to make such accusations plausible. Brissot, the most prominent opponent of the proslavery colonists, was, as we have seen, fatally prone to making such accusations himself, and Robespierre, his mortal enemy, was equally susceptible to such beliefs. The "patriot" colonists' success in spreading their conspiracy explanation of the Saint-Domingue revolt also owed a good deal to the chaotic state of French radical politics. Jean-Daniel Piquet has shown that there were some French Jacobins other than Brissot's circle who defended the slaves' right to take up arms to obtain the enjoyment of the rights that the revolution had granted to citizens in France, but these radical French supporters of the blacks' cause were unorganized and the issue was never at the top of their agenda.[23]

While the radical advocates of abolition were disorganized and fearful of being tarred with the Brissotin brush, the "patriot" defenders of colonial slavery were well organized and single-mindedly determined to achieve their goals. This group, headed by Pierre-François Page and Jean-Augustin Brulley, two representatives sent to France from Saint-Domingue in mid-1792, successfully recast the colonial debate in terms that led many Jacobins to embrace their cause. They were able to take advantage of the fact that the black insurrectionists in Saint-Domingue had originally proclaimed themselves supporters of Louis XVI: in August 1793, Toussaint Louverture, then in the employ of Spain, was still writing to the republican leaders in the colony to tell them, "We know there is no more king because you republican traitors had him killed on a shameful scaffold."[24] But Page and Brulley also made a case for their position in terms of the French revolutionaries' own principles. Speaking to the Convention deputies in early 1793, Page admitted that that body had "declared that man is born free; it cannot decree enslavement, without being in opposition to its own principles." But he found a way to defend the colonists' position in equally republican terms: "If the Convention has recognized the rights of man, it cannot ignore the rights of the people, and since no one owes obedience to a law he hasn't helped make, or freely consented to personally or through his representatives . . . the Convention cannot make any law for [the colonies], without at the same time legitimizing the resistance that they might put up, if the law was disastrous for them."[25]

The colonists' victory was not merely one of words. Even before the committee hearings just mentioned had been concluded, they had claimed the head of one of their enemies, the disgraced royal governor Blanchelande.[26] The sans-culotte *journée* of May 31–June 2, 1793, marked the defeat of the colonists' *bête noire*, Brissot. This was not, however, a total victory for the Saint-Domingue "patriots": on June 3, 1793, the Jacobin Club welcomed a delegation of free coloreds, and on June 4, a petition calling for the immediate abolition of slavery was presented to the Convention. But the colonists enjoyed another victory on July 16, 1793, when the Convention voted for the recall and arrest of commissioners Léger-Félicité Sonthonax and Étienne Polverel, even though abbé Henri Grégoire gained a point for the antislavery forces a week later, when the Convention voted the abolition of subsidies for the slave trade.[27]

Thanks to the effects of the British naval blockade, the recall decree did not reach Saint-Domingue for another eleven months, by which time the general emancipation of the slaves had been carried through in Saint-Domingue and endorsed by the Convention. Even as their world was crumbling back home, however, the "patriot" colonists continued to hold their own in France. In September 1793, the white colonists joined the radical sans-culottes in demanding "prompt justice . . . for Brissot and all his accomplices, destroyers of the colonies." They were duly gratified on this point in the following month when the Montagnard Amar, speaking on behalf of the Committees of Public Safety and General Security, formally accused the Girondins of having "lost our colonies" and of having "disguised their own perfidious projects under the veil of philanthropy, just as they long concealed the plan of resuscitating monarchy in France under the forms of the republic."[28] The "patriot" colonists also joined in the prosecution of Barnave, who concluded that his role in colonial issues was "the real reason for my downfall." He pointed out that the Revolutionary Tribunal had just condemned Brissot for destroying the colonies and that since Brissot's opinions on the issue had been "diametrically opposed" to his own, he could hardly be guilty of the same crime, but this argument did him no good.[29] The colonists succeeded in having Julien Raimond, the leading spokesman for the free coloreds of Saint-Domingue, imprisoned, and complained regularly throughout the Terror period that he was never put on trial. The anti-Girondin hysteria in the fall of 1793 had the effect of discrediting the antislavery cause; in November 1793, even Robespierre, who in earlier debates had shown his opposition in principle to slavery, endorsed the "patriot" colonists' position that "the same faction which, in France, wanted to reduce the poor to the condition of helots and put the people under the aristocracy of the rich, wanted to suddenly emancipate and arm all the negroes to destroy our colonies."[30]

The situation changed with the arrival in Paris of three deputies—one white, one of mixed race, and one black—who were sent to the Convention from the republican sector of Saint-Domingue controlled by Sonthonax. The delegation brought news of the general emancipation of the slaves in Saint-Domingue proclaimed by Sonthonax in August 1793, which meant that any further endorsement of slavery in France would commit the Republic to reimposing the institution on a population that had already been freed and was fighting for the French cause. As Yves Benot has shown in a detailed dissection of the debate, the abolition of slavery was nevertheless not passed in a sudden burst of humanitarian enthusiasm. The debate occupied four sessions of the Convention, and the Jacobin allies of the "patriot" proponents of slavery tried several maneuvers to ward off a decision, either by referring the issue to the Committee of Public Safety (whose members were absent from the Convention during the key day of the debate because they were holding a private meeting with Page and Brulley!) or by postponing its implementation until the Constitution of 1793, which had been adopted in June 1793 but had been suspended until the peace, was put into effect.[31] There would be good grounds for a post-Thermidorian antislavery delegation to tell the Convention that they could produce "witnesses who will testify to the coalition of Page and Brulley with Robespierre and Fouquier[-Tinville]."[32]

The abolition decree of 16 Pluviôse II was certainly a defeat for the "patriot" colonial lobby, even if it was not as unequivocal as it has sometimes been made out to be. A skeptic might note that at the moment it was passed, the Convention's vote did not actually free any slaves: those in Saint-Domingue had already been emancipated by the commissioners Sonthonax and Polverel, those in Guadeloupe and Martinique were soon under British occupation, and the representatives of the French islands in the Indian Ocean succeeded in getting its implementation there suspended.[33] In Saint-Domingue, the question of whether abolition was anything more than a desperate effort to ward off defeat still hung in the balance: between September 1793 and May 1794, the British took over a third of the colony, while the Spanish invaded other parts of it.[34] Now that revolutionary France had committed itself to the abolition of slavery however, it was harder to make the case that the defense of slavery was patriotic. Numerous public festivals were held in France to celebrate the abolition decree, which the Jacobins presented as proof that republican France was the only true country of liberty.[35] On 16 Ventôse II (March 7, 1794), a month after the decree's passage, the Committee of Public Safety ordered the arrest of Page and Brulley, followed two days later by a general order for the arrest of all the proslavery colonists. In the port city of Brest, the deputy on mission, Prieur de la Marne, who was a member of the Committee of Public Safety, organized a commission to investigate the roles of the hundreds of Saint-Domingue refugees who had finally reached France with the so-called Vanstabel convoy in June 1794. The commission's work resulted in indictments against a large number of them, although they were never tried because the final report was not completed until after Thermidor.[36] At the same time, however, the Convention was still fearful of "Brissotins." The decree for the arrest and recall of Sonthonax and Polverel was maintained, and the antislavery colonist Claude Milscent was sent before the Revolutionary Tribunal and executed on the basis of testimony from proslavery witnesses.[37]

Not only did the passage of the abolition decree fail to end the destructive effect of the Montagnards' fear of conspiracies related to the colonies, but the association between the abolition of slavery and the high point of the Terror also laid the seeds of future political turmoil over the issue. During the Thermidorian period, the proslavery colonists nearly succeeded in discrediting the abolition of slavery as one more utopian folly engendered by the Revolution. After Robespierre's fall, the "patriot" colonists were released from prison and promptly resumed their campaign. In October 1794, the Thermidorian Convention approved their demand for public hearings on their charges against the commissioners Sonthonax and Polverel, and a par-

liamentary commission began taking testimony on 4 Pluviôse III. The colonists spared no effort in their determination to assimilate Sonthonax and
Polverel to the deputy Carrier, the prosecutor Fouquier-Tinville, and the
other agents of the Terror who had been executed after Thermidor. "France
must know that its overseas citizens had . . . its tyrants, its Carriers and its
Robespierres," one of them told the commission.[38] If the Commission had
accepted the colonists' arguments, the abolition of slavery would have been
categorized as a part of the Terror and the reinstitution of slavery would
have become a necessary part of the post-Thermidorian return to order.
The fact that the Convention appointed Brissot's former ally J. P. Garran to
chair the commission and named the abbé Grégoire and the former terror-
ist "proconsul" Fouché as members suggests that the outcome of the hearings was determined in advance. Nevertheless, the proceedings, commonly
if misleadingly referred to as "the trial of Sonthonax," were allowed to go on
for six months and the colonists were given every opportunity to broadcast
their charges.[39] The hearings were widely covered in the press and constituted the most detailed airing ever carried out of any aspect of revolutionary policy during the Terror period. They were thus a major part of the
process by which France "came out of the Terror," as Bronislaw Baczko has
put it.[40]

After six months, the exhausted commission members closed the debates
and referred the matter back to the Convention, which voted against indicting
Sonthonax.[41] In a narrowly political sense, this was a victory for the abolitionist cause and for the commissioner, who was reappointed to Saint-Domingue
in early 1796.[42] Whether Sonthonax won the battle for public opinion is less
certain. The newspaper press, dominated since Thermidor by barely disguised
opponents of the revolution, sympathized with the colonists.[43] A published
summary of the proceedings, which is much more readable than the nine volumes of transcripts, slanted the story against Sonthonax. Its author reported
that "on the one side were all those whom the hope for booty, the thirst for
pillage, crime, [and] debauchery, [and] the love of blood and of murder had
assembled around Polverel and Sonthonax," while on the other side were those
who believed in "the interest of the country, order, justice, reason, humanity,
duty, law, the love of the public good." Sonthonax's straightforward assertion
that "he needed nothing less than unlimited power, to control a country full
of counter-revolutionaries" made him sound like an acolyte of Robespierre at
a time when any association with the Incorruptible had become a dangerous
liability.[44] The Directory's decision to reappoint Sonthonax thus risked associating the regime itself with memories of the Terror.

Although the Thermidorian reaction had permitted the proslavery colonists to inject themselves into French politics again, the Constitution of
the Year III, which was socially conservative with respect to the metropole,

incorporated a radical position on the empire. It was the deputy Boissy d'Anglas, who had strongly defended the restriction of voting rights in France to wealthy property-owners, who insisted that there could be no return to the notion that the colonies could be allowed to exempt themselves from any provisions of the constitution. "The revolution that you are bringing to its conclusion was not just for France, it was for the universe," Boissy told his colleagues. Admittedly, Boissy's arguments were more utilitarian than principled. Europeans had become too dependent on colonial products to do without them, he said, and the alternative to France's possessing its own colonies would be not their independence but rather their seizure by the British. He did not need to remind the deputies that the British still held Martinique and a good part of Saint-Domingue and that France's only chance of reconquering its possessions was to rely on the black troops recruited through its emancipation policy who had liberated Guadeloupe and who were fighting the British in Saint-Domingue.[45]

The debate over the colonies in 1795 thus produced a decision in favor of a republican empire in which slavery was outlawed everywhere and in which there were ostensibly no distinctions between the legal regimes of the metropole and the colonies. The colonies continued to be represented in the assemblies of the Directory, which meant that black legislators such as J. B. Belley, who had arrived from Saint-Domingue in 1794, participated actively in debates about colonial issues. The breaking of the color bar cannot be credited only to the Convention during its most radical phase: it was consolidated during the Thermidorian reaction, out of a combination of idealism, a pragmatic realization that there was no other strategy that held out any hope of keeping Saint-Domingue French, and a fear that condemning Sonthonax would open the door to further attacks on anyone who had supported the radical republic. Only with the end of the "trial of Sonthonax" did the advocates of colonial slavery finally abandon the hope of seeing their position accepted as a republican one. From early 1796 onward, the politics of the empire reverted to the situation of 1789–1792, in which advocacy of colonial slavery was an integral part of right-wing opposition to revolutionary principles.

Most of the "patriot" agitators who had worked with Page and Brulley from 1792 through the Sonthonax hearings now faded from the scene, but their place was taken by new spokesmen, many of them figures who had been associated with the proslavery cause during the early years of the revolution. They were an integral part of an increasingly aggressive right-wing coalition that hoped to use the Republic's own institutions to subvert the revolution. The colonial issue was ready-made for their purposes, allowing them to denounce the government for violating property rights and pose as patriotic defenders of France's overseas possessions while accusing their opponents of defending unrealistic schemes that harked back to the Terror period. The Directory's failure to react when the colonists in the Mascareigne islands prevented the implementation of abolition in 1796 emboldened the right-wingers, and they put the colonial issue at the top of their agenda after their victory in the legislative elections of April 1797.[46] In a stormy weeklong debate in June 1797, they vociferously played the "race card," denouncing the government for favoring blacks over whites. "The owners must be able to reclaim their plantations. The blacks should not be slaves; but the whites have an equal right not to be deprived," one speaker insisted. The debate was also an opportunity to reopen the attack on Sonthonax, who had been absolved, according to another deputy, "at that disastrous epoch when the members of the Convention, in danger of being proscribed themselves, did not want to expose themselves and give their enemies a pretext, by accusing a man they wanted to protect."[47] The republican coup d'état of 18 Fructidor V (September 4, 1797) ousted the right-wing deputies and ended the immediate threat of a repudiation of abolition, but not before one anti-abolition pamphleteer had outlined the strategy that Napoleon would actually adopt in 1802: a secret decision to reestablish slavery, the sending of a military expedition to occupy Saint-Domingue and then announce the decree, and the elimination of any black who had held a position of authority since the start of the insurrection there. "To avoid the spilling of blood," the author disingenuously concluded, "one could propose to send them back to their families" in Africa.[48]

The Fructidor coup brought a reaffirmation of republican militancy in France, marked in the colonial domain by the issuance of Garran-Coulon's massive four-volume report on the findings of the Colonial Commission of 1795; the passage of the law of 12 Nivôse An VI, which specified how the constitution would be applied in the colonies; and the revival of the Société des Amis des Noirs, which had stopped meeting in 1791. Garran's report stated unequivocally that the insurrection that began in 1791 was not the result of a political conspiracy but rather the inevitable consequence of the oppressive nature of slavery. "One would have little understanding of human nature, if one were to believe that . . . the blacks needed any inspiration other than that irresistible impulsion for all living beings which . . . speaks perhaps even more to the hearts of those who are closest to nature," he wrote.[49] The law of 12 Nivôse VI was meant to install civil government in place of the emergency military regime that had prevailed in Saint-Domingue since 1794 and to consolidate the rights granted to the former slaves.[50] The Société des Amis des Noirs et des Colonies, the first public organization specifically devoted to colonial affairs since the disappearance of its ancestor in 1791, brought together politicians, government officials, and intellectuals, including several women members. It was part of a broader resurgence of republican club activity following Fructidor, but it fell apart in early 1799 as the post-Fructidor republican coalition began to separate into hostile neo-Jacobin and authoritarian camps.[51]

Just as the right-wing deputies of 1797 had seized on the supposed catastrophe of republican colonial policy as a way of attacking the regime, the republicans of 1797–1799 used the supposed success of their policy in Saint-Domingue as a means of legitimizing their rule at home, particularly at a time when all traces of republican idealism seemed to have disappeared from the "great nation's" policy toward the "sister republics" in Europe. Annual parliamentary sessions commemorating the abolition of slavery in 1794, for example, were occasions for highlighting the presence of a "tri-color" colonial delegation of black, mixed-race, and white deputies in the French legislature. Meanwhile, however, the divisions in Saint-Domingue's own internal politics, particularly the power struggle between Toussaint and the free colored leader André Rigaud, were projected into French politics as each recruited colonial deputies to defend his position.[52]

Some recent historians have seen this period of the "Second Directory" as a moment of lost possibilities in the colonial domain, suggesting that there could have been a mutually beneficial alliance between a genuinely multiracial Saint-Domingue under Toussaint Louverture's leadership and a French republic finally freed from the danger of counterrevolutionary subversion after Fructidor.[53] This notion depends on an optimistic reading of Toussaint's conduct and an equally optimistic assessment of the degree of support for neo-Jacobin policies in France. The republican colonial camp suffered from at least two major weaknesses. One was its inability to show that the Republic could actually assert any control over the powerful black general. By the end of 1798, after Toussaint had negotiated his own peace treaty with the British forces, imitating the conduct of young General Bonaparte, who had made his own peace with the Austrians in April 1797, most of the republicans interested in the colonies turned against him, including Sonthonax, who had returned to France as one of Saint-Domingue's deputies. The other weakness of the republicans was their inability to satisfy those who adhered to the utilitarian notion that colonies existed to promote the economic and political interests of the metropole. Although some white plantation owners returned to the island, they were unable to regain control of their property, and the modest revival in colonial production in these years was not nearly enough to offset the losses suffered since 1791.

When Napoleon overthrew the Directory on 18 Brumaire An VIII, he thus inherited a "colonial problem" that had affected every successive government since 1789. His engagement in the Egyptian campaign had clearly indicated his interest in expanding French power overseas, and he quickly made one major decision bearing on the colonies: he saw to it that the new Constitution of the Year VIII, which no longer included a declaration of rights, specifically exempted the colonies from metropolitan constitutional law. This was a return to the principles of the Constitution of 1791 and a renunciation of the unified concept of the empire reflected in the Directory's constitution; it clearly opened the door to the reintroduction of slavery in the colonies. Napoleon also allowed a number of proslavery figures who had been active in the right-wing resurgence of 1797 to regain positions of influence. So long as France remained at war with England, there was little Napoleon could do about the colonies, but as peace negotiations neared success in 1801, he made it clear that he took the colonies as seriously as any previous revolutionary government by readying a massive military expedition to Saint-Domingue and a smaller force for Guadeloupe. They set sail in late 1801 and early 1802. Meanwhile, at home, Napoleon presented his hand-picked legislature with the law of 30 Floréal An X. Ostensibly, the law simply authorized the maintenance of slavery in colonies where it had not been abolished—the Mascareignes, Martinique (where the British occupation had prevented the implementation of the 1794 abolition decree) and, significantly, the Louisiana territory, which Spain had just retroceded to France. In fact, it was clearly intended to pave the way for the reimposition of slavery in Guadeloupe, where General Richepance issued a decree to that effect on July 16, 1802, and in Saint-Domingue, as well as in French Guiana.[54]

In *La démence coloniale sous Napoléon*, Yves Benot has rightly insisted that Napoleon must bear personal responsibility for the decision to reimpose slavery in the colonies, but the alacrity with which merchant and shipping interests rushed to resume the triangular trade in 1802 shows that he had considerable support.[55] By the standards of the Napoleonic period, however, the measures taken in 1802 also encountered a fair amount of opposition. Even after the systematic purge of liberals in the Tribunate, the vote for the reintroduction of slavery was only 54 to 27, and there seems to have been little enthusiasm for the series of edicts restricting the rights of blacks in metropolitan France issued in conjunction with the restoration of slavery.[56] The restoration of slavery followed closely on the heels of the Concordat with the Catholic Church, and, like the Concordat, it represented a deliberate repudiation of what had come to be accepted as a central aspect of the revolutionary legacy. In both cases, Napoleon sought to consolidate an alliance between his own rule and the hierarchical institutions of the old regime. The famous story of how French troops were perturbed by hearing their own republican songs being sung in the camp of their black opponents in Saint-Domingue, to the point that they asked themselves "Have we become servile instruments of politics?" underlines the depth of the breach with 1789 and 1793 that Napoleon's colonial policy created.[57]

It is clear that the colonies, especially Saint-Domingue, were a presence in every phase of the French revolutionary drama, from the effervescence of the pre-revolutionary crisis to Napoleon's effort to restore a regime based on hierarchical principles that ignored the egalitarian tenets of the republicans. One does not need to go to the extreme of claiming that the colonial tail wagged the metropolitan dog to recognize that passions rooted in these colonial debates often helped make revolutionary politics even more explosive than they otherwise would have been. Admittedly, colonial issues never became the basis for a mass movement in France. Agitation over the colonies in revolutionary France was largely confined to revolutionary political elites, to the representatives of the colonists, and to those who had a direct economic stake in overseas commerce. In effect, the revolution precluded the development of a mass movement because it gave the metropolitan population too many other problems to worry about. When the population took to the streets during the revolution, it did so in the name of causes closer to home. The one colonial-related issue that provoked a major demonstration, the riots against the high price of sugar in Paris in February 1793, was a sans-culotte consumer protest, not a movement against slavery or colonialism.[58] Concern with the colonies and slavery was even more remote from the French peasantry. Despite the efforts of the abbé Grégoire, the Catholic church was completely incapable of playing the mobilizing role on these issues that religious groups did in England and the United States: Catholic energies were fully engaged in the struggle over religion in France itself. Paradoxically, the revolution, whose principles made engagement with colonial problems and slavery inevitable, also created a situation in which too many other things were going on to allow colonial issues to become the center of public debate.

However, the absence of mass mobilization around colonial issues by no means meant that these problems were marginal to French revolutionary politics. Even in a revolution, it is not just the masses who count. Colonial issues mattered deeply to many of those engaged in revolutionary politics. From 1789 to 1802, accusations related to the colonies were deadly weapons in revolutionary political combat. The fighting that followed the outbreak of the Saint-Domingue insurrection was interpreted in France itself as a struggle against the counterrevolution, and if it is true, as Georges Lefebvre famously said, that "the war upset the plans of everyone" involved in the revolution, it is important to recognize that the period of revolutionary warfare began in the colony in August 1791, not in Europe in April 1792.[59] The execution of Governor Blanchelande in April 1793 made him the first French military commander to be put to death on suspicion of political disloyalty and heralded the approach of the Terror. The "disasters of Saint-Domingue" helped doom the Girondins, and colonial activists succeeded in tying the Montagnards in knots during 1793–1794, until the arrival of the republican deputies from Saint-Domingue led to the passage of the epochal 1794 decree abolishing slavery. After Thermidor, the "trial of Sonthonax" was a critical moment in defining the limits of "de-Jacobinization." In 1796 and 1797, the resurgent counterrevolutionary right turned the colonial issue against the republicans, whereas after Fructidor, the republicans used it to demonstrate the genuineness of their progressive credentials. Ironically, only the Napoleonic regime, which actually did lose Saint-Domingue along with more than 50,000 French troops, escaped domestic repercussions from its colonial policy. The suppression of open political debate in France enabled Napoleon to drive criticism underground and divert attention to his successes in Europe.

Nevertheless, the existence of the empire drove the revolutionaries to face the fundamental question of whether the rights so ringingly declared in 1789 could be limited by race and geography. Initially, the answer given by the National Assembly was that they could. Like the American revolutionaries, the French found a variety of practical reasons why the apparent implications of their principles could not be put into practice. The empire, while it gave the revolution in France a global dimension, militated against the realization of its universalist potential. Under the pressure of events, however, the revolutionaries did change their minds, first with the granting of rights to some people of mixed race in May 1791 and (more comprehensively) in April 1792, and then with the abolition of slavery in February 1794. Incomplete and short lived as these measures were, they nevertheless created an historic precedent. From the revolutionary era onward, those who claimed to see individual liberty and equality as the ultimate bases of the social and political order had to recognize that those principles implied the abolition of slavery and the recognition of the rights of at least the male members of all races. Later, notions like that of the "mission civilisatrice" would provide pretexts for the denial of rights to colonial populations, but at the same time the idea of France's civilizing mission implied that the final goal of the colonial enterprise was to create conditions in which those populations could someday exercise their rights. Today, when people of color sit in the legislatures of western European countries and in the Congress of the United States, it is appropriate to remember that the National Convention and the Directorial assemblies were the first such bodies to break the color bar.

Although it is appropriate to acknowledge the French Revolution's contribution to the campaigns against slavery and racial prejudice, it is equally important to recognize the other side of the coin. Even at the height of the Jacobin ascendancy in 1794, the principles enshrined in the decree of 16 Pluviôse II were never fully implemented or universally accepted. The dynamics of revolutionary France's imperial system gave groups with vested interests in the colonies and slavery ample opportunities to defend themselves. By appealing to patriotic sentiments, economic considerations, the rights of property, the injustice of arbitrary rule, and the principle that citizens had a right to consent to laws affecting their interests, defenders of the colonial status quo were frequently able to enlist the metropolitan government on their side.

The struggles over Saint-Domingue during the 1790s foreshadowed the colonial crises of France's Fourth Republic a century and a half later. In Indochina and Algeria in the 1950s, as in the France of the 1790s, arguments about the need to maintain France's place in the world; defend the country's commerce, industry, and investments; and protect the rights of France's overseas citizens led to protracted military engagements that ended in humiliating military defeats. France, with its long republican and democratic traditions, fought more stubbornly to retain its possessions than did any of the other European imperial powers. Revolutionary France's legacy with respect to colonialism and issues of race was thus a deeply ambivalent one.

Notes

1. The starting point for the recent literature on this topic is Yves Benot, *La Révolution française et la fin des colonies* (Paris: La Découverte, 1989), together with the more recent but not always equally convincing account in Jean-Daniel Piquet, *L'émancipation des Noirs dans la Révolution française (1789–1795)* (Paris: Karthala, 2002). Fundamental for understanding the fate of slavery after the passage of the abolition law of 1794 is Claude Wanquet, *La France et la première abolition de l'esclavage 1794–1802* (Paris: Karthala, 1998).

2. Léon Deschamps, *Les colonies pendant la Révolution. La Constituante et la Réforme coloniale* (Paris: Perrin, 1898), 3.

3. David Armitage, *The Ideological Origins of the British Empire* (Cambridge: Cambridge University Press, 2000); Arthur L. Stinchcombe, *Sugar Island Slavery in the Age of Enlightenment: The Political Economy of the Caribbean World* (Princeton, N.J.: Princeton University Press, 1995).

4. For an analytical model of the conflicts built into colonial-metropole relationships during this period, see Stinchcombe, *Sugar Island Slavery*, 180–182.

5. Catherine Duprat, *Le temps des philanthropes: La philanthropie parisienne des Lumières à la monarchie de juillet* (Paris: C.T.H.S., 1993), 125; Marcel Dorigny, "La Société des Amis des Noirs: antiesclavagisme et lobby colonial à la fin du siècle des Lumières (1788–1792)," in *La Société des Amis des Noirs 1788–1799*, ed. Marcel Dorigny and Bernard Gainot (Paris: Editions UNESCO, 1998), 40.

6. Dorigny and Gainot, eds., *Société des Amis*, 218, 223, 231.

7. On the Saint-Domingue planters' campaign for admission to the Estates-General, see Prosper Boissonnade, *Saint-Domingue à la veille de la Révolution et la question de la représentation coloniale aux Etats Généraux (janvier 1788—7 juillet 1789)* (Paris: Paul Geuthner, 1906); and Blanche Maurel, *Cahiers de doléances de la colonie de Saint-Domingue pour les Etats-généraux de 1789* (Paris: Librairie Ernest Leroux, 1933). A copy of the group's proceedings in 1788 is in Ms. MMC 2671, U.S. Library of Congress.

8. Jérôme Mavidal, et al., eds., *Archives parlementaires de 1787 à 1860*, première série (1787–1799), 82 vols. (Paris, 1867–1913), session of June 27, 1789, 8:165.

9. Mavidal, *Archives parlementaires*, 8:186–190. After the decision on Saint-Domingue, seats were also allotted to deputies from the other colonies.

10. *Courrier de Provence*, August 20–21, 1789, cited in Dorigny and Gainot, *Société des Amis*, 242n–243n. Emphasis in the original.

11. The fundamental work on the Club Massiac remains Gabriel Debien, *Les colons de Saint-Domingue et la Révolution: Essai sur le Club Massiac (août 1789-août 1792)* (Paris: Armand Colin, 1953).

12. Bonnemain, *Régénération des colonies, ou moyens de restituer graduellement aux hommes leur état politique, et d'assurer la prospérité des nations* (Paris: Cercle social, 1792), 93–96.

13. Benot, *Révolution française et la fin des colonies*, 65; Dorigny and Gainot, *Société des Amis*, 245.

14. Jacques-Pierre Brissot, *Discours de J. P. Brissot, député, sur les causes des troubles de Saint-Domingue, prononcé à la séance du premier décembre 1791* (Paris: Imprimerie nationale, 1791), 59.

15. For a sample of these petitions, inspired by articles in Brissot's newspaper, the *Patriote françois*, see *Lettres des diverses sociétés des Amis de la Constitution, qui réclament les droits de citoyen actif en faveur des hommes de couleur des colonies* (Paris: Imprimerie du *Patriote françois*, 1791).

16. Benot, *Fin des colonies*, 75–76, 79–82; and Piquet, *L'émancipation des noirs*, 71–95. The most extended account in English is E. D. Bradby, *The Life of Barnave*, 2 vols. (Oxford: Clarendon Press, 1915), 2:57–74.

17. Bradby, *Life of Barnave*, 2:238–253.

18. Deschamps, *Colonies pendant la Révolution*, 141–145.

19. Gibbon to Sheffield, December 28, 1791, in Edward Gibbon, *The Letters of Edward Gibbon*, ed. J. E. Norton, 3 vols. (London: Cassell and Company, 1956), 3:240.

20. Letter of November 1791, in Dxxv 79, d. 775, Archives Nationales, Paris (hereafter AN).

21. Jacques-Pierre Brissot, *Discours sur un projet de décret relatif à la révolte des Noirs, prononcé à l'Assemblée nationale, le 30 octobre 1791, par J. P. Brissot, député* (Paris: Imprimerie nationale, 1791), 8, 12.

22. Brissot, *Discours de J. P. Brissot*, 48, 49, 67, 70.

23. Piquet, *L'émancipation des noirs*, 161–176.

24. Toussaint Louverture to Chanlatte, August 27, 1793, in CC9A/8, Centre des Archives d'Outre-mer, Aix-en-Provence (hereafter CAOM). On the "royalism" of the slave insurrection, see David Geggus, *Haitian Revolutionary Studies* (Bloomington: Indiana University Press, 2002), 12. For background on one important document that helped spread this impression, see Jeremy Popkin, "Facing Racial Revolution: Captivity Narratives and Identity in the Saint-Domingue Insurrection," *Eighteenth-Century Studies* 36 (2002–2003): 511–533.

25. *Développement des causes des troubles et désastres des colonies françaises, présenté à la Convention nationale, par les commissaires de Saint-Domingue, sur la demande des comités de Marine et des Colonies, réunies, après en avoir donné communication aux colons résidens à Paris, & convoqués, à cet effet, le 11 juin 1793, l'an 2 de la République* (N. p., n. d.), 51.

26. Dxxv 69, d. 697, pièce 37, AN.

27. Piquet, *L'émancipation des noirs*, 254–262.

28. Dxxv 80, September 29, 1793, AN. The Amar citation is in Piquet, *L'émancipation des noirs*, 282.

29. Gérard Walter, ed., *Actes du Tribunal révolutionnaire* (Paris: Mercure de France, 1968), 310–311.

30. Robespierre, speech of 27 Brumaire An II, quoted in Piquet, *L'émancipation des noirs*, 275.

31. Yves Benot, "Comment la Convention a-t-elle voté l'abolition de l'esclavage en l'An II?" *Annales historiques de la Révolution française*, nos. 293–294 (1993): 349–361.

32. Anon., *Pétition des citoyens de couleur des colonies, sur la conspiration et la collation des colons avec les Anglais, lu, le 5 vendémiaire [An III], à la barre de la Convention* (Paris: Pain, 1794), 10.

33. On the sequence of measures leading to general emancipation in Saint-Domingue in 1793, see Robert Louis Stein, *Léger-Félicité Sonthonax: The Lost Sentinel of the Republic* (Rutherford, N.J.: Fairleigh Dickinson University Press, 1985), 85–95; and Laurent Dubois, *Avengers of the New World: The Story of the Haitian Revolution* (Cambridge, Mass.: Harvard University Press, 2004), 59–65. For the Mascareignes, see Wanquet, *La France et la première abolition*, 133. Emancipation was carried out in Guadeloupe when the French reconquered the island in June 1794. See Laurent Dubois, *A Colony of Citizens: Revolution and Slave Emancipation in the French Caribbean, 1787–1804* (Chapel Hill, N.C.: University of North Carolina Press, 2004), 192–200.

34. David Geggus, *Slavery, War and Revolution: The British Occupation of Saint-Domingue 1793–1798* (Oxford: Clarendon Press, 1982), 114.

35. Jean-Claude Halpern, "Les fêtes révolutionnaires et l'abolition de l'esclavage en l'An II," in *Les abolitions de l'esclavage: De L. F. Sonthonax à Victor Schoelcher 1793 1794 1848*, ed. Marcel Dorigny (Paris: Editions UNESCO, 1995), 187–198.

36. Claire Blondet, "Quand les 'terroristes' font le procès du colonialisme esclavagiste les thermidoriens organisent son oubli," in *Périssent les colonies plutôt qu'un principe!: Contributions à l'histoire de l'abolition de l'esclavage 1789–1804*, dir. Florence Gauthier, (Paris: Société des études robespierristes, 2002), 43–65.

37. Piquet, *L'émancipation des noirs*, 430–437; Sophie Piollet, Nathalie Piquionne, and Delphine Roux, "Milscent créole historien de la Révolution de Saint-Domingue 1790–1794," in *Périssent les colonies plutôt qu'un principe!: Contributions à l'histoire de l'abolition de l'esclavage 1789–1804*, dir. Florence Gauthier (Paris: Société des études robespierristes, 2002), 23–42.

38. *Débats entre les accusateurs et les accusés, dans l'affaire des colonies, imprimées en exécution de la loi du 4 pluviôse*, 9 vols. (Paris: Imprimerie nationale, An III), 1:170. On the political stakes of the Carrier trial, see Bronislaw Baczko, *Comment sortir de la Terreur* (Paris: Gallimard, 1989), 191–254.

39. The hearings were not judicial procedures; if the charges against Sonthonax had been sustained, he would still have had to be tried. These hearings, documented in the nine published volumes of proceedings, have not yet received a thorough study. There are brief accounts in Stein, *Sonthonax*, 113–120; and Yves Benot, "Le procès Sonthonax, ou les *Débats entre les accusateurs et les accusés dans l'affaire des colonies* (an III)," in *Léger-Félicité Sonthonax*, ed. Marcel Dorigny (Paris: Société française d'histoire d'outre-mer, 1997), 55–63.

40. Bronislaw Baczko, *Ending the Terror: The French Revolution after Robespierre*, trans. Michael Petheram (Cambridge: Cambridge University Press, 1994).

41. Stein, *Sonthonax*, 119–120.

42. Stein, *Sonthonax*, 128.

43. On the right-wing domination of the press in this period, see Jeremy D. Popkin, *The Right-Wing Press in France, 1792–1800* (Chapel Hill, N.C.: University of North Carolina Press, 1980).

44. Guillois, *Analyse des débats, entre les accusateurs et les accusés, dans l'Affaire de la colonie de Saint-Domingue, conformément aux décrets de la Convention Nationale; par le Citoyen Guillois, l'un des tachygraphes nommés par la Convention Nationale, pour recueillir les débats* (Paris: Chevet, 1795), 113, 61. Although the author's partiality for the colonists comes through clearly, he also made it evident that Sonthonax's enemies damaged their cause by wasting the first four months of the hearings pursuing vague and irrelevant issues. Only when the commission finally demanded that they present a specific set of accusations and then stick to them did the debates take on some semblance of coherence. Guillois, *Analyse des débats*, 39.

45. Wanquet, *La France et la première abolition*, 248–255 (quote on p. 253).

46. Wanquet, *La France et la première abolition*, 301–377.

47. *Réimpression de l'ancien Moniteur* (Paris: Bureau central, 1843), 28:720–721.

48. *De l'affranchissement des noirs*, 29.

49. Jean Philippe Garran, *Rapport sur les troubles de Saint-Domingue, fait au nom de la Commission des Colonies, des Comités de Salut Public, de Législation, et de Marine, réunis*, 4 vols. (Paris: Imprimerie nationale, 1797–1798), 1:194.

50. On the ambiguities of the law's attempt to reconcile the granting of citizenship with the perceived necessity to restore the colony's workforce, through a system of coerced labor if necessary, see Bernard Gainot, "Métropole/Colonies: Projets constitutionnels et rapports de forces 1798–1802," in *Rétablissement de l'esclavage dans les colonies françaises 1802: Aux origines d'Haïti*, dir. Yves Benot and Marcel Dorigny (Paris: Maisonneuve et Larose, 2004), 19–20.

51. On the Société des Amis des Noirs et des Colonies, see Bernard Gainot, "Introduction," in *La Société des Amis des Noirs1788–1799*, ed. Marcel Dorigny and Bernard Gainot (Paris: Editions UNESCO, 1998), 301–327; and Marcel Dorigny, "The abbé Grégoire and the *Société des Amis des Noirs*," in *The Abbé Grégoire and His World*, ed. Jeremy D. Popkin and Richard H. Popkin (Dordrecht: Kluwer, 2000), 34–39.

52. Bernard Gainot, "La députation de Saint-Domingue au corps législatif du Directoire," in Dorigny, ed., *Léger-Félicité Sonthonax*, 95–110.

53. This argument has been made most forcefully in Florence Gauthier, *Triomphe et mort du droit naturel en Révolution 1789–1795–1802* (Paris: Presses Universitaires de Paris, 1992).

54. For accounts of Napoleonic policy on the colonies, see Yves Benot, *La démence coloniale sous Napoléon* (Paris: La Découverte, 1991), 57–99; and Thomas Pronier, "L'implicite et l'explicite dans la politique de Napoléon," in *Rétablissement de l'esclavage dans les colonies françaises 1802: Aux origines d'Haïti*, dir. Yves Benot and Marcel Dorigny (Paris: Maisonneuve et Larose, 2004), 51–67. Laurent Dubois, in *Avengers of the New World*, 252–261, argues that Napoleon may not have made up his mind about restoring slavery in Saint-Domingue as thoroughly as other historians imply.

55. See, for example, Eric Saugera, *Bordeaux, port négrier: Chronologie, économie, idéologie XVIIe-XIXe siècles* (Paris: Karthala, 1995), 125–129.

56. Benot, *La démence coloniale sous Napoléon*, 92, 96.

57. Pamphile de Lacroix, *La Révolution de Haïti* (original title: *Mémoires pour servir à l'histoire de la Révolution de Saint-Domingue*) (Paris: Karthala, 1995), 333.

58. On the riots against the high price of colonial products in February 1793, see Susanne Petersen, *Lebensmittelfrage und revolutionäre Politik in Paris 1792–1793* (Munich: Oldenbourg, 1979), 196–208.

59. Georges Lefebvre, *The French Revolution from Its Origins to 1793*, trans. Elizabeth Moss Evanson (New York: Columbia University Press, 1962), 227.

Speaking of Haiti
Slavery, Revolution, and Freedom in
Cuban Slave Testimony

Ada Ferrer

AT THE END OF THE EIGHTEENTH CENTURY, A WORLD BUILT UPON SLAVERY, COLONIALISM, AND RACIAL HIERARCHY WAS TURNED UPSIDE DOWN IN THE SMALL BUT PROSPEROUS COLONY OF FRENCH Saint-Domingue. The events that shook Saint-Domingue from 1791 to 1804 converted Europe's most profitable colony into an independent nation ruled by former slaves and their descendants. This new society, born of a process never before contemplated, lay right in the middle of the Caribbean Sea, a short sail from islands ruled by European governors and inhabited, sometimes overwhelmingly, by enslaved Africans.

Less than fifty miles from Saint-Domingue's western coast was the island of Cuba. As slavery and colonialism collapsed in the French colony, Cuba underwent transformations almost the mirror image of Haiti's. In Cuba, sugar planters and colonial authorities saw the devastation of their neighboring colony and looked at their own society with fresh eyes. Publicly and privately, they professed fear and terror that the scenes of the Haitian Revolution would be repeated in their own territory. But for the most part, the men with the power to decide the future course of the Spanish colony resolved to live dangerously. Working with the colonial state, Cuban planters and merchants rushed to fill the void left by Saint-Domingue's collapse. They imported an ever-growing number of slaves and amassed greater and greater wealth in sugar. "The hour of our happiness has arrived," predicted one planter, looking ahead to the boom that would turn Cuba into the world's largest producer of sugar. But the planters' vision had a catch: they sought to follow in their French neighbors' footsteps and reproduce a prosperity built on sugar, slavery, and colonialism but to stop emphatically short of the upheaval caused by

223

those same institutions in Saint-Domingue. They sought, in other words, to emulate Saint-Domingue but to contain Haiti.

The example of Haiti, however, was not easy to contain, especially in Cuba, where the Haitian Revolution felt immediate and urgent. The passage between the two islands was short and well traveled. Throughout the revolution, slave-owners from the French colony arrived by the thousands, seeking refuge with their slaves and telling stories of black vengeance and physical desolation. French forces defeated by former slaves evacuated via Cuba as local residents watched and discussed their presence with great interest. In the decades that followed Haitian independence, Cubans heard repeated rumors about potential Haitian incursions into Cuban territory. And just as planters learned about Haitian happenings, so too did enslaved and free people of color. They knew the events of the revolution as if by memory, claimed a contemporary newspaper.[1] Among them, said one official, the names of Haitian leaders resounded like those of invincible heroes and redeemers of slaves.[2] Cuban plantations increasingly resembled their Saint-Dominguan predecessors, where slaves were subjected to increasingly brutal labor and disciplinary regimes and where they sometimes responded by envisioning risings like the ones of their counterparts in Haiti. To look at Cuba in this period with Haiti in mind is thus to glimpse the overlapping stories of freedom and slavery being made and unmade—simultaneously and each within view of the other.

This chapter explores how this keen awareness of the Haitian Revolution shaped the transformation of slavery in Cuba. It asks how the entrenchment of slavery in Cuba might have been shaped by the fact that this process occurred precisely as its protagonists watched the unraveling of the world's foremost slave society not far from their coasts. To undertake this exploration, I begin with a brief discussion of the thinking on slavery and freedom among the planter elite who conceptualized and oversaw the transformation of Cuban slavery. The heart of the chapter, however, has to do with the much less documented question of how enslaved men and women in Cuba might have come to understand the Haitian Revolution and its connection to their own enslavement and liberation. Though this question is framed here as a specific one about the response of Cuban slaves to revolution in Haiti, it has broader roots and implications. In 1979, Eugene Genovese made the bold claim that the Haitian Revolution propelled a revolution in black consciousness. In 1986, Julius Scott pioneered the effort of interpreting how that revolution might have taken place, documenting the ways in which black people in the hemisphere came to know about and understand the Haitian Revolution. More recently, Laurent Dubois has reissued the call in bold terms, asking us to write an intellectual history of the enslaved in the Age of Revolution and Enlightenment. This chapter takes up the challenge posed by these important works. The point here is not to argue that slaves had an intellectual history—that is, a history of thinking through ideas about liberty, rights, power, and so forth; that point should be fairly self-evident. The chapter, rather, is a methodological and conceptual exercise to assess how we might go about exploring and writing histories of that intellectual and political engagement.[3]

Transformations in Cuban Slavery

At the beginning of the Haitian Revolution, approximately 153,000 people were living in slavery in Cuba. The number was already growing, especially after the planter elite negotiated to have the slave trade to Cuba opened to Spaniards and foreigners in 1789. Then came the Northern Plain uprising in August 1791. With the decision on renewing the open slave trade in the king's hands just as news of the Saint-Domingue rebellion reached Europe, Cuban planters worked to make sure that news of slaves' burning of plantations did not discourage the growth they so desired. Francisco Arango—prominent planter, creole politician, and the most eloquent voice for the planters' vision of economic growth—addressed the king to dispel any trepidation and to argue for the continued expansion of slavery in Cuba. The slave rebellion, he argued, was not cause for fear but rather cause for shrewd political and economic calculation. Without much effort, Arango drew the conclusion that confirmed the path on which he and his colleagues had already embarked. The revolution, he said, represented "the opportunity to give our agriculture a definitive advantage over the French."[4] He went on to reiterate the case for expanding the slave trade and to repeat his vision of a profitable Cuban colony based on large-scale commercial sugar production sustained by the labor of more and more captured Africans.

Arango's plea was persuasive. The king acceded, and over the next two decades the growth was dizzying. Approximately 325,000 Africans were legally brought to Cuba as slaves between 1790 and 1820 (more than four times the number brought in during the previous thirty years). The demand was great because the number of sugar mills kept growing, almost doubling from 1790 to 1806, while the average output of sugar per estate in the same period more than doubled. By 1820, the planters' vision had materialized and Cuba had come to occupy Saint-Domingue's old role as the premier colony of the new world and the largest producer of sugar on the globe.[5]

In the course of this expansion, its architects continually had to confront the specter of the Haitian Revolution. Even as they rejoiced at the opportunities and happiness that (for them, at least) abounded, they frequently challenged one another to think about how to ensure that the slave trade and the economy it sustained would continue to flourish while avoiding a rebellion that would annihilate the growth they were just achieving. In the substantial writings of the planter elite—many of whom served in one capacity or another in the colonial administration—this tension emerges as a recurring theme.

The Real Consulado's Junta de Fomento, one of the most influential institutions in colonial Cuba, was created in 1794 under the guiding hand of the planter elite to encourage economic growth through the expansion of agriculture and the liberalization of trade.[6] But if that was its general mission, its most pressing concern on its creation was to reconcile the economic growth that slavery produced with continued peace and order. As one of the junta's members recalled in 1799, it was the slave revolution in Saint-Domingue that had most impact on the creation of the junta, and the body's foundational task was to explore methods by which they could combine the growth in the slave population with the preservation of its tranquility and obedience.[7]

The argument Arango and the other members of the Real Consulado advanced most often was that a growth in the slave trade could be reconciled with the security of the colony. Arango asserted this from the start, arguing in November 1791 shortly after learning of the outbreak of revolution in Saint-Domingue that the events that were destroying the French colony could not be repeated in Cuba. The turmoil in the French colony resulted not from any quality inherent in the institution of slavery but rather from the political irresponsibility of French revolutionaries and officeholders and the irresponsibility of French masters toward their slaves. Spanish loyalty was stronger and Spanish slavery more benign than its French counterpart. On the basis of these differences, he argued, there was no cause for fear in Cuba.[8] His fellow planters and statesmen agreed. As one member of the Real Consulado explained, at the time of the body's creation in 1794, its members judged that "the risk of insurrection was not imminent here because our slaves were in a different situation. That is, they enjoyed civil privileges that their neighbors did not, which, with the [added] handicap of being far less numerous than the free population, led us to believe that they would not, on their own, conceive of rebelling, nor be able to sustain a rebellion. We therefore agreed that, since the urgent need for laborers for our fertile lands was so clear, we would quickly seek out all means available to encourage [the slave trade]."[9]

As they worked to expand that trade, however, they urged utmost vigilance. They commissioned and wrote reports to assess the dangers, examine the racial balance or imbalance of the population, advocate immigration from Spain, study the coasts and fortifications in those areas closest to Saint-Domingue, and reform the system for defeating maroons, whom they feared might someday join invading black forces from rebellious Saint-Domingue. It was in part the caution provoked by the example and proximity of the Haitian Revolution that led the creole elite in Havana to embark on what are usually seen as projects of state- and nation-building: surveying distant

national territory, counting and classifying the population, devising programs for settlement in sparsely populated regions.[10] In fact, one of the first
plans for the establishment of rural schools in Cuba arose in this context of
thinking about white security in a post-Haiti world. The junta's report on
the methods for assuring slaves' subservience speculated that the desire for
freedom on the part of slaves was natural, in fact, inextinguishable and that
it need not be feared in and of itself. But, they cautioned, the very organization and nature of the Cuban sugar estate was encouraging a willingness to
attempt to achieve that freedom by force. The problems they identified began
not with slaves but with masters, who, they said, exercised "absolute authority" in a context that encouraged only "abuse and excess." Overseers, they
argued, were often worse, men of "known rusticity" whose only means of
getting slaves to work were the machete and the whip.[11] The solution to such
problems, said the report's authors, was to try to better educate masters and
overseers on these questions, but not by legally reducing the power or right
of the master, which they suggested would be as dangerous as the problem
itself. Better educated masters and overseers would be more likely to respect
the humanity of slaves, to recognize their right to marriage or free time or
provision grounds. If owners were less focused on the question of immediate profit and more attuned to questions of long-term viability, they would
be more willing to purchase women, who would serve to limit violence and
conspiracy. In their view, the creation of rural schools would reform those
who exercised authority over slaves, thus minimizing the slaves' willingness
to make a violent bid for freedom.

In such ruminations, the same planter-statesmen who had insisted early
on that they were safe because Spanish slavery was different in practice than
French slavery were gradually beginning to concede, implicitly at least, that
their own zeal to supplant French Saint-Domingue had diminished that
essential difference and with it one source of their original confidence in
their safety. Especially as the decade of the 1790s advanced, their confidence
seemed increasingly shaken. The planter elite continued to engage in their
intellectual and pragmatic reflections on balancing profit and survival, but
increasingly these reflections became less abstract. And increasingly they
were motivated by moments of crisis, brought on less by events in Saint-
Domingue than by more immediate events in Cuba itself. By the late 1790s,
the junta was prefacing its discussions of security with anxious discussions
about the presence of turmoil on its own soil. Though its members continued
to advocate the path of sugar and slavery, they now admitted that there was
cause for fear. The cause for this shift—and all the speculation and reflection
on slavery that it produced—can be found (as they themselves admitted) in
the growing resistance of enslaved men and women on the island. They noted
with displeasure and alarm the appearance and increase of unrest among the

enslaved, who they said were acting with greater and greater "organization and achievement."[12] In 1798, in one of its numerous reports on methods for ensuring the tranquility of slaves, the Junta de Fomento lamented that "five attempts at, or signs of, insurrection of a more or less serious nature have appeared in the short space of three years, which leaves no doubt that the seed of rebellion has evidently been planted among our slaves."[13]

How can we read the planters' repeated statements that slaves, seeing the example of revolution in Saint-Domingue, had become infested with the "seed of rebellion"? To pose this question is to suggest two avenues of inquiry, one relatively straightforward, the other significantly more challenging. The first avenue involves attempting to gauge the extent to which instances of conspiracies and outright rebellions were increasing in Cuba in the wake of the Haitian Revolution. Given how vigilant authorities and planters tried to be, the question is relatively easy to answer, with one possible caveat. With all the recent (and not-so-recent) controversy regarding the existence of conspiracies, we are reminded that just because authorities took voluminous testimony from slaves suspected of conspiring, we cannot always be sure whether the appearance of a conspiracy was the result of gossip, rumor, paranoia, and torture or in fact the product of concerted planning on the part of slaves. Still, we are certainly able to see if cases of alleged conspiracy were on the rise, and even more clearly can we identify cases of actual rebellion.

It is easy to corroborate the planters' claims that the subordination of the island's slaves had been deeply disturbed. Conspiracies or rebellions of various dimensions were in fact uncovered at fairly regular intervals: in 1795 in Bayamo and Puerto Príncipe; in 1796 in Puerto Príncipe; in 1798 in Trinidad, Güines, Mariel, Santa Cruz, and again in Puerto Príncipe; in 1802 in Managua; in 1803 in Río Hondo; in 1805 in Bayamo; in 1806 in Güines; in 1809 in Havana and Puerto Príncipe; and in 1811–1812 in Puerto Príncipe, Bayamo, Holguín, Remedios, and Havana.[14]

The list alone makes the statements of the Havana Consulado members seem at the very least plausible. The nature of these incidents varied tremendously. In Trinidad in 1798, for example, the problem seemed to involve mostly loose talk among enslaved men, yet there were enough of them and the talk was of an alarming enough nature that a wide repressive net was cast. Several slaves were executed and others were banished from the island. Despite authorities' eagerness to punish the alleged wrongdoers, the testimony in fact says very little about a concerted plan for rebellion. Most suspects denied taking part, and the two who confessed to conspiracy said they had done so only out of ignorance and begged for mercy. The ambitiousness of the scheme and the imagined links with revolutionary Saint-Domingue seemed to come more from the minds of anxious planters and authorities than from the slaves, and no rebellion ever ensued. By contrast, in

Puerto Príncipe just one month earlier, rebels managed to launch a rebellion in which they murdered whites on three farms and put others in the stocks before most of them were caught some days later.[15] It thus seems possible to relate white anxiety to an escalation of rebellion and conspiracy.

The second, related, avenue of inquiry is notably more difficult. The planters' assertion that in the aftermath of revolution in Saint-Domingue the seeds of rebellion had been internalized by the slaves, which is a claim about the slaves' interior world. It is a claim perhaps not unlike Genovese's statement that the "revolution in Saint-Domingue propelled a revolution in black consciousness throughout the New World."[16] Such an argument forces us to grapple with the intellectual and cognitive effects the example of Haiti had in the Atlantic World. In the sections that follow, I will try to address this question, first focusing on some of the impediments and limitations to any attempt to answer it and then seeing what we can learn from posing that question despite very real and substantial methodological obstacles.

Slavery and Freedom in Cuban Slave Testimony

The question of what slaves might have been thinking was likeliest to produce written documentation in moments of crisis—that is, in moments of rebellion or suspected conspiracy. In those moments, slaves were asked in very power-laden contexts to reveal their thoughts and recount the talk in which they had engaged. Usually after being apprehended by force and often under threat of torture, they were asked to testify in a language perhaps not their own. Then their words were recorded by a scribe who paraphrased them in the third person. This leaves us with perennial doubts not only about the veracity or completeness of what has come down to us as slave testimony but also with a much more basic doubt as to whether the words before us— "0 liberty," for instance, or "Haiti"—were actually the words spoken by the slave in question. Despite these inherent problems, scholars have tended to rely on existing testimony because it is one of the few written sources that comes close to capturing conversations among slaves and where slaves are asked to reflect on their servitude and their imagined or planned liberation.[17]

In the case of Cuba, the available slave testimony is voluminous. In almost all the cases of alleged conspiracy and rebellion noted above—as well as in many others—authorities rounded up suspects and took extensive testimony. Most often, the sequence went something like this: a slave on an estate would reveal to his master or overseer that he had been recruited to rebel and had rejected the invitation. That slave would be brought before authorities to be questioned; then the slaves he or she named as recruiters and organizers would be brought in and questioned as well. The net would invariably widen as individual slaves named other recruiters and recruits on their own and on neighboring estates. Before authorities and with a scribe present, they would answer questions under oath—if baptized, an oath taken by the sign of the cross, if not baptized they would be admonished to tell the truth or, in at least one instance, allowed to take an oath by the "god [they] adore[d]."[18]

From testimony to testimony, the questions would proceed routinely. The suspect would give his or her name, which often contained an ethnic marker (as in Mariano Congo, Genaro Lucumí, José Criollo), as well as age, status, place of birth and residence, occupation, name of master, and so on. Depending on the scale of the threat posed (or imagined), interrogators would ask enslaved witnesses about arms and about potential allies among whites and free people of color. In all cases, however, slaves would be asked to recount details of meetings and conversations with other slaves, to describe the specific plans for rebellion, and to divulge the names of everyone involved, in particular the names of leaders. In the process of answering such questions, enslaved witnesses incidentally revealed much about their daily life in enslavement—about work rhythms, about relationships among slaves and between slaves and free people, about slave participation in ethnic *cabildos*, about material culture and the informal slave economy, about festive gatherings, and especially about daily patterns of mobility that took them off their plantations to roads, towns, and other estates in the region.[19] Yet despite the testimony's richness, enticing bits of information—and even glaringly basic questions—were passed over as interrogators plowed forward, interested only in what they already knew they wanted to know.[20]

If the suspect appeared to have had any involvement at all in the conspiracy or rebellion, the questioning would become more intense. He or she would be brought back for questioning numerous times. Apparent contradictions were addressed by bringing in other witnesses to confront the suspect directly, and the written record paraphrases these public conversations (*careos*) before authorities. Denials would be met by explicit, sometimes aggressive, incredulity from interrogators, who countered slaves' denials with questions such as "how can he persist in his denials when it is clear that . . ." followed by a recitation of imputed meetings and conversations. At some point authorities almost always asked why witnesses had not informed their masters or authorities of the plot, because in the vast majority of cases they had not. Much of the testimony, particularly when officials believed the witness was implicated in any way, tended to end with a question that was probably more rhetorical than substantive, more about asserting authority than gathering information: Hadn't they realized the seriousness of their acts and the severity of the punishments reserved for those who engaged in them? So, in 1812, slave witnesses were asked "if [they] did not know that it is a most outrageous crime to promote, acquiesce in, or contribute to such rebellions, and even more outrageous when done with the resolute intention of killing people, nor is it less so to burn houses in the town, causing inexpressible havoc, and [did they not know] that the law has punishments established to teach a lesson to the commissioners of such crimes."[21]

If the structure of so much of the testimony is formulaic because of the repetition of questions from witness to witness, there is also a way in which the content of the testimony—and the answers given by the enslaved—can be almost equally formulaic. Denials were customary and the form they took completely predictable: he said he was asked to join but refused. Even the confessions of those who admit participation often seem pat and scripted, as they confessed plans to rise up, burn the plantation, kill the whites, march on the town, take control of arms in the forts, and gain their liberty and the land. Of course variations exist, but even the variations tend to take on the same form. For example, while there always seemed to be a generalized plan to kill the whites—"to clear the whites as one clears grass," in the words of one enslaved man—there were often disagreements about sparing or targeting particular masters, mistresses, children, or priests.[22] Sometimes amid stock talk about killing all the whites, witnesses elaborated on conversations about plans to kill specific people, sometimes in very specific ways. José Miguel González, identified as Mandinga, apparently one of the principal leaders of the January 1812 rebellion in Puerto Príncipe, for example, testified that Calixto, one of the co-organizers, had told him that "by the faith of a *Carabalí Vivi*, three individuals were going to pay: the first was his master whose flesh he would use to make a drum; the second was Mr. Reg . . . [illegible], and the third the governor, and their heads were going to dance."[23] But overall, the general outlines—and sometimes even the particular details—that emerge seem remarkably similar, even routine.

On the one hand, the repetitive (and voluminous) nature of the testimony can be overwhelming. On the other, its very sameness becomes a potential object of inquiry. If we think back to the planters' worries about the growing incidents of conspiracy and rebellion, we are reminded that is not just the specific answers and questions that are getting repeated over and over again, but rather the very ritual of slaves being brought before authorities to speak and explain. Over and over, authorities listened to denials that must have sounded scripted, as the vast majority of slaves under interrogation admitted that they had been asked to join a movement but said they had declined to do so. It is difficult to know whether the listeners, hearing very similar denials from one witness after another, would have been likelier to feel relieved that so many slaves rejected the call to insurrection or profoundly suspicious that among so many denials some at least may have been false.

By reading and listening carefully, however, we can move beyond the pat denials. For while most enslaved witnesses trumpeted their refusal of insurrection, they almost always went further and—unasked—volunteered the reasons for their refusal to rebel. Occasionally, enslaved witnesses explained that they did not join the movement because they were content with the treatment they received from their masters—because, in other words, they were loyal. This was a perhaps unsurprising answer given the context of a trial in which a verdict of guilty—for which the threshold was pretty low—resulted in certain public and painful death. In an 1806 conspiracy in Güines, for example, one slave testified that he declined to join because he had been born among whites, lived well, and was loyal to his mistress, to whom he had to hand over only a part of his daily wage. Yet the vast majority of slaves questioned explained that they had rejected the call to rebellion not out of loyalty but for much more pragmatic considerations. Mariano Congo claimed to have said no because he believed all the blacks would die, Juan Bautista because he believed the slaves to be outnumbered by whites and free people of color, José [Miguel] Catalina because his leg was injured, Tomás for fear of being killed, Rafael because, he said, he was a miserable old man.[24] Few rejected the inherent appeal and the justice of a rebellion to win their freedom; most simply judged that at that moment the forces against them were too powerful. Their refusal, they seemed to admit, was not necessarily for want of desire.

Authorities heard slaves paraphrase conversations among themselves that often blurred in their sameness, conversations in which names—of slaves, plantations, and towns—varied but in which the structure of the narrative remained remarkably consistent. In the back and forth between slaves and interrogators, one thing came across clearly in all the muddle: Talk of possible rebellion was a regular feature of this slave society, where fantasies of liberation seem to have found frequent voice. The repetition of such descriptions in the testimony referred to numerous similar conversations on plantations, on roads, and in towns. A slave who reported a conspiratorial conversation in detail might then, in passing, describe it as typical of the "chatter" (habladurías) that went on among slaves all the time. One slave in Trinidad in 1798 recounted a conversation with another slave in which they commented that the current conspiracy "was getting more serious and wasn't the same as every year"—an indication of the likely routine nature of such conversations.[25] Suggesting not only the constancy of such talk but also its universality among the enslaved, another witness, Calixto (the same person who allegedly talked about making a drum out of his master's flesh) admitted that he had been willing to help the rebels and had failed to warn the authorities. According to testimony, "he confessed to the charge made against him, but in order to clear his conscience, he warns that all the slaves as much inside as outside the town have the same disposition and that they are generally involved in this conversation, not specifying who those are because it would be a procedure ad infinitum."[26]

For authorities listening to such testimony the implications might have seemed daunting: a dense parade of enslaved witnesses describing one after another an endless number of conversations that referred to another indeterminate number of conversations, many of them about conspiracy, rebellion, and self-liberation. From both the volume and the repetitive content of the testimony a terrain emerges in which the enslaved seemed to be almost always imagining war and the freedom that would result from it.

In this light, the warnings and anxieties of the planter elite can be understood less as an abstract reaction to unprecedented news arriving from Haiti than as a reaction to the world that was revealed before them in judicial testimony. My point here is not that planters invariably reacted with fear or that slaves were always actually plotting a real rebellion but rather that in a context in which the Haitian Revolution (or Haiti itself) loomed large and in which the enslaved repeated over and over descriptions of conversations always about the same thing, local slave rebellion became part of the daily fabric of possibility. These conversations, imperfectly recorded later in judicial testimony, serve as a backdrop for the claims of white authorities about a world awash in danger, a world inhabited by slaves who had internalized the seeds of rebellion and authorities who were forced to adopt a posture of extreme vigilance to avert the budding of other Haitis.

The recitation of plans that always seemed the same, however, did more than affect the way such testimony might have been heard at the time. It may also affect the way the testimony is read by us as scholars. The testimony, consisting of hundreds of pages of similar conversations recounted with varying names, works in a way to decontextualize the speech of the enslaved. Confronted with answer after answer, one can forget whether one is reading about a conspiracy or rebellion in Cuba or the U.S. South or Brazil or Venezuela. Except for when there are references in the testimony to specific events such as the Haitian Revolution, one cannot tell if the discussion concerns a rebellion in, say, 1736 or the aftermath of the unprecedented events of 1791.

The consistency in the conception and description of plans for rebellion hint at a possible continuity of opportunities, strategies, and motivations for achieving freedom across New World societies. But that very sameness, although interesting and important as evidence of continuities across time and space, can also function to transport slaves' actions, their thoughts, and their words out of their time and place and—in a word—out of history. In so doing, the testimony tends to obscure the intellectual work in which slaves engaged as individuals and as communities as they learned of events around them and weighed their changing options and the relative merits of striking out or hanging back at a very particular moment in time. One of our tasks, then, in reading such testimony is to apprehend and move beyond its apparent sameness, to open up the spaces in which we can glimpse the cognitive world in which slaves lived, to see them interpreting the world around them and making political judgments about the possibilities of freedom.

For our purposes, one of the most important examples of historical context working its way into slave testimony is, perhaps not surprisingly, the regular references to the revolution in Saint-Domingue and, after 1804, to Haiti itself. Even if there were times—as in the 1798 Trinidad conspiracy—when the example of Haiti was more often cited by fearful authorities than it was by the enslaved, there were a greater number of instances when enslaved men and women themselves brought up Haitian events, suggesting that the example set there was very much on their minds as they contemplated their own fates and possibilities.

Speaking of Haiti

Let us turn now to slaves' invocations of Haiti. These took myriad forms in slave testimony. First, Haiti came up as goal, as a desired end. If planters and authorities insisted that enslaved people around them were seeking to emulate Haiti, slaves themselves often testified to just that. These are the most general references to Haiti found in slave testimony from this period. Slaves testified that in conversations among themselves they talked about Haiti and held up that revolution as an example. This was the case in Güines in 1806 in a conspiracy whose leaders were three enslaved men. One was a Saint-Domingue–born slave who allegedly boasted to others that he had participated in that revolution, another was a Cuban creole who could read and write, and another a Kongolese man more recently arrived. Slaves confessed to saying that if they rose up, killed the whites, and took the fort in town, they would be free like their counterparts in Haiti, who had taken back the land from the whites. Those men were now "absolute masters of the land." Sometimes this kind of invocation became a sort of dare: If the French slaves could do it, why not them? They needed, recruiters said, to have "balls," as the slaves of Saint-Domingue had shown.[27] For these slaves, Haiti signified not only the murder of whites or the end of slavery but a more general victory as well: the forceful taking of the land and the exercise of total mastery.

Often when slaves spoke about what happened in Haiti, they tried to divine what might have accounted for the success of the rebellion there, perhaps to explore the extent to which that success might be reproducible on their home turf. For example, in Puerto Príncipe, two enslaved men, one Mandinga, the other Carabalí, saw one possible source of success in the "faith" of Haitian rebels. One demanded of the other "if he didn't see what the blacks had done in Le Cap, where as long as they failed to take action and finish off the whites they didn't deserve victory and did not succeed in getting a king, [whereas] now everything that will happen here is ordained by God and so we will win." To this the other concurred that if those from France had "accomplished so many feats, it was because they defended the faith of Christ."[28] If the explicit reference to Christ here was somewhat unusual in the testimony, the general outlines of the conversation were not: Haiti was taken up as a model, and direct links between what happened there and what might happen in Cuba were boldly imagined. Even when they weren't talking about Haiti as ultimate goal, they appeared to have talked about the revolution in general and about the feats of their Haitian *compañeros* in particular.[29]

In fact, enslaved men (we have no evidence here about women) seemed to know quite a bit about particular Haitian counterparts. In numerous conspiracies and rebellions, slaves testified to having been recruited with promises that they could serve as captains, as had Toussaint Louverture or Jean-François in the revolution in Saint-Domingue. Thus, in Bayamo in 1805, slaves confessed that they had been lured by promises that they would have roles comparable to these leaders. Such statements seemed to echo the claim of the Cuban captain-general in 1795 that the names of such leaders resounded among the population of color in Havana like the names of well-known conquerors. Even when suspects denied any participation in rebellion or conspiracy, they admitted that they did in fact engage in sustained conversations about men like Toussaint and Jean-François, both former slaves turned generals. For example, a lot of the recruiting that went on for the Aponte conspiracy in 1812 in Havana appears to have involved talk of Haitian leaders, as Aponte and others shared images of Toussaint and Christophe and another took on the name and persona of Jean-François.[30] Even farther afield in Remedios, the lawyer for a free person of color suspected of participating in a conspiracy that was perhaps related to Aponte's rebellion defended his client by arguing that all he had done was "to talk with other blacks about the political status of those of his class on the island of Santo Domingo and of the coronation of Christophe." The lawyer then asked why it should seem strange "that this man should talk about events so worthy of capturing one's attention by virtue of their rarity."[31]

Haiti also comes up in another way. In many of these alleged conspiracies and rebellions, the accused made regular reference to aid coming directly from Haiti. This claim—present not only in Cuba but elsewhere in the Atlantic World—was not a vague expression of sympathy or admiration for Haiti, as we have seen in some of the examples above, but rather a concrete (if generally unfounded) assertion that they believed the Haitian republic they so much admired stood ready to commit money, arms, and forces for their own liberation. Sometimes the alleged aid was in the form of a ship waiting off the coast with men and munitions. Other times it was in the form of emissaries of Haitian leaders bringing proclamations of freedom for local slaves. Such assertions in the testimony allow us to glimpse a potentially strong sense of solidarity in which enslaved people in Cuba (or elsewhere) imagined themselves to be, on the one hand, emulators of Haitian rebels and, on the other, objects of

Haitian benevolence and an activist Haitian foreign policy.

Together these three modes of reference to Haiti—expressions of general admiration, mention of specific Haitian leaders, and assertions of imminent Haitian assistance—provide further evidence in support of what numerous scholars have argued: that knowledge of the Haitian Revolution circulated among slaves and free people of color across the Atlantic World. But we can take these Haitian references further. Rather than simply point out that local slaves invoked Haiti, I suggest we do more to interrogate why, when, and how they did so. To simply list Haitian references that appear in a range of local incidents makes Haiti seem like a vague ahistorical constant that could be invoked at any time after 1791. To some extent, this may be true; that is, enslaved people could invoke it as example and model without much elaboration, using vague allusions to serve their purposes.[32] But I think there is also a way in which invocations of Haiti were often not vague but specific and historically contingent. In the sections that follow, I examine one specific type of invocation of Haiti in Cuban slave testimony in order to suggest that such invocations were part of an active engagement with the intellectual and political currents then circulating in the Caribbean and Atlantic worlds.

The theme of Haitian aid for rebels recurred in a number of locations in Cuba and elsewhere, beginning with a little-known conspiracy in 1805 on the island of Trinidad, where a suspect-turned-informer testified that conspirators had been collecting money and arms for two years under the direction of Haitian agents. Denmark Vesey's much more notorious (alleged) conspiracy in Charleston in 1822, the Aponte conspiracy in Cuba in 1812, and the Escalera conspiracy in 1843–1844 all produced statements about imminent Haitian assistance for local efforts to win freedom. Historians have generally approached such claims from one of two viewpoints. They have accepted and incorporated such claims into narratives about an unwavering Haitian commitment to an expansive New World freedom, despite a glaring lack of evidence. Or they have dismissed them as spurious, products of either overactive imaginations or loose or drunken talk. Proponents of this latter view emphasize the noninterventionist claims made in the early Haitian constitutions, all of which renounced the idea of Haiti as "an incendiary torch" in the region. Such proponents also argue that Haitian leaders could not have risked secretly supporting or fomenting revolution in the Caribbean. To have done so would have been to risk provoking a maritime blockade or invasion. The very politics of survival suggest that Haiti could not (and therefore did not) pursue an activist antislavery foreign policy.[33]

It is impossible at this point to prove that Haitian help was destined for any of the post-1804 conspiracies in which such allegations surfaced. But it is equally true that disproving the possibility of secret Haitian assistance is also a formidable task, especially given the relative scarcity of Haitian state sources for the immediate post-independence period.[34] Rather than focus on the question of the reality of Haitian assistance, it may be more fruitful to explore when, why, and under what specific circumstances Cuban (or other) slaves believed Haitian assistance was coming. Was this merely a ploy by slave leaders to entice recruits with visions of a powerful supporter for their endeavors? Perhaps, but that would suggest that we would find this assertion in more conspiracies than we do. In fact, though it recurs, it is not nearly universal. What allowed such assertions to emerge in particular moments and places? If we shift the focus and try to contextualize slave testimony, to recreate a world of news, references, and rumor to which slaves had access in the periods immediately before or during the alleged conspiracies, then we can read their claims about Haitian aid in a new light. The point here is to understand those claims and to explain what might have made them plausible enough for slaves to restate them to each other and before a court. The claims, then, can be read less as true or false statements about Haitian foreign policy than as windows into the intellectual and political world inhabited by enslaved and free people of color in Cuba.

One time when claims about Haitian aid gathered considerable momentum was during the 1812 Aponte rebellion, the most widespread and ambitious conspiracy in Cuba in this period.[35] Its leader was a free black carpenter who recruited slaves and free people, showing them pictures in a book that he had made, which included images of scenes and people from Saint-Domingue. Others who were implicated appear to have seen or carried printed pictures of Henri Christophe. One conspirator took on the name of one of the most important slave rebels of the early revolution in Saint-Domingue—Jean-François, usually identified in the record as Juan Fransuá. Conspirators thus drew bold and explicit links between their efforts and both the history (Jean-François) and present state (Christophe) of Haiti. But they also went further, asserting that this link was reciprocal: they emulated Haiti, yes, but Haiti itself stood behind them, prepared to aid them in their endeavor. Several key witnesses testified that 5,000 Haitians were under the orders of two Haitian officers waiting in the hills of Monserrate (Havana) ready to swoop down and fight for the freedom of Cuban slaves as soon as the rebellion began.[36] The claim, needless to say, is hard to believe. As hard as it is to document systematically the actions of early Haitian governments, it is not plausible to think that Christophe could have sent an army of 5,000 to Spanish territory without some other trace surviving in the historical record.

The claim that two Haitian officers were present in Havana lobbying for the freedom of Cuban slaves was especially widespread. It appeared not only in the testimony of free leaders of color but also in the testimony of slaves from the rural countryside around Havana. Slaves—some of them apparently coachmen—seem to have discussed the presence in Havana of two Haitian officials sent by Christophe, identified usually as the king of Haiti or the king of the blacks, in order to request or demand their freedom from the captain-general.[37] This is the kind of claim that would be easy to dismiss. There were no formal relations between Spain and Haiti at this time. Whatever his desire to end slavery outside of Haiti, Christophe was not very likely to send officials to negotiate the end of slavery in Cuba, given his own international vulnerability and the growing strength of Cuban slavery at the time. But rather than dismiss the slaves' claims as false or as wishful thinking and rather than leave things there and point simply to the power of Haiti in the thinking of these slave witnesses, I suggest we take the claim further, trying, if even in a speculative manner, to interrogate its possible origins and meanings.

Might such claims have referred to anything specific? Interestingly, after some correspondence between Christophe and Havana's Governor Someruelos, the latter received a royal order from Spain instructing him to send a Spanish agent or emissary to Christophe in order to cultivate good rela-tions. But the Havana governor, after thinking it through, came to the conclu-sion that if he were to send an emissary to Christophe, then Christophe would expect to send one of his own in return, as might Pétion in the south as well. The prospect of high-ranking Haitian officials moving around Havana seemed so potentially dangerous that Someruelos decided not to comply with the royal order, a refusal eventually approved by his superiors in Spain.[38] It is, of course, impossible to know the extent to which this back and forth about potential emissaries of Christophe circulated beyond the governor and his immediate circle. But we do know that the governor's personal coachman was one of the first men questioned and implicated in the Aponte conspiracy in Havana and that the rumor about the two Haitian agents sent by Christophe circulated intensively among black coachmen who testified. It is not impossible that a connection existed, but we are still a long way from understanding a certain origin for the assertions about the pair of Haitian officials demanding freedom for Cuban slaves from the governor.

One possibility is that such claims referred instead to one of the conspir-ators in the plot, Juan Barbier, a freed slave who appears to have spent time in Charleston and in Saint-Domingue and who in Cuba in 1811–1812 took on the name, persona, and sometimes the uniform of Jean-François. He tried to recruit slaves by presenting himself as someone now in Havana to fight for their freedom.[39] There were also other "French" figures in Havana at the time of the conspiracy. Men who had served under the real (although by that time dead) Jean-François in Saint-Domingue in 1793–1795 and who had been exiled from the island were in 1811–1812 returning to Santo Domingo and claimed to have stopped in Havana en route. During their several-month stay in Havana they appear to have had contact with local people of color, who, according to the testimony of the sojourners, displayed great interest in their military uniforms. Between the elusive Barbier/Fransuá and the former officers of the real but deceased Jean-François, there seem to have been flesh-and-blood referents for the vague but persistent testimony that two Haitian officers were working for freedom in Havana.

In the testimony, however, the pair of Haitian officers work for freedom at the behest of Henri Christophe, as officials sent by the Haitian state to meet with the highest authorities in Cuba to demand the freedom of Cuban slaves. Meanwhile, the specific testimony about Juan Fransuá and the black officers en route to Hispaniola never makes mention of such a mission. So what made witnesses so sure that Haitian figures officially represented a Haitian state engaged in a policy of international antislavery that aimed at securing their own freedom? It would certainly be possible to read the slaves' belief in this Haitian mission as an expression of wishful thinking. It would be even more plausible to read it simply as a powerful appropriation of the memory of the Haitian Revolution to serve the interests and desires of Cuban slaves at a particular moment. I think, however, that it makes more sense to read this belief as part of slaves' sustained interpretation of recent Haitian acts and interesting Haitian news then circulating in Havana.

Many of the slaves who testified in the Aponte case (and free people as well) clearly knew that Christophe was the ruler of Haiti, and most of them further knew that he had been recently crowned. Most referred to him as the king of Haiti or Guarico or the blacks. Some specifically recalled discussing the news of his coronation, which occurred on June 2, 1811. But beyond his very existence, was there anything concrete that might have made Cuban slaves and free people of color think that he was willing to bring freedom to their own land?

As we have seen, the early Haitian state beginning in 1804 explicitly eschewed the possibility of taking freedom to the colonies and islands of the region by force. In a provocative discussion of the early Haitian constitutions, Sibylle Fischer has noted that such statements should be read in conjunction with constitutional provisions regarding the boundaries of citizenship. These, she argues, became increasingly broad in their conception: from the 1805 constitution, in which Haitians who left the island lost their citizenship, to Christophe's 1807 constitution, which stated simply that every resident of Haiti was free, to Pétion's 1816 constitution, which stated that all Africans and Indians who came to live in Haiti would enjoy full citizenship rights after one year of residence. The very vagueness and increasing scope of these provisions can be read as a "trace of the transnational nature of radical antislavery" and can thus be fruitfully juxtaposed with the articles that promise Haitian noninvolvement in the affairs of neighboring colonies and states.[40]

The vague provisions regarding citizenship can also be fruitfully read alongside other Haitian acts and laws regarding residency. Just days after the declaration of independence, Dessalines passed a law that provided for payment to American ship captains for the return of people of color who had been removed from Saint-Domingue and now wished to return. Over the next decade or so, Haitian leaders returned to this idea regularly. In 1809, for instance, Pétion sent a ship to Cuba to bring back Haitians who wanted to return and requested permission to keep sending such ships, since potential passengers were not likely to have the resources to organize return trips on their own.[41] Pétion had to have known that those interested in such policies might, in fact, be held as slaves by other refugees or by Spanish or Cuban slaveholders who had purchased them from French refugees years earlier. Thus, in the period of significant conspiracy and rebellion, Haitian ships arrived hoping to take back refugees (who by then of course were local residents) to freedom in Haiti, and black officers in uniform stopped in Cuba en route to Santo Domingo.

But other black people as well were ending up in Haiti in this period, and slaves in Cuba were hearing all about it. Early in 1811, news began arriving in Havana about new and daring acts by Christophe in the north, who was intercepting slave ships bound for Cuba, liberating the Africans on board, bringing them to Haitian soil as ostensibly free men and women, and sending the crews and empty ships on their way. In 1810–1812, such was the fate of at least three ships: the *Nueva Gerona*, an unnamed Portuguese ship en route with 440 Africans from Rio to Havana, and the *Santa Ana*, whose shipment of 205 slaves was liberated and taken by Christophe's forces to the port of Gonaïves. In addition, the Havana Junta Consular referred to the capture of "various slave ships" prior to the interception of these three, news of which, they said, was circulating in Havana.[42] Fox example, Francisco Xavier Pacheco, allegedly one of the principal conspirators in the Aponte rebellion in Havana, confessed shortly before his execution that when Aponte showed him a portrait of King Christophe, he had explained "that England was intercepting the ships that came loaded with blacks because it no longer wanted slavery, sending them to [Haiti] to be governed by the black king."[43]

If such news circulated, we can be sure that one of its key points of transmission was the docks, where the arrival of empty slave ships whose original human cargo had been taken to Haiti would have found a most attentive audience. As is well known, many of the figures questioned in association with the Aponte conspiracy were men who frequented the docks as workers or simply as residents of a bustling port city. Many further testified to having heard news of the current conspiracy and of Haiti itself at the docks. It was in fact at the docks where Haitian artifacts and images circulated from hand to hand, including perhaps one in which Christophe stood over a caption that said *"Cumple lo mandado"* ("Execute what is ordered"). It was in this world that slaves and free people of color talked about Christophe's commitment to their freedom—a world where men and women who would have been enslaved alongside them had through the intervention of Christophe reached free soil.[44]

Conclusion

If we think back now to our original question of what slavery and freedom looked like from a colonial Cuba inescapably in the orbit of the Haitian Revolution, we see that some of the usual categories and concepts used to analyze such questions seem somehow inadequate. It is hard, for example, to apply simple dichotomies of fear and greed to the planter-statesmen who choreographed the turn to sugar and slavery. These men, notwithstanding their greed, thought very hard about things that scared them and about threats to the wealth they were creating. It was from these efforts to reconcile rapid growth based on slavery with immediate and long-term security that some of their most serious intellectual efforts ensued. These efforts, moreover, did not emerge in a vacuum. Their willingness and urgency in taking up such matters resulted precisely from the actions of the enslaved, who made the planters' initial predictions about security seem facile and forced them to think about the potential perils of emulating Saint-Domingue. The actions of local slaves were thus very much a part of the intellectual and social field in which Cuban and Spanish planters and politicians operated.

But what of the enslaved and their place in a post-Haiti Cuba? Undoubtedly the example of the Haitian Revolution gave local resistance, conspiracy, and rebellion new momentum. Even though no rebellion came close to assuming the proportions of the Haitian example and even though in most cases actual rebellion was thwarted, it is clear that the Haitian Revolution, and Haiti itself, became part of the cognitive world of the enslaved, who assumed it as metaphor, possibility, and goal.

Here, however, it is important to remember that Haiti was also more than a symbol, more than a vague memory or invocation of revolution available for the taking. Though slaves and free people clearly invoked it as a metaphor for freedom or radical change, they also engaged it as a living active agent. They consumed and thought about the most current information available to them, developing and sharing interpretations with one another about the meanings of Haitian events in relation to their own world. The traces of this intellectual process are audible in the voluminous slave testimony. And the traces of those conversations, as fragmentary and mediated as they are, leave further traces of an engagement with Haiti as a state whose presence was in some way felt in their lives; as a state capable, for example, of freeing captives bound for Cuba; as a state whose very existence and whose actions (based on what they heard in Cuba) might in some way contribute to their own liberation. In this light, slave testimony about Haiti emerges less as vague abstraction or groundless hope. It can be seen, rather, as the product of slaves' sustained intellectual and political engagement with the tumultuous world of the Age of Revolution, a world that—based on their evidence and interpretation—might produce enough openings to help them generate freedom in their own lifetime.

Notes

Vincent Brown, Laurent Dubois, Sibylle Fischer, Alejandro de la Fuente, David Geggus, Martha Hodes, and Louis Perez commented on the paper at different points; I am grateful for all their suggestions and input. I am also grateful to Ana Dopico, Aisha Finch, Rebecca Scott, Julius Scott, and Walter Johnson for many instructive conversations about the problems treated in this essay.

1. *Gaceta de Madrid,* May 18, 1804.

2. Las Casas to Príncipe de la Paz, December 16, 1795, Estado, leg. 5B, exp. 176, Archivo General de Indias, Sevilla (hereafter AGI).

3. See Eugene Genovese, *From Rebellion to Revolution: Afro-American Slave Revolts in the Making of the Modern World* (Baton Rouge: Louisiana State University Press, 1979), 96; Julius Scott, "The Common Wind: Currents of Afro-American Communication in the Era of the Haitian Revolution" (Ph.D. diss., Duke University, 1986); and Laurent Dubois, "An Enslaved Enlightenment: Rethinking the Intellectual History of the French Atlantic," *Social History* 31, no. 1 (2006): 1–14.

4. Francisco Arango y Parreño, "Representación hecha a S.M. con motivo de la sublevación de esclavos en los dominios franceses de la Isla de Santo Domingo," November 20, 1791, in *Obras de D. Francisco de Arango y Parreño* (Havana: Ministerio de Educación, 1952), 1:111–112.

5. Figures are from Manuel Moreno Fraginals, *El ingenio* (Havana: Ciencias Sociales, 1978); and Laird W. Bergad, Fe Iglesias Garcia, Maria del Carmen Barci, *The Cuban Slave Market* (Cambridge: Cambridge University Press, 1995).

6. On the founding of Havana's Real Consulado, see Peter J. Lampros, "Merchant-Planter Cooperation and Conflict: The Havana Consulado, 1794–1832" (Ph.D. diss., Tulane University, 1980); and Maria Dolores González-Ripoll Navarro, *Cuba, la isla de los ensayos* (Madrid: CSIC, 1999), 182–194.

7. "Copia del expediente no. 134 sobre proponer al Rey un plan para asegurar la tranquilidad y obediencia de sus siervos en esta Colonia en Representacion de 10 de Julio de 1799," in "Expediente sobre el fomento de la poblacion blanca en esta Ysla," Real Consulado y Junta de Fomento (hereafter RCJF), leg. 184, exp. 8330, Archivo Nacional de Cuba, Havana (hereafter ANC). Alexander von Humboldt must have had a copy of this document when he wrote his famous *Ensayo Político Sobre la Isla de Cuba,* for much of his chapter on slavery is taken verbatim from it. See Humboldt, *Ensayo Político* (Paris: Jules Renouard, 1827), 276n. For a recent and fresh perspective

on Humboldt's writings on Cuban slavery based on newly discovered manuscripts, see Michael Zeuske, "Comparando el Caribe: Alexander von Humboldt, Saint-Domingue y los comienzos de la comparación de la esclavitud en las Américas," *Estudos Afro-Asiáticos* (Rio de Janeiro) 26, no. 2 (2004): 381–416.

8. Arango, "Representación hecha a S.M. con motivo de la sublevación de esclavos."

9. "Copia del expediente no. 134 sobre proponer al Rey un plan para asegurar la tranquilidad y obediencia de sus siervos en esta Colonia en Representacion de 10 de Julio de 1799," in "Expediente sobre el fomento de la poblacion blanca en esta Ysla," RCJF, leg. 184, exp. 8330, ANC.

10. Ada Ferrer, "Cuba en la sombra de Haití: Noticias, sociedad y esclavitud," in María Dolores González-Ripoll, Consuejo Naranjo, Ada Ferrer, Gloria Garcia, and Josef Opartný, *El rumor de Haití en Cuba: Temor, raza y rebeldía, 1789–1844* (Madrid: CSIC, 2004), especially 203–214.

11. O'Farrill, López, and Patrón to Conde de Santa Clara, August 18, 1798, in "Expediente relativo a las precauciones y seguridad," RCJF, leg. 209, exp. 8993, ANC.

12. "Copia del expediente no. 134 sobre proponer al Rey un plan para asegurar la tranquilidad y obediencia de sus siervos en esta Colonia en Representacion de 10 de Julio de 1799," in "Expediente sobre el fomento de la poblacion blanca en esta Ysla," RCJF, leg. 184, exp. 8330, ANC.

13. O'Farrill, Lopez, Patron, to Conde de Santa Clara, August 18, 1798, in "Expediente relativo a las precauciones y seguridad en orden a los Negros en Gral y en particular a los introducidos de las colonias extranjeras," RCJF, leg. 209, exp. 8993, ANC.

14. Evidence of uprisings and conspiracies is in the following sources: For Serapio Recio's slaves in Puerto Príncipe, see Estado, leg. 5A, exp. 15, AGI; [Viana] to Las Casas, June 14, 1795, RCJF, leg. 209, exp. 8993, ANC; and in Cuba, leg. 1463B, AGI. For French slaves in Puerto Príncipe in 1796, though evidence is not compelling, see Alfonso Viana to Las Casas, May 19, 1796, RCJF, 209, 8993, ANC. For Güines, Mariel, and Santa Cruz in 1798, CM Morales, T. 6, no. 10, Biblioteca Nacional José Martí, Havana (hereafter BNJM). For Puerto Príncipe in 1798, see Vidal Morales y Morales, *Iniciadores y primeros mártires* (Havana, 1901), 132. For Managua in 1802, see Junta Consular to Capitán General, June 9, 1802 (may be 1803), RCJF, leg. 150, exp. 7407, ANC. For Río Hondo in 1803, see Real Consulado to Someruelos, February 24, 1803, Cuba, leg. 1651, AGI. For Bayamo in 1805, see "Testimonio de la criminalidad," Cuba, leg. 1649, AGI. For Havana (free people of color against French) and Puerto Principe in 1809, see CM Arredondo, BNJM. For the Aponte rebellions and conspiracies in 1811–1812, see Matt Childs, *The 1812 Aponte Rebellion in Cuba and the Struggle against Slavery* (Chapel Hill: University of North Carolina Press, 2006).

15. See "Testimonio de autos seguidos de oficio criminal contra varios negros de los ingenios de Trinidad sobre el levantamiento que intentaban contra los blancos," July 25, 1798, Asuntos Políticos (hereafter AP), leg. 7, exp. 30, ANC.

16. Genovese, *From Rebellion to Revolution*, 96.

17. For some important Cuban examples of work on slave testimony, see Gloria García, *Conspiraciones y revueltas: La actividad política de los negros (1790–1845)* (Havana: Editorial Oriente, 2003); and Manuel Barcia, *A Colossus in the Sand: The Guamacaro Slave Revolt of 1825*, forthcoming; Aisha Finch, "Insurgency at the Crossroads: Cuban Slaves

and the Escalera Conspiracy" (Ph.D. diss. in progress, New York University). There has also been a recent revival of interest in the Aponte conspiracy, which has brought scholars of different disciplines to the judicial testimony in that case. See Childs, *The 1812 Aponte Rebellion*; Sibylle Fischer, *Modernity Disavowed: Haiti and the Cultures of Slavery in the Age of Revolution* (Durham, N.C.: Duke University Press, 2004); and Stephan Palmié, *Wizards and Scientists: Explorations in Afro-Cuban Modernity and Tradition* (Durham, N.C.: Duke University Press, 2002).

18. Oaths taken by the sign of the cross appear in the vast majority of testimonies of both free and enslaved. Among non-Christian slaves, the reminder to tell the truth in testimony appears in testimony of José Agustín, Cuba, leg. 1780, f. 107, AGI. An oath by non-Christian gods appears in testimony of Joaquín in "Bautista y Juan Antonio sobre la conjuración que intentaban contra el Pueblo y sus moradores," [Bayamo], 1805, Cuba, leg. 1649, AGI.

19. For a sense of the rich material contained in such testimony, see Gloria García, *La esclavitud desde la esclavitud* (Havana: Ciencias Sociales, 2003). For a particularly fruitful mining of testimony for this kind of information on the everyday life of slavery and its links to instances of rebellion and conspiracy, see Finch, "Crossroads of Insurgency."

20. My thinking on working with slave judicial testimony has been influenced by several historians: by Winthrop Jordan's insistence that we do our best to listen to, contextualize, and attend to the details in slave testimony, resisting the temptation to force that testimony into generalizing narratives more important to historians than to the witnesses involved; by Carlo Ginzburg's attention to the ways in which the assumptions of interrogators shape the testimony produced in judicial encounters; and by Martin Lienhard's cautions about the need to examine carefully the production of the written testimony itself and the interplay between the oral and the written at work in its production. See Jordan, *Tumult and Silence at Second Creek* (Baton Rouge: Louisiana State University Press, 1995); Ginzburg, *Night Battles* (New York: Penguin, 1983); and Lienhard, *Testimonios, cartas y manifiestos indígenas* (Caracas: Biblioteca Ayacucho, 1992).

21. Testimony of Nicolás, f. 86, Puerto Príncipe, January 22, 1812, Cuba, leg. 1780, AGI.

22. The quote is "*bamos* [sic] *a chapear blancos como se chapea llerba*," which comes from the testimony of Bartolomé (negro, casta Mandinga, esclavo), who attributed it to Nicolás, January 18, 1812, Cuba, 1780, ff. 48v–49, AGI. The phrase also appears in the testimony of José, casta Congo, who attributes it to Nicolás and four other slaves from the same plantation. Ibid., ff. 16–17v.

23. Testimony of José Miguel Gonzáles, January 25, 1812, Cuba, leg. 1780, ff. 72v–73v, AGI.

24. "Expediente criminal contra Francisco Fuertes y demas negros . . . sobre levantamiento en el pueblo de Güines," AP, leg. 9, exp. 27, ANC.

25. Testimony of Jose María Peña, alias Curazao, Trinidad, 1798, AP, leg. 7, f. 31v, exp. 30, ANC.

26. Testimony of Calixto, January 21, 1812, Cuba, leg. 1780, ff. 82v–84v, AGI.

27. "Expediente criminal contra Francisco Fuertes y demas negros . . . sobre levan-

tamiento en el pueblo de Güines," AP, leg. 9, exp. 27, ANC. For a more detailed discussion, see Ada Ferrer, "La société esclavagiste cubaine et la révolution haïtienne," *Annales* 58, no. 2 (2003): 333–356.

28. See testimony of José Miguel Gonzáles describing conversation with Calixto, January 25, 1812, Cuba, 1780, ff. 73–73v, AGI.

29. If the reference to Jesus Christ is somewhat unusual, more general references to faith are not. For example, Juan Barbier, also know as Juan Francisco or Jean-François, was said to recruit slaves by telling them that he was fighting "for faith and liberty" ("*que venía a tomar la Habana no peleando por otra cosa que por la fé y por la livertad*"). AP, leg. 13, exp. 1, ANC.

30. On the figure of Jean-François in the Aponte rebellion, see Childs, *The 1812 Aponte Rebellion*, chapter 5.

31. "Consulta de los autos seguidos por la . . . ordinaria contra varios negros por sublevacion," April 30, 1812, AP, leg. 12, exp. 27, ANC.

32. See Ferrer, "La société esclavagiste cubaine et la révolution haïtienne."

33. For examples of the first view, see St. Victor Jean-Baptiste, *Le fondateur devant l'histoire* (1954; repr., Port-au-Prince: Editions Presses Nationales d'Haïti, 2006), chap. 5; and Jean Fouchard, "Quand Haïti exportait la liberté aux Antilles," *Revue de la Société Haïtienne de Histoire et de Géographie* 143 (1984): 41–47. On the second view, see David Geggus, "Slavery, War, and Revolution in the Greater Caribbean," in *A Turbulent Time: The French Revolution and the Greater Caribbean*, ed. D. B. Gaspar and D. Geggus (Bloomington: Indiana University Press, 1997), 1–50.

34. On early Haitian foreign policy, see Maurice Lubin, "Les premiers rapports de la nation haïtienne avec l'étranger," *Journal of Inter-American Studies* 10, no. 2 (1968): 277–305; Jean Coradin, *Histoire diplomatique d'Haïti, 1804–1843* (Port-au-Prince: Edition des Antilles, 1988); and Eddy Etienne, *La vraie dimension de la politique extérieure des premiers gouvernements d'Haïti (1804–1843)* (Quebec: Naaman, 1982).

35. For recent work on Aponte, see Childs, *The Aponte Rebellion*; Fischer, *Modernity Disavowed*; and Palmié, *Wizards and Scientists*. The early work of José Luciano Franco is indispensable. See especially *Las conspiraciones de 1810 y 1812* (Havana: Ciencias Sociales, 1977); and *Ensayos históricos* (Havana: Ciencias Sociales, 1974).

36. See, for example, the *careo* (judicial confrontation) between Aponte and Ternero, March 25, 1812, AP, leg. 12, exp. 18, ANC; and that between Aponte and Chacón, March 19, 1812, AP, leg. 12, exp. 14, ANC. There is an interesting variation in this *careo* in which one of them reminds the other to recall that he had even given the names of the two officers: "*siendo hijos de la Havana que habían ido al Guarico para incorporarse al Exército del Rey Cristoval.*"

37. In addition to the testimony above, see testimony of the following slaves: moreno Damaso Mina, esclavo de los bienes de D Antonio de Quintana; moreno José Antonio Lucumí, esclavo de los bienes de D. Antonio Quintana; moreno Gabriel (Mandinga), esclavo de D. Esteban León; negro Joaquín, esclavo del Pbro. D. Domingo José Pérez; and Juan, negro esclavo de José Reguiferos; all in AP, leg. 12, exp. 26, ANC. See also the testimony of Salvador Ternero, AP, leg. 12, exp. 14, ANC.

According to the testimony of several slaves, the captain-general seemed almost willing to grant slaves their freedom, but the move was successfully opposed by Sres.

Conde Barreto and Peñalver. Why these slaves would have mentioned these two prominent Havana families is unclear. Both were part of the Havana establishment and members of each family held prominent posts, from vicar of Havana to mayor. Just three years before these events, Barreto had made himself the most vocal critic of Francisco Arango y Parreño's effort to create an independent junta, which had been done elsewhere in Spanish America in response to the Napoleonic invasion of Spain. In light of the fact that some of the Aponte conspirators pinned what has been called a declaration of independence on the captain-general's door, it is interesting to think of rumors circulating among slaves about opposition to emancipation coming from the same figure who vocally opposed an independent junta. At this point such connections must remain speculative, but at the very least it suggests that enslaved witnesses managed to connect their knowledge of the Haitian Revolution with knowledge about their specific local political setting. Perhaps more immediately relevant is the fact that of the fifteen men executed in Havana in connection with the Aponte rebellion, six were slaves owned by a member of the Peñalver family and one was a free black of the same last name.

The story about Barreto and Peñalver appears in the testimonies of Damaso Mina, José Antonio Lucumí, Joaquín, and Juan, all in AP, leg. 12, exp. 26, ANC. For information on Barreto and Peñalver, see Francisco Calcagno, *Diccionario biográfico cubano* (New York, 1878); and Allen Kuethe, *Cuba, 1753–1815* (Knoxville, Tenn., 1986), 160, 169.

38. See the 1809 correspondence between Christophe, Someruelos, and multiple Spanish authorities in Estado, leg. 12, exps. 57, 50, 51, 54, AGI. On Christophe sending agents to meet with Spanish authorities in Philadelphia, see Estado, leg. 12, no. 54, AGI.

39. This claim is repeated many times in the testimony. See especially AP, leg. 13, exp. 1, ANC.

40. Fischer, *Modernity Disavowed*, chap. 11; quote appears on p. 241.

41. The 1804 law appears in *Lois et actes sous le règne de Jean-Jacques Dessalines* (Port-au-Prince: Editions Presses Nationales d'Haïti, 2006), 13–14. On Pétion's policy, see the correspondence between Pétion and Santiago de Cuba's governor Sebastián Kindelán, between Kindelán and Havana governor Someruelos, and between Someruelos and Secretario de Estado, Madrid, in AP, leg. 213, exp. 41, ANC; AP, leg. 209, exp. 144, ANC; and Estado, leg. 12, exp. 54, AGI.

42. On these three examples, see Junta Consular to Capitán General, February 23, 1811, and June 26, 1811, CM Morales, Tomo 79, nos 23 and 26, respectively, BNJM; and Claudio Martínez Pinillos to Real Consulado, March 24, 1812, AP, leg. 106, exp. 21, ANC. Haitian interception of slave ships is discussed briefly in José Luciano Franco, *Comercio clandestino de esclavos* (Havana, 1996), 106–107. The fate of the Santa Ana, which was taken to the port of Gonaives, may be linked to the history of the famous village and ritual center of Souvenance, a few miles from that city. A possible connection to Souvenance at this point is speculative. In oral and popular history, the origins of the place are associated with a slave ship whose human cargo was liberated and taken to that area in roughly this period. Personal communication from Patrick Tardieu, November 2006, and Michel Hector and Jean Casimir, February 2007.

To my knowledge, no one has worked on the Haitian capture of slave ships, and it is thus impossible at this point to know how widespread or rare the practice was, whether it affected other slaveholding powers, the extent to which such acts were carried out by north or south, or the fate of Africans aboard the ships captured. Years later, Christophe, in correspondence with British abolitionist Thomas Clarkson, appears to deny involvement in such practices, writing on March 20, 1819, "Though it is only with the greatest grief that I can bear to see Spanish vessels engaged in the slave trade within sights of our coasts, it is not my intention to fit out ships of war against them." This was in reply to Clarkson's recommendation that he consider doing just that. See Earl L. Griggs and Clifford Prator, eds., *Henry Christophe and Thomas Clarkson: A Correspondence* (New York, 1968), 128, 115–117. For this same period, José Luciano Franco briefly discusses an 1819 case in which Boyer's naval forces (on the warship *Wilberforce*) intercepted a Cuban-bound slave ship and freed and took its hundreds of captives to Port-au-Prince; *Comercio clandestino de esclavos*, 107.

43. Here the testimony seems to echo the interpretation of the events advanced by the Real Consulado to the captain-general that Haiti was intercepting slave ships with the protection of the British. The quote is from the testimony of Francisco Xavier Pacheco in "Autos sobre el incendio de Peñas Altas," AP, leg. 13, exp. 1, f. 291, ANC.

44. The ongoing work of Sue Peabody and Keila Grinberg on the evolution of the free soil idea prompts us to think of a related vernacular, as opposed to juridical, concept of Haiti as free soil, an association perhaps encouraged by Haitian policies such as the interception of slave ships whose captives were liberated "to" Haiti and the extension of Pétion's activist definitions of Haitianness (and thereby freedom) to black and brown people in other territories who might come to reside in Haiti. On the legal concept of free soil, see Sue Peabody and Keila Grinberg, "Free Soil: An Atlantic Legal Construct," presented at the conference Rethinking Boundaries: Transforming Methods and Approaches in Atlantic History, New York University, February 9–10, 2007. On the circulation of vernacular Atlantic concepts of rights, see also Rebecca Scott, "Public Rights and Private Commerce: A Nineteenth-Century Atlantic Creole Itinerary," *Current Anthropology* 48, no. 2 (Spring 2007): 237–256.

The Saint-Dominguan Refugees and American Distinctiveness in the Early Years of the Haitian Revolution

Ashli White

REFUGEES FROM SAINT-DOMINGUE BROUGHT THE HAITIAN REVO-
LUTION TO AMERICAN DOORSTEPS, EVERYWHERE FROM NEW YORK TO
CHARLESTON, AS THEY BEGAN TO ARRIVE IN SIGNIFICANT NUMBERS
in the early 1790s. In shows of sympathy rooted in transatlantic racial solidarity, white Americans raised funds in support of the displaced migrants. Yet at
the same time, residents scrutinized the exiles' flight and found the departure
of thousands of able-bodied white men problematic. By all accounts, the slaveholding colonists of the French Caribbean island should have been winning
the war. They faced adversaries—black and colored Saint-Dominguans—
who, according to the dominant racist notions of the age, were inferior. In
addition, the U.S. government had sent supplies and munitions to help to
crush the rebellion. How, observers wondered, could well-equipped white
men lose to such a foe?

In response to this question, white Americans set aside transnational
racial ties and looked for answers that were purportedly unique to the
French colony. They highlighted the differences between themselves and
their Caribbean counterparts in order to dismiss the possibility of a similar
rebellion in the United States. In other words, as the Haitian Revolution
challenged slavery and racism in increasingly universal terms, white U.S. residents particularized the causes of the revolution, concocting explanations
that would absolve their country from the same fate. Throughout the 1790s
and early 1800s, white Americans adopted assorted strategies to achieve
this end and did so with varying degrees of conviction. In this manner, the
Haitian Revolution became the basis of yet another claim for the distinctiveness of the United States.

Typically, when scholars talk about the emergence of U.S. national senti-ment in this era, they focus on internal sources of inspiration and consolidation: political tracts, patriotic symbols, parades, and commemorations, among oth-ers. Sometimes they include European (usually British and French) influences. But the Saint-Dominguan refugees demonstrate how the Caribbean shaped the articulation of national difference as well.[1] In the case of the exiles, the discussion about distinctiveness took place in fits and starts, as papers reported the latest news from the French colony, Americans tried to interpret it, and the refugees chimed in with their views. The reactions of white Americans were rife with inconsistency and hairsplitting logic: they both sympathized with and upbraided the refugees (sometimes in the same article), and they condemned slavery and racism in Saint-Domingue but not in the United States. These explanatory gymnastics reveal the difficulties of maintaining the fiction of American singularity under the pressure of the Haitian Revolution.

The treatment of white male refugees also shows how gender was central to attempts to mark national difference in the Atlantic context. Before 1794, white Americans laid part of the blame for the rebellion in Saint-Domingue at the feet of white male colonists. White men were held responsible for protect-ing and preserving the colony, and their failure to do so cast doubt on their abilities and character. Observers pointed to two factors that destabilized these men and, by extension, the island: their depravity and their prejudices—vices from which Americans were, at least compared to the Saint-Dominguans, immune. A vociferous lot, the white refugees did not take these criticisms sit-ting down. But refuting these accusations was a delicate operation, for many male exiles relied on American aid. The refugees, therefore, had to resuscitate their reputations in such a way that neither Americans nor Saint-Dominguans lost face. In newspapers, memoirs, and other writings, white male refugees told their own versions of the revolution in Saint-Domingue, stories that empha-sized their honor without threatening the carefully constructed position of white Americans.

This conversation about the culpability of white refugees was most evident in the first few years of the revolution—from about 1789 to 1794. After the French National Assembly abolished slavery in 1794, white Americans found that they could not indict the male colonists so cavalierly. Emancipation changed the terms of discussion fundamentally because at that moment the slave rebellion became a legitimate arena of republican revolution. However, the initial sporadic debates over the refugees demonstrate how the Haitian Revolution (and the Atlantic world more generally) affected the rhetoric of American distinctiveness in a criti-cal period—just after the ratification of the U.S. constitution—when ideas about the new nation and its citizens were fluid and uncertain.

In the early years of the Haitian Revolution, American appraisals of the white male refugees were informed by notions about how a respectable late-eighteenth-century man should behave. A man of honor commanded respect and embodied attributes such as bravery, self-control, and integrity. These qualities were confirmed by the positions men held, the clothes they wore, and the words they chose. By these standards, many white male refugees considered themselves honorable men. In Saint-Domingue some had been patriarchs with large estates, distinguished posts, and cultural and social prominence. But these indicators had been compromised by the revolution: families had been separated, slaves had rebelled, fortunes had been lost, and prestigious appointments had been rescinded.

Furthermore, the definition of masculine honor was in flux in the Atlantic world. Previously, honor had been associated with aristocracy and court culture, yet with the age of revolutions, it became aligned with republican sentiments. In this new configuration, aristocracy was associated with luxury, vice, and intrigue, while republicanism implied virtue and reason. This shift was uneasy because the elite connotations of honor did not match well with the egalitarian and democratic impulses of republican politics.[2] Nevertheless, white Americans applied these benchmarks to incoming white male refugees.

One conspicuous site for appraisal was military service, and on this score, white Americans found Saint-Dominguan men wanting. In 1792 and early 1793, even as U.S. newspapers lamented the "horrors of St. Domingo," some chalked up the failure of white men to protect the colony to laziness, charging that military service during the rebellion was "not performed with very great ardour on the part of the citizens."[3] Exile itself represented an extreme form of indolence, as white male inhabitants abandoned "their public duty" by emigrating to the United States. The anonymous author of these comments directed his criticism at the largest proprietors, the very ones who, because of their elevated social and economic status, were supposed to spearhead the campaign to defeat the insurrection. The writer hinted that by leaving the island, these men had shirked the responsibilities of leadership.[4]

This dereliction of duty contrasted with what Americans remembered (somewhat rosily and selectively) as their own spirited response to the call to arms during the American Revolution. Although military service had long been significant as a measure of manly honor, it became politically charged in the age of Atlantic revolutions. A republican model emerged that presented military struggles in a moral light. Victories demonstrated *not* the winning side's superior firepower but its soldiers' moral supremacy. From the American perspective, the Saint-Dominguan colonists' defeats indicated personal corruption.[5]

To explain the source of this wantonness, Americans drew on long-standing stereotypes of New World men. For decades, residents of the Western Hemisphere had smarted from European theories that the American environment produced inferior plants, animals, and humans.[6] Yet U.S. commentators were themselves more than willing to see evidence of so-called creole degeneracy elsewhere as they insisted on the strength and virtue of their new nation and its citizens. Prior to the U.S. Revolution, "creole" and "American" were virtually synonymous (both terms denoting any person born in the New World), yet after the Revolution, citizens of the United States tried to redefine and claim "American" almost exclusively for themselves. As part of this process of revision, white Americans contended that nowhere was creole corruption more evident in the early 1790s than in Saint-Domingue. The sultry climate was reputed to enfeeble men physically, and this bodily debilitation, coupled with misguided social practices, frayed the moral fiber of creoles. Observers maintained that the demise of Saint-Dominguan men began at a very early age, as creole parents coddled their children, indulging every whim and fancy. Consequently, they grew up with appetites for amusement that knew no bounds, and Saint-Dominguans were renowned for the luxury with which they surrounded themselves. According to the Philadelphia magazine *The American Museum*, this lavish living "eradicate[d] every principle of virtue from the mind of the Creole." Not even the oft-prescribed Enlightenment cure for depravity—education—curbed the vice of Saint-Dominguan men.[7]

The moral and physical infirmity of Saint-Dominguan men had serious implications for the colonial body politic. For decades, American writers had argued that the individual decadence of citizens could lead to the demise of entire countries, and this refrain persisted in the 1790s. "Oranoak" warned in an editorial in the *New-York Journal* that "it is well known, luxury and intemperance enervates both mind and body; as was exemplified in the fall of the Roman empire. At this period her citizens were strangely depreciated; instead of being fired with an active spirit, and a manly fortitude, they sunk under the burthen, and fell like an emaciated effeminate race."[8] In the minds of some, the lesson of Rome was being illustrated again by the white landowners' feeble response to the war in Saint-Domingue. White Americans on the mainland, although they had to remain vigilant, could breathe a sigh of relief that they were more disciplined than their Caribbean neighbors.

Despite these perceived differences, Americans shared one important trait with Saint-Dominguans: both lived in slave societies. Reluctant to criticize the institution of slavery, white Americans looked to widespread notions about Caribbean masters in order to draw a distinction between the United States and Saint-Domingue. Well before the Haitian Revolution, cartoons and articles lampooned West Indian slave-owners for their entourages of bondsmen, ready to cater to the most absurd and capricious demands. Creole planters were seen as being so dependent on slaves that they were unable to perform simple tasks for themselves. Reliance, in turn, bred "the passion of arbitrary dominion over slaves," and this despotism, even if aimed at slaves, provided more proof of moral corruption.[9] In an age that celebrated men as reasonable and self-controlled, this recklessness contributed to damning Saint-Dominguan masters to the dishonorable ranks.

Writers in the United States used these characterizations of Caribbean slavery to distance their peculiar institution from that of the West Indies. They envisioned themselves as moderate men and hence "good" masters who reared obedient slaves. With this rationalization, white Americans tried to dispel fears about a slave rebellion erupting on their own soil.[10]

The Haitian Revolution, however, was not just a war between white masters and black slaves. Free people of color were integral actors on the island, and strikingly, in the early years of the revolution, U.S. newspapers often criticized Saint-Dominguan white men for their bias against the free *gens de couleur*. This censure was framed differently from the condemnation of the supposedly effete white Saint-Dominguan slave-owning class. Accounts of missteps in relations between white and free colored men identified the problem as one of politics and prejudice.

In the decades before the Haitian Revolution, white Saint-Dominguans were aggressive in their attempts to restrict people of color. Colonial courts passed an increasing number of discriminatory measures that segregated public spaces, barred men of color from certain professions, and instituted racialized sumptuary laws.[11] Given these efforts to harden the color line in Saint-Domingue, white colonists reacted fiercely to the French legislature's efforts in 1791 and 1792 to expand and guarantee the legal, political, and civil rights of free men of color. When violence erupted between white and free colored Saint-Dominguans, U.S. commentators averred that the stubborn biases of the white Saint-Dominguans brought on their suffering. As a report in the *Pennsylvania Gazette* stated bluntly, "The miserable fate of the whites may in great measure be attributed to their obstinate hatred and opposition of every law and every attempt made by the commissioners to restore the free mulattoes to the natural rights of citizenship."[12] The white colonists' bigotry flew in the face of reason. Articles contended that they were "determined to bury themselves and the colony in ruin . . . rather than renounce the prejudices of color."[13] Not even self-interest and self-preservation could vanquish prejudice—further evidence to Americans that white Saint-Dominguans were beholden to senseless and self-destructive passion.

Considering the pervasive and institutionalized racism in the United States, this denunciation of prejudice is very surprising. After all, white Americans were at least as discriminatory toward black and colored people as their Saint-Dominguan counterparts. Even in states that had begun the process of gradually emancipating slaves, free and enslaved African Americans lived daily with the harsh effects of rampant racism, and few, if any, enjoyed the full rights of citizens.[14] Yet white Americans saw the situation in another light: the exiles' bigotry was particularly heinous and distinct because it stemmed from "aristocratic" tendencies. As a committee in Philadelphia solicited donations from the public to aid the white refugees, it also criticized the exiles on this score: "They [the committee members] are convinced that their [the refugees'] prejudice and their aristocracy of colour, not less absurd and prejudicial to mankind than the heretofore French nobles, have been the principal cause of all the evils which now assail them."[15] The Philadelphia committee paraphrased the French revolutionaries' denunciation of colonial planters, and French officials and many Americans believed that the white refugees were sympathetic to the ancien régime (as indeed many were), which added more credence to the indictment.[16]

This argument must have been a sore spot for the refugees because they became victims of their own rhetorical machinations. Before the revolution, white colonists in Saint-Domingue had attributed to free men of color the damaging characteristics of aristocracy. As John Garrigus points out, white Saint-Dominguan men depicted their colored peers as morally and physically effeminate, borrowing from the increasingly negative language applied to French court culture. The characterization was intended to justify and bolster white dominion in the colony, but with the revolution the white refugees found themselves on the defensive.[17]

Similar to the contentions about creole corruption and slavery, the linking of aristocracy and prejudice conveniently distanced Saint-Dominguan society from that of the United States. The condemnations of white colonists intimated that had they been honorable men (rational, moral, and republican), they could have prevented the calamities that befell Saint-Domingue and so avoided exile. By extension, white Americans could take comfort in the thought that their nation would endure because of its diligent, upstanding citizens. Of course, residents still harbored doubts about their virtuous character and the viability of their republic; nevertheless, they held themselves above Saint-Dominguans.[18]

The refugees did not suffer this derision quietly. Rather than attempt to undercut white Americans' contorted logic, the exiles emphasized their New World character. Given the nasty traits associated with the label "creole," this was a hard sell. But their colonial credentials offered white Saint-Dominguan men a way to distinguish themselves from continental French contemporaries. This differentiation was important since the colonists blamed French officials, not slaves and free people of color, for the war on the island. (To credit black and colored Saint-Dominguans for the revolution would have implied that they were men who were responsible for their actions, and white Saint-Dominguans did not want to cede this point.)[19] They had to convince

Americans that it was French officials in Saint-Domingue, not colonists, who were dishonorable men bent on the destruction of the colony.

To make this distinction, the refugees deployed the same disparaging terms that had been directed against them, namely charges of prejudice and corruption. Inhabitants ascribed their mistreatment to the French hatred of the colonists. In self-sponsored newspapers and the U.S. press, Saint-Dominguans went on the offensive in the fall of 1793 and spring of 1794. In an editorial, a refugee fumed that "every thing was attempted to depicture the colonists, not as men, but as unnatural monsters; and they have been treated as such as a consequence of it."[20] According to the white refugees, the new republican government in Saint-Domingue took every opportunity to detain, harass, and imprison white colonists. Exiles complained that they were refused fair trials and were deported from the island without just cause and that these deplorable practices stemmed from the prejudice of continentals against white colonials.[21] The refugees went on to accuse French ministers in the United States of colluding with administrators in Saint-Domingue to heap more misery on the white colonists. Frustrated by the lukewarm (if not antagonistic) reception from Edmond Charles Genet, the French minister to the United States, an exile exclaimed, "It may easily be perceived that the whites are not the men of law—it is necessary to be either a negro, or a mulattoe, to be protected by a *negrophile* minister."[22] In the refugees' view, French officials in both Saint-Domingue and the United States were forsaking republican tenets (the rights of citizens and the rule of law, for example) to persecute colonists because they were white. This, they argued, was a new kind of "aristocracy of the skin."

In challenging French officials specifically, the exiles repudiated the charges against them, but perhaps more important, they avoided confronting American opinions directly. Echoing arguments from the U.S. Revolution, the colonist—in the refugees' version—became the defender of liberty, imbued with virtue, and the European became its corrupter. White male exiles turned to a similar line of reasoning in their defense of slavery in Saint-Domingue, arguing that the Frenchman, not the creole, was the despotic master. As a refugee priest in Baltimore declared in a sermon to recently arrived exiles that circulated in the U.S. press, "You were . . . almost the sovereigns of a race of people, over whom you never became tyrants."[23] One exile attested that creoles rarely carried out the atrocious slave punishments that made Saint-Domingue infamous. Instead, "it is always done by a European, a Philosopher upon arrival, but a cruel Master two months later! The Creole makes a point of honor of being gentle and indulgent."[24] The implication was clear: corruption was imported, not homegrown.

However much white refugees blamed French republican officials and continental Frenchmen generally, they needed to account for the successes of black and colored Saint-Dominguans on the battlefield. To do so, white exiles fell back on racist notions about slaves and free people of color. Colonists denied that black and colored men were real soldiers—a position that required some finessing since Saint-Domingue, along with other Caribbean colonies, had a long history of employing free black, mulatto, maroon, and enslaved men in militias as both laborers and soldiers. As late as 1789, free colored and black militia companies constituted 104 out of a total of 156 units in Saint-Domingue.[25] White colonists had always claimed that military service failed to imbue black and colored men with honor, but in light of the French revolutionaries' claims to the contrary, the refugees' assertion acquired greater urgency.[26]

White exiles argued that former slaves were governed by passions and irrationality that made them less than human. They were commonly referred to as "cannibals," "unchained tigers," "savages," and "monsters."[27] While the most animalistic appellations were reserved for former slaves, men of color did not fare much better. A refugee in Philadelphia named Bernard-Bernabé O'Shiell published a history of the revolution that insisted that men of color were "the true assassins of St. Domingo," emphasizing "the heinousness of their race and their crimes."[28] The word "assassin" is significant, insinuating that colored Saint-Dominguans were killers for hire rather than men fighting for their own cause. At best, white exiles maintained, black and colored soldiers were mercenaries, defying morals and honor, and at worst, they existed outside the boundaries of society, if not humanity.

Sustaining this view was especially important after the French civil rights laws of 1791–1792 and Sonthonax's emancipation decree in 1793. The laws acknowledged that black and colored Saint-Dominguans had their own goals (and noble ones at that). The refugees, however, denied that black and colored men fought for liberty and the rights of citizens and decried the French measures. Boston's *Columbian Centinel* featured a letter from a colonist in Jérémie who encapsulated the sentiment: "Great is our desolation; endless are our woes; and all that, because the offspring of ourang outangs strive to become men."[29] No law and no uniform could transform these ignoble characters into men, let alone citizens.

White Saint-Dominguan men contended that the *ways* that former slaves and men of color fought further proved their degradation—and the refugees' innocence. Accounts of the war written in exile charged that black and colored men routinely violated the honorable conduct of war by raping women, bayoneting children, killing the elderly, and leaving the wounded to languish.[30] Rather than facing white soldiers in open fields, black and colored Saint-Dominguans waged a guerrilla war. Although white colonists admitted that this mode of fighting was effective, they saw it as evidence of the rebels' innate cowardice, not their savvy. A member of the militia put his opinions into verse: "Each tree, each hole, each piece of rock / Hid from our unseeing eyes a cowardly assassin, / Who, if undiscovered, came to pierce our breasts;

/ But who fled or begged for mercy / When we found him face to face."[31] As the final couplet suggests, colonists averred that their foes crumbled when engaged in "honorable" battle.

White colonists met with another obstacle when battling black Saint-Dominguans—their deceit. In a Boston newspaper, a colonist told how a commander in the northern part of the island had experienced "a new instance of treachery from the Brigands." A group of black soldiers promised to surrender, but when they were brought into the colonists' camp, they revolted in conjunction with an attack from outside.[32] Colored soldiers were noted for similar underhanded maneuvers. In one instance narrated by a white refugee, a colored militia professed to repent its alliance with black forces, but once "by dint of guile they had dulled the vigilance of the Whites," they killed and robbed them.[33]

The characterization of these actions as "treacherous" is revealing, but not with regard to race. As Karen Kupperman has demonstrated in her work on charges of Indian treachery, anyone—black, white, colored, Indian, European, creole—could be denounced as treacherous. (And white refugees were quick to condemn French officials as "republican traitors."[34]) Typically treachery was reserved for interactions between men, and (and this is important to this consideration) the word suggests a betrayal of trust.[35] It implies a personal relationship based on reciprocity in which the honorable one is the victim. Through the language of treachery, white refugees indicated that they had entered into relationships with black and colored men in good faith and had been deceived.

It is crucial to note that not all black and colored Saint-Dominguan soldiers were seen as treacherous. Colonists were careful to distinguish between rebellious and loyal ones in the U.S. press, praising black men who fought on their behalf. The *Baltimore Daily Intelligencer*, for example, ran an article in the spring of 1794 about the black leader Jean Kina who carried out a counterattack against republican forces near Jérémie. White locals lauded his success: "This brave Negro . . . behaved like a hero, and is every day acquiring new claims to the gratitude of the whites."[36] These kinds of reports served the exiles' purposes, broadcasting that there was a sizable slave population still loyal to their masters and hence that all was not lost in Saint-Domingue—if it was left in the right hands.

Relations were uncertain with free men of color as well. White colonists depended on them, declaring that "the mulattoes have been our most faithful citizens, and have borne a great part of our military burdens."[37] But other articles noted that alliances between white and colored citizens were prone to collapse at the least provocation.[38] One refugee explained that the free men of color in his regiment had been "faithful up to now," yet he predicted that they "would cease to be so." Instead of honoring their ties, he surmised that colored soldiers had "placed a price on their allegiance" that other parties were more than willing to pay.[39]

Not surprisingly, the refugees usually downplayed the courage of black and colored soldiers in favor of celebrating the gallantry of white ones. Under the right conditions, one creole boasted, "one single white could put to rout twenty of these poor wretches."[40] But the colonists' battlefield heroics were not without complication: in their attacks on black and colored Saint-Dominguans, white soldiers admitted to tactics reminiscent of those of "treacherous rebels." In one raid the colonists blackened their faces and hands, and upon entering the enemy camp, they revealed themselves and seized the leader and his troops.[41] In the minds of these colonists, perhaps blackface permitted the transgression of treacherous devices, separating the man from the action.

Faced with a dastardly enemy and rogue officials, white Saint-Dominguan men portrayed themselves as victims, not perpetrators, of prejudice and corruption. In terms that echoed the language of American revolutionaries a decade or so before, the exiles made a case for the virtue of the New World over the Old. By their own estimation, they were the true defenders of republican liberty on the island. This assertion was difficult for white Americans to swallow in the early 1790s. Many still saw the French Revolution as the validation of the American one and hence were reluctant to accept the refugees' arguments wholesale. In addition, the exiles' claims of colonial virtue ran contrary to the American enterprise of national mythmaking.

Yet after 1794 white Americans retreated from their outspoken criticism of white male refugees. To some extent, they may have been persuaded by the exiles' defenses, but the timing seems more significant. The 1794 emancipation proclamation gave white Americans pause, including both those for and against slavery. Suddenly, slaves were free citizens—a radical move that few white Americans could condone. In their view the French government had taken a rash step, and many, quite frankly, wanted to see immediate abolition fail. The white exiles' allegations seemed a little less reactionary and the exiles themselves a little less culpable than they had appeared to be in the first years of the rebellion.

For the remainder of the Haitian Revolution, white Americans tested out other ways to explain events on the island and their implications for the U.S. republic. Opinion about the revolution split as relations with France became increasingly contentious toward the end of the decade. Federalists showed some approval of Toussaint Louverture's designs, while Jeffersonians worried about how this sympathy might undermine institutionalized racism and slavery in the United States. As the Jeffersonians carried the day in the aftermath of Haitian independence, so, too, did their views on the second republic in the New World. On this score they borrowed heavily from the rhetoric of the refugees, especially its characterization of black and colored soldiers as "brutal" and "dishonored." Throughout the antebellum era, the refugees' spin on the revolution turned up repeatedly as proslavery advocates alluded to the violence and "treachery" of the Haitian Revolution (and the victimization of white male inhabitants) in their arguments against abolition. Here again, white Americans looked to the Haitian Revolution to justify their nation's distinctiveness. In this case, however, exceptionalism was rooted in the U.S. refusal to abolish slavery in the face of widespread emancipation in the Atlantic world.

Notes

The author thanks the John Carter Brown Library, the American Philosophical Society, and the Library Company of Philadelphia for fellowships that supported research for this essay. She is also grateful for the helpful comments and suggestions from Eduardo Elena.

1. On the anti-Atlantic character of studies of the early republic, see Joyce Chaplin, "Expansion and Exceptionalism in Early American History," *Journal of American History* 89, no. 4 (March 2003): 1431–1455. Two recent and notable exceptions include Sean Goudie, *Creole America: The West Indies and the Formation of Literature and Culture in the New Republic* (Philadelphia: University of Pennsylvania Press, 2006); and Marie-Jeanne Rossignol, *The Nationalist Ferment: The Origins of U.S. Foreign Policy, 1789–1812*, trans. Lillian A. Parrot (Columbus: Ohio State University Press, 2004).

2. Joanne B. Freeman, *Affairs of Honor: National Politics in the New Republic* (New Haven: Yale University Press, 2001), xvi, xx.

3. *Virginia Herald and Fredericksburg Daily Advertiser*, January 24, 1793. On the question of the "enfeebled" soldier in eighteenth-century England, see Philip Carter, *Men and the Emergence of Polite Society, Britain 1660–1800* (Harlow, England: Pearson Education Limited, 2001), 130–131.

4. *Virginia Herald and Fredericksburg Daily Advertiser*, August 23, 1792.

5. On the moral rhetoric of military service in the United States, see John Wood Sweet, *Bodies Politic: Negotiating Race in the American North, 1730–1830* (Baltimore: Johns Hopkins University Press, 2003), 188, 198. For the disparity between rhetoric and practice, see Charles Royster, *A Revolutionary People at War: The Continental Army and American Character, 1775–1783* (Chapel Hill: University of North Carolina Press, 1979). For a similar trend among continental Frenchmen during the French Revolution, see Robert A. Nye, *Masculinity and Male Codes of Honor in Modern France* (Berkeley: University of California Press, 1992).

6. For a famous retort to these claims, see Thomas Jefferson, *Notes on the State of Virginia*, ed. Frank Shuffelton (New York: Penguin Books, 1999).

7. "Character of the Creoles of St. Domingo," *The American Museum* 6 (Philadelphia: printed by Matthew Carey, November 1789); 360. Also see Leonard Tennenhouse, "Caribbean Degeneracy and the Problem of Masculinity in Charles Brockden Brown's *Ormond*," in *Finding Colonial Americas: Essays Honoring J. A. Leo Lemay*, ed. Carla Mulford and David Shields (Newark: University of Delaware Press, 2001).

8. *New-York Journal and Patriotic Register,* January 4, 1792.

9. "Character of the Creoles of St. Domingo," 360. For a fictionalized account of brutality in Saint-Domingue, see "The Negro Equalled by Few Europeans," *The American Museum* 9–10 (1791). On men's self-control and violence in eighteenth-century England, see Elizabeth Foyster, "Boys Will Be Boys? Manhood and Aggression, 1660–1800," in *English Masculinities, 1660–1800,* ed. Tim Hitchcock and Michèle Cohen (London: Addison Wesley Longman Limited, 1999).

10. Slave-owners in Cuba made similar arguments to differentiate Cuban from Saint-Dominguan slavery and discount the possibility of a rebellion in Cuba. Matt Childs, "A Black French General Arrived to Conquer the Island: Images of the Haitian Revolution in Cuba's 1812 Aponte Rebellion," in *The Impact of the Haitian Revolution in the Atlantic World,* ed. David P. Geggus (Columbia: University of South Carolina Press, 2001).

11. John Garrigus, "Colour, Class and Identity on the Eve of the Haitian Revolution: Saint-Domingue's Free Coloured Elite as *Colons Américains,*" *Slavery and Abolition* 17, no. 1 (April 1996): 26.

12. *Pennsylvania Gazette* (Philadelphia), July 10, 1793. For similar accounts see *Virginia Herald and Fredericksburg Advertiser,* January 24, 1793; and *Virginia Chronicle* (Norfolk), July 28, 1792.

13. *Baltimore Daily Intelligencer,* November 13, 1793.

14. Joanne Pope Melish, *Disowning Slavery: Gradual Emancipation and "Race" in New England, 1780–1860* (Ithaca: Cornell University Press, 1998); James Kettner, *The Development of American Citizenship, 1608–1870* (Chapel Hill: The University of North Carolina Press, 1978), chapter 10.

15. *Pennsylvania Gazette* (Philadelphia), July 17, 1793.

16. Laurent Dubois, *Avengers of the New World: The Story of the Haitian Revolution* (Cambridge: Harvard University Press, 2004), 82; Ashli White, "'A Flood of Impure Lava': Saint-Dominguan Refugees in the United States, 1791–1820" (Ph.D. diss., Columbia University, 2003), chapter 4.

17. John Garrigus, "Redrawing the Colour Line: Gender and Social Construction of Race in Pre-Revolutionary Haiti," *Journal of Caribbean History* 30, nos. 1–2 (1996): 28–50.

18. On this wavering dynamic in the early republic more generally, see Robert Ferguson, *Reading the Early Republic* (Cambridge: Harvard University Press, 2004), 7.

19. For an eloquent exploration of the refusal to acknowledge the Haitian Revolution as a political act by slaves, see Michel-Rolph Trouillot, *Silencing the Past: Power and the Production of History* (Boston: Beacon Press, 1995).

20. *American Star* (Philadelphia), February 18, 1794.

21. *American Star* (Philadelphia), February 11, 1794; C. C. Tanguy de la Boissière, *Proposals for Printing a Journal of the Revolutions in the French Part of St. Domingo* (New York[?], 1793), 6.

22. *American Star* (Philadelphia), February 6, 1794. For another attack on Genet along these lines, see *Baltimore Daily Intelligencer,* December 12, 1793.

23. Reported in the *City Gazette and Daily Advertiser* (Charleston), September 13, 1793.

24. Althéa de Puech Parham, ed. and trans., *My Odyssey: Experiences of a Young Refugee from Two Revolutions by a Creole of Saint-Domingue* (Baton Rouge: Louisiana State University Press, 1959), 44 (hereafter *My Odyssey*).

25. Peter M. Voelz, *Slave and Soldier: The Military Impact of Blacks in the Colonial Americas* (New York: Garland Publishing, Inc., 1993), 111, 113, 122–123, and 378; Stewart King, *Blue Coat or Powdered Wig: Free People of Color in Pre-Revolutionary Saint-Domingue* (Athens: University of Georgia Press, 2001), 63.

26. Laurent Dubois, "Citizen Soldiers: Emancipation and Military Service in the Revolutionary French Caribbean," in *Arming Slaves: From Classical Times to the Modern Age,* ed. Christopher Leslie Brown and Philip D. Morgan (New Haven: Yale University Press, 2006), 233–254.

27. Mary Hassal (also known as Leonora Sansay), *Secret History; or, the Horrors of St. Domingo, in a Series of Letters, Written by a Lady at Cape Francois, to Colonel Burr, Late Vice-President of the United States, Principally during the Command of General Rochambeau* (Philadelphia: Bradford & Inskeep, 1808), 147; *My Odyssey*, 40, 42; and John Thomas Carré to Charles Wilson Peale, ca. 1792, Sellers Family Papers, American Philosophical Society, Philadelphia, Pennsylvania.

28. As cited in a letter to the editor of the *American Star* (Philadelphia), March 18, 1794.

29. *Columbian Centinel* (Boston), August 14, 1793.

30. On how these atypical stories became archetypal, see Dubois, *Avengers of the New World*, 111.

31. *My Odyssey*, 30–31.

32. Quotation from a report in the *Boston Gazette*, January 14, 1793.

33. *My Odyssey*, 69.

34. De la Boissière, *Proposals for Printing a Journal of the Revolutions in the French Part of St. Domingo*, 4.

35. Karen Kupperman, "English Perceptions of Treachery, 1583–1640: The Case of the American 'Savages,'" *Historical Journal* 20, no. 2 (1977): 263–287. Many thanks to Michael LaCombe for bringing this article to my attention. In a quick survey of the *Pennsylvania Gazette* from 1750 to 1800, I found only one case of a woman accused of treachery, taken from the Roman historian Livy (*Pennsylvania Gazette*, April 12, 1786).

36. *Baltimore Daily Intelligencer*, May 31, 1794. For more on Jean Kina, see David Geggus, *Haitian Revolutionary Studies* (Bloomington: Indiana University Press, 2002), 137–151; and during the revolution more generally, see Geggus, "The Arming of Slaves in the Haitian Revolution," in Brown and Morgan, *Arming Slaves: From Classical Times to the Modern Age*.

37. *New-York Journal*, September 26, 1792; *Baltimore Evening Post*, September 29, 1792.

38. See, for example, *New-York Journal*, September 19 and October 13, 1792, and March 20, 1793; *Baltimore Evening Post*, September 29, 1792; *Virginia Herald and Fredericksburg Advertiser*, August 23, 1792; and *Columbian Herald* (Charleston, S.C.), August 17, 1793.

39. *My Odyssey*, 69, 81.

40. *My Odyssey*, 31.

41. *My Odyssey*, 62.

"Free upon higher ground"
Saint-Domingue Slaves' Suits for Freedom
in U.S. Courts, 1792–1830[1]

Sue Peabody

THE MANY HISTORIANS WHO HAVE STUDIED THE SAINT-DOMINGUAN OR HAITIAN DIASPORA OF THE REVOLUTIONARY ERA HAVE GENERALLY CONCENTRATED ON THE WHITE REFUGEES, who are the most readily recovered in the historical record.[2] All support Ashli White's recent assessment that "it remains difficult to learn much about the intentions of black and colored Saint Dominguan exiles in the United States,"[3] in part because documentary evidence for nonwhites is more fragmentary but also because some historians have been more entranced with the cultural contributions of Francophone whites. More recent work, however, by such historians as Gary Nash, Paul Lachance, Ashli White, and Darrell Meadows has done much to move forward our understanding of the enslaved and free nonwhite refugees from Saint-Domingue in the United States and throughout the Atlantic/Caribbean region. Indeed, this chapter would not be possible without the considerable work already done by these and other historians.[4]

In this chapter I investigate a source of information hitherto unexamined by historians of the first Haitian diaspora: lawsuits for freedom by nonwhite refugees in U.S. courts. I am interested in what they tell us about the experience of slaves and free people of color in the United States but also about a wider Atlantic process: the ways that freedom was constructed through judicial institutions in the Age of Revolution. In the course of justifying a particular individual's free status, court documents not only narrate the story of that person's life but also reflect the competing state regulations regarding slave and free status. Refugees from Saint-Domingue, as migrants traversing the boundaries of multiple state authorities, provide dynamic illustrations of how states and individuals negotiated free status as old systems of status and privilege were overturned in multiple revolutions. In this way, I hope to contribute to a growing understanding of the role of the judiciary in constructing, defining, and regulating national citizenship in the modern world.[5]

Sources

Evidence concerning slaves' suits for freedom can turn up in a wide range of documentary collections. Gary Nash makes use of Philadelphia vagrancy dockets and the minutes of the Pennsylvania Abolition Society.[6] I have found Helen Catterall's well-indexed compendium of U.S. legal cases very helpful as well as the Academic Universe Lexis/Nexis database of state case law.[7] However, the Catterall and Lexis/Nexis sources typically catalog only the state appeals or superior court decisions, which means that (for the moment) my evidence is restricted in two ways: 1) many more Haitian slaves' suits for freedom probably exist in archival records of the lower municipal and district courts; and 2) a good deal more can be learned from other documentation, such as the slaves' and masters' original petitions, the depositions of witnesses, and so forth. There is still much to do in state and local archives to recover a fuller picture of these people's lives and their judicial struggles.[8]

The scattered nature of these sources makes quantitative assessment difficult. For this chapter, I have identified thirty-one individuals from Saint-Domingue or Haiti who sued for their freedom in four U.S. states: Pennsylvania (14), Maryland (11), Louisiana (4), and Tennessee (2). This list of states contains some surprising omissions, including New York, Virginia, North and South Carolina, and Georgia, all of which received hundreds of enslaved refugees from the beginning of the slave revolt through the first decade following Haiti's independence. It is likely that these latter states are not represented in my sampling for several reasons: 1) many Haitian refugees may have resolved their cases in the lower district courts (in New York, for example); 2) the legal terrain for slaves in most southern states (for example, Georgia, Virginia, and the Carolinas) was not favorable to lawsuits for freedom;[9] 3) the legal and financial assistance of abolitionists in northern and border states was crucial to helping slaves to bring their suits; and 4) Saint-Domingue slave masters often attempted to evade freedom suits by relocating to southern states with stronger legal infrastructures to support masters' property rights.

The outcome of these cases—whether they resulted in freedom or continued enslavement—is almost evenly split. Of the thirty-one slaves in this sampling, eleven won their freedom in lawsuits, eleven lost their cases, and the outcome in the remaining nine cases is unknown.[10] Although the small sample size and number of unknown outcomes enjoins caution, two clear tendencies can be seen. The strongest tendency was temporal: slaves were more likely to win their freedom from 1792 to 1815 than was the case thereafter, when the courts in all states became more restrictive and denied freedom to the majority of petitioners. Another strong correlation is by state: enslaved refugees in Pennsylvania won the majority of their cases; those in Maryland and Louisiana were less likely to win.

Slave Motivation

What can we learn from these freedom suits? One of the strengths of legal documentation is the light it sheds on the actions and sometimes the intentions of nonliterate and otherwise underdocumented people. Some historians have speculated about enslaved refugees' motivation during the initial flight from Saint-Domingue. Nash believes that the unusual age profile and the absence of large enslaved families is evidence that the enslaved refugees were coerced to flee and otherwise would likely have stayed to join the insurgency. The enslaved refugees were very young, with a median age of about 15, and very few—especially the men—were over the age of 24. According to Nash, "The black Saint-Dominguans . . . came overwhelmingly as parentless children and childless parents."[11]

Yet it is interesting to compare this Philadelphia population with the enslaved domestic servants that French colonists brought with them to Paris during the late eighteenth century. The standard profile of blacks registered in Paris between 1777 and 1789 closely parallels Nash's Philadelphia congregation of young black men. Although the historian Pierre Boulle has shown that the profile of colonial nonwhites in Paris changed somewhat over this twelve-year period (for example, the mean age for males rose from 15.7 to 20.7), this was likely a response to French legislation requiring slaveholders to return their enslaved domestic servants to the colonies, leaving an older, more stable free nonwhite population in Paris. Furthermore, Nash's analysis omits a systematic tally of the reported racial characteristics of each manumitted slave. In late-eighteenth-century Paris, 63 percent of the registered nonwhite population was listed as *nègre* and 28 percent as *mulâtre/mulâtresse*, with the remaining categorized as *quarteron, sauvage, indien, métiz,* or merely *créole* (9 percent).[12] If Philadelphia and Paris groups had a similar racial composition (including a relatively high proportion of people of mixed racial heritage), this might suggest that some refugee slaveholders were bringing their concubines and children with them, which changes Nash's picture of "parentless children and childless parents."

Nash further notes that "not one scrap of documentary evidence has been discovered to gauge feelings of hundreds of young slaves as their masters and mistresses escorted them to the Philadelphia magistrates who certified their release from slavery and signed their lengthy indentures."[13] While I have not been able to find materials in the slaves' own words, the court cases do shed some light on their motivations.

Ashli White proposes that some slaves followed their masters into exile out of loyalty while others were intimidated or forced onto ships.[14] Undoubtedly some of both occurred, but the freedom suits, for what they are worth, tend to portray the slaves as uncommonly devoted to their masters. For example, when her mistress fled the Saint-Domingue slave revolt to a boat anchored in the harbor, the slave Bernardine reputedly swam to it, following her first to Cuba and then to New Orleans when the Saint-Domingue refugees were expelled from Cuba in 1809.[15] Others, such as 35-year-old Pierre Lewis, responded to the summons of his dead master's brother, Payen Boisneuf, in Maryland, accompanying two enslaved children, Fillette (age 8) and Lambert (age 5) on a ship from Saint-Domingue to Georgetown in 1793.[16] In no case was a slave represented as being forced to leave Saint-Domingue, but the evidence from these freedom suits cases is admittedly skewed; it was important for blacks' lawyers to portray their clients as "deserving" of the freedom they sought in the courts.

Justifying Freedom in U.S. State Courts

The freedom suits also illustrate the complex and dynamic legal framework that regulated free status for nonwhites in the Atlantic world. In attempting to compare the progress of Haitians' freedom suits in U.S. courts, we run into the problem of multiple axes of freedom: each state designed its own policies regarding freedom, and in this period of the early republic, most states' freedom policies were fluid, under revision or renegotiation in response to the spread of abolitionist sympathies or crises such as slave revolts. To some degree, then, the early U.S. republic is a microcosm of the multiple judicial structures of freedom in the Atlantic world as a whole.

Slaves' grounds for claiming freedom in U.S. courts can be compared to justifications for freedom in other parts of the Atlantic world. In eighteenth-century Paris, more than two hundred slaves sued for their freedom on the grounds of the Freedom Principle, the legal maxim that setting foot on free soil was sufficient to win freedom for a slave. Certain courts such as the Admiralty Court of France and the Parlement of Paris accepted these arguments, despite royal legislation designed to make exceptions for slave-holding colonists.[17] In other parts of the world, the rationales were not so simple. For example, Keila Grinberg, in her study of Brazilian freedom suits, examines the arguments offered on behalf of 400 slaves and their masters by their lawyers in nineteenth-century Rio de Janeiro. There, seven specific arguments were employed: a letter granting freedom (31.5 percent); "maintenance of freedom," in which freedmen were suing to protect themselves

against others' claims to re-enslave them (16.25 percent); purchase of freedom (13.75 percent); "maintenance of slavery," in which masters initiated
suits against their former slaves (11.25 percent); "free womb," where the slave
was descended from a free, often indigenous Indian woman (10.75 percent);
violence or abuse, which in Brazil was sufficient grounds to terminate slavery (4 percent); or arrival after the legal abolition of the slave trade in 1850
(2 percent).[18] Several of these rationales (including violence, the free womb
argument, and the abolition of the slave trade) were established by specific
acts of legislation while others followed customs that arose out of long-standing practices in Portugal or Spain or their American colonies (self-purchase,
letter of manumission, etc.).

This study of Haitian slaves' suits for freedom in U.S. courts reveals that
American lawyers expanded their justifications for slaves' freedom as the
abolitionist movement took hold in the early republic. Through the second
decade of the nineteenth century, judges in Pennsylvania and Maryland justified their decisions for or against a particular slave's freedom by referring to
specific local state laws. Beginning in Tennessee in 1809 and subsequently in
Louisiana, and finally in Maryland, courts considered whether laws external
to the republic, such as Spanish slave law or France's general emancipation
act of 1794, could authorize the freedom of refugees from Saint-Domingue
in the United States.

The primacy of local legislation in determining freedom is clear in half a
dozen cases from the border states of Maryland and Pennsylvania between
1794 and 1820.[19] In each of these cases, judges justified their decisions
regarding free or enslaved status by referring to specific state legislation.

As Gary Nash has demonstrated, abolitionists took an active role in creating a legal climate favorable to freedom in Pennsylvania, especially Philadelphia.
Their first legislative success, the state's 1780 act for gradual emancipation,
permitted masters who brought their slaves into the state to retain them for
only six months; thereafter the slaves were legally free. In response to this
legal framework, many slaveholders from Saint-Domingue manumitted their
slaves upon arrival but bound them to a term of indentured servitude; these
manumissions were recorded by the Pennsylvania Abolition Society (PAS).
According to the society's papers, of the approximately 816 slaves who arrived
in Philadelphia from Saint-Domingue from 1791 to 1794, 659 (81 percent)
were freed in this way.[20]

Pennsylvania freedom suits reveal that Philadelphia's legal system tended
to justify freedom in terms of the 1780 gradual emancipation law. For example, Joseph, "a negro lad" about 13 years old, came from Saint-Domingue to
Philadelphia with his master's family in the spring of 1793. Several months
later, Joseph's master, Peter Boudineau, left Philadelphia for France. The following year, on June 13, 1794, Madame Boudineau, who must have intended

to keep Joseph under her authority but could only do so legally through indenture, arranged a contract with Joseph whereby he would "learn the arts of cook and housewaiter." According to the terms of the indenture, he would remain with her for twelve years, until June 13, 1808 (i.e., an approximation of his 28th birthday). However, on April 1, 1795, Madame Boudineau assigned Joseph's indenture to David H. Conyngham. Nine years later, in 1804, she left for France. Some time after Madame Boudineau's departure, Joseph, now in his mid-twenties, decided to sever his relationship with Conyngham. He made his independence known, whereupon Conyngham had him arrested and jailed in the Philadelphia County jail as a "runaway servant." Abolitionists intervened on Joseph's behalf, filing a writ of habeas corpus to challenge his imprisonment as unlawful. The judge ruled that because Joseph's indenture was not originally filed within six months of his arrival in the state, as required by Pennsylvania's 1780 gradual emancipation act, the contract was void and he did not owe any further service to Mr. Conyngham.[21]

Not all slaves brought to Pennsylvania were so lucky. Some Saint-Dominguan slaveholders sought to evade the state's gradual abolition scheme by removing their slaves to states that were more amenable to slavery. For example, a Madame Chambre brought her two women slaves, Magdalen and Zare, to Philadelphia after fleeing from the "conflagration" of Cap-Français, probably in 1793. After residing in Philadelphia for five months and three weeks, Madame Chambre moved with them to Burlington, New Jersey, specifically to avoid freeing or registering her slaves as required by Pennsylvania's 1780 law. Magdalen and Zare thereupon took matters into their own hands, fled Madame Chambre, and returned to Philadelphia to claim their freedom. Their lawyers argued that the period of residency amounted to "six lunar months," citing five precedent decisions (none of which bore directly on the condition of slavery). However, the Pennsylvania Supreme Court justices unanimously ruled that the statute indicated calendar months, not lunar months, and that the women should be returned to Madame Chambre.[22] Apparently the Pennsylvania Supreme Court justices were not so opposed to slavery in 1794 that they would stretch the commonsense interpretation of the law. Magdalen and Zare's fate suggests what may have happened to some of the 157 slaves who we know were brought to Philadelphia but whose masters did not bind them to indenture. Their masters may simply have taken them elsewhere to avoid emancipating them. In any event, it is noteworthy that both the abolitionist lawyers and the high court judges apparently confined their discussion of the women's status to the interpretation of Pennsylvania statutes.[23] There is no reference in the decision to France's recent proclamation of February 4, 1794, abolishing slavery throughout its territories, word of which would certainly have reached Philadelphia by September of that year.

Maryland's economy was more deeply tied to slavery and its legislature more divided on the question of general emancipation. Hence, Maryland's law of freedom shifted considerably over the decades following the American Revolution. In 1664, Maryland's colonial assembly had legislated that all Africans brought to the colony would be servants *durante vitae*, that slave status would pass from mother to child, and that mixed-race children born to white female servants would remain servants until the age of 31.[24] Maryland courts interpreted this law as a presumption that all blacks were slaves unless they could prove free status (for example by descent from a white or American Indian woman). A century later, a series of new laws regulated the entry of slaves into the state of Maryland. The act of 1783 prohibited anyone from importing slaves for sale or for residence, although it made an exception for "any person traveling through this state, or sojourning therein for a short time."[25] In 1792, the flood of refugees from Saint-Domingue pushed the Maryland legislature to pass a new law specifically aimed at the "slaves of certain French subjects"—that is, the refugees of Saint-Domingue.[26] This law specifically permitted refugee slaveholders from the French islands to bring and maintain in Maryland a maximum of three to five slaves if they registered them with the county clerk.[27]

One early case from 1794, *John G. de Kerlegand v. Negro Hector*, dealt with Saint-Domingue slaveholders who arrived with slaves prior to the act of 1792. According to the anti–slave trade law of 1783, if foreign immigrants brought their slaves to Maryland, the slaves were automatically freed. But by 1792, the legislature clearly intended for them to be able to retain a small number of slaves.[28] What would happen to those immigrants who arrived prior to the December 23, 1792, passage of the law?

The appeals court judge's lengthy opinion reviewed the circumstances of the immigrants' arrival, dwelling on the meaning of the words "sojourning" and "residence," since if the refugees' stay was only temporary they were entitled to keep their slaves. Following this review, the court affirmed that according to the *letter* of the law, the "Negro Hector" was entitled to his freedom. But the rhetorically complex decision offers a stunning reversal. One can imagine Hector and his supporters' initial relief as the judge read out his decision to the courtroom. The first half of the opinion clearly upholds Hector's freedom. However, the judge went on to declare that because the *spirit* of the 1792 Maryland act was to extend the right of French refugees to bring their slaves to Maryland, Hector would remain enslaved. The slaveholders' discomfort with the initial portion of the decision must have given way to smug satisfaction as the judge laid out his reasons for deliberately overturning the traditional legal principle that no law should have a retroactive effect.[29]

In 1796, the Maryland legislature consolidated and revised the state slave code as An Act Relating to Negroes.[30] This version expanded some of the rights of free blacks in the state but tried to curb runaways and limit slaves' suits for freedom in the courts.[31] In 1797, during a conservative reaction against "French Negroes," Maryland politicians repealed the act of 1792, presumably to discourage new immigrants from bringing slaves into the state from war-torn and rebellious Saint-Domingue. Moreover, citing the French slaves' "disorderly conduct . . . dangerous to the peace and welfare of the city of Baltimore," the new law instructed Baltimore's mayor to expel any "negro or mulatto French slave" suspected of being "dangerous to the peace and welfare" of the city to another state or sell such slaves to "any one of the West-India islands" at the city's expense. The French slaveholders were to receive the sales price of the slaves sold on their behalf.[32]

Yet two years later, the tide had turned against white French émigrés in Maryland. In 1799, a slave from Saint-Domingue, Pierre Lewis, sued for his freedom in the Frederick County court. His former master, Pierre Payen, a creole colonist of Saint-Domingue, had died in 1791. Payen's brother and the executor of the estate was one Boisneuf, also creole, but he had moved to France in 1786, purchased property, and served in the revolutionary Constituent Assembly. Boisneuf left France for Saint-Domingue in June 1793 but settled instead in Maryland. Soon thereafter, he arranged for three of Payen's slaves—Pierre Lewis (aged 35), Fillette (8), and Lambert (5)—to be transported from Saint-Domingue to Maryland. The three landed in Georgetown in the fall of that year. When, in 1799, Pierre Lewis sued for his freedom, the jury found in his favor. Boisneuf appealed to the Maryland General Court justices, but they upheld the lower court's ruling. The court's opinion was terse, emphasizing that the act of 1792 applied only to "French emigrants from any of the *French islands*." Apparently the court held Boisneuf to be a resident of France, not of the islands, and thus ineligible as an heir to retain his slaves under Maryland law.[33]

New Arguments

The early cases (1794 to 1808) from Pennsylvania and Maryland follow a similar pattern: lawyers argued for their clients' freedom solely on the basis of local state laws. They apparently ignored the cataclysmic innovation of the French and Haitian revolutions: the emancipation of all slaves, first within the French colony of Saint-Domingue (1793) and then throughout the French empire with the National Convention's emancipation decree of February 4, 1794. However, beginning in Tennessee in 1809 and 1813, then in Louisiana in 1818–1820, and finally in Maryland in 1820, slaves' lawyers introduced a new argument for freedom. They began to argue that their clients were entitled to freedom not only because of local legislation but also because of the general French emancipation of 1794. These lawyers, many of whom were activists for abolition, argued that U.S. courts should recognize French emancipation as transferable into the new context.

Two Tennessee cases are especially interesting. They concern a light-skinned woman, Clarissa, and her "deep yellow" son, Seac.[34] According to Clarissa, who was the wife, widow, or concubine of a ship captain, they were creoles from Guadeloupe.[35] Around 1797, Clarissa gave birth to Seac.[36] The available records are silent as to precisely when they arrived in Alexandria, Virginia, from an unspecified locale somewhere in the West Indies, but it is plausible that they arrived in 1809 among the Cuban exiles. There they were sold by one "Lambert" to William Edwards, who then brought them to Tennessee. According to a witness, Lambert "had several persons of color . . . all of whom were [presumed] slaves."[37] Yet Clarissa's lawyer pointed out that ever since her arrival in the United States, she had insisted in numerous conversations that she was free.[38]

In 1809, Clarissa sued for her freedom in the Rutherford County (Tennessee) court, alleging assault, battery, and imprisonment by her puta-tive master, Edwards. As part of her case, Clarissa invoked "a decree of the French Convention . . . which abolished slavery in the West India islands."[39] Witnesses also testified that prior to 1794, "the greater part of persons of her color were free" and that by 1795 "all persons at that time were free [in Guadeloupe]."[40] Clarissa's lawyer also submitted a work of history, "Stephen's history of the wars, which grew out of the French Revolution, which con-firmed the [Guadeloupean] emancipation decree of March 25, 1794."[41] The jury, apparently impressed with such erudite testimony, ruled in favor of Clarissa's freedom.

Edwards's subsequent appeal to the Tennessee Supreme Court was unsuc-cessful. Judge John Overton set aside Edwards's claims to have purchased Clarissa and her son in Virginia, for even if the sale had occurred, it was not certain that the seller, Lambert, had legitimate title.[42]

Four years after Clarissa's successful suit for freedom, however, her son, Seac, found himself again at odds with Edwards, who continued to claim the youth as his slave. As in Clarissa's suit, much evidence was presented on each side. Seac's lawyers produced a document signed by Edwards that apparently emerged in conjunction with Clarissa's earlier suit:

> I, William Edwards, do hereby relinquish all claim to a yellow boy named Seac, now in my possession, on the principle of his being free, and do hereby direct my wife Nancy Edwards to deliver the said boy to Hinchey Pettway, or any other person by whom this writing may come. Given under my hand and seal this 19th day of May, 1808[43]

Yet Edwards countered with evidence showing that he had maintained his possession of Seac from the original Virginia sale until November 19, 1809, six months after the decision in Clarissa's favor.[44] Moreover, while the court reviewed France's historic 1794 emancipation decree, Edwards's lawyers insisted that the decree was invalid, since: 1) Guadeloupe had been under English occupation when the decree was promulgated there in July 1794; and 2) the French government had revoked the emancipation in 1802. Invoking the U.S. Constitution, Edwards' lawyers insisted that the French abolition was invalid "because it was a violation of private property."[45]

Seac's lawyers countered that if Clarissa was free at the time of Seac's birth, then her son too must be free. Since Seac was born between the 1794 emancipation decree and the restoration of slavery in 1802, his free status could not be in doubt. However, the lawyers had to wrestle with the retroactive impact of the Napoleonic restoration of slavery, and their reasoning reflects the incendiary rhetoric of the abolitionist cause:

> We contend that [the 1802 decree] did not mean to reduce those to
> slavery who before were free; but only to tolerate slavery thereafter in
> that island. If it goes further than this, it is very questionable how far it
> can affect persons subject to the former decree. We utterly condemn the
> idea that any nation has the right to make a slave of a free man without
> his own consent. Freedom, when once acquired, is a privilege of which
> no man can be divested, unless by the strong arm of power. . . . It would
> be folly to suppose that the inhabitants of St. Domingo are subject to
> the decree of 1802. Reducing those unfortunate people again to a state
> of servitude, must depend solely upon the power of the sword; and there
> cannot be a possibility that a court in a country like ours, can be found
> corrupt enough to lend the arm of the law to assist mere acts of power
> in a foreign government to deprive a human being of his liberty.[46]

Yet despite such eloquence, Supreme Court Justice Overton—the same judge who had granted Clarissa's freedom four years earlier—ruled against Seac's freedom. His decision apparently focused on a technical error: he felt that the lower court judge's instructions to the jury—that the verdict for the mother's claim to freedom necessarily supported the son's claim—was erroneous. And since the date of Clarissa's emancipation was never firmly established (and might have occurred after Seac's birth), he reversed the lower court decision, maintaining Seac's status as a slave.

These two Tennessee cases are the first evidence I have found in which a U.S. court deliberated the impact of France's emancipation decree on nonwhite immigrants to the United States. The contradictory rulings are ambiguous, especially emanating from a single judge, the eminent Tennessee pioneer John Overton, a land magnate and friend of Andrew Jackson.[47] Moreover, though the lawyers on both sides were willing to debate the impact of foreign emancipation acts on immigrants to the United States, the judge delicately avoided the topic in both his decisions.

By contrast—and perhaps not surprisingly—the next justifications for freedom based on foreign law come from refugees' cases in Louisiana courts. In 1818, the Louisiana Supreme Court, Eastern District, used Spanish law to deny free status to Adelaide Metayer, a woman of color. In Saint-Domingue, she had been the slave of Charles Metayer. In 1803, she left Cap-Français, settling first in Baracoa, Cuba, and then, in 1809, in New Orleans. While in Cuba, Adelaide lived, by all accounts, as a free woman. However, in 1810, shortly after her arrival in New Orleans, creditors seized her against the debts of her former master. Six years later, in 1816, Jean Pierre Metayer, the son of Adelaide's former master, caught up with her in New Orleans and claimed her as his slave. Two years later she sued for her freedom in the parish court of New Orleans. While this lower court ruled in her favor, the Louisiana Supreme Court overruled the decision, finding insufficient proof of manumission by her original owner. In his decision, Judge Derbigny noted that although Adelaide had proved that she had lived as a free woman for a period of time, it did not meet the Spanish legal standard of twenty years in the master's absence.[48]

However, Adelaide's story does not end there. Six months later, she stood before the same Louisiana Supreme Court judge, asserting her freedom once more.[49] This time, after debate, the court determined that Jean Pierre Metayer was indeed Charles Metayer's only son and heir. However, Adelaide's lawyer introduced a key new line of reasoning: Adelaide was free not because Charles Metayer had manumitted her but because

> she was in Hispaniola when the general emancipation was proclaimed by the commissioners of the French government, and remained there until after the evacuation of the island by the French in 1803, a period of about ten years. It is further proved that she continued in the enjoyment of her freedom, without interruption, until 1816; so that she has lived as a free person during twenty-three years.[50]

In other words, based on the French emancipation, her life as a free woman had exceeded the Spanish threshold of twenty years. Jean Pierre's lawyer countered that since "the abolition of slavery [on Hispaniola] was an act of violence," the years she resided there should not count toward the requisite twenty. However, Judge Derbigny ruled that

> if the abolition of slavery by the commissioners of the French republic has been maintained by the successive governments of the island, no foreign court will presume to pronounce that unlawful which, through a course of political events, has been sanctioned by the supreme authority of the country.[51]

This decision, therefore, marks a formal recognition in Louisiana courts of Haiti's sovereignty and its legitimacy as a state without slavery—forty-three years before the United States government would officially recognize the independent state of Haiti in 1862.

The last instance I want to explore of this new line of judicial reasoning—that the French general emancipation of 1794 should extend to Haitian refugees in the United States—appears in a particularly complex and fascinating case that spans three states and involves more than a score of slaves. In 1797, Madame Jeanne Mathusine Droibillan de Volunbrun fled Saint-Domingue, arriving in New York with at least nineteen of her slaves.[52] She established herself there for several years, allegedly managing a house of prostitution.[53] Since the late 1780s, antislavery activists had worked on many fronts to abolish slavery in New York. A 1788 law made it illegal for New York residents to sell their slaves out of state.[54] In 1799, they successfully pressured the New York legislature to free all children born to slaves (though girls would have to serve their masters until the age of 25 and boys until 28). In 1801, for reasons that are not entirely clear, Volunbrun decided to send her slaves to Norfolk, Virginia.[55] Upon getting wind of Volunbrun's plans, the New York Manumission Society began legal proceedings against her. Members of New York's black community, however, decided to take more immediate action. Twenty black men from Saint-Domingue, armed with clubs, gathered in front of her house on Eagle Street in lower Manhattan. According to witnesses, they threatened "to burn the house, murder all the white people in it and take away a number of black slaves."[56] Eventually, some 200 blacks—both Americans and émigrés from Saint-Domingue—gathered outside her house on Eagle Street to protest, only to be dispersed by fifty members of the city watch. Although the Manumission Society won a temporary release of the slaves, perhaps because of the riot, the abolitionists did not continue to push for the slaves' freedom and Madame de Volunbrun resumed custody of them.[57] While New York historians' accounts of de Volunbrun and her slaves end there, a Maryland case of 1820 sheds light on subsequent events.

According to Maryland appeals court records, in 1802 (that is, shortly after the riot), de Volunbrun "finding the climate unfavorable to her health . . . removed to the city of Baltimore, with the petitioners [i.e., Baptiste and an unspecified number of additional blacks] as part of her family." According to historian Steven Whitman, by 1813, Madame de Volunbrun was "Baltimore's richest business woman," with twenty-two slaves (ten men, nine women, and three children) constituting 80 percent of her wealth. She invested her fortune in cigar sales and, presumably, manufacture.[58] Some time after their arrival in Baltimore, according to de Volunbrun, several of her slaves attempted to escape and return to Saint-Domingue; records show that four or five of them filed a "petition for freedom" in the Baltimore City Court in 1818.[59] In response, de Volunbrun had them forcibly removed to New Orleans, where they were sold separately to new owners. The Baltimore City Court denied their petition for freedom. In 1820, they appealed the case to the Maryland Court of Appeals.[60]

The case is interesting for several reasons. First is the length of time; the events unfolded over more than two decades from the move from Saint-Domingue in 1797 to the Maryland ruling of 1820. Second, it is further evidence of slaveholders' flight from abolitionism. Like slaveholders in earlier cases from Pennsylvania, de Volunbrun made use of variations in the slave laws in different states to maintain ownership of her slaves. In both 1801 and 1818, by removing them further south she avoided northern abolition laws.[61] Finally, Baptiste's case can be seen as a form of "negotiation" between slaves and their mistress, with considerable assistance from abolitionists and other allies. De Volunbrun's efforts to move her slaves to a southern state in 1801 met with collective action: the riot. Somehow she managed to move them, not to the Deep South but to Baltimore, a city with slavery but also with a policy for gradual emancipation. The case documents do not make it entirely clear which came first, Madame de Volunbrun's intention to relocate Baptiste and the others to New Orleans or their threatened flight to Saint-Domingue. But in any event, it is clear that the blacks felt sufficiently strong in their claims—again, with abolitionist help—to challenge her authority over them, first with the threat of flight and then through the courts.[62]

In court, the lawyer for Baptiste and the others introduced two familiar lines of reasoning to justify their freedom.[63] He argued that by Maryland law, Baptiste and his compatriots were free. Building upon the laws that informed the prior Maryland decisions of *de Kerlegand v. Hector* (1794), *Boisneuf v. Lewis* (1799), and *De Fontaine v. De Fontaine* (1818), he argued that according to Maryland law, it was illegal for anyone but "travellers and sojourners" to transport slaves into the state and that Madame de Volunbrun could not be considered a sojourner—no matter how great her desire to return to her own country at some future date—by virtue of the fact that she had remained in the state for some sixteen years.[64]

Yet the blacks in question, according to their lawyer, were also free "upon higher ground." He insisted that as residents of Saint-Domingue in 1797, their freedom was already established by the abolition decree of 1794.[65] As evidence, the lawyer read an excerpt from another book, "Bains's history of the wars of the French revolution," which included "a decree of the National Convention of the 25th of April [sic] in the second year of the French republic,'which declares, that negro slavery, in all the colonies, is abolished.'"[66] For the second time in these case records, lawyers introduced historical works as evidence of French abolition on behalf of their clients. This move allowed Baptiste's lawyer to counteract the 1664 Maryland law stipulating that, in the lawyer's words, "the African race are presumed to be slaves" by limiting the scope of Maryland law. According to the lawyer:

> When it is proved, or admitted, that a person has been brought to
> this state from a foreign country, there can be no presumption of slavery
> arising from the color of his skin. Such would be a most violent and
> unnatural presumption, more especially when it is known that the
> person has been brought from a country where slavery does not exist.....
> But in a country [such as the United States] where this abominable
> traffic is condemned and prohibited under the severest penalties, where
> man's natural right to freedom is recognised, and proclaimed in the
> most solemn manner, for a court of justice to presume, merely from
> the complexion, without any other proof whatever, that a man is a
> slave, would be so repugnant to natural law, common sense, and
> common justice, as . . . to shock natural reason.[67]

Once again, it is clear that abolitionist lawyers in the United States used the French precedent of general emancipation to try to secure freedom for their clients. But unlike Adelaide Metayer's Louisiana lawyer, Baptiste's attorney did not try to invoke subsequent Haitian constitutions affirming general emancipation.

However, the four judges of the Maryland Court of Appeals, refer-encing their decision in a prior case,[68] rejected the claims of Madame de Volunbrun's slaves to freedom on several grounds. First, they felt that she had not come into the state voluntarily. According to the opinion drafted by Justice Buchanan, she "was driven to this country from St. Domingo by an insurrection of the negroes. . . . She was compelled to come by necessity." He also claimed that "she moved from New York to Baltimore, in consequence of the climate being injurious to her health. She therefore had no choice."[69] Moreover, the judges found that de Volunbrun's assertions that she never embraced U.S. citizenship and fully intended to return to her country as soon as she could do so safely were sufficient to qualify her residence in the U.S. as a temporary sojourn, thus entitling her to retain the petitioners as her slaves under Maryland law. Finally, the judges were unimpressed by the historical work of Bains that contained the text of the French emancipation act. According to them, Baptiste and his companions never qualified as slaves under French law:

> As foreign laws are facts, which, like other facts, must be proved before
> they can be received as evidence in courts of justice, the decree of the
> National Convention must be considered as not [germane?] in the case,
> not being proved in any other way than by the book from which it was
> read, and no attempt to obtain an authentication of appearing it to have
> been made. It is not, therefore, necessary to inquire, what would be the
> effect of that decree, if it was properly before us.[70]

In this way, the Maryland judges rejected the claims of Madame de Volunbrun's slaves to freedom, dismissing the historian's publication as unreliable.[71]

Following the de Volunbrun case, French emancipation disappears as a justification for freedom in U.S. courts. In the only subsequent lawsuits for freedom
concerning Haitian refugees that I have been able to find, French emancipation
does not seem to have been introduced by lawyers.[72]

Conclusion

What have we learned from this brief survey of U.S. judicial decisions on
Haitian refugees' free or enslaved status?

First, this inquiry clearly suggests the potential fruitfulness of judicial
documents in getting at the aims and experiences of some nonwhite immigrants to the United States. Further research, especially into the local court
archives, should uncover rich information about participants in the Haitian
diaspora, especially in petitions, legal arguments, and lower court decisions.

Second, these freedom suits suggest further lines of interpretation. I am
struck by the prominence of women—white, black, and brown—in these stories. There are Magdalen and Zare, spirited away from Philadelphia to New
Jersey by the ruthless Madame Chambre. There is Clarissa of Guadeloupe, who
persuaded a Tennessee judge that she likely lived as the free wife or partner of
a ship captain, though the judge seems to have had second thoughts about her
son. Finally, there is the indomitable Madame de Volunbrun, who managed
to maintain her authority over a large retinue of enslaved men, women, and
children in clear violation of Maryland legal limits until they sought to return
to newly independent Haiti, whereupon she sold them to new owners in New
Orleans. While this clearly posed the gravest harm to Baptiste and the other
slaves, it also marked a net loss of status for de Volunbrun herself, reducing the
number of her slaves.[73]

Third, the stories can undermine our assumptions about who might sue for
freedom in U.S. courts. Initially I thought that most freedom suits would involve
slaves who achieved their freedom when they reached northern states or by virtue
of the 1794 French emancipation act. While this applies to many of the people
examined in this chapter, other people of color, such as Clarissa, apparently lived
free in the French colonies but were subjected to unscrupulous capture and sale
as slaves when they entered the United States. How many of these cases were
dependents seeking upward mobility through personal emancipation and how
many were free people of color fighting attempts to enslave them?

Finally, by closely examining the arguments put forward by lawyers and
judges to justify or deny free status, we can begin to see the outlines of a
new transnational discourse on freedom, violence, and the state in the revolutionary era. Each of the cases invoking the 1794 emancipation act also
wrestles with the problem of violence in legitimizing freedom. For example,
in 1813, Seac's lawyers argued that no state could legitimately reduce a free

person to slavery, except perhaps by conquest.[74] Conversely, the Louisiana lawyer opposing Adelaide Metayer's freedom in 1819 framed French abolition as an act of violence against slaveholders, denying it could legitimately confer her freedom:

> The time during which the defendant remained in Hispaniola, ought not to be included in this calculation, because the abolition of slavery in that island was an act of violence.[75]

But the judge in Adelaide's case rejected this argument because "successive governments of the island" had maintained the abolition of slavery. Subsequent state sanction overrode the question of whether violent insurgency could legitimately establish legal principles. Finally, the Maryland judges ruling over the fate of Madame de Volunbrun's slaves portrayed her as a victim of violence:

> It cannot be presumed, that the legislature contemplated the extreme case of fugitives for their lives from the horrid scenes of slaughter in St. Domingo, during the servile wars in that island. . . . The law will never intend, that he who is forced to fly from his country, by causes not within his control, and with his slaves seeks refuge here, brings them either for sale or to reside [two actions prohibited by Maryland law]. . . . The defendant in the case before us was driven to this country from St. Domingo by an insurrection of the negroes, and brought with her the petitioners, as her slaves; she was compelled to come by necessity, a vis major, which she could not resist, and that necessity is her protection. But it is said, that she first arrived at New York, and though she may have been driven by necessity from St. Domingo, the same necessity did not pursue her, after she reached New York, where she might have remained in safety, and that her coming into this state was a voluntary act. The answer to that argument is, that it appears, from the case stated, that she moved from New York to Baltimore, in consequence of the climate of the former being injurious to her health. She therefore had no choice, between becoming a sacrifice to the climate of New York, and going to some other place better suited to her constitution.[76]

It is ironic that the judges' decision overlooks the fact that Madame de Volunbrun's departure from New York was equally prompted by violence (the riot when she made it known that she would move her slaves to the South rather than free them), and that that violence, in turn, consisted of African Americans' efforts to enforce New York State's fragile emancipation act. Today we are more likely to see the New York rioters as performing a "just war" of liberation, inspired by the revolt in Saint-Domingue. It seems to me that this transformation in consciousness is truly the legacy of the Haitian Revolution.

Notes

1. When a historian of France and its Atlantic colonies makes the leap to the North American mainland, she inevitably experiences a certain loss of bearings. Especially helpful in this project, in addition to the published works listed below, have been the generous advice and assistance of Ashli White and T. Stephen Whitman. I also wish to offer special thanks to David Taft Terry, Research Specialist in the History of Slavery and African American History at the Maryland State Archives, for helping me locate several cases and for orienting me to the tremendous online offerings of the Maryland State Archives.

2. In this paper I often use "Haitian diaspora" or "Haitian refugees" instead of the more technically correct "Saint-Dominguan" because it is more familiar to U.S. audiences and a little less awkward. Of course, virtually all of the people mentioned in this chapter fled the colony of Saint-Domingue prior to the January 1, 1804, declaration of Haitian independence and hence are not technically refugees from "Haiti."

3. Ashli White, "The Politics of 'French Negroes' in the United States," *Historical Reflexions/Reflexions historiques* 29, no. 1 (2003): 105.

4. Frances Sergeant Childs, *French Refugee Life in the United States, 1790–1800: An American Chapter of the French Revolution* (Baltimore. Md.: Johns Hopkins University Press, 1940), includes the Saint-Domingue refugees as part of its subject but contains fewer than a dozen passing references to slaves and "Negroes" who migrated to the United States and no sustained inquiry into their experience. Winston C. Babb's doctoral dissertation, "French Refugees from Saint Domingue to the Southern United States: 1791–1810" (Ph.D. diss., University of Virginia, 1954), contains more direct discussions, but slaves and former slaves always appear as background characters to the more centrally figured white colonists. His only chapter that directly discusses the experience of black refugees in the United States focuses on their participation in slave revolts, which was not the norm. Paul Lachance's phenomenal demographic work has helped fill in the important Louisianan experience: "Were Saint-Domingue Refugees a Distinctive Cultural Group in Antebellum New Orleans? Evidence from Patterns and Strategies of Property Holding," *Revista Interamericana* 29, nos. 1–4 (1999): 171–192; Lachance, "The 1809 Immigration of Saint-Domingue Refugees to New Orleans: Reception, Integration and Impact," *Louisiana History* 29, no. 2 (1988): 109–141, reprinted in *The Road to Louisiana: The Saint Dominguan Refugees, 1792–1809*, ed. Carl A. Brasseaux and Glenn R. Conrad (Lafayette: University of Southwestern Louisiana, 1992). This latter volume also includes important essays by Gabriel Debien and Thomas Fiehrer on refugees in Cuba and Louisiana. In "Saint Domingue in Virginia: Ideology, Local Meanings and Resistance to Slavery, 1790–1800" (*The Journal of Southern History* 63, no. 3 [1997]: 531–552), James Sidbury does a good job of trying to reconstruct the perspective of the enslaved in Virginia and the impact on both whites and blacks of the arrival of "French Negroes." See also Gary Nash, "Reverberations of Haiti in the American North: Black Saint Dominguans in Philadelphia," *Explorations in Early American Culture: A Special Supplemental Issue of Pennsylvania History* 65 (1998): 44–73. R. Darrell Meadows's insightful "Engineering Exile: Social Networks and the French Atlantic Community, 1789–1908" (*French Historical Studies* 23, no. 1 [2000]: 67–102) explores how social networks—and the absence thereof—affected white and nonwhite refugees of both the French and Haitian

revolutions. Three additional essays on refugees, by Susan Branson and Leslie Patrick, Paul Lachance, and David Geggus, appear in *The Impact of the Haitian Revolution on the Atlantic World*, ed. David P. Geggus (Columbia: University of South Carolina, 2001). See also Geggus, "The Slave Leaders in Exile: Spain's Resettlement of Its Black Auxiliary Troops," in his *Haitian Revolutionary Studies* (Bloomington: Indiana University Press, 2002), 179–203. I have found Ashli White's recent work especially valuable: "'A Flood of Impure Lava': Saint Dominguan Refugees in the United States, 1791–1820" (Ph.D. diss., Columbia University, 2003).

5. Participants in this scholarly conversation are numerous. Interested readers might begin with The Law in Slavery and Freedom: A Collaborative International Research and Teaching Project, under the direction of Rebecca Scott, Martha Jones, Jean Hébrard, and Michael Zeuske, available online at http://sitemaker.umich.edu/law .slavery.freedom/home.

6. According to Nash, the Vagrancy Dockets are housed in the Philadelphia City Archives, but he was able to access computerized printouts provided by Billy G. Smith of Montana State University. See Nash, "Reverberations of Haiti in the American North," 57–58 and 71nn61–64.

7. Helen Tunnicliff Catterall, *Judicial Cases Concerning American Slavery and the Negro* (Washington, D.C.: Carnegie Institution, 1926–1937; reprint, Buffalo, N.Y.: W. S. Hein, 1998).

8. A vast quantity of historical data is now available online. In addition to the many judicial decisions that can be found via the Academic Universe Lexis-Nexis subscription service, this chapter makes use of the extremely valuable and publicly accessible project Archives of Maryland Online, available online at www.aomol.net.

9. As early as 1792, South Carolina prohibited the importation of all slaves, and it prohibited the entry of free blacks and mulattoes soon thereafter; Florida, Georgia, and North Carolina also banned slaves' arrival from the "West Indies." Virginia is the only southern state not to have issued such a ban. See Winthrop Jordan, *White Over Black: American Attitudes toward the Negro, 1550–1812* (Chapel Hill: University of North Carolina Press, 1968), 382.

10. These simple numbers belie more complicated situations. For example, a case decided in favor of freedom by a jury might be overturned upon appeal (e.g., Clarissa v. Edwards, 1 Tenn 393, 1813) or the same litigants might be involved in multiple cases (e.g., 1818–1819, Louisiana). One case, from Maryland in 1820, included twenty-three slaves who lost upon appeal. See *Baptiste et al. v. de Volumbrun*, 5 H. & J. 86, 1820 Md. Lexis 18 (Court of Appeals of Maryland, June 1820). See the related cases of *Metayer v. Noret* and *Metayer v. Metayer*, cited in notes 48 and 50 below.

11. Nash, "Reverberations of Haiti in the American North," 52–53.

12. Pierre Boulle, "Les gens de couleur à Paris à la veille de la révolution," in *L'image de la révolution française*, ed. Michel Vovelle (Paris, New York: Pergamon Press, 1989), 1:161–162. Interestingly, the Parisian nonwhite population changed markedly over the course of the eighteenth century; it became older, more of its members were free, and a greater proportion of its members were racially mixed. Compare Boulle's figures with data compiled in Sue Peabody, *"There Are No Slaves in France": The Political Culture of Race and Slavery in the Ancien Régime* (New York and Oxford: Oxford University Press, 1996), 75–87.

13. Nash, "Reverberations of Haiti in the American North," 55.

14. White, "'Flood of Impure Lava,'" 33–35.

15. The date of the original departure from Saint-Domingue is omitted from the judge's decision. *Bernardine v. L'Espinasse*, 6 Mart. (n.s.) 94, 1827 La. Lexis 103 (Supreme Court of the State of Louisiana, Eastern District, 1827), accessed via Academic Universe, Lexis/Nexis, http://web.lexis-nexis.com/universe (hereafter Lexis/Nexis).

16. *Boisneuf v. Lewis*, 4 H. & McH. 414, 1799 Md. Lexis 33 (Court of Appeals of Maryland, General Court, 1799), accessed via Lexis/Nexis. Another legal case involving Saint-Domingue refugees, though not a suit for freedom, suggests a willing departure: In 1809 "the defendants [56 French emigrants] were banished from Cuba, and all their property (excepting the negroes . . . who followed their master) had . . . been . . . confiscated." See *Debora v. Coffin and Wife*, 1 Mart. La. 40, Fall 1809, in Catterall, *Judicial Cases Concerning American Slavery and the Negro*, 3: 446.

17. Peabody, "'There Are No Slaves in France.'"

18. The remaining 9.75 percent of the cases did not specify the grounds for the case. See Keila Grinberg, "Manumission, Gender and the Law in Nineteenth-Century Brazil: Liberata's Legal Suit for Freedom," paper presented at the Conference on Manumission in the Atlantic World, College of Charleston, South Carolina, 2000; and Grinberg, *Liberata—A lei da ambiguidade: as ações de liberdade da Corte de Apelação do Rio de Janeiro no século XIX* (Rio de Janeiro: Relume Dumará, 1994).

19. *Kerlegand v. Hector*, 3 H. & McH. 185, 1794 Md. Lexis 3 (Court of Appeals of Maryland, General Court, May 1794); *Commonwealth v. Chambre*, 4 U.S. 143 (1794), 1 L.Ed. 776, 1794 U.S. Lexis 107, 4 Dall. 143 (Supreme Court of Pennsylvania, September 1794); *Boisneuf v. Lewis*; *Respublica v. Lambert Smith*, 4 Yeates 204, 1805 Pa. Lexis 15 (Circuit Court of Pennsylvania, Union Town, March 1805); *Fulton v. Lewis*, 3 H. & J. 564, 1815 Md. Lexis 30 (Court of Appeals of Maryland, May 1815); *De Fontaine et al. v. De Fontaine* (Court of Appeals of Maryland, June 1818). From a footnote in the case: *Baptiste et al. v. de Volunbrun*, 5 H. & J. 86, 1820 Md. Lexis 18 (Court of Appeals of Maryland, June 1820). All accessed via Lexis/Nexis.

20. Nash, "Reverberations of Haiti in the American North," 44–73.

21. *Respublica v. Lambert Smith*.

22. *Commonwealth v. Chambre*.

23. I say "apparently" because the only documentation I have been able to consult is the decision, which is fairly terse. It is possible that the lawyers introduced other arguments that were ignored by the justices.

24. Jonathan L. Alpert, "The Origin of Slavery in the United States: The Maryland Precedent," *American Journal of Legal History* 14 (1970): 195.

25. "An Act to Prohibit the Bringing of Slaves into this State," April 1783, ch. 23, in *Hanson's Laws of Maryland, 1763–1784* (Annapolis: Frederick Green, 1787), 203:350, accessed via Archives of Maryland Online, http://www.mdarchives.state.md.us/megafile/msa/speccol/sc2900/sc2908/html/codes.html. The law also exempted slaveholders who might immigrate to Maryland from another state.

26. "An Act Respecting the Slaves of Certain French Subjects," December 23, 1792, ch. 56, in Thomas Herty, *A Digest of the Laws of Maryland* (Baltimore: printed for the editor, 1799), MSA SC M 3150, p. 1699, accessed via Archives of Maryland Online, http://www.mdarchives.state.md.us/megafile/msa/speccol/sc2900/sc2908/html/codes.html.

27. "The emigrants from any of the French islands, who seek an asylum in this state, may import and keep their domestic slaves, to the number of five, if a master of a family; but if a single man, the number of three. . . . Every such French emigrant who shall or may thereafter import any such slave or slaves as aforesaid, shall, within three months thereafter, deliver and lodge, with the clerk of the county into which the same shall first be first brought or imported, a list of such slaves so imported, and shall at the same time elect and notify in the said list to the said clerk, which of the said slaves he will retain as his domestic or house slaves, which list shall be recorded by the said clerk." The original full text of this law does not appear in Herty's *Digest of the Laws of Maryland* but was quoted in the opinion of the General Court of Maryland in *Boisneuf v. Lewis*.

28. Putting slaves to productive work would potentially keep both the slave and the master off the poor rolls.

29. *Kerlegand v. Hector*.

30. "An Act Relating to Negroes, and to Repeal the Acts of Assembly Therein Mentioned," December 31, 1796, in *Session Laws* 105:249, accessed via Archives of Maryland Online, http://www.mdarchives.state.md.us/megafile/msa/speccol/sc2900/sc2908/html /laws2.html.

31. David Skillen Bogen, "The Maryland Context of *Dred Scott*: The Decline in the Legal Status of Maryland Free Blacks, 1776–1810," *American Journal of Legal History* 381 (1990): 393–395.

32. "An Act to Repeal an Act Entitled, 'An Act Respecting the Slaves of Certain French Subjects,' and for Other Purposes Therein Mentioned," [November 1797], ch. 75, in Herty, *Digest of the Laws of Maryland*, 1992–1993, accessed via Archives of Maryland Online, http://www.mdarchives.state.md.us/megafile/msa/speccol/sc2900/sc2908/html/codes. html, May 18, 2004.

33. Emphasis in original text. *Boisneuf v. Lewis*. Another Maryland case, *De Fontaine v. De Fontaine*, was decided on the basis of the Maryland 1796 code (5 Har. and John 99n, June 1818, cited in Catterall, *Judicial Cases Concerning American Slavery and the Negro*, 4:66).

34. I infer that Clarissa was light-skinned from her lawyer's statement: "This woman's color was presumptive evidence of freedom" (*Clarissa v. Edwards*, 1 Tenn. 393, 1809 Tenn. Lexis 14, 1 Overt. 393 [Supreme Court of Tennessee, Mero District, May 1809], accessed via Lexis/Nexis). Seac was described as "deep yellow" in his later freedom suit (*William Edwards v. John P. M'Connel*, 3 Tenn. 304, 1813 Tenn. Lexis 20, 1 Cooke 304 [Supreme Court of Tennessee, Nashville, 1813], accessed via Lexis/Nexis).

35. The court noted that Clarissa's origins in Guadeloupe could not be ascertained with certainty but cited corroborating evidence: "her speaking French, being a good seamstress, and having in her possession letters written by the captain of a trading vessel, whom she stated was her husband, dated [from] about [1793]"; *William Edwards v. John P. M'Connel*.

36. *William Edwards v. John P. M'Connel*.

37. *Clarissa v. Edwards*.

38. *Clarissa v. Edwards*.

39. *William Edwards v. John P. M'Connel*. This summary of Seac's case describes the evidence as it first appeared in Clarissa's 1809 suit.

40. *William Edwards v. John P. M'Connel.*

41. *William Edwards v. John P. M'Connel.* This undoubtedly refers to James Stephen, *The Crisis of the Sugar Colonies, or, An Enquiry into the Objects and Probable Effects of the French Expedition to the West Indies* (London, 1802).

42. *Clarissa v. Edwards.*

43. *William Edwards v. John P. M'Connel.* It appears that John P. M'Connel stood as guardian for the 16-year-old Seac. For narrative ease, I refer to his counsel as "Seac's lawyers." These attorneys explained that Edwards had "executed" this "release" in 1809 in exchange for Clarissa's forgoing of claims for back wages upon winning her freedom.

Hinchey Pettway signed as a witness to the Treaty of Tellico between the United States and the Cherokee Nation on October 24, 1804 (www.cherokee.org). He appears in later historical records as a Harpeth Academy trustee (1811), a Williamson County lottery manager (to raise $3,000 to pave the roads, 1813), and a Franklin bank superintendent (1815). See Tennessee State Library and Archives, Historical and Genealogical Information, Acts of Tennessee, 1796–1830, available at http://www.state.tn.us/sos/statelib/pubsvs/actindex.htm, May 20, 2004.

44. *William Edwards v. John P. M'Connel.*

45. *William Edwards v. John P. M'Connel.*

46. *William Edwards v. John P. M'Connel.*

47. Records of the Tennessee State Library and Archives suggest that Overton manumitted one of his slaves, Rachel Moyers, in 1829, four years before his death. See Tennessee State Library and Archives, Historical and Genealogical Information, Acts of Tennessee, 1796–1830, accessed via http://www.state.tn.us/sos/statelib/pubsvs/actindex.htm, May 20, 2004.

48. *Metayer v. Noret*, 5 Mart. (o.s.) 566, 1818 La. Lexis 47 (Supreme Court of the State of Louisiana, Eastern District, June 1818), accessed via Lexis/Nexis. The Spanish standard was apparently ten years if the master was present.

49. Whether by fluke or design, Adelaide Metayer was able to have two supreme court rulings on her status. In the first case (1818), Adelaide sued Noret, identified as Jean Pierre Metayer's attorney, who had arrested and imprisoned Adelaide on Jean-Pierre's behalf. In the second suit (1819), Jean Pierre Metayer sued Adelaide, trying to establish his rights over her.

50. *Metayer v. Metayer*, 6 Mart. (o.s.) 16, 1819 La. Lexis 98 (Supreme Court of the State of Louisiana, Eastern District, January 1919), accessed via Lexis/Nexis.

51. *Metayer v. Metayer.*

52. *Baptiste et al. v. de Volumbrun*, 18 Md.App. (1820), 1820 Md. Lexis 18, accessed via Lexis/Nexis. The fullest account of the events in New York, including de Volunbrun's full name, is in Paul Gilje, *Road to Mobocracy: Popular Disorder in New York City, 1763–1834* (Chapel Hill: University of North Carolina Press, 1987), 147–150. Gilje uses newspaper accounts, notes from the New York City Manumission Society, and the New York City Court of General Sessions to reconstruct the events surrounding Madame de Volunbrun's slaves in New York City. Shorter references to the events appear in Shane White, *Somewhat More Independent: The End of Slavery in New York City, 1770–1810* (Athens: University of Georgia, 1991), 144–145; and Leslie M. Harris, *In the Shadow of Slavery: African Americans in New York City, 1626–1863* (Chicago: University of Chicago

Press, 2003), 92. Most recently, Martha Jones has uncovered new archival documentation for the litigants in Maryland and Louisiana in "*Baptiste v. de Volunbrun*: Atlantic Encounters in Baltimore City," in *Santo Domingo/Saint-Domingue/Cuba: 500 años de esclavitud negra y transculturación en las Américas*, ed. Thomas Neuner and Michael Zeuske (Berlin: LIT-Verlag, forthcoming).

53.　Timothy J. Gilfoyle, "Strumpets and Misogynists: Brothel 'Riots' and the Transformation of Prostitution in Antebellum New York City," *New York History* 68, no. 1 (1987): 48–49. However, Shane White questions whether the documented riot had anything to do with prostitution; see *Somewhat More Independent*, 251–152n99.

54.　Harris, *In the Shadow of Slavery*, 62.

55.　Gilje, *Road to Mobocracy*, 149.

56.　Gilje, *Road to Mobocracy*, 149. It is not clear which source Gilje is quoting in this passage. He cites *People v. Marcelle Sam et al.*, October 9, 1801, New York City Court of General Sessions; *Gazette, New-York*, August 24 ad October 15, 1801; and *American Citizen*, October 15, 1801.

57.　Gilje adds that "twenty-three blacks were arrested, convicted of riot, and sentenced to sixty days in jail," an unusually harsh punishment for rioting at the time. *Road to Mobocracy*, 149–150.

58.　T. Stephen Whitman, *The Price of Freedom: Slavery and Manumission in Baltimore and Early National Maryland* (Lexington: University of Kentucky Press, 1997) 23, 183n52.

59.　Jones, "*Baptiste v. de Volunbrun*: Atlantic Encounters in Baltimore City."

60.　*Baptiste et al. v. de Volunbrun*.

61.　Gary Nash mentions similar cases in 1796 and 1797; see "Reverberations of Haiti in the American North," 58nn62–63.

62.　I lose track of Baptiste and company once they were banished to New Orleans. Madame de Volunbrun does not appear in Judith Kelleher Schafer's two books, and the only name identifying her slaves, Baptiste, is too common to track in Francophone Louisiana. See Judith Kelleher Schafer, *Slavery, the Civil Law and the Supreme Court of Louisiana* (Baton Rouge: Louisiana State University Press, 1994); and Schafer, *Becoming Free, Remaining Free: Manumission and Enslavement in New Orleans, 1846–1862* (Baton Rouge: Louisiana State University, 2003).

63.　The case summary lists the slaves' lawyer merely as "Raymond." It seems likely that this was the antislavery pamphleteer Daniel Raymond, who, according to Stephen Whitman, was born in Connecticut, moved to Baltimore around 1814, and attacked slavery in pamphlets on political economy and the Missouri question. Stephen Whitman, *Price of Freedom*, 212n3.

64.　*Baptiste et al. v. de Volunbrun*.

65.　*Baptiste et al. v. de Volunbrun*.

66.　*Baptiste et al. v. de Volunbrun*. Martha Jones identifies Bains's work as Edward Baines, *History of the Wars of the French Revolution* (London, 1817). The work circulated widely in the United States. See Martha S. Jones, "*Baptiste v. de Volunbrun*: Law, History, and the Re-Making of the Haitian Revolution," unpublished paper presented at the meeting of the French Colonial History Society, La Rochelle, France, June 7, 2007.

67.　*Baptiste et al. v. de Volunbrun*.

68. *De Fontaine v. De Fontaine*, Court of Appeals of Maryland, June 1818. A fuller discussion of the case appears in a footnote to *Baptiste et al. v. de Volunbrun*.

69. *Baptiste et al. v. de Volunbrun.*

70. *Baptiste et al. v. de Volunbrun.*

71. Martha Jones has uncovered evidence that de Volunbrun did not even bother to wait for the Maryland court's ruling before she sold her slaves in New Orleans. According to Jones, "In the spring and summer of 1819, months before the court issued its final ruling, Madame Volunbrun, by her agent, William Papillon, sold her slaves Jean Baptiste, Louis dit Cadet, Gentas and Jean Joseph in the city of New Orleans." In New Orleans notarial records, Jones traces each slave to its new owner, one of them a free man of color born decades earlier in colonial Saint Domingue. See *"Baptiste v. de Volunbrun:* Atlantic Encounters in Baltimore City."

72. Both cases involve enslaved women in New Orleans who accompanied their owners from Saint-Domingue and Cuba during the two general exoduses. In each case the master promised to free the slave but heirs (or an executor) took possession after the owner's death. In one case, the judge ruled for the woman (*Bernardine v. L'Espinasse*, 6 Mart. [n.s.] 94; 1827 La. Lexis 103 [Supreme Court of the State of Louisiana, Eastern District, 1827], accessed via Lexis/Nexis). In the second, the judge dismissed the woman's petition and she remained a slave (*Prudence v. Bermodi et al.*, 1 La. 234, April 1830, cited in Catterall, *Judicial Cases Concerning American Slavery and the Negro*, 3:489. I have not been able to find this case in Lexis/Nexis.

73. Darrel Meadows's thoughtful essay prompted me to see Madame de Volunbrun in this light. See Meadows, "Engineering Exile," esp. 83.

74. *William Edwards v. John P. M'Connel.*

75. *Metayer v. Metayer.*

76. *Baptiste et al. v. de Volunbrun.*

REPERCUSSIONS OF THE HAITIAN REVOLUTION IN BRAZIL, 1791–1850

João José Reis and Flávio dos Santos Gomes

EMORY OF THE HAITIAN REVOLUTION WAS RECALLED IN BRAZIL AT VARIOUS CRITICAL MOMENTS WHEN SLAVE REBELLIONS ERUPTED AND MORE GENERALLY WHEN THERE WERE TENSIONS AND CON-flicts within the free population. In the former case, it was feared that localized slave revolts would lead up to a major rebellion, at least a regional revolt, and slave-owners and authorities generally accused each other at such times of not meeting their obligations effectively enough to keep the slaves under control. On other occasions, when there was political conflict, observers, who were often visitors and foreign representatives, warned contentious free citizens that if they were divided, they would be creating a favorable environment for a Haitian-style rebellion.

Imaginary or real expressions of social revolt involving blacks and "people of color," free or slave, were often labeled *haitianismo*, or Haitianism. We could not establish precisely when this rather vague term was first coined, but it became current in the Brazilian political vocabulary, especially in the press, after the country declared its independence from Portugal in 1822, and was associated with different situations that somehow evoked the Haitian Revolution or an aspect of it. Fears of *haitianismo* bolstered the arguments of critics of the slave trade and in some cases of those who opposed the institution of slavery itself. They argued that because rebellions produced by African-born slaves were a constant threat, massive importation of Africans would only increase the danger presented by the already large African-born population.

Indeed, the growth in the volume of the transatlantic slave trade was one of the long-term repercussions of the Haitian Revolution in Brazil because more slaves were needed to produce tropical products such as sugar and coffee, of which the French colony had been a major supplier to the international

284

market. Sugar exports from Bahia, for example, more than doubled from 1789 to 1795, from 500,000 *arrobas* to more than 1 million *arrobas* (1 *arroba* = 14.746 kilograms, or 32.4 pounds). The number of slaves imported into that region increased from 20,300 in 1786–1790 to 34,300 in 1791–1795. For Brazil as a whole, the number of slaves increased from 97,800 in the first period to 125,000 in the second. During the first half of the nineteenth century, Portuguese and Brazilian slave ships transported at least 2,119,300 captives, almost all of them to Brazil.[1]

Nevertheless, the slave population was not the only cause for concern. Local authorities also paid a great deal of attention to the growing population of mixed African/European descent, who were enjoying some social mobility and seeking new political opportunities at the time. They numbered some 406,000 in 1798 and between about 2.5 and 3 million by 1847, respectively 12.4 percent and approximately 46 percent of the population.[2] These groups of free colored people were often charged with desiring to imitate the revolutionary island. Both free and freed blacks or mulattoes, some of whom were of good social and political standing, were accused of having Haitianist leanings. In addition, two kinds of travelers haunted Brazilian authorities: Haitians who visited Brazil and Brazilians who visited Haiti.[3] Unfortunately, information about them is scant in the documents that have been uncovered so far.

This chapter presents, in the first place, a broad but far from exhaustive overview of the perception that slaves and free blacks or mulattoes had of events in Haiti. Given what was known in Brazil, the question remains of to what degree this information fueled ideas of rebellion or simply stimulated dreams of freedom and equality. We also map out the use of fears of a Haitian-style rebellion as part of the rhetoric intended to strengthen political control in Brazil. We then present the special case of a border region between Brazil and French Guiana where those fears seemed especially amplified. Finally, we follow the footsteps of a Catholic priest arrested in this very region who had been to Haiti and was accused of inciting slaves to rebel.

The Haitian Revolution and Brazil: the Reception from Below

The revolution in Saint-Domingue began in 1791 with a slave rebellion and reached its climax in 1804, when the French colony became an independent nation called Haiti. In Brazil the event had an almost immediate effect. In June 1792, the governor of Pernambuco wrote Portuguese authorities in Lisbon about the need to prevent the ideas that inspired the revolution in Saint-Domingue from reaching Brazil. According to him, revolutionary clubs in France were ready to send agents to spread the "abominable and destructive principles of liberty and equality." He reminded Lisbon that this kind of "propaganda," as he called it, had ignited "the fire of revolt and insurrection, making slaves rise up against their masters" in the French colony, where they had "committed the most atrocious cruelties."[4]

These nightmares almost became reality with the so-called Tailors' Conspiracy, which took place in Bahia in 1798. The aborted movement involved free mulatto soldiers and artisans as well as slaves and included as its objectives putting an end to Portuguese colonialism and racial discrimination and, albeit timidly, abolition of the institution of slavery itself. When the conspiracy was exposed, four rebels were hanged, all free mulattoes. Saint-Domingue was not mentioned in the movement's manifestoes, in the interrogation records, or in the literature found in the possession of the conspirators. Nor did it appear in the vast written records produced by local and by Portuguese metropolitan authorities. Nevertheless, references to French revolutionary principles were present throughout the investigation. A mulatto soldier named João de Deus declared, "It was fitting that all should be like Frenchmen, to live with equality and plenty . . . eliminating the difference between the colors white, black, and brown . . . [who should be] invited and admitted to all ministries and posts."[5] It is notable that Deus referred to "*Frenchmen*," not to Dominguans. He was also said to have declared that Bonaparte, not Toussaint, should be counted as a potential ally of the "República Bahiense" or "Bahian Republic."[6]

It is possible that the authorities were maintaining a strategic silence about Saint-Domingue to avoid alarming a society where the sugar-plantation economy was thriving and increasingly depended on slave labor, or it may be that the conspirators themselves suppressed their true inspiration in order to appear less dangerous than they already seemed. It is unlikely that well-informed literate Bahian mulatto artisans and soldiers were unaware of the meaning of the Saint-Domingue revolution for the world in which they lived. In any case, following Robin Blackburn's argument that it is important to consider the impact of the Haitian Revolution on France, we conclude that the aspects of the French Revolution that so inspired the mulattoes of Bahia were the declaration of equality between *gens de couleurs* and *blancs* in April 1792 and the abolition of slavery in February 1794 in all the French colonies, including Saint-Domingue.[7] Thus, the Haitian Revolution was in fact silently present in the Bahian conspiracy by way of France. The "Frenchness" of Bahian mulattoes was in some ways similar to that of creole slaves in Virginia in the 1790s, in that freedom and racial equality were appropriated ideologically as French principles.[8] Of course it is ironic that Bonaparte, the would-be ally of Bahian rebels in 1798, would four years later, in May 1802, revoke the abolition of slavery in the middle of a massive attack against Haitian revolutionary forces.

The first explicit allusion (that we know of) to Haiti as a symbol of black resistance in Brazil—or at least as a matter for black pride—dates from

1805. The unknown author of a petition to the Portuguese crown against the slave trade reported that when he arrived in Rio de Janeiro in 1805, he was informed that a few days earlier the general magistrate of the city "had ordered that the Portrait of Dessalinas [*sic*], Emperor of the Blacks of the Island of S. Domingos, be ripped from the chests of some manumitted *cabras* [dark-skinned mulattoes] or Creoles, and what is most remarkable is that these same [persons] were employed in the troops of the city's Militia, where I saw them skillfully handling artillery."[9] Clearly, news circulated quickly across the Black Atlantic, for Dessalines had adorned the chests of those soldiers only one year after he had declared Saint-Domingue independent from France, proclaiming himself emperor of the island. The medallions were probably brought to Brazil from Haiti on board a ship. The petitioner believed that it was dangerous that black soldiers in the colonial Portuguese army and subjects of the Portuguese crown should idolize the great military strategist of the Haitian Revolution, a successful black general-turned-emperor who was responsible for the humiliating defeat of the French army and for the massacre of maybe several thousand unarmed whites.[10] He cited this episode among other examples of threats to law and order in which free, freed, and enslaved blacks and mulattoes played a leading role. In the case of Bahia, he referred to the 1807 conspiracy of Hausa slaves, which the government had discovered and suppressed shortly before he arrived there on his way to Portugal, just before the flight of the Portuguese court to Brazil in November of that year. Nothing indicates, however, that the Hausa rebels were in any way inspired by events in Haiti.[11]

Nevertheless, seven years later, also in Bahia, African slaves, a majority of whom were Hausa, were accused of speaking about Haiti in the context of a major uprising. On that occasion, which took place in February 1814, hundreds of slaves escaped from Salvador, the capital of Bahia, and gathered in a nearby *quilombo* (maroon settlement) before descending on coastal whaling posts. Slave fishermen joined the rebels after killing an overseer and members of his family and setting fire to fishing nets and storehouses. The rebels then set off for a fishing village, where they killed about fifty people and burned to the ground more than 100 houses. The uprising was ultimately brought under control when the rebels were making their way to the Recôncavo, the region where sugar plantations and most of the slave population were concentrated.[12]

The governor of Bahia at the time, Count dos Arcos, took a critical view of Brazilian slavery and had his own style of slave control. He believed that masters meted out unnecessarily harsh punishments to slaves, overworked them, curtailed their leisure hours, and fed them poorly. He felt that slaves should be allowed enough free time to alleviate their sufferings under slavery and time as well to remember their particular cultural origins by engaging in the rituals of their own ethnic groups. Dividing the slaves through the force of their own cultures—rather than uniting them by the force of the whip—was for the enlightened governor the right formula for preventing united rebellions.[13] This led Count dos Arcos into direct conflict with slave-owners, who had accommodated to the rigid style of controlling slaves introduced into Bahia between 1806 and 1809 by the previous governor, the Count da Ponte. They attributed the increase in slave rebellions to Arcos's liberal views and decided to confront him through several petitions to the acting monarch, Prince Regent João. In one petition, written in April 1814, after yet another violent plantation uprising, the "citizens of the City of Bahia," headed by the merchants, warned that revolts were becoming increasingly violent and pointed to the bloodshed in February as proof.[14]

The signatories made two references to Haiti, which they insisted on calling São Domingos, as if refusing to accept the reality of an independent black nation. In one, they argued that the government's policy on controlling slaves plus their large numbers in the population was an explosive combination that created the ideal circumstances for another Haiti in Bahia. They suggested that the weakening of white control caused by the revolution in France had favored the black uprising in the French colony. Later, they added that "blacks can be seen gathering in the streets at night, just as they did before [the February revolt], conversing about anything they please in their own languages with constant whistling and other signs; they make so bold that, using our own language, they criticize each other for having acted too soon, before the date planned for their insurrection. They speak and know of the fatal success on the island of São Domingos, and other rebellious speeches are heard, [saying] that by St. John's day, there will be no whites or mulattoes left alive."[15] The charge that the slaves talked about Haiti was a denunciation not heard in Bahia before, despite the combativeness of its slave population.

Bahians feared both what they understood and what they did not understand of conversations and other forms of communication between Africans. African languages gained the dimension of an independent protected cultural territory associated with other secret codes, such as whistles. The cultural estrangement between masters and slaves fed the climate of fear, but even when they understood each other, the news was not good. That some African slaves were mentioned as speaking the masters' language is an indication that acculturated, or rather *ladino*, slaves were involved in the movement. They discussed their rebellion using the language of white folks, which suggests a dialogue between members of different ethnic groups who had to speak Portuguese to understand one another. Another passage of the petition mentions that other African nations had joined the Hausas in the February uprising. Haiti figured as a theme in this interethnic dialogue, which was an American inspiration, not one that belonged to traditions brought from

Africa, such as Islam, which was a major factor in the February 1814 uprising. The reference to the Haitian Revolution thus may be interpreted as a
sign of African creolization. The choice of St. John's festival as the date for the
next rebellion points in the same direction, since it was a decision based on
familiarity with the local culture. St. John was and still is a very popular saint,
celebrated every year on June 23–24 with bonfires and firecrackers, fire being
the main means of destruction used by African rebels during their uprisings.

There are further indications of Haitian principles in the February
rebellion's battle cry, "Liberty; long live the blacks and their king ... death to
whites and mulattoes." There was a king in Haiti, and rebels there had carried out massacres. The last point was haunting. Imagined and real scenes of
massacres of whites, including "innocent children," were mentioned several
times in the Bahian petition.

The petitioners also reported an incident involving a slave who tried
to persuade a group of recently arrived Africans, who were about to be
reshipped, to rebel, "making sure that there were few whites about, for [the
rebels] had killed a large number, and that they should not set sail, but stay
to help them ... and they would be the masters of everything." Having lost
the war on the battlefield, the rebels tried to resume it as war propaganda.
And here again the scene is one in which a *ladino* African slave attempted
to mobilize recently arrived Africans who were still shocked and physically
weakened by the Middle Passage. The call for arms did not work, but it was
dangerous nonetheless. The signatories concluded with a warning to the
prince regent: "In fact, Your Highness will lose [Brazil] and we our lives and
plantations" if the governor was not compelled to change his slave control
policy.[16] Just as France had lost Saint-Domingue, Portugal would lose Bahia;
just as the French white colonials had lost their wealth and lives, so would the
Portuguese. Clearly the fear was of another Haiti in the making.

If slaves in Bahia discussed Haiti, we do not know exactly what they
said. They may have been interrogated about it in 1814, but records of the
full investigation have not been found. It is possible that slaves did not refer
to Haiti at all, and, as the Count dos Arcos would argue, that Bahian slave-
owners were inventing the Haitian threat to strengthen their demands for an
official crackdown against the slave population. If slaves did talk about Haiti,
their information may have been vague, although it probably included news
about successful massacres of whites and the formation of a nation ruled by
blacks. In fact, one of the most striking aspects of the numerous slave revolts
and conspiracies in Bahia prior to and following 1814 was the rebels' alleged
aim of exterminating whites.

A reference was made to Haiti in this context several years later by a slave
involved in the Muslim revolt of 1835. This uprising took place in the city
of Salvador, where hundreds of Africans took control of the streets for a few

hours. Most were Yoruba speakers or Nagô, led by white-clad Muslims wearing protective amulets around their necks containing verses from the Qur'an and other prayers rather than medallions bearing portraits of Dessalines. After the revolt was defeated, a slave named Paulo—a sedan-chair porter and leader of a slave-for-hire work group—was said by a witness to have complained that Africans in Bahia were incompetent rebels, for "in Havana blacks had risen and killed all whites, and that only in Havana blacks knew how to injure whites."[17] Paulo may have gotten the wrong island, but he got the right story. He was another *ladino* speaking about Haiti. He said that he had been living in Bahia since the time of Count dos Arcos's government and declared that he was punished for participating in a previous uprising. Paulo may have been talking about Haiti since 1814, and he was certainly not talking to himself.

Apparently, slaves in Brazil learned about Haiti in the same way those in the Caribbean and other parts of the Americas learned about it—from Haitian sailors and travelers, from foreign visitors to the island, probably also from people who could read newspapers and books and pass on the news, and finally from listening to conversations between literate whites.[18] There are indications that Haitian sailors were present in Bahia within two years of the 1814 revolt. After yet another uprising, a petition was sent to Rio de Janeiro in 1816 signed by thirty-seven Recôncavo sugar planters alleging that there was direct Haitian involvement in Bahia's slave rebellions. According to them, revolts were "generalized among the entire class of slaves and mainly incited by those in the city, where the ideas of liberty communicated by black seamen from São Domingos are widespread." These ideas were easily disseminated in the city because thanks to the governor's tolerance, slaves could gather "at any time of day or night." But "the ideas of liberty" reached plantations through "emissaries" from the city, particularly freed blacks. This passage was followed by a detailed proposal for more control over the black population in general and not just slaves. The planters suggested that freedpersons should be allowed to travel in the plantation districts only with a pass issued by the police. In addition to controlling the movements of ex-slaves, this measure would prevent fugitive slaves from passing themselves off as free.[19]

An earlier petition that same year by 179 residents of the Recôncavo demanded the importation of families of European workers to settle in the region, which would serve to counterbalance the greater number of black people. The petitioners were worried because only 21.6 percent of the region's 411,190 inhabitants were said to be white, the rest were "ignorant or barbaric mulattoes and blacks."[20] It is interesting that unlike the petition written two years earlier, the "enemy ranks" this time included mulattoes, a shadow of the Tailors' Conspiracy. Viewed together or separately, slaves and freed or free persons of color were a main focus of concern in different historical contexts.

Haiti was the watchword during the process of decolonization in Brazil between 1817 and 1824, both in the fears of a slave revolt made possible by the divisions among freemen and by the movements staged or supported by free and freed blacks and mulattoes. News of the Haitian link often appears in small doses and was often controversial hearsay unrelated to formal political rhetoric. During the anticolonial rebellion of 1817 in Pernambuco, a free mulatto, a tailor like the Bahian conspirators of 1798, asked a white man who had been to Haiti about the revolution and received as an answer that the rebels had "destroyed and ruined everything the French, their masters, built, and if the British had not sponsored them, the devil would have taken them long ago." The mulatto responded with an ironic tone: "So it is only whites who preserve things intact?"[21]

The specific scenario for expressions of sympathy with Haiti varied, but the context was usually one of political tensions. More evidence of this can be found in other episodes of Luso-Brazilian disputes. In 1821 in São Luís, the capital of Maranhão province, the mostly black and mulatto military, who opposed a newly created pro-Portuguese local junta, were accused of attempting to incite slaves to rebel. Leaflets were spread in the city that said "Arm yourselves [slaves] for your freedom!" and "Death to the whites." During the inquiry, a witness declared he heard "some blacks" speak of São Domingos.[22]

Evidence that Haiti was in the minds of blacks and mulattoes came from different corners of the country. In 1824, after independence, guests at an anti-Portuguese dinner party in Larajeiras, in the province of Sergipe, shouted "Long live the King of Haiti!" and "São Domingos, the Great São Domingos!" Allegedly among the guests was Antonio Pereira Rebouças, a respectable mulatto lawyer who was secretary of the provincial government of Sergipe and would go on to a successful career as a politician and jurist. Accused of being sympathetic to the Haitian Revolution, Rebouças vehemently denied it, alleging that he was the victim of political enemies who objected to seeing a mulatto occupy a high office in the government of a province dominated by white sugar planters. His interest in Haiti, however, is apparent from an inventory of his library carried out forty years later, which lists such titles as a two-volume *Histoire de Haïti* by an unknown author and *Saint-Domingue* by Abbé Dominique de Pradt, maybe an extract of his 1817 *Des colonies et de la Révolution actuelle de l´Amérique* or *L´Europe et l´Amérique en 1822 et 1823*. De Pradt's works circulated in Brazil at the time, but this loyal subject of Napoleon and bishop of Malines certainly did not praise revolutionary Haiti, even if he preached a controlled transition from slavery to freedom.[23] Rebouças would not have become a convert to the Haitian cause from reading de Pradt. In any case, the Brazilian political elite believed him and continued to support him. Two years later, the 1824 incident was brought up in an anonymous accusation against Rebouças, now a provincial councilor of Bahia, which charged that he "was the head of a revolt of freed blacks and slaves, whose objective was the general massacre of whites, and the institution of the horrendous regime of the Island of São Domingos."[24]

It is unlikely that Rebouças was sympathetic to Haiti in the sense of wanting to see a slave revolution in Brazil—he owned slaves himself—or wanting to see a massacre of whites, many of whom were his allies and benefactors. However, Rebouças may have been a Haitianist in the sense that he preached the abolition of racial prejudice and demanded equal rights for freemen of his color. He liked to say that any black or mulatto could become a general as long as he had the talent for it.[25] It is interesting that he chose to mention a general, for Haitian generals were more than once remembered as role models by black and mulatto militiamen in Brazil. That same year (1826), the mulatto general Jean-Pierre Boyer ruled Haiti, having united the two warring parts of the country and, with the 1822 conquest of Santo Domingo, the whole island of Hispaniola.[26] These events may have inspired Rebouças' enthusiasm, if any, for post-revolutionary Haiti.

In 1824, Rebouças was probably better informed about the Haitian situation than his less-educated colored brethren in Pernambuco. That year, during the unrest that preceded the declaration of the so-called Equator Confederation—a liberal revolt that contested the authority of Emperor Pedro I—a battalion of mulatto soldiers accompanied by a large crowd of ordinary civilians tried to loot Portuguese-owned stores. On that occasion, they chanted:

> Qual eu Imito a Cristovão / Thus I Imitate Christophe
> Esse Imortal Haitiano / That Immortal Haitian
> Eia! Imitai ao seu povo / Hey! Imitate his people
> Oh meu povo soberano! / Oh my sovereign people![27]

Clearly the militiamen in Rio back in 1805 were not alone among men in uniform in their admiration for Haitian leaders. This time mulatto soldiers promised to emulate another famous general and asked the people of Pernambuco to act like Haitians. By the time he was hailed this way in 1824, Henri Christophe, who in 1811 proclaimed himself King Henri I of Haiti, had committed suicide (in 1820) after being deposed in a popular revolt. The power vacuum in the north allowed Boyer to occupy the region and unify the country under his leadership. But it was Christophe who became "immortalized" in the verses of Pernambuco's common folk. It is ironic, however, that although the mulatto soldiers cheered a black Haitian general, a black battalion commander prevented them from looting shops.[28]

The leader of the mulatto troops involved in this incident was Major Emiliano Felipe Benício Mundurucu, who was the son of a Catholic priest and was a veteran of the 1817 movement. He later fled the country to become a revolutionary adventurer in the Americas. By 1826, he was in the service of General Antonio Peláez in Caracas, where he published a short pamphlet describing some of his wanderings after he left Brazil two years earlier. In it, he did not discuss racial demands or the problem of slavery but professed his republican and liberal faith. He wrote that he had visited Boston, gone from there to Haiti, and soon returned to the U.S. city, from where he traveled down to Puerto Cabello in Venezuela, which was then part of Gran Colombia. He said he was "very well received" in the United States and Venezuela but kept silent about his apparently quick sojourn in Haiti. Possibly, when seen first hand, Haiti no longer presented an example worth being followed by Brazilians. What he saw was a postrevolutionary country struggling to survive, trying to establish normal commercial and diplomatic relations with reticent European nations. Not even the control of the Haitian government by the mulatto elite seemed worth noting by this Brazilian mulatto.[29]

Pernambuco, a province significantly shaken by liberal and federalist revolts from the 1820s through the 1840s in which there was notable popular participation, was the site of the first and only direct mention of Haiti that we know of in which the black republic figured in what can be considered a clear call for rebellion. In 1846, a free black man named Agostinho José Pereira was arrested in Recife, the capital of Pernambuco. Known as the "divine Teacher," he was a Christian preacher with a numerous following. He was accused of deserting the army, founding a "religious sect," and conspiring to incite a slave rebellion which was intended to span several provinces, including the once-inflamed Bahia. When the police searched his house they found a copy of the Bible in which Old Testament passages on freedom from slavery had been marked. They also confiscated a sheet of verses that praised the "*Moreno* (Brown) race" and protested against the enslavement of Africans. The verses preached that Christ was black and demanded freedom for His children and made threatening reference to the example of Haiti. This finding strengthened official suspicion of the literate black man.[30] This is the only known document to explicitly mention Haiti that was found on someone accused of rebellion. The Haitian connection, however, did not go beyond rhetoric.

Politics of Fear: Haiti as Conservative Argument

Perhaps more than nourishing dreams of freedom in the slave quarters and proposals for racial equality among free Afro-Brazilians, Haiti was the stuff of nightmares in the mansions and government palaces. This was in itself a disservice to the Brazilian slaveholding order, in that it disrupted the masters' peace of mind. Amid the anti-Portuguese agitation in Brazil in the early nineteenth century several voices warned, in private and in public, that the Haitian Revolution could repeat itself there if the rift between the Portuguese

and Brazilians widened. A Portuguese army commander used this argument to persuade rebel landowners involved in the 1817 Pernambuco revolution to give up fighting the crown.[31] But it was in the 1820s, when the
anti-Portuguese fever increased, that fears of Haitian-style rebellions—large,
violent, and bloody—heightened. The voices of law and order asked for unity
and leadership on the part of the white elite. In the city of Rio de Janeiro in
1823, a group of planters urged that support for Emperor Pedro I "would
greatly influence the security of this Country and help to control its numerous slaves in such critical times in which it is presumed that slave insurrections are being promoted, and then [there will be seen] the disastrous scenes
of São Domingos."[32]

Foreign visitors also argued that whites had to unite to prevent the repetition of Haiti in Brazil. Frenchmen, among them businessmen who had fled
from Saint-Domingue, were particularly sensitive to events in Brazil.[33] In
Bahia, where a war of independence was in progress in 1822–1823, a consul,
an admiral, and a spy for Portugal—all of them French—shared a similar
opinion. Educated by events in their former colony, they warned that the ideals of liberty and equality had already "infected" Brazilian blacks and mulattoes
and were gradually reaching *ladino* Africans, who were no longer obeying their
masters as they once did. With the Haitian precedent in mind, the French spy
recommended in a secret report that *gens de couleur* should join forces with
les blancs against slaves to prevent a massacre of both groups.[34] Other foreigners elsewhere in Brazil echoed these fears. On the eve of independence,
Maria Graham, an English traveler, wrote in her diary that the Portuguese
were "aware of the prodigious inconvenience, if not evil, they have brought on
themselves by the importation of Africans, and now no doubt look forward
with dread to the event of a revolution, which will free their slaves from their
authority, and, by declaring them all men alike, will authorize them to resent
the injuries they have so long and patiently borne."[35]

Foreigners were not alone in their fears. When news of the Luso-
Brazilian conflicts reached him in Portugal through letters from his sister in Salvador, José Garcês reflected that "if the [Portuguese] troops
should fail, it will be another São Domingos." This was also the thinking
of the editor of *Semanário Cívico*, a pro-Portuguese weekly published in
Salvador, in a critique of the provisional Bahian government established
in the Recôncavo which had declared support for independence and
now contested the authority of the Portuguese military commander in
Salvador. The weekly predicted that emigration of the Portuguese from
the capital would put the few white Bahians left behind at the mercy of
the abundant "races of color." And then, "Could the horrendous scenes
of São Domingos not recur? This is something for those madmen of the
Recôncavo to ponder." The Portuguese commander, Madeira de Mello,

resorted to the same rhetoric to weaken the resistance of local planters, pointing to agitators of slaves who were pushing Bahia close to reproducing "the horrendous picture presented by the Island of São Domingos." One month later Madeira insisted that separation of Brazil from Portugal would promote strife "among the diverse elements of the population, maybe repeating the sinister scenes of the Island of São Domingos."[36]

After independence was won in Bahia, the anonymous author of a brochure published in 1824 warned that in looking for an enemy more attention should be given to Africans than to the Portuguese. "If the love of Independence has agitated the colonies to emancipate themselves," he wrote, "an even more energetic love agitates the hearts of slaves to recover their freedom." Africans had lost their respect for the "white color" because they were allowed to insult the "defeated Portuguese," which had "destroyed that idea of inequality, so necessary to the maintenance of order in a country where there are free people and slaves, and differences of [skin] color." The scenario was then set for a Haitian last act: "a terrible carnage which will fall upon us perpetrated by African and barbarous slaves who, certain of their strength, will not be long in seizing the opportunity to set themselves free."[37]

Throughout the 1820s and particularly the 1830s, the fledgling nation of Brazil was plagued by separatist and liberal revolts, many of which recruited large masses of free Afro-Brazilians and, in some cases, slaves. There were strong traces of a race war during the Balaiada revolt in the northern province of Maranhão in the late 1830s.[38] In particular, the issue of controlling slaves and free and freed blacks reared its head throughout Brazil after the January 1835 Muslim uprising in Bahia. This revolt had several points in common with Haitianism, particularly the accusation that the rebels planned to kill the entire white population, a favorite theme of those devoted to the slaveholding order. Repercussions of this revolt in other areas of Brazil strengthened the specter of Haiti. On the south coast of Bahia in the village of Camamu, a justice of the peace wrote to the president of the province in March 1835, complaining about escaped slaves who were ambushing travelers on the roads and robbing and killing people. Even in the view of this village justice, both the recent revolt in Salvador and the local slave unrest were due to the authorities' "remarkable indifference" to the "tragic scenes that had taken place with blood and fire in earlier times on the Island of Haiti." In addition to calling for stricter control of the slave population through the creation of a local police force, the magistrate implied that the slave trade, which had been illegal since 1831, should be actively suppressed.[39] As in 1814 and on other occasions, control of slaves and suppression of the slave trade were recurring themes when associating Brazil and Haiti.

After the 1835 revolt, Haiti was invoked again and again all over Brazil. In São Luís, the capital of Maranhão, the question of controlling slaves was associated with that of also controlling freed Africans. After all, African slaves *and* freed persons had joined forces in Bahia. In São Luís, the houses of freed persons who hosted festivities and African religious rituals were put under police surveillance in April 1835. The chief of the municipal guard assured his superiors that so far the gatherings did not appear to be subversive, but he warned that although most slaves who attended them were submissive, some were "impertinent" because of their overly indulgent, usually wealthy masters. Like a soldier who appreciates great historic battles, the police officer wrote, "The scenes that took place on the main island of the Antilles, where the forces of one of the greatest European powers, commanded by the wise and valiant Leclerc, could not triumph over those who raised the banner of insurrection [that] should be indelible in the memory of those who [indulge their slaves in this manner]." After warning slave-owners of the dangers of a slave rebellion, he pointed out the threat presented by freedpersons, whom he considered "delirious and bad individuals" who presumed to be "equal to Kings" simply because they possessed some civil rights. "It seems that this class is pushing to step beyond its place, where it should be kept for the sake of social order," he wrote. He concluded his report by saying, "The slightest problem they have is accompanied by that common notion of equality, and no one is [considered] better than them."[40]

These words confirm that the events in Haiti were a source for reflection not only on slave unrest but also on the behavior of ex-slaves. Frequently, as in 1835 and on prior occasions, the ex-slaves formed rebellious alliances with slaves, but another kind of subversion had to do with the aspiration of freedpersons to full citizenship, which had been clear since the 1798 Bahian movement. The Maranhão police officer agreed with those who argued that ex-slaves should not have political rights. He explicitly stated that they should be content with paragraph 13 of article 179 of the Brazilian Constitution of 1824, which stated that the law "will be equal for all." Implicitly he suggested that they should overlook the paragraph following, which stated, "All Citizens may be admitted to Public Office, Civilian or Military, without distinction, other than their talents and virtues."[41] Rebouças may have been thinking about that paragraph when he wrote that blacks and mulattoes could be generals. When the Constitutional Assembly discussed the matter in 1823, assemblymen used Haiti as an argument both to defend and attack the proposal to grant freedpersons full civil rights. According to some, giving them equal rights would represent, in a way, the constitutional Haitianization of Brazil, but others felt that it would help prevent Haitianization because freedpersons would be more strongly committed to the new order. The solution was a compromise: freedpersons born in Brazil would have full civil rights but not political rights. African-born ex-slaves were not included in any plans for full or even partial citizenship.

They were, legally speaking, just "foreign negroes," as Manuela Carneiro da Cunha puts it.[42] It was precisely this that freedpeople in Maranhão, such as Rebouças, wanted to see changed.

Shortly after the Bahian uprising, the national government gave the same priority to controlling slaves as it did to the control of other groups that could help them rebel. No precaution was too great in Rio de Janeiro, a city that was not only the center of imperial power but also had an enormous black population that included 46,000 slaves (about half of the total population). They made the city the location of the all-time largest concentration of slaves in the Western hemisphere.[43] The measures taken, particularly vigilance over West African or "Mina" slaves and freedpersons, aimed to "ease the minds of residents of this Capital who fear the possibility that the horrific scenes that took place in Bahia due to the African insurrection might recur here."[44] The "horrific scenes" so often associated with the Haitian Revolution were now being linked to the Muslim revolt. According to British representative H. S. Fox, "the intelligence of this revolt has spread more uneasiness in Rio de Janeiro, than any other public disturbance which has occurred for many years."[45] Two days later, he informed the Foreign Office that the Brazilian minister of justice had assured him that "more than usual precautions have been adopted . . . to watch the coloured population; more particularly the free blacks and mulattos, from whom, if from any class of African and mixed races, mischievous designs might be apprehended."[46] The "coloured population" that was to be carefully controlled meant not only supposedly dangerous slave and freed Africans but also free Brazilian-born blacks and mulattoes. The British representative considered the heavy atmosphere in Rio as a warning that despite Brazil's "amazingly great" riches, "a servile or St. Domingo revolution could dry up these natural sources of public wealth."[47]

The Provincial Legislative Assembly of Rio de Janeiro passed a law that facilitated household searches and authorized the president of the province to deport freed Africans, a measure that had already been taken in Bahia. The law also banned secret associations such as Masonic lodges, a right guaranteed by the Constitution, when their membership included "foreigners of color." In this case, the foreigners in question were not freed Africans but would-be agents of a kind of black international that the government believed was inciting slave revolts throughout the Atlantic basin.[48] Such concerns were not new, and as in the case of Bahia in 1816, suspicions fell on Haitian sailors and travelers. Since 1831—a year of unrest all over Brazil that led to emperor Pedro I's abdication—the police had investigated "blacks from the Island of São Domingos" who had landed in Rio and were seen gathering "in the midst of many [local] blacks." A certain Pedro Valentim (probably Pierre Valentin) was investigated, but no proof of conspiracy was found.[49]

In 1835, there were reports about a Haitian named Moiro (Moor) who was encouraging slaves in several villages of the interior to rise up in arms, saying that about 7,000 captives had already been recruited for the conspiracy. The Haitian man's nickname, Moor, represented an immediate connection between Muslim culture and the Haitian Revolution. He was arrested and did not deny the charges, "but he said he was only joking," according to a police report. Joke or not, he was duly expelled from the country.[50] One year later, commenting on the confiscation from a slave of handwritten Muslim prayers, a police officer warned that "without taking many more measures . . . we will all be the victims of the black clouds that continually threaten us." He concluded, "The example of São Domingos is before us, we should not forget it."[51]

The 1835 uprising illustrated another danger that came from the sea—Africans imported by the trans-Atlantic slave trade. Since at least the beginning of the century, criticism of the slave trade had spread throughout Brazil, and these condemnations often referred to Haiti as a warning against the concentration in the country of African-born slaves, who were always considered more dangerous than creole slaves.[52] Fifteen years later an experienced British diplomat in Rio de Janeiro pointed out that it was only after the Bahian revolt that the Brazilian government started "to look with some anxiety to the increase of the Negro population, and the danger arising from it."[53]

It was not only the government that changed. After 1835, proposals multiplied in favor of stricter measures to combat the illegal trade in African slaves. Declarations opposing the very institution of slavery also appeared.[54] For example, the Haitian Revolution was remembered in a series of newspaper articles published in Bahia in 1836. Its author was an opponent of slavery, although he argued that it should not be terminated abruptly, a common thought at the time. He believed that slavery was immoral, an "inhuman practice established by blind avarice" and also "entirely impolitic" because slaves could have no "affection" for a country where, among other things, the laws did not protect them. What slaves wanted was to destroy such a state, together with the whole "social body." Nevertheless, the anonymous writer established a basic difference between African and creole slaves. In his view, creoles were more complacent because they were born into slavery and had developed an affection for their masters and native land. This was not the case with Africans, who represented a growing majority in the slave population. All they lacked was a leader, he argued, echoing Abbé Raynal: "If a Spartacus should appear in America, what will the Africans do? The terrible example of Haiti would not be the only one in the history of the New World." This author was both antislavery and anti-Haitianism, of course, and he suggested that abolition should be declared before the slaves decided to impose it by force.

Repercussions in the Northern Borderlands and the Brazilian "Bishop of São Domingos"

In the 1790s, fears of sedition on Brazil's frontier with French Guiana were rampant and were reinforced by the disputes over control of the region.[55] Several chroniclers and historians who discuss these disputes have emphasized that the combined fear of foreign invasion and slave unrest permeated the entire period from the beginning of the eighteenth until the first decades of the nineteenth century. Although diplomatic historiography is silent on this subject, it was blacks and Amerindians, whether they were escaping, migrating, or forming maroon settlements, who laid the foundations for establishing the borders in this region.

In 1791, before the Haitian Revolution began, the governor of Grão-Pará, which included the Amazon region, wrote of the danger that "could still be introduced in that area—that malignant vertiginous spirit that has unfortunately consumed the [French]."[56] The movement of slaves and deserters across international borders and the possibility that ideas might move with them were viewed as potentially explosive. After the Haitian Revolution, these fears were confirmed. In 1795, the need for ships to guard the border was discussed by the colonial government in view of the growing number of fugitive slaves, "now that in Cayenne [slaves] will obtain their freedom,"[57] a reference to the abolition of slavery in the French colonies the year before. The greatest concern was the possibility that this "abominable doctrine" had already been introduced into Portuguese America, and if so, how to avoid further damage. This could be done by taking "more opportune and effective measures to advise against and prevent any kind of communication between these inhabitants with those of that restive nation." The French were said to be "flattering the slaves with the idea of pretended liberty and equality" and encouraging the maroons, who were inducing other slaves to abandon their masters.[58] It was feared that French agitators might be influencing slaves in Portuguese territory, and there were even suspicions that "they brought books, manuscripts, and pamphlets" to further their plans.[59] Secret orders were issued by the Portuguese crown expressly recommending "great vigilance over all those individuals who, through words or secret assemblies and particularly demonstrations, spread the false and disastrous principles that have infested all of Europe."[60]

Emissaries and spies who sent reports to the Portuguese authorities observed that "in the streets of Cayenne, one hears nothing but the words 'Convetion [sic], Nation, Citayen [sic] and Egalité' and this from the mouths of those same blacks who are very full of pride because they deem themselves armed to fight against the Portuguese."[61] Those were truly dangerous expressions for a monarchy based on divine right in a colony inhabited by subjects (not by citoyens), an ancien régime, and a slave-based society.

War in Europe led to the French occupation of Portugal in late 1807 and the transfer to Rio de Janeiro of the Portuguese royal government, which attacked and occupied Cayenne the following year. The Portuguese minister, Count de Galvêas, recommended that at all costs, the new governor of Cayenne should prevent "the system of slave insurrection" from establishing itself there. He stressed that "in São Domingos the bloody voice of Freedom" had been raised among the slaves, "a voice that decided, amidst the most horrendous sufferings, the fates of almost all the white inhabitants who lived on that island."[62] Cayenne's treaty of surrender included the requirement that slaves from both sides be disarmed and returned to their masters. As for the "French blacks" enlisted "into service during the war" or freed by the Portuguese government, they should be "ordered to leave the colony because they cannot be anything in the future but a source of disturbance and discord."[63] The Portuguese insisted that "these characters, who until now have supported us, now disquiet us most extremely: they have rebelled in nearly all parts of the Colony and looted some homes."[64]

In this politically charged atmosphere, Cayenne was the setting for a drama involving a curious and enigmatic character who, although exceptional, aptly illustrates how experiences related to Haiti were disseminated in the Atlantic world. He was Joaquim de Souza Ribeiro, a Catholic priest born in Bahia in the mid-eighteenth century and arrested in Cayenne in 1814, the same year a Hausa slave rebellion shook Bahia. Appearing dressed in "an episcopal habit with a crucifix in his hands," he declared he had been appointed "Bishop of São Domingos." He was then 59 years old. Considered mentally deranged, Ribeiro was interned in the military hospital, where he was personally interrogated by the Portuguese governor of Cayenne, João Severiano Maciel da Costa. Besides being labeled a lunatic and an impostor, Ribeiro was later charged with attempting to incite to revolt the slaves who served him. According to testimony, he "greatly deplored their [i.e., the slaves'] fate, telling them they were the children of God and that there was no reason for them to be the slaves of whites, citing the example of [the slaves] of São Domingos, who had even become Kings, as he said he witnessed."[65] Finally, he was charged with trying to incite the soldiers, many of whom were probably mulattoes if not blacks, lamenting the treatment they received and accusing the military commander and the governor of being "freemasons and thieves."[66] During the investigation to determine his guilt, he told a colorful tale about his life to that point.

In 1783, already a priest, Ribeiro went to Portugal, where five years later he graduated in law at Coimbra University and began a life of constant travel.[67] He returned to Bahia at an uncertain date and revisited Portugal in 1791. He claimed to have been sent to Maranhão with the "title of assistant and future successor of the Reverend Bishop of that Captaincy."

A colonial magistrate relieved him of his duties, however, because, taking advantage of the prelate's old age, Ribeiro had made the latter appoint him as interim bishop. Ribeiro sought refuge in Grão-Pará, but was arrested and sent to Portugal in 1794 for trial by an ecclesiastical court.[68] He was imprisoned for an unknown number of years and when released, he visited Spain, then Rome (where he said he received Saint Felix's relics from the pope), then returned to Spain to ask permission to do missionary work in Spanish America. Instead of being sent on a mission, he was sent to prison for unknown reasons, and he ended up banished to Havana. Soon after, he reappeared in Jamaica, where he obtained a British passport, and went on to St. Thomas. His ship docked at the island of Saint-Domingue at an uncertain date in the middle of the Revolution.

According to Ribeiro, at the invitation of André Rigaud, the mulatto governor of southern Saint-Domingue, and of "the people of the island," he remained there to "instruct them in the aims of religion." He also claimed to have attended the "consecration ceremony of the Black King," probably Jean-Jacques Dessalines, who became Jacques I in 1804. However, he said that he remained in Saint-Domingue only "for two years establishing churches, [and] arranging priestly vestments [and] sacred vessels, until the said governor [was] supplanted by General Toussaint Louverture due to reverses in the civil war."[69] This narrative puts his departure from Haiti in 1800, when Rigaud was defeated and sent into exile to France. But if it is true that he witnessed the coronation of Dessalines, which happened in early October 1804, he spent at least four years in Haiti, not two, as he claimed.

It is curious that the Brazilian priest claimed that he was hired by the secular Rigaud and not by Louverture, a devout Catholic. The clergy had never been a strong presence in the island, in part due to the opposition of colonists and colonial authorities to any effective evangelization of slaves, which was considered dangerous. And indeed, at least in the north, many priests adhered to the rebel cause. In the south the clergy was apparently less supportive of the revolution, but both there and in the north Catholicism was relevant to the rebellious masses. It is possible that Rigaud, recognizing the role of religion as a mechanism of social control, may have responded to demands to reorganize the local church and that Father Ribeiro became part of his plans.[70]

Leaving immediately after Rigaud's defeat or sometime later, Ribeiro fled the island after having been accused of stealing religious silver vessels. He made it to St. Thomas and then Philadelphia. Knowing of his presence in Philadelphia, the Haitian government announced in the local newspapers that it would pay "five thousand cruzados[71] to whoever presented the head of the Portuguese priest who had escaped," according to an official in Lisbon who interrogated Ribeiro when he landed there from Philadelphia.

From Portugal, Ribeiro went to Spain, where he was arrested again and expelled sometime in 1805 after signing a document promising he would never return there. On this occasion he supposedly visited different places in Europe and North Africa: Cadiz, Faro, Gibraltar, Tangier, Tarifa, Algeciras, Paris, Marseille, Nice, Lyon, Genoa, Leghorn, Malta, and, more than once, Rome. It would have been on one of his trips to Rome that he was allegedly appointed bishop of São Domingos. He started to sign documents as such in about 1808. He apparently made another attempt to reach Paris at an uncertain date, intending to get permission from Napoleon to go to Haiti, a claim that does not fit with his later statement that he knew that the colony had become independent. He gave up going to France only when he learned of the occupation of Portugal by the French. As a Portuguese citizen, he considered that he might not be welcome in France. But he also considered renouncing his Portuguese citizenship to become a French citizen, and indeed a copy of a letter he wrote to Napoleon to that end was found among his belongings in 1814.[72]

Instead of going to France, Ribeiro traveled to England in an attempt to return to the Caribbean through one of the British colonies, which he managed to accomplish only in 1814. He embarked from Portsmouth and after a brief stop in Madeira, reached Barbados in April or May, when he was informed that, in his own words, "São Domingos was divided between three parties, and each one had chosen a Bishop; the blacks had a great Archbishop, the Mulattoes a Bishop, and the Spaniards another." Convinced that the island already had too many bishops, he gave up the idea of sailing to Haiti, deciding instead to return to Brazil. Before doing this, however, he baptized and confirmed several people in Barbados, but his main glory was his success in converting "a Moorish woman from Turkey" to Catholicism.[73] After that, he left for Brazil where, he declared, he intended to spend the rest of his life in peace.[74]

Father Ribeiro left Barbados on July 6 and arrived in Cayenne on August 31, 1814, after a tormented journey, according to a diary he kept of this trip. In it he accused captain and crew of torturing him physically and psychologically, besides stealing from his belongings and attempting to kill him several times with poison. Much of what he wrote seems to have been the product of his fertile imagination. However, his diary also contained convincing descriptions of the seamen's religiously irreverent culture in the Atlantic world of that period. Sailors ridiculed the Catholic mass, Mary's rosary, and the Holy Trinity, and the captain and pilot read "the most execrable of books [written] by the freemasons."[75] The kind of irreligious language he heard from the seamen gained a strong politically subversive dimension within a Portuguese colonial world that rulers were trying hard to keep under control. No wonder the investigation of the 1798 conspiracy in Bahia looked for signs of irreligion and anticlericalism, besides political deviation, among the mulatto rebels. The passage in Ribeiro's diary about the language of seamen may represent the part of this new revolutionary world that, as a priest, he abhorred. Louverture himself and his successor Dessalines were both devout Catholics, and they would probably have agreed with the priest on this point.

The curious narrative by Father Joaquim de Souza Ribeiro about his travels and the conviction with which he declared himself the "Bispo de São Domingos" is almost surreal, but in the heavy atmosphere of the northern frontier, accusations of sympathy for the Haitian Revolution, no matter how delirious, were taken seriously. It should be stressed that the initial charges against Father Ribeiro regarding his allegedly seditious conversations with slaves were levied by João Severiano Maciel da Costa, governor of Portuguese-occupied Guiana (1809–1819), who later wrote an anti–slave trade tract in which the Haitian Revolution was characterized as a "fearsome shadow" looming over Brazil.[76] Insistent rumors of slave sedition shaped Maciel da Costa's thinking during his time in Guiana, even before he accused Father Ribeiro of sedition. When he returned to Rio de Janeiro in 1820, images of revolutionary Saint-Domingue were still fresh in his mind. He then went on to Lisbon with João VI as a member of the king's council, where he published his booklet against the slave trade. Father Ribeiro must have been one of those "fanatical philanthropists" who sold "moral and political blasphemies," as the former governor described the preachers of "equality" in his brochure.[77]

When Ribeiro was arrested in Cayenne, Maciel da Costa personally interrogated him and decided that the prisoner's tales "lacked consistency and verisimilitude," that they were even "extraordinary." Paradoxically, the governor also considered him a "dangerous evildoer," especially after reading his travel diary, in which the priest included detailed commentaries and cited the names of "people of high stature" he had allegedly met—including generals, admirals, counts, princes, judges, bishops, archbishops, and even the pope—some of whom he accused of "the most enormous crimes."[78] One of the chapters in Ribeiro's story that shocked the governor the most was precisely his impersonation of a high ecclesiastical authority. So much subversion of the established social hierarchy, albeit symbolic or imaginary, could not be tolerated, especially when added to Ribeiro's attempt to incite slaves to follow the Haitian path. This terrified Maciel da Costa, who sent "the Bishop of São Domingos" to Rio as a prisoner, together with his considerable luggage and papers, after precisely seventy-eight days in Cayenne.[79]

Ribeiro was lucky, for in Rio de Janeiro he seemed much less dangerous. Investigations by the capital's police could find no evidence against the priest. Regarding the charge of Haitian sympathy, the police intendant claimed that Maciel da Costa had not sent sufficient proof. Quite the opposite: "He handled this business too hastily, although it was in fact highly essential, giving me neither the information nor the rudiments needed to conduct an investigation."

The intendant believed that Ribeiro was an "impostor," yes, but primarily "a lost mind." What could be said of a man who claimed to be a saint and to be impervious to knives, firearms, and poison?[80] The priest himself cleverly used the allegation that he was weak in the head to defend himself. Under interrogation in Rio, he rejected accusations of incitement of a slave rebellion by saying "it was all false, because there had never been any such conversations with blacks, and it would have been impossible because he had landed at eight in the evening and was taken to the Military Hospital where he was treated like a lunatic, and held incommunicado."[81]

The police investigation ended with a recommendation that Ribeiro be sent to Portugal for internment in an ecclesiastical prison. It also recommended that he should be allowed to carry with him "all the papers in which he confides so much," referring to, among other things, the diary in which the priest narrated part of his "extraordinary and extravagant" adventures in two continents and on the ocean that separates them.[82] We are still looking into how, where, and when Ribeiro ended his days and if he added new imaginary or real adventures to his already amazing life.[83]

Conclusion

The experience and the words of a character like Joaquim de Souza Ribeiro encapsulate several of the themes discussed in this chapter and add a few others. Whether it was entirely true or not, his story made tremendous sense in the historical context in which it was told—it contained every element needed to make slave-owners and authorities tremble. Ribeiro had not only visited Haiti but worked for its government, and that alone made him threatening. He had then been found inciting slaves to follow the revolutionary island's example. The priest represented one of those characters of the Age of Revolution who challenged established limits by preaching the transformation of the Atlantic world across several geopolitical and cultural frontiers.[84] In a highly original way Ribeiro brought Haiti closer to the rest of the world, Brazil included, by suggesting that the principles of racial equality and black power brandished by the Haitian Revolution were not bad by definition. In the whirlwind of words he wrote and spoke, we search in vain for a condemnation of the revolution. Even if Ribeiro's tale was largely a fable, we can still view it as a rare example of the Haitian Revolution's impact on the Brazilian imagination—the revolution as the theme of a tormented man's delirium.

Governor João Severiano Maciel da Costa's ideas about the slave trade were neither as imaginative nor as original as Joaquim Ribeiro's narrative, in the sense that his memoir was part of an established trend, dating back to the early nineteenth century, that associated an increase in the African population with the dangers of Haitianism. However, Maciel da Costa sided with the more conservative part of that trend, which, long before it was proposed by racial theorists toward the end of the century, in a way invented the ideology of racial whitening in Brazil through European immigration.[85] This might be one of the most interesting repercussions of the Haitian Revolution on the mentality of Brazilian whites in the first half of the nineteenth century. When Maciel da Costa died in 1833 with the important title of marquis, he had had the satisfaction of seeing the transatlantic slave trade to Brazil abolished two years earlier, although he never realized that the law was, in a term coined at the time, *para inglês ver* ("strictly for British consumption"). The traffic would continue illicitly until 1850 because fears of another Haiti were overwhelmed by the desire and need for fresh African labor. In this regard, José Antonio Saco's description of Cuba is fitting for Brazil: "But amid the fears caused by the destruction of Santo Domingo, amid the flames of that blaze, [the Cubans] still craved for blacks, believing that there could be no prosperity for Cuba without them."[86] Both in Cuba and in Brazil, the slave trade was an attractive and lucrative business that mobilized small and large fortunes despite the British cruisers. Even so, it is worth noting that the final years of the traffic were marked by rumors from several parts of Brazil regarding slave rebellions that may have influenced the definitive prohibition of the slave trade.[87] Although the pressure of the British navy was probably a greater factor, the Haitian Revolution, having originally stimulated the slave trade to Brazil, also had something to do with its final elimination.

As for the deployment of the Haitian Revolution as a rhetorical tool to justify more control over the black population, the effectiveness of that device reflected fears of a real threat pervading Brazilian society. Expressions such as "atrocious cruelties," "disastrous scenes," "tragic scenes," "horrendous scenes," "horrific scenes," "terrible carnage," and "most horrendous sufferings" that were paraded in the writings of white Brazilians were not produced by ideology alone; they reflected a collective mentality, a sentiment of danger. Fear of another Haiti was a valuable political commodity because it had plenty of potential customers. Although from today's perspective the threat may appear remote, back then, after Haiti and Bahia, the potential for disaster seemed much closer. It seemed possible because rebellions staged by slaves and freedmen were firsthand demonstrations of what could happen—"horrendous scenes," "terrible carnage," and so forth—when whites were not only in the minority but were also divided.[88]

Yet many factors militated against a repetition of the Haitian experience in Brazil. As we have mentioned, black troops impeded mulatto troops from looting Portuguese stores in Pernambuco in 1824. The same was observed in Bahia that year, when black soldiers protected public buildings threatened by a rebellious battalion largely formed by mulatto soldiers.[89] Within the slave population there was animosity between African-born and creole slaves, who never joined the former in any of the more than thirty rebellions and conspiracies in Bahia. In some of them, plans to massacre whites also included plans to massacre creole blacks and mulattoes. The Africans themselves were divided by nations that rarely joined together in revolt.[90] Along with the fear that served to unify Brazilians against Africans in general, these internal divisions within many subaltern groups were frequently mentioned as one of the guarantees of order in Brazil. One of the main architects of Brazil's independence, José Bonifácio, suggested that this political configuration greatly inhibited the opponents of the new political regime. He wrote that the "fear of Blacks and the rivalry among the diverse castes are the safeguard against political revolutions."[91] Even when "political revolutions" spread in the 1820s and 1830s, that same fear and rivalry prevented them from receiving wider support from the free people and thus prevented the radicalization of the rebels' plans.

Finally, there are the different ideological leanings of the slave rebels in Brazil and Haiti. When they rose up in arms, Africans in Brazil did so inspired primarily by ideas, symbols, and rituals they had brought from Africa,[92] although they were not absolutely indifferent to events in the Caribbean. Given the evidence so far assembled, the Haitian Revolution seems to have appealed more often to free blacks and mulattoes born in Brazil, who, until at least the mid-nineteenth century, were not necessarily abolitionists. And it made sense that Haiti was praised by these people, for they had read or heard about the free blacks and mulattoes who were a key factor in the Haitian revolutionary process. Slave or free, mulattoes or blacks, in Brazil none of these groups seems to have planned a movement entirely based on, or specifically inspired by, the Haitian model.

Notes

We wish to thank members of the discussion group Escravidão e Invenção da Liberdade of the History Department, Universidade Federal da Bahia, and participants of the Latin American History Workshop, University of Chicago, for their comments on an earlier version of this chapter. Parts of this text were translated by Sabrina Gledhill.

1. Bert J. Barickman, *A Bahian Counterpoint: Sugar, Tobacco, Cassava, and Slavery in the Recôncavo, 1780–1860* (Stanford, Calif.: Stanford University Press, 1998), 35; David Eltis, "A participação dos países da Europa e das Américas no tráfico transatlântico de escravos: novas evidências," *Afro-Ásia* 24 (2000): 49; David Eltis, *Economic Growth and the Ending of the Transatlantic Slave Trade* (New York: Oxford University Press, 1987), 243. On the Bahian slave economy and society, besides Barickman, see Stuart B. Schwartz, *Sugar Plantations in the Formation of Brazilian Society: Bahia, 1550–1835* (London: Cambridge University Press, 1985). On the Bahian slave trade, see Pierre Verger, *Flux et reflux de la traite des nègres entre le Golfe de Bénin et Bahia de Todos os Santos, du XVIIe au XIXe siècle* (Paris: Mouton, 1968). For a recent evaluation of the

substantial increase in the number of slave ships leaving Bahia in the 1790s through the early 1800s, see Alexandre Vieira Ribeiro, "O tráfico atlântico entre a Bahia e a Costa da Mina: flutuações e conjunturas (1683–1815)," *Estudos de História* 9, no. 2 (2002): 15.

2. Manuela Carneiro da Cunha, *Negros, estrangeiros: os escravos libertos e sua volta à África* (São Paulo: Brasiliense, 1985), 20. For the growth of the free Afro-Brazilian population in nineteenth-century Brazil, see Herbert Klein, "Nineteenth-Century Brazil," in *Neither Slave Nor Free: The Freedmen of African Descent in the Slave Societies of the New World*, ed. David W. Cohen and Jack P. Greene (Baltimore, Md.: Johns Hopkins University Press, 1972), 309–334.

3. These are some, although not all, of the questions raised about the impact of the Haitian Revolution in the Americas by David Geggus. See "Preface," in *The Impact of the Haitian Revolution in the Atlantic World*, ed. David Geggus (Columbia, S.C.: University of South Carolina Press, 2001), x.

4. D. Tomás José de Mello to Martinho de Mello e Castro, Recife, June 4, 1792, Caixa 181, documento 12605, Arquivo Histórico Ultramarino, Lisbon (hereafter AHU). Kenneth Maxwell, *Conflicts and Conspiracies: Brazil and Portugal, 1750–1808* (New York: Routledge, 2004), chap. 8; and Kenneth Maxwell, *Naked Tropics: Essays on Empire and Other Rogues* (London: Routledge, 2003), chap. 7, discuss the impact of the French and Haitian revolutions on Portuguese colonial thought and policies.

5. Quoted in Ignácio Accioli de Cerqueira e Silva, *Memórias históricas e políticas da Província da Bahia*, ed. Braz do Amaral (1835–1837; repr., Bahia: Imprensa Oficial do Estado, 1931), 1(ii):17n86.

6. On the Bahian movement, see Katia M. de Queirós Mattoso, *A presença francesa no movimento democrático baiano de 1798* (Salvador: Itapoã, 1969); Luís Henrique D. Tavares, *História da sedição intentada na Bahia em 1798* (São Paulo: Pioneira, 1975); Luís Henrique D. Tavares, *Da sedição de 1798 à revolta de 1824 na Bahia* (Salvador: EDUFBA; Campinas: UNESP, 2003); Ístvan Jancsó, *Na Bahia contra o império: história do ensaio de sedição de 1798* (São Paulo/Salvador: Hucitec/EDUFBA, 1996); Ístvan Jancsó, "A sedução da liberdade: cotidiano e contestação política no final do século XVIII," in *História da vida privada no Brasil: cotidiano e vida privada na América Portuguesa*, ed. Laura de Mello e Souza (São Paulo: Companhia das Letras, 1997), 1:387–438; and Carlos Guilherme Mota, *Atitudes de inovação no Brasil, 1789–1801* (Lisboa: Horizonte, n.d.).

7. Robin Blackburn, *The Overthrow of Colonial Slavery, 1776–1848* (London: Verso, 1988), chap. 6; Robin Blackburn, "The Force of Example," in Geggus, *The Impact of the Haitian Revolution in the Atlantic World*, 16.

8. See James Sidbury, *Ploughshares into Swords: Race, Rebellion, and Identity in Gabriel's Virginia, 1730–1810* (Cambridge: Cambridge University Press, 1997), 39–49.

9. Quoted in Luiz Mott, "A escravatura: a propósito de uma representação a El-rei sobre a escravatura no Brasil," *Revista do Instituto de Estudos Brasileiros* 14 (1974): 133n3. Luiz Mott pioneered the discussion on the repercussion of the Haitian Revolution in Brazil with the article "A revolução dos negros do Haiti e o Brasil," *História: questões e debates* 3, no. 4 (1982): 55–63.

10. On these massacres, see Laurent Dubois, *Avengers of the New World: The Story of the Haitian Revolution* (Cambridge, Mass.: Belknap Press, 2004), 300; and Thomas

O. Ott, *The Haitian Revolution, 1789–1804* (Knoxville: University of Tennessee Press, 1973), 190–191.

11. On this episode, see João Reis, "La révolte haoussa de Bahia en 1807: résistance et contrôle des esclaves au Brésil," *Annales: histoire, sciences sociales* 61, no. 2 (2006): 383–418.

12. On this rebellion see João Reis, *Rebelião escrava no Brasil* (São Paulo: Companhia das Letras, 2003), 81–89; and Stuart B. Schwartz, "Cantos e quilombos numa conspiração de escravos haussás," in *Liberdade por um fio: história dos quilombos no Brasil*, ed. João Reis and Flávio Gomes (São Paulo: Companhia das Letras, 1997), 373–406.

13. See Reis, *Rebelião escrava*, chap. 3.

14. Petition by the Merchants' Association and Other Citizens of Bahia to His Royal Highness, ca. April 1814, Biblioteca Nacional do Rio de Janeiro (hereafter BNRJ), II, 34, 6, 57. Carlos Ott reproduces the full text in *Formação étnica da Cidade do Salvador* (Salvador: Manu, 1955), 2:103–108.

15. Petition by the Merchants' Association and Other Citizens of Bahia to His Royal Highness, ca. April 1814.

16. Petition by the Merchants' Association and Other Citizens of Bahia to His Royal Highness, ca. April 1814.

17. The Trial of Paulo, of the Nagô nation, slave of Rita Paixão, Insurreições, maço 2849, fl. 12, Arquivo Público do Estado da Bahia, Salvador (hereafter APEBA).

18. See Julius S. Scott, "The Common Wind: Currents of Afro-American Communication in the Era of the Haitian Revolution" (Ph.D. diss., Duke University, 1986).

19. Alexandre Gomes Ferrão Castelbranco et al to d. João, March 15, 1816, SM, DB, C9, 5, BNRJ.

20. Petition to the Crown, February 24, 1816, SM, DB, C9, 5, BNRJ.

21. Quoted in Carlos Guilherme Mota, *Nordeste 1817* (São Paulo: Perspectiva, 1972), 118. The reference to the British probably had to do with their considerable economic influence in the northern, wealthier part of independent Haiti, then ruled by the black King Henry I. The southern, poorer region was a republican state ruled by a mulatto president, Alexandre Pétion.

22. See Iara Lis Carvalho Souza, *A pátria coroada: o Brasil como corpo político autônomo, 1780–1831* (São Paulo: Editora da UNESP, 1999), 150–152.

23. *L´Europe et l´Amérique*, for instance, is mentioned in an anonymous publication precisely in 1824, the same year de Pradt's book came out, which indicates how fast European publications reached and were read in Brazil. See *Memória sobre a crise da Província em 1824 por hum brasileiro* (Bahia: Typ. Da Viúva Serva, e Carvalho, 1824), 11. The 1827 catalogue of the Plancher bookstore in Rio de Janeiro lists both *L'Europe et l'Amérique* and *La France, l'émigration et les colons* by de Pradt, the latter also published in 1824. See Marco Morel, "Duas revoluções e três abades," unpublished paper, 2006, in authors' possession. We thank Marco Morel for letting us read and cite this paper here.

24. Luiz Mott, *Escravidão, homossexualidade e demonologia* (São Paulo: Ícone, 1988), 11–18; Keila Grinberg, *O fiador dos brasileiros: cidadania, escravidão e direito civil no tempo de Antonio Pereira Rebouças* (Rio de Janeiro: Civilização Brasileira, 2002), ch. 2, quote on p. 81.

25. Grinberg, *O fiador*, 86.

26. For an overview of Boyer's government, see David Nicholls, *From Dessalines to Duvalier* (Cambridge: Cambridge University Press, 1979), 60ff. On Boyer's government's economic difficulties, which included payment of indemnification to French property holders in exchange for the recognition of independence by France, see Blackburn, *The Overthrow of Colonial Slavery*, 480, 539–540.

27. Marcus Joaquim M. de Carvalho, "Hegemony and Rebellion in Pernambuco (Brazil), 1824–1835" (Ph.D. diss., University of Illinois Urbana-Champaign, 1989), 66–67; Glacyra Lazzari Leite, *Pernambuco 1824: a Confederação do Equador* (Recife: Massangana, 1989), 101–103.

28. Leite, *Pernambuco 1824*, 102.

29. Mundurucu's leaflet is reproduced in Vamireh Facon, ed., *Da Confederação do Equador à Grã-Colômbia: escritos políticos e manifesto de Mundrucu* (Brasília: Senado Federal, 1983), 194–199. See also Flávio Gomes and Marco Morel, "Trajetórias atlânticas: dois brasileiros no Haiti no início do Oitocentos," in *História cultural: experiências de pesquisa*, ed. Sandra Jatahy Pesavento (Porto Alegre: Editora da UFRGS, 2003), 37–64.

30. Marcus J. M. Carvalho, "'Que crime é ser cismático?' As transgressões de um pastor negro no Recife patriarcal, 1846," *Estudos Afro-Asiáticos* 36 (1999): 109, 111, 114; Marcus J. M. Carvalho, "'Fácil é serem sujeitos, de quem já foram senhores': o ABC do Divino Mestre," *Afro-Ásia* 31 (2004): 327–334.

31. Mota, *Nordeste 1817*, 119.

32. January 1823, GIFI 5 B 214, Arquivo Nacional, Rio de Janeiro (hereafter ANRJ). On fear of Haitianismo, see Flávio Gomes and Carlos Eugênio L. Soares, "Sedições, haitianismo e conexões no Brasil: outras margens do Atlântico negro," *Novos Estudos CEBRAP* 63 (2002): 131–144; and Gomes, "Experiências transatlânticas e significados locais: idéias, temores e narrativas em torno do Haiti no Brasil Escravista," *Tempo* 13, no. 1 (2002): 209–246.

33. Glacyra Lazzari Leite, "A Confederação do Equador no processo de independência do Brasil: aspectos das relações internacionais (1822–1825)," in *Confederação do Equador*, ed. Manuel Correia de Andrade (Recife: Massangana, 1988), 34.

34. João Reis, "O jogo duro do Dois de Julho," in João Reis and Eduardo Silva, *Negociação e conflito* (São Paulo: Companhia das Letras, 1989), 90–91, 94.

35. Maria Graham, *Journal of a Voyage to Brazil and Residence There etc.* (1824; repr., New York: Praeger, 1969), 126.

36. Antônio Pinto d'Oliveira França, ed., *Cartas baianas, 1821–1824* (Rio de Janeiro: Companhia Editora Nacional, 1980), 36, 42, 49, 60; *Semanário Cívico* 83 (October 3, 1822): 1; Proclamation by Madeira, March 29, 1822, Juizes, maço 2860, APEBA. Madeira's second quote refers to a proclamation dated 2 Abril 1822, quoted in Souza, *A pátria coroada*, 165.

37. *Memória sobre a crise da Província em 1824*, 11.

38. Maria Januária Vilela Santos, *A Balaiada e a insurreição de escravos no Maranhão* (São Paulo: Ática, 1983), 82, 110–111.

39. Justice of the Peace Marcelino Gomes da Silveira to the President of Bahia Province, March 31, 1835, Juizes de paz, maço 2298, APEBA.

40. "Relação das casas habitadas por negros libertos, e que por se juntarem em algumas delas escravos, devem ser conhecidas das autoridades e vigiadas pela Polícia,"

[April 2, 1835], Guarda Municipal Permanente, 0331, Mapoteca 01, Gaveta 4, Arquivo Público do Estado do Maranhão, São Luís. We thank Mundinha Araújo for sharing this document with us.

41. *Constituição política do Império do Brasil* (Rio de Janeiro: Typ. de Silva Porto, 1824), 63.

42. Article 6, paragraph 1 and article 93, paragraph 2 of the constitution. See also José Honório Rodrigues, *A Assembléia Constituinte de 1823* (Petrópolis: Vozes, 1974), 122–137, esp. 130–137; Jaime Rodrigues, *O infame comércio: propostas e experiências no final do tráfico de africanos para o Brasil (1800–1850)* (Campinas: Editora da UNICAMP/CECULT, 2000), 52–54; and Cunha, *Negros, estrangeiros*, 62–100.

43. On the slave population in Rio, see Mary Karasch, *Slave Life in Rio de Janeiro, 1800–1850* (Princeton, N.J.: Princeton University Press, 1987), 61.

44. Justice of the Peace of São José District to Chief of Police, February 20, 1836, Códice 334, Correspondência reservada da Chefia de Polícia da Corte, fl. 2v, ANRJ.

45. H. S. Fox to the Duke of Wellington, February 11, 1835, FO 13/117, fl. 59v, British National Archives (hereafter BNA).

46. Fox to Wellington, February 13, 1835, FO 13/117, fl. 208–208v, BNA.

47. Fox to Wellington, April 13, 1835, FO 13/117, fl. 250, BNA.

48. Regência, cód. 334, fls. 9v, 11, 14, 15, and 19, ANRJ.

49. Mott, *Escravidão*, 18; Karasch, *Slave Life*, 327.

50. Justice of the Peace of São João do Príncipe to the Vice-President of Rio de Janeiro Province, May 30, 1835, JAP, Fundo PP, coleção 80, Arquivo Público do Estado do Rio de Janeiro (hereafter APERJ); Vice-President of Rio de Janeiro Province to the Minister of Justice, May 18, 1835, Minister of Justice to the Chief of Police, n.d., *Correspondência citada*, Cód. 334, fl. 12v, ANRJ.

51. Justice of the Peace of São José to Chief of Police, May 5, 1835, GIFI, pacote 5, B, 515, ANRJ.

52. See, for instance, the opinion of two powerful contemporary politicians writing in the early 1820s: João Severiano Maciel da Costa, "Memória sobre a necessidade de abolir a introdução dos escravos africanos no Brasil," in *Memórias sobre a escravidão* (Rio de Janeiro: Arquivo Nacional, 1988), 22, 27; and José Bonifácio de Andrada e Silva, "Representação à Assembléia Geral Constituinte e Legislativa do Império do Brasil sobre a escravatura," in *Memórias sobre a escravidão*, 63, 64–65, 67, 69, 77n4, 70, and 75. (For Maciel da Costa's opposition to extending citizenship to freed Africans, see Rodrigues, *A Assembléia Constituinte*, 133–135.) For a discussion of Bonifácio's ideas on slavery and the slave trade as obstacles to the development of Brazil, see Ana Rosa Cloclet da Silva, *Construção da nação e escravidão no pensamento de José Bonifácio, 1783–1823* (Campinas: Editora e Centro de Memória da UNICAMP, 1999), 133–135. See also Maxwell, *Naked Tropics*, 163–164. Both Maciel da Costa and Bonifácio, in addition to other critics of the slave trade at the time, urged the immigration of European settlers to counter the disproportionate number of blacks in Brazil.

53. Reis, *Rebelião escrava*, 527–536. British diplomat William Ouseley quoted in Dale Graden, *From Slavery to Freedom in Brazil: Bahia, 1835–1900* (Albuquerque: University of New Mexico Press, 2006), 17.

54. Reis, *Rebelião escrava*, 527–536.

55. Rosa Acevedo Marin, "A Influência da Revolução Francesa no Grão-Pará," in *Ecologia, desenvolvimento e cooperação na Amazônia*, ed. José Carlos C. da Cunha (Belém: UNAMAZ/UFPA, 1992), 35–40; Flávio Gomes, "Other Black Atlantic Borders: Escape Routes, Mocambos, and Fears of Sedition in Brazil and French Guiana (Eighteenth to Nineteenth Centuries)," *New West Indian Guide* 77, nos. 3–4 (2003): 253–287.

56. D. Francisco de Souza Coutinho to Martinho de Mello e Castro, March 1, 1791, Documentação Rio Branco, Cód. 340-1-3, Arquivo Histórico do Itamaraty, Rio de Janeiro (hereafter AHI).

57. D. Francisco de Souza Coutinho to Martinho de Mello e Castro, January 10, 1795, Coleção Manoel Barata, Instituto Histórico Geográfico Brasileiro, Rio de Janeiro.

58. D. Francisco de Souza Coutinho to Martinho de Mello e Castro, July 8, 1792, Coleção Manoel Barata, Instituto Histórico Geográfico Brasileiro, Rio de Janeiro.

59. See Flávio Gomes, "Nas fronteiras da liberdade: mocambos, fugitivos e protesto escravo na Amazônia Colonial," *Anais do Arquivo Público do Pará* (Belém: APEPA, 1996), 258ff.

60. Antônio Ladislau Monteiro Baena, *Compêndio das eras da Província do Pará* (Belém: UFPA, 1969), 232.

61. Marcos José Monteiro de Carvalho to Francisco Xavier Azevedo Coutinho, Belém, October 3, 1794, Documentação do Ministério anterior a 1822, Pasta 9, Lata 172 e maço 2, AHI.

62. "Parecer" by Conde de Galveas on Cayenne Convention, March 1, 1809, I-32, 18, 3, BNRJ.

63. Cited in Arthur César Ferreira Reis, *Limites e demarcações na Amazônia Brazileira* (Rio de Janeiro: Imprensa Nacional, 1947), 289–291.

64. D. Francisco de Assis Mascarenhas to Conde de Linhares, May 14, 1809, Códice 7, 4, 83, BNRJ.

65. The documents pertaining to Father Joaquim de Souza Ribeiro are in the Arquivo Nacional do Rio de Janeiro (GIFI, pacote 6, I, 79, ANRJ). We are grateful to Isadora Mota, who called our attention to and copied these documents.

66. Maciel da Costa to Caetano Pinto de Miranda Montenegro, Cayenne, November 21, 1814, GIFI, pacote 6, I, 79, ANRJ.

67. Father Ribeiro, born in Bahia and son of Manuel de Sousa Ribeiro, is listed as a student at Coimbra in "Estudantes brasileiros na Universidade de Coimbra (1772–1872)," *Anais da Biblioteca Nacional do Rio de Janeiro* 62 (1940): 175.

68. Martinho de Mello e Castro to the Governor and Capitain-General of Maranhão, Lisbon, January 30, 1794, GIFI, pacote 6, I, 79, ANRJ.

69. João de Mattos Vasconcellos Barbosa de Magalhães to the Prince Regent, Lisbon September 24, 1813, GIFI, pacote 6, I, 79, ANRJ.

70. Adolphe Cabon, *Notes sur l'histoire religieuse d'Haiti: de la Révolution au Concordat (1789–1860)* (Port-au-Prince: Petit Séminaire Collège Saint-Martial, 1933), esp. 71–74; Laënnec Hurbon, "The Church and Slavery in Eighteenth-Century Saint-Domingue," in *The Abolitions of Slavery: From L. F. Sonthonax to Victor Schoelcher, 1793, 1794, 1848*, ed. Marcel Dorigny (New York: Berghahn Books, 2003), 55–68; Gabriel Debien, *Les esclaves aux Antilles françaises (XVIIe–XVIIIe siècles)* (Basse-Terre: Societé d'Histoire de la Guadeloupe, 1974), chap. xiv, esp. 279–295.

71. One cruzado is equivalent to 400 réis, the real being the Portuguese currency. Five thousand cruzados was a small fortune that could buy sixteen slaves in Rio de Janeiro in 1810. For slave prices, see Manolo Florentino, "Slave Trading and Slave Traders in Rio de Janeiro, 1790–1830," in *Enslaving Connections: Changing Cultures of Africa and Brazil During the Era of Slavery*, ed. José Curto and Paul Lovejoy (Amherst, N.Y.: Humanity Books, 2004), 63.

72. For the last two paragraphs, see Alexandre Joseph Ferreira Castello to João de Mattos V. B. de Magalhães, General Intendant of Políce, Lisbon, October 9, 1813; João da Silva Moreira Payzinho to João de Mattos V. B. de Magalhães, Lisbon, October 14, 1813; and Magalhães to Prince Regent, Lisbon, September 24, 1813, all in GIFI, pacote 6, I, 79, ANRJ.

73. Ribeiro, "Diário de Lisboa até Londres e Barbados," ms. annexed to the inquiry made in Rio de Janeiro in 1814–1815, GIFI, pacote 6, I, 79, ANRJ.

74. Interrogation of Father Ribeiro, Cayenne, September 2, 1814, GIFI, pacote 6, I, 79, ANRJ.

75. Ribeiro, "Diário de Lisboa até Londres e Barbados."

76. Da Costa, "Memória," 22.

77. Da Costa, "Memória," 22.

78. Maciel da Costa to Marquis de Aguiar, Cayenne, November 21, 1814, GIFI, pacote 6, I, 79, ANRJ.

79. Ribeiro's belongings are described in a document signed by him in February 1, 1815, entitled "Nota do que se achou em sette Bahus do Padre Joaquim de Souza Ribeiro." There is also a receipt dated November 22, 1814, signed by Maciel da Costa, attesting that he received 26,700 réis from Ribeiro related to expenses incurred during his stay at the military hospital. GIFI, pacote 6, I, 79, ANRJ.

80. Paulo [illeg.] to Marquis de Aguiar, Rio de Janeiro, May 1, 1815, GIFI, pacote 6, I, 79, ANRJ.

81. "Auto de perguntas feitas ao Pe. Joaquim de Souza Ribeiro," Rio de Janeiro, April 13, 1815, GIFI, pacote 6, I, 79, ANRJ.

82. Paulo [illeg.] to Marquis de Aguiar, Rio de Janeiro, 1 May 1815.

83. The authors are writing a book on Father Ribeiro.

84. For other contexts, see Scott, "The Common Wind." See also Peter Linebaugh and Marcus Rediker, *The Many-Headed Hydra: Sailors, Slaves, Commoners, and the Hidden History of the Revolutionary Atlantic* (Boston: Beacon Press, 2000).

85. See, for example, Lilia Schwarcz, *O espetáculo das raças: cientistas, instituições e a questão racial no Brasil, 1870–1930* (São Paulo: Companhia das Letras, 1993).

86. José Antonio Saco, *História de la esclavitud de la raza africana en el Nuevo Mundo y en especial los paises américo-hispanos* (La Habana: Cultural S. A., 1938), 3:29.

87. *Correio Mercantil*: March 8, 1848 and October 7, 1848; Afonso Cláudio, *A insurreição do Queimado* (1884; repr., Vitória: Editora da Fundação Ceciliano Abel de Almeida, 1979). See also Robert Slenes, "'*Malungu Ngoma Vem*': África encoberta e descoberta no Brasil," *Revista USP* 12 (1991–1992): 64–66; Dale T. Graden, "An Act 'Even of Public Security': Slave Resistance, Social Tensions, and the End of the International Slave Trade to Brazil, 1835–1856," *Hispanic American Historical Review* 76, no. 2 (1996): 249–282. For an opposite view, see Jeffrey Needell, "The Abolition of the Brazilian Slave

Trade in 1850: Historiography, Slave Agency and Statesmanship," *Journal of Latin American Studies* 33 (2001): 681–711.

88. For a perspective that emphasizes the rhetorical use of Haiti for social control purposes, see Rafael Bivar Marquese, "Escravismo e independência: a ideologia da escravidão no Brasil, em Cuba e nos Estados Unidos nas décadas de 1810 e 1820," in *Independência: história e historiografia,* ed. Ístvan Jancsó (São Paulo: Hucitec, 2005), 809–827.

89. For the Bahian episode, see Tavares, *Da Sedição,* 187–238.

90. Although not so decisive as the divisions between blacks and mulattoes, tensions and conflicts between black creoles and Africans also punctuated the Haitian revolutionary process and became acute during the French invasion in 1802, when creole blacks adhered to the French and African-born ex-slaves fought them after Toussaint's arrest in what Michel-Rolph Trouillot calls "*a* war within *the* war." *Silencing the Past: Power and the Production of History* (Boston: Beacon, 1995), 40. See also Carolyn Fick, *The Making of Haiti: The Saint-Domingue Revolution from Below* (Knoxville: University of Tennessee Press, 1990), 231–232. The negative views that many nineteenth-century Haitian intellectuals had of Africa and the Africans are discussed in Nicholls, *From Dessalines to Duvalier,* 41–46.

91. José Bonifácio de Andrada e Silva, *Projetos para o Brasil,* ed. Miriam Dollnikoff (São Paulo: Companhia das Letras, 1998), 151.

92. As suggested in Schwartz, *Sugar Plantations,* 479.

PART FOUR

REPRESENTATIONS
OF THE REVOLUTION

THE SPECTER OF SAINT-DOMINGUE
AMERICAN AND FRENCH REACTIONS TO THE HAITIAN REVOLUTION

Alyssa Goldstein Sepinwall

The Negroes are burning and destroying everything before them.
—*New York Daily Gazette*, 1791

Qui oserait encore plaider la cause des noirs, après
les crimes qu'ils ont commis?
—F.-R. Chateaubriand, *La génie du christianisme*, 1802

THE HAITIAN REVOLUTION AROUSED FEAR AMONG WHITES THROUGH-OUT THE ATLANTIC WORLD. THE FIRST SUCCESSFUL REBELLION BY SLAVES AFTER 300 YEARS OF AFRICAN SLAVERY IN THE AMERICAS, the revolution in colonial Saint-Domingue sent shock waves throughout the New World and back to the European metropoles. For slave-owners and their allies, the world was turned upside down; the very words "Saint-Domingue" conjured up a terrifying alternative universe in which whites could lose their power, their fortunes, and even their lives. For enslaved peoples around the Atlantic, on the other hand, the Haitian Revolution had a different meaning: it served as a flicker of inspiration and hope as they imagined a world in which the scourge of slavery could be eradicated.

It would not be an overstatement to call the Haitian Revolution's international effects cataclysmic. For the French, Haitian independence meant the loss of the empire's most important colony, the pearl of the West Indies. More important, it signaled the end of French imperial grandeur, at least until the invasion of Algeria and the new imperialism of the later nineteenth century. For the young United States, the Haitian Revolution was also of crucial national significance, even if this is often forgotten today. Indeed, many scholars have claimed that it was France's loss of Saint-Domingue that enabled the United States to expand westward. After defeat in the Seven Years' War followed by the

317

loss of Saint-Domingue, France's vision of an American empire was finished, and there was no need to keep Louisiana. Other scholars have pointed to a more nefarious consequence of the Haitian Revolution: white Americans' fears about possible domestic imitators led to heightened enforcement of slavery in the South as slave-owners turned more repressive at any sign of resistance. The anxiety of Americans and Frenchmen had a concrete effect on Haiti itself: in order to crush the aspirations of American or West Indian blacks who might wish to emulate their Haitian brothers, the United States placed an embargo on trade with the new nation and Frenchmen agitated for a reconquest of the island. Though the American embargo was often flouted and later allowed to lapse and the French eventually abandoned hopes for reconquest, it was only by agreeing to pay a staggering indemnity that Haiti received recognition from France in 1825 and was allowed to join the community of nations. This sum, 150,000,000 francs, turned Haiti's de facto political independence into a crippling financial dependency.

For an event of such importance, the revolution's memory has not been well preserved, in either the United States or in France. In this chapter, I offer an overview of how historians of the United States and France have looked at the aftermath of the Haitian Revolution. Though the historiography is growing, it is still too early to make authoritative comparisons between how each of these countries reacted to the revolution. Indeed, while the American historiography has become rather voluminous in the past twenty years, more work needs to be done on the French side before one can make confident generalizations. However, by presenting a survey of existing work on the topic, I hope to identify some questions that remain to be answered by scholars and offer insights on the interplay between history, memory, and ideas of race, for Americans as well as for the French. The growing concern in American historiography with the Haitian Revolution, I believe, stems from Americans' heightened consciousness about the problem of race, while the lesser attention to Haiti in French historiography stems from the rejection of the concept of race in French public discourse and the peculiar place of the Haitian Revolution in French history.

In 1940, the American historian Ludwell Lee Montague wrote: "Haiti lies only six hundred miles from Florida.... It is [therefore] remarkable that the land and its people should be so little known to Americans. Although Haitian history has been closely related to that of the United States for more than two centuries, to the American mind Haiti remains a land of foreboding and mystery—terra incognita."[1] These words, penned sixty-four years ago, could practically have been written today. Despite the proximity of Haiti to the United States, very little scholarship was produced on the relations between the two nations until the American occupation of Haiti, which lasted from 1915 to 1934. In the wake of this invasion, American scholars looked back in time to understand the background of U.S.-Haitian relations. Four studies appeared between 1916 and 1941, written by Mary Treudley, Charles Tansill, Ludwell Lee Montague, and Rayford Logan.[2] These authors pointed out that in the eighteenth century, Saint-Domingue was the main trading partner of the American colonies. As John Adams said in 1783, "We are necessary to them, and they are to us."[3] The American War of Independence in fact strengthened ties with the island by giving the newly styled Americans even greater freedom to choose French sugar, coffee, and molasses over these same commodities produced by the British.

Logan and Montague remarked that Haiti and the United States had much in common. Both were born of rebellions against rulers in Europe who refused to extend to their colonies the liberties enjoyed in the metropole. Whereas in the North American colonies grievances centered on trade restrictions and taxation without representation, in Saint-Domingue, free and enslaved people of color sought to combat the racial oppression that persisted in spite of the new discourses of liberty and equality. A further point of similarity was that each revolution was led by a general who became both a civilian leader and a national icon: George Washington in the United States and Toussaint Louverture in Haiti. Despite these parallels, Americans would prove unwilling to recognize the independence of their southern neighbor, even after France had done so. While Charles X reached agreement on recognizing Haiti in 1825, the United States withheld recognition from the island nation until 1862.

One task facing American historians who study the aftermath of the Haitian Revolution has been to explain this prolonged refusal to grant diplomatic recognition. Why did the United States wait so long to accept the fact of Haitian independence? To solve this puzzle, the first generation of post-invasion scholars focused on high politics, trade, and diplomacy. They depicted American policy toward Saint-Domingue as part of efforts by the United States to balance the power of Britain and France and carve out its own sphere of influence in the Americas. These scholars cited figures such as John Quincy Adams, who suggested that it would be ideal if Saint-Domingue and other French colonies were "free and independent, in close alliance and under the guarantee of the United States." At the same time, these authors asserted, Americans were anxious not to jeopardize permanently their relations with either great power by being the only nation to recognize the island's independence; they feared that this might provoke the complete blockage of American-Caribbean commerce.[4]

Not all Americans were of one mind regarding Saint-Domingue/Haiti, however. Northern merchants, though uncomfortable with the French National Convention's abolition of slavery in 1794 and later with the prospect of a black-led state, were primarily concerned with continuing the commerce—"low-grade fish for cheap molasses"[5]—that was their lifeblood. Southern planters, in contrast, were more anxious about the impact of the Saint-Domingue rebellion on their own slaves.

American policy therefore went through a number of shifts, depending on the relative strength of the North and the South, the president in power, and particular events in Haiti and in France. For example, where George Washington's first instinct was to supply arms, provisions, and money to the beleaguered white colonists when violence flared on the island in 1790–1791, John Adams sought a way to continue commerce with Saint-Domingue even under Toussaint. During Adams's presidency, hostility to the French republicans and controversies such as the XYZ Affair bolstered the northern merchants' position that commerce with Saint-Domingue should be sustained no matter who was in power there and regardless of the French reaction.

Under Jefferson's presidency, the planters gained ascendancy. The United States not only refused to recognize the new nation, it also imposed a trade embargo on it (though this was flouted by northern merchants who carried on a clandestine commerce). The embargo was allowed to lapse in 1809, but southern planters continued to block any suggestion of recognition. Even after France recognized Haiti in 1825 and other nations followed suit, the United States persisted in its refusal. As Robert Y. Hayne of South Carolina argued in the U.S. Senate in 1825, "Our policy with regard to Hayti is plain. We can never acknowledge her independence." Similarly, his colleague from Missouri, Thomas Hart Benton, commented that

> our policy towards Hayti . . . has been fixed . . . for three and thirty years. We trade with her, but no diplomatic relations have been established between us. . . . We receive no mulatto consuls, or black ambassadors from her. And why? Because the peace of eleven states will not permit the fruits of a successful negro insurrection to be exhibited among them. It will not permit black ambassadors and consuls to . . . give their fellow blacks in the United States proof in hand of the honors that await them for a like successful effort on their part. It will not permit the fact to be seen, and told, that for the murder of their masters and mistresses, they are to find friends among the white people of these United States.[6]

In not recognizing Haiti even when other maritime powers did, the United States angered the Haitian government, which responded by cutting ties with American commercial agents and levying tariffs on American goods and ships.

Why, then, was recognition finally granted in 1862? According to these authors, the onset of the Civil War and the South's secession changed political circumstances. With southern senators no longer balancing the demands of northern merchants, commercial motives could now prevail. By the 1860s, although some senators from border states continued to argue that Washington was not ready for the arrival of black diplomats, abolitionists were in a much stronger position. Senator Charles Sumner, the noted abolitionist from Massachusetts, argued that recognizing Haiti was a matter of simple justice, especially since it had already been independent for nearly six decades. Lincoln also hoped that recognizing Haiti would win support for the North from British and French liberals.[7]

After this initial burst of post-invasion scholarship in the United States between 1915 and 1941, interest in Haiti waned. In the rest of the 1940s and into the 1950s, work on early American attitudes towards Haiti was rare and was focused primarily on the experiences of white refugees from Saint-Domingue arriving in the United States.[8]

With increased interest in questions of race among American historians after the 1960s, however, a new wave of scholarship on U.S.-Haitian relations was sparked. Some of this work has continued to focus on diplomacy and trade even while modifying some of the assumptions of the earlier studies. Tim Matthewson has argued, for example, that the split between northerners and southerners was not absolute, pointing out that some northern merchants sided with southern planters against recognition, especially after the violence that marked Dessalines's rule. Matthewson cited the case of one Boston congressman who argued that "American merchants should not trade with a people 'it is in the interest of the United States to depress and keep down.'"[9] Matthewson has also suggested that not all northerners based their arguments on commercial interests. He pointed to the northern radical Abraham Bishop, who launched a full-scale defense of the Haitians' right to revolt against their oppressors. In 1791, Bishop wrote, "We believe that Freedom is the natural right of all rational beings. . . . Let us be consistent Americans, and if we justify our own conduct in the late glorious Revolution, let us justify those, who, in a cause like ours fight with equal bravery." "The blacks are entitled to freedom, for we did not say, all *white* men are *free*, but *all men* are free."[10]

Another subject of contention in recent scholarship has been the attitudes toward Haiti of Thomas Jefferson, a man who has become emblematic of America's tortured history of race relations. Where some scholars have given a sympathetic account of Jefferson wrestling with issues of race and liberty, Michael Zuckerman has taken a much harsher view of Jefferson's attitudes on Haiti. He argues that "color countermanded everything for Jefferson" and that "the similarities in the struggles of the American and San Domingan rebels caused Jefferson not a moment's pause."[11]

This new wave of scholarship has not limited itself to explaining the U.S. stance on recognition or to expounding upon elite white Americans' fears of the Haitian example. On the contrary, new work has focused, as has other scholarship written since the 1960s, on the ideas and actions of non-elites and on the revolution's broader cultural meaning. Alfred Hunt's *Haiti's Influence on Antebellum America* is the most comprehensive study in this regard. Building on work by others, Hunt has shown how the Haitian Revolution further strengthened the institution of American slavery. At a time when the idea of gradual emancipation was taking hold among reformers throughout the Atlantic world, American defenders of the slave regime invoked the Haitian experience to warn of the dangers of emancipation, gradual or not. As Hunt argued, "Vivid reports of the massacres in St. Domingue convinced southerners that the only thing they could expect from freed slaves was vicious retaliation."[12] Similarly, David Brion Davis has argued that in the short term, the Haitian Revolution set back the American abolitionist movement: "Abolitionists were increasingly portrayed as inciters of violence. . . . [and] found it difficult to escape the stigma of Saint-Domingue."[13]

Even as this new wave of scholarship has noted that the Haitian Revolution had a chilling effect in the short term on the persuasiveness of American abolitionism, it has also pointed out that the revolution had a very different impact over the long term on American blacks, free and enslaved. Davis has noted that even while the United States remained a slave society, the Haitian Revolution showed American blacks that "bondage was not an inevitable and eternal fate." In 1893, for example, Frederick Douglass attributed worldwide abolition to the impact of "the brave stand taken by the black sons of Haiti ninety years ago." Similarly, Hunt has found that "the founding of a black republic in the New World . . . contributed to the development of a sense of black nationalism." He has focused particularly on the figure of Toussaint Louverture, who was venerated by American blacks as both a hero and a refutation of the argument that blacks could not govern themselves.[14]

Several recent studies have examined additional aspects of the influence of Haitian events on American blacks.[15] These works mention the impact of the Haitian Revolution on the earliest slave rebellions in the United States and on the colonization movement. This ultimately unsuccessful experiment sent free blacks to Haiti in the 1810s and 1820s. Whites hoped that exporting free blacks would help solve the problem of racial coexistence, while black participants hoped for a new start in a free black society. Despite the failure of this program, Haiti remained a symbol for American blacks into the twentieth century and the Harlem Renaissance, as can be seen in work of various writers and in the paintings of African American artists like Jacob Lawrence.[16]

The last half-decade has spawned even more fascinating scholarship in this growing field. A number of studies have focused on the arrival of black and mixed-race Saint Dominguans in the United States or on the impact of the Haitian Revolution in particular American cities. In one seminal study on Philadelphia, Gary Nash argued that the arrival of white refugees from Saint-Domingue indirectly hampered the growth of free black institutions in that city and that white philanthropists who had pledged to fund an African church there instead directed their dollars toward a relief fund for the new white immigrants. Meanwhile, Nash noted, the arrival of free Saint-Dominguans of color made white Philadelphians anxious that they would bring racial conflict with them, and expressions of sympathy with the Saint-Domingue Revolution became scarcer. Nevertheless, Nash maintains, the uprising in Haiti had a profound effect on American blacks' sense of themselves and their possibilities, providing a "symbol of black autonomy and equal rights for many decades."[17]

Important new research is also being done on the effects of the revolution in Louisiana. Though not all scholars agree on the extent to which losing Saint-Domingue spurred Napoleon's decision to sell Louisiana to the United States, the revolution affected Louisiana in many important ways. These range from creating new agricultural opportunities there to inspiring slave revolts and new restrictions on slaves. Paul Lachance has also suggested that arriving émigrés solidified the French character of the region and its distinctive three-color social structure.[18]

As Michel-Rolph Trouillot has remarked, most Americans are ignorant about the Haitian Revolution because such an important event in what is now a poor country remains profoundly "unthinkable." Still, the scholarly study of the effects of the Haitian Revolution on the United States has now become a mature field—encouraged not only by the modern interest in race but also by the current vogue for Atlantic world scholarship. Although many questions remain to be resolved, the field has reached a level of detail that transcends facile generalizations, showing the effects of the Haitian Revolution not simply on whites in general but on whites in different regions and political parties, and not simply on whites alone but also on free blacks and slaves.[19] Scholarship has also extended along a variety of methodological avenues, turning from high diplomacy and politics to cultural and social approaches and to literary study.

In France, in contrast, the field is not quite as developed. A number of historians and literary critics have produced fascinating studies in recent years, but there is much we do not yet know about the French reaction to the Haitian Revolution. Before surveying what does exist, it is useful to reflect on the reasons for the lesser attention to Haiti within French historiography. This can be explained, I would like to argue, by differences in American and French attitudes toward the idea of race and by the special place of Haiti in French history.

Though both the United States and France share slaveholding pasts, the two nations have had different trajectories in both their national histories and their historiographies. In the United States, a civil war and a civil rights movement have made Americans acutely conscious of race, even if they have not always agreed on how to regard its historical legacy. Studies of race have become a staple of university history curricula, utilizing the hundreds of new works published each year on the topic. Meanwhile, candidates who study race or colonialism have become desired commodities on the American academic job market. While Americans know woefully little about Haiti, public interest in race relations more generally is high, as is evidenced by the observance each winter of both Martin Luther King Day and Black History Month, which are accompanied by television programs and public ceremonies. The growing scholarly attention to U.S.-Haitian relations, a prime vehicle for studying American ideas of race over two centuries, stems from this larger cultural climate.

In France, on the contrary, there has been what Yves Benot has called a national *oubli* (forgetting) about the history of slavery by both lay people and scholars.[20] Part of this amnesia stems from the obvious fact that both colonial expansion and the plantation system took place outside of mainland France, making the history of slavery less central to the nation's national past. At the same time, the very recent traumas of modern decolonization—particularly the Indochinese and Algerian wars—have further prevented postcolonial approaches from taking root in the French academic establishment, with the exception of particular campuses, such as the Universities of Paris-VII (Denis Diderot) and Paris-VIII (Saint-Denis).

French republican identity also affects how slavery is discussed. Crucial to the French self-image is the idea that the French Republic is historically universalist and that all distinctions between people were eradicated in 1789. Slavery is thus remembered only when it can be inscribed within a narrative of republican liberation, with ideals of liberty sweeping from Paris through the French empire and the whole world. This narrative was predominant in 1989 (when the French celebrated the bicentennial of the French Revolution and portrayed it as having liberated people around the world), in 1994 (when the bicentennial of the first French abolition of slavery was feted), and in 1998 (the 150th anniversary of the second abolition of slavery).[21]

When aspects of the actual history of slavery threaten this narrative, however, they have generally been ignored. Despite the public celebrations of 1994 and 1998, most French scholars (excepting the circle around Benot and Marcel Dorigny) were loathe to commemorate 2002—the bicentennial of Napoleon's reimposition of slavery and the very reason a second abolition was needed.[22] Most people in France are not even aware that Napoleon reversed the abolition proclaimed by the revolutionary government in Paris in 1794 or that racism continued to underlie republican policies long after 1789, as in Jules Ferry's famous 1883 declaration that French colonialism was necessary since "superior races have rights over inferior races."[23]

The disparity between American and French scholarship on slavery and on Haiti can also be explained by the fact that the concept of race is anathema in contemporary French discourse. Since World War II, when both Nazis and enthusiastic Vichy collaborators murdered French citizens on the grounds of their "Jewish race," French citizens across the political spectrum (excepting the far right) have insisted that race is an unscientific category. They consequently refuse to use it to classify people, either in governmental affairs or in public discourse, and are shocked when Americans use terms like "blacks" to refer to people's "racial identity." To them, the American system of affirmative action is absurd; studying the place of race in French history seems not only illogical but also dangerous. The result, however, has been a woeful underattention to France's slaveholding and colonial past. Recognizing the artificiality of the idea of race in discussions today does not obviate the truth that the category was long treated as valid and that it shaped power relations in multiple ways. In contrast to the United States, the history of slavery is generally omitted from both school and university curricula in France, and books on the history of race have difficulty finding publishers because the topic is seen as scandalous.[24]

Much of the scholarship on issues of race in French history has consequently been produced only in the last thirty years and typically by researchers outside of metropolitan France, whether in the West Indies or in North America. Of course, there are exceptions. The 1920s and 1930s saw a flowering of work in the field by African American and Caribbean scholars. A few like-minded writers in mid-twentieth-century France also published on issues of slavery, often motivated either by anticolonialism or the leftist antiracism of the Nazi and post-Shoah periods. Still, most of the twentieth-century scholarship on the French Caribbean focused more on colonial Saint-Domingue or on French abolitionism than it did on the Haitian Revolution and Haitian independence, which were much more traumatic subjects in the French consciousness.[25]

Indeed, as a number of recent studies have suggested, Haiti has been the subject of a special amnesia in French national memory. Unlike in the American case, the Haitian Revolution was a direct blow against the French nation; the story of Haitian independence exposes both the weakness of the French colonial army and the hypocrisy of the French civilizing mission. As Francis Arzalier has pointed out, if the French Revolution was as liberating as its place in national mythology implies, why would the people of color of Saint-Domingue have needed to revolt against it? Haiti was thus best forgotten, as scholars like Trouillot, Myriam Cottias, and Christopher Miller have recently suggested. Indeed, according to Catherine Coquery-Vidrovitch, not until 1962 did the publication of Aimé Césaire's *Toussaint Louverture* shock certain French intellectuals into remembering Haiti. Nevertheless, for most French people, as for their American counterparts, Haiti has remained a subject of general ignorance, brought into the news periodically to show the French generously helping to stabilize a country that cannot seem to achieve peace on its own.[26]

In this context, it is not surprising that little work was done on the French reaction to the Haitian Revolution until recently. As compared to the American case, in which no less than eleven monographs cover the American reaction, there is only one monograph devoted to early French-Haitian relations. The first scholars to work on the subject were not French but Haitian, the nineteenth-century writers Beaubrun Ardouin and Thomas Madiou, whose epic chronicles of Haitian history included numerous sources related to early French-Haitian relations. Their presentations were more narrative than analytical, however, and few of their twentieth-century successors were anxious to write critically about the topic.[27] Especially in the wake of the American invasion of Haiti, intellectuals in that country were more concerned with gaining support from French counterparts for their country's plight than with alienating them; they therefore wrote surprisingly rosy accounts of past relations between the two countries.[28]

Not until the 1950s and 1960s did scholars turn seriously to the subject of the French reaction to Haitian independence. Like the first wave of scholarship in the United States on relations with Haiti, these early studies focused on diplomatic relations between France and its rebellious former colony. Building on the foundations laid by Ardouin, Madiou, and scholars of U.S.-Haitian relations, the Haitian historians Ghislain Gouraige and Maurice Lubin seem to have been the first to write detailed analyses of early Haitian-French relations. Gouraige's study, written as a thesis at Haiti's Institut Diplomatique and published in 1955, used printed and archival sources to trace the protracted and complicated negotiations between France and Haiti, both before and after the recognition agreement. However, despite the impressive research and level of detail in Gouraige's study, most scholars are unaware of it, and citations of it are rare.[29]

Lubin's essay, which is more frequently cited, was published in 1968. It focused on Haitian foreign policy during the first years after independence was declared and discussed Haitian leaders' attitudes toward their former colonizers as well as efforts by the French government to ensure that Haiti remained an international pariah. Just as Dessalines declared that the French were a "barbarous people" and that Haitians would never forget the crimes they had suffered at the hands of the French, the French continued to seethe with anger at their defeat. Refusing to use the name "Haiti" and referring instead to Saint-Domingue, which implied that the territory was still rightfully theirs, some French authors called the inhabitants of Saint-Domingue savage "enemies of France" who had performed "the most criminal acts."[30]

Lubin also traced the efforts of France to persuade the other major powers not to recognize the independence of Saint-Domingue. He noted that Haitian leaders, in an effort to allay the fears of the slaveholding nations, had pledged not to try to spread revolution to neighboring colonies. Dessalines's 1804 independence proclamation warned his fellow citizens, "Let us ensure that the spirit of proselytism does not destroy our work. Let us leave our neighbors in peace . . . and not become arsonist-revolutionaries who, appointing ourselves the legislators of the West Indies, make our glory consist of troubling the tranquility of neighboring islands." French fears were not assuaged, however, and the government urged other "white nations" to choke the rebellious colony. In 1805, for instance, Talleyrand told the United States that by allowing its merchants to continue to trade with Haiti, it was "only helping arsonists and assassins."[31]

In the 1970s, another Haitian historian, Benoît Joachim, expanded on Gouraige's and Lubin's work. Focusing on the Restoration period in France, he used pamphlet and archival sources to explain why France ultimately changed course and recognized Haiti. He argued that France normalized relations after realizing it was not strong enough to reconquer the island and because it feared that Haiti might indeed export rebellion to Guadeloupe and Martinique. Economic factors also drove this decision. By the 1820s, French industrial production was taking off but France had a trade deficit and needed new markets. The Monroe Doctrine and Britain's aggressive attempts to expand its trade in the Americas fed French worries that they might be shut out from New World commerce. An agreement with Haiti promised them access not only to Haitian consumers but also to nearby Latin American ones who had just freed themselves from Spanish control. As other nations began to make overtures toward Haiti, France worried that a competitor might capture Haiti's trade for itself.[32]

Nevertheless, Joachim noted, members of the Restoration government were not of one mind about how to deal with Haiti. Some continued to hope to reconquer the island or to neutralize it in some other way. Eventually, the government settled on being indemnified, an idea first proposed by Pétion in 1816. The French believed that Haitian coffers were full and that the 150,000,000 francs could be paid within five years. This assumption was mistaken, however, and the pressure to pay off the indemnity plus accumulating interest on the balance turned out to have a crushing effect on postcolonial Haiti. Indeed, Joachim held up Haiti as an early model of the postcolonial condition in which a former colony gained political independence but was rendered economically dependent by its former colonizer.[33] Recent scholarship by François Blancpain (from France) and Gusti Klara Gaillard-Pourchet (from Haiti) has provided further information on the indemnity and its effects.[34]

The contributions of these scholars have been invaluable in revealing the economic and diplomatic aspects of the French government's response to Haitian independence. As in the American case, scholarship on the impact of the Haitian Revolution in France has also pushed in new directions in the last three decades. In this case too, much of it has been produced by scholars outside France, whether in the Caribbean or in North America. One trajectory of this new scholarship has focused on diplomatic history, while shifting from an examination of the French attitude toward recognition in favor of contemporary Haitian attitudes about it.[35] Another trajectory has looked beyond the metropole to see how inhabitants in other French colonies, both free and enslaved, reacted to Haitian independence.[36]

Literary studies, particularly those on "representations," have been another rich source of new work in the field. Two pioneering studies in the 1970s by Léon-François Hoffmann and Régis Antoine traced depictions of blacks and of Haiti in nineteenth-century French literature. Hoffmann has paid particular attention to Alphonse Lamartine's play *Toussaint Louverture*, which by 1850 was one of the only favorable depictions of Haiti in France. Although it attracted hostility from contemporary critics, it seemed patronizing to twentieth-century writers like Frantz Fanon. Scholars like J. A. Ferguson and George Tyson have examined other representations of Toussaint Louverture in French literature. Recently, Christopher Miller has begun new work on the French literary reaction to the Haitian Revolution. He focuses on how abolitionists, in an effort to prove slaves' worthiness for freedom, endeavored to turn the French public's attention away from Haitian violence and instead toward the black civilizations of ancient Africa.[37]

Other important works on depictions of the Haitian Revolution by white French men and women have been published by Joan Dayan and Jeremy Popkin. Dayan has analyzed representations of the revolution through modern times, focusing especially on depictions of Haitian religion. Meanwhile, Popkin has drawn attention to the captivity narratives written by whites in the immediate aftermath of the revolution. He argues that these sources can help illuminate the trauma suffered by white Frenchmen suddenly ejected from power as the foundations of the colonial Atlantic were shaken.[38]

One of the most fertile—and contested—areas of study concerns the impact of the Haitian Revolution on the early-nineteenth-century French abolition movement. Some scholars have suggested that the memory of Haitian violence continued to haunt the French public through the middle of the nineteenth century, pushing abolitionists to moderate their demands while discrediting even the notion of gradual emancipation. Myriam Cottias has written that "until 1848, Saint-Domingue was an omnipresent reference in abolitionist texts."[39] Lawrence Jennings has agreed that the memory of Saint-Domingue was "still alive" in France of the early 1830s and that "negative references to Saint-Domingue were especially prevalent in the discourse of French colonial spokesmen, who remained prepared to muster every possible demonic vision in their campaign against slave liberation." Nevertheless, Jennings has argued that caution is necessary before overgeneralizing about the effects of the Haitian Revolution on French abolitionism:

> The negative consequences of Saint-Domingue upon the French abolitionist movement from the mid-1830s on should not be exaggerated. It is far too facile to overemphasize the effects of Saint-Domingue on French consciousness and overlook far more important and complex

elements hindering French anti-slavery. In the late 1830s and
especially in the 1840s, all evidence indicates that this memory
had faded considerably. References to Saint-Domingue declined
markedly after the British experience showed that emancipation
could be achieved without violence.

Jennings argues that the relative ease with which the second abolition of slavery
was passed in 1848 reflected the British experience of abolishing slavery in the
1830s, which made the memory of Saint-Domingue less relevant. Yves Benot
has contributed further to our knowledge of how early nineteenth-century
French abolitionists and politicians responded to Haitian independence.[40]

Despite the mounting contributions of these new studies, there is much
we could still learn about the French reaction to Haitian independence.
Among the many avenues open to further exploration, one concerns the
exiled colonists' reaction to independence. Although it is well known that
they pushed the French government to compensate them for their lost property and that they wanted France to reconquer Haiti, more work could be
done to examine the arguments they used to press their case and to explore
how these arguments were refigured as France shifted from the Napoleonic
regime to the Bourbon Restoration. These issues can be explored both
through the documentation of colonists' demands for restitution (preserved
in the Archives nationales) and through the pamphlet literature they produced, now available in American and French research libraries.[41] Given the
flowering of scholarship on the reintegration of the *pieds noirs* (former French
colonists in Algeria) into the French mainland after Algerian independence,
it would also be valuable to learn more about how France's first postcolonial refugees, the colonists of Saint-Domingue, adjusted to their new life in
France that was foreign to many of them.

More research could also be done on the reception of the colonists'
arguments by the French public and on how they continued to demand that
"Saint-Domingue" be punished and that recognition be retracted. An 1829
poem provides a vivid example of their frustrations with the arrangement
reached by the French government:

> En élevant nos destructeurs
> Jusques aux suprêmes grandeurs;
> En leur prodigant nos richesses
> Sous l'appât de vaines promesses,
> C'était cimenter vos bienfaits
> Du sang de cent mille Français. . . .
>
> Mais pour nous, pauvres orphelins!
> Reconnaître des souverains
> Dans les meurtriers de nos pères,
> Semblait le comble des misères. . . .

As the writer indicated, colonists viewed Haitians as murderers who were being rewarded by the French government for their crimes. Other writings protested the recognition decision into the 1830s.[42]

Another promising area for further study concerns how government attitudes toward Saint-Domingue changed in the transition from Napoleonic to Bourbon rule. More research could be done to extend the findings of Gouraige, Joachim, and Benot regarding Restoration-era debates about whether to recognize Haiti or to continue treating it as a pariah. Diplomatic correspondence, for instance, reveals how the Bourbons, in an effort to restore their control over Saint-Domingue, tried to persuade Haitians that their revolution had not been a revolt against the French but against Napoleon, a common enemy of both Haitians and Bourbons.[43] Further analysis of Restoration discursive strategies and how they led to the indemnity agreement would be extremely helpful to scholars. Similar research might be done on the Haitian side, extending the work begun by Haitian historians and by David Nicholls to examine how Haitians responded to French propaganda, from the diatribes of the colonists to the Bourbons' initiatives for rapprochement.

Another useful area of research concerns the ideas of those abolitionists who did not try to divert public attention from independent Haiti but instead continued to praise it. In writings like *De la littérature des nègres* (1808), the abbé Henri Grégoire focused more on the achievements of Africans in the classical world and within modern Europe than he did on those of Haitians. Nevertheless, he continued to feel that Haitians were being unfairly vilified in European discourse, and he defended the young nation even as it became increasingly unfashionable to do so. When the ex-colonists and their allies recounted the "crimes" of Saint-Domingue blacks, Grégoire and other sympathetic abolitionists responded that white slave-owners had brought their downfall upon themselves and that not enough attention was paid to their brutality.[44]

Though more work can profitably be done on both the American and French reactions, what we do know from existing scholarship is that Haitian independence provoked anger and anxiety on both sides of the Atlantic. Acting on the basis of these feelings, white Americans and Frenchmen attempted to isolate Saint-Domingue and to prevent slaves elsewhere from being tempted to emulate its example. These long-ago efforts, forgotten by most citizens of these countries today, continue to affect the lives of Haitians. In these troubled times in Haiti, we can only hope that our collective efforts to disseminate more information on its history—and the role of the United States and France in influencing it—might spur a greater sense of responsibility for crises that we contributed to bringing about. Of course, American and French historians must always guard against minimizing the effects of Haitian agency on Haitian history. Nevertheless, we must acknowledge that the specter that continues to haunt Haiti is one that we helped to create.

Notes

Epigraphs: *New York Daily Gazette*, 14 November 1791, quoted in David H. Jackson, Jr., "American Reactions to the Haitian Revolution, 1791–1804," *Consortium on Revolutionary Europe: Selected Papers* (1998), 222; and François-René Chateaubriand, *Essai sur les révolutions; Génie du christianisme; texte établi, présenté et annoté par Maurice Regard* (Paris: Gallimard, 1978), 1000 (part IV, bk. IV, ch. VII) ("Who would dare now to plead the cause of the blacks, after the crimes that they have committed?"). I am grateful to Dominique Rogers, Christopher L. Miller, Elizabeth Colwill, and Laurent Dubois for their input on this essay, especially on the section covering the French reaction to the Haitian Revolution. For a fuller discussion of the historiography on the American reaction to the revolution, see my "La Révolution haïtienne et les États-Unis: Étude historiographique," in *1802. Rétablissement de l'esclavage dans les colonies françaises: Aux origines de Haïti*, ed. Yves Benot and Marcel Dorigny (Paris: Maisonneuve et Larose, 2003), 387–401.

1. Ludwell Lee Montague, *Haiti and the United States, 1714–1938* (Duke University Press, 1940; repr., New York: Russell & Russell, 1966), ix, 4.

2. See Mary Bosworth Treudley, *The United States and Santo Domingo, 1789–1866* (Ph.D. diss., Clark University, 1916); Charles Callan Tansill, *The United States and Santo Domingo, 1798–1873: A Chapter in Caribbean Diplomacy* (Baltimore: Johns Hopkins Press, 1938); Montague, *Haiti and the United States*; and Rayford Whittingham Logan, *The Diplomatic Relations of the United States with Haiti, 1778–1841* (Chapel Hill: University of North Carolina Press, 1941). See also James A. Padgett, "Diplomats to Haiti and their Diplomacy," *Journal of Negro History* 25 (July 1940): 265–330.

3. Montague, *Haiti and the United States*, 29–30.

4. Compare Treudley, *The United States and Santo Domingo*, 129–130 and passim; and Tansill, *The United States and Santo Domingo*, 13–14, 68–69 and passim.

5. Montague, *Haiti and the United States*, 45.

6. These infamous passages are quoted in Montague, *Haiti and the United States*, 53–54 and in the other works.

7. See Logan, *The Diplomatic Relations of the United States with Haiti*, 298–302.

8. See Frances Sergeant Childs, *French Refugee Life in the United States: An American Chapter of the French Revolution* (Baltimore: Johns Hopkins University Press, 1940); Winston C. Babb, "French Refugees from Saint-Domingue to the Southern United States: 1791–1810" (Ph.D. diss., University of Virginia, 1954); and the two translated memoirs published in these years, *Moreau de St. Méry's American Journey, 1793–1798*, trans. and ed. Kenneth Roberts and Anna M. Roberts (Garden City, N.Y.: Doubleday, 1947); and *My Odyssey: Experiences of a Young Refugee from Two Revolutions, by a Creole of Saint Domingue*, trans. and ed. Althéa de Puech Parham ([Baton Rouge]: Louisiana State University Press, [1959]). Also published during this era was Alain Turnier, *Les États-Unis et le marché haïtien* (Washington: n.p., 1955), which built upon the American scholarship of the invasion period and may be the earliest full-scale work by a Haitian author on the subject of U.S.-Haitian relations (Turnier was a Haitian diplomat educated in the United States). For more recent treatments of white refugees in the United States, see R. Darrell Meadows, "Engineering Exile: Social Networks and

the French Atlantic Community, 1789–1809," *French Historical Studies* 23, no. 1 (2000): 67–102; and Ashli White, "'A Flood of Impure Lava': Saint Dominguan Refugees in the United States, 1791–1820" (Ph.D. diss., Columbia University, 2003).

9. Tim Matthewson, "Jefferson and the Nonrecognition of Haiti," *Journal of Negro History* 140, no. 1 (1996): 22–48 (quote on 30). See also Matthewson's "Slavery and Diplomacy: The United States and Saint Domingue, 1791–1793" (Ph.D. diss., University of California-Santa Barbara, 1976); "George Washington's Policy toward the Haitian Revolution," *Journal of Negro History* 3, no. 3 (1979): 321–336; and *A Proslavery Foreign Policy: Haitian-American Relations during the Early Republic* (Westport, Conn.: Praeger, 2003).

10. Matthewson, "Abraham Bishop, 'The Rights of Black Men,' and the American Reaction to the Haitian Revolution," *Journal of Negro History* 67, no. 2 (1982): 148–154. Compare Michel-Rolph Trouillot, *Silencing the Past: Power and the Production of History* (Boston, Mass.: Beacon Press, 1995), 88, which elides the existence of such discourse in 1791, even though Trouillot is correct to portray most Americans as hostile to it. Other recent work on diplomatic relations or the reactions of American whites comes from Yves L. Auguste, a Haitian scholar who taught in the United States; see *Haïti et les États-Unis:1804–1862* (Sherbrooke, Québec: Éditions Naaman, 1979). See also Donald R. Hickey, "America's Response to the Slave Revolt in Haiti, 179–1806," *Journal of the Early Republic* 2 (1982): 361–379; Hickey, "Timothy Pickering and the Haitian Slave Revolt: A Letter to Thomas Jefferson in 1806," *Essex Institute Historical Collections* 120, no. 3 (1984): 149–163; and Simon Newman, "American Political Culture and the French and Haitian Revolutions: Nathaniel Cutting and the Jeffersonian Republicans," in *The Impact of the Haitian Revolution in the Atlantic World,* ed. David Patrick Geggus (Columbia: University of South Carolina Press, 2001), 72–89.

11. Michael Zuckerman, "The Power of Blackness: Thomas Jefferson and the Revolution in St. Domingue," in *Almost Chosen People: Oblique Biographies in the American Grain* (Berkeley: University of California Press, 1993), 175–218, esp. 204–205, 213. See also Matthewson, "Jefferson and the Nonrecognition"; Peter S. Onuf, "'To Declare Them a Free and Independent People': Race, Slavery, and National Identity in Jefferson's Thought," *Journal of the Early Republic* 18, no. 1 (1998): 1–46, esp. 37; Hickey, "Timothy Pickering and the Haitian Slave Revolt," 149–163; and Yves Auguste, "Jefferson et Haïti," *Revue d'histoire diplomatique* 86, no. 4 (1972): 333–348.

12. See Alfred N. Hunt, *Haiti's Influence on Antebellum America: Slumbering Volcano in the Caribbean* (Baton Rouge: Louisiana State University Press, 1988), 2 and passim; Matthewson, "Jefferson and the Nonrecognition," 37; John Baur, "International Repercussions of the Haitian Revolution," *The Americas* 25, no. 4 (1969): 394–418, esp. 412–413. Brenda Gayle Plummer's *Haiti and the United States: The Psychological Moment* (Athens, Ga.: University of Georgia Press, 1992) also covers some of these issues, but its primary focus is on a later period.

13. See Davis's unpublished essay on the influence of the Haitian Revolution on the United States (copy courtesy of author), which is an expanded version of his "Impact of the French and Haitian Revolutions," in *The Impact of the Haitian Revolution in the Atlantic World,* ed. David Patrick Geggus (Columbia: University of South Carolina Press, 2001), 3–9. In revised form, this essay will be a chapter in Davis's forthcoming *The Problem of Slavery in the Age of Emancipation.* The typescript pages are unnumbered.

14. Davis, unpublished essay, last page; Davis, "Impact of the French and Haitian Revolutions," 3; and Hunt, *Haiti's Influence on Antebellum America*, 3.

15. See Monroe Fordham, "Nineteenth-Century Black Thought in the United States: Some Influences of the Santo Domingo Revolution," *Journal of Black Studies* 6 (1976): 115–126; James O'Dell Jackson, III, "The Origins of Pan-African Nationalism: Afro-American and Haytian Relations, 1800–1863" (Ph.D. diss., Northwestern University, 1976); Julius Sherrard Scott, "The Common Wind: Currents of Afro-American Communication in the Era of the Haitian Revolution" (Ph.D. diss., Duke University, 1986); Chris Dixon, *African America and Haiti: Emigration and Black Nationalism in the Nineteenth Century* (Westport, Conn.: Greenwood Press, 2000); and Leon D. Pamphile, *Haitians and African Americans: A Heritage of Tragedy and Hope* (Gainesville: University Press of Florida, 2001). For a counterweight to the argument about Haitian influence on free blacks, see Bruce Dain, "Haiti and Egypt in Early Black Radical Discourse," *Slavery and Abolition* 14 (December 1993): 139–161.

16. See for example Montague, *Haiti and the United States*, 66–80; Hunt, *Haiti's Influence on Antebellum America*, 163–181; Dain, "Haiti and Egypt in Early Black Radical Discourse," 141–142; Arthur O. White, "Prince Saunders: An Instance of Social Mobility among Antebellum New England Blacks," *Journal of Negro History* 60 (1975): 526–535; Dixon, *African America and Haiti*; J. Michael Dash, *Haiti and the United States: National Stereotypes and the Literary Imagination* (New York: St. Martin's Press, 1988); and Walter Dean Myers and Jacob Lawrence, *Toussaint L'Ouverture: The Fight for Haiti's Freedom* (New York: Simon & Schuster Books for Young Readers, 1996), which contains reproductions of Lawrence's 1930s *Toussaint* series.

17. Gary Nash, "Reverberations of Haiti in the American North: Black Saint Dominguans in Philadelphia," *Pennsylvania History* 65 (supp. 1998): 44–73. See also Susan Branson and Leslie Patrick, "Étrangers dans un Pays Étrange: Saint-Domingue Refugees of Color in Philadelphia" (which offers an alternate reading of the Philadelphia case) and Robert Alderson, "Charleston's Rumored Slave Revolt of 1793," both in *The Impact of the Haitian Revolution in the Atlantic World*, ed. David Patrick Geggus (Columbia: University of South Carolina Press, 2001), 192–208 and 93–111, respectively; David H. Jackson, Jr., "American Reactions to the Haitian Revolution, 1791–1804," *Consortium on Revolutionary Europe: Selected Papers* (1998): 220–227; Ashli White, "The Politics of 'French Negroes' in the United States," *Historical Reflections/Réflexions historiques* 29, no. 1 (2003): 103–121; and Sue Peabody, "'Free upon Higher Ground': Saint-Domingue Slaves' Suits for Freedom in U.S. Courts, 1792–1830," in this volume.

18. Paul Lachance, "Repercussions of the Haitian Revolution in Louisiana," in *The Impact of the Haitian Revolution in the Atlantic World*, ed. David Patrick Geggus (Columbia: University of South Carolina Press, 2001), 209–230; and Robert L. Paquette, "Revolutionary Saint-Domingue in the Making of Territorial Louisiana," in *A Turbulent Time: The French Revolution and the Greater Caribbean*, ed. David Barry Gaspar and David Patrick Geggus (Bloomington: Indiana University Press, 1997), 204–225. See also Carl A. Brasseaux and Glenn R. Conrad, *The Road to Louisiana: The Saint-Domingue Refugees, 1792–1809* (Lafayette, La.: Center for Louisiana Studies-University of Southwestern Louisiana, 1992); François Latortue, *Haïti (ex Saint-Domingue) et la Louisiane: leurs liaisons passées et leurs rôles dans l'émergence du colosse américain* (Port-au-Prince: Imprimeur II, 2001).

19. Trouillot, *Silencing the Past*. On the gaps in existing historiography, see especially David P. Geggus, "Epilogue" and Seymour Drescher, "The Limits of Example," both in *The Impact of the Haitian Revolution in the Atlantic World*, ed. David Patrick Geggus (Columbia: University of South Carolina Press, 2001), 247–252 and 10–14, respectively.

20. See Yves Benot, *La Révolution française et la fin des colonies* (Paris: La Découverte, 1987), ch. 10; and Benot, *La démence coloniale sous Napoléon* (Paris: La Découverte, 1991), ch. 11. See also the updating of Benot's list of major works ignoring slavery by Léon-François Hoffmann in his edition of Alphonse de Lamartine, *Toussaint Louverture* (Exeter: University of Exeter Press, 1998). I focus here on the issue of memory in the metropole among non-Antilleans, since the subject of how slavery is remembered in the Antilles and among Antilleans in France is a complex one which has been treated elsewhere. See, for instance, David Beriss, *Black Skins, French Voices: Caribbean Ethnicity and Activism in Urban France* (Boulder: Westview Press, 2004).

21. The next few paragraphs offer generalizations about American and French ideas on race, drawing upon several years of participation in Franco-American conferences and sustained dialogue with French scholars and laypeople. For a fuller analysis of the origins of French thinking about difference, see Alyssa Goldstein Sepinwall, *The Abbé Grégoire and the French Revolution: The Making of Modern Universalism* (Berkeley: University of California Press, 2005), esp. ch. 4 and Epilogue. A more general comparison of French and American ideas about race is offered in George M. Fredrickson, "Race, Ethnicity and National Identity in France and the United States: A Comparative Historical Overview," paper presented at the conference Collective Degradation: Slavery and the Construction of Race/Fifth Annual Gilder Lehrman Center International Conference, Yale University, New Haven, Connecticut, November 7–8, 2003, available at http://www.yale.edu/glc/events/race/Fredrickson.pdf (accessed June 2, 2004).

22. To break the silence about this more notorious bicentennial, Benot and Dorigny organized a major conference in 2002 called Ruptures et continuités dans la politique française coloniale. They gathered scholars from around the world and convinced UNESCO, the French Culture Ministry, and Radio France Outre-Mer to provide funding. Nevertheless, to my knowledge, the only media outlets or politicians who noted this anniversary were the Communist newspaper *L'Humanité*; the socialist mayor of Paris, Bertrand Delanoë, who invited conference participants and West Indian constituents to an opening reception for the conference in City Hall; and Radio France Outre-Mer.

23. Jules Ferry, speech to Chamber of Deputies, 28 July 1883, translation from *Modern Imperialism, Western Overseas Expansion, and Its Aftermath, 1776–1965*, ed. Ralph A. Austen (Lexington, Mass.: Heath, 1969), 107.

24. While the French rejection of the idea of race has admirable intentions, it has not wiped out racism. The result has been not merely a whitewashing of France's colonial past but also the perpetuation of inequities between "native French" and so-called children of immigration. When American scholars published a volume on the history of race in France (Sue Peabody and Tyler Edward Stovall, *The Color of Liberty: Histories of Race in France* [Durham: Duke University Press, 2003]), a French scholar lamented to me that such a volume could never find a publisher in France, the very notion being an affront to republican identity. For more on the absence of slavery from French national memory, see the Benot essays cited in note 20 and Christine Chivallon, "L'émergence récente de

la mémoire de l'esclavage dans l'espace public: enjeux et significations," *Cahiers d'histoire. Espaces Marx* 89 (4e trim. 2002): 41–60.

25. Classic French studies of eighteenth-century slavery or Saint-Domingue include Lucien Pierre Peytraud, *L'esclavage aux Antilles françaises avant 1789 d'après des documents inédits des archives coloniales* (Paris: Hachette, 1897); P. Boissonnade, *Saint-Domingue à la veille de la révolution et la question de la représentation coloniale aux États généraux (janvier 1788–7 juillet 1789)* (Paris: J. Geuthner, 1906); Pierre de Vaissière, *Saint-Domingue: la société et la vie créoles sous l'ancien régime (1629–1789)* (Paris: Perrin, 1909); Blanche Maurel, *Cahiers de doléances de la colonie de Saint-Domingue pour les Etats-generaux de 1789* (Paris: E. Leroux, 1933); Gaston Martin, *Histoire de l'esclavage dans les colonies françaises* (Paris: Presses universitaires de France, 1948); Gabriel Debien, *Les esclaves aux Antilles françaises, XVIIe-XVIIIe siècles* (Basse-Terre: Société d'histoire de la Guadeloupe, 1974); Yvan Debbasch, *Couleur et liberté. Le jeu de critère ethnique dans un ordre juridique esclavagiste* (Paris: Dalloz, 1967); and Pierre Pluchon, *Nègres et juifs au dix-huitième siècle. Le racisme au siècle des Lumières* (Paris: Tallandier, 1984). Pioneering works produced in the early twentieth century by scholars in the United States or West Indies on these topics include Anna J. Cooper, "L'attitude de la France à l'égard de l'esclavage pendant la Révolution" (Thèse de doctorat, Université de Paris, 1925), translated and reprinted as *Slavery and the French Revolutionists (1788–1805)*, trans. Francis Richardson Keller (Lewiston, N.Y.: Edwin Mellen Press, 1988); C. L. R. James, *The Black Jacobins: Toussaint Louverture and the San Domingo Revolution* (London: Secker and Warburg, 1938); Carl Ludwig Lokke, *France and the Colonial Question: A Study of Contemporary French Opinion, 1763–1801* (New York: Columbia University Press, 1932); Edward Derbyshire Seeber, *Anti-Slavery Opinion in France during the Second Half of the Eighteenth Century* (Baltimore: Johns Hopkins University Press, 1937); Mercer Cook, *Five French Negro Authors* (Washington, D.C.: Associated Publishers, Inc., 1943); Shelby T. McCloy, "Negroes and Mulattoes in Eighteenth-Century France," *Journal of Negro History* 30 (1945): 276–292; Philip D. Curtin, "The Declaration of the Rights of Man in Saint-Domingue, 1788–1791," *Hispanic-American Review* XXX (May 1950): 157–175; and Léo Elisabeth, "Les problèmes des gens de couleur à Bordeaux sous l'ancien régime (1716–1787)" (Maîtrise, Faculté des Lettres, Université de Bordeaux, 1954).

26. See Catherine Coquery-Vidrovitch, "Révolution française, mouvement révolutionnaire de Saint-Domingue-Haïti et colonisation française en Afrique," and Francis Arzalier, "La révolution haïtien dans l'imaginaire français," both in *La Révolution française et Haïti: filiations, ruptures, nouvelles dimensions*, ed. Michel Hector (Port-au-Prince: Société haïtienne d'histoire et de géographie/Editions H. Deschamps, 1995), 334–347 and 348–357, respectively; Trouillot, *Silencing the Past*, 101 and passim; Myriam Cottias, *D'une abolition à l'autre: anthologie raisonnée de textes consacrés à la seconde abolition de l'esclavage dans les colonies françaises* (Marseille: Agone, 1998), esp. 7; and Christopher L. Miller, "Forget Haiti: Baron Roger and the New Africa," *Yale French Studies*, no. 107 [*The Haiti Issue: 1804 and Nineteenth-Century French Studies*, ed. Deborah Jenson] (2005): 36–69.

27. Ghislain Gouraige, *L'indépendance d'Haïti devant la France* (Port-au-Prince: Impr. de L'Etat, 1955); also Thomas Madiou, *Histoire d'Haïti* (1847; repr., Port-au-Prince, Haiti: H. Deschamps, 1987); B. Ardouin, *Etudes sur l'histoire d'Haïti suivies de la vie du général J.-M. Borgella*, 2d ed. (1853; repr., Port-au-Prince: F. Dalencour, 1958).

28. For a perfect example of this tendency, see the address by the Haitian diplomat A. Firmin to a group of Frenchmen in Firmin, *La France et Haïti* (Paris: Librairie Cotillon, 1901). After a short overview of the Haitian struggle for independence in the 1790s and 1800s, Firmin added, "All of this is history . . . history that goes back nearly a century. Since then, Haitians and Frenchmen have learned to understand each other better . . . than they were able to under the ancien régime. All of the memories of the fight for independence have slowly died down. Haiti, far from holding a grudge against France, turns its gaze instead towards it as if towards its *ancienne mère* [former mother] and *féconde éducatrice* [honored teacher]." See also the glowing accounts of Jean Price-Mars (otherwise a critic of Europhilia in Haiti) in "La position d'Haïti et de la culture française en Amérique," *Journal of Inter-American Studies* 8, no. 1 (1966): 44–53 (speech originally given in 1956); and Association France-Haïti, *Haïti et la France* (Paris: [1956?]) (available at the New York Public Library). One important twentieth-century exception was the article by Leslie Manigat discussed below, though that aimed more to revise Haitian founding myths than to criticize the French themselves.

29. Gouraige, *L'indépendance d'Haïti*. That Gouraige's study, produced in Haiti, has fallen into obscurity in France and the United States is unfortunately symbolic of how Haitian cultural efforts are often received abroad.

30. Maurice A. Lubin, "Les premiers rapports de la nation haïtienne avec l'étranger," *Journal of Inter-American Studies* 10, no. 2 (1968): 277–305, quotes from 278–280, 282. See also the brief discussion in Debbasch, *Couleur et liberté*, 253–259.

31. Lubin, "Les premiers rapports de la nation haïtienne avec l'étranger," 282, 279; see also Madiou, *Histoire d'Haïti*, III:148.

32. Benoît Joachim, "La reconnaissance d'Haïti par la France (1825): Naissance d'un nouveau type de rapports internationaux," *Revue d'histoire moderne et contemporaine* 22, no. 3 (1975): 369–396; and Joachim, "L'indemnité coloniale de Saint-Domingue et la question des rapatriés," *Revue Historique* 246, no. 2 (1971): 359–376. Compare Gouraige, who saw France's interests in New World trade and the desire to keep Jean-Pierre Boyer (seen as an Anglophobe) in power as the factors that propelled France to enter into recognition negotiations; *L'indépendance d'Haïti*, 143–144.

33. Joachim, "La reconnaissance"; and Joachim, "Le néo-colonialisme à l'essai: la France et l'indépendance d'Haïti," *La pensée* 156 (1971): 35–51.

34. François Blancpain, "L'ordonnance de 1825 et la question de l'indemnité," and Gusti Klara Gaillard-Pourchet, "Aspects politiques et commerciaux de l'indemnisation haïtienne," both in *1802. Rétablissement de l'esclavage dans les colonies françaises: Aux origines de Haïti*, ed. Yves Benot and Marcel Dorigny (Paris: Maisonneuve et Larose, 2003) (Paris: Maisonneuve et Larose, 2003), 221–230 and 231–237, respectively. See also Blancpain, "Note sur les 'dettes' de l'esclavage: le cas de l'indemnité payée par Haïti (1825–1883)," in *Haïti: première république noire*, ed. Marcel Dorigny (Paris: Société française d'histoire d'outre-mer, 2003), 241–245; and Blancpain, *Un siècle de relations financières entre Haïti et la France, 1825–1922* (Paris: L'Harmattan, 2001). Before the fall of Jean-Bertrand Aristide's government, there was an effort to persuade France to pay reparations to Haiti for having forced the indemnity payments; see Sharifa Rhodes-Pitts, "Reparation Day: A Call for $21 Billion from France Aims to Lift Haiti's Bicentennial Blues," *Boston Globe*, January 4, 2004, C1.

35. See especially Leslie Manigat, "Le délicat problème de la critique historique. Un exemple: les sentiments de Pétion et de Boyer vis-à-vis de l'Indépendance Nationale," *Revue de la société haïtienne d'histoire de géographie et de géologie* 25–26, nos. 95–96 (1954–1955): 29–59; David Nicholls, *From Dessalines to Duvalier: Race, Colour and National Independence in Haiti* (Cambridge: Cambridge University Press, 1979), esp. 47–53; and Nicholls, "Pompée Valentin Vastey: Royalist and Revolutionary," in *La Révolution française et Haïti: filiations, ruptures, nouvelles dimensions,* ed. Michel Hector (Port-au-Prince: Société haïtienne d'histoire et de géographie/Editions H. Deschamps, 1995), 419–434.

36. See for example the articles by Lucien René Abenon, Serge Mam Lam Fouck, Frédéric Régent, and Jacques Adélaïde-Merlande in *1802. Rétablissement de l'esclavage dans les colonies françaises: Aux origines de Haïti,* ed. Yves Benot and Marcel Dorigny (Paris: Maisonneuve et Larose, 2003); as well as Adélaïde-Merlande, *La Caraïbe et la Guyane au temps de la Révolution et de l'Empire, 1789–1804* (Paris: Karthala, 1992); and Laurent Dubois, *A Colony of Citizens: Revolution and Slave Emancipation in the French Caribbean, 1787–1804* (Chapel Hill: Omohundro Institute of Early American History and Culture/University of North Carolina Press, 2004).

37. Léon-François Hoffmann, *Le nègre romantique; personnage littéraire et obsession collective* (Paris: Payot, 1973); Régis Antoine, *Les écrivains français et les Antilles: des premiers Pères blancs aux surréalistes noirs* (Paris: G. P. Maisonneuve et Larose, 1978); Hoffmann's edition of Lamartine's *Toussaint Louverture,* cited above (which also contains an extensive bibliography of other works on Lamartine's play and on representations of slavery on the nineteenth-century French stage); J. A. Ferguson, "Le Premier des Noirs: The Nineteenth Century Image of Toussaint Louverture," *Nineteenth Century French Studies* 15, no. 4 (1987): 394–406; George F. Tyson, *Toussaint L'Ouverture* (Englewood Cliffs, N.J.: Prentice Hall, 1973), 60–78; and Miller, "Forget Haiti: Baron Roger and the New Africa." See also Gérard Gengembre, "From Bug-Jargal to Toussaint Louverture: Romanticism and the Slave Rebel," in *The Abolitions of Slavery: From Léger Félicité Sonthonax to Victor Schoelcher, 1793, 1794, 1848,* ed. Marcel Dorigny (New York: Berghahn Books, 2003), 272–279.

38. Joan Dayan, *Haiti, History, and the Gods* (Berkeley: University of California Press, 1998); Jeremy D. Popkin, "Facing Racial Revolution: Captivity Narratives and Identity in the Saint-Domingue Insurrection," *Eighteenth-Century Studies* 36, no. 4 (2003): 511–533. On images of Saint-Domingue in the Napoleonic press, see also Michel L. Martin and André G. Cabanis, "Ignorance et malentendus: L'indépendance d'Haïti devant l'opinion en France sous le consulat et l'empire," in *La Révolution française et Haïti: filiations, ruptures, nouvelles dimensions,* ed. Michel Hector (Port-au-Prince: Société haïtienne d'histoire et de géographie/Editions H. Deschamps, 1995), 358–374. Elizabeth Colwill's forthcoming work on ritual, gender, and slavery in the Haitian and French Revolutions will explore how French men and women represented abolition and the Haitian Revolution in popular festivals.

39. See Cottias, *D'une abolition à l'autre,* 7; also Serge Daget, "Les mots esclave, nègre, Noir, et les jugements de valeur sur la traite négrière dans la littérature abolitionniste française de 1770 à 1845," *Revue française d'Histoire d'Outre-Mer* LX, no. 221 (1973): 534; and Marcel Dorigny, "Sismondi et les colonies: un maillon entre Lumières et théoriciens du XIXe siècle?" in *1802. Rétablissement de l'esclavage dans les colonies fran-*

çaises: *Aux origines de Haïti*, ed. Yves Benot and Marcel Dorigny (Paris: Maisonneuve et Larose, 2003), 471–484.

40. Lawrence C. Jennings, *French Anti-Slavery: The Movement for the Abolition of Slavery in France, 1802–1848* (New York: Cambridge University Press, 2000), 120–121; Benot, *La démence coloniale*, esp. 21–31, 77–88, 93–99, 117–128, 173–176, 202–210, and 256–266.

41. See "Indemnité de Saint-Domingue" collection, 7SUPSDOM and 8SUPS-DOM, Dépôt des papiers des colonies, ANSOM (Archives nationales, section Outre-Mer, Aix-en-Provence). For subtle changes in the pamphlet literature, compare for instance René Périn, *L'incendie du Cap; ou, Le règne de Toussaint-Louverture* (Paris: Chez les Marchands de Nouveautés, 1802); Chotard, *Origine des malheurs de Saint-Domingue, développement du système colonial, et moyens de restauration* (Bordeaux: Dubois et Coudert, [1805]); and Drouin de Bercy, *De Saint-Domingue: de ses guerres, de ses révolutions, de ses resources, et de moyens à prendre pour y rétablir la paix et l'industrie* (Paris: Chez Hocquet [etc.], 1814). Fortunately, scholars have recently begun to work on some of these questions; see R. Darrell Meadows, "The Planters of Saint-Domingue, 1750–1804: Migration and Exile in the French Revolutionary Atlantic" (Ph.D. diss., Carnegie Mellon University, 2004); and Jennifer J. Pierce, "Discourses of the Dispossessed: Saint-Domingue Colonists on Race, Revolution and Empire, 1789–1825" (Ph.D. diss., Binghamton University, 2005).

42. Piton du Spiral, *Épitre au roi de France, sur le non-payement de l'indemnité de St.-Domingue* (Nouvelle-Orléans: Chez A. L. Boimare, 1829), 3: "In elevating our destroyers / To the pinnacle of greatness, / In being lured to lavish our riches upon them / In exchange for vain promises, / You cemented your kindness / With the blood of a hundred thousand Frenchmen. . . . / For us, poor orphans! / Calling the murderers of our fathers "sovereigns" / Seemed the height of misery." See also M. Coustelin, *Sur l'émancipation de Saint-Domingue* (Paris: Le Normant, 1825); Victor Alexis Désiré Dalloz, *Consultation de MM. Dalloz, Delagrange, Hennequin, Dupin jeune et autres jurisconsultes, pour les anciens colons de St-Domingue* (Paris: De l'imprimerie de Madame veuve Agasse, 1829); and the texts excerpted in Cottias, *D'une abolition à l'autre*.

43. See *Pièces relatives à la correspondance de MM. les commissaires de S.M. Très-Chrétienne, et du président d'Haïti, précédées d'une proclamation au peuple et à l'armée* (Port-au-Prince: De l'Imprimerie du guvernement, 1816), 2–3 and passim; and Pompée-Valentin Vastey, *An Essay on the Causes of the Revolution and Civil Wars of Hayti . . .* [*Translation of Essai sur les causes de la révolution et des guerres civiles d'Hayti*] (Exeter: Western Luminary Office, 1823).

44. See Henri Grégoire, *De la littérature des nègres, ou Recherches sur leurs facultés intellectuelles, leurs qualités morales et leur littérature . . .* (Paris: Maradan, 1808), esp. 56–58; Benot, *La démence coloniale*, 256 -266; and Sepinwall, *The Abbé Grégoire and the French Revolution*, esp. chs. 7 and 8. For an example of another abolitionist defending Haiti, see Civique de Gastine, *Lettre au Roi, sur l'indépendance de la République d'Haïti, et l'abolition de l'esclavage dans les colonies françaises* (Paris: Chez le marchands de nouveautés, 1821), 3–5.

Representations of the Haitian Revolution in French Literature

Léon-François Hoffmann

The historians usually never realize the importance
of San Domingo...

—Alec Waugh, *Wheels within Wheels* (1933)

A S FAR AS THE MAJORITY OF NINETEENTH- AND TWENTIETH-CENTURY
FRENCH HISTORIANS ARE CONCERNED, THE HAITIAN REVOLUTION
WOULD APPEAR TO BE A PERPLEXING AND AT ANY RATE SECONDARY
incident. Even historians with progressive convictions dispose of it in a few
hasty lines, if they mention it at all.[1] Those who at least record the basic
facts usually do not delve into their crucial consequences for the evolution of
the French Revolution, for Napoleonic foreign policy, for ideological debates
during the Restoration and the July Monarchy of 1830–1848, for subsequent French colonial policy, for the manifestations of racism, and for an
understanding of the general issues of slavery and its abolition.[2]

Regrettable as it is, this discretion is understandable for the first half of
the nineteenth century. Before Waterloo, imperial censorship ensured that the
first defeat of a Napoleonic army (one might rather speak of military disaster, since the French expeditionary force lost 40,000 men and was practically
wiped out) received as little publicity as possible. When it was mentioned, the
emphasis was put on the heroism and abnegation of the French troops and on
the perfidy of the British who undercut their efforts to restore order among
the savages.[3] Partisans of the ancien régime laid responsibility for the loss of
Saint-Domingue at the door of the 1789 revolutionists and so did Napoleon,
who was engaged in suppressing their democratic achievements. In September
1811, the *Mercure de France* asserted:

> The source of the evils suffered by France and by her American posses-
> sions is the same: it is the revolutionary spirit which, under the hollow
> name of Freedom, flooded with blood and tears lands formerly so
> beautiful, so peaceful and so happy.

Slavery was reimposed by Bonaparte and maintained in the colonies by his
Restoration and July Monarchy successors. Since it was still enforced in the
French West Indies, it remained injudicious if not downright subversive to
publicize the Haitian emancipation and independence struggle, let alone celebrate it, even after the grudging recognition of Haitian independence by the
government of Charles X in 1825. Not long after the definitive abolition of
slavery in their overseas possessions by the provisional government of the
Second Republic in 1848, the French embarked on colonial expansion in
Africa and elsewhere. Once again, to remind the public of the first overthrow
of European imperial rule by the ancestors of those very Africans who were
the recipients of the "civilizing mission" of the Third Republic would have
been gauche and might have been considered unpatriotic.

What can only be termed a conspiracy of silence has lately begun to be
dispelled in France, first during the celebration of the bicentennial of the
storming of the Bastille, then on the occasion of the 150th anniversary of
the abolition of slavery, and finally by the worldwide celebration of the bicentennial of the Declaration of Haitian Independence. To mark these events,
conferences and colloquia were held throughout France and elsewhere and
a number of monographs as well as scholarly and popular articles were published, although scholars from the Hispanic- and English-speaking worlds
contributed as much if not more than their French colleagues to this long
overdue reevaluation, or perhaps we should say revelation.

If the reading public was kept (or even made) aware of the Haitian Revolution once the Napoleonic adventure was over, it was for a time through the
numerous booklets and pamphlets published by the former plantation owners
and their salaried spokesmen. They were hoping to persuade public opinion to
pressure the government into mounting another military expedition with the
goal of returning the land and slaves to "their rightful owners." These pamphlets
celebrated the industry of the erstwhile planters, downplayed their exploitation
and mistreatment of Africans, and painted a horrifying picture of the depreda-
tions and atrocities committed by the rebelling slaves. The destruction, murder,
and rape by "African savages," which was described in gory detail, supported
the conclusion that they were neither ready for nor deserving of freedom, let
alone independence. In several of these works lurid evocations of what came to
be known as the Bois-Caïman Vodou ceremony appeared, which supposedly
launched the uprising. (It quite probably never actually took place and was the
invention of an evicted French planter writing in 1814.) It was first mentioned
by a Haitian writer, Hérard Dumesle, in 1824.[4] Yet, surprisingly, the alleged

events at Bois-Caïman eventually came to be accepted uncritically as historical fact by most European, American, and Haitian historians. It is indeed regrettable that the latter have been just as guilty as the former of depicting the country's history as a form of what the Cuban novelist Alejo Carpentier called "marvellous realism" or what the Haitian novelist Fernand Hibbert referred to as "a gory operetta" (*une opérette sanglante*).

During the first quarter of the nineteenth century, the events in Saint-Domingue were also exploited by a handful of French writers of fiction, who have sunk into well-deserved oblivion. I have found four such works, all of them with ideologically explicit titles, all of them presenting themselves as factual accounts. In point of fact, as Hans-Jürgen Lüsebrink has pointed out, "the boundaries between fictional and pragmatic texts remain hazy" in the first texts dealing with the Haitian revolution.[5] The works in question are Jean-Baptiste Berthier's *Félix et Éléonore, ou les colons malheureux* (*Felix and Eleonore, or the Ill-starred Planters*) in 1801; René Perrin's *L'incendie du Cap ou règne de Toussaint Louverture* (*The Destruction of Cap-Français, or the Reign of Toussaint Louverture*) in 1802; Mademoiselle de Palaiseau's *L'histoire de Mesdemoiselles de Saint-Janvier, les deux seules blanches conservées à Saint-Domingue* (*History of the Saint-Janvier Young Ladies, the Only Two White Women Saved in Saint-Domingue*) in 1812; and finally Laisné de Tours's *L'insurrection du Cap ou la perfidie d'un noir* (*The Cap-Français Insurrection, or a Black Man's Perfidy*) ten years later in 1822. These scribblers, most of whom wrote during the reign of Napoleon, understandably avoided the noble term "revolution" and spoke instead of "revolts," "mutiny," "uprisings," "perfidy," "sedition," and "criminal plots" on the part of "barbarian ingrates" and "ferocious Africans." Their efforts, along with those of the former planters, dispelled for a time French abolitionist sympathy for the plight of black slaves. As Chateaubriand, the father of French Romanticism and future minister of foreign affairs, wrote in *Le génie du christianisme* (*Genius of Christianity*) (IV, vii, 1802): "Who could still dare to argue in favor of the blacks after the crimes they have committed?"

In 1825, King Charles X finally bowed to the inevitable and "granted" independence to the Haitians. After his government recognized the new republic, other nations followed suit. Haiti and its revolution were no longer topical once France had disengaged politically. For all intents and purposes, after slavery was abolished and the specter of a repetition of the Saint-Domingue tragedy in Martinique and Guadeloupe was also dispelled, Haiti faded from the metropole's collective memory and consequently from her literature. Since primary and secondary education still do not include the loss of Saint-Domingue in their history manuals, it is hardly exaggerated to suggest that today even well-educated Frenchmen remain all but unaware of the Haitian saga.

For the second quarter of the nineteenth century, I could find only nine works of fiction inspired by the Haitian Revolution. Most are authored by third-rate hacks but two are signed by shining lights of French Romanticism whose writings have always been studied in their country and abroad. They are Victor Hugo's 1826 short novel *Bug-Jargal* and Alphonse de Lamartine's 1850 drama *Toussaint Louverture*,[6] both of which have been translated into English and other languages. Two inconsequential stage parodies of these major publications have also been performed.[7]

While most critics have justifiably stressed the ideological dimensions of the work of Hugo and Lamartine, it should be added that both authors were influenced to a substantial degree by the aesthetic conventions of the melodrama, a form of popular entertainment much in favor at the time they were composing. A brief summary of both works follows.

Bug-Jargal takes place in Saint-Domingue in 1791. D'Auverney, a young man lately arrived from France at his uncle's plantation is betrothed to the uncle's daughter, Marie. One of the plantation slaves, Bug-Jargal, is also in love with Marie. He saves her life when she is about to be devoured by an alligator and thus earns the gratitude of the young lovers. On their wedding day, the slaves revolt under the joint leadership of a reluctant Bug-Jargal, the cruel Biassou, and the sinister dwarf Habibrah. D'Auverney is captured and taken to the rebel camp. Bug-Jargal spares him and brings him to the French camp so he can take leave of his bride before returning, as he has promised Biassou, to face execution. He entrusts Marie to Bug-Jargal, who is secretly in love with her, but the French, under the impression that d'Auverney has been killed by Bug-Jargal, threaten to shoot ten black prisoners if he does not give himself up. He does and is executed. Marie eventually dies at the hands of the rebels. D'Auverney returns to France and falls heroically on the battlefield.

In Lamartine's *Toussaint Louverture*, the principal action takes place when General Leclerc's expeditionary force lands in 1802 to convince Toussaint Louverture to submit to French rule. Toussaint hesitates but finally realizes that Bonaparte intends to reimpose slavery, which had been abolished by the French Republic in 1794. At the end of the play, he calls his comrade to arms and the war begins.

Within this frame, several secondary plots unfold. The drama of paternity: Louverture's two sons, who were being educated in France, land with Leclerc's expeditionary force. The elder encourages his father to cooperate with the French, while his brother suspects their real intentions. Pathetic scenes take place between the black leader and his elder son, who finally chooses French "civilization" over Haitian independence. (In actual fact as well as in Lamartine's fiction, both sons were educated in France and one of them, Isaac, the youngest, did side with his mentors, while Placide, the elder, opted to stand by his father.)

The recognition plot: Toussaint's right arm is his mulatto niece Adrienne, the daughter of his sister, who was raped and abandoned by the white overseer Salvador. Unaware that he has fathered a daughter, Salvador goes back to

France and eventually returns with Leclerc's army. Since Adrienne refuses to betray Toussaint, Salvador has her jailed in a prison for fallen women. Thanks to a medallion (that indispensable prop of melodramas), he realizes that the girl is his daughter just before she falls victim to French bullets.

The melodramatic disguise: In order to learn Leclerc's intentions, Toussaint disguises himself as an old beggar and attends a French Army war council. When Toussaint realizes that his nephew Moïse is about to betray the cause, he knifes him and escapes through the window. Not unreasonably, the Parisian public and critics found this scene outlandish and regrettable.

Twenty-five years separate the publication dates of the two works. One is a novel written by a 23-year-old beginner, the other a play composed in alexandrine verse by a mature, 50-year-old man of letters and statesman. Lamartine's eponymous hero is of course a historical figure and Hugo's hero a figment of the author's imagination, although in *Bug-Jargal* as well as in *Toussaint Louverture* many historical figures appear as secondary characters. Some scholars have argued, unconvincingly, it seems to me, that Toussaint served as the inspiration for Bug. Both Hugo and Lamartine lamented the loss of France's richest colony, but while the novelist blamed it on the cynical ambition of bloodthirsty native leaders and the misguided ideology of revolutionary France, Lamartine put the primary responsibility on Bonaparte's duplicity and his decision to reinstate slavery. These differences suggest the different ways in which this momentous event in national and world history was interpreted by the French collective imagination during a time of rapid political, social, and intellectual change. To be sure, young Victor Hugo, at the time a royalist conservative, meant his short novel to be an argument against republican ideology, the quixotic idealism of abolitionists, and the naïve affirmation of racial equality. While Hugo eventually evolved into a world spokesman for democratic principles, he never repudiated *Bug-Jargal* or his other reactionary juvenilia.

However, *Bug-Jargal* was probably designed primarily to satisfy the reading public's new interest in exoticism and its partiality for the sort of grandiose hero whose many virtues were no protection against a tragic destiny. In the same way, Lamartine's play was a courageous attempt to celebrate the political leader betrayed and murdered by Napoleon and to explain and justify his decision to oppose the French. By including the decision of one of Toussaint's sons to throw in his lot with the enemy, he gave him a human dimension (one might even say a superhuman one, since he was played by the famous Frédérick Lemaître, an actor renowned for his melodramatic interpretations of larger-than-life heroes). *Toussaint Louverture* constituted the century's only literary justification of the Haitian fight for independence. Predictably, several reactionary critics accused the author of a lack of patriotism.

Melodramas typically have four main stock characters who are little more than caricatures and show hardly any psychological complexity: the hero, the heroine, the villain, and the comic relief. The hero is a compendium of

appealing traits and virtues: he is young, good-looking, courageous, resource-
ful, honest, faithful, and altogether exemplary. Such is Hugo's eponymous
hero who despite being black (but fine featured and the son of an African king,
as are most nineteenth-century black heroes in Western literatures) is admirable in every way. As far as blacks are concerned, he is the exception, which
young Hugo uses to confirm the rule of their iniquity. Lamartine's Toussaint is
more complex but just as praiseworthy; his sole motivation is the love of liberty
and family and the welfare of his countrymen. Only patriotism and the defense
of human rights compel him to execute Moïse and start the war.

Complementing the hero is the heroine, who is young, beautiful, chaste,
tenderhearted, pious, and devoted to her parents and to her betrothed. She
represents the ideal woman according to the petty bourgeois ideology of the
time: she is obedient, not very intelligent, prone to childish alternations of
despair and delight, a frequent shedder of tears, a homebody not very good
at taking initiatives, and generally dependent on the man in her life. Such is
Marie in Bug-Jargal. Adrienne, in Toussaint Louverture, is slightly more complex and does at times serve as the hero's advisor. But her sentimentality, ado-
lescent love pangs, and tearful lamentations place her in the ranks of typical
melodrama heroines.

An indispensable stock character of French melodramas is the villain,
who, in contradistinction with the hero, is the incarnation of all evil traits
. . . and is of course all the more fascinating for it. In Hugo's novel, practically any of the rebel chiefs, except Bug-Jargal himself, could play the role,
but the deformed dwarf Habibrah is the most sinister, vengeful, and cruel.
His grotesque appearance (Hugo's lifelong fascination with the grotesque
is well known) is symbolic of his twisted mind. In Toussaint Louverture,
the despicable Frenchman Salvador is the obvious villain. One would otherwise be hard put to justify his presence, which is irrelevant to the main
action. It would appear that Lamartine borrowed this character from the
repertory of the melodrama to cater to the taste of the less sophisticated
among his public.

There is actually not much comic relief in the two works under consideration. In the case of Bug-Jargal, d'Auverney's aide-de-camp, the Polish soldier
Thadée, provides what little there is: his gushing devotion to his master, his
childish credulity, and his blustery manner of expression may bring at least a
smile to the face of the reader. Lamartine's play, on the other hand, still owes
much to classical aesthetics, which forbade the coexistence of the dramatic
with the comic. In some ways, Toussaint Louverture, although written for the
stage, is actually less influenced by the melodrama than is Hugo's novel.

Most melodramas include music (the word comes from the Greek melos,
melody) and dancing. Toussaint Louverture opens with Haitian children
singing "La Marseillaise des noirs," which, to the tune of the French national

anthem, calls for peace and universal brotherhood. In *Bug-Jargal*, half-naked screaming witches obscenely bumping and grinding in Hugo's phantasmal conception of a Vodou ritual, taunt young d'Auverny while he awaits execution at the hands of the rebellious slaves.

An obligatory convention of the French melodrama is that it should have a happy ending. The villain does not necessarily have to perish, but at the very least he should be dragged to prison by the constabulary. The lovers must be reunited and joined in holy matrimony, and the curtain usually falls on happy revelers celebrating the triumph of virtue and justice. This obviously does not apply to *Bug-Jargal* in which, as is not unusual in Hugo's works, the main characters end up dead, nor does it apply to *Toussaint Louverture*, where in the last scene Adrienne dies and war breaks out. It is often the absence of a happy ending (and a more refined style) that differentiates the noble drama, as a genre, from the lowly melodrama.

Both Lamartine and Hugo had lofty literary ambitions, and both attained great popularity. Hugo became a famous playwright and attempted to reach a wide audience; his quip *"Vive le mélodrame où Margot a pleuré!"* ("Long live the melodrama that made Maggy shed a tear!") is well known. But it could be argued that this popular genre had as much influence on his novels as on his dramatic works, if not more. Lamartine wrote just two plays in his life, and only *Toussaint Louverture* was ever performed. After considering calling it a "modern tragedy," a "tragedy," a "dramatic and popular poem," a "drama in five acts and in verse," he finally settled on "dramatic poem" (*poème dramatique*). There is no evidence that he ever considered "melodramatic poem," but such a choice would not have been ludicrous.

It seems evident that the traits we tend to identify primarily with the melodrama, a specific theatrical genre, in fact suffused the sensibility not only of the masses but also, to a considerable extent, that of the cultured elites of bourgeois France. It would be easy, if tedious, to show that melodramatic traits are therefore also found to a degree in all the admittedly few works of fiction that deal with the Haitian Revolution composed after the expulsion of the French. In these works, the hero is often a young Frenchman just arrived in Saint-Domingue, shocked at first by the treatment of slaves but soon realizing that blacks are not ready for emancipation. His betrothed heroine is in constant danger of being outraged by the villain or villains and depends entirely on the hero for rescue. The villain is either a brutal and libidinous white overseer (often of foreign origin) or a bloodthirsty black leader. A faithful and feeble-minded African can provide comic relief with his naïveté and childish way of speaking French.

As far as ideology is concerned, two main patterns are almost always present. The first, which goes back to eighteenth-century abolitionist fiction, castigates cruel masters and is designed to move the reader to pity the poor slaves who are

subjected to inhuman living and working conditions and are put to the lash for
the least infraction. This criticism, however, seldom questions the principle of the
peculiar institution itself, which at best is considered an unfortunate economic
necessity that is bound to disappear when its black victims reach the level of civilization required for full citizenship. Nor do they excuse those blacks who, tired
of waiting for that blessed day, take matters into their own hands and resort to
violence. In a children's book published as late as 1874, Julie Gouraud's *Les deux
enfants de Saint-Domingue*, we do find the following lines:

> [The slaves] have been driven to revolt by the cruel way they were treated.
> Isn't it hateful to be sold as vile cattle? You can clearly see that there are
> beautiful souls among the Negroes, and that they are men just like us![8]

But the author specifies that these words do not represent her own convictions;
they are spoken by *l'orateur du village*, of which, she adds condescendingly,
"there's always one around." In fact, the two children in question were saved
by a devoted mulatto slave from death at the hands of Toussaint Louverture,
who "hates the whites and wants to kill them all." The faithful slave pays for
his devotion with his life; the frustrated Toussaint stabs him to death with his
own hands.

Another novel, also intended for the edification of children, Madame
Fresnau's 1888 *Thérèse à Saint-Domingue*, is the story of a French family who
lands in Saint-Domingue in 1789. The young daughter asks her mother:

> [Negroes] are men quite like us, despite their ugly black skin, aren't
> they, maman?
> Of course, my child, and we have no right to treat them differently
> than the servants you have seen in France, although God has generally
> given them less intelligence than to whites. But they often are very virtu-
> ous, they are capable of devotion towards those who are good to them,
> and their good qualities then replace their lack of intelligence.[9]

The intellectual inferiority of Africans and their descendants, universally
accepted well into the twentieth century as scientific fact, was therefore postu-
lated in all good conscience, as was their ugliness according to Caucasians' aesthetic standards. Little Thérèse finds black skin ugly. In Jules-Berlioz d'Auriac's
La guerre noire, souvenirs de St Domingue, first published in 1862, and in its
ninth edition in 1913, Bono-Joko, the faithful slave is described as:

> not handsome unfortunately; of the Negro race he had, in exaggerated
> form, the flat nose, the thick lips, the receding forehead; his inordinately
> long arms were a great help to him for climbing trees, but did very little
> for his attractiveness; his feet, hard as rocks and always naked, had the
> rare and strange ability to grab with their toes, just as hands do with
> their fingers. The whole of his person embodied the unflattering aspect
> of an orangutan.[10]

And Bono-Joko is a faithful slave; it can be imagined how unfaithful ones are depicted.

The second characteristic trait, which would become dominant for a long time, is the focus on the inhuman cruelty and corruption of the revolted slaves and the obscene tortures they inflicted on white planters (and especially on their wives and daughters). Up until quite recently, these descriptions were not as graphic as when permissiveness in these matters became pervasive. They have by now become staples of a production of specialized erotica, not to say pornography, and are still inspired, as they were in the nineteenth century, by the supposedly personal experiences of white survivors. A case in point is Robert Gaillard's 1971–1972 tetralogy with the revealing titles: *La luxure du matin* (*Morning Lust*), *La volupté et la haine* (*Sensuality and Hatred*), *Désir et liberté* (*Desire and Freedom*), and *La chair et la cendre* (*Flesh and Ashes*). By describing flayings, burnings, eviscerations, and rapes perpetrated indiscriminately by whites on blacks and by blacks on whites, such works obviously cater to the racist and the sadist who slumber in every reader.

But the above remarks apply to the depiction of blacks in general, whether in Haiti or in the French West Indies or, when the French grabbed their portion of Africa to its colonized natives. The Haitian revolution specifically has inspired few French writers of fiction, far fewer than the number of English-speaking authors. There are two obvious reasons. First, historical novels have never been nearly as popular with the French reading public as with the "Anglo-Saxons," who have made a specialty of the genre created by Sir Walter Scott. And second, while the French do not particularly enjoy writing and reading about an inglorious defeat at the hand of black slaves, neither English nor American novelists have such qualms.

To the meager corpus of works of generally scant literary quality that we have rapidly analyzed could be added those of several Haitian, French West Indian, and African authors writing in the French language in the aftermath of decolonization. Yet apart from being composed in French, they have little in common, ideologically or aesthetically, with those of the metropole. For those black writers and for their compatriots, the Haitian revolutionary epic has far more personal and dignifying connotations than for the French from the Hexagon. Their works richly deserve a separate study. Strangely enough, a systematic investigation of the depiction of the saga of independence in Haitian literature still awaits scholarly attention.[11]

Notes

1. On the silence of French historians, see Yves Benot, *La Révolution française et la fin des colonies* (Paris: La Découverte, 1989); Francis Arzalier, "La Révolution haïtienne dans l'imaginaire français," in *La Révolution française et Haïti*, ed. Michel

Hector (Port-au-Prince: Société haïtienne d'histoire et de géographie & Éditions Henri Deschamps, 1995), 2:348–357; Myriam Cottias, "Le Silence de la nation," *Outre-Mers* 90, no. 338–339 (2003): 21–45.

2. See Michel L. Martin and André G. Cabanis, "Ignorance et malentendus: l'indépendance d'Haïti devant l'opinion en France sous le Consulat et l'Empire," in *La Révolution française et Haïti*, 2:358–374.

3. See, among many others, Jacques Thibeau, *Le temps de Saint-Domingue: l'esclavage et la Révolution française* (Paris: J. C. Lattès, 1989); and Yves Benot, *La démence coloniale sous Napoléon* (Paris: Éditions La Découverte), 1991.

4. Hérard Dumesle, *Voyage dans le nord d'Haïti* (Les Cayes: Imprimerie du Gouvernement, 1824). The first mention of the Bois-Caïman ceremony was made in Antoine Dalmas' *Histoire de la révolution de Saint-Domingue* (Paris: Mame frères, 1814). See also my "Histoire, mythe et idéologie: la cérémonie du Bois-Caïman," *Études créoles* 13, no. 1 (1990): 9–34.

5. Hans-Jürgen Lüsebrink, "Mise en fiction et conceptualisation de la révolution haïtienne: la genèse d'un discours littéraire (1789–1848)," in *Proceedings of the Xth Congress of the International Comparative Literature Association* (New York: Garland Publishing, 1985), 228–233, quote on 229.

6. A shorter story by Hugo with the same title appeared in *Le Conservateur littéraire* in 1820; the much amplified "definitive" version was published in Paris in book form by Urbain Canel. A stage adaptation of Hugo's novel by Pierre Bonnier and Richard Lesclide was published in 1886 but seems never to have been performed. Lamartine's play was published in Paris by Michel Lévy frères. Beside Varin and Labiche's, another parody of *Toussaint Louverture, Tout-Serin-la-Clôture*, by Coquenard fils, closed after only one performance and was never published. On the ideology of both works, see my "Victor Hugo, les Noirs et l'esclavage," *Francofonia* 31 (Autumn 1996): 47–90; and the introduction to Alphonse de Lamartine, *Toussaint Louverture* (Exeter: University of Exeter Press, 1998).

7. *Bugg ou les Javanais*, by Benjamin Antier, F. Coizy, and Hyacinthe de Flers (1828), and *Traversin et Couverture*, by Victor Varin and Eugène Labiche (1850). Eugène Labiche (1815–1888) went on to be a very successful playwright and was elected to the Académie française. Some of the 175 light comedies attributed to him are still performed today.

8. Julie Gouraud, *Les deux enfants de Saint-Domingue* (Paris: Hachette, 1874), 42. "*Ils ont été poussés à la révolte par les mauvais traitements. N'est-il pas odieux d'être vendus comme de vils troupeaux? Vous voyez bien qu'il y a parmi les nègres de belles âmes, et qu'ils sont des hommes comme nous!*"

9. Armand Fresnau, *Thérèse à Saint-Domingue* (Paris: Hachette, 1888), 16. "*Thérèse: Ils sont tout à fait des hommes comme nous, n'est-ce pas, maman, malgré leur vilaine peau noire?*

Madame de Vernoux: Certainement, mon enfant, et l'on n'a pas le droit de les traiter autrement que les domestiques que tu as vus en France, quoique Dieu leur ait donné en général moins d'intelligence qu'aux blancs. Mais ils ont souvent beaucoup de coeur, sont capables de s'attacher à ceux qui leur font du bien, et leurs bonnes qualités remplacent alors chez eux l'intelligence qui leur manque."

10. Jules-Berlioz d'Auriac, *La guerre noire, souvenirs de St-Domingue* (Paris: Putois Cretté, 1862), 80. "*Malheureusement il n'était pas beau, et, de la race nègre, il avait conservé, en les exagérant, le nez épaté, les lèvres charnues, le front fuyant; ses bras, d'une longueur démesurée, lui étaient d'une utilité incomparable pour grimper aux arbres, mais ils ne*

contribuaient que médiocrement à l'embellir: ses pieds, toujours nus et durs comme la corne, avaient la rare et singulière faculté de saisir presque comme des mains à l'aide de leurs doigts. L'ensemble de sa personne réalisait le type peu flatteur de l'orang-outang."

11. Two interesting preliminary studies have been published: Wolfgang Bader, "Tradition et décolonisation: Fonction et image de la révolution haïtienne dans la littérature des Caraïbes après la seconde guerre mondiale," in *Proceedings of the Xth Congress of the International Comparative Literature Association* (New York: Garland Publishing, 1985), 234–239; and Arlette Chemin-Defrange, "Bicentenaire de la Révolution et Affranchissement," in *Révolution française, peuple et littératures*, ed. André Peyronie (Paris: Klincksieck, 1991), 343–355.

Bibliography

Primary Works

A. "Augustin, ou la révolte des Noirs." In Pierre-Philippe Baignoux and A., *Amelina, Godefroy et Augustin, ou les trois époques d'Haïti*. Tours: R. Pornin et Cie, 1844.

Anonymous [Eugène Chapus?]. *Oxiane, ou la Révolution de St-Domingue*. 3 vols. Paris: Corbet, Pigoreau, 1826.

Antier, Benjamin, F. Coizy, and Hyacinthe de Flers. *Bugg, ou les Javanais, mélodrame en 3 actes*. Paris: Quoy, 1828.

Augustin, Marie. *Le Macandal. Épisode de l'insurrection des noirs à St. Domingue. Par Tante Marie*. New Orleans: G. Müller, 1892.

Auriac, Jules-Berlioz d'. *La guerre noire—souvenirs de St-Domingue*. Paris: Putois Cretté, 1862.

Béraud, Louis et Joseph Rosny. *Adonis, ou le bon Nègre, mélodrame en 4 actes*. Paris: Glisau, an VI [1798]. (Stage adaptation of Piquenard's novel of the same name).

Berthier, Jean-Baptiste. *Félix et Éléonore, ou les colons malheureux*. 2 vols. Paris: Maradan, 1801.

Bonnier, Pierre Elzéar, and Richard Lesclide. *Bug-Jargal, drame en 7 tableaux*. Paris: Barbé, 1886.

Chenu, Charles Marie. *Tragédie créole*. Paris: Fayard, 1955.

Furcy de Bremoy, H. *Évrard; ou, Saint-Domingue au dix-neuvième siècle*. 2 vols. Paris: Pillet aîné, 1829.

Fresnau, Mme Armand, née de Ségur. *Thérèse à Saint-Domingue*. Paris: Hachette, 1888. (American trans. 1889.)

Gaillard, Robert. *La chair et la cendre*. Paris: Fleuve noir, 1972.

———. *Désir et liberté*. Paris: Fleuve noir, 1972.

———. *La luxure du matin*. Paris: Fleuve noir, 1971.

———. *La volupté et la haine*. Paris: Fleuve noir, 1971.

Gilles, Bernard, and Serge Quardu. *Le Chouan de Saint-Domingue*. Paris: Presses de la Renaissance, 1979.

Gouraud, Melle Julie [Louise d'Aulnay]. *Les deux enfants de Saint-Domingue*. Illustrated with 54 engravings by Émile Bayard. Paris: Hachette, 1874.

Hugo, Victor. *Bug-Jargal*. Paris: Urbain Canel, 1826. (English trans. 1833.)

Laisné de Tours, E. V. *L'insurrection du Cap, ou la perfidie d'un noir*. Paris: Aurélien Fleuriau, 1822.

Lamartine, Alphonse de. *Toussaint Louverture*. Paris: Michel Lévy frères,1850. (English trans. 1875.)

Marsollier des Vivetières, Benoît-Joseph. *La mort du colonel Mauduit, ou les anarchistes du Port-au-Prince, fait historique en un acte et en prose*. Paris: Cailleau, an VIII [1800]. (Written in 1792; never performed.)

Palaiseau, Melle de. *L'histoire de Mesdemoiselles de Saint-Janvier, les deux seules blanches conservées à Saint-Domingue*. Paris: Blaise, 1812.

Perrin, René. *L'incendie du Cap, ou règne de Toussaint Louverture*. Paris: Marchand, An X [1802].

Picquenard, Jean-Baptiste. *Adonis, ou le bon nègre*. Paris: Impr. Didot jeune, l'an VI [1798].

———. *Zoflora, ou la bonne négresse: anecdote coloniale*. Paris: Imprimerie de Didot jeune, An VIII [1800].

Pigault-Lebrun, Charles. *Le blanc et le noir, drame en quatre actes*. Paris: Mayeur, An IV [1795].

Rémusat, Charles de. *L'habitation de Saint-Domingue ou l'insurrection*. Paris: CNRS, 1977. (Written in 1824.)

Saillet, Alexandre de. *Lucile de Saint-Albe, épisode de la révolution de Saint-Domingue*. Paris: P. C. Lehuby.

Varin, Victor et Eugène Labiche. *Traversin et couverture*. Poissy, Arbieu, 1850.

Critical Studies

Antoine, Régis. *Les écrivains français et les Antilles*. Paris: Maisonneuve et Larose, 1978.

Arzalier, Francis. "La Révolution haïtienne dans l'imaginaire français." In *La Révolution française et Haïti*, ed. Michel Hector, 2:348–357. Port-au-Prince: Société haïtienne d'histoire et de géographie and Éditions Henri Deschamps, 1995.

Bader, Wolfgang. "Tradition et decolonisation: Fonction et image de la révolution haïtienne dans la littérature des Caraïbes après la seconde guerre mondiale." In *Proceedings of the Xth Congress of the International Comparative Literature Association*, 234–239. New York: Garland Publishing, 1985.

Benot, Yves. *La démence coloniale sous Napoléon*. Paris: Éditions La Découverte, 1991.

———. *La Révolution française et la fin des colonies*. Paris: La Découverte, 1989.

Chemin-Degrange, Arlette. "Bicentenaire de la Révolution et affranchissement. Recherches francophones en théâtralité." In *Révolution française, peuples et littératures*, ed. André Peyronie, 343–355. Paris: Klincksieck, 1991.

Cottias, Myriam. "Le silence de la nation." *Outre-Mers* 90, no. 338–339 (2003): 21–45.

Gengembre, Gérard. "De *Bug-Jargal* à *Toussaint Louverture*: le romantisme et l'esclave révolté." In *Les Abolitions de l'esclavage, Actes du colloque international de Paris VIII, 3–4–5 février 1994*. Paris: Presses Universitaires de Vincennes and Éd. UNESCO, 1995.

Halpern, Jean-Claude. "L'esclavage sur la scène révolutionnaire." *Annales historiques de la Révolution française*, no. 293–294 (1993): 409–420.

Hoffmann, Léon-François. "Histoire, mythe et idéologie: la cérémonie du Bois-Caïman." *Études créoles* 13, no. 1 (1990): 9–34.

————. "Victor Hugo, les Noirs et l'esclavage." *Francofonia* 31 (Autumn 1996): 47–90.

Lüsebrink, Hans-Jürgen. "Mise en fiction et conceptualisation de la révolution haïtienne: la genèse d'un discours littéraire (1789–1848)." In *Proceedings of the Xth Congress of the International Comparative Literature Association,* 228–233. New York: Garland Publishing, 1985.

Martin, Michel L., and André G. Cabanis. "Ignorance et malentendus: l'indépendance d'Haïti devant l'opinion en France sous le Consulat et l'Empire." In *La Révolution française et Haïti,* ed. Michel Hector, 2:358–374. Port-au-Prince : Société haïtienne d'histoire et de géographie and Éditions Henri Deschamps, 1995.

Thibau, Jacques. *Le temps de Saint-Domingue: l'esclavage et la Révolution française.* Paris: J.C. Lattès, 1989.

Neoclassicism and the Haitian Revolution

Carlo Célius

THE ARTISTIC TREND THAT IN 1880 WAS DUBBED NEOCLASSICISM FIRST MADE ITS MARK 150 YEARS EARLIER, IN THE MIDDLE OF THE EIGHTEENTH CENTURY. CENTERED ON ROME, WHERE ITS FIRST theoreticians, Anton Raphael Mengs and Johann J. Winckelmann, made their home, it celebrated freedom, heroism, and civic virtue as well as an idealized beauty. It thus anticipated French revolutionary ideology, in which the mania for Classical antiquity occupied a central position.[1] Because of its ties to the French Revolution, the Haitian Revolution was also concerned with these issues, and the question arises as to where this revolutionary craze for antiquity fits in the development of the Haitian Revolution's own system of symbols. In addressing this question, I would like to trace the establishment of the basic symbolic machinery through which official memory was formed in Haiti.

Freedom for All and Revolutionary Symbolism

On July 14, 1793, the civil commissioners Léger-Félicité Sonthonax and Étienne Polverel decided to celebrate "Bastille day" by transforming the holiday into a consecration of the emancipation they had recently proclaimed of slaves who had agreed to become armed defenders of the Republic. The nineteenth-century historian Beaubrun Ardouin describes the scene:

> That day, surrounded by all the servants of the state from the civil and military sectors, all the troops, and all the citizens of Cap-Français, the civil commissioners went to the Champ-de-Mars where an altar was erected to the homeland. *The tree of liberty*, the majestic palm of the West Indies, was planted *for the first time*; the Phrygian cap, also dedicated to freedom, was placed on top of a pike. Polverel gave a speech that day in which he reminded the crowd of the eternal struggle of the oppressed

against the oppressors. He ended it by vowing "to be faithful to the French Republic, to duly execute all the laws made by the National Convention and those that the Convention might produce in the future, to wage *a war unto death against all kings*, against all the enemies of liberty and equality."[2]

That same day, a great number of citizens took home the cap of freedom. Beaubrun Ardouin observes that "this ceremony inaugurated all those of the same nature that took place in the country thereafter; every government believed that it was bound to do this, and perhaps they may have gone too far."

This commemorative operation was quickly extended to the whole colony, where on the parade grounds of the cities and towns the tree of liberty was planted next to a pike topped by the Phrygian cap. Not surprisingly, a few years later, in the late 1790s, a small circular Greco-Roman temple was erected to commemorate the granting of general liberty. Although the site where the temple stood cannot be located with certainty, its existence was made known in 1805 by Marcus Rainsford. It was probably destroyed in 1802 during the Leclerc expedition. Vergniaud Leconte reckons it to have measured 6.5 meters in height and 9 meters in circumference. The temple consisted of seven Tuscan columns supporting a dome. Steps led to an altar on which stelae were placed and on these was inscribed an extract from the proclamation of general liberty. In the center was a spear topped by a Phrygian cap surrounded by "small olive branches."[3] (Fig. 18.1.) Rainsford visited the monument around 1799 (all visitors had access as long as they agreed not to touch the Phrygian cap). It is quite probable that it was conceived earlier, perhaps at the time of Sonthonax's second mission to the colony. The commissioner, who had to go back to France in 1794 to respond to allegations brought against him by the colonists, returned on May 11, 1796, as a member of a new civil commission, only to leave again on August 23, 1797, because he was at odds with Toussaint. Thereafter he occupied a seat as a deputy of Saint-Domingue in the Council of Five Hundred.

If Toussaint was extremely popular, so, too, was Sonthonax, as several sources confirm. "The farmers called him father and his name was a talisman for them."[4] "The children were taught, in all the black families, to say a prayer requesting blessings from heaven for Sonthonax, who had given them their freedom."[5] The early Haitian historian Thomas Madiou noted in the conversations he had with elderly people "the enthusiasm with which" they "spoke of Sonthonax's negrophilia." Several told him that Sonthonax "was the right man to regenerate the newly freed men."[6]

It may well be that the initiative to erect the temple came, as Rainsford suggested, from the newly freed men, which perhaps suggests that they appropriated the French revolutionary symbolism introduced by the commissioners. But if Toussaint went to great lengths to get rid of Sonthonax, he did not give up this symbolism. A coin dating from the time of Christophe's

government but in fact made from a cast used during Toussaint's administration testifies to this; the goddess of liberty appears on it.[7]

The commissioners had thus already decided upon the meaning that would be attributed to general emancipation long before their proclamation of it—a liberation granted by France and not one wrested in battle by the slaves. This conception of emancipation would prevail in the metropole following the Convention's decree of abolition in February 1794, which was perceived not as a confirmation of what had already been accomplished in Saint-Domingue but as the founding act of the freedom of the blacks.

For Neoclassical art and the arts of the French Revolution in general, slave emancipation was not a major event. In this respect, the silence of the painter Jacques-Louis David is particularly telling. As the main figure of Neoclassicism, he was producing politically engaged work even before 1789, and he became a political actor during the revolution. A member of the Jacobin Club by December 1790, he was elected to the National Convention in September 1792 as a representative for Paris. He served as president of the Jacobins in June and July 1793 and as president of the Convention in January 1794. Closely associated with Robespierre, he was arrested after Robespierre's overthrow in August 1794 but was released in late December 1795. On November 20, 1796, the Directory made him a member of the painting section of the Institute of Sciences and Arts created in October 1793. In February 1800, he turned down an appointment as official government painter, but he remained in the entourage of Napoleon and was in charge of painting the coronation ceremony of December 2, 1804. He went into exile under the Bourbon Restoration.

David is the archetype of the committed artist. A planner of revolutionary celebrations and a reformer of the arts, a painter of effigies and of commemorations, for him aesthetics and politics were part of the same combat in the service of freedom. Yet Saint-Domingue and slave emancipation did not inspire him at all. As a Jacobin, David could not have been unaware of the abolitionist campaign of the Friends of the Blacks and the debates concerning Saint-Domingue. As a deputy in the Convention, the demand for slave emancipation sent to the assembly in 1793 by some men of color could not have escaped his notice. He undoubtedly heard his colleague Camboulas announce with the arrival of the deputation from Saint-Domingue on February 3, 1794, the end of "the aristocracy of skin color". He witnessed the adoption of the emancipation decree, and perhaps saw during the December 13, 1794, session Pierre Jean Boquet offer the Convention his painting *View of the Forty-Day Burning of the Plantations of the Plain of Cap-Français which Occurred on August 23, 1791*.[8] Regardless of all this, the cause of the blacks did not inspire David. At its highest level, neoclassicism refused to celebrate slave emancipation as the major event that it was.

Admittedly, the emancipation decree did prompt the production of a whole series of prints. These depict the freed slave decked out in symbols of the French Revolution. He wears the Phrygian cap (as did the new freedmen of Saint-Domingue) or even the mason's level around his neck as a sign of equality. Little black men and little white men tread on the serpent of discord and embrace each other under the protection of Fraternity. Nature nurses a black child and a white child. A few rare images set themselves apart from this type of production. For example, *The Armed Negro* of Mlle Rollet, based on a work by Fougéa, exalts the martial virtues of the new fighters of freedom. The hero, armed with a rifle, bids farewell while holding his child in his arms; his wife, in the background, bursts into tears. Marcel Chatillon perceives a relationship between this drawing, which is Neoclassical in flavor, with one by Fabre from the same period representing Hector's farewell to Andromache.[9]

A drawing from 1794 merits longer scrutiny. It is, to this day, the only attempt at a graphic representation of the moment the decree of 16 Pluviôse Year II was adopted. The drawing, by Nicolas-André Monsiau (or Charles Thévenin), is in the bombastic style of the times, for which David's *Tennis Court Oath* (*Le serment du Jeu de paume*) constitutes a reference model. The crowd is set in motion at the moment the decree is adopted. A black man breaks away to go and hug the president of the assembly, who is white. In the foreground, to the right, a black male or female raises a baby in the direction of the podium— an element taken from other compositions of the period. But the most significant motif is placed at the very forefront, almost in the center of the drawing. A black man on his knees is being helped up by a white figure, who is dressed in the attire of Classical antiquity. Here we find a formula widely circulated by abolitionist imagery. The artist is careful to place this action in the forefront by isolating it distinctly from the crowd as if it were an easily recognized sign (abolitionist imagery was, in fact, widely distributed), placed there to explain (the gesture of the figure is in this sense quite evocative) what is going on in the background. By doing so, the artist offers a reading of the 16 Pluviôse decree as the triumph of the abolitionist struggle. (Figs. 18.2 and 18.3.)

Two portraits are to be understood in this same perspective. The first, of Civil Commissioner Sonthonax, belongs to the Musée du Panthéon in Port-au-Prince. Unsigned and undated, it is attributed to the school of David. Sonthonax, wearing clothing from the period of the Directory,[10] holds in his right hand the proclamation of August 29, 1793, and points with his left hand to the Code Noir crumpled on his work table. He is alone in the privacy of his study, perhaps waiting to deliver the proclamation he has just written, which will destroy the Code that has been in effect in the colonies since 1685. (Possibly the scene takes place after the proclamation but there is no doubt that it represents the destruction of the Black Code.) No source of inspiration

[**Fig. 18.2**]

Nicolas-André Monsiau (or Charles Thévenin), *Abolition de l'esclavage par la Convention, Le 16 Pluviôse an II* (1794), pen-and-ink drawing, 32 × 24 cm. Musée Carnavalet, Paris. All rights reserved by Agence Photographique Roger-Viollet.

Soyez libres et citoyens (1789), drawn by P. Rouvier, engraving, 20 × 12 cm. Frontispiece of Benjamin-Sigismond Frossard, *La Cause des esclaves nègres* . . . (Lyon, 1789). Courtesy of the John Carter Brown Library at Brown University.

is suggested, nor are the circumstances that led the official to take this step. It is an entirely personal act, dictated by the sole will of the republican hero.

The portrait of the black deputy Mars Belley is, on the other hand, well known as the work of Anne-Louis Girodet, a student of David. Belley was elected in September 1793 as one of Saint-Domingue's deputies to the Convention, and he held a seat in the Council of Five Hundred under the Directory until May 1797. He posed for Girodet around the time he was getting ready to leave France. The portrait has an antithetical structure in which the painter carries out a sort of inversion. One recalls those seventeenth- and eighteenth-century paintings where a little black page wearing the collar of servitude accompanies a high society lady. On the formal level, the presence of the "black" makes the "white" complexion more vivid, a formula that would endure and reappear notably in the *Olympia* of Manet (1863). Girodet portrays someone who is his own man, who has come out of servitude standing tall. Although the artist has recourse to the usual black/white contrast, he places Belley in the forefront. He inverts an established pattern of the plastic arts in the interest of a symbolic statement that relates everything to abolitionism. The abbé Raynal, in the guise of a Classical philosopher, stands out as an imposing and inspirational figure. As proud and dignified as Belley may appear, he nonetheless owes his dignity and his pride to the philosopher and his thought—and, in the end, to abolitionism.

An essential distinction can be made between the two portraits. In contrast to Belley, Sonthonax is represented as completely independent in thought and action. Such autonomy will be later seen in Richard Evans's portrait of Henry Christophe. Admittedly this work belongs to the tradition of pageantry portraits, but what is important is that the ruler of the kingdom of Haiti is portrayed just like any other king. The conditions in which the work was realized (political context, art sponsorship, ideological underpinnings) were no longer the same.

Political Rupture and Symbolic Reinvestment

During the war against the forces of Napoleon, the army of Saint-Domingue called itself the "indigenous army." Then, shortly before the final campaign, it gave itself its own rallying symbol: a flag was born.[11] Once victory was won in November 1803, two other symbolic acts took place: Dessalines, the general-in-chief, chose January 1, 1804, for the proclamation of independence,[12] thus making the beginning of the new state's official existence coincide with the first day of the new year. This was to clearly signify the break with an old order and the beginning of a new era. At the same time, the idea arose of renaming the country. The ancient Taino name for the island was adopted: Haiti. This was not simply paying homage to the Tainos. It was an assertion that the Tainos and the Africans reduced to slavery shared a common fate, that the victory over the colonists was the outcome of a battle begun by the aborigines themselves, and that the land that had just been conquered belonged to the oppressed, who were the only ones who made it bear fruit. It was a symbolic justification of the process of reappropriating the territory and an act of becoming once again indigenous. Haiti was reborn, with the island's history and memory incarnated legitimately in a new people.

This act of symbolization shows that the victory over the French troops created a new situation that was experienced as a radical break. It was a moment of great intensity that created—before, during, and after the proclamation of independence—a community bound together by emotion.[13]

The proclamation of independence purports to be an act of foundation accompanied by all the usual celebratory trappings. The celebration of victory and of a liberty acquired by conquest established a date and also a model of commemoration consisting of official speeches, religious and civic events, and popular merrymaking. In this way an official memory was organized after 1804 that was very different from what had been put in place from 1793 onward. However, the revolutionary symbolism introduced at that time was not completely done away with.

It is important to remember that the French visual arts were not unknown in the colony, where they overshadowed other plastic arts expression, that from Taino (in the form of material remains) and from African cultures (in a residual state). The metropolitan artistic forms imposed and appropriated, sometimes in a very active manner, both religious and secular imagery and even became a stake in the struggle for self-valorization by the new emerging elite.[14] It is these same dynamics that help us understand the maintenance of French revolutionary symbolism.

Liberty and equality are two key concepts of revolutionary ideology in France. Originating in Greco-Roman culture, they thus are related to the revolution's enthusiasm for Classical antiquity which derived from a cultural movement under way in French society at least since the middle of the eighteenth century.[15] The same cannot be said of Saint-Domingue society. However, these disseminated ideas corresponded to the actual battles fought by the colony's oppressed socioracial groups. The concepts of liberty and equality allowed those groups to name their actions and give meaning to them when confronting their adversaries. The "freed men of color" were fighting for "equality" and the slaves for "liberty" first and foremost. The notion of fraternity acquired its full meaning in the decisive phase of the war of independence, when the rival factions found they had to combine their forces to defeat a common threat. This threat was the restoration of the old order, of slavery and racial discrimination, to be precise. At this time of crisis, when a horrendous battle without mercy began, the slogans "liberty or death" and "live free or die"—derived from metropolitan revolutionary ideology—lost all of their foreign characteristics and acquired a particular resonance and efficacy. The same was true of the Phrygian cap, previously worn by the freed slave and therefore a symbol of freedom. This symbolic device acquired an entirely renewed meaning in 1804. The necessity of having to struggle against a metropole that had initially advanced these principles and symbols revealed the truth that it was now on the soil of Saint-Domingue, not France, that the universalization of the great revolutionary principles was accomplished. The boundaries of universality (or what was considered as such) were thus being expanded by universalizing one's own self-interested battles.

Herein lies Haiti's main line of defense throughout the entire nineteenth century, which consisted of emphasizing the humanity of all men, including those born in slavery. The Haitian Revolution created and legitimized the whole anthropological substance of Haitian thought in the nineteenth century. By going back in time, one can understand the choice of the slogan "liberty, equality, fraternity," the mottoes "liberty or death" (Dessalines), "liberty, equality" (Pétion), "liberty, independence" (Christophe) at the end of the Haitian war for independence as well as the adoption of the elements that constitute the arms of the new state. In spite of their origins in ancien régime iconography and their readaptation in French revolutionary symbolism, these slogans and icons express the realization of Haitian revolutionary ideals.

After independence had been proclaimed and the collective vow to live free or die was pronounced on the altar of the homeland, such altars received a new investiture. Imbued with emotion, they marked the landscape of Haiti's cities and towns throughout the nineteenth century. At first only podiums of wood but later more permanent structures, they were sites of power and of collective memory, sacred ground where people gathered regularly to remember great deeds and renew the civic oath of the founders.

Civic festivities featured allegorical figures that represented the "Homeland and Liberty," or "Fame and Abundance." As described by the historian Madiou, President Jean-Pierre Boyer's planned visit to Saint-Marc on his triumphal return from newly annexed Santo Domingo in 1822 provides a good example:

> In this town, the authorities and the population prepared a great national celebration to greet him. The district and town commanders wrote to ask that he let them know the day when he would be arriving at Drouillard, located about a league from the capital. A program for the celebration was inserted in the *Télégraphe*. The procession which was to greet him was to be formed of a mounted figure representing Renown, decorated in white and the national colors, followed by four trumpeters, also on horseback, a squadron of mounted national guards, three floats, one carrying the goddess of Liberty, the other the goddess of Justice, and the third the goddess of Abundance. In each float,

beside each of the goddesses, there was a young man, one representing
Agriculture, another Commerce, and the other, Strength. Nineteen
young men on horseback, representing the nineteen years of independence,
were to be divided into four squads. One was charged with carrying a
banner on which was written: North, South, East, West, united by
friendship. The young woman who was to represent Liberty, one of
the most beautiful girls of the town, had already been chosen.[16]

Goddesses representing "Freedom and the Republic" would appear on stamps
and on coins,[17] in prints and paintings, and as statues. (Fig. 18.4.)
     During the nineteenth century, the idea arose of erecting commemora-
tive columns. On August 20, 1816, in his northern kingdom, King Henry
Christophe published a decree ordering the erection of a monument on the
parade ground of the Citadel. The document's preamble reads:

> In our desire to give the Haitian people a striking proof of our love of
> freedom and independence, which they have conquered by their energy
> and courage, and the most noble and generous sacrifices; in our desire to
> consecrate with a long lasting memorial, this act of the national will, and
> to perpetuate its memory down to the last of our nephews; and consider-
> ing it our duty, and that we must take pains to nourish the feelings and
> the passion of our people for glory, to rouse the emulation that gives birth
> to great men, and to repress crimes, by marking with shame and infamy
> the memory of those who renounced honor and betrayed justice.[18]

The five articles of the act follow. The first one indicates that a column to
Liberty and Independence will be erected in the middle of the parade ground of
the Citadel-Henry. The second makes provisions for the Act of Independence
to be engraved on a bronze plaque. The third article states that the names of
the signatories will be engraved in the same order as on the original act (with
some exceptions, to which I will later return). Article five makes provision for
pronouncing every year on the anniversary of independence, at the foot of the
monument, a funeral eulogy of the warriors killed in combat or who died under
torture defending freedom and independence. Madiou states that "the figura-
tive and descriptive plan of this memorial was presented to the king by the
minister of finance and of the interior, and the director-general of the Corps of
Engineers, and that while waiting for the plan to be carried out with its bronze
base, Christophe had a wooden facsimile erected."[19] We do not know if the full
monument was put up before Christophe's death in 1820.
     The existence at the beginning of the 1840s of a commemorative col-
umn not far from Gonaïves was recorded by Victor Schoelcher during his
visit to Haiti.[20] Another was erected for the centennial of independence
in 1904.[21]
     A different type of construction that requires discussion is the triumphal
arch. When President Boyer journeyed to the southern city of Les Cayes in 1820

[Fɪɢ. 18.4]

Statue of Alexandre Pétion in Port-au-Prince, 1904. CIDIHCA Archives, Montréal.

to ratify the end of Goman's insurrection, he found a triumphal arch erected in his honor on the bridge at the entrance to the city. He let it be known that he considered the pacification of the Grande Anse a duty accomplished for the Republic and that he had done nothing but reunite with society citizens and brothers of the same family. They were not vanquished enemies. Yet Boyer was forced to pass under the memorial. When he came back from Les Cayes, another triumphal arch awaited him at the south entrance to the capital. He accepted the compliments of the inhabitants but declined the honors of this inopportune triumph by repeating the same arguments he had put forward in Les Cayes.[22] When he came back from the eastern part of the island in March 1822, people lined the road from Quartier-Morin to Cap-Haïtien. At the edge of the Fort-Liberté district, a triumphal arch that was erected by farmers, according to Madiou, awaited him as well. The inhabitants of Le Cap built two at the gates of their city. "The one at La Fossette measured 24 feet high and 18 feet wide. It was richly decorated and had on its outward side the allegorical attributes of freedom with the slogan, "The Nation thanks Jean-Pierre Boyer, President of Haiti." The inside bore the attributes of commerce and displayed another motto on a ribbon in national colors, "Token of love from the residents of Le Cap." The second triumphal arch "was erected at the entrance to the ferry. The slogans were, on the city-side, 'He sheltered the ship of state from storms' and, on the other side, 'His charity and his virtues earned him everyone's heart.' The city was splendidly illuminated and fireworks were set off until very late in the night."[23]

This practice of erecting temporary triumphal arches was maintained until recently. Coming back from a tour in the country in 1852, Faustin Soulouque returned to the capital under a triumphal arch. The entrance of General Antoine Simon into Port-au-Prince on December 5, 1908, took place under the same type of structure. As late as the 1940s, some shopkeepers of Port-de-Paix erected one in honor of Elie Lescot. These constructions were not always temporary, as is shown by the one still standing at the entrance to the city of Fort-Liberté. (Figs. 18.5 and 18.6.)

The reference to Greco-Roman antiquity is evident in other types of construction, such as, in the realm of official architecture, the National Palace[24] or a more discreet structure built in 1938 to house the national museum, which is now occupied by the National Bureau of Ethnology. In the domain of funerary architecture, the chapel intended to receive the remains of Pétion (the construction of which did not receive Boyer's assent) was conceived in 1840 by the architect Rouanez "following the style of the Greek temples of Paestum."[25]

Successive governments also developed the tendency to commission copies of works of Classical antiquity. We thus find in the National Museum collection (1938–1982) *The Bather*, *The Medici Venus*, *The Venus de Milo*, *The Player of Cymbals*, and *Two Wrestlers*.[26] Also noteworthy are the great

[Fig. 18.5]

The entry of Faustin Soulouque into Port-au-Prince through a temporary triumphal arch.
L'Illustration (Paris), February 21, 1852. Private collection.

[Fig. 18.6]

The entry of General Antoine Simon into Port-au-Prince in 1908 beneath a triumphal arch. CIDIHCA Archives, Montréal..

number of copies of ancient statues commissioned for the Bicentennial Exhibition in Port-au-Prince in 1949–1950.[27] It is hardly surprising to find the same Greco-Roman model as the basis for drawing classes planned in school curricula of the nineteenth century.[28]

Recourse to this model is linked, as we have seen, to the process of universalization in accordance with the revolutionary ideal, although domestically it has played the role of a social marker. But let us ponder a while the political stakes involved in the development of official memory. Let us tackle the problem from the angle of hero-making, given that heroism is linked to neoclassicism and that the portrait of the hero is central to the apparatus of power in Haiti.

Cult of Freedom, Cult of Heroes

Haitian nationalism takes the form of a heroic nationalism, in which the hero occupies a significant, even central, place. The national pantheon, nevertheless, took time to form. It was definitively completed toward the end of the nineteenth century, but it can be glimpsed in the earlier period when the organization of official memory crystallized around the cult of freedom. This pattern continued while taking on aspects of the cult of heroes. Already in the nineteenth century, under the exterior of the cult of freedom, a real struggle over official memory was under way involving candidates for "hero-ship."

Article 3 of the royal edict of 1816 concerning the commemorative column intended for the Citadel's parade ground stipulated that the names of the signatories of the Act of Independence were to be engraved on a bronze facsimile in the same order as in the original document, except for the names of traitors, which would be omitted for having betrayed the cause of freedom and independence. Article 4 entrusted the Grand Council of State with the responsibility of submitting a report to the king listing whose names would be inscribed and whose omitted. Alexandre Pétion and the generals of the west and the south were excluded because they refused to recognize Christophe's rule. Pétion, for his part, entrusted the French painter Barincou junior, who arrived in Port-au-Prince in 1817, with the task of painting portraits of Haitian military leaders in the war of independence, which were intended to decorate the main room of the national palace in Port-au-Prince. Those excluded were the men of the north and the Artibonite with the exception of General Magny, who in 1812 submitted to the Republic.[29] Each ruler thus sought to expunge the other from official memory while securing his own place and conducting his own "heroization." This process of self-heroization was in line with the cult of the leader that was tied to the authoritarian structure of state power then being established. Heroization was already at work under Dessalines, who considered himself a hero[30] and was acclaimed as such while he was alive. On the occasion of the emperor's birthday in 1805, Roumage jeune, the principal administrator of the Northern division, declared at the imperial palace in Le Cap, "Thanks be to the Divinity for having preserved our hero, whose days are so precious to us! You are the real founder and savior of our freedom and our immortal independence; you, who have sacrificed everything for our homeland to shield her from the tyranny under which others wanted to immerse her once more."[31] But the hero was assassinated on October 17, 1806. The mutilation of his body, abandoned on Government Square, and the refusal for some time to give him a proper burial signify a true rite of desecration. Moreover, a new date of commemoration was instituted, at least in the west: October 17 meant from then on the end of tyranny. From the perspective of official memory, Dessalines was consigned to purgatory, where Christophe joined him in 1820. The king's suicide during an uprising against him was followed by the looting of his palaces. He had to be buried at night and in great haste, under a pile of limestone in the Citadel, where he remained some time without a real tomb. The country was then reunited under the authority of the men of the west. In this way, Christophe, upon his death, also missed the entrance gate to the pantheon, in contrast to Pétion, who benefited from more favorable circumstances. It is reported that "the people in its entirety" mourned his passing.[32]

It is true that Boyer refused to execute the law of 1818 calling for the erection of a mausoleum to Pétion's memory, that he opposed the building of a monument commissioned by Joute Lachenais (ex-companion of Pétion and companion of Boyer) destined to house the coffins of Pétion and his daughter Célie, and that he rejected the bill voted by the legislature in 1840 appropriating an amount of 70,000 piastres to build a chapel to contain the remains of his predecessor. Nevertheless, Pétion was the first Haitian head of state whose remains were placed in a public space. His heart, placed in an urn, can be found in a tomb on the square near the national palace known during the colonial era as Place d'armes, Champ-de-Mars, or Place du gouvernement, which later became Place Pétion. His entrails are buried in one of the forts overlooking the capital, the Fort National. When, in fear of a new French invasion, the government planned to move the capital to a new site, the Coupe-Charbonnière (law of September 23, 1831), the new town was given the name of Pétion (Ville-Pétion, then Pétionville). The process of pantheonization of the former president began at the moment of his death. An engraving printed for the occasion underscores this. The explanatory caption reads,

> The image of Alexandre Pétion appears in the midst of his tomb; two
> *fasces*, emblems of the union of the Haitian family, support his sarcophagus;
> two of his soldiers guard the monument dedicated to posterity. From
> Liberty and Equality emanate the rays of his glory; Justice and the
> constitution form the source of these rays. The bas-relief represents

[Fig. 18.7]

Tombeau d'Alexandre Pétion. Undated (ca. 1818?), artist unknown. Bibliothèque nationale de France, Paris, Estampes.

> Time comforting the Republic by showing her, on Mars's shield, the
> name of he whom her children have chosen to preside henceforth over
> her Felicity and Happiness.

It is also worth noting the inscription at the bottom of the medallion: "He
never caused anyone to shed a tear." (Fig. 18.7.)

Boyer's name appears on Mars's shield and his initials on the *sabretache*[33] of
the soldier to the right. This discreet presence would soon expand, as painted
and engraved portraits of the new president multiplied.[34] A painting was commissioned from Barincou junior to celebrate his accession to power. The work
was sent from France in 1821 and hung upon its arrival in the senate meeting
room. The painting was probably completed in a context different from the one
in which it was first commissioned. The country was reunified in 1821 with
the prospect of integrating the eastern part of the island. Barincou, it seems,
wanted to take this into account. The outcome was an ambiguous work, to
say the least, if we are to judge from the explanatory leaflet that accompanied
it.[35] The title of the painting is *The Republic of Haiti, Being Reborn from Her
Ashes*—an inversion of Christophe's slogan "I am reborn from my ashes." It is
no longer the king, whose person is one with state, who is being reborn, but
the Republic itself, and it is the Republic that grants power."From her victorious and protective hand, [she] entrusts her weapons to the immortal Boyer,
whom the nation unanimously has called upon to preside over her great destiny." In this way, the difference between the two political regimes is conveyed
as well as the triumph of one over the other.

This message is not entirely unambiguous, however. If the Republic was
"reborn from its ashes," it had supposedly been destroyed. It rises over the
debris of tyranny and it triumphs over a regime that it had preceded and was
superior to but of which it was also a victim. The split between the north
and the west, the political battles that led to it and those that it generated,
are therefore not seen as merely confining Pétion's republican project to one
part of the national territory but as having destroyed it. As it happens, Boyer
inherits Pétion's republic. Of course, on rising from the ruins of tyranny, the
Republic turned its first gaze of gratitude toward the picture of its illustrious founder. But the importance of descent is not emphasized. This filiation
is not direct and would not be achieved smoothly. On the engraving of the
death of Pétion, the tearful Republic is consoled by Time, who points out
Boyer's name inscribed on the shield of Mars. From now on, the Republic,
which had been supposedly destroyed, is suddenly resurrected and her victorious hand entrusts Boyer with military power. It is a question of establishing, thanks to new circumstances, Boyer's own leadership and of carrying
out his heroization, a self-heroization, given that the painting was officially
commissioned. Boyer is already "immortal" side by side with the "brave and

immortal defenders of freedom and national independence" who perished and whose funerary monuments are shown.

This heroization, or self-heroization, of Boyer does not quite rise to the occasion, however, as is suggested by other pictures commissioned during the same period. This is especially true of a relatively well-known series of engravings that illustrate certain historical episodes in chronological order. Their captions read as follows:

—"The young Ogé, realizing that the National Convention would not recognize the civil rights of his fellow countrymen, embarks for England, from where he sails to America, and after a long detour arrives in Le Cap on October 12, 1790. His brother Chavanne, and other friends come to greet him. He places himself at their head and is the first to unfurl the flag of liberty." (Fig. 18.8.)

—"General Toussaint L'Ouverture handing two letters to the English general, who had come to see him in his camp. The first had been written to him by one of the French commissioners to urge him to seize the English general; the second was his response, which contained a noble refusal, and which ended in the following manner: 'The trust that the English general has in my good faith has committed him to place himself in my hands, and I would forever be dishonored if I followed your advice. I am totally devoted to the cause of the Republic, but I would never serve her against my conscience and my honor.'" (Fig. 18.9.)

—"On July 1st, 1801, Governor-General Toussaint L'Ouverture, accompanied by the legally assembled delegates entrusted with the authority of the Haityan people, and in the presence and under the auspices of the Almighty, proclaims the Constitution of the Republic of Haity." (Fig. 18.10.)

—"General Toussaint Louverture, to whom General Leclerc had sent his children to urge him to abandon the cause of the blacks, sends them back after embracing them. The pleas of his wife and his children could not shake his resolve, and he walks away from them telling his children's guardian, who had brought them to him, 'Take back my children since it has to be this way. I wish to be faithful to my brothers and to my God.'" (Fig. 18.11.)

—"Toussaint L'Ouverture dies in the prison of the Castle of Joux in the sole presence of his servant, April 27, 1803. Thus ended the life of a great man. His talents and his virtues earned him the gratitude of his countrymen; posterity will place his name among those of the most virtuous and patriotic generals and legislators." (Fig. 18.12.)

[FIG. 18.8]

Le jeune Ogé déployant l'étendard de la Liberté (1822), drawn by François Grenier, lithograph by Villain. Musée d'Aquitaine. ©Mairie de Bordeaux, photograph by J. M. Arnaud.

[FIG. 18.9]

Entrevue de Toussaint Louverture et du Général Maitland (1821), drawn by François Grenier, lithograph by Villain. Élie Lescot, Jr., Collection, Paris.

[FIG. 18.10]

Toussaint Louverture proclame la constitution de 1801, undated (ca. 1822?), artist unknown, lithograph by Villain. Archives départementales de la Gironde..

[FIG. 18.11]

Entrevue de Toussaint Louverture et de ses enfants, undated (ca. 1822?), artist unknown, lithograph by Villain. Musée d'Aquitaine, ©Mairie de Bordeaux, photograph by J. M. Arnaud.

[FIG. 18.12]

Mort de Toussaint Louverture, undated (ca. 1822?), artist unknown, lithograph by Villain.
Élie Lescot, Jr., Collection, Paris.

Quite obviously, this series of pictures, which may or may not be complete, was ordered by the government, as is attested by the official stamp of the arms of the Republic that they bear. At least one of the images, *The Interview with General Maitland*, dates from 1821.[36] It was signed by François Grenier, as was *The Young Ogé*, which is dated 1822.[37] The others, anonymous, might be dated from the same period—probably from 1822.

Four of the five engravings depict episodes from the life of Toussaint. This cannot fail to catch our attention if we bear in mind how, in the early 1840s, Victor Schoelcher railed against the fate of Toussaint's memory under Boyer's government. Also relevant is historian David Nicholls's meticulous reconstruction of the mulatto elite's consolidation of its hegemony and the subsequent instrumentalizing of color ideology under Boyer.[38] Nevertheless, Fritz Daguillard argues that Boyer was "the first Haitian head of state to celebrate the memory of Louverture. Daguillard further indicates that, as a young officer, Boyer had met Toussaint, who impressed him very much with his dignity and his sense of historical mission."[39] These considerations, however, are not enough to explain the existence of these pictures. A more conclusive political motive needs to be to be found.

These pictures of Toussaint have a precedent. In the villa built by Pétion at Volant-le-Thor (inaugurated on December 24, 1815), which became the property of Joute Lachenais, one could read in the main salon, "written in gold letters, the glorious names of *Ogé, Chavanne, Pinchinat, Bauvais, Lambert, Rigaud, Toussaint Louverture, Villatte*, all descendants of the African race and appearing with honor in our national history, by the side of those Europeans who distinguished themselves by their efforts and their feelings in favor of this race: *Ferrand de Baudière, Raynal, H. Grégoire, Wilberforce.*" This sitting room was "adorned with portraits of four great captains of Antiquity: *Thémistocle, Alexandre, Annibal and César.*"[40] The choice of glorious names from the nation's history is of great significance—they are principally those of mulattoes. The order in which they appear, which in all likelihood is the same order as in the salon inscription, is not fortuitous. Toussaint is in second to last place, ahead of Villate. He is there, nonetheless, and thus made it into the gallery of great men conceived by Pétion. But with the engravings of 1821–1822, it is no longer a simple matter of a name in golden letters confined to a private space. Furthermore, Toussaint is situated after Ogé, credited for being the first to unfurl "the flag of freedom." Toussaint, as a virtuous hero, is thus presented as his successor who pursues the struggle summarized in four stages. He displays a noble character and great loyalty toward General Maitland, whose surrender makes his control of the colony complete. Stubborn, courageous, visionary, Toussaint proclaims the constitution of 1801, the ultimate achievement of his struggle. Resolute and stoic, he chooses, in a last heroic act, his cause over his family. It is a fatal gesture announcing his tragic end; the hero accepts the supreme sacrifice, that of his life. Toussaint is therefore a martyr of freedom and, after Ogé, Haiti's first national hero. It is truly a version of the great national narrative in progress that is being proposed here.

The confrontation between the symbols on the flag held by Ogé and the arms of the Republic placed below the image shows the distance that had been covered. It reconstructs the origin of the struggles and the principles that guided them and the making of their symbols, as well as their end result and its symbolic representation. Interrelationship and evolution can be read into the kinship ties and the specificity of each of the symbols. The constitution of 1801, a decisive document, is represented as already Haitian. Similarly, in the scene representing Toussaint meeting his children, there appears on the wall behind the hero a barely noticeable map, identified not as a map of Saint-Domingue but as a map of Haiti. The explanatory caption of the engraving of Toussaint's death describes him as a great man, a model for his "countrymen" that posterity will have to place among the great generals and the most virtuous and patriotic legislators.

Since he himself did not rank among the leading generals of the War of Independence, Boyer was able, at this time of self-heroization, to designate in an act of publicity Haiti's first two national heroes. The works described above are not great paintings intended for state buildings but lightweight pictures printed in a certain number and therefore destined for distribution.[41] The precise circumstances surrounding the ordering of the pictures, how many were distributed, and by what means, all remain unclear. Yet one thing is certain: this was 1821–1822, a moment dominated by the reunification with the north. How should the newfound unity be celebrated? How could it be expressed in a manner acceptable to everyone, especially when, for the first time, the head of state had not himself been a major figure in the "indigenous army"? Reviving the memory of great figures of the past became imperative. But who should be chosen? At least someone with whom the former opposing parties could identify. Christophe was the tyrant who had just been overthrown and it was hard to remove Dessalines from purgatory, given the complicity in his assassination of the men of the west, chief among them Pétion. The figure of Toussaint was essential. He was the only one who could be offered to the old supporters of Christophe and Dessalines. Boyer would go so far as to more or less identify himself with him by means of a double portrait, effectively a pledge to unite the two colors.[42]

These events were in fact all played out against a background of color ideology, the critical importance of which is revealed in the Darfour affair that occurred, significantly, in 1822, between late August and early September. Darfour, an African journalist practicing in Haiti, sent a petition to the legislature in which he denounced, most notably, the mulattoes' monopoly of power. He was sentenced to death and executed. At the time reunification was being celebrated, it was considered seditious to denounce the use of color ideology. This was a seemingly opportune moment for the Guadeloupe-born artist Guillaume Guillon-Lethière to offer the Haitian government his painting *The Oath of the Ancestors*. Completed in September 1822 and given to President Boyer by the son of the painter at the beginning of 1823, the work celebrates reconciliation, the founding union of blacks and mulattoes, represented by Dessalines and Pétion. In reality, this exceptional gift proved rather out of place. (Fig. 18.13.)

Some questioned the artist's motives with regard to France, where he lived.[43] Emphasis is often put on the fact that France had not yet recognized Haiti's independence, without noting, however, that at the beginning of the 1820s a positive current of opinion was developing, led mostly by merchants who publicly expressed their support for the recognition of Haiti's independence.[44] In 1822, when Lethière produced his painting, some French legislators clearly favored this solution,[45] and he had had plenty of time to adopt this position. But let us focus on how the painting was received. There were three main possible destinations: the presidential palace, the Senate, and the House of Representatives, places where other paintings commissioned by the government were already hung. This painting was offered instead to the metropolitan cathedral. It would be taken back eighty-one years later (a ripe old age!) by the government of Alexis Nord, which hung it in the Palace of the Centennial (or Palace of Independence), a veritable pantheon-museum founded in 1904 to honor the memory of the ancestors, with Dessalines as its dominant theme. In 1918, Father Jean-Marie Jean reclaimed the painting to place it in the brand-new cathedral.[46]

The decision to offer the painting to the metropolitan cathedral seems to signal it was favorably received in that the work was placed in a highly frequented site. Religious life was intense at this time. Furthermore, main political events and national holidays were usually accompanied by religious services. Yet we should note that the Senate and the Chamber of Deputies were also open to the public. There is reason to believe that the government found it difficult to hang in a state building a work that recognized Dessalines as an ancestor and founder of the nation equal to Pétion. They preferred to champion a vision of Pétion that clearly differentiated him from Dessalines as the exclusive father of the nation. As the founder of the republican regime in Haiti, he was thus able to pass from the Father of the Republic to "*the* Father of the Fatherland."

> From March 29 to 31 [following his death in 1818], the body of Pétion remained on display on a ceremonial bed in the great hall of the palace converted into a chapel of rest; and day and night, the people of the city and the countryside came to pray in deep contemplation at the feet of he whom everyone called the Father of the fatherland.[47]

[FIG. 18.13]

Guillaume Guillon-Lethière, *Le serment des ancêtres* (1822), oil painting, 334 × 228.9 cm.
Courtesy of the Musée du Panthéon National Haïtien.

It was only with the fall of Boyer that Dessalines's memory reappeared in the public arena. In his January 1844 speech, the new head of government, Charles Hérard, Sr., declared: "It is to the glorious Dessalines and to his immortal companions that the fatherland owes the new era on which it has embarked. Public teachers, the hope of the country is entrusted to your learning and to your patriotism." Catts Pressoir considers that since then, "the cult of the memory of the founder of the Haitian nation has been indestructible. Already in March 1845," Pressoir notes, "23 citizens of Gonaïves sent an address to the government asking that it join the city's population in commemorating the memory of Dessalines. And the answer was positive."[48] However, the proposition in 1861 to erect a memorial to Dessalines started a heated controversy in the periodical *L'Opinion Nationale*, with color ideology as a backdrop.[49] It then became apparent why a law passed in 1847 concerning the erection of a series of statues celebrating the great figures of national history had not been enforced.[50] This was clearly a sign of the times. In 1872, there could be seen in the National Assembly the portrait of Pétion next to one of Christophe, along with those of John Brown and William Wilberforce.[51] Quite obviously, a change was under way, which is best illustrated by the initiative of President Michel Domingue in 1875 in building a national pantheon. On October 18, 1875, he laid the first stone of the monument in compliance with the March 23 law passed by the National Assembly the same year. The choice of date for this event is quite telling. It was initially chosen for October 17, the anniversary of the death of Dessalines, and then was carried over to the next day. It was around the figure of the first emperor that the pantheon was to be organized, as is attested by the speech made on this occasion by Thomas Madiou. October 17 was no longer a shameful date, marking the end of tyranny; Dessalines was rehabilitated in official memory. Madiou strongly supported this position. "Let us show that we have a memory," he said; "it is time we did so. We of this century shall not incur the reproach of posterity which, in repairing our wrongs, would not fail to pass judgment on us." It was "a duty," Madiou stressed, to talk about Dessalines, "the man of the past, the serf who became an emperor."[52]

> Giant of Antiquity, he raised his monument by sweat and blood alone. His work is the result of this profound conviction that only independence would make the people of our island happy. He slew all those who, even among his own, resisted his efforts. Never backing away from any obstacle, he remained inflexible on every occasion that he had to strike. Shuddering with horror and admiration, we do not know whether to condemn or absolve him. Moral standards condemn him, but does not the logic of public salvation cleanse him from blame? The enemies of independence saw in him a merciless being. The very incarnation of the principle of freedom, he was barbaric in the face of colonial barbarism.[53]

Madiou ended his speech by announcing that "the remains of DESSALINES and those of PETION . . . will be solemnly transferred [to the pantheon] and those two principal heroes of Independence lying close to each other, will form the symbol of our indissoluble union." The memorial, which was ordered, could not be erected. Nevertheless, the collective state of mind had changed and in official memory, the Haitian national pantheon was from then on composed of its most important figures. Lethière's painting found its full legitimacy once again. Alexis Nord would hang it some years later in the Palace of the Centennial.

The five engravings and the painting of Lethière follow the principle decreed by Lessing according to which the activity of the painter consists less in the choice of the subject than in the choice of the moment, the "pregnant" moment where the past is summarized and the future is announced. Each of the pictures presents a moment deemed significant, which makes heroes out of actors on a stage, offering them as a model to the community.

Considered in its totality, the series of engravings presents an obvious unity. The desire of those who commissioned it to present a coherent story partly accounts for this. Other factors contribute as well: the stamp of the lithograph, the fact that all the images bear the arms of the Republic and that four of them depict the same hero. There is also the structure of the images, at least of the first four, where a hero is confronted with a group and there is a great deal of expressiveness in gestures and attitudes.

The first two episodes, which are the only ones that are signed, are attributed to the same artist. Some characteristics are common to all: main character versus group; meeting on a threshold (tent, shore); an expanse (camp, ocean); the clothing and poses of the heroes virtually identical. Evidently the posture of the speakers differs; Ogé is greeted as a savior, even with some attitudes of entreaty and gazes directed toward the sky. Those same gestures are found in the pictures of the proclamation of the constitution and of the meeting of Toussaint and his sons. Note that the action in this last picture also takes place on a doorstep (although on the inside, where a departure is suggested, whereas the other two cases concern an arrival).

These two episodes drawn by Grenier chronologically preceded the others, but were the pictures drawn first? Did they serve as models for the others? There are similarities in Toussaint's facial features in the five engravings, but with certain nuances. The face of the Toussaint with his family is quite close to that of the figure at the Fort de Joux, but it differs noticeably from that of the hero proclaiming the constitution, and this seems due to the artist's personal touch. This picture's different construction is revealed in comparing the woman with child seated in the right foreground with the wife in the family scene. The drawing is less angular, the volume more pronounced and better rendered. One can see it in the more ample modeling of the anatomy and the greater mastery in the treatment of the drapery.

This female figure, which we find again in *L'esclave révolté* by Mlle Rollet, is a constituent element of the neoclassic staging of heroism: the imploring or weeping woman facing the stoic attitude of the man responding to his civic duty. The scene where Toussaint meets his children is therefore typical of this device, a stylistic trait that stands out better when the picture is compared to another dealing with the same subject. (Fig. 18.14.)

The artist carries out a compression of time to give the chosen moment all its dramatic intensity. There were two meetings between Toussaint and his sons, Isaac and Placide. The first occurred in the presence of their tutor, Coisnon, who was delivering a message from Napoleon. In the second, Coisnon was absent and it was his sons who delivered a letter from General Leclerc, provoking Toussaint to ask them to choose between him and France. The picture synthesizes the two meetings by showing us Coisnon witnessing the pleas to Toussaint by his wife and children. The historian Beaubrun Ardouin was very cautious about that scene, which could have been embellished by Pamphile de Lacroix, who reported it. Authentic or not, it provided the elements for endowing Toussaint with the stature of a Classical hero, a real Brutus choosing the homeland in spite of, and at the expense of, the family. It was a necessary and decisive act befitting the founder of a nation—as is attested by the map of Haiti on the wall behind the hero.

The Toussaint of François Grenier (the meeting with Maitland) shows a very different perspective. If the accent is on virtue, there is in all likelihood no reference to a model of Classical drama. This is subtle heroism without heartbreak, taken right out of daily life, that of a military leader on campaign, of course, but one who is already a victor. We find examples in Grenier's series *Conquests and Victories*, devoted to Napoleon Bonaparte, from which the artist borrows many an element for his Toussaint: the confrontation of the figures, their poses, their attitudes, and the landscape.[54]

In the work of Lethière, a Neoclassical painter, we find diverse influences. From a general standpoint, he would be closer to Poussin than he is to David, although it is David whom he emulates. The God who blesses in his *Oath of the Ancestors* was supposedly inspired by an element of the monumental décor of the Annunziata chapel in Rome's Quirinal Palace attributed to Guido Reni (1611). And in the background of the painting, one glimpses some hints of Goya. However, the principal elements of revolutionary symbolism are present, beginning with the work's title. There is, in fact, no evidence of a pledge between Pétion and Dessalines, and to judge from the dictionaries of Moïse and Oriol, the circumstances of their meeting have not been clearly determined.[55] As with *The Oath of the Horatii*, the oath as such cannot be found in the historical record. Yet the title sounds accurate. The custom of pledging was common during the revolutionary period, in France as in Saint-Domingue. The title is not only plausible, it also forcefully

TOUSSAINT LOUVERTURE REÇOIT
UNE LETTRE DE BONAPARTE.

Tom. III.

[FIG. 18.14]

Toussaint Louverture reçoit une lettre de Bonaparte, in Georges Le Gorgeu, *Étude sur Jean-Baptiste Coisnon: Toussaint Louverture et Jean-Baptiste Coisnon* (Paris, 1881), engraving with watercolor from a previous original; artist unknown. Élie Lescot, Jr., Collection, Paris.

expresses and felicitously synthesizes the coalition of forces in the making, which proved decisive in Haiti's war of independence. Lethière discovered here a founding moment equivalent to David's *Serment du Jeu de paume*.

Lethière does not fail to evoke the allegory of fraternity as it was portrayed during the revolution. His painting also recalls the black figure dashing toward the president of the Assembly in the drawing by Monsiau (or Thévenin), and the reference to David is obvious because of the three figures in the foreground of the *Serment du Jeu de paume* and because of its drapery blown by the wind that Lethière evokes.

But why this divine figure of the God who blesses? It constitutes one of the elements of the three-part device of the allegorical figure of fraternity. Lethière perhaps found it more convenient to place the "colored brothers" under the protection of Yahweh rather than under that of a Greco-Roman goddess, especially as the Haitians never ceased to present themselves as Christians in their constitutions and elsewhere. Moreover, the God who blesses also appears in one of the five engravings of 1821–1822, that depicting Toussaint's proclamation of his constitution. In his speech on that occasion, July 18, 1801, Toussaint declared:

> Oh, my fellow citizens of all ages, of all states, and of all colors, you are free, and the constitution which was given to me today will eternalize your liberty! Let us first bow down before the Creator of the Universe to thank him for such a precious gift. . . . This constitution guarantees each individual the enjoyment of his rights. It demands from each citizen the practice of virtue, just as it summons to our land the rule of morality and the divine religion of Jesus Christ. . . . For my part, I promise under the eyes of heaven, to do all in my power, if God allows me, to preserve the unity, peace, and public tranquility, and therefore the happiness of my fellow citizens. I promise to execute what is prescribed to me by the colonial constitution. Swear likewise, before the Supreme Being and before me, that you will submit to these laws which will bring you happiness and consolidate your freedom.[56]

After Toussaint spoke, the president of the Le Cap civil court made a speech, and then everyone went to church. The Constitution of 1801 was proclaimed under the auspices of divine protection; this is what the engraving is intended to show. It may well be that Lethière had seen this picture printed in France, probably before September 1822.

Lethière places the two protagonists of his painting at the center of the altar of the fatherland, where a stela stands, at the foot of which lies the chain of bondage, broken, and trampled on like the Serpent of Discord in the allegory of fraternity. The platform rises above a camp and some combatants witness the oath. The brothers-in-arms seem to be without any control over their decision and their action. They are not faithfully shaking hands as the two figures do in the foreground of *Le Serment du Jeu de paume*. They are not looking at each other, nor do they embrace. They touch with their eyes turned heavenward listening to and, it would seem, repeating the oath decreed by the Almighty. The inscriptions on the stela appear to reveal the contents of the oath. The following words can be read: Freedom, Religion, Laws, Constitution." One can make out "Strength through unity," "Live free or die."

In many ways, the painting is in perfect resonance with the engraving of the episode of 1801: the eyes turned toward heaven, the figures behind the altar of the fatherland and those placed behind the general-in-chief and the prelate, as well as the fact that Lethière's painting concerns laws and a constitution. The arms of the Republic are visible on the *sabretache* of the black forefather; like those appearing on the engravings, they write the painting into the national history. The episode of 1801, an official picture, might well have encouraged Lethière in his decision to place the scene under divine authority, to clearly signify the sacred dimension of the foundational union in the eyes of the Haitian authorities.

Haitian revolutionary symbolism derives essentially from *anticomanie*, an obsessive interest in the rhetorical codes of Classical art. Introduced initially as a simple extension of the metropolitan revolutionary ideal into the colonial space, this system of symbols would be actively appropriated because it served as a vehicle for the great principles of which the struggles taking place in Haiti promised full realization. The victory over the French troops was instantly understood for its universal implications. These helped to ground the defense of the new state, which was an unwelcome arrival in a world that was still colonialist and proslavery. One can therefore appreciate what was at stake in the pictures commissioned by the Haitian authorities as opposed to those created through the initiative of foreigners.

A final example is provided by President Boyer's acceptance of Charles X's decree that recognized Haiti as independent, which inspired a series of engravings authorized by the French government.[57] This still-unstudied corpus includes many portraits of Boyer himself. Two deserve attention. One shows the president greeting the delegation charged with bringing him the edict. It depicts a supplicatory Boyer, in distinct contrast to *Son Excellence Jean-Pierre Boyer, président de la République d'Haïti, en grand costume*, a work commissioned from Barincou. A lithography of this work, executed by Langlumé, was put on sale November 5, 1825. Another picture, signed A. Cheyère, had appeared earlier on September 3, 1825, and simply bears the title of *Indépendance d'Haïti*. It echoes other pieces from the corpus and would merit a lengthy commentary. Let us simply note how it evokes Rouvier's engraving of 1789. (Figs. 18.15 and 18.16.)

[**Fig. 18.15**]

Le 11 juillet 1825. L'ordonnance de S. M. Charles X qui reconnut l'indépendance d'Haïti, est reçue par le Président Boyer, aux acclamations de toutes les classes d'habitans de l'Ile, undated, drawn by C. Develly, Musée de Bordeaux, photograph by J. M. Arnaud.

INDÉPENDANCE D'HAÏTI.

[FIG. 18.16]

Indépendance d'Haïti, September 3, 1825, artist unknown, lithograph by A. Cheyère.
Élie Lescot, Jr., Collection, Paris.

But even the works ordered by the Haitian authorities were subject to internal political constraints. With an official national memory in the making, it was impossible to avoid internecine struggles, and political interests dictated how the past would be manipulated. This was occurring even as public memory was crystallizing around the cult of freedom, notably in the context of designating the heroic figures who were to embody this cult. The case of Lethière's painting is emblematic in this regard. The work quite obviously bespeaks great friendship for Haiti, and it may have been conceived in a moment of enthusiasm for the country's reunification. Yet it originated, when all is said and done, in a misunderstanding; for Dessalines was still languishing in the antechamber of Haiti's national pantheon.

Notes

1. See, among others, Claude Mossé, *L'Antiquité dans la Révolution française* (Paris, 1989).

2. Beaubrun Ardouin, *Études sur l'histoire d'Haïti*, 11 vols., ed. François Dalencour (1853–1860; Port-au-Prince, 1958), 2:43. Ardouin's italics.

3. It is important to note a difference between the engravings printed in the English and Dutch editions. Only Roman numerals appear on the stelae in the English edition, shown here, whereas a text is suggested in the Dutch version. See Marcus Rainsford, *An Historical Account of the Black Empire of Hayti* (London, 1805), and *St. Domingo, of Het Land der Zwarten in Hayti en Deszelfs omwenteling* (Amsterdam, 1806), vol. 1, pl. 2, between 376 and 377. Vergniaud Leconte was inspired by the 1805 version (*Henri Christophe dans l'histoire d'Haïti* [Paris, 1931], pl. 2, between 24 and 25), and this is the one reproduced in Michèle Oriol, *Images de la Révolution à Saint-Domingue* (Port-au-Prince, 1992), 69.

4. Report by Marec quoted in Victor Schoelcher, *Vie de Toussaint-Louverture* (1889; Paris, 1982), 191.

5. Pamphile de Lacroix, cited in Schoelcher, *Vie de Toussaint-Louverture*, 311.

6. Schoelcher, *Vie de Toussaint-Louverture*, 191–192.

7. Edmond Mangonès, "Numismatique haïtienne," *Cahiers d'Haïti* 3 (October 1943): 24–27, and 5 (December 1943): 58–61.

8. See the reproduction of two engravings by Jean-Baptiste Chapuy based on this painting in *Regards sur les Antilles. Collection Marcel Chatillon* (Bordeaux, 1999), 229–230nn183–184.

9. *Regards sur les Antilles*, 225.

10. According to an explanatory note on the portrait (printed on the cover) in Marcel Dorigny, ed., *Léger-Félicité Sonthonax. La première abolition de l'esclavage. La Révolution française et la Révolution de Saint-Domingue* (Saint-Denis/Paris, 1997). The picture is therefore slightly anachronistic, since it concerns an event that took place under the Convention.

11. On the flag or flags of the Indigenous Army, see Claude B. Auguste et Marcel B. Auguste, *Pour le drapeau. Contribution à la recherche sur les couleurs haïtiennes* (Quebec, 1982).

12. Following the capitulation and evacuation of French troops, a "Preliminary declaration of independence" was signed on 29 November 1803, to use the expression of H. Pauléus Sannon (*Histoire de Toussaint Louverture* [1933; Port-au-Prince, 2003], 3:288). For an updated commentary on this first proclamation of independence, see Leslie F. Manigat, "Une brève analyse-commentaire critique d'un document historique. Esquisse d'une analyse de texte historique: la première proclamation officielle et publique de notre indépendance," *Revue de la Société Haïtienne d'Histoire et de Géographie* 221 (avril–juin 2005): 44–56.

13. See especially Thomas Madiou, *Histoire d'Haïti* (1847–1848; Port-au-Prince: Éditions Henri Deschamps, 1988–1989), 3:142–153.

14. Carlo A. Célius, "Les enjeux de la représentation. Portraits de noirs et de mulâtres pendant la révolution à Saint-Domingue (1789–1804)," in *Negros, Mulatos, Zambaigos. Derroteros africanos en los mundos ibéricos*, ed. Bertas Ares Queija and Alessandro Stella (Seville, 2000), 313–360.

15. See, among others, Mossé, *L'Antiquité dans la Révolution française*.

16. Madiou, *Histoire d'Haïti*, 4:308. The celebration did not take place. Having heard the news of the nomination of new deputies according to procedures that did not suit him, Boyer rushed back to Port-au-Prince without informing the local authorities who were waiting for him.

17. See Léon Montès, *La timbrologie haïtienne, 1881–1954* (Port-au-Prince, 1954), 21–30.

18. Madiou, *Histoire d'Haïti*, 5:337–338.

19. Madiou, *Histoire d'Haïti*, 5:338.

20. Victor Schœlcher, *Colonies étrangères et Haïti. Résultats de l'émancipation anglaise* (Paris, 1842–1843), 1:175.

21. Antoine Augustin, *1804–1904. Les fêtes du centenaire aux Gonaïves* (Port-au-Prince, 1905), 49–53.

22. Ardouin, *Études sur l'histoire d'Haïti*, 8:92–93.

23. Madiou, *Histoire d'Haïti*, 6:306–307.

24. See Daniel Élie, "Le Palais national au coeur de l'architecture néoclassique," in Georges Corvington, *Le Palais national de la République d'Haïti* (Port-au-Prince, 2003), 115–127.

25. Georges Corvington, *Port-au-Prince au cours des ans. Tome II. La métropole haïtienne du XIXe siècle, 1804–1915* (Montreal, 2003), 103.

26. See Stephen Alexis, *Catalogue du Musée national* (Port-au-Prince 1941); Luc Dorsinville, *Catalogue du Musée national d'après le dernier inventaire* (Port-au-Prince, 1953).

27. According to the historian of Port-au-Prince, Georges Corvington, these marble and bronze statues were a loan from the Metropolitan Museum of Art in New York, renewable every three months, granted to Haiti for the Bicentennial Exposition (celebrating the founding of Port-au Prince). In the 1960s almost all the works were taken back by the museum because of the state of neglect they were in.

28. See "Loi sur l'instruction publique," in *Recueil général des lois & actes du Gouvernement d'Haïti depuis la proclamation de son indépendance jusqu'à nos jours*, ed. Linstant de Pradine (1818–1823; Paris, 1860), 3:290–297. See especially Sténio Vincent et L. C. Lhérisson, *La législation de l'instruction publique en Haïti (1804–1895)* (Paris, 1895).

29. Madiou, *Histoire d'Haïti*, 5:339.

30. See "La proclamation du Général en chef adressée au peuple," January 1, 1804, in Madiou, *Histoire d'Haïti*, 3:146.

31. Madiou, *Histoire d'Haïti*, 3:291–292.

32. See the description of the funeral in Madiou, *Histoire d'Haïti*, 5:484–489.

33. A type of flat bag which hung from the belt of certain cavalry uniforms.

34. The Duplessis catalogue of the print department of the National Library of France has thirteen portraits of Boyer, one of which dates from 1820, six from 1825, one from 1841, and one from 1857. The remaining four are not dated. *Catalogue de la collection des portraits français et étrangers conservée au Département des estampes de la Bibliothèque Nationale rédigé par Georges Duplessis* (Paris, 1897), 2:55. The number of portraits of Boyer dating from 1825 rises to nine in the *Bibliographie de la France*, which contains announcements published weekly from November 1811 until the end of 1830. The notices are transcribed in George D. McKee, *Introduction to the Image of France, an Index of the Record of Prints Authorized for Public Distribution, 1811–1830*, available at http://humanities.uchicago.edu/orgs/ARTFL.

35. Barincou fils, *La République d'Haïti renaissant de ses cendres. Sujet allégorique d'un tableau national* (Paris, 1821). The text is published and commented on by Carlo A. Célius, "La République d'Haïti renaissant de ses cendres (1821). Un tableau historique de Barincou fils," *Pour Haïti* 44 (April–June 2003): 32–39. A revised and extended version was published in issue of the *Revue de la Société Haïtienne d'Histoire et de Géographie* 220 (January–March 2005): 29–43.

36. M 24 3046, Estampes, Bibliotheque Nationale de France (hereafter BN).

37. M 24 2947, Estampes, BN.

38. David Nicholls, *From Dessalines to Duvalier. Race, Colour and National Independence in Haiti* (London, 1979).

39. Fritz Daguillard, *Mystérieux dans la Gloire. Enigmatic in his Glory. Toussaint Louverture (1743–1803)* (Port-au-Prince, 2003), 44.

40. Ardouin, *Études sur l'histoire d'Haïti*, 8:66.

41. If the distribution of the pictures has yet to be well documented, it is, in any event, attested to since the colonial period. It was common in the field of religion. In the political domain there is the well-known case of the portrait of Vincent Ogé, which was sent from Paris to be distributed everywhere in the colony so he could be recognized and arrested. See Célius, "Les enjeux de la représentation."

42. It is very likely that the double portrait came after the series being examined here. The face of Toussaint bears a resemblance to a "portrait" of him done to illustrate the travel narrative of Alcide D'Orbigny in America (Oriol, *Images de la Révolution à Saint-Domingue*, 76). It is similar in inspiration to the famous Toussaint by Maurin (see Célius, "Les enjeux de la representation"), whereas the traits of the Toussaint of the official series should be compared to those of one of the "portraits" of Bonneville and some others from 1802. One notes, even so, that the figure's general traits are not too different from those of Ogé.

43. For further information on Lethière and other interpretations of the painting, see Geneviève Capy, "Guillaume Guillon-Lethière" (Thèse de doctorat, Université de Paris-Sorbonne, 1998); *Le serment des ancêtres, Guillaume Guillon-Lethière, Sainte-Anne (Guadeloupe), 1760–Paris, 1832*, textes de Christiane Naffah, Geneviève Capy, Florent

Laballe, Florence Delteil, Jean-François Bardez. Document de présentation du tableau après restauration par le laboratoire du Louvre, du 4 février au 9 mars 1998, Musée du Louvre, Hall Napoléon; Mario Valdes, "Guillaume Guillon-Lethière," available at http://www.pbs.org/wgbh/pages/frontline/shows/secret/famous/lethiere.html. See also Helen Weston, "The Oath of the Ancestors by Lethière "le mulâtre": Celebrating the Black/Mulatto Alliance in Haiti's Struggle for Independence," in *An Economy of Colour: Visual culture and the Atlantic world, 1660–1830*, ed. Geoff Quilled and Kay Dian Kriz (Manchester, 2003), 176–195.

44. Leslie Manigat, "Une occasion perdue: la reconnaissance de l'indépendance haïtienne par la France était possible en 1821," in *Éventail d'histoire vivante. Des préludes à la Révolution de Saint-Domingue jusqu'à nos jours (1789–1999). Une contribution à "la Nouvelle Histoire" haïtienne. Traité d'Histoire d'Haïti* (Port-au-Prince, 2001), 1:261–277.

45. Madiou, *Histoire d'Haïti*, 6:312–318.

46. Georges Corvington, *Port-au-Prince au cours des ans. La capitale d'Haïti sous l'occupation 1915–1922* (Port-au-Prince, 1984), 271. In an earlier publication, Corvington evokes the painting of Lethière, which he situated behind the master altar of the cathedral: *Port-au-Prince au cours des ans. La métropole haïtienne du XIXe siècle, 1804–1888* (Port-au-Prince, 1974), 63–64. This was repeated in Michel-Philippe Lerebours, *Haïti et ses peintres de 1804 à 1980. Souffrances et espoirs d'un peuple* (Port-au-Prince, 1989), 1:103 and 123n56. However, the authors of *Le serment des ancêtres* commented, "Before 1991, the existence of the painting was known only to a few historians but, since 1900, neither it nor its provenance have ever really been identified." [39] (citing *Le Nouvelliste*, Port-au-Prince, June 29, 1900).

47. Madiou, *Histoire d'Haïti*, 5:486.

48. Catts Pressoir, *L'enseignement de l'histoire en Haïti* (Mexico, 1950), 30.

49. Nicholls, *From Dessalines to Duvalier*, 86.

50. See Justin Dévot, *Le centenaire de l'indépendance nationale d'Haïti* (Paris, 1901).

51. Edgar La Selve, *Le pays des nègres. Voyage à Haïti ancienne partie française de Saint-Domingue* (Paris, 1881), 231.

52. Thomas Madiou, "Documents inédits: Thomas Madiou rend hommage à l'Empereur. Pose de la première pierre d'un Panthéon national par le président Domingue, le 18 octobre 1875," *Revue de la société haïtienne d'histoire et de géographie* 145 (décembre 1984): 10.

53. Madiou, "Documents inédits."

54. See, for example, François Grenier, *Victoires et conquêtes* (Paris, 1818), Ie-36-fol., Estampes, BN, *Affaire dans le camp anglais* (XIV, 54) or *Affaire sur la côte de Damiette* (XII, 114), for the trees, tents, and the panorama in its entirety. See *Retour de Bonaparte au Kaire* for the same elements but also for the meeting of the leader and a group; and *Bataille de Millesimo* (V, 181) for the figure who is keeping guard behind Toussaint.

55. Compare the entries on Pétion and Dessalines in Claude Moïse, ed., *Dictionnaire historique de la Révolution haïtienne (1789–1804)* (Montréal, 2003); Michèle Oriol, *Histoire et dictionnaire de la Révolution et de l'indépendance d'Haïti* (Port-au-Prince, 2002).

56. Sannon, *Histoire de Toussaint Louverture*, 3:29–30.

57. See George D. McKee, *Introduction to the Image of France*.

Epilogue

Robin Blackburn

WITH THIS FINE VOLUME AND SEVERAL OTHER RECENT COLLECTIONS ON THE HAITIAN REVOLUTION AND RELATED TOPICS, PLUS NEW SINGLE-AUTHORED STUDIES, THE "SILENCING" OF HAITI'S PAST has ended.[1] Of course there was always a literature on Haiti and its revolution, one to which Haitian historians themselves made an important contribution. The "silencing" had more to do with the near-absence of Saint-Domingue, the slave uprisings, and the Haitian Revolution from general accounts of the revolutionary epoch and, on the occasions they did gain a mention, the resort to a few hackneyed stereotypes that denied to Haitian history the meaning and resonance that attached to other struggles for independence and freedom.[2] The revolts in Saint-Domingue and Haiti confronted the Atlantic governments with revealing contrasts between their principles and the realities of slavery, racism, and colonialism. There was much moral capital at stake and few in the civilized world were disposed to award it to Haiti.[3]

It is still too early to say how Haiti will figure in the textbooks reflecting the new Atlantic history, but one can be fairly sure it will not be ignored. There could even be a danger that icons of the black revolution will be adopted simply as a new symbol of political correctness, with little substantive connection to what was truly remarkable and revolutionary. Fortunately the excellent research and the fresh argument of the present volume are animated by a quite different spirit and will serve, should it be necessary, as an antidote.

Jacques de Cauna vividly sketches the context of the New World's richest slave colony, its moldering sugar works and aqueducts still visible today (about which more below). At the center of the volume is the simple fact that this was the setting for the largest and most successful slave revolt in history, one which was consolidated by general emancipation and the birth of a new state based on this liberation. Anyone tempted by the thought that such a colony was bound eventually to explode in freedom would, however, soon discover their error. While there are pre-revolutionary intimations of a dormant volcano, there is abundant evidence of busy people, both statesmen and private citizens, who seemingly could not imagine a future without property in slaves. As late as June 1793, the official subsidy to slave traders was still being paid and slaves were still being advertised for sale in the official press.

Saint-Domingue's royal officials and *habitants* warned one another that they were perched on barrels of gunpowder, but the very fear of revolt and racial mayhem helped to cement every New World slave system. David Geggus insists on the striking absence of large-scale slave revolts or conspiracies in Saint-Domingue for several decades prior to 1791. French planters and officials may also have been misled by the actual absence of slave uprisings during the Independence War in North America (escapes were less visible and less disturbing). Sometimes colonists who warned of danger referred to conflicts within the free population rather than, in the first instance, to the threat of slave revolt.

Several studies here underline the special position of the free people of color. The very tangible evidence that Dominique Rogers supplies of the social integration of free people of color, notwithstanding colonial racism, has large implications, as does the evidence supplied by John Garrigus for not only a wealthy colored planter class but also a regional subculture of black or mulatto military experience in the North. The growing significance of the free people of color had also sparked racializing resistance from self-described "American patriots," something that could make *anciens libres* welcome metropolitan recognition (April 1792) at one stage and the ending of slavery at another.

If some of these outstanding essays bring home the political potential of the free people of color and, by extension, the creoles, others stress the huge African component of the ultimately successful revolution. The African-born were, after all, in a majority among the slave population. They supplied many, perhaps most, grassroots leaders and soldiers at every stage, but especially in the resistance to Napoleon in 1802–1803. Carolyn Fick makes the argument and supplies the names.

Intense factional disputes within the colonial elite gave an opening to the great slave uprising of August 1791. Yves Benot's illuminating account of the ideas animating the uprising is sadly one of the last texts written by this valiant historian, who died in 2005 at the age of eighty-five. For decades, and sometimes almost single-handedly, Benot challenged the reluctance of French historians to register the huge significance of Saint-Domingue and Haiti for France itself, let alone for the rest of the world.[4] Benot's study of surviving accounts of the uprising in the north highlights a very significant phrase, one that echoes revolts in other parts of the colony. The leaders proclaim their intention to "seize the country," echoing a French soldier's letter, quoted by Carolyn Fick, that said of rebels in the south: "They come and treat us as if we were the brigands and tell us: '*nous après tandé zaute*,' which is to say, 'we had expected you, and we will cut off your heads to the last man; this land is not for you; it is for us.'"[5]

But with his customary scruple, Benot is not constructing a picturesque *image d'Épinal* of the slave rebel. These leaders had not yet committed themselves to ending slavery and many were willing to enlist with a Spanish monarch who upheld it. In the first year or two very tangible objectives—such as three free days a week, the freedom of this person or that, the fate of this garden or plot—had more purchase and meaning than French legal categories. But the notion of kingship and a willingness to exploit it for a variety of ends were, as Gene Ogle explains, common to African and French political culture. The willingness of the rebels to invoke the king against local masters, unworthy officials, and racist colonists is not difficult to understand.

Despite the occasional presence of the fleur-de-lys, the diffuse royalism of the black leaders is not easily interpreted as fidelity to a particular king. The French republicans who so persistently sought to portray the slave rebellion as a traitorous Vendée, as Ghachem recounts, were dupes of their own conceit if they failed to notice that the British—the Republic's most dangerous enemy—responded in a very different way toward these two revolts, encouraging the Vendée in France while attempting to put down the slave uprising at the cost of the lives of thousands of British soldiers. Jeremy Popkin quotes an observation by the deputy Garran-Coulon, who admitted that slave rebels might have an agenda of their own: "One would have to have little understanding of human nature, if one were to believe that ... the blacks needed any other inspiration than that irresistible impulsion of all living beings which ... speaks perhaps even more to the hearts of those who are closest to nature."

Beneath the legal and political terminology was the reality of a massively exploitative slave system, a system that exposed any black or colored person to abuse and that was only held in place by force—that of the militia, *maréchaussée*, overseers, and elite slaves, including slave drivers. Once a degree of disorder reigned, the reliability of the slave elite was likely to vanish. Eventually all political actors had to explain whether they wished to maintain, reform, or abolish this regime.

Most abolitionists and black leaders, including two key actors, Sonthonax and Toussaint, wished to replace slavery with other work disciplines and guarantees of future plantation labor. The philosopher Condorcet himself had insisted as much in his 1781 scheme of emancipation—and his measures for ending slavery were extraordinarily timid and protracted.[6] The grandeur of Sonthonax and Toussaint is that they were willing, as no abolitionist had been before, to end slavery immediately, without delay, compromise, or compensation. The fact that they committed themselves to general emancipation separately but on the same day—29 August 1793—points to a common inspiration, namely the great assembly of the Commune at Le Cap on 25 August and its vote for general emancipation.[7]

Elizabeth Colwill supplies us with a series of superbly vivid tableaux that culminate in this crucial turning point: the civil commissioners' shunning of Governor Galbaud, their celebration of interracial conviviality, the republican marriages, Galbaud's recoil from these transgressive events, and the parade of the Republican forces in Le Cap (100 whites, 300 mulattoes, and 6,000 blacks). A fascinating detail here is that Sonthonax was still making minor adjustments to the offer of freedom through matrimony only a week before the adoption of general emancipation by the great assembly. These assemblies were often stage-managed. Perhaps this one was not or perhaps the commissioner himself went for the strong solution at the last moment. In any event, the assembly of some 15,000 new and old citizens on the 25th called for general emancipation, leaving Sonthonax and Toussaint to echo it on the 29th.

While these events and pronouncements have their own powerful significance, they do so partly because they point us elsewhere—to what was happening in the countryside, hills, and towns throughout the colony. The appearance of Eugénie on the commissioner's arm, the oath taken by the African commander Louis Pierrot in the colonial capital, the rescue of Sonthonax by Jean-Baptiste Belley and his men, and the parades and concerts in Le Cap all signal the emergence of a new racial order in response to counterrevolution, the British threat, and the surging tide of slave revolt. Yet it was far from inevitable that the Republic would catch this tide rather than being crushed by it. The sweeping proclamations and the insistent ceremonies were devices for transforming both the Republic and the slave insurgency. They were tributes to the pressure of the slave rebellion but, as such, they were still very incomplete—the Convention had not spoken—and the commissioners were in competition with Toussaint's simultaneous appeal for the ending of slavery.

Jeremy Popkin is surely right to draw attention to the Convention's decision to seat black and brown representatives from Saint-Domingue. These delegates had been arrested at the prompting of so-called patriots, and their release and seating itself represented a blow to the upholders of slavery and the "aristocracy of the skin." These decisions led directly to the debate on, and passage of, the motion of 16 Pluviôse to do away with slavery in the French colonies. This was certainly another transformative moment and one that was once again overdetermined by the insurgency. There are rare occasions when a text redefines context and subtext because it is establishing a new horizon.

The motion of the Convention read as follows: "The National Convention declares slavery abolished in all the colonies. In consequence it declares that all men, without distinction of color, domiciled in the colonies, are French citizens and will enjoy all the rights assured under the Constitution." The words perhaps say less than they appear to. Since the Constitution was suspended, the precise import of the last promise was not clear, while the phrase "domiciled in the colonies" could be linked, via regulations that had already been reported, to continuing labor obligations. But while some dubious proslavery patriots may have comforted themselves with such interpretations, the plain meaning of the motion is what counts and what counted at the time.[8] It was an offer of alliance to the black insurgents and to the sizeable slave populations of the colonial territories still controlled by the royalist planters and their allies, the British.[9] The decree was understood in this way by Toussaint when he declared for the Republic a few months later. Governor Laveaux's promotion of the black general, the sending of 30,000 muskets from France, and the offensive of the forces of Victor Hugues in the Eastern Caribbean all helped to spell out the meaning of the decree of 16 Pluviôse.

It has always been clear that the French commitment to revolutionary emancipation gained support because it constituted a response to the large-scale British expedition to seize the French islands. But it cannot be dismissed as mere realpolitik. While emancipation fitted well with resistance to Britain, it also posed a great strategic risk—that of antagonizing the "sister republic," the United States, France's erstwhile ally. Some of the hesitations of Robespierre and the Committee of Public Safety about enforcing the decree may have stemmed from this consideration, although the blind spots of republican discourse and the obsession with plots also contributed. Whatever the case, the Committee of Public Safety was showing boldness, not narrow calculation, when it swiftly dispatched an expedition conveying the decree of 16 Pluviôse to the New World.

France's antislavery offensive lasted for a relatively brief period, from mid-1794 to late 1799, with a few wobbles. Given its boldness, the surprise should be that it lasted so long. The Directory, notwithstanding the predictable hostility of the United States, backed the emancipationist strategy and reappointed Sonthonax. The radical antislavery policy gave a vital breathing space to the new black power in Saint-Domingue and inflicted large-scale losses on Britain. British losses in the Eastern Caribbean were as great as in Saint-Domingue, and Britain lost more troops in the Caribbean than in Europe. If the British had not been defeated or if the Republic had not backed emancipation, perhaps the new black power would have triumphed anyway. But this is far from certain. Slavery did continue within the British-occupied part of Saint-Domingue. Systems of slavery have usually survived, though not unscathed, even after huge revolts, such as those associated with Spartacus or the Zanj in eighth-century Mesopotamia.

But if the Republic should be given its due, the cause of black emancipation still had to triumph against it in its perverted Napoleonic form. As Benot and Fick make clear, the black revolt contained germs of independence from the outset. Toussaint's agreement with General Maitland on British withdrawal, his acceptance of U.S. aid in crushing Rigaud, and his constitution of 1801 were acts of independence. Yet it remains significant that Toussaint did not declare a formal breach with the French republic—not even in his last battle with Leclerc.

Nationalism has generally not been very strong in the Caribbean, and where it exists it has often been tinged with universalism and filled with social content. Hence Aimé Césaire and the "overseas departments," Frantz Fanon or, in the Anglophone Caribbean, C. L. R. James and Eric Williams, and a variety of labor parties that testify to the worker militancy of the late colonial era. In the Spanish-speaking Caribbean, we have Simón Bolívar and Fidel Castro, on the one hand, and Puerto Rico with its anarchists, nationalists, and status as an "associated state," on the other. Toussaint's intransigence regarding slavery but willingness to accept the French link is, perhaps, of a piece. The Caribbean still has many colonies yet is also the source of the most ambitious anti-imperial ideas.

Can we pinpoint the historic moment when a new principle of human rights became embodied in a state? Florence Gauthier has urged that the decisive moment came with Toussaint's response to Napoleon's first attempt to deceive him and the people of Saint-Domingue by insisting that he recognized their liberty. Louverture responded: "It is not an ad hoc liberty, conceded simply to ourselves, that we wish; it is the absolute commitment to the principle that any man, whether born red, black or white, cannot become the property of another such man."[10] This principle was enshrined in Toussaint's constitution of 1801. But Toussaint himself did not get round to suppressing slavery in the eastern half of the island prior to the arrival of Leclerc. So this leaves us with the founding of the Republic of Haiti in 1804, after which, whatever the very great problems that Haitians had to contend with, slavery really had been defeated, never to return.

If Napoleon had been willing to accept black freedom and a large measure of colonial autonomy, he would have avoided a humiliating defeat and might have made great gains. Consider the following. In 1798, Mississippi's territorial governor, Winthrop Sergeant, warned Secretary of State Pickering that if France regained Louisiana, "a few French Troops with a Cordial cooperation of the Spanish Creoles, and arms put into the hands of Negroes, would be formidable indeed."[11] So formidable that the United States would have had great difficulty seizing Louisiana *manu militari*, something the New Englanders would have opposed anyway. In some French official correspondence it is hinted that the real aim of the huge expedition to Saint-Domingue was to make a reality of the retrocession of Louisiana, something that was on the cards ever since Spanish weakness had become apparent in 1795.[12] But the first consul spurned this immense prize and, thanks to his own prejudices and the temptations dangled in front of him by the British and American governments, decided to restore slavery. Talleyrand and sundry bankers, colonial lobbyists, and land speculators were all busy in the background. Several of the Republic's best-informed military and political figures—Admiral Truguet,

General Laveaux, and Colonel Vincent—opposed the reckless abandonment of a successful and promising strategy.[13] As Popkin points out, the normally supine institutions of the Consulate saw a significant vote against the law restoring slavery.

Napoleon's miserable attempt led to a situation in which the revolution in Saint-Domingue could only defend its amazing social conquest—the suppression of slavery—by adopting the form of a nation state. In setting up such a state, the generals proclaimed principles of representation that were just as momentous, in their implications for slavery and race, as any other documents of the Age of Revolution.[14] But as the Haitian achievement is registered, we should extend the temporal horizon by a couple of decades, since it was not until the 1820s that a unified Haitian state emerged and it became evident to all that there would be no going back to slavery or colonial rule.

It is widely recognized that the defeat inflicted on the British, the Spanish, and the French by the insurgent blacks had an immediate impact. It favored a moderate abolitionist objective—ending the slave trade—but it also led to security measures and political arrangements that greatly reinforced the slave order, a process documented in various ways by Ada Ferrer, João José Reis and Flavio Gomes, Ashli White, and Alyssa Goldstein Sepinwall. In the short run the encouragement given to some slave conspiracies and revolts was certainly of greatly lesser significance. Sue Peabody cites some interesting attempts to incorporate French or Haitian emancipation into U.S. law, but it seems that they generally failed. Reis and Gomes explain the phenomenon of *haitianismo*, usually a scarecrow, not a tribute and hence comparable with *pardocracia*, the heresy which overassertive black commanders were supposed to be guilty of in the eyes of paler South American patriots.

The panic set off by Haiti may have stimulated racial feeling and planter vigilance in ways that helped the slaveholders, but it also showed them how their social order could disintegrate. The events in Saint-Domingue had shown that the slave order was vulnerable to division and controversy, that in an extreme military or political crisis it could be jettisoned, and that the mass of the enslaved and free people of color would use any opening to unite against a regime that upheld racial oppression. Fear of white treachery and black vengeance could lead slaveholders to acts that compounded their problems, the secession movement in the U.S. south being an outstanding example.

The large amount of blood shed in the course of the eventual victory and the publicity and credulity extended to any atrocity story had the effect of stimulating planter vigilance and putting abolitionists on the defensive. But in the longer term those who upheld the slave system could not conceal that its daily operation relied on naked violence and terror. While there was much horrible violence in Saint-Domingue, Laurent Dubois is right to remind us that Toussaint and a number of the other generals made significant efforts to channel and control it. Once a united Haitian Republic emerged, it experienced some decades of peace and recovery.

Official Haiti presented itself to the outside world in Neoclassical heroic garb, as Carlo Célius explains, but it was a significant achievement that the large peasantry and small middle class managed to develop their own more hybrid culture, with its *méringues* and modest but brightly adorned dwellings. While Africa seems everywhere, France has not disappeared either from the music or from the pattern of property. (As Dominique Rogers explained to me at the conference at Brown, many notaries and clerks had been free people of color in colonial Saint-Domingue, and they went on applying French law in the Republic of Haiti.)

Two great and bloody conflicts helped seal the fate of racial slavery in the American hemisphere—the Haitian revolution and the American Civil War. It would have been much better if slavery could have been ended without unleashing the pent-up violence inseparable from a slave order. British West Indian slave revolt and emancipation have their own importance but occurred on a greatly lesser scale, in part thanks to Haiti. It is extraordinarily difficult to see how the immensely valuable slave regimes of the Americas could all have been peacefully suppressed. In any event, such a peaceful emancipation did not come to pass in the United States and 600,000 persons lost their lives. Abraham Lincoln and Toussaint Louverture both had to contend with partisans of a slave order that was not ready to cede without a struggle.

There is a certain parallel between the hostile portrayals in the standard historiography of the French Directory, the Haitian Republic, and Radical Reconstruction. The real blemishes on these attempts to build racial equality have been played up and exaggerated to hide or discredit real successes, achieved against all odds. Haiti's revolution should not be accorded special favors by the historian. But neither should it—or these other important episodes in the war against slavery—be held to a different and more demanding standard than is applied to other major protagonists of the age.

At the outset I observed that national historiographies relating to slavery and abolition have often been animated by a desire to claim moral capital, just as abolitionists and political leaders themselves sometimes were. Much stranger were constructions of the nation and the patriotic that shunned or belittled the great turning points in the struggle for racial equality. As indicated above, there were Jacobins and "neo-Jacobin" officials who were and remained committed to the cause of slave emancipation, and their actions had real impact.[15] At the same time we have to explain the narrow and deceptive patriotism that targeted the emancipationists, of which Popkin cites examples.

L.-F. Hoffman's reading of the evidence of literature is very illuminating, but we should also be aware that republican emancipationism did not disappear without trace from French political culture. Its most eminent representative was Victor Schoelcher, who wrote a serious life of Toussaint Louverture and who, when appointed colonial secretary in 1848 (by Lamartine), enacted the second French emancipation. While Schoelcher's antislavery credentials were good, he became a misleading symbol of French colonialism.

There is so much of interest in these essays—and in the rediscovery of the Haitian Revolution—that I can mention only a few, somewhat arbitrarily selected topics. While matters are improving and "silence" no longer holds, there is still much work to be done, both on the interaction of national stories and in such areas as religion and music, popular architecture and planta-tion archaeology, family and sexuality and in understanding the perversity of French and American proslavery patriotism. As the philosopher put it, *Français, encore un effort . . .*

In conclusion, I would like to suggest an idea prompted by Jacques de Cauna's account of the dilapidated and vulnerable condition of Haiti's historic built environment. Might the scholarly community abroad—in close collabora-tion with Haitian historians, curators, and archivists—play a role in help-ing to preserve Haiti's past, its written records, and historic buildings? And more generally, might it work to ensure appropriate conditions in Haiti for the study of the country's remarkable history? Western governments have too often mistreated Haiti, and their direct interventions have usually been very misguided. But financial and material help to assist Haitians to preserve their history and to offer their own conclusions arising from it would per-haps be a tangible act of reparation.

Notes

1. Michel-Rolph Trouillot, *Silencing the Past: Power and the Production of History* (Boston, 1995), 88–107.

2. Recent works include Laurent Dubois, *Avengers of the New World: The Story of the Haitian Revolution* (Cambridge, Mass., 2004); Laurent Dubois, *A Colony of Citizens: Revolution and Slave Emancipation in the French Caribbean, 1787–1804* (Williamsburg, Va., 2004); Sibylle Fischer, *Modernity Disavowed: Haiti and the Cultures of Slavery in the Age of Revolution* (Durham, N.C., 2004); David Geggus, *Haitian Revolutionary Studies* (Bloomington, Ind., 2002); David Geggus, ed., *The Impact of the Haitian Revolution in the Atlantic World* (Columbia, S.C., 2001); David Barry Gaspar and David Patrick Geggus, eds., *A Turbulent Time: The French Revolution and the Greater Caribbean* (Bloomington, Ind., 1997); Yves Benot and Marcel Dorigny, eds., *Rétablissement de l'esclavage dans les colonies françaises, 1802* (Paris, 2003). Of some relevance are Frédéric Régent, *Esclavage, métissage et liberté: la Révolution française en Guadeloupe, 1789–1802* (Paris 2004); and Marcel Dorigny, ed., *Esclavage, résistances et abolitions* (Paris 1999). Examples of the impact of Haiti include Nelly Schmidt, *L'abolition de l'esclavage* (Paris,

2005); Gary Wills, *The Negro President: Jefferson and the Slave Power* (Boston, 2003); and Adam Hochschild, *Breaking the Chains* (London, 2006). But problems certainly remain; see Régis Debray, *Haïti et la France* (Paris, 2004).

3. I use the term in the sense suggested in Christopher Brown, *Moral Capital: Foundations of British Abolitionism* (Chapel Hill, N.C., 2006).

4. A tribute from Roland Desné and Marcel Dorigny and a bibliography of Benot's writings appear in a new collection of essays: Yves Benot, *Les Lumières, l'esclavage, la colonisation* (Paris, 2005). They reveal that Benot was involved with the Surrealists as a young man, that he worked as a political journalist in Nkrumah's Ghana, and that he used several noms de plume.

5. Carolyn Fick, *The Making of Haiti* (Knoxville, Tenn., 1990), 156.

6. Louis Sala-Molins, *The Dark Side of the Light: Slavery and the French Enlightenment* (Minneapolis, 2006). Notwithstanding its exaggerations, this book does convey the great timidity of even the best abolitionist thinking before the uprising in Saint-Domingue. In order to contemplate general revolt and emancipation, Louis-Sébastien Mercier had to place it in *L'an 2440* (the year 2440). For a stress on the positive contribution of the Lumières, see Sunkar Mutho, *Enlightenment against Empire* (Princeton, N.J., 2003).

7. For these crucial events, see also Dubois, *Avengers of the New World*, 156–163; and Florence Gauthier, ed., *Périssent les colonies plustot qu'un principe! Contribution à l'histoire de l'abolition de l'esclavage, 1789–1804* (Paris, 2002), 108. Polverel decreed emancipation in the west on August 27, so perhaps he should be given more credit.

8. The attempt of proslavery forces to somehow amend or stymie the motion is explained by Yves Benot, "Comment la Convention a-t-elle voté l'abolition de l'esclavage en l'an II," in *Les Lumières, l'esclavage, la colonisation*, 252–263. See also Jean-Daniel Piquet, "L'Emancipation des Noirs dans les débats de la Société des Jacobins de Paris (1791–94)," in *Esclavage, résistances et abolitons*, ed. Marcel Dorigny (Paris: Comité des travaux historiques et scientifiques, 1999), 187–198.

9. For the persistence of a slave order in several parts of Saint Domingue in 1794, see David Geggus, *Slavery, War and Revolution: The British Occupation of Saint Domingue, 1793–1798* (Oxford, 1982).

10. Florence Gauthier, *Triomphe et mort du droit naturel en révolution* (Paris, 1992), 288.

11. Quoted in Adam Rothman, *American Expansion and the Origins of the Deep South* (New York, 2004), 16.

12. Napoleon's maneuvers are traced in Robert L. Paquette, "Revolutionary Saint-Domingue in the Making of Territorial Louisiana," in *A Turbulent Time: the French Revolution and the Greater Caribbean*, ed. David Barry Gaspar and David Patrick Geggus (Bloomington, Ind., 2003), 204–225.

13. Bernard Gainot, "Metropole/Colonie. Projets constitutionnels et rapports des forces," in *Rétablissement de l'esclavage dans les colonies françaises, 1802*, ed. Yves Benot and Marcel Dorigny (Paris, 2003), 13–28.

14. A point stressed and documented by Laurent Dubois in *Avengers of the New World*, 240–246.

15. Bernard Gainot and Jean Daniel Piquet have documented this, including in the texts cited above.

CONTRIBUTORS

YVES BENOT is recently deceased. He is the author of *La Révolution française et la fin des colonies* (1988) and *La démence coloniale sous Napoléon* (1992), among many other works.

ROBIN BLACKBURN is Professor of Sociology at the University of Essex. He is the author of *The Making of New World Slavery: From the Baroque to the Modern, 1492–1800* (1997) and *The Overthrow of Colonial Slavery, 1776–1848* (1988).

JEAN CASIMIR teaches courses on the Culture and Society of Haiti at the Université d'État d'Haïti and is the author of *La cultura oprimida* (1980), *La Caraïbe, une et divisible* (1991), and *Pa bliye 1804, Souviens-toi de 1804* (2004). From 1991 to 1997, he was ambassador of the Republic of Haiti to the United States and Permanent Representative of Haiti to the Organization of American States.

JACQUES DE CAUNA teaches history at the Université de Pau et des Pays de l'Adour, France. He is the author of *Au Temps des Isles à Sucre* (1987) *Haiti, l'eternelle Revolution* (1997), and *Toussaint Louverture et l'indépendance d'Haïti* (2004), among many other works. He was cultural attaché at the French embassy in Haiti.

CARLO A. CÉLIUS, a historian and research scholar at CELAT, Université Laval (Québec), is the author of *Langage plastique et énonciation identitaire. L'invention de l'art haïtien* (2007) and editor of *Situations créoles. Pratiques et représentations* (2006).

ELIZABETH COLWILL is Associate Professor of Women's Studies at San Diego State University, California. Her publications include "Pass as a Woman, Act Like a Man: Marie-Antoinette as Tribade in the Pornography of the French Revolution," reprinted in *Marie-Antoinette: Writings on the Body of a Queen* (ed. Dena Goodman, 2003) and "State Ritual, War, and Freedwomen's Politics in Post-Emancipation Saint-Domingue," in *Gender, War, and Politics: The Wars of Revolution and Liberation—Transatlantic Comparisons, 1775–1820* (ed. Karen Hagemann, forthcoming).

LAURENT DUBOIS is Professor of History and Romance Studies at Duke University. He is the author of *A Colony of Citizens: Revolution and Slave Emancipation in the French Caribbean, 1787–1804* (2004) and *Avengers of the New World: The Story of the Haitian Revolution* (2004).

ADA FERRER teaches history at New York University. She is the author of *Insurgent Cuba: Race, Nation, and Revolution, 1868–1898* (1999) and "La société esclavagiste cubaine et la révolution haïtienne," *Annales* 58, no. 2 (2003).

CAROLYN E. FICK teaches history at Concordia University in Montreal, Quebec, Canada. She is the author of *The Making of Haiti: The Saint Domingue Revolution from Below* (1990) and "The Haitian Revolution and the Limits of Freedom: Defining Citizenship in the Revolutionary Era," *Social History* 32, no. 4 (2007).

JOHN D. GARRIGUS teaches history at the University of Texas at Arlington. He is the author of *Before Haiti: Race and Citizenship in French Saint-Domingue* (2006) and (with Laurent Dubois) *Slave Revolution in the Caribbean, 1789–1804: A Brief History with Documents* (2006).

MALICK W. GHACHEM is an attorney at the Boston office of Weil, Gotshal & Manges LLP. He is the author of a forthcoming book entitled *The Old Regime and the Haitian Revolution* and editor of a special volume of *Historical Reflections/Réflexions Historiques* entitled "Slavery and Citizenship in the Age of the Atlantic Revolutions" (Spring 2003).

FLÁVIO DOS SANTOS GOMES teaches history at the Universidade Federal do Rio de Janeiro, Brazil. He is the author of *Histórias de quilombolas: Mocambos e comunidades de senzalas no Rio de Janeiro—século XIX* (2006) and *A hydra e os pântanos: Mocambos, quilombos e comunidades de fugitivos no Brasil—séculos XVII–XIX* (2005).

Emeritus professor LÉON-FRANÇOIS HOFFMANN taught French and Haitian Literatures at Princeton University. He is the author of *Le Nègre romantique* (1973) and coordinated the *Œuvres complètes de Jacques Roumain*.

GENE E. OGLE teaches history at John Cabot University, Rome, Italy. He is the author of "Slaves of Justice: Saint Domingue's Executioners and the Production of Shame," *Historical Reflections/Réflexions Historiques* 29 (2003) and "Natural Movements and Dangerous Spectacles: Beatings, Duels and 'Play' in *Saint Domingue*," in *New World Orders: Violence, Sanction, and Authority in the Early Modern Americas, 1500–1825* (ed. Thomas J. Humphrey and John Smolenski, 2005).

SUE PEABODY is Professor of History at Washington State University, Vancouver. She is the author of *There Are No Slaves in France: The Political Culture of Race and Slavery in the Ancien Régime* (1996), co-editor (with Tyler Stovall) of *The Color of Liberty: Histories of Race in France* (2002), and co-editor (with Keila Grinberg) of *Slavery, Freedom and the Law in the Atlantic World* (2007).

JEREMY D. POPKIN, T. Marshall Hahn, Jr., Professor of History at the University of Kentucky, is the author of *Facing Racial Revolution: First-Person Narratives of the Haitian Insurrection* (2007) and a number of books on the press in the revolutionary era, including *Revolutionary News: The Press in France, 1789–1799* (1990).

JOÃO JOSÉ REIS teaches history at the Universidade Federal da Bahia, Bahia, Brazil. He is the author of *Slave Rebellion in Brazil: The 1835 Muslim Rebellion in Bahia* (1993) and *Death Is a Festival: Funeral Rites and Rebellion in Nineteenth-Century Brazil* (2003).

DOMINIQUE ROGERS teaches history at the Université des Antilles et de la Guyane, Schoelcher, Martinique, FWI. She is the author of "De l'origine du préjugé de couleur en Haïti" in *Haïti, première république noire* (ed. Marcel Dorigny, 2004) and "Présences noires en Aquitaine au XVIIIème siècle, une question à redécouvrir," *Institut Aquitain d'Etudes sociales*, bulletin 76 (2001). She is a member of the Centre International de Recherches sur les Esclavages (CNRS).

ALYSSA GOLDSTEIN SEPINWALL teaches history at California State University, San Marcos. She is the author of *The Abbé Grégoire and the French Revolution: The Making of Modern Universalism* (2005).

ASHLI WHITE teaches history at the University of Miami. She is the author of the forthcoming work *Revolution and Refuge: Saint-Dominguan Exiles in the United States*.

INDEX

Page numbers in italics indicate illustrations.

David Patrick Geggus teaches history at the University of Florida, Gainesville. He is author of *Slavery, War and Revolution* (1982) and *Haitian Revolutionary Studies* (2003), co-editor (with David Barry Gaspar) of *A Turbulent Time: The French Revolution and the Greater Caribbean* (1997), and editor of *The Impact of the Haitian Revolution in the Atlantic World* (2001). A former Guggenheim, Mellon, and NEH fellow, he has worked extensively on the Caribbean in the Age of Revolution.

Norman Fiering is the author of two books, *Moral Philosophy at Seventeenth-Century Harvard: A Discipline in Transition* (1981) and *Jonathan Edwards's Moral Thought and Its British Context* (1981). The two works together won the Merle Curti Prize for Intellectual History, awarded by the Organization of American Historians. From 1983 to 2006, Dr. Fiering was the director and librarian of the John Carter Brown Library, an independently funded and administered institution for advanced research located at Brown University.